FRANK APPLEGATE OF SANTA FE:
ARTIST AND PRESERVATIONIST

BY
DARIA LABINSKY
& STAN HIERONYMUS

FRANK APPLEGATE OF SANTA FE:
ARTIST AND PRESERVATIONIST

BY
DARIA LABINSKY
& STAN HIERONYMUS

LPD PRESS ❖ ALBUQUERQUE
2001

For information: LPD Press
2400 Rio Grande Blvd NW PMB 213
Albuquerque, NM 87104-3222
Telephone: (505) 344-9382
www.nmsantos.com

Book and cover design by Paul Rhetts & Barbe Awalt

Library of Congress Card Number 00-112266

ISBN 1-890689-02-5 (hardcover)
ISBN 1-890689-11-4 (softcover)

10 9 8 7 6 5 4 3 2 1

Cover painting, *Hopi Katcina Dance*, first exhibited in 1923. Private collection.

Contents

A tribute to Gretchen Hieronymus Beall

FRANK APPLEGATE
OF SANTA FE

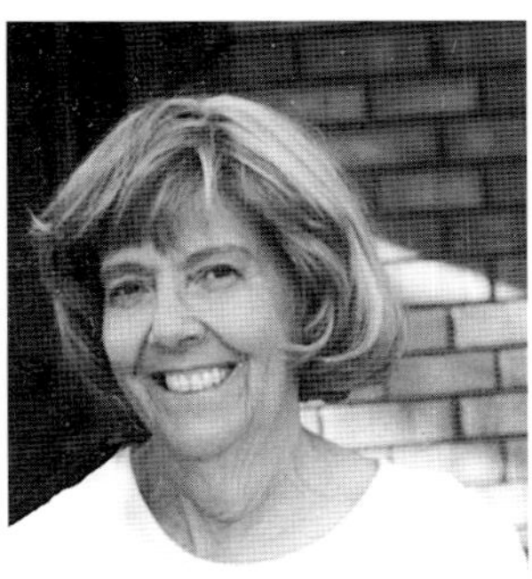

Gretchen Hieronymus Beall, Ph.D., daughter of Frank Applegate's youngest sister, Ruth Hieronymus, was the guiding force behind this book. Beall had considered writing a book about her regionally renowned uncle years ago, and with such a project in mind she took notes during conversations with her cousin, Applegate's daughter, Ruth Elizabeth "Betty" Applegate McClung. She also sought out relatives who had known Frank and had them write down or tell her their memories of him. Many of these individuals have since passed on, so it is only by Gretchen's foresight that we are able to have their recollections to share.

Gretchen also conducted initial research into Frank Applegate's life and kept track of many of his personal papers, which she shared with us. She tracked down pieces of his artwork that are housed in private collections across the country. She worked with us on the manuscript over a period of years, amiably putting up with our constant questioning, rereading the text and offering suggestions, and connecting us to people who provided additional assistance. She has been extremely generous with both time and resources. This book could not have been written without her, and it is as much her book as it is ours.

Acknowledgements

Researching Frank Applegate's life required extensive investigation into many different subject areas, and we relied on advice, encouragement, and information supplied by people all across the country. We would like to thank other members of the Applegate family who shared their memories and artwork with us. They include Muriel Stanley, Richard Applegate, Thomas Hieronymus, Albert Hieronymus, Susan Hill, Katherine Harris, Dorothy Morse, Sally Cushman, Thomas Morse, Doug Morse, Donald Applegate and his children, and Mark and Jill Hieronymus.

Our most valuable sources for studying Applegate's early years were the Logan County Public Library and the

Atlanta Public Library and Museum, both in Illinois. The University of Illinois Library and the staff at the University Archives provided valuable material and assistance, as did the staff of the Peoria (Illinois) Public Library. Much of the information about the decade Applegate spent in Trenton, New Jersey, was found in newspaper accounts housed at the Trenton Public Library and New Jersey State Library. Joan and Richard T. Ashton sent us correspondence and photos from the first home Applegate built, in Morrisville, Pennsylvania.

The archives and staffs at art museums around the United States proved very helpful, especially the Archives of American Art, Smithsonian Institution, Washington, D.C.; Albright-Knox Art Gallery, Buffalo, N.Y.; Pennsylvania Academy of the Fine Arts, Philadelphia; Art Institute of Chicago; Brooklyn Museum; Fred Jones Jr. Museum of Art, University of Oklahoma, Norman; Museum of Fine Arts, Houston; Los Angeles County Museum of Art; Denver Art Museum; Colorado Collection, CU Art Galleries, University of Colorado at Boulder; Colorado Springs Fine Arts Center; Metropolitan Museum of Art, New York; and Corcoran Gallery of Art, Washington, D.C.

Other libraries whose archives and staff proved valuable include the Houghton Library, Harvard University; Bancroft Library, University of California at Berkeley; Beinecke Rare Book and Manuscript Collection, Yale University; Library of Congress; Harry Ransom Humanities Research Center, University of Texas at Austin; Missouri Historical Society Library, St. Louis; Braun Research Library, Southwest Museum, Los Angeles; Van Pelt Library, University of Pennsylvania. Our research also took us to the Illinois State University Library, Bradley University Library, Denver Public Library, Albuquerque Public Library, Santa Fe Public Library, Chicago Public Library, and New York Public Library. Special recognition must be given to the Huntington Library in San Marino, Calif., especially Sara Hodson; Leslie Calmes at the Center for Creative Photography at the University of Arizona, Tucson; the staff at the Ansel Adams Publishing Rights Trust, Greenbrae, Calif.; and the Center for Southwest Research at the University of New Mexico, Albuquerque.

In Santa Fe we received help from the libraries and staff at the New Mexico State Records Center and Archives, New Mexico State Library, the Museum of New Mexico History Library and Photo Archives, the Museum of Fine Arts, the School of American Research, the Museum of International Folk Art, the Spanish Colonial Arts Society, and the Laboratory of Anthropology. Others who gave permission to have material quoted in this book are *New Mexico Magazine, Southwest Review,* HarperCollins Publishers, University of Tennessee Press, Witter Bynner Foundation, Paul Beekman Taylor for Mrs. A.R. Orage, and Thomas B. Catron III. This book could not have been produced without the help of Gerald Peters and his staff at the Gerald Peters Gallery, especially Catherine Whitney. Others who provided art and information include Barbe Awalt and Paul Rhetts, Rey Móntez, Sotheby's, Rose Gibbs, Nancy Briggs, Larry Ballard, Eugene Coombs, Herbert and Margaret Pickworth, the Karotkin Collection, Ken and Becky Phillips, Chuck and Jan Rosenak, Nick Herrera, Raymond Bal, and David Rasch and Donna Pierce of the Spanish Colonial Arts Society.

Richard Schwarz of Boulder, Colorado, provided the initial inspiration for this book. He was one of Applegate's earliest admirers, and he encouraged Gretchen Beall and later, the authors, to investigate Applegate's life and career. We would also like to thank the following people who offered us scholarly advice, assistance, and information: Lonn Taylor, Brenda Romero, Maria Mathes, Evaline Foley, Katharine Bartlett, Catherine Hathaway, Marc Simmons, Charles M. Carrillo, Robert R. White, Sue Widdows, Orlando Romero, the curators at the Saint-Gaudens National Historic Site, Cornish, N.H., Diane Greenlee, Howard Applegate, Robert R. White, William Wroth, Theresa Salazar, Robin Farwell Gavin, Christine I. Oaklander, and Thomas J. Steele, S.J.

Editors' Note: Where known, all measurements for art are height by width.

Dedication by Gerald P. Peters

While I never had the good fortune of knowing Frank Applegate personally (he was one of the first Santa Fe Art Colony artists to pass away, dying in 1931), my career and family life have been greatly enriched by his legacy. Representing Applegate's estate and living in his former home for more than two decades has brought me closer to this overlooked artist's passion and spirit. Applegate was somewhat of a paradox because he was both a staunch defender of traditional Hispanic and Native American arts and a maverick who painted in a modernist style, keeping his hand on the pulse of the burgeoning art scene in Santa Fe during the Roaring Twenties.

Applegate's love of Santa Fe's tricultural character is preserved in the place that was closest to him: the historic de la Peña House. This dwelling, which he began renovating in 1926 without compromising its eighteenth century Spanish Colonial core, was his Santa Fe home. It has also been the place my family and I have called home for more than twenty years, and it is through this shared framework that I have gleaned passing impressions of Applegate's passions and historical importance. Existing photographs of this property taken by his friend, photographer Ansel Adams, and others show that Applegate decorated his adobe home sparsely with Spanish Colonial decorative arts and furniture as well as Native American pots and textiles. My wife, Katie, and I share his tastes and have continued this tradition by decorating our home with Indian pots and textiles, Spanish Colonial furniture, and by hanging our walls with the best examples from the Santa Fe Art Colony and Taos Society painters – Applegate's watercolor landscapes among them.

Even the former location of the Gerald Peters Gallery at 439 Camino del Monte Sol has Applegate's stamp upon it. While it served us well from the 1970s through the late 1990s, it is still known to some as the "Mary Austin House," and was called by Austin herself Casa Querida, or "Beloved House." Austin was Applegate's good friend, neighbor, and fellow arts advocate who housed artists and intellectuals such as Ansel Adams, Willa Cather, and D.H. Lawrence and helped to found the Indian Arts Fund and Spanish Colonial Arts Society. Austin and Applegate were also active in the local theater scene and friendly with local painting legends such as Andrew Dasburg, Gerald Cassidy, and William Penhallow Henderson, among others.

Given the numerous connections I have with Applegate's legacy, it goes without saying that I am thrilled to see this long-overdue tribute to one of Santa Fe's greatest talents come to fruition. My thanks and admiration go out to Daria Labinsky and Stan Hieronymus for their initiation of and devotion to this project, as well as for their thorough research and compelling manuscript. Barbe Awalt and Paul Rhetts of LPD Press are also to be commended for their editorial, financial, and passionate support of this historic project. These people were the true hearts and brains behind this publication. My thanks also go out to all the lenders to this show as well as to the collectors who permitted their works to be photographed by our staff photographer, Joe D'Alessandro. I was flattered to be asked to participate in this project and am proud to sponsor the exhibition, under the direction of Catherine Whitney, which honors the printing of this publication and the seventy-fifth anniversary of the Spanish Colonial Arts Society. It has been a pleasure to work with everyone involved and to "get to know" Frank Applegate a little bit better as a result of this project.

Gerald P. Peters

Frank Applegate of Santa Fe

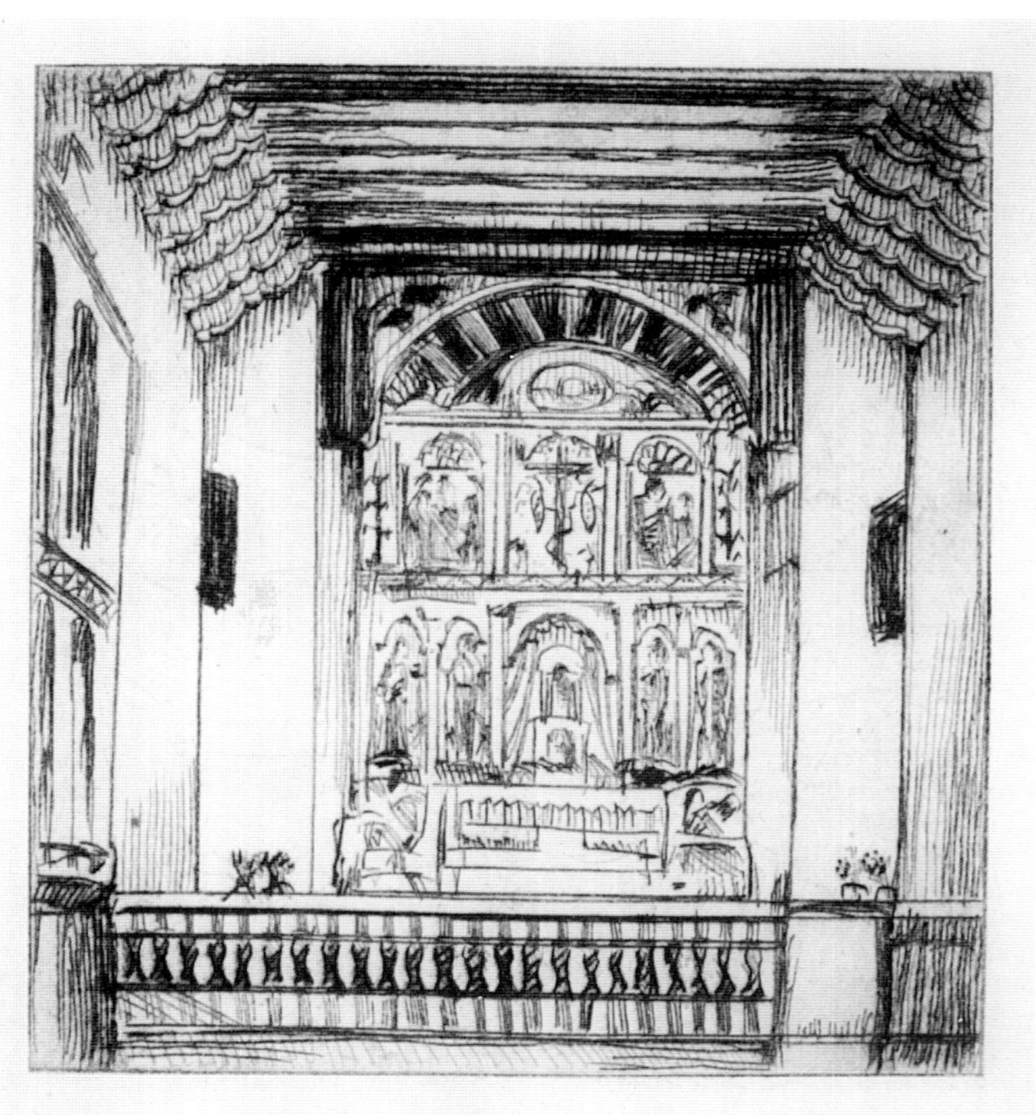

Untitled (*Altarpiece*), etching by Frank Applegate. 4" x 4". Collection of Gerald Peters Gallery. Photograph courtesy of Gerald Peters Gallery, Santa Fe. This is an etching of the altarscreen at Santa Cruz de la Cañada.

Foreword by William Wroth

Some Sources for the Ideas of Frank Applegate

One of the apparent contradictions of the century through which we have just passed is that the movement in the arts called modernism was actually quite conservative: It sought to preserve what is of the essence and to dispense with the superficial. A powerful tendency in modernism was the search for essential forms in nature and in traditional and so-called primitive arts. Frank Applegate, as made amply clear in the present book, was thoroughly a modernist in his painting and sculptural work and simultaneously he was attracted to the Indian and Hispanic cultures of New Mexico. Like many of his contemporaries who were drawn to New Mexico, he saw that these indigenous cultures still retained much of their traditional character. Artists like Applegate saw the values and forms of these cultures as a restorative against the alienation of modern American life and as an inspiration for their own work.

Within two years of his arrival in New Mexico in 1921 Applegate became an eloquent advocate for both Pueblo Indian and Hispanic culture, and he began a systematic program for preservation and revival of traditional Hispanic crafts. His virtually instant advocacy for these arts suggests that he was well prepared for what he found in New Mexico. In this essay I want briefly to consider some of the intellectual influences which led Applegate to play such a prominent role in the birth of the Hispanic crafts revival in New Mexico.

Frank Applegate and his friend and collaborator Mary Austin were immersed in the philosophical movement which has latterly been labeled "antimodern." This movement found its roots in the reaction against industrialism which began at the end of the 1700s with the Romantics such as Blake and Wordsworth and was elaborated by John Ruskin and by William Morris and others attached to the Arts and Crafts movement of the late 1800s. While much of the Arts and Crafts movement was bent on reviving European crafts, there also began a gradual revaluation of indigenous and folk arts in other parts of the world, which in the throes of industrialism and Victorian civilizationism had previously been denigrated and ignored.

One of the leading proponents of the new appreciation and revival of traditional arts was the thinker, artist, and art historian Ananda Coomaraswamy. Starting in 1905 in Ceylon and India with an eloquent series of articles, books, and exhibitions, he portrayed the deadening effects of colonialism on local communities and the need to nurture and revitalize handcraft traditions. Other Indian nationalists advocated local craft production as a bulwark against economic and political control of Indian life by the British, but at the heart of Coomaraswamy's thought was the need for spiritual and cultural preservation and revival. Only by preserving core values which recognized the beauty and meaning in traditional Indian forms could a true nationalist movement be based, a movement that could free itself not only from Western economic and political domination but also from cultural domination. Following the lead of Ruskin and Morris, Coomaraswamy decried the mediocrity and uniformity of machine-made products as well as the sapping effects of factory work upon laborers and the meaninglessness of an industrial culture no longer based upon spiritual traditions. Coomaraswamy's ideas helped set the stage for the full-scale incorporation of handcrafts into the Indian nationalist movement led by Mohandas Gandhi.

The close parallels between the ideas espoused by Coomaraswamy in the early 1900s and those of Frank Applegate and Mary Austin in the 1920s suggest intriguing possibilities of intellectual influences. It is likely that John and Mary Mowbray-Clarke in New York were an important conduit for some of these revivalist and anti-industrialist ideas. As well documented in the present book, the Mowbray-Clarkes were close friends of Frank and Alta Applegate. Applegate first met the sculptor John Mowbray-Clarke in 1914 and appeared with him in several group exhibitions. He was a frequent visitor to Mary Mowbray-Clarke's New York bookstore and gallery, The Sunwise Turn, and he and Alta often visited the Mowbray-Clarkes at their Rockland County home.

The Mowbray-Clarkes were also among Ananda Coomaraswamy's first and closest friends after he moved to the United States in 1917. Coomaraswamy's frequent visits to New York centered around the lively atmosphere at The Sunwise Turn, and he also often stayed with the Mowbray-Clarkes at their country home. In 1918 Mary Mowbray-Clarke published under The Sunwise Turn imprint Coomaraswamy's impor-

tant book, *The Dance of Shiva*, which included much discussion of his ideas about cultural preservation and revival. Alta Applegate owned this book; her copy (signed by her on the front flyleaf) was until recently in the possession of the present writer. In 1919 The Sunwise Turn published a catalogue of John Mowbray-Clarke's sculpture, with text by Coomaraswamy, and in 1920 they published Coomaraswamy's *Twenty-eight Drawings*, an exhibition of which came to Santa Fe in the same year. We don't know if Applegate and Coomaraswamy ever met, but all of these Sunwise Turn publications came out while the Applegates were still living in the East, prior to their move to New Mexico and while they were in frequent contact with the Mowbray-Clarkes.

Meanwhile Coomaraswamy himself had visited New Mexico in the summer of 1917. An article in *El Palacio* in 1920 concerning the show of Coomaraswamy's drawings at the Fine Arts Museum in Santa Fe discusses his visit three years earlier when he had been the guest of William Penhallow and Alice Corbin Henderson, later neighbors and close friends of the Applegates: "It is worth noting, incidentally, that Mr. Coomaraswamy ... was one of the first to appreciate the work of the Pueblo Indian artists, which has recently excited so much interest in New York. He purchased at the time, from Mrs. Abbott at the Rito, two of the water colors by Alfonso Roybal [San Ildefonso Pueblo artist Awa-Tsireh] whose work is perhaps the finest and most progressive of the Indian artists, and who was, in fact, the initiator of the 'movement.'" Writing in 1945 Alice Corbin Henderson recalled her and Coomaraswamy's visit in 1917 to Bandelier National Monument, where through Mrs. A.J. Abbott they discovered Awa-Tsireh's watercolors, which Coomaraswamy immediately purchased. Coomaraswamy, then a well-known art historian just hired by the Boston Museum of Fine Arts, clearly helped to spark interest in Awa-Tsireh and other Pueblo artists, just as he had years earlier supported the work of young painters in India working in traditional styles. He was also one of the first to recognize the significance of Navajo Indian sandpainting and later wrote: "The Amerindian sand-paintings, considered intellectually, are superior in kind to any painting that has been done in Europe or white America within the last several centuries."

Prior to moving to the United States Coomaraswamy was a leader in the English Arts and Crafts movement, and he had a close relationship with two prominent anti-industrialists, A.R. Orage and Arthur J. Penty. Orage and Penty were proponents of "guild socialism," a movement to restore the means of production to workers through revival of handcraft production along the lines of medieval guilds. Coomaraswamy contributed several articles to Orage's weekly, *The New Age*, and in 1914 he collaborated with Penty in editing the book *Essays in Post-Industrialism*. Penty later credited Coomaraswamy with coining the term "post-industrialism," and he was strongly influenced by Coomaraswamy's much earlier discussions of handcraft production in India under the guild system, such as his 1908 publication, *The Indian Craftsman*. As the authors discuss in the present work, Orage had a later influence on Frank Applegate, when in the 1920s he established a Gurdjieffian group in Santa Fe which met weekly at the home of the Applegates and also at their neighbors, the Hendersons. It is likely that Applegate had long been familiar with the work of Orage and Penty through *The New Age*, and through Penty's several books on the philosophy of guild socialism. One of these books, *A Guildsman's Interpretation of History*, was published in America by Mary Mowbray-Clarke under The Sunwise Turn imprint in 1919.

Arriving in Santa Fe in 1921, Frank Applegate quickly immersed himself in both Indian and Hispanic cultures and began building an important collection of "Spanish colonial" arts and crafts, focusing particularly on religious images. Within a short period of time he and Mary Austin conceived the idea of the Society for the Revival of Spanish Colonial Arts (later the Spanish Colonial Arts Society) to preserve historical pieces and promote revival efforts among rural Hispanics in New Mexico. Applegate's ideas at this time clearly reflect those outlined earlier by Coomaraswamy and Penty. Writing in the 1920s (an essay which he sent to the Mowbray-Clarkes), he noted that Hispanic crafts had reached near extinction due to "the American traders and exploiters who by their superior aggressiveness forced their machine-made civilization on them. Now cheap colored lithographs are taking place of the old gesso on wood paintings. Cheap cotton goods are replacing their wonderful weavings." The efforts of the arts society and its leaders, like those of Coomaraswamy, went beyond the crafts revival to recognize other important aspects of traditional Hispanic rural culture, such as music, poetry, and religion.

One of the most essential of Coomaraswamy's ideas in dealing with the situation in India was the notion of "svadharma," which may be rendered in English as "true vocation": every being can and should do work that is in conformity with his or her own nature. This ancient concept is of great significance, for it allows individuals to bring to fruition what is deepest in themselves and in their cultural heritage. In the modern era svadharma inevitably comes in conflict with industrialism, which in the name of economic efficiency ignores the innate skills as well as the cultural traditions of workers and treats them as anonymous cogs in the industrial enterprise, enslaving them in deadening factory work. Through revival of crafts, individuals could continue to be artists and artisans in their own traditions instead of being forced into factory work. In Coomaraswamy's terms, a crafts revival could realize not only svadharma but also "svaraj," that is "self-rule" or "own country," the regaining of economic and political autonomy by the local community.

In Hispanic New Mexico a colonialist situation prevailed that was very similar to India. Since the arrival of the Anglo-Americans in the mid-1800s, local communities had lost their autonomy; their former self-sustenance had been replaced by reliance upon products made and sold by the colonizers. Like Coomaraswamy in India, the Hispanic revival movement also envisioned a larger revitalization of village life, reversing the process of depopulation and loss of economic viability. These concepts were at the root of the ideas of Frank Applegate and Mary Austin, and to large degree they were realized over the succeeding decades after the deaths of these two pioneers: first in the blossoming of the Hispanic crafts revival in the 1930s and later in the present crafts revival which began in the 1970s. Thanks in part to the efforts of Applegate and Austin many Hispanic artisans in New Mexico today live comfortably from their art, and in so doing they fulfill Coomaraswamy's concept of svadharma: "Being a vocation, his art is most intimately his own and pertains to his own nature, and the pleasure that he takes in it perfects the operation. There is nothing he would rather work at than his making; to him the leisure state would be an abomination of boredom."

William Wroth
Bloomington and Santa Fe
October 2000

[**Bibliographic notes**. Among Ananda Coomaraswamy's early writings on cultural and crafts revival in Ceylon and India are: *Mediaeval Sinhalese Art* (1908); *Essays in National Idealism* (1909); *The Indian Craftsman* (1909); and *Art and Swadeshi* (1911). Frank Applegate's friendship with John and Mary Mowbray-Clarke is documented in the present work; see especially Chapter 3 below. Biographical information about Coomaraswamy, including his friendship with the Mowbray-Clarkes, is found in Roger Lipsey, *Coomaraswamy 3: His Life and Work* (1977). The notice of his 1917 visit to Santa Fe is in *El Palacio*, 8:5-6 (May-June, 1920), 129-130. Alice Corbin Henderson's account of her and Coomaraswamy's discovery of Pueblo artist Awa-Tsireh appears in her article "Indian Artists of the Southwest" in *The American Indian*, 2: 3 (Spring 1945), 24. Coomaraswamy's discussion of Navajo sandpaintings appears in "Sir Gawain and the Green Knight: Indra and Namuci," *Speculum* 19 (1944), 124-125. Applegate's unpublished essay on the loss of Hispanic craft traditions, which is now in the Mowbray-Clarke Papers, is cited below in Chapter 12. Coomaraswamy's definition of svadharma is found in "Figure of Speech or Figure of Thought?" reprinted in Roger Lipsey, ed. *Coomaraswamy 1: Selected Papers. Traditional Art and Symbolism* (1977), 29.]

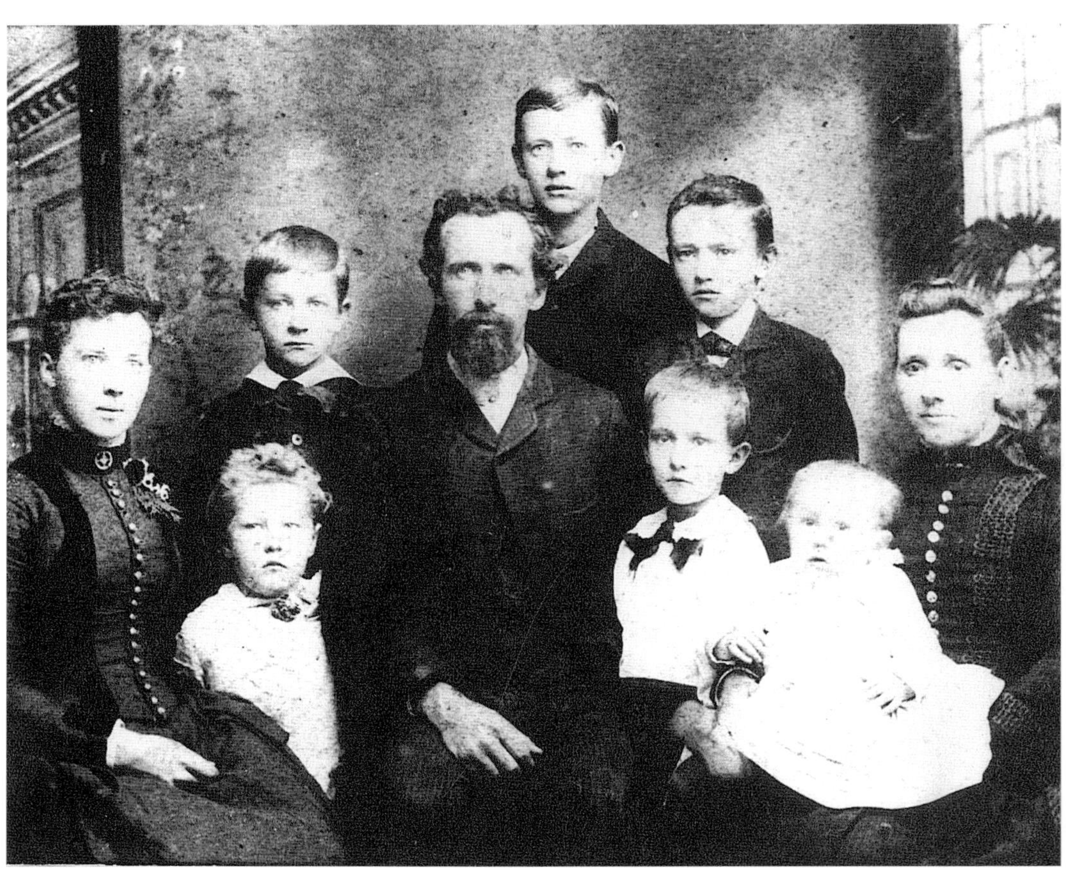

The Applegate Family, 1887 (before the birth of Bert and Ruth). From left: Mabel, Anne, Frank (age 6), father Albert Alonzo, Alpheus, Arthur (small boy in white shirt), Archie, Linn, and mother Clara Angelina. Photograph courtesy of the Applegate family.

Introduction

The artists' colony that flourished in Santa Fe in the 1920s is remembered as much for its colorful characters as for the art created there. Enduring stories recall the energetic young painters known as "Los Cinco Pintores," poet Witter Bynner and his Prohibition-era "tea" parties, writer Mary Austin, whose domineering manner earned her the nickname "God's mother-in-law," and many others.

Few stories have been told about one of the most important art colony members. Frank Applegate lived in Santa Fe for only a decade, but he had a profound impact on the city and the cultural region. The things that make Santa Fe a "city different" today, such as the Pueblo Revival architecture, the intermingling of Spanish, Indian, and Anglo cultures, and the celebration of art, are the very things Applegate admired and defended.

Who was Frank Applegate? An editorial eulogizing him in the *Santa Fe New Mexican* called Applegate "a lover and preserver of beauty":

> His contribution to the sum total of those things which make living in Santa Fe a privilege and a pleasure was tremendous. The renaissance of beautiful native Spanish and Indian arts; the architectural movement which has made Santa Fe a city unique in the world; the literature of the south-west, the 'little theater' movement, painting,—all these owe Applegate a heavy debt. He was in the widest and best sense an artist. His fight for landscape beauty was deter-mined and persistent; he was a consistent enemy of the ugly and the sordid, and his stu[r]dy and kindly personality was a tower of strength to every one interested in these causes. ... Applegate's capable, busy, and tireless hands used pen and brush, trowel and chisel with equal facility. He molded adobe and clay, wood and metal, the thoughts of those around him, public sentiment, into forms of grace and beauty. He was in the highest sense a builder, and a strong and helpful friend.[1]

This eulogy only touched the surface of Applegate's life. He managed both to epitomize his era as a defender of the handmade over the mass-produced and a proponent of modern art and to tran-scend it as a visionary who fought to curb the ever-increasing impact of modern civilization on the Southwest and its indigenous cultures. He actively supported causes that are still debated today, ranging from historic preservation to the rights of Native Americans to govern themselves. Once one begins to examine Applegate's life, it is difficult to understand his relative obscurity, be-cause he did important work in so many areas.

Of all the Santa Fe art colonists, none had a wider variety of interests than Applegate did, and scholars who are familiar with a single aspect of his life are often unaware of its other facets. Books on American arts and crafts note his efforts to revive Spanish Colonial art but make no mention of his own studio pottery or his work with Hopi potters. Likewise, scholars who have read his books of Southwestern folklore know nothing about his fine woodcarving. Museum curators who admire his contributions to their collections of Indian pottery and Spanish Colonial art are often unaware of his devotion to Pueblo Revival architecture.

Applegate was foremost an artist, and his work received much recognition and praise during his lifetime. He was a lifelong student who developed not only an admiration for various art forms but an interest in their origins and compositions. As an educator, he took pleasure in sharing information with others, first through teaching and later through writing. An ambitious man with a healthy ego, Applegate's path crossed those of historical figures known to modern audiences, including philanthro-pist John D. Rockefeller Jr.; sculptor and art patron Gertrude Vanderbilt Whitney; sculptors William Zorach and Charles Grafly; Andrew Dasburg, Ernest Blumenschein, and the other New Mexican painters; Presidents Theodore Roosevelt and Harry S Truman; and photographer Ansel Adams.

In the article "Santa Fe in the Twenties," Ruth Laughlin summed up Applegate in a few sentences: "Frank Applegate stopped over on a cross-country trek and stayed the rest of his life. His versatile gifts included ceramics, painting, writing, and collecting primitive art in bultos and santos. He bought land on the Camino [del Monte Sol] opposite the Hendersons and encouraged a group of young artists to mix adobes and build their homes on that hillside."[2] This book will elaborate upon that simple tribute by documenting a life filled with many worthwhile accomplishments that left Santa Fe and New Mexico better for one man's having lived there.

Endnotes

[1] *Santa Fe New Mexican*, Feb. 13, 1931, 4.
[2] Laughlin, "Santa Fe in the Twenties." *New Mexico Quarterly Review* 19 (Spring 1949): 63.

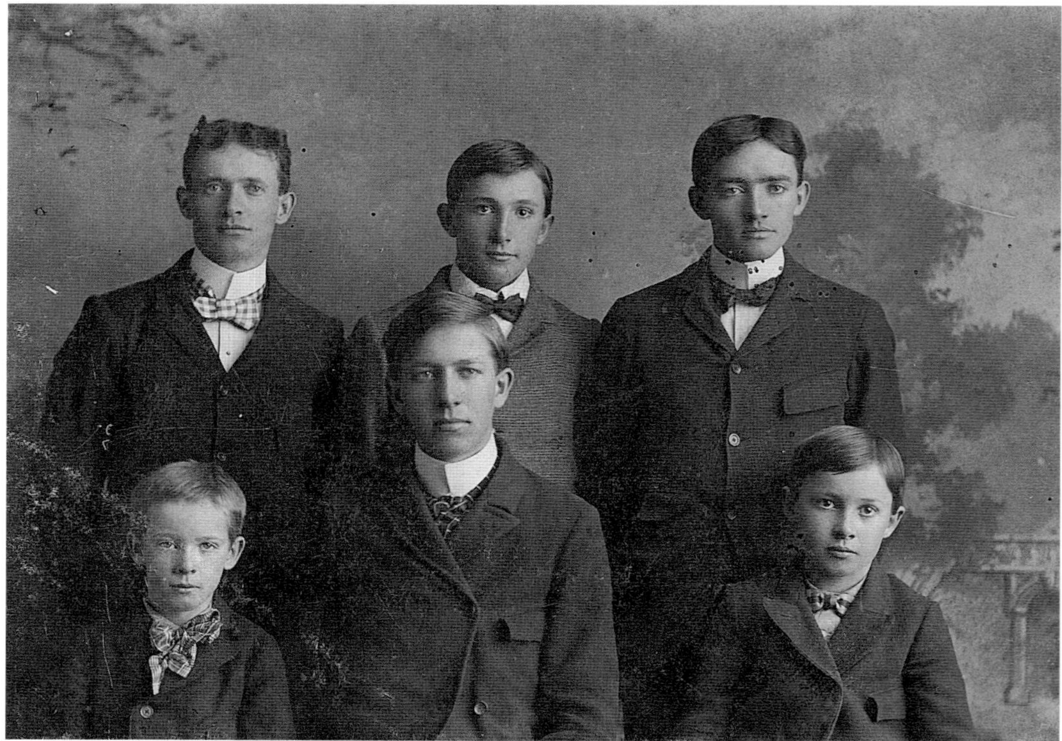

The Applegate boys, ca. 1894. Top row, left to right: Alpheus, Arthur, and Archie. Bottom row, left to right: Albert, Frank, and Linn. Photograph courtesy of the Applegate family.

1 A Farmer's Son

The life of Frank Guy Applegate may have cast a longer shadow than that of his father, Albert Augustus Applegate, but he was no more extraordinary a man. A.A. Applegate, as he was known, was a berry farmer who worked atypically poor Illinois farmland and never lived more than 30 miles from where he was born, but he helped rear nine children who went to college during an era when a high school education was still uncommon.

The Applegate family arrived in the United States not long after the Pilgrims. In 1625 A.A.'s paternal ancestors, Thomas and Elizabeth Wall Applegate, left England and settled in Braintree, Massachusetts, where Thomas operated a river ferry. Their descendants eventually moved to Cincinnati, and Halstead Applegate, Frank's grandfather, was born in Hamilton, Ohio, in 1817. He graduated from the Eclestis Medical Institute in Cincinnati and moved to Illinois in 1839, where he divided his time between homeopathy and farming. Halstead married Mary Jane Linn in 1841, and they had three sons—Alpheus, who died in infancy, Alonzo, who lived to age 38, and Albert Augustus, who was born May 8, 1849. A year after his birth, the family moved to Eminence Township, located 40 miles northwest of the state capital, Springfield.

Albert was just 2 years old when his father died, and his mother married Jordan Bruner, a successful Eminence farmer, a few years later. A.A. lived a typical farm boy's youth, working in the fields, hunting and fishing, attending church and school, and studying.[1]

The town of Atlanta sits on the prairie about five miles east of Eminence, on the Chicago-to-St. Louis highway of commerce through the heart of the state. In A.A.'s youth, a trip to Atlanta was a major outing, and one to the county seat of Lincoln was extraordinary. In 1905, A.A. recalled one such trip he had made with his uncles: "We sat for two hours on the north side of the old court house and listened to Abraham Lincoln discuss 'The Dred Scott Decision,' and the 'Missouri Compromise,' and crack jokes on his opponent, Stephen A. Douglas."[2]

A.A. was quite impressed with Lincoln. "To have told us at that moment that he was the greatest and best production of the 19th century would have been no revelation," he wrote. "We have attended many political gatherings since and listened to many noted men, but prize the memory of those two hours and their vivid impressions of that strong, intellectual face with its wonderful depth of earnestness and determination; and yet the shades as they flitted over his rugged countenance spoke of the kind, loving, patriotic heart within."[3]

Albert grew into a man with bright blue eyes, curly black hair, and dreams of becoming a writer, but his stepfather's death in 1868, while Albert was attending an academy in Normal, Illinois, changed his plans. Quite ill himself, probably with rheumatic fever, he left school at 18 and never returned.[4]

A.A. married Clara Angelina Miller, a diminutive, cheerful, brown-eyed woman known as Lina, in 1872. According to family members, A.A. and Lina met at a "singing school" convention. Churches held singing schools for their members in order to teach them to read music, so as to improve their hymn singing. Lina's family had been in the New World probably as long as the Applegates had. Family stories hold that her mother walked behind a wagon from Virginia to Kentucky and later on to Illinois. Her grandfather was the first town clerk in Eminence, and her twin brother, Arthur, was a successful Atlanta businessman.[5]

The couple first lived in Hartsburg, not far from Eminence. "We wrote up the items (for the *Lincoln Times*) from Hartsburg when that metropolis was still in its infancy," A.A. remembered in a later newspaper column. "In those days we organized the first Hartsburg Sunday School." They also lived in Midland City, where A.A. briefly tried being a merchant, but the store failed as a result of arson.[6]

The Applegates returned to Eminence and purchased an 80-acre farm. A.A. also found employment as a correspondent for two local newspapers, the *Lincoln Daily Courier* and the *Atlanta Argus*. He often was more gossip columnist than reporter, writing about who was visiting whom, upcoming marriages, and anything else he found interesting. Frank saw his father toil long over his words, for A.A. loved puns and a well-turned phrase. He worked hard to keep his reports from being boring.

Occasionally, A.A. inserted a paragraph or more of his own thoughts, but often he enlivened his reportage with a mere sentence or two. He had a talent for writing humorously, which Frank would inherit:

> The [Spanish-American] war is the general topic of conversation in our town. Woe unto the Spanish Armada that dares to sail up Sugar Creek.

> Some very crooked tracks, a lady's fan that looked as if broken in a struggle, and a torn, crumpled love letter in the highway near our domicil Monday morning was evidence that we had missed an interesting item. We shall have to adopt a flashlight system in our observatory.

> We have been asked of late if we are an expansionist. We wouldn't dare express an opinion until our wife returns, as she reads the *Courier*. Just now we are an imperialist, but are ready at any time to lay down the sceptre and submit to our former government.[7]

A.A. and Lina had nine children over the course of 20 years, beginning with Edith Mabel in 1873. Alpheus Miller was born in 1874, Archie Bligh in 1878, Frank Guy on February 9, 1881, Arthur Leslie in 1882, Annie Mary in 1885, Vern Linn in 1887, Albert Angelo in 1889, and Ruth Pauline in 1893.[8] All lived to adulthood, a rather unusual occurrence in those days.

It was not easy caring for such a large family. Although he and Lina raised hogs and poultry, grew corn and grapes and owned fruit trees, A.A. was best known for his berries, and nobody got rich growing berries. Most of his children had gone off to college when these thoughts appeared in the *Lincoln Daily Courier*:

> We fully realize how unequally the blessings of life are bestowed and how destitute some worthy people are of the most common necessities when we were told that our friend, Mr. Curry, had recently applied to a charitable institution for the gift of one small boy. For many years we have enjoyed the luxury of a houseful of the genuine domestic article without giving thought to the utter destitution of some of our neighbors. How much they must have missed of the interesting economic problems of life.

We have often seen the subject "How to keep the boys on the farm," discussed in the papers, but the writers have always missed the vital point. To us the unsolved question has always been what shall they eat, what shall they drink, and wherewithal shall they be clothed. If there were half a dozen fathers in a family and one boy, the cost of clothing theory might suffice, but where the order is reversed, one father and six boys, it is but a small factor. When we note the cast-off piles of old boots everywhere in evidence in the fence corners and waste places, ranging from the little No. 1 copper toe to the huge No. 11 cowhide, we begin to calculate how many extra acres we might have owned had we not invested so largely in boot leather and ready made clothing.[9]

Indeed, the Applegates' life was difficult. Occasional reports in the *Atlanta Argus* hint at hard times in the early 1890s. A late freeze could mean a loss of hundreds of dollars in income for the family, as it did in 1895. The paper carried frequent reports of sickness in both animals and humans, for everyone knew how grave a slight illness could become. A.A. himself had a double hernia and a heart condition, and Lina was frequently bedridden by a crippling illness that made her lame.[10]

Yet, even in hard times, the door of their home remained open to others. "Our home seemed to be the mecca for itinerant preachers, back-pack peddlers, tramps, or men just down on their luck," son Albert Applegate recalled years later in an essay. "Father and mother provided food and lodging one winter for three men, who made posts, or chopped wood for no wages, although Father provided them with tobacco and Mother made mittens for them." The Applegates were charitable toward neighbors as well. After a local man committed suicide, A.A. "went, literally, to the rescue" of his German immigrant family, Bert wrote. "It seemed to us children that whenever there was trouble, Father was in the midst of it." Often, A.A. invited two or three other families over for Sunday dinner, which never pleased the children, since they had to wait until everyone else had eaten before they could eat.[11]

A.A. often read to the children, and he had "a feeling for the dramatic," as Bert put it. He vividly remembered hearing his father read Dickens' works: "The books were paperback, cheap, fine print, two columns to a page, and Father had to hold the book close to the lamp to see the print. He had black curly hair and a fiery red beard, and as he read it looked, sometimes, as if his beard would catch fire, with the light shining through it." Lina also read voraciously. When she was in her 80s, she would send one of her granddaughters to the library to pick up six or eight books at a time, and within a week she would be ready for more.[12]

Music also played an important role in the Applegate household. A.A. "had a beautiful, high tenor voice," and Alpheus once heard him hit a high C. Lina was a "powerful soprano," and together, Bert said, "they made a good duo."[13]

A.A. was also "a good raconteur [who] … loved to talk," as Bert recalled. "Father would tell me about things that occurred in his boyhood, or stories he had heard from earlier generations—of the Mormons who had passed through, the gang of desperadoes who robbed drovers … of fishing at night because his stepfather would not let him go during the day, and many others."[14] Years later, Frank Applegate would garner praise for his own storytelling skills.

Brother Applegate was an elder in the Eminence Christian Church, who conducted many Sunday School activities and often was asked to deliver the sermon at a child's funeral. He was also an active Prohibitionist and frequently spoke out against saloons and drinking; as the *Atlanta Argus* colloquially put it, "Mr. Applegate don't drink nor kuss." Although there is no record of Frank's stand on prohibition, he inherited A.A.'s temperance views on a personal level.[15]

Temperance on A.A. Applegate's part did not translate into intolerance, however. "Father was not orthodox in his beliefs," Bert wrote. "In a day when fundamentalism was the only way of believing, Father had read and enjoyed [Darwin's] *Origin of Species*, Ingraham's

Natural Life in the Spiritual World, and quoted Emerson the way some of the itinerant preachers quote the Old Testament."[16] He freely quoted from a host of literary references in his newspaper columns.

The elder Applegates believed in the importance of education and saw to it that the children were well educated. "Every township should have high school privileges at public expense," A.A. wrote. "The time was when a common school education was sufficient for all practical purposes, but the present high standard of intelligence required in all lines of work, agriculture not excepted, calls for something more than 'the 3 R's.'"[17] The Applegates sent eldest child Mabel to an academy before the nearby town of Atlanta opened its high school and she later went to college. The other eight children all graduated from Atlanta High School and went on to the University of Illinois on scholarships won in competitive county exams.

Although the Applegates' life was hardly cosmopolitan, it was never intellectually limited. In addition to the weekly *Argus* and daily *Courier,* they subscribed to the *St. Louis Globe-Democrat* and *Bloomington (Ill.) Pantagraph.* The children traveled with their father when he went to preach on Sundays, and Frank would often set out with one of his older brothers to visit relatives in nearby towns. While attending the university, the children often brought professors home to visit.

Frank was an inquisitive sort from early on, and family members recall that he tried to culture pearls by putting grains of sand in clams and tried to raise pet owls. One of his first paintings, a portrait, was executed on the granary door of a barn. As he got older, he tried his hand at woodworking, crafting furniture for the family home and making a checkerboard, among other things. He remained a woodworker and furniture-maker throughout his life.[18]

Hunting was another popular pastime. The local papers often reported a bit of hunting prowess by one of the boys, and when they were grown and returned to Eminence as visitors, their excursions included fishing, boating, and hand-catching fish. Years later Frank Applegate would hunt wild turkeys to share with his Santa Fe neighbors.

The Applegate children differentiated themselves from others in the Atlanta-Eminence community, sometimes to their neighbors' displeasure. The *Atlanta Argus* mentioned that Alpheus Applegate and some of his friends were considered "stuck up" because they "had a noble ambition to know something." When telephones came to Eminence in 1901, party lines let everybody know everyone else's business. The Applegates' solution was to speak to one another in foreign languages. Such tricks were not popular with the neighbors, and A.A. put tongue in cheek when he wrote: "We trust at the next meeting of our telephone directors they will pass a ruling making it obligatory on all to speak English over the lines. It is so disappointing for one to slip up at a neighbor's call for a few minutes' eavesdropping and find them speaking in a unknown tongue." The reputation of "those queer Applegates" even spread to neighboring towns. [19]

Although the family was close-knit, the children began to distinguish themselves from each other early on. All inherited or learned musical skills from their parents, and Frank and three of his brothers sang informally as "the Applegate quartet"; however, Alpheus and Ruth were the most gifted musically.[20] Alpheus studied voice in Chicago, toured the nation with the Mendelssohn Quartet of Cincinnati after graduation, went on to further study in New York, and eventually settled there and sang professionally. Ruth's singing was always in demand at church and civic events. She became a homemaker, while Archie, three years older than Frank, was the star farmer. Anne and Bert went on to become college professors, Linn became a farmer, and Arthur worked in a variety of occupations, including farming.

The Atlanta Fair was the town's most important annual event, featuring exhibitions, horse races, and scores of competitions. From the fair results come the first records of Frank's artistic skills. He won two blue ribbons in 1897, when he was 16 years old, for a portrait in charcoal and a pencil drawing. In later years he would pick up first- and second-place awards for work in pencil, oils, charcoal, crayon, and watercolor, with landscapes, portraits, still lifes, and casts dominating his entries.

Frank occasionally showed these skills in other ways. A favorite Applegate family story concerns the time he molded the form of Icy Frost (his sister Mabel's friend and daughter of Jack) on a sandbar along Sugar Creek. A township resident heading home after a long evening in one of Atlanta's saloons is said to have seen the sculpture, exclaimed, "My God, it's a dead woman," and scurried off as fast as his legs could carry him.[21] As the incident indicates, Frank loved a good joke. His brother Archie's daughter, Dorothy Morse, remembered him as a prankster, and decades later in Santa Fe he was still playing practical jokes.[22]

Frank displayed an array of talents early in his life. In a family of storytellers, singers, and linguists, Frank was all of those and an artist besides. "Originality is one of his strongest characteristics," the *Atlanta Argus* said of him early on. Nephew Albert Hieronymus recalled, "He dominated family gatherings—he had to defer to Alpheus and Ruth in singing, but to no one in storytelling." By his teen years, Frank had made it clear he did not intend to spend his life on the farm. "From the beginning he ignored some sibling mutterings," Dorothy Morse recalled. "I think he avoided farm work as much as possible. Naturally, that did not go over well with those who were stuck with it." Yet, as his nephew Thomas Hieronymus heard it, Frank worked faster than any of the others, once he put his mind to it.[23]

At 6-foot-4 and with feet so large they drew comment, it seemed Frank had somehow been sent to the wrong family. A.A. was 5-foot-10 and wore a size 5-1/2 shoe when he could find it, and he was as tall as any of his children except Frank.[24] Dorothy Morse remembered Frank as long, lanky, and loose of limb, slow-moving and speaking with a drawl, which is common in rural Illinois. When Atlanta High School formed its first football team in the fall of 1901, Arthur started at quarterback and Frank at left guard.[25]

Frank graduated from Atlanta High School in May 1902, when he was 21 years old. Such late graduations were not uncommon in those days, for children frequently started school at a late age, and boys took leaves of absence from school to help on the family's or a relative's farm.[26]

In June Frank passed the state scholarship exam, and in another two months he was off to the University of Illinois. Frank would return home often and eagerly but never stayed very long, for his ambitions quickly stretched far beyond his hometown.

Endnotes

[1] *History of Logan County, Illinois*, 1886, 697. "Applegate Family" and "John Linn and Ann Marie (Westerinen) Applegate," *History of Logan County, Illinois*, 1982, 163.
Some of the information in this chapter comes from "Recollections of A.A. Applegate," by Albert Applegate (Frank Applegate's brother), a typewritten essay on file at the Atlanta, Illinois, Public Library. Recollections are written in two parts; Part 1 is an insert on Halstead Applegate, while Part 2 is Bert's recollections of his father. Other information on the family, in this and subsequent chapters, comes from family members, especially Gretchen Hieronymus Beall, daughter of Frank Applegate's sister Ruth, whom the authors interviewed numerous times from 1992-1999.
[2] Applegate, A.A., "Old Time Talks by an Old Timer," *Lincoln (Ill.) Times-Courier*, Jan. 14, 1905, 2. This would have been in 1858, when Lincoln and Douglas were opponents for a seat in the U.S. Senate and were stumping all around the state. The historic Lincoln-Douglas debates were but a few of the many times the two men spoke together that year. Lincoln, Illinois, was named for Abraham Lincoln in 1853.
[3] Ibid.
[4] *History of Logan County, Illinois*, 1886, 697. "Applegate Family" and "John Linn and Ann Marie (Westerinen) Applegate" in *History of Logan County, Illinois*, 1982, 163.
[5] Beall written notes, Applegate Papers.
[6] *Lincoln (Ill.) Daily Courier*, Jan. 1, 1907, 5. Applegate, Albert, "Recollections of A.A. Applegate," 2:12.
[7] *Lincoln (Ill.) Daily Courier*, April 22, 1898, 6; July 29, 1898, 6; Jan. 13, 1899.
[8] Birthdates as recorded in the family Bible, in a letter dated July 1984 from Roberta Grace Applegate to the Atlanta Public Library, inserted in Applegate, Albert. The Bible is in a family member's possession. Frank's birth year is listed erroneously as 1882 in many reference books. His obituary in the *Atlanta Argus*, Feb. 20, 1931, 1, verifies the above date.
[9] *Lincoln (Ill.) Daily Courier*, Dec. 23, 1902.

CHAPTER 1:
A
FARMER'S
SON

[10] *Lincoln (Ill.) Daily Courier,* Dec. 23, 1898, 7. Applegate, Albert, 2:2, 3.

[11] Applegate, Albert, 2:8-10. Authors' interviews with Gretchen Beall.

[12] Applegate, Albert, 2:1. Beall written notes.

[13] Applegate, Albert, 2:1-2.

[14] Applegate, Albert, 2:4.

[15] *Atlanta (Ill.) Argus,* July 29, 1897.

[16] Applegate, Albert, 2:6-7.

[17] *Lincoln (Ill.) Daily Courier,* May 21, 1904, 6.

[18] Richard Applegate to Gretchen Beall, Jan. 17, 1988, Applegate Papers.

[19] *Atlanta (Ill.) Argus,* July 6, 1900. *Lincoln (Ill.) Daily Courier,* Feb. 12, 1904, 3. Beall written notes.

[20] "Notable Family Reunion," *Atlanta (Ill.) Argus,* Sept. 14, 1928, 4.

[21] Family members offer several versions of this story. This one comes from Richard Applegate (son of Frank's brother Linn) as written in the article "Richard Paul Applegate," in *History of Logan County, Illinois,* 1982, 163-164.

[22] Morse, "Memories of Uncle Frank," 3, Applegate Papers.

[23] *Atlanta (Ill.) Argus,* Feb. 19, 1915, 4. Beall written notes. Morse, 6. Interview with Thomas Hieronymus.

[24] Applegate, Albert, 2:3. Authors' interviews with Gretchen Beall.

[25] Morse, 1. *Atlanta (Ill.) Argus,* Oct. 11, 1901.

[26] Frank may have been embarrassed by his advanced age. His enrollment records at the University of Illinois give his year of birth as 1883, and as mentioned above, many biographical references place his birthdate as 1882.

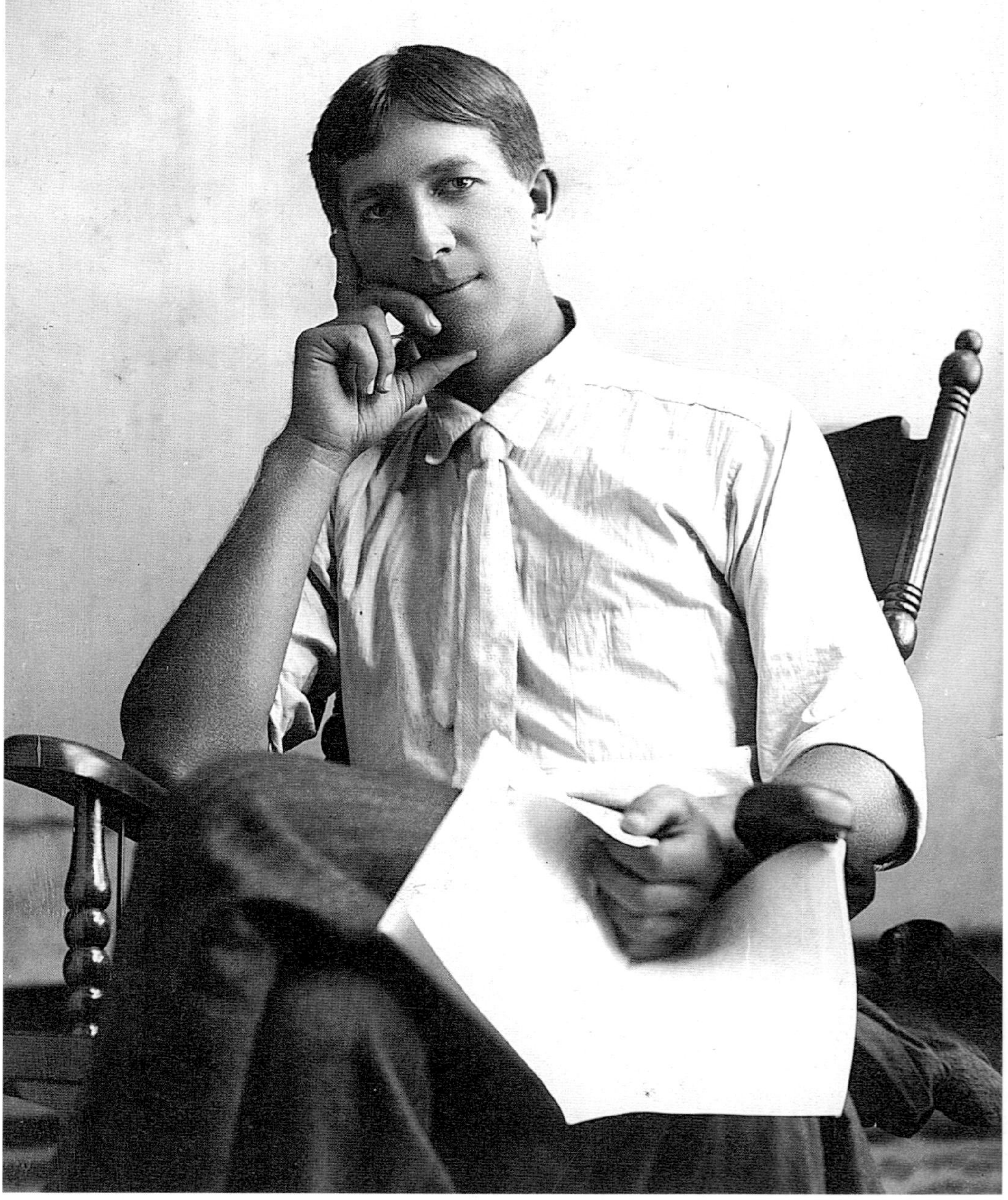

Frank Applegate, ca. 1906-1907. Applegate Papers.

2 'Genius' in the Making

Frank Applegate arrived at the University of Illinois in the fall of 1902 with 50 cents in his pocket. He saw a picture of the university president in a bookstore, bought some plaster of Paris, made a bas-relief in the likeness of the president, sold it, and was in business making more.[1]

So began his career as a sculptor, and soon he was busy studying "art designing and literature."[2] He also played on the freshman football team, which won the class championship. According to family stories, Frank went out for football in the hopes that he would be fed at the training table and save himself money. Although he never did make the training table, he continued to play on the football team in 1903 and part of 1904.

During his first three years, Applegate's studies included eight art and design courses, among them freehand drawing, portrait or still life in oil, and modeling. He applied some of these skills outside the classroom by contributing cartoonish drawings to the school yearbook, *The Illio* (p. 19).[3]

In 1904 his work was exhibited at the Louisiana Purchase Exposition in St. Louis. The State of Illinois' exhibit in the Palace of Education "was one of the most extensive, embracing every line of work in the public schools, normal institutes, colleges, and universities." The University of Illinois' College of Literature and Arts had its own exhibit area, and within it the department of art and design offered one of the most elaborate and attractive displays.[4]

It is likely that Applegate attended the fair, which would have been a broadening experience for a college student. The display of arts and crafts outside the college section was quite impressive. "For the first time at an international exhibition, the applied arts, or 'original products of Art workmanship' as they were described in the catalog, were segregated from mechanically made goods. ... Within the halls of the [Palace of Arts] 'applied' arts were treated as equal with 'fine' arts." The Palace of Arts housed 1,100 examples of art workmanship, including 400 examples of porcelain, pottery, and tiles.[5] Additionally, the exposition showcased the Cliff Dwellers, the Zunis, and the Hopis of Walpi, with whose work Applegate would become intimately familiar in later years.

While some family and historical references indicate that he majored in architecture, Applegate graduated in 1906 with a bachelor's degree in "general course" from the College of Liberal Arts. He did take three general engineering drawing courses called "elements of drafting," and one of his art and design classes was architectural modeling. He also did "considerable work in the cement laboratories" while at the university, and during his final year there, the school began providing instruction in ceramic technology.[6]

Other classes included rhetoric, advanced newspaper writing, physiology and physics, zoology, history, botany, education, and six language courses. By the time he graduated, Applegate had studied French, Italian, Greek, Spanish, and German, and he had already studied Latin in high school.[7] He seemed to be preparing himself for a trip to, or perhaps a life in, Europe, and there he headed.

His first stop was Paris. In December 1906, A.A. Applegate reported: "We publish the following out of respect for the boy's father: Frank Applegate left home the eighth of this month for a tour of Europe. He goes via New Orleans, from whence he sails for Italy, where he will tarry several months studying art and the language of the country. He will visit Spain, Germany, and France for the purpose of getting a better knowledge of the different languages. He expects to be away two or three years."[8]

Applegate studied at Academie Julian, the largest and most popular private art school in Paris. Founded in 1868 by a minor painter and former wrestler named Rodolphe Julian, "the academy catered to foreigners, who often had trouble getting into the École des Beaux-Arts, the official government school. ... (It) offered a certain freedom from regimentation—a freedom that was decidely absent at the École des Beaux-Arts."[9] Taos, New Mexico, artists Ernest Blumenschein, Bert Phillips, and Joseph Henry Sharp were among earlier students at the academy.

Applegate provided a vivid picture of the Academie Julian in a letter that appeared in the *Atlanta (Illinois) Argus*:

> This particular studio is situated about half way down an old, narrow, crooked street running off the main boulevard in the Latin quarter and is entered through a large doorway and court. The school consists of several large rooms, each able to accommodate a hundred students or more. The walls are frescoed with caricatures and hung with canvasses and the shelves filled with clay and plaster studies done by ambitious students in the past hundred years. In the room where I work there are two models posing, one for the class in painting and one for the class in sculpture. At present, there are about 50 students working in the two classes. ...

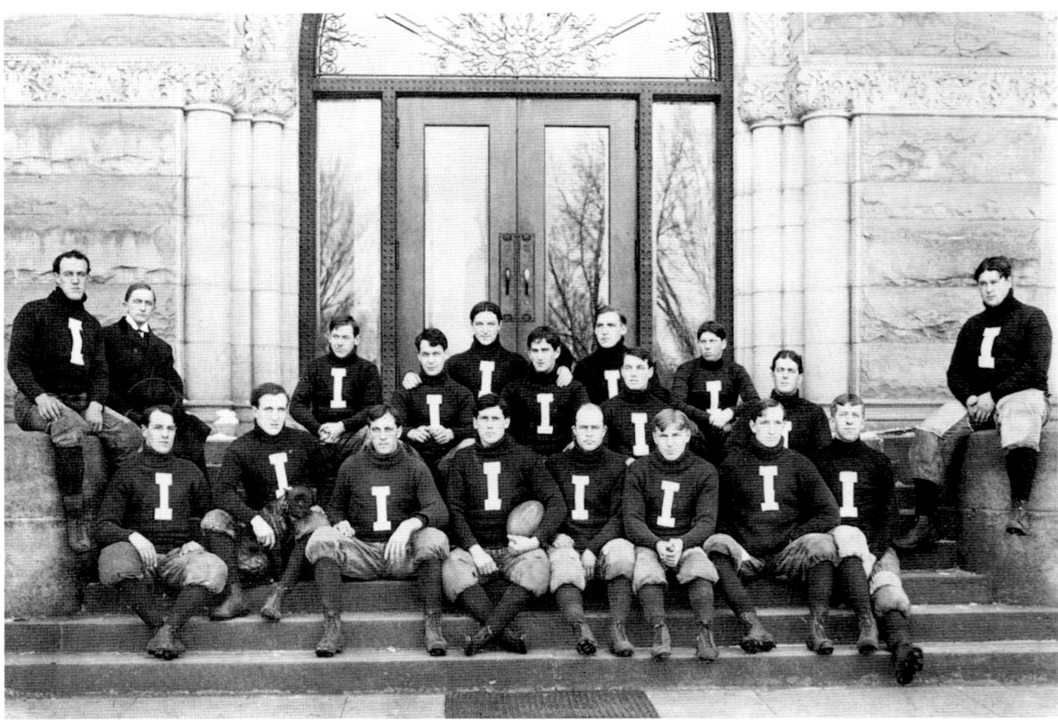

1903 University of Illinois Football Team from 1904 *Illio*. Frank Applegate is seated second from the right. Photograph courtesy of the University of Illinois.

When I came into the room the first morning every one gave me a long, steady stare, then they gathered around me and most of them in a very haughty manner shook hands with me but never speaking a single word more than if I'd been a wooden image. ... As the day passed I could hear groans and all sorts of grunts, etc., around me but I was not molested any more. The next morning was the same only everyone was a trifle more impudent if anything and soon there were more groans, then mumbling, then everything that

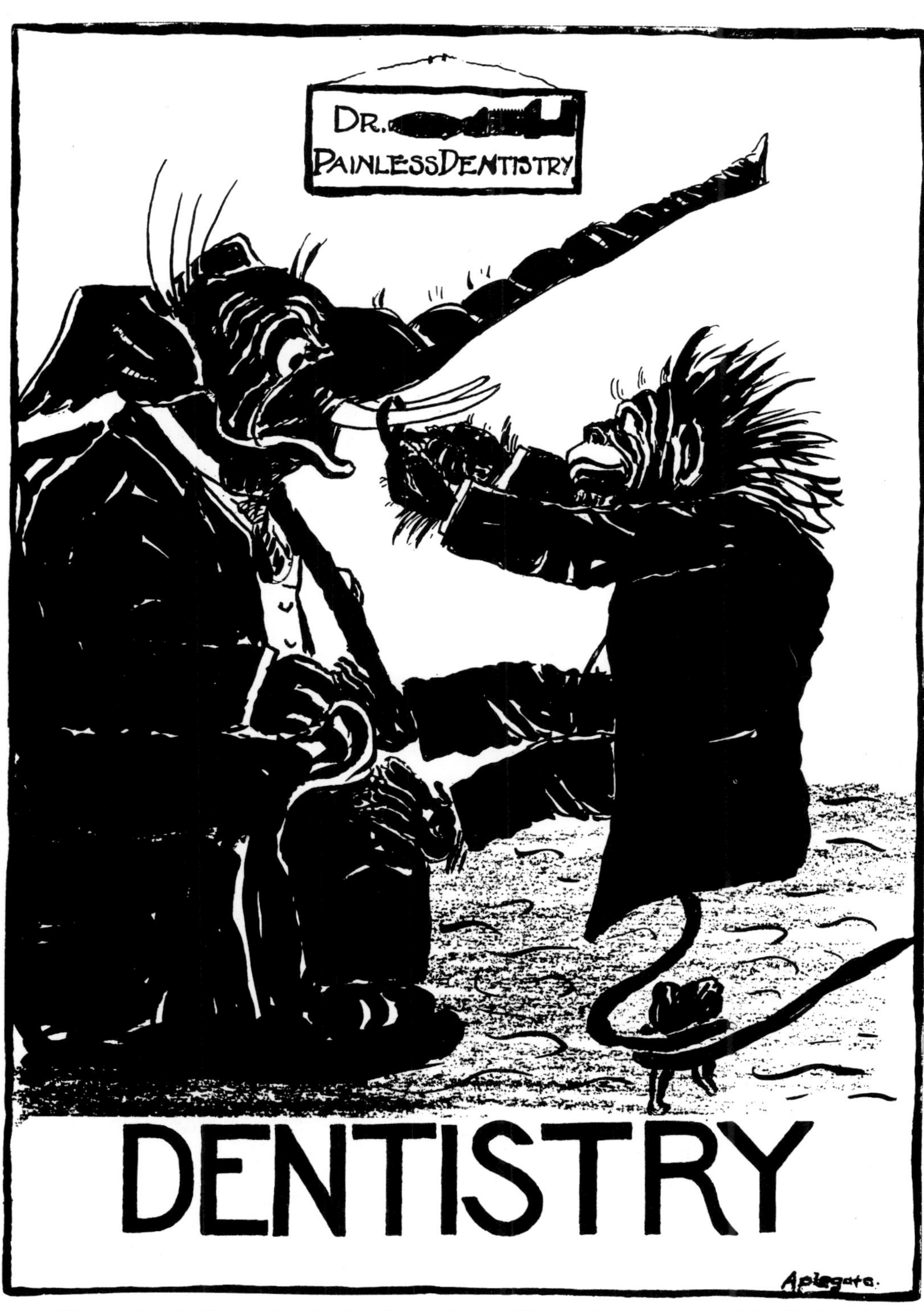

1906 *Illio* yearbook illustration by Frank Applegate. Illustration courtesy of the University of Illinois.

CHAPTER 2:
'GENIUS'
IN THE
MAKING

could be employed to make a noise was put in to commission, then a hiss and all was silent again and suddenly some fellow said "a boire" (drink) "Je soif" (I'm thirsty). … Then the whole lot started for me. When they got a little too close, I yelled "a boire." At that they gave a shout and gathering up whatever they could find in their haste, threw it over the two models and carrying them on their shoulders made for the cafe on the corner, yelling and singing. … they made themselves at home and raised all the rough house possible till they had their drink. Then back again they went to the studio, carrying the models. I was left behind to settle the bill. …

Back at the studio everything was all changed. Now every one came around to shake hands with me and tell me he was my friend and so forth. All were jolly and even our model wanted me to kiss her. But aside from the little exuberance of spirits the students indulge in, there is a great deal of serious work done.[10]

Frank's letters home frequently appeared in the *Atlanta Argus*. Although he was a recent college graduate not long removed from the central Illinois prairie, he was also 25 years old and well prepared to explore the world. "So long as a fellow is here he ought to see it all," he wrote.[11] As a result, his letters often foreshadowed themes he approached in some of his later artwork.

While he sometimes wrote humorous travelogues about European farming techniques and tourist attractions, he also sent back descriptions that painted Europe much differently than it appeared on postcards:

Paris shelters everything. … [It] is the home of the very highest civilization and the lowest. It is the combination of the best and the rottenest. There are places so low and dirty that the word hell conveys but a very faint idea of this loathsomeness and horror. …

When honest, respectable Paris goes to sleep the slums pour from its holes and dens, its population crawls around seeking what they may devour. The thieves and robbers of Paris are the most dangerous in the world. … They hunt in small packs, slipping up on their victims and attacking them from behind. I've stayed out three whole nights making the rounds of the worst districts of Paris to see for myself how the underworld lives. More than once I have run across these "Apaches" but wearing an old cap with a handkerchief around my neck and keeping in the shadow I did not look unlike one of their own number. Frenchmen have told me I was a fool for doing it and that nothing would tempt them to enter those places after 11 o'clock p.m. However I've sat in their cafes and talked with them and drank their wine. Every morning with a fellow's coffee is served up news where they have killed and robbed a half-dozen people.

But to me this element of the slum life does not appeal in such a tragic manner as the extreme poverty and filthiness of the inhabitants. Near the great markets is one of the dirtiest slums. There is one house on a side street where over one thousand people pass the night. They get a bowl of soup and a place to lie down for 4 cents. An old mouldy looking place it is and the people lying around on the floor resemble bundles of rags. They not only sleep on the upstair floors but down in the damp earthy cellars and the odors that come from those rooms would do credit to a breath from hell. But many poor wretches in the slums are too poor to even get lodgings in this hole or other similar ones and are obliged to pass the night lying on the streets under carts or leaning against some wall. …

I went into another large cafe about 2 o'clock a.m. The air was so foul I could hardly enter. Here they serve only the vilest liquor at 2 cents a glass. Old women were sitting at the tables with their heads full of absinthe cursing and howling in language too foul to even repeat in thought. Old men were too dirty to describe, grinning at the women. Everything was indescribably miserable and awful. I went out of here and turned up a side street where even the pavement stunk and things like dead snakes seemed to mash under my feet. Old gray rats scampered everywhere diving in old drain holes or else looking boldly at me as I passed. In another hole in this quarter, old men were assorting cigar and cigarette stubs. No sooner does a fellow enter one of these places than he is surrounded by half a dozen old hags, who beg for cigarettes or snatch the stub out of his mouth and go on smoking it. There are also dance halls and other vile resorts worse however than in most American cities and also the people who frequent them are much younger but all have that pale, pasty, dirty complexion that marks the wretched awful poor. The climax of all things horrible may be seen at the morgue down back of Notre Dame. For here day by day many of the habitues of those horrible resorts are carried. … If you want to know how the lowest keep from starving go along the streets early in the morning when the garbage boxes and cans are set out to wait for the carts and see the poor fighting with the dogs for bones from which they can gnaw a little gristle or marrow, or old scraps of dry mouldy bread and other food.[12]

It is obvious from this chilling narrative that Applegate was developing a social conscience far beyond the impressions of his bucolic youth. He also wrote of the poverty in Naples, where "a cigar or cigarette stump never any more than strikes the ground until it is pounced upon by some poor, barefooted wretch." He saw three bloody fights, including a knife fight, in Rotterdam.[13] Dark images such as these would haunt him and return to his thoughts when he became a professional sculptor.

Applegate's sense of the importance of heritage and of preserving heritage was also apparent. From Rome he wrote:

It takes a fellow with a pretty strong imagination to re-build the old Roman forum to his satisfaction in all its original glory. There are a few old columns to mark the position of the temple of Castor and Pollux, a pile of brick and marble to show where the rostrum stood, a pedestal showing where Caesar said "et tu Brute," and old

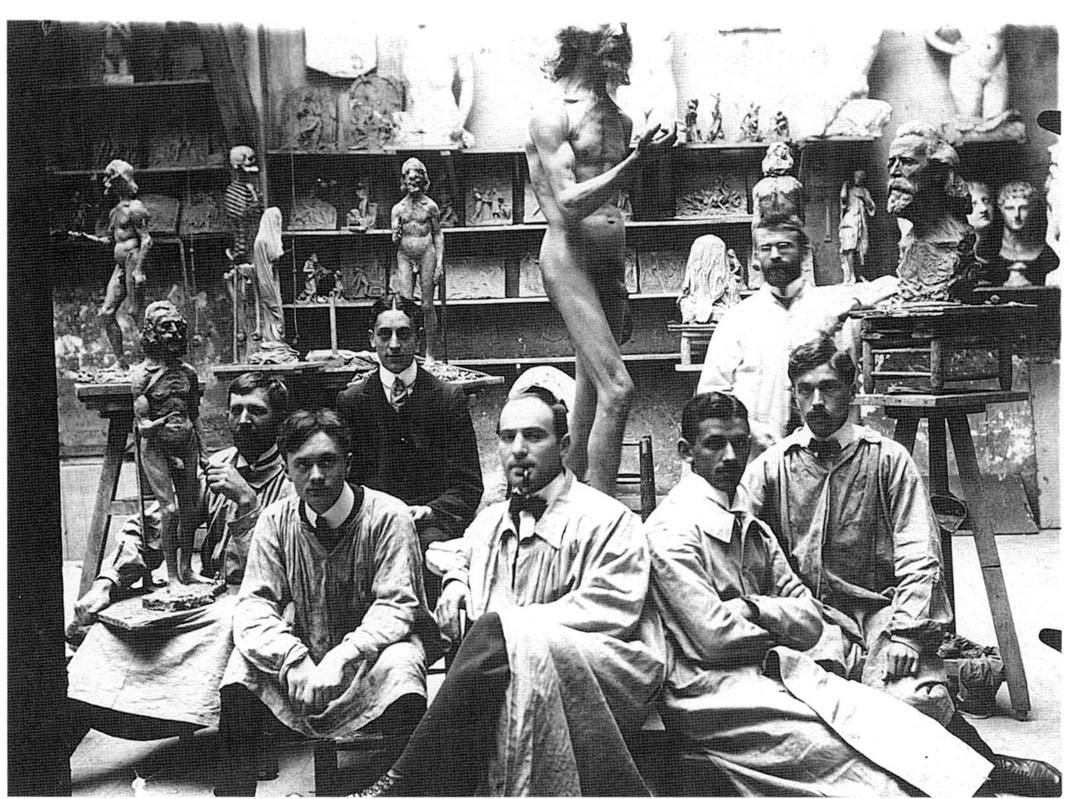

Frank Applegate, far left, in a class at the Academie Julian. Applegate Papers.

capitals, pieces of marble, broken arches, mosaics, and columns showing where magnificent buildings once stood. On going through the old forum on a fine day with the sunshine lighting up these old ruins and reflecting from the old paving stones on which the Caesars once walked, a fellow feels rather awed.[14]

While Rome lived up to his expectations, he was disappointed with what he found in the French countryside:

> The people seem to know nothing about the early history of their country. Almost everywhere are old ruins dating back many centuries, but the common people know absolutely nothing about their history and do not take the least interest in it. At first I visited every cemetery I saw, expecting to find much that would be of interest on the monuments and stones, but to my surprise but few of them were more than one hundred years old. One day I asked a fellow where his great grandfather was buried, and he said "up there on the hill where you see that vineyard." The fellow built his house out of the tombstones, and now he drinks wine raised over the graves of our fathers.

He traveled from Paris to Nice on foot, delighting at the reactions of the French people toward him:

> It was better than a circus to see the people stare at me as I would pass through a sleepy little mountain town singing in English at the top of my voice. The country people here seldom see a foreigner, and at once spot me as a German. I have been arrested about once a day. When they call for my papers I usually show them a copy of the *Argus* which I carry with me, next my sketch book, in which I have a number of sketches of places of interest. Then they think I am a German spy. I usually laugh and coax them out of the notion, but one fellow got me late in the evening and locked me up for the night. The next morning when I was taken before the chief he was profuse in his apologies and insisted on paying for my breakfast.

The weather was stormy and miserable as he walked through the Rhone Valley toward Nice:

> To add to the discomfort of my trip, my feet got sore and my shoes went to pieces. I began to try at every little town to buy a pair, but fellows with feet of such liberal proportions as mine seem to be scarce in France. I finally found two torture chambers that would go over my feet. Certainly the Spanish inquisition never invented anything more cruel than those French shoes. It's no wonder the French people are deceminating [*sic*]. When I reached Nice I had eleven blisters on one foot.[15]

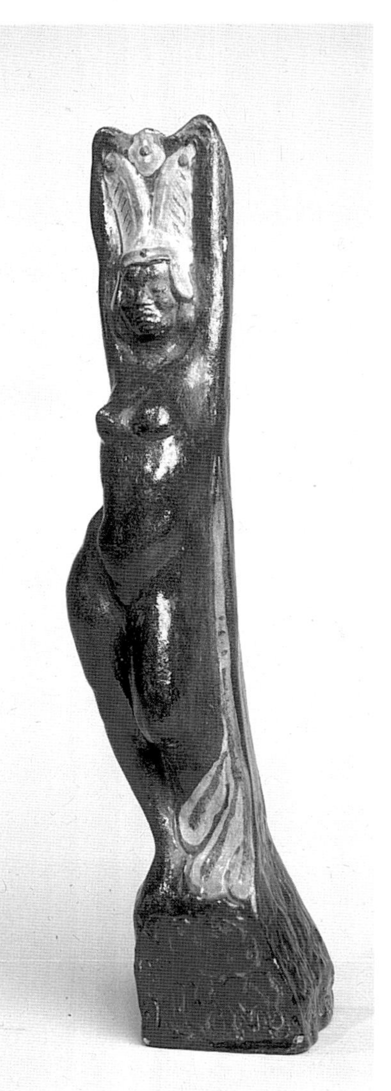

Ceramic figure. Collection of Gerald Peters Gallery. Photograph courtesy of Gerald Peters Gallery, Santa Fe.

According to oft-repeated family stories, Applegate traded artwork for food and lodging as he traveled. He mentioned such in a letter from Rome, saying he had arrived there with just over a dollar to his name and in three weeks had made about $10.

"The first day in Rome, I felt a little blue," he wrote, "but the next day I made a sketch of St. Peter's and two or three nuns and some Russian Jews staying at the same inn where I do immediately got interested with the result that most of their countrymen in Rome, including their Ambassador and Consul, have some of my sketches. I have been doing very well while my agents, the Jews, have been living like millionaires and are trying to get me to stay in Rome all summer."[16]

Instead, he returned to France, then went on to Holland, Belgium, and England. While the *Argus* originally reported Applegate expected to be gone for two to three years, he returned home in August. A.A. Applegate wrote: "Our wandering boy pulled up at home the last of the week, whiskers and all. He expects to be at home until after the Atlanta fair. Mr. Applegate will teach art the coming year at an art school in Trenton, N.J."[17]

Applegate had taken a position as the head of the modeling department at the School of Industrial Arts in Trenton. Dr. Frank Forrest Frederick, who was a professor of art and design at the University of Illinois when Applegate was enrolled there, was the school's director and induced him to take the position. The *Trenton (N.J.) Sunday Advertiser* noted Applegate's employment and stated he "studied modeling and its part in the industrial supremacy of European products" during his trip abroad. The article added, "He has been very successful with portrait busts and expects to take commissions here."[18]

Frank's shortened stay in Europe may have been due in part to his father's increasingly poor health. Although A.A. never hinted of it in his columns, his health had begun to fail by the early 1900s. "From the time I was 12 or 13 years old [1901 or 1902] we could see the beginning of Father's failing health," Bert Applegate recalled.

He stilll rose at 4 o'clock, but he tired more easily and had to rest more frequently. But an interesting side of him developed. He shaved his beard, trimmed his mustache, and bought a stick of mustache wax which he applied each Sunday. Mother kept him dressed in white shirts, too, and he wore his hat at a jaunty angle. It seems, as I look back on it now, as if he were defying time and ill health. We boys did more of the actual labor with the fruit, with Father assigning us our duties. ... By the time Linn was graduated from high school, Father had discontinued raising so much berry fruit. ... Sometimes at night, Father's feet and ankles would be badly swollen, and it fell to me to try to rub the swelling away, rubbing away from the feet. ... We tried to persuade Father to rest more, but he seemed to be driving himself to have things about the farm in order. Mother, of course, knew better than we children, what was in father's mind, and although she kept up a cheerful front, I know her heart was breaking.[19]

Finally, in October 1907, A.A. Applegate publicly acknowledged that he was seriously ill. "We perhaps owe an explanation to our *Courier* friends for our continued silence," he wrote.

It is not that we have forgotten the importance of the Eminence news nor our obligations to our paper, but it is simply a case of the "spirit being willing but the flesh is weak." For nearly 60 years we have met in the busy arena of Eminence life nearly every form of labor and care and responsibility that usually confronts the small farmer who is endeavoring to maintain a family that even Teddy [the prolific Roosevelt] would respect at least for numerical attainments and until the last two months we had never lowered our arm in the fight.

...

All of a sudden we felt like an old washtub with half the hoops off and the bottom dropped out. ... Wearily we wended our way to the doctor's private office. We will omit the pleasant odor of drugs that met our nostrils and the cheering sight of the bright cold steel instruments that adorned the walls and tables. Suffice it to say we were soon laid out on the operating table like a "stiff" in the dissecting room and the learned man with an instrument with long hooks which he put in his ears proceeded to listen to our "internal workings." …

Finally after other processes too numerous to remember we were told that our affliction was not consumption, kidney trouble, indigestion, paralysis, nor even fits, nor dozens of other things we had imagined but simply "nervous prostration." All we needed was complete rest physically and mentally and careful diet. Now we are looking for some smart man to tell us how a fellow with a wife and nine kids is to attain complete rest. But already we are dealing better and rather enjoy being waited on. Our Irish blood is again bringing out the bloom on our nose and we have a growing hope that some "sweet day" we'll make good.[20]

A.A. felt better only briefly. On November 13, 1907, the *Lincoln Daily Courier* reported that A.A.'s condition was very serious and his children had been sent for. "There was no definite time we could say Father's illness began. He simply became weaker by the day," Bert wrote. "Finally, Aunt Lina Bruner came to help care for him, and Anne came home from the university for a few weeks. … She, Aunt Lina, and I took turns fanning Father as sometimes he struggled for breath. Then, as Anne gave over the fan to Aunt Lina he whispered, 'In about two minutes I'll be gone.' And he was."[21]

Albert A. Applegate died on November 16, with the cause listed as "an affection of the heart." Although the *Atlanta Argus* seldom ran pictures, his obituary was accompanied by a reproduction of a relief cast Frank had made of him.[22]

Frank returned to Trenton, where he only recently had started working at the School of Industrial Arts. His new boss and former instructor, Frank Forrest Frederick, proved a superb administrator

and publicist, and the school enrollment grew from 100 students in 1906 to 454 in 1911. By 1909 Frederick also had increased the faculty from eight members to 18. Frederick was an accomplished landscape painter whose work was displayed nationally even before he left the University of Illinois. He published many articles and several books on art-related subjects, including architectural drawing, perspective, and plaster casting. Before assuming his post in Trenton, Frederick had spent a year touring industrial arts schools in France and England. He was adamant that art should be inclusive and studied by the masses. Speaking of Trenton, he once said: "It is true that we are not, as a city, as much interested in painting and sculpture as some of us wish, but considering the question broadly, it is safe to say that the people of Trenton are artistic. Art is not confined to painting and sculpture; it has to do with everything we produce or use." Frank Applegate must have been listening, for he adopted this credo early on. Applegate paid tribute to Frederick by making a cast relief of him. He showed the portrait, along with the cast relief of his father, at his first major exhibition, the Pennsylvania Academy of the Fine Arts spring exhibition in February 1908.[23]

In 1908 Trenton was a city of more than 90,000 where, as Applegate wrote shortly after he arrived, "the Italians grind street organs and sell bananas and peanuts. The Hebrews run the clothing store, the Germans run the saloons and butcher shops, the negroes clean the streets and do the other duty [sic] work while the Americans do anything that comes along that will help them get along whoever or whatever it may be."[24]

For someone interested in ceramics, Trenton of the early 1900s offered unlimited opportunities. It was one of the centers of potterymaking in the United States, with about 50 potteries in 1911. The area along the Delaware River, like many others in the state, boasted a variety of different clays suitable for potterymaking. In 1907 Trenton's potteries produced more than $30 million worth of pottery. It was first among New Jersey cities, and only Ohio surpassed

New Jersey in pottery production.[25] The School of Industrial Arts offered both vocational and artistic training, and the potteries sent their employees to study at the school.

The early 1900s were characterized by an awakening interest nationally in pottery as an art form. At this time art schools such as the School of the Art Institute of Chicago and the Pennsylvania Museum School of Industrial Arts began offering classes in throwing, glazing, and china and underglaze painting. In 1898 the innovative ceramicist Charles F. Binns became the director of the Trenton School of Technical Science and Art (later the School of Industrial Arts). "Binns spurned the painting of decorative designs on ceramic bodies. As an alternative, he advanced the 'purest' school, in which the 'fire itself was the decorator.'"[26] Although Binns moved on to Alfred University in 1900, seven years before Applegate arrived in Trenton, Applegate adopted the ideas Binns championed and spent many hours experimenting with various clays and perfecting glazes.

Binns and other artist-potters also supported the Arts and Crafts movement, which had its beginnings in England with the teachings of John Ruskin and William Morris in the mid- and late 1800s. The movement united the fine and applied arts by touting the superiority of handcrafted pottery, furniture, glassware, metalwork, and other artifacts over factory-made objects. Morris aimed to create design firms dedicated to the principles of the medieval craft guilds in the hopes that "the emphasis on the individual craftsman would bring about the reforms necessary to an overly industrialized society."[27] Arts and Crafts furnishings were showcased at the 1904 Louisiana Purchase Exposition in St. Louis. Applegate soon donned the mantle of Arts and Crafts, and theories similar to those of Morris would guide many of his actions when he later worked with Indians and Hispanics in New Mexico.

While commercial firms such as Cincinnati's Rookwood Pottery produced exquisite examples of art pottery at this time, a committed group of artist-potters were setting to work in private studios.

Many of them also taught, and secure employment as teachers contributed to their artistic freedom and financial stability. These ceramic artists developed innovative approaches to the medium, expressing themselves through clay and glaze, as Binns advocated, rather than through decorative painting.[28]

Applegate became one of these artist-potters. The School of Industrial Arts proved ideally matched to his ambitions, at least at the start. His schedule afforded him the opportunity to be both artist and teacher, with mornings free for his own pottery and ceramic work and afternoons and evenings devoted to his classwork in freehand drawing, modeling, and ornament.[29] The location gave him ready access to a variety of clays, and he worked almost entirely with the local material.

Applegate quickly set about installing a first-rate ceramics production center and coordinating exhibitions of his students' and his own work. A new kiln was installed at the school in 1908 and debuted with an exhibition attended by local ceramics experts. "The work in ceramics was commented on very favorably," a newspaper reported. "All the art objects made by the students at that time were fired in the local plant of the Lenox Inc. Co. With the new kiln, the firing will be under the direct supervision of Instructor Applegate, and the varied stages of finishing will be studied by students."[30]

A few months later a newspaper reported on the modeling department: "Workmen and youths employed in the pottery trades are beginning to look into and appreciate the work the school is accomplishing in advancing its students. … Instructor Frank G. Applegate has been visiting all the potteries and machine shops explaining, at the request of employers, the results attained in the school."[31]

Applegate's fellow faculty members included several renowned painters. R. Sloan Bredin, director of the life class, was linked to the New Hope, Pennsylvania, school of American impressionism and best known for his portraiture and landscape paintings. In 1908 he painted a portrait of Applegate that was shown at the National Academy of Design in New

York.[32] H.R. "Henry" MacGinnis was known for his landscape work and portraiture, and New Hope impressionist Daniel Garber also taught at the school for a while.

Applegate completed his first year of teaching in May 1908, and the *Trenton Sunday Advertiser* reported that during the summer vacation he would be "visiting the Western country for a long rest. He will also work on some models for next year's work."[33] He spent the summer in Atlanta, Illinois (considered the West), and returned to Trenton with a bride.

Alta Bertha Chenoweth was working as Atlanta's librarian when she agreed to marry Frank Applegate. Little is known of their courtship, but she was the close girlhood friend of Edna Verry, who had married Frank's brother Archie in 1902. The Chenoweth family was well regarded throughout the area. Alta's father, Dr. Alfred W. Chenoweth, was a Civil War veteran, a dentist, and an optician. He held various municipal offices including alderman and mayor.[34] Alta's mother, Agnes, was one of Atlanta's first professional photographers.

Although Alta and Frank were about the same age, Alta completed high school three years before he did. She was active in school and church activities, a member of the Atlanta Women's Club and a sought-after singer and musician. It was she who sang the solo "Jesus Saviour Pilot Me" at A.A. Applegate's funeral. Alta attended Illinois Wesleyan University in Bloomington and completed the teachers' course in 1905.[35] The couple married on August 25, 1908, and soon after settled in Trenton.

Frank Frederick was an enthusiastic supporter of the arts, and in 1908 he and others on the school faculty, including Applegate, formed the Arts Society of Trenton. The society's goals were to provide a forum for the discussion of matters of art, including education and the integration of art into civic undertakings. Frederick also convinced Applegate and others to help him organize an exhibition of 20 paintings by celebrated American artists (including Edward Potthast and Albert Groll), an innovative undertaking for the working-class city. Visitors paid 10 cents a ballot to vote for their favorites, with the money raised going toward purchasing the winning

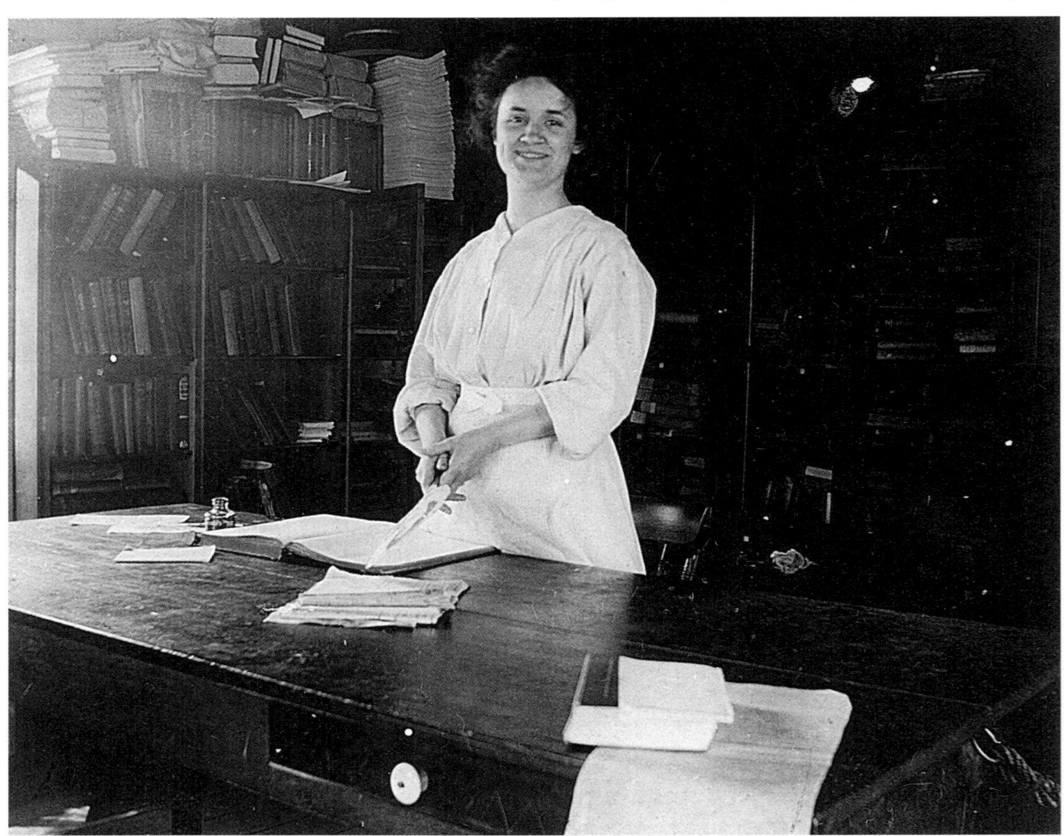

Alta Chenoweth working in the Atlanta Public Library. Applegate Papers.

painting. Unfortunately, the 1,444 ballots cast did not raise enough money to cover expenses for the event. When the exhibition opened in February 1909, a newspaper commented: "It is not intended as any unkind reflection upon Trenton to say that it is a thoroughly commercial city, given over for the most part to the pursuit of success in industrial lines. Trenton has never aspired to become a center of culture, but has remained content hitherto to produce its iron and steel, its wire and rubber, its pottery and oilcloth without concerning itself much with aesthetic ideals."[36]

The relationship between professional potteries and the School of Industrial Arts strengthened as the years progressed. A story in the *Trenton Sunday Advertiser* in May 1911 noted that some manufacturers made attendance at the school compulsory for apprentices because it had become a technical school of science as well as an art school.[37]

Frederick described the school's department of ceramics in a journal article, explaining that students were taught using equipment contributed by the manufacturers of Trenton and the vicinity. The four-year program was conducted in the evenings because all the students enrolled worked in potteries during the day. To receive a diploma, a student was required to produce a "'masterpiece,' in which either artistic quality or technical workmanship, or both, is shown, or … [develop] an invention or a device that will improve some process of clay manufacture." Each man in the class weighed his own mix, did his own preparation, threw or pressed a piece of pottery, prepared it for kiln, and after the burn applied a glaze.[38]

Applegate's stature as an artist sprouted quickly in Trenton. The *Crockery and Glaze Journal* hailed his work with a story headlined, "Marvels of Modeling from Pellets of Clay: Frank Guy Applegate of the Trenton School of Industrial Arts, Astonishes Clay-Modelers by Productions That Evince Positive Genius." The article's proclamation of Applegate's "genius" no doubt strengthened what family members recall was already a healthy ego. The story extrava-

gantly praised Applegate throughout, and offered valuable insight into his methods:

> In the modest little combined studio and workshop of the ceramic department of the Trenton (N.J.) School of Industrial Arts there are being wrought some highly artistic and interesting figures in clay which evoke expressions of surprise and enthusiastic commendation from visitors versed in the art of modeling and designing. Men who are broad-gauged in the world of ceramics—artists who have visited the museums and salons of world famous Europeon cities—unhesitatingly exclaim that never before have they seen plastic clay under the rapid manipulation of the

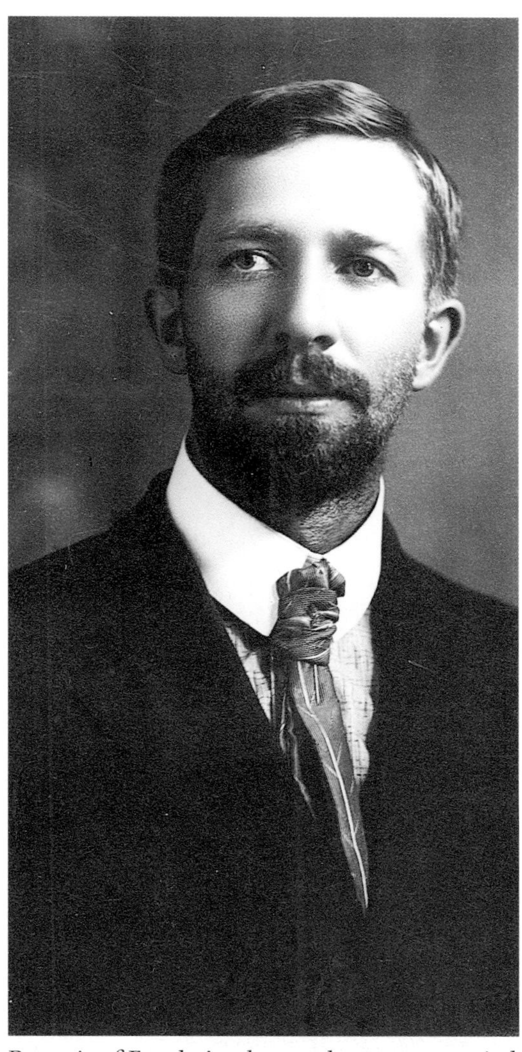

Portrait of Frank Applegate that accompanied an article in the *Crockery and Glaze Journal*, 1909. Applegate Papers.

hands of the modeler evolve into such life-like figures and fascinating groups.

Frank Guy Applegate, practically unknown as yet in the commercial field of modeling, is the artist responsible for the work above referred to. He may be said to be just at the beginning of his career—he is but twenty-seven—and it would seem, from the pieces he has turned out, that if he continues to apply his remarkable talent in the same direction as at present he will some day occupy a niche in the hall of immortal modelers.

Mr. Applegate proceeds along altogether original lines in his work. He uses no instrument nor tool in fashioning his figures, but takes pellets of clay in his hands and after working them up for a time as one might go through the process of softening putty, builds them up little by little. As a masterpiece upon canvas reveals its full beauty to those who behold it a few paces removed, so Mr. Applegate's work presents a softening of outline and a new and indefinable attractiveness when viewed in perspective. It seems almost incredible that an artist could exert with fingers mechanically unaided such complete mastery over soft and yielding clay as does Mr. Applegate.

Modelers in wax resort to use of concealed supports to aid in retaining the pose of a figure or group which they wish to perfect; but Mr. Applegate employs no such aids. A striking example of his success in this regard is present in one of the illustrations ["The Combat," which was pictured]. Two workmen are shown in mortal combat. The right hand of each, grasping a murderous dirk, is held powerless and momentarily inert in the grasp of the other's remaining hand. The disarranged clothes and the strained muscles standing out upon the necks and exposed parts of the bodies of the foemen convey at once to the beholder an idea of deadly furious onslaught. No details calculated to simulate the strenuous activity of the duellists have been overlooked, and yet the gravity-defying posing of the figures presents perhaps the most remarkable aspect of the piece. The bodies of the antagonists—one bearing down upon the other—would seem from sheer weight of the mass of unsupported soft clay to make impossible the successful drying out and firing of the piece. Yet with such finesse has the artist calculated in this regard that here is not even the suggestion of warping or drooping.

"The Derelicts" is the title of a group worked up by hand by Mr. Applegate, and many who have seen his productions of this character regard the work as his masterpiece. Four men, ragged and unkempt, are sitting upon a park bench. One is leaning over with his face buried in his hands; another is reading a paper, while the third is glancing at the sheet and listening attentively to the recital of the news of the day. The fourth derelict, with hat cocked upon the side of his head and hands clasped lazily over his paunch, is dozing peacefully. The attitudes of the men are for all the world such as one may see in the parks of the city any morning when the unemployed sit idly planning for the day that has just begun, or at the noon hour when they gather upon the benches to rest from the morning's wanderings. This group Mr. Applegate has been urged to have placed in the French Salon.[39]

Applegate had seen the slums of New York and much of Europe by the time he crafted "The Derelicts," but he pointed out that the inspiration came when he passed through New Orleans. There he "saw groups of white men, whose jobs had been taken by cheaper negro laborers, lounging despondently in the public squares."[40]

Applegate's interest in depicting this gritty urban reality sprang up at the same time as members of a group called The Eight were invoking the realism of New York City in their own work. Led by painter and teacher Robert Henri and his students John Sloan, William Glackens, Everett Shinn, and George Luks, the group introduced a uniquely American "urban realism" to the canvas. They portrayed people living in slums, sky-scrapers, and tenement buildings, sweaty-browed boxers and working girls. Along with painters Arthur B. Davies, Maurice Prendergast, and Ernest Lawson, the artists exhibited as The Eight at New York's Macbeth Gallery in February 1908, and the show was greeted with strong opinions by visitors and media alike. The exhibition of work by The Eight traveled to Philadelphia for the winter of 1908-09. The sculptures discussed in the *Crockery and Glaze Journal* article indicate Applegate likely attended the show (either in Philadelphia or in New York) and was influenced by it.

In the summer of 1910 Applegate returned to the Academie Julian to study with pre-eminent sculptor and teacher Raoul Charles Verlet, whose work is in the Louvre and Musee du Luxembourg. Verlet's classical sculpture evoked "modern realism in all its glory." Frank and Alta shared a belated, 3-1/2-month-long honeymoon trip to Europe with Alta's sister, Olive Chenoweth, and Frank's sister Anne, who stayed on in Paris to study. The group split up for a time, with Frank and Olive visiting Germany, Holland, Belgium, and France and Anne and Alta journeying to Italy and Switzerland. They met up in Paris, where Applegate reported he was "busy at work now in the Julian academy, modeling from life, while the rest of the party are busy sight seeing."[41] Wherever he went, Applegate collected fodder for stories:

> One day we were loitering about in a tiny village, near Paris, looking for local color, when we saw a sign up on a farmyard gate which read, "Fumier for sale" (understand farmers live in villages). We did not know what fumier was but thought it must be something good to eat. As we were rather hungry I said I'd buy a few sous worth and we'd sample it. I told the man who came to the door in answer to my knock what I wanted, so he came back soon with something done up in a small paper bag.
>
> We were of course very anxious to reach some secluded spot where we could sample its contents and kept sniffing at the bag to see if we could determine what was inside. Being familiar with the odor of the native cheese which is ripened by being buried in the stable a year, I declared for that. Alta said "Rochefort," while Olive simply turned up her nose in a way that meant more than words. Finally we opened the bag and behold its contents! Manure, common, ordinary, such as any farmer in

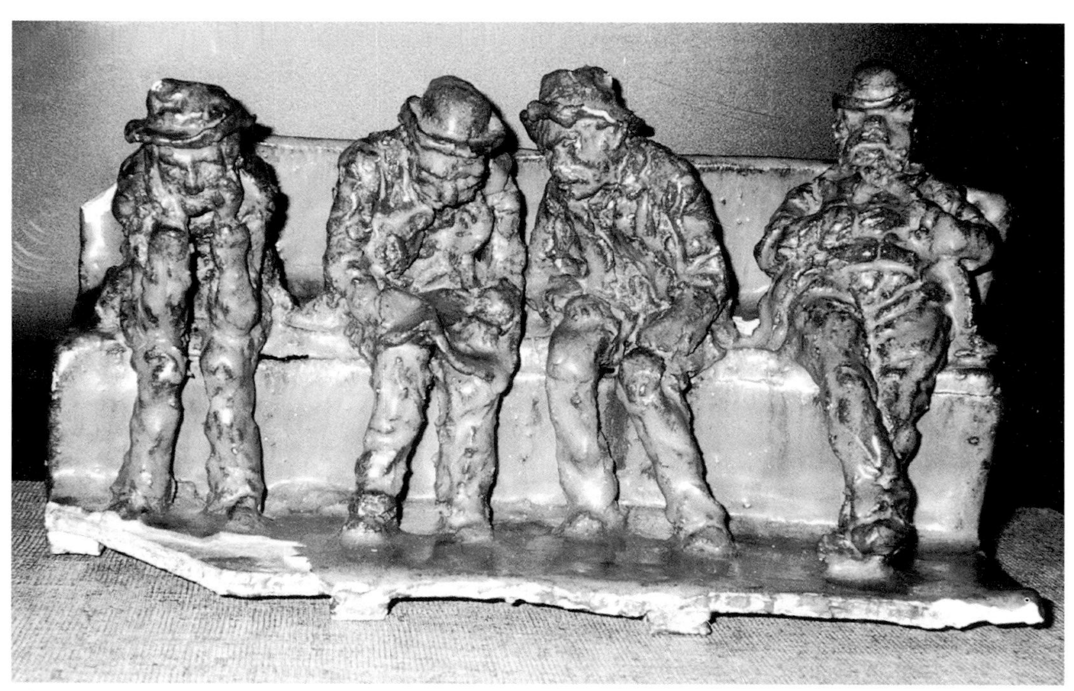

The Derelicts, ceramic. Private collection. Photograph courtesy of the owner.

Illinois spreads so profusely on his fields and thinks nothing of it. Then it suddenly dawned on my mind how they sold it here in France. … Yes, they sell it like we sell sugar, ice cream or oysters.

We had almost a pound of the "precious." What should we do with it? We couldn't eat it. Mrs. A. wanted to abandon it exactly where we discovered its nature. I'd heard my father say it was fine on strawberries, but we didn't have any with us, besides the rest of the party said they preferred cream and sugar and I'm no volunteer. I wished to take it home to Arthur so he could have some of the genuine imported article once, for I had no doubt he'd know how to use it. … [Unable to come up with any alternative,] I dropped the paper and its contents into the hat of a passing beggar and made him rich.[42]

The letters home are full of other tourist stories—about a huge airplane race outside Paris, touring the sewers of the city by boat and electric car, visiting Stratford-on-Avon, watching windmills in Holland, etc. The group traveled to Brussels for the Brussels International exposition, which Frank described as "the poorest sight we've seen since we've been over here."

"It was one grand advertising affair," he wrote, "and in the different exhibits they tried to sell us everything from a Singer sewing machine to a Chinese god. And they still persisted even when I told them we were Esquimaux or that I was Captain Peary and had no use for anything they had."[43]

The highlight of the trip was an excursion on the Rhine, where the tourists were on the lookout for castles. "Soon Olive espied an old glue factory all in ruins and was quite on the point of going into raptures over it when she learned its disgraceful, noxious career so that it needed the ruins of a very fine castle indeed to call forth her enthusiasm a second time. As one bend of the river after another revealed one fine, old castle after the other, they became after a while as common a sight as grain elevators on the I.C.R.R. … The only thing that marred the whole trip was a large sign of

Quaker Oats placed in a conspicuous position below one of the old castles."[44] Applegate's aversion to advertising presaged a cause he would take up later in life, the fight against the proliferation of outdoor advertising.

Not every letter read like a travelogue. At times Applegate moved the tourists to the foreground, such as in this letter, which foreshadows an essay he would write about tourists in the Southwest and their approach to art years later:

It is great sport to be in one of the great galleries like the Louvre and watch a bunch of tourists go by, headed by their energetic guide. There are about eight miles of galleries in the Louvre, and it take a pretty well seasoned bunch of tourists to do it in a half a day in warm weather. We will be standing in one of the picture galleries and all will be tranquil and quiet, with everyone studying their favorite pictures, when hark! in the distance there is a sound like rumbling of thunder, mingled with escaping steam.

Everyone glances around with apprehension. The noise comes nearer. It is now a terrific clatter, mingled with high pitched voices and puffing. Everyone looks terrified. "Bon Dieu, it must be the 'Cooks,'" exclaims someone, and some who would cross a street in front of a dozen oncoming autos or buses sought a place of safety, while the bravest stepped aside and watched the entrance in a fascinated, expectant attitude. Suddenly the cause of the disturbance bursts upon us, the guide in front and the stronger of his flock close behind, while others in all stages of exhaustion lag behind.

Now the guide stops before a renowned picture. "Attention, ladies and gentlemen," he shouts, and those who are nearest crowd around and look up with a "Now what" expression on their faces, while he tells them what they ought to appreciate in the picture. But they only have time to wipe the perspiration from their faces, take two breaths, and make a cross opposite the name of the picture in their guide books before the untiring guide, who has undertaken to conduct the party through the Louvre in three hours, is on his way again.

"What is it," says some of the party, who have just managed to drag themselves up as the guide starts on. "Oh, that picture of Di Vinci's [*sic*]; there it is. Do hurry up and mark it in your book and come on. All you want is to say you've seen it anyway." And so they go stampeding on and finally the last sound of them dies away in the distance like the rumbling of thunder after a storm. All come out from their hiding places and all is once more tranquil and so quiet that the scratching of the sandpaper on the canvas of a painter, who is trying to reproduce an old master, sounds quite out of proportion to the cause.[45]

The point of other stories was more subtle, and illustrate that Applegate had spent years mastering the literary device of the "eavesdropping observer" by the time he came to use it in his books *Native Tales of New Mexico* and *Indian Stories From the Pueblos* in the late 1920s and early 1930s. He began one such story, "In the studio this morning at rest period, I lost five minutes listening to another conversation between the two other American students. After this I am going to take care to sit out of earshot of them or I'll be losing too much time listening to them chatter."[46]

Applegate's studies in Paris introduced him to the forefathers of modern art, revolutionary artists whose work was still unknown in the United States. Most American artists of the early 1900s were grouped in either the academic traditionalist or impressionist schools, and unless one traveled to Europe, one had no opportunity to see the works of Paul Cézanne, Pablo Picasso, Henri Matisse, or other pioneer modernists. But several American artists, gallery owners, and collectors were about to change that. First came the aforementioned show by The Eight, featuring work that was considered realistic in a modern way. Although it was a far cry from the "radicalism" taking place in the European art world, it was a direct challenge to the status quo–art that was approved by the National Academy of Design.

Then in late 1911 a group of artists in New York organized the Association of American Painters and Sculptors. Led by painters Arthur B. Davies and Walt Kuhn and sculptor John Mowbray-Clarke, the artists began to develop plans for the International Exhibition of Modern Art, better known as the Armory Show. The show opened February 17, 1913, in New York, and went on to Chicago and Boston. It would go down in history as "the most important single exhibition ever held in America."[47]

Endnotes

[1] Morse, "Memories of Uncle Frank," 4, Applegate Papers.
[2] *Lincoln (Ill.) Daily Courier*, Oct. 17, 1902.
[3] See *The 1904 Illio*, 380; *The 1906 Illio*, 87, 126, 138.
[4] Los Cinco Pintores," *El Palacio* 13:10 (Nov. 15, 1922): 131. Bennitt, ed., *History of the Louisiana Purchase Exposition*, 351. "The College of Literature and Arts at the Louisiana Purchase Exposition," *University of Illinois Press Bulletin*, Feb. 22, 1904, 1.
[5] Brandt, " 'Worthy and Carefully Selected': American Arts & Crafts at the Louisiana Purchase Exposition, 1904," *Archives of American Art Journal* 28:1 (1988): 2-3; 11.
[6] "Applegate Voiced Protest Against Statue Immediately," *Santa Fe New Mexican*, Oct. 19, 1927, 2. Parmelee, "History of Ceramic Education at the University of Illinois," *Journal of the American Ceramic Society* 6:1 (January 1923): 98. Another indication that Applegate studied architecture is the fact that Frank Forrest Frederick, his mentor (who hired Applegate to work at the School of Industrial Arts in Trenton, N.J.), taught architecture at the University of Illinois. General "art and design" courses included architecture as part of their curriculum.
[7] Student records, University of Illinois. By 1909 he was considered fluent in Italian, French, German, and Spanish; see "Marvels of Modeling From Pellets of Clay," *Crockery and Glaze Journal*, May 28, 1909, 22.
[8] *Atlanta (Ill.) Argus*, Dec. 14, 1906, 1.
[9] Homer with Organ, *Robert Henri and His Circle*, 40.
[10] *Atlanta (Ill.) Argus*, July 22, 1910, 2.
[11] "Paris, As Seen by Frank Applegate," *Atlanta (Ill.) Argus*, July 12, 1907, 1.
[12] Ibid.
[13] "Letter From Rome," *Atlanta (Ill.) Argus*, May 24, 1907. "Holland, As Seen by Frank Applegate," *Atlanta (Ill.) Argus*, July 19, 1907, 1.
[14] "Letter From Rome."
[15] "In France," *Atlanta (Ill.) Argus*, April 19, 1907, 1.
[16] "Letter From Rome."
[17] *Atlanta (Ill.) Argus*, Aug. 9, 1907.

18 "Marvels of Modeling From Pellets of Clay,"
Crockery and Glaze Journal, May 28, 1909, 22.
Trenton (N.J.) Sunday Advertiser, Sept. 22, 1907, 11.
Various newspaper accounts placed Applegate's
position in the ceramics department or pottery
department; apparently the three departments
were closely linked.
19 Applegate, Albert, "Recollections of A.A.
Applegate," 2:11.
20 *Lincoln (Ill.) Daily Courier*, Oct. 17, 1907.
21 *Lincoln (Ill.) Daily Courier*, Nov. 13, 1907, 5.
Applegate, Albert, 2:12.
22 *Atlanta (Ill.) Argus*, Nov. 22, 1907, 1.
23 *Trenton (N.J.) Sunday Advertiser*, Feb. 21, 1909,
May 14, 1911. Dowdell, "Art Instructors Hold an
Exhibit," n.d., H.R. MacGinnis Papers. "Dr.
Frederick, Art School Head, Dies," *Trenton (N.J.)
Times*, June 2, 1942. Falk, ed., *The Annual Exhibition Record of the Pennsylvania Academy of the
Fine Arts, Vol II*, 70. It is likely that there was a
connection between Frederick's visit to Europe and
Applegate's, which would account for Applegate's
having a job waiting for him in Trenton.
24 "Frank Applegate Writes From Trenton," *Atlanta
(Ill.) Argus*, n.d., Applegate Papers.
25 *Trenton (N.J.) Sunday Advertiser*, Feb. 12, 1911, 19.
"Over 30 Million Dollars' Worth of Pottery Made
Here," *Trenton (N.J.) Sunday Advertiser*, Oct. 4,
1908, 15.
26 Levin, *History of American Ceramics*, 112. "Origin
of the School of Industrial Arts," *Trenton (N.J.)
Sunday Advertiser*, Jan. 26, 1908, 8. Keen, *American
Art Pottery, 1875-1930*, 66.
27 Levin, 49.
28 Keen, 67.
29 *Trenton (N.J.) Sunday Advertiser*, Sept. 19, 1909,
5.
30 "Art School Pins Here; Also New Pottery Kiln,"
Trenton (N.J.) Sunday Advertiser, Nov. 8, 1908, 1.
31 "Potters Like Course at the Art School," *Trenton
(N.J.) Sunday Advertiser*, Jan. 24, 1909, 1.
32 "Art School Notes," *Trenton (N.J.) Sunday
Advertiser*, March 15, 1908, 3. The whereabouts of
the portrait are unknown.

33 "Vacation of Art Teachers," *Trenton (N.J.) Sunday
Advertiser*, May 17, 1908, 8.
34 *Atlanta (Ill.) Argus*, Dec. 15, 1905, May 2, 1924.
35 *Lincoln (Ill.) Daily Courier*, June 16, 1905.
36 "Arts Society Is Now a Reality," *Trenton (N.J.)
Sunday Advertiser*, March 1, 1908, 1. "Fine Arts
Exhibit to Be Given in Trenton," *Trenton (N.J.)
Sunday Advertiser*, Oct. 18, 1908, 1. "Fine Pix Here
for Art Exhibition," *Trenton (N.J.) Sunday Advertiser*, Jan. 31, 1909, 1. *Trenton (N.J.) Sunday
Advertiser*, March 7, 1909, 5. "Trenton's Art
Exhibition," *Trenton (N.J.) Sunday Advertiser*, Feb.
7, 1909, 6.
37 "School of Industrial Arts: Important Feeder to
Trenton's Force of Skilled Artisans," *Trenton (N.J.)
Sunday Advertiser*, May 14, 1911, 25.
38 Frederick, "School of Industrial Arts, City of
Trenton," *Journal of the American Ceramic Society*
6:1 (January 1923): 115.
39 "Marvels of Modeling From Pellets of Clay,"
Crockery and Glaze Journal, May 28, 1909, 21-22.
The whereabouts of "The Combat" are unknown.
"The Derelicts" is in a private collection. The article
also included a photograph of a Toby jug of
Bacchus, whereabouts unknown. Note that
Applegate was said to be 27, indicating he gave his
birthdate as 1882, not 1881.
40 Ibid.
41 Taft, *Modern Tendencies in Sculpture*, 33. "Letter
From Paris," July 22, 1910.
42 "Some Foreign Notes From Frank Applegate,"
Atlanta (Ill.) Argus, Aug. 19, 1910, 2.
43 "Letter From Frank Applegate," *Atlanta (Ill.)
Argus*, July 15, 1910, 1.
44 Ibid.
45 "Some Foreign Notes From Frank Applegate." See
Chapter 6 for more on "Tourists and Art."
46 "Frank Applegate's Letter," *Atlanta (Ill.) Argus*,
Sept. 2, 1910, 2.
47 Brown, *American Painting, From the Armory
Show to the Depression*, 47.

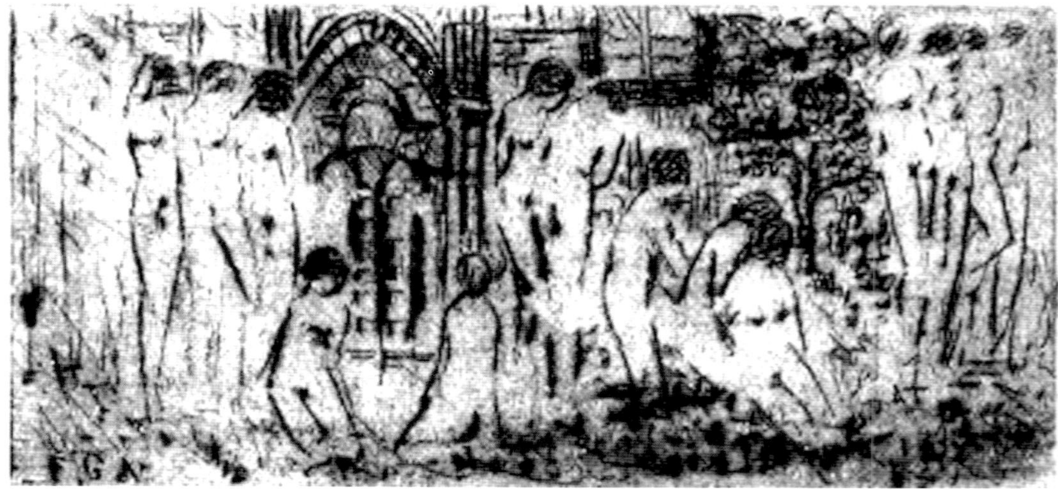

Group of females, etching. Private collection. Photograph courtesy of the owner.

3 East Coast Artist

It is not known whether Frank Applegate attended the Armory Show, but given his frequent trips to New York where his brother Alpheus lived and his later use of modernist techniques in painting and sculpture, it seems highly probable. His daughter, Betty Applegate McClung, recalled that her father "was always going to New York or Philadelphia to see things." She also remembered being "dragged" to art galleries at an early age.[1]

Ceramic sculpture and other studio pottery were underappreciated and little-known art forms in the early 1900s. Sculptors worked in bronze, stone, or plaster, and the great ceramic artists who created masterpieces in art potteries generally operated within the constraints of a factory. Studio potters such as Applegate were rare; however, the fact that his work appeared during the 1910s in major galleries and sculpture shows and at museums including the Metro-

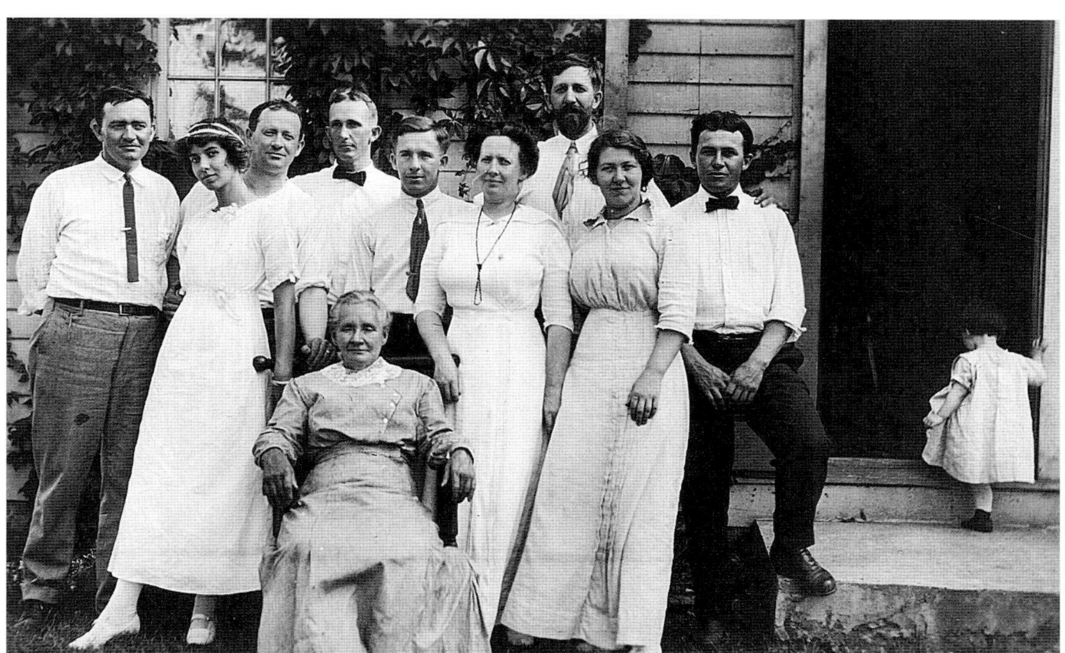

The Applegate family, ca. mid-1910s. Top row, left to right: Archie, Ruth, Alpheus, Arthur, Albert, Mabel, Frank, Anne, and Linn. Bottom center, mother Lina. Betty Applegate is at the doorway. Applegate Papers.

politan Museum of Art, the Carnegie Institute, and the Art Institute of Chicago undoubtedly helped the field of ceramic sculpture gain recognition.

Throughout the teens Applegate lived the life of the potter-teacher. Teaching freehand drawing and ceramics at the Trenton School of Industrial Arts paid the bills, the class load left ample free time to work on his own ceramics, and the school's studio gave him access to kilns and tools. Looking back on this period of his life in the mid-1920s, Applegate stated, "I worked at ceramics on the side, you might say, to earn my living so I could work at art." By 1914 he was lecturing on pottery at the Pennsylvania Academy of the Fine Arts, explaining the different glazing processes, the Chinese and English methods of glazing, and the use of oxides.[2]

Alta Applegate gave birth to the couple's only child, Ruth Elizabeth, known as Betty, on August 6, 1911, while visiting family members in Decatur, Illinois. Ever the joker, Frank sent relatives a picture of a child with elephantiasis to announce the new arrival.[3] A few months before Betty's birth, the Applegates purchased land in Morrisville, Pennsylvania, across the Delaware River from Trenton and within walking distance of the School of Industrial Arts. The property was on a hill overlooking the Pennsylvania Canal, in an area called "The Greystones" for the huge boulders that jutted out of the hill. "The Greystones" had been William Penn's first land purchase in what would become Pennsylvania, and Penn's manor house, Pennsbury, is located a few miles south.

The site was ideal for commuting to Trenton, and Applegate expanded his holdings twice, in 1916 and 1920. Aided by relatives, he built a large house overlooking the canal. He uncovered the remains of an Indian amphitheater, arrowheads, and other artifacts while excavating for the foundation, and some of the artifacts were sent to the Peabody Museum.[4]

The Applegate home and grounds were something of a showplace, and the *Trenton State Gazette* described "Professor Applegate's Park" thus:

> Part of the grove, with its little ravine, winding stone walk, gushing spring with rugged stone walled runway and miniature waterfall, amid towering chestnut trees and screens of shrubbery, has been made a veritable little park by Prof. Applegate, whose shingled cottage lies far back from the street, nestled upon one of the largest of the historic "Graystones." Life and finishing touches to the rustic have been added by artistic cement benches, pieces of statuary and other creations of the sculptor's art placed about the grounds. The view … is a superb one, overlooking western Trenton.[5]

Frank showed a preference for hills and mountains over flat Illinois prairieland early on. He once wrote of his hometown, "The country directly around here is not particularly interest-

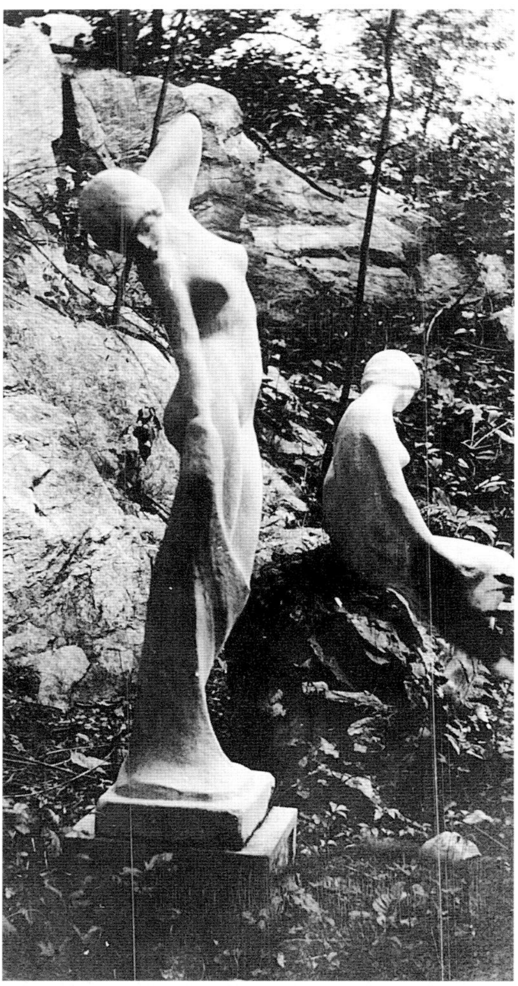

Sculpture made by Frank Applegate for his Morrisville, Pennsylvania, yard. Applegate Papers.

ing, all maize and wheat fields and quite level, the center of the 'Corn Belt.'" Illinois was still home, however, and he, Alta, and Betty returned to visit occasionally. His niece Dorothy Applegate Morse said his visits home were "always a special time for [my brother] Donald and me. … We envied … his casual way of dressing, especially the bare feet which distressed my mother, but would only elicit a slow grin when she tried vainly to scold him." She recalled "singing around the piano in our parlor, the chuckle that seemed to sit comfortably in his throat ready to express itself, and the fun lurking in his eyes."[6]

Applegate studied life modeling at the prestigious Pennsylvania Academy of the Fine Arts in Philadelphia during the 1913-1914 school year. The sculpture department was chaired by Charles Grafly, who at the time was considered the country's foremost teacher of sculpture. Grafly started sculpting in a stoneyard, then studied with Thomas Eakins and William Anshultz at the Pennsylvania Academy of the Fine Arts and at the Academie Julian and École des Beaux-Arts in Paris. His most notable works were symbolic nudes and portrait busts, and he is best known for the General Meade Memorial in Washington, D.C. Grafly's work tended toward the classical, and he "preferred to work with the ideal figure in images that expressed some basic element of human existence." A fervent believer in the idea (which Applegate came to share) that great art comes from within and cannot be produced "on demand," he frequently created pieces without the benefit of a commission. Grafly's symbolism often proved exasperating to critics, for he used icons that he alone understood. Nevertheless, his ability was highly praised, especially with regards to portraiture.[7] He was a superb modeler, and his nudes show the power of the human body with its taut, rippling muscles. They were more idealistic than realistic, perfect specimens of human anatomy.

Applegate was one of only two pupils accepted into Grafly's life modeling class that year. His classmate, Fiske Boyd, gained fame as an engraver and painter and studied under John Sloan in New York. Another student enrolled in the academy at the time was scholarship winner Theodore Van Soelen, whose path later would cross Applegate's in New Mexico.[8] Applegate's studies with Grafly continued during the first term of the 1914-15 school year.

Most of the artists teaching at the Academy of the Fine Arts during Applegate's time there were conservatives. American impressionists, including Phillip Hale, Daniel Garber, J. Alden Weir, and William Merritt Chase, led the

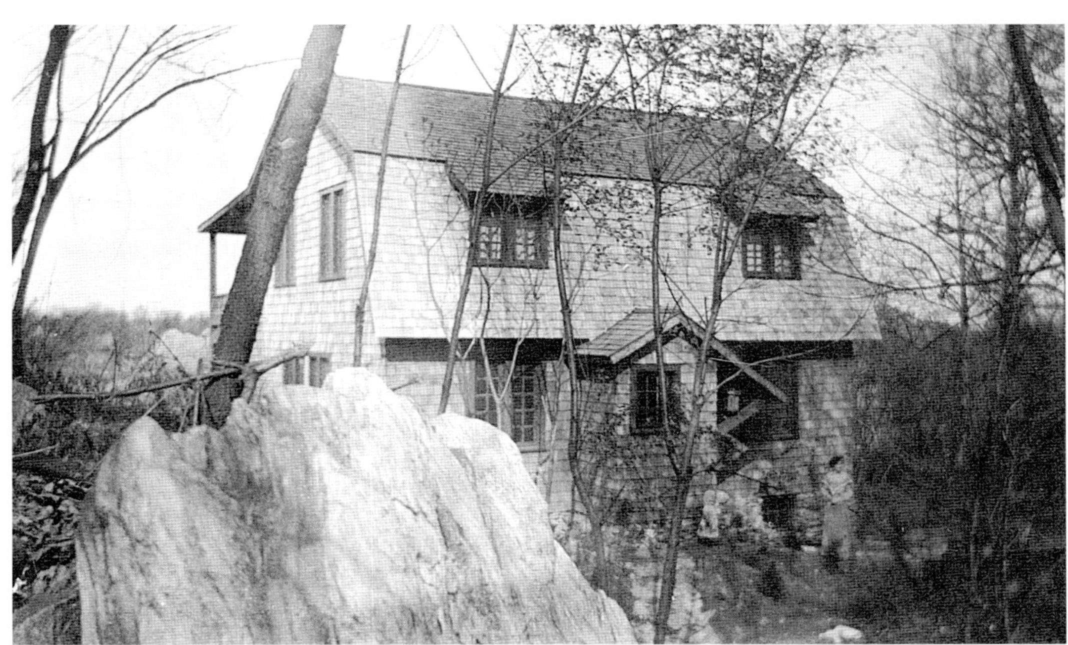

The Applegates' Morrisville, Pennsylvania, home. Applegate Papers.

faculty, with Hugh Breckenridge one of the few "moderns" employed. John Sloan, William Glackens, Everett Shinn, Robert Henri, and George Luks had studied at the academy, and the exhibition of works by The Eight appeared there, but it would be several years before conservative styles no longer dominated the school curriculum.[9]

Although modern art had little bearing on Grafly's work, he had been a friend of Henri's since the 1880s and had great respect for Henri's work.[10] While Grafly did not use his own talents to portray "urban realism," he likely taught his students about it. Realists such as Henri, George Bellows, and Sloan reflected the strong emotions and hurried pace of the increasingly urbanized world in their art. The work was decidedly unromantic, and their portraits often depicted members of the lower classes.

While many of Applegate's earliest sculptures such as "The Derelicts" were realistic social commentaries, pieces he completed during and after his study with Grafly celebrated muscular beauty and grace, human and animal power. Some of his works depicted the graceful flow of a woman's body in motion, while others revealed a distended stomach or emaciated torso, combining realism with classicism. Although critics called his work "modern" throughout the 1910s, he probably did not cross over from realism into abstractionism until late in the decade.

From early on, Applegate was passionate about his artwork and about having people see it. He sometimes was reluctant to sell pieces to private collectors, preferring that they remain on public display.[11] He exhibited in Trenton regularly, and in 1914, Applegate gained an entrance into "the big time" New York's modern art galleries.

Applegate met a sculptor named Howard Kretz Coluzzi, who went by both his father's name, Kretz, and his mother's, Coluzzi. Coluzzi had studied at the National Academy of Design, had shown several paintings and drawings in the Armory Show, and was included in an exhibit of Armory Show veterans organized by Arthur B. Davies in February 1914. In May 1914, at Coluzzi's suggestion, Applegate wrote to sculptor John Mowbray-Clarke, the vice-president of the Association of American Painters and Sculptors, who had helped Davies and Walt Kuhn produce the Armory Show. Mowbray-Clarke's work bore some similarity to Applegate's in that both used their art for social commentary and neither shied away from the more brutal aspects of the world they saw. His "Aphrodite," for example, was a depiction of a London whore.[12]

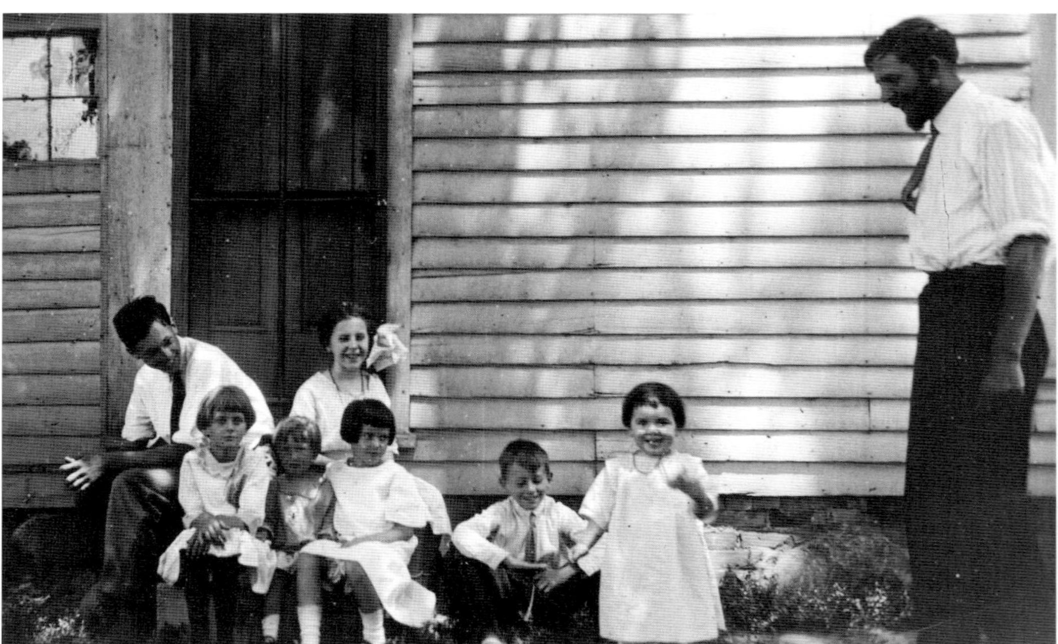

Frank Applegate, far right, with some of the extended family's children. Betty Applegate is next to her father, Frank. Applegate Papers.

Applegate asked to meet with Mowbray-Clarke during an upcoming visit to his brother Alpheus' home in New York. "I had a letter from Howard Kretz [Coluzzi] saying that you were going to exhibit at the MacDowell Club next autumn and that I might get to exhibit there too if I'd write to you about it first," he wrote. "I was afraid my stuff might not be up to a point where you'd care to have it on exhibit with yours. My work would be mostly terracotta glazed and unglazed and nothing very large."[13] Applegate's humble letter belied his ambition, but it worked. Mowbray-Clarke asked Applegate to send him photographs of his work.

The Applegates left for Illinois when school ended. "I am doing some work out here this summer, tho [*sic*] nothing of great importance," Applegate told Mowbray-Clarke. "I hope to get a few good things." This was the last summer Applegate spent in Atlanta, although he returned for visits, and his hometown newspaper continued to report on his life. As his career progressed, he found it advantageous to stay and work in the East. He spoke disparagingly of the provincialism of central Illinois in a letter to Mowbray-Clarke, writing, "People out here are mostly rather indifferent to anything in art. Their greatest ambition seems to be to have an automobile a little larger than the other fellow and to get out and tear around through the dust and heat in it."[14]

Mowbray-Clarke apparently responded positively to Applegate's work, for in November 1914 Frank took part in his first New York show, at the MacDowell Club. The MacDowell Club shows were jury-free, organized either by a representative who selected the fellow artists or by a group of artists who decided whether to include others.[15] Applegate's and Mowbray-Clarke's sculptures were exhibited along with the paintings of Armory Show committee

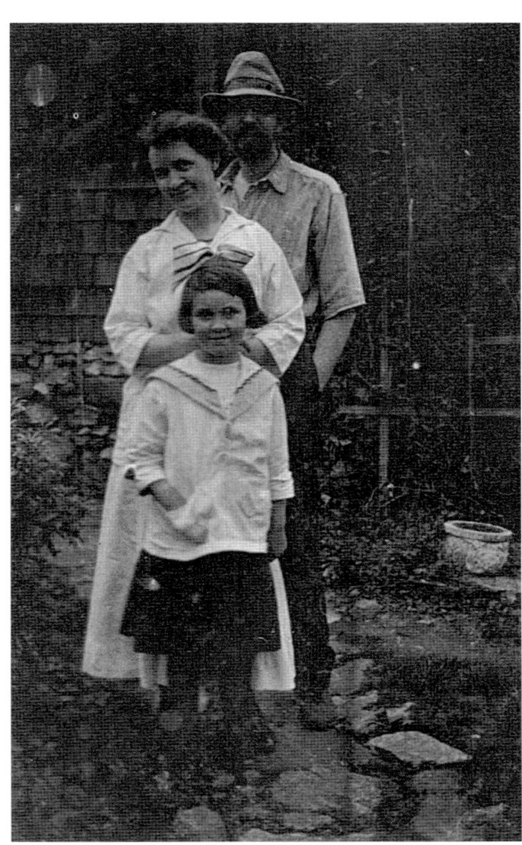

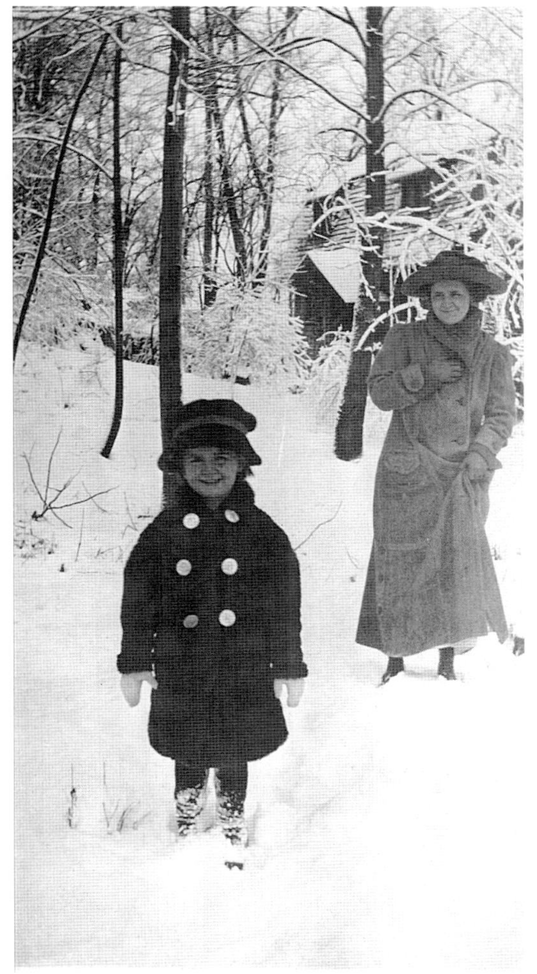

Left: Frank, Alta, and Betty Applegate in Pennsylvania, ca. mid-1910s. Right: Alta and Betty in the snow with the Applegates' Pennsylvania home in the background. Applegate Papers.

members and exhibitors Karl Anderson, D. Putnam Brinley, and Allen Tucker, Armory Show exhibitor Sidney Dale Shaw, and painters Charles Reiffel and Lydia Gibson.

The New York Times praised the show in its review and printed an article specifically on Applegate's work. The piece the *Times* reviewer considered most worthy of note was a tiny, terra cotta mouse (p. 105):

> A mouse is now on exhibition at the MacDowell Club. A somewhat undersized mouse that gives, nevertheless, an impression of stalwart competency. Frank G. Applegate modeled it from the soil of New Jersey, and nothing could speak more eloquently for Mr. Applegate's power to treat a little common subject in a large sculptural style. … When a mouse in the prime of his mousehood and at the fullness of his powers is vigorously nibbling a spilled fragment of predigested breakfast food, its strong young jaws moving with ease and certainty, its sinewy claws securely grasping its prize, we may well imagine it as feeling itself more than an ordinary mouse, an embodiment rather of the mouse ideal of capacity and natural force. This is what Mr. Applegate shows in his heroic little terra cotta figure less than two inches long.

The reviewer considered his other pieces as well: "When the same sculptor undertakes to symbolize the strife and strength of love he goes about it in the same fashion. His entwined figures are creations of Euripides, all stark emotion. When he makes two laborers bearing a burden from the kilns on bent backs, he hints at the imprisonment of energy by a back-breaking task in the rhythm of their step, and the holes by which he balances his masses are as interesting and well considered as the fenestration of a cathedral front. In a word, he is a true sculptor." In addition to modeling clay with his hands, Applegate also made molds and produced multiple copies of the same piece, varying the colors and glazes.[16]

Applegate began to exhibit his work regularly after the MacDowell Club show. The 10th annual Pennsylvania Academy of the Fine Arts exhibition of February-March 1915 featured a group of his terra cotta figures. A Trenton newspaper said his work "promises to not only add fame to the maker but also to the local institution with which he is connected. … Every piece of work offered by Mr. Applegate was accepted, and he was requested to bring still another specimen."

The article goes on to reveal that Applegate had aligned himself with modern art, if not modernism *per se*, by

The invitation to Frank Applegate's first exhibition in New York in 1914.

this time: "The work of the local artist is something new in modeling, and it was because of this that he was awarded a special place in the exhibition. The designs are all modern in spirit and original in conception. In his work, Mr. Applegate has endeavored to get away from the academic style of other artists. … From the tremendous advancement he is making in the world of artists, he bids fair to become one of the leading sculptors in the country."[17]

The next show in which he participated drew a great deal of publicity. It ran from late March to late April at the Montross Gallery, one of the few galleries in New York (along with Alfred Stieglitz's Photo-Secession gallery and the Daniel Gallery) that was actively promoting modernist art in the teens. *Arts and Decoration* speculated, "People go to the Montross Gallery to see the Montrossities and to laugh," but the magazine acknowledged Newman E. Montross' ability to predict what would become popular and thus to succeed at selling modern art.[18] Applegate's association with Montross continued on and off for many years.

Artists whose work appeared in the show along with Applegate's read like a who's who of the contemporary New York art world. In addition to Mowbray-Clarke and Coluzzi, two other exhibitors, Arthur B. Davies and Walt Kuhn, assumed a minor degree of importance in Applegate's life. Davies is best known for paintings that used heavy brushwork and deep, rich colors to portray fairy-lands filled with dancing, classically inspired nymphs who frolicked through fantastic landscapes and waterfalls. In the years immediately following the Armory Show, however, Davies experimented with cubism. He was also a printmaker, an etcher, and a sculptor in wood and bronze. Most of his sculptures reflected the fairy figures of his best-known paintings, although he was showing cubist pieces in the mid-1910s.[19] One notices a similarity in subject matter and style between Davies' sculpture and Applegate's. Both often portrayed a romantic image of the female form, although Applegate's women were sometimes more realistic than fantastic.

Later, as a painter, Applegate shared Davies' fondness for deep color and heavy strokes.

Davies visited the family in Morrisville and they took this to be a great honor, according to Betty Applegate McClung. She embarrassed her parents by draping some of Davies' nude sculptures with dolls' clothing. Applegate acquired two of Davies' etchings, both portraying his world of fantasy. At some point, Applegate also made Davies-like etchings (pp. 32, 66, 88, 189).[20]

Less important but still significant was Applegate's acquaintance with Walt Kuhn. Kuhn's greatest work was as a portrait painter, and he is best known for his vivid, forthright interpretations of stage and circus folk. Kuhn's paintings, like the work of Davies and Applegate, were admired for their graceful virility. Applegate shunned portraiture when he became a painter, but his legacy from Kuhn may be the bold brushwork and heavily applied paint that characterizes much of his work.[21]

The remaining artists in the Montross Gallery show (with the exception of painter and illustrator Alfred J. Frueh) were also Armory Show alums: painter and Armory Show organizer Henry Fitch Taylor; Man Ray, then a painter, who would achieve great fame as an avant-garde photographer; Frank Nankivell, best known as an illustrator (and one of Davies' printers); William Glackens and Maurice Prendergast, both formerly of The Eight; painter Charles Prendergast; Brinley and Tucker from the MacDowell Club show; impressionist Elmer McRae; and modernists Charles Sheeler and Morton Schamberg. The Armory Show's long-lived notoriety and Davies' and Kuhn's promotional skills guaranteed crowds, and the ensuing publicity helped propel Applegate's career. Conventional art critics considered the exhibit quite radical, and several of them panned it, but 32 pieces sold on the first day.[22]

Applegate debuted a ceramic piece called "Damn," a small, indigo depiction of evil incarnate, laughing and rubbing its paws (p. 109), which drew considerable attention. The *New York Herald* headlined its review of the show: "Damn!' Says Sculpture, at Extreme American Art" and ran a photograph of the piece. The review called the artists "American extremists," and continued, "On one wall is a large decoration by Arthur B. Davis [*sic*], entitled 'Dances,' with prismatic figures suggesting human beings going through hectic measures. … In another corner … looking at Mr. Davis' latest picture, is a symbolic figure by F.G. Applegate, carrying a wofully [*sic*] wry face and labelled 'Damn!' So there you are!" Of the exhibition as a whole, the *Herald* said it was "mitigated by the saving grace of American humor. Each artist seems to be chuckling over the jolt he is giving to established ideals." Applegate also showed a dramatic piece titled "Wounded Lion Charging" here (p. 235). *The New York Times* reviewer said Applegate's terra cotta pieces were "touched by the vivifying comic spirit."[23]

On the heels of this critical acclaim, Applegate chose to work in Trenton during the summer of 1915 while Alta and Betty visited Illinois. He labored hard that summer, as he told Mowbray-Clarke:

> I intended answering your letter before this but have been very busy lately and too tired at night to write. I keep two or three things going all the time this summer and have a model a couple of times a week. I'm doing a number of things this summer but don't know how they will show up to others when I get them in the terra cotta. I'm going to carry out further experiments soon too in crushed stone and cement. … I'll be glad to see you when you can get over and I expect to be over sometime this autumn.[24]

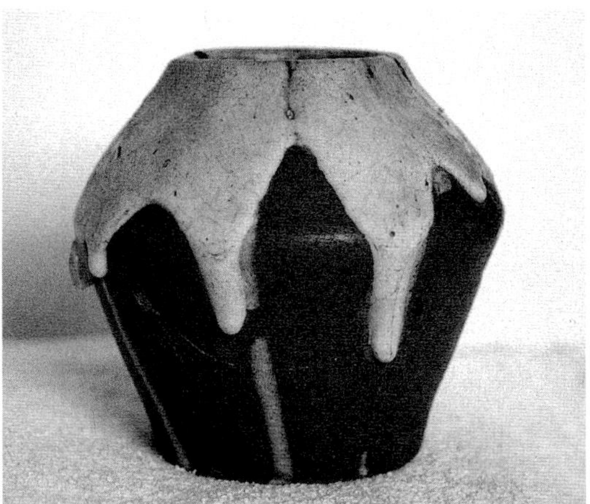

Ceramic pot. Private collection. Photograph courtesy of the owner.

It is often difficult to date Applegate's artwork because the pieces seldom carried a distinguishing title. From the statement about having a model, however, one can infer that some of his nudes date from this summer. This also may be the period when he started creating sculptures of graceful women wearing drapes or long, flowing skirts (p. 105). He often caught the women in motion, much as Davies' dancers flowed on the canvas of his paintings. Applegate created garden sculpture for his back yard in Morrisville in this style (p. 34). One small statue is of a seated, nude woman. Her features are indistinguishable, but her pose is pensive and dreamy, and her lower body melds into the base of the sculpture. Graceful, dancing women, arms overhead and skirts flowing, decorate a large concrete pot.[25] Applegate also designed tiles depicting these graceful figures (p. 111). His figurals convey a sense of movement having just happened or about to happen, while similar mass-produced works by factory art potters seem static and frozen by comparison. Judging from his letter and the descriptions of the pieces shown at the Montross Gallery, Applegate had not yet embraced modernism. But at some point in the 1910s he started adding cubist attributes to his figures, perhaps in response to Davies' cubist sculptures.

Applegate's friendship with John Mowbray-Clarke and his wife, Mary, continued throughout the teens, and he, Alta, and Betty visited the couple and their son at their Rockland County, New York, estate. The foreword to the catalog for Mowbray-Clarke's 1919 show at the Kevorkian Galleries described him as "a mystic, a man of his hands, to other usages than those of Art—an out-of-doors-man, keen on play and apt at manly sports, a reader of the stars and of men's palms, a willing listener and an incomparable counsellor, on whose insight and … wisdom his friends have learned to lean."[26] It is obvious that Applegate's love of the outdoors and sports meshed with Mowbray-Clarke's; less apparent is whether Frank showed an interest in mysticism. Given some of his acquaintances in later years, however, it would not be surprising.

Mary Mowbray-Clarke was the co-owner of a Manhattan bookstore, gallery, and decorating shop called The Sunwise Turn, which was a "rendezvous of leaders in the worlds of painting, sculpture, and literature." Her clients and friends included visual artists Rockwell Kent, Henry Varnum Poor, Marcel Duchamp, and B.J.O. Nordfeldt and writers Roger Fry, Eugene O'Neill, Ernest Hemingway, and Witter Bynner.[27]

Applegate's participation in the New York shows and his friendship with the Mowbray-Clarkes opened doors for him. He visited Albert Rosenthal, a noted painter, collector, and art expert who lived in New Hope, Pennsylvania, about 30 miles from Morrisville. Applegate also met the Lewisohn sisters, Alice and Irene, who founded the Neighborhood Playhouse in 1915. Another significant acquaintance was Elizabeth Sage Hare, wealthy art collector, progressive thinker, and a great supporter of art, particularly modern American art. As a historian noted, "She was rich, she was witty, she was energetic, she was imperious, and her close friends included every far-out intellectual worth knowing in New York and Europe." Applegate and Howard Kretz Coluzzi also remained friends, although Coluzzi was notoriously unreliable and mysterious. Applegate often inquired after him in letters to Mowbray-Clarke, saying in one, "He said he'd be down in June or July but didn't come."[28] Irene Lewisohn, Elizabeth Hare, and Coluzzi all reconnected with Applegate in New Mexico.

Many of his acquaintances shared Applegate's interest in social reform and in using art for the greater good. Applegate had the opportunity to make an artistic social statement in late 1915, when he entered a piece in the "Immigrant in America" competition. The contest was sponsored by wealthy sculptor Gertrude Vanderbilt Whitney and organized by her right-hand woman, Juliana Force. It was the brainchild of Frances Kellor of the Society for the Americanization of Immigrants in America and was designed to attract attention to the 13 million unnaturalized, foreign-born residents of the United States. The society's goal was assimilation, something the Frank Applegate of later years would decry as it applied to Native Americans and Spanish-Americans.

The competition targeted foreign-born young artists, a category for which Applegate hardly qualified. Its stated goal was for the artist to show "the meaning of America to the Immigrant and the Immigrant to America." Among the judges were painters Robert Henri and John Sloan, illustrator Charles Dana Gibson, and sculptors Paul Manship and James E. Fraser.[29]

Four hundred paintings, sculptures, and drawings were submitted, and about 100 of those were accepted for the exhibit. Applegate's piece took third place, behind a sculpture by Beniamino Bufano and a painting by Mary Bayne, and he won $100. His sculpture, called "Hope," was described as "a group showing a figure of 'Hope' leading a man and a woman carrying their earthly goods toward the West." One review said the sculpture "represents the Immigrant, with all his power and rugged strength, led by an ideal which appears to be symbolical of freedom." From these

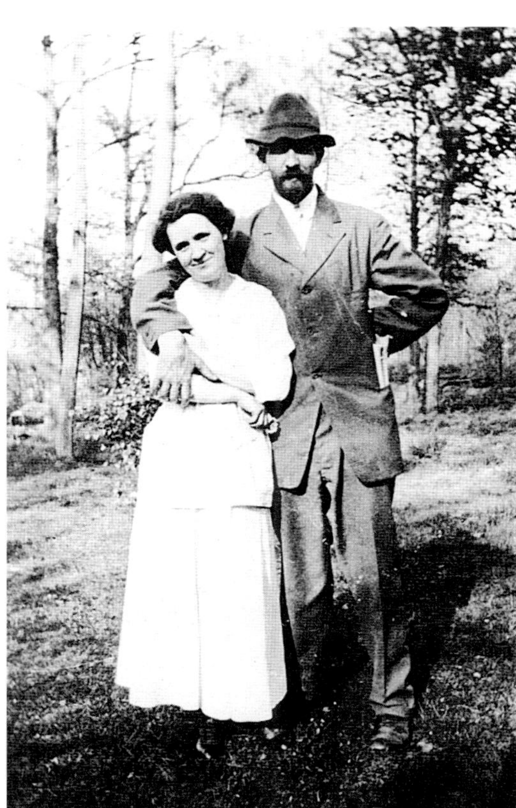

Frank and Alta Applegate in Pennsylvania. Applegate Papers.

descriptions, it sounds like something Charles Grafly might have created, a symbolic depiction of an abstract concept; yet the reference to "power and rugged strength" is distinctly Applegate.[30]

The "Immigrant in America" exhibition initially drew about 250 people a day on weekends, a respectable attendance.[31] The show became a circus, however, after former President Theodore Roosevelt paid it a visit in early December. Roosevelt's reaction to the show underscored the dichotomy between popular art and modern art. *The New York Times* recorded the scene in entertaining detail:

> He did not agree with the awards made by the jury … There were 90 sculptures, paintings, and things in the display, all designed to portray the spirit which animates the immigrant on his arrival in the United States. With the first award, the Colonel had no quarrel. …
>
> "Wonderful work," exclaimed the Colonel. "Great. Very good!" … Suddenly the glance of the supplemental jury fell upon a painting representing pallid and twisted wraiths winding themselves into knots over a bleached fire.
>
> "What's that?" he asked.
>
> "Hope," they told him gently, almost in a whisper.
>
> "Why not 'Despair'?" demanded he. "Vampires and corpses, I should say."
>
> Again his gaze swept the place and lighted upon a mass of grotesque figures amalgamated into a coal black wave. "If I had not seen it here," the Colonel said, turning his glass, "I should have said that those were devils."
>
> Then suddenly he discovered what to him seemed a most convincing work of sculpture, a noble and classic Egyptian figure, and demanded why it had not been put among the four prize winners. The immigration from the Ptolemaic period to which it belonged is not very heavy just now, but all the same the Colonel thought it typified aspiration to a very great degree.

After a few choice comments on other pieces, the *Times* reported, Roosevelt had his picture taken with Bufano, Bufano's sculpture, and the Egyptian piece, and "went away entirely delighted." Roosevelt's visit turned the exhibition into "an unqualified triumph, in terms of the number of visitors, attention focused on unnaturalized residents, and publicity for the Whitney Studio."[32]

Applegate was invited or accepted into exhibitions of increasing prestige following the "Immigrant in America" show. His sculptures appeared in the Pennsylvania Academy of the Fine Arts exhibitions of 1916 and 1917. He had 17 small sculptures in the 1916 exhibition, and a Trenton paper noted "his placings are most advantageous." As always, the pieces were modeled from Delaware Valley clay. Many of the items he showed at the academy that year went to a show at Trenton's Contemporary Club, along with the work of Applegate's friend Henry MacGinnis, a painter who headed the School of Industrial Arts' department of design. "A display of this sort is quite new in Trenton," a local paper commented.[33]

From June to October 1916, Applegate exhibited eight pieces in the Exhibition of Contemporary American Sculpture at the Buffalo Fine Arts Academy's Albright Art Gallery. Organized by the National Sculpture Society, this was the "greatest exhibition of American sculpture ever presented in the United States" up to that time, and was a result of the success of sculpture at the 1915 Panama-Pacific International Exposition in San Francisco. As art director Cornelia B. Sage noted in the catalog, it was "a real sculpture exhibition, not the usual affair in which the sculptors play but an incidental part." It included the works of 168 sculptors. Many of the pieces had been shown at the Pan-Pacific Exposition, and others, including Applegate's, were solicited for acceptance by a jury. In the first month, the exhibit drew more than 61,000 visitors. Applegate's pieces went on to the Annual Exhibition of American Paintings and Sculpture at the Art Institute of Chicago.[34]

Applegate exhibited at the Carnegie Institute in Pittsburgh, the Herron Art Institute in Indianapolis, and other major museums during the 1910s.[35] His ceramic and terra cotta sculpture, which critics termed "modern," reflected both the realism of The Eight and the romanticism of art nouveau. Pieces ranged from classically influenced vases, urns, and bowls to intricately colored tiles to works that were solely decorative. He focused on animals—elephants, ducks, tiny mice, stalking panthers (p. 110); and on women—nude women, women wearing cloth or feathers, women dancing together and alone, a woman draped over a harp (pp. 89-90, 105, 108). And in a combination of the two, he sculpted Europa riding on the back of the bull Zeus (p. 111).

He experimented with glazes, often using several colors on a single small piece. Sculptures of tigers bore glaze-created stripes of dark brown on their fierce, muscled bodies (p. 49). Especially striking are the various shades of blue he was able to create, from palest sky blue to aqua and turquoise to deep indigo.[36]

Applegate's reputation began to attract art students to the School of Industrial Arts, and his work with the local potteries drew their full-time employees to the school. By 1916 the school's enrollment had risen to 926, having more than tripled since Applegate's first year there, 1907. Despite the increased class sizes, the course work allowed Applegate sufficient time to work on his art. "I have just three weeks' vacation yet this year, but my work is not hard here at the school and I have much time to work during the winter months," he told John Mowbray-Clarke.[37]

One of Applegate's most significant friendships during the latter half of the 1910s was with Clara Sidney Potter Davidge Taylor, the wife of artist and Association of American Painters and Sculptors board member Henry Fitch Taylor and the daughter of Episcopal Bishop Henry Codman Potter, a crusading social activist. The Armory Show was hatched and incubated at her Madison Gallery, and historian Milton Brown called Clara "one of the unsung heroes of the Armory Show."[38]

Open from 1909 to 1912, the Madison Gallery showcased the work of progressive artists whom other galleries turned away. All Clara Davidge (she married Taylor in 1913) asked "was a personal attitude in the work and that the man himself be driven by a sincere purpose." Walt Kuhn said of Davidge and Taylor, "They are absolutely honest but non-commercial. They make no effort to sell pictures whatsoever. She treats me fine and always says, 'I hope you will not desert us, Mr. Kuhn, because we are not selling, but our idea is to get a reputation for the very finest.' … The gallery is certainly gaining in reputation every day." Clara also steered wealthy art collectors Kuhn's way.[39]

Clara Taylor was described as "a small, mercurial creature … brown-eyed and vivacious; a patrician, with race in every line; a hostess … a rebel against convention and Episcopalianism." Her interests were not restricted to the visual arts. One of her most successful protégés was poet Edwin Arlington Robinson, for whom she built a studio behind her Washington Square home. She took Robinson into La Tourette, her old brick mansion on Staten Island, and attempted to cure him of alcoholism.[40]

Mabel Dodge Luhan, who would move her New York salon to Taos, New Mexico, in the late 1910s, wrote about "Aunt Clarissa," as she called her, in her memoir, *Movers and Shakers:*

> She had a fringe like ruffled brown feathers and the brightest of brown eyes. Animated, eccentric, rattle-brained Clarissa! Always dressed like the doll of any little girl of ten who has had recourse to the family ragbag and secured bits of gay silk, fur, and lace, she was warmhearted, rather bad-tempered, and fond of expressing herself in a loud, high-pitched voice in a language rich with her own variations. She collected. She collected old furniture and promising artists. Having transferred the family sense of excellence from worldliness and religion to poetry and paint and antiques, she furnished her house with spinning wheels, Cape Cod china, four-post bedsteads, a painter, and a poet.

Luhan's catty description of Clara Taylor was inaccurate: photographs prove her quite attractive, and she wore antique clothing, not "rags."[41]

Luhan titled the chapter about Clara Taylor "Psychic"; apparently Taylor, like John Mowbray-Clarke, strongly believed in psychic phenomena. "She believed that we are surrounded by subjective Mind which is waiting for us to impress it with our wishes so that it may carry them out," Luhan wrote. "Every wish, every thought consciously directed, is marked upon the sensitive surrounding ether, and is carried into form, materialized, brought to being, by Mind. This was called New Thought." The Taylors' "mind impressions" apparently worked on Edwin Arlington Robinson, because he lost his desire to drink.[42]

Clara Taylor was in her 50s when she "collected" Applegate as a protégé and friend. In the summer of 1918 she offered him the use of Echo Farm in Plainfield, New Hampshire, which was part of the art colony of Cornish. Founded by Augustus Saint-Gaudens, the great American sculptor, Cornish was one of the best-known and most influential of the country's art colonies. It is set in the shadow of Mount Ascutney, along the Connecticut River, and was "a blue-jean if not homespun community long before the days of hippy communes." In the early 1910s painter Willard Metcalf stayed in the abandoned mill Taylor had renovated, and other full- or part-time colonists in the teens included painters Maxfield Parrish, Everett Shinn, and Kenyon Cox, sculptor Paul Manship, and writers Norman Hapgood, Winston Churchill (the American best-selling novelist), and Witter Bynner.[43]

Applegate spent his first summer in New Hampshire without Alta and Betty. There he met the artists William and Marguerite Zorach, two more of Clara Taylor's protégés. The Zorachs had stayed at Echo Farm in 1917 and were living in another house loaned by Clara Taylor in the summer of 1918. At the time, Marguerite was best known for her intricate tapestries, while William was painting, drawing, and experimenting with woodcarving.

Echo Farm was not a country estate but an abandoned farm. William Zorach described it as being "in a hollow among wooded hills—five miles from a village—no neighbors, desolate, empty and mosquito-ridden." He recalled the summer of 1918 in his autobiography, *Art Is My Life:* "Mrs. Taylor brought up a man named Applegate, a potter. He built a kiln out of an old stove and some fire brick, and we all played with ceramics." Applegate later recalled that he made the kiln "by taking an old heavy sheet iron heating stove, setting it up on brick piers, then building a brick cone up around it with [an] arch to put fuel in around and under the stove."[44]

Zorach remembered, "We sat up all night firing the kiln, cooking hot dogs, singing songs, and stoking the fire. It was wild and exciting. Awful things happened; our work blew up from not being properly dried, bricks blew up and wrecked the kiln and everything in it. Something always went wrong. We had a lot of fun and experience but only one or two pieces survived." Applegate learned from his mistakes and later noted, "You must start very slowly with your clay and bring [the] heat up gradually to as high a temperature as possible" with this kind of kiln. Zorach's introduction to ceramics furthered his abandonment of painting for sculpture, the medium that would bring him worldwide fame. In Applegate's kiln Zorach created his first ceramic sculpture in the round, "First Steps."[45]

Zorach also alleged that pottery was not the only thing on Applegate's mind:

> That summer there was Nettie May. Applegate asked Mrs. Taylor to have her up, and Mrs. Taylor suggested she stay with us. … Nettie May wasn't beautiful. She was sensitive and charming and delightful and a little fey. There was something rare and out of this world about her. And she was very young. I think she was a student of Applegate's. He had fallen in love with her and was looking forward to an affair with her away from the eyes of his family. Nettie May was not in love with Applegate but wondered if she should have an

affair with him. We were horrified. He looked like a very old man to us; he must have been 45. …

Men fell for Nettie May. Mo Moskowitz [an Australian pianist who was staying with the Zorachs that summer] was so intrigued he couldn't be persuaded to leave. An artist friend staying in the village haunted our swimming pool. I was very intrigued myself, being always susceptible to feminine charms. But it is a little complicated when the charmer lives in the house with you and your family and is pursued by various males. I found myself in the position of protector from the wolves. … Yet, she had her own method of protection: she thought she was in love with an artist in New York, a protégé of Arthur B. Davies.

Zorach ended his story of the summer of 1918 there, so Applegate and the elusive Nettie May apparently did not have an affair.[46]

Clara Taylor offered Echo Farm to Applegate as a gift, and he accepted. One condition of the generous offer was that he create ceramic pieces for her, and Applegate brought a better kiln to the farm. Alta and Betty accompanied him for the summers of 1919 and 1920. During the years in Plainfield, Applegate became acquainted with Augustus Saint-Gaudens' widow, Augusta, his brother, Louis, and Louis' wife, Annetta, both of whom were sculptors. Dorothy Morse, Applegate's niece, recalled visiting the Applegates and meeting Augusta St. Gaudens. One of Applegate's ceramics students was Louis and Annetta's son, Paul, who worked with Applegate and Zorach on that first kiln. Paul traveled to Trenton to study with Applegate at the School of Industrial Arts. In 1921 Paul and his mother founded Orchard Kiln Pottery in Cornish. He went on to become a highly regarded ceramicist admired for his glazes.[47]

Applegate showed 15 pieces of sculpture, three tile panels, and six pieces of pottery in the 36th annual Architectural League Exhibition, held in the Metropolitan Museum of Art in the spring of 1921. *The New York Times* said of the exhibition, "It is apparent at even a first glance that a good deal of the so-called modernist art has been admitted and declines to hide its light." Applegate was by this time a member of the New York Society of Keramic Arts. He gave lectures as a ceramics expert, addressing women's clubs, arts organizations, and pottery societies in Trenton and New York, and was a consultant to the Cement Manufacturers Association when it published a book on cement aggregates and colors. "A kiln in every back yard" was his motto; he believed that every householder who was so inclined should make and fire the pottery used in his own home. The Minton potteries of Stoke-on-Trent, England, were so taken with his work that they offered him a job. According to one article, "The representatives of the Minton China Potteries said that the work of Mr. Applegate in glazes has exceeded all results in the country or in Europe. He was offered great inducement … to go to England with the Minton people."[48]

But Applegate had begun corresponding with Gerald Cassidy, a painter who lived in New York City and Santa Fe, New Mexico, and his wife, writer Ina Sizer Cassidy. It is not known how they met, but a letter from Gerald Cassidy, most likely written in 1920, apparently spurred the friendship. In the letter Cassidy wrote of his and Ina's concern over the declining quality of the clays being used by Pueblo Indians and wondered if Applegate might be able to help them. The Cassidys also had heard of his "pro-kiln" manifesto and asked for advice on kiln-building.[49]

Applegate responded with a detailed description and drawings of a kiln they could build. He asked them to forward samples of the Indian clay for him to analyze. "I've always had a curiosity as to the composition of the clay the Southwest Indians used. This will be a chance to find out," he wrote. Applegate's interest in Indian pottery may have been triggered by his excavations a decade before on his Morrisville land and by his visit to the St. Louis World's Fair, and he had ample opportunity to examine Indian pottery at Trenton and big-city galleries. He already knew something about the Indians' clay, for he told

Cassidy, "most of the clays the Indians used had quite a good deal of lime in them."[50]

Clara Davidge and Henry Fitch Taylor likely contributed to Applegate's interest in New Mexico clay. Clara noted in a letter written in 1919 that she and Henry planned to move to Santa Fe because Henry wanted to examine clay deposits there. According to art historian Christine I. Oaklander, in 1920 the Taylors sold off all their possessions and planned to go to Santa Fe to establish a commune based on potterymaking and spiritualism.[51]

In subsequent correspondence the Cassidys enclosed several clay samples. Applegate performed tests on the clay, firing it at different temperatures and examining its composition, and was convinced he could help the Indians. In the summer of 1920 the Cassidys sent him a program for the Santa Fe Fiesta, a multicultural pageant that drew visitors to Santa Fe, and likely encouraged him to visit. By that time, Ina Cassidy was referring to Applegate as one of many "especial friends of ours, or those whom we know reasonably well."[52]

Meanwhile, the School of Industrial Arts continued to grow. The ever-increasing school enrollment, which by January 1920 numbered more than 1,100, necessitated the construction of yet another building. By the fall of 1920 Applegate decided that the current school year would be his last, and he gave notice. He planned to spend a year traveling around and studying the native clays of various regions, after which the family intended to spend winters in either Santa Fe, New Mexico, or Pasadena, California, and summers in Plainfield, New Hampshire, or New York City. "It is possible he will establish a studio in Pasadena or in or near New York City, as conditions warrant," a Trenton paper reported. Pasadena had a thriving art colony and was a center for the American Arts and Crafts movement, and his brother Archie had spent several months there in 1919 and had been favorably impressed with the city.[53]

In June 1921 Applegate showed his work for a final time in the School of Industrial Arts' annual exhibition. His pieces represented a wealth of knowl-edge and talent, an accumulation of a variety of techniques and styles that had taken a decade to distill. A ceramics authority said in a Trenton newspaper, "This is the best example of modern art pottery exhibited in recent years—the beauty of the glazes equals that of the ancient Egyptian and Persian craftsmen." One vase, which depicted a female figure with two other bent-kneed figures seated on either side, was noted for its "barbaric abdominal and breast marking." "[It] certainly would arouse the murderous greed of an ancient Egyptian king, who gleefully would poison a whole tribe of his subjects for its possession," the reviewer said.

Other pieces were described as "heavily glazed vases which have the appearance of being dug from the ruins of some long-forgotten city." The reviewer said the exhibit included several small pieces for "futuristic faddists," an indication that Applegate had started making modernist or even abstract sculpture by then. "These figures, or whatever they may be called, are handled in a subdued tonal manner," the article stated. Other more conventional shapes bore one of Applegate's "new glazes, a gold flake on red-brown background. As the piece is turned in the hand these 'crystals' reflect myriad flashes of light which are very pleasing."

Among the other glazes mentioned were a pearly opalescence, "a rarity in the potter's art, although much used by the old Venetian glassmakers," and deep, rich blues and greens "prized by Professor Applegate, as they represent long-continued effort, finally crowned by success in reproducing the Egyptian and Persian potters' finest work." He was called "one of the few modern potters who had produced the honey-colored glaze, if not the only one (p. 106)." The paper also noted that most of Applegate's "turquoise pieces" (p. 106) had been sold.[54]

Despite Applegate's achievements throughout the 1910s, the work of the studio potter was still underappreciated at the decade's end. Nor was the market for art pottery as sound as it had been earlier in the century, for the great art potteries, such as Rookwood, Van Briggle, and Weller, were on the wane.

By 1920 their financial stability relied increasingly on the production of mass-produced "industrial" pottery, and the skilled art pottery specialists were forced out. It took another decade, and the creation of the Robineau Memorial/ National Ceramic Exhibition, before studio ceramics earned recognition as a legitimate art form.[55]

The School of Industrial Arts administrators wrote to the Pennsylvania Academy of the Fine Arts to inquire where they could find an instructor to replace Applegate. The academy responded that "the best man they knew of in the country for such work was Frank G. Applegate, of Morrisville, Pa.," and advised the faculty to contact Mr. Applegate. According to a Trenton newspaper, Applegate "told [this] story with keen enjoyment."[56]

The Applegates packed up their belongings and equipped their Model T Ford for an extended camping trip, for Frank planned to visit some remote regions out West. They spent several weeks in Atlanta, heading west from Illinois in August. While they had no way of knowing what profound changes awaited in Santa Fe, like the pioneers of decades past, the Applegates were ready to write a new chapter in their lives.[57]

Endnotes

[1] Greenlee, "An Untitled Watercolor by Frank Applegate in the Colorado Collection at the University of Colorado, Boulder" (Unpublished paper, University of Colorado, n.d.), 28. Authors' interviews with Gretchen Beall.

[2] Murray, "Art in the Southwest," *Southwest Review* 11:4 (July 1926): 287. *Atlanta (Ill.) Argus*, March 6, 1914, 4, reprinted from the *Philadelphia News*.

[3] Morse, "Memories of Uncle Frank," 3, Applegate Papers.

[4] Land records, Bucks County, Pa., Book 398, p. 390, Book 450, p. 336, Bucks County Courthouse. Podmore, "A Little Journey to Picturesque Morris Heights," *Trenton (N.J.) State Gazette*, May 27, 1921.

[5] Podmore.

[6] FGA to John Mowbray-Clarke, July 7, 1914, Mowbray-Clarke Papers, Archives of American Art (AAA), Reel D169A. Morse, 1-2.

[7] Pennsylvania Academy of the Fine Arts student records, Pennsylvania Academy of the Fine Arts Archives. Taft, *History of American Sculpture*, 511, 579. Craven, *Sculpture in America*, 438, 439.

[8] Loughery, *John Sloan: Painter and Rebel*, 367. Pennsylvania Academy of the Fine Arts faculty minutes, Oct. 30, 1913, Pennsylvania Academy of the Fine Arts Papers, Archives of American Art.

[9] Boyle, in National Collection of Fine Arts, *Pennsylvania Academy Moderns, 1910-1940*, 10.

[10] Loughery, 23. Perlman, *Painters of the Ashcan School: The Immortal Eight*, 28.

[11] "F.G. Applegate Has Five Canvases in Los Angeles Museum Exhibition," *Trenton (N.J.) State Gazette*, n.d., probably July 1923, Applegate Papers.

[12] Brown, *Story of the Armory Show*, 210, 232. Wolff, "John Mowbray-Clarke and His Work," Mowbray-Clarke Papers. It is not known how Coluzzi and Applegate met.

[13] FGA to Mowbray-Clarke, May 29, 1914, Mowbray-Clarke Papers.

[14] FGA to Mowbray-Clarke, July 7, 1914, Mowbray-Clarke Papers.

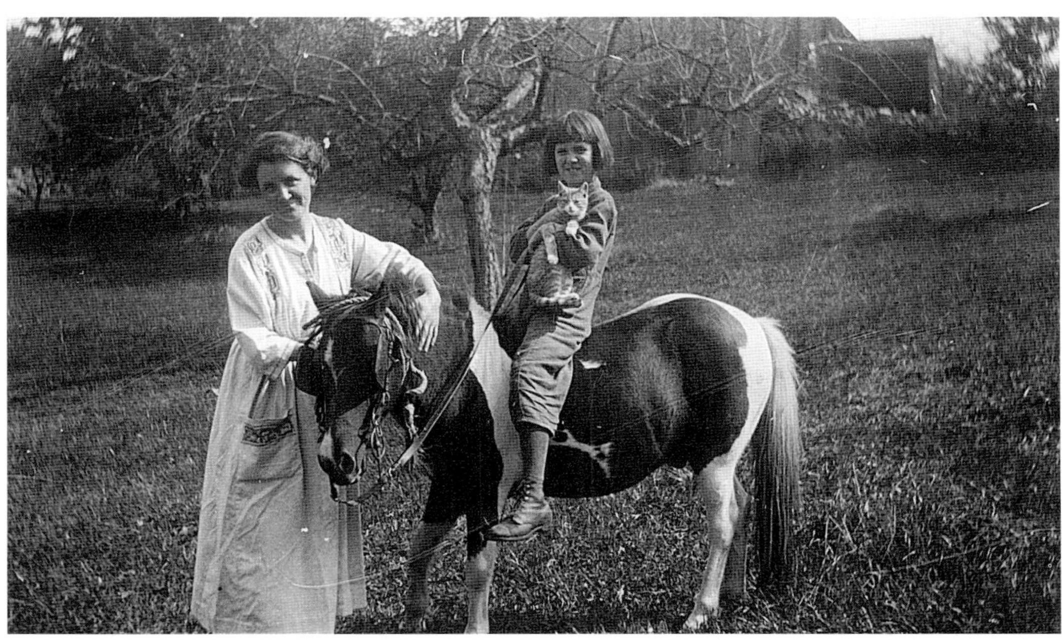

Alta and Betty Applegate, ca. late 1910s. Applegate Papers.

[15] Homer with Organ, *Robert Henri and His Circle*, 165.

[16] "Art Notes," *The New York Times*, Nov. 20, 1914, sec. 8, 7. Applegate made many mice, drawing his initial inspiration from a small, commercially made ceramic one that today is owned by the Gerald Peters Gallery.

[17] "Applegate's Terra Cotta Work Adding Fame to Art School, As Do Pupils Under Bourne," *Trenton (N.J.) Sunday Times-Advertiser*, Feb. 7, 1915.

[18] "Who's Who in American Art: N.E. Montross," *Arts and Decoration*, July 1915, 435.

[19] "Moderns at the Montross Gallery," *Arts and Decoration*, May 1915, 286.

[20] Beall written notes, Applegate Papers. "Exhibits of Etchings and Prints," *El Palacio* 20:2 (Jan. 15, 1926): 51-52; see also Chapter 6.

[21] Scant evidence has been found of Applegate's acquaintance with Kuhn. See Applegate obituary, *Santa Fe New Mexican*, Feb. 13, 1931, 1, also a postcard from Santa Fe believed to be from Sully Lewis to Walt Kuhn, undated but apparently sent in December 1923, when a painting of Kuhn's was on exhibit at the Museum of Fine Arts, Santa Fe; in Kuhn Papers, Archives of American Art, Reel D240.

[22] "Damn!" Says Sculpture, at Extreme American Art," *New York Herald*, March 26, 1915.

[23] Ibid. "Art Notes," *The New York Times*, March 26, 1915, 12. Two versions of "Wounded Lion Charging" are owned by the Gerald Peters Gallery. Two copies of "Damn" are in private collections. An undated clip from an unidentified Trenton newspaper in the Applegate Papers indicates he showed sculptures at the Montross Gallery another time in the 1910s. The clip says Applegate had "25 pieces of sculpture of the modern school and is the only display of sculpture in the exhibition." No other information about this exhibit has been found.

[24] FGA to Mowbray-Clarke, Aug. 30, 1915, Mowbray-Clarke Papers.

[25] Thanks to Richard T. Ashton of Morrisville, Pa., for providing the authors with photographs of Applegate's garden decorations.

[26] Alta Applegate to "Bumper" Mowbray-Clarke, Aug. 6, 1916. Murray, in catalog of Mowbray-Clarke show at Kevorkian Galleries, May 7-June 7, 1919, Mowbray-Clarke Papers.

[27] "Mary Mowbray-Clarke Is Dead," *The New York Times*, Nov. 21, 1962, 33. Sunwise Turn business receipts, Mowbray-Clarke Papers. While there is no evidence to indicate that Applegate met his future friends and colleagues Nordfeldt and Bynner before moving to Santa Fe, N.M., it is worth considering.

[28] FGA to Rosenthal, Jan. 27, n.d., Gratz Collection, Historical Society of Pennsylvania, AAA, Reel P22. Sprague, "Colorado Springs Fine Arts Center, Its Formative Years," in *Colorado Springs Fine Arts Center: A History and Selections from the Permanent Collections*, 18. FGA to John Mowbray-Clarke, Aug. 30, 1915, Mowbray-Clarke Papers. According to historian Lonn Taylor, Applegate had a studio in New Hope at one time, but the authors have been unable to corroborate this fact. See Taylor, "Arts and Crafts in the Santa Fe Style," 29.

[29] Berman, *Rebels on Eighth Street*, 117. "East Side Artist Wins Exhibit Prize," *The New York Times*, Nov. 3, 1915, 15.

[30] Ibid. "Mrs. Whitney's Prize to Italian Sculptor," *New York Tribune*, Nov. 13, 1915, 11. "Immigrant in America Competition," *American Art News*, Nov. 20, 1915, 7. Bufano (1898-1970) is best known for his public sculptures in the San Francisco Bay area. His most famous works include the statue of Sun Yat-sen in the city's Chinatown and "Peace" at the San Francisco International Airport. He made about 150 sculptures of St. Francis of Assisi. Bayne (1889-?), also known as Mary Bayne Bugford, studied with George Bellows at the Art Students League and exhibited throughout New York and New Jersey. According to Cassidy, "Art and Artists of New Mexico: Frank G. Applegate" (*New Mexico Magazine* 12:6 (June 1934): 51), "Hope" was installed at Ellis Island; however, no record or pictures of it have been found.

[31] Berman, 118.

[32] "Colonel's Big Stick Batters Cubist Art," *The New York Times*, Dec. 3, 1915, 11. Berman, 120.

[33] "Trenton Artists Gain Added Fame," undated clip from unidentified Trenton newspaper, Applegate Papers. "Art Exhibit at the Contemporary," *Trenton (N.J.) Evening Star*, n.d., MacGinnis Papers, AAA, Reel 75. Falk, *Annual Exhibition Record of the Pennsylvania Academy of the Fine Arts, Vol. III*, 70.

[34] Buffalo (N.Y.) Fine Arts Academy, "Exhibition of Contemporary Sculpture at the Albright Art Gallery," *Academy Notes* 11:3 (July 1916): 67, 92. Buffalo (N.Y.) Fine Arts Academy, *Catalogue of an Exhibition of Contemporary American Sculpture*, 6. Falk, ed., *The Annual Exhibition Record of the Art Institute of Chicago, 1888-1950*, 68.

[35] "Los Cinco Pintores," *El Palacio* 13:10 (Nov. 15, 1922): 131.

[36] The Gerald Peters Gallery, Santa Fe, N.M., owns more than 60 pieces of Applegate's pottery, including "Europa."

[37] "Art School Now Nearing Capacity," *Trenton (N.J.) Sunday Advertiser*, Feb. 6, 1916. FGA to Mowbray-Clarke, Aug. 30, 1915, Mowbray-Clarke Papers.

[38] Brown, *Story of the Armory Show*, 72.

[39] "Mrs. Henry Fitch Taylor," *The New York Times*, Nov. 19, 1921, 12. Walt Kuhn to Vera Kuhn, Dec. 7, 1911, Dec. 12, 1911, Kuhn Papers, AAA, Reel D240. Oaklander, "Clara Davidge's Madison Art Gallery: Sowing the Seed for the Armory Show," Archives of American Art Journal 36: 3-4, 20.

[40] Hagedorn, *Edwin Arlington Robinson*, 233. Neff, *Edwin Arlington Robinson*, 152, 165-166.

[41] Luhan, 123. Oaklander, 20, 25. Authors' correspondence with Oaklander.

[42] Luhan, 124-125, 128.

[43] Wade, *Brief History of Cornish*, 45, 54, 73, 89. Van Buren, "The Artists and Their Works," in *A Circle of Friends: Art Colonies of Cornish and Dublin*, 49, 96.

[44] Zorach, "The Background of an Artist, Part 2," *Magazine of Art*, May 1941, 237. Zorach, *Art Is My Life*, 50. FGA to Gerald Cassidy, n.d., (April 29, 1920). Quoted by permission of The Bancroft Library, owners of the Cassidy Family Papers, [ca. 1897-1965]. BANC MSS 67/1 p.

[45] Zorach, *Art Is My Life*, 50-51. FGA to Gerald Cassidy, n.d.

[46] Zorach, *Art Is My Life*, 51. Zorach added that Nettie May died later that year, having gone mad after being rejected by the artist she loved.

[47] Colby and Atkinson, *Footprints of the Past: Images of Cornish, New Hampshire and the Cornish Colony*, 173, 378, 449. Authors' interviews with Gretchen Beall. *Atlanta (Ill.) Argus*, June 6, 1919, 5, July 23, 1920, 4. Morse correspondence with Gretchen Beall, Applegate Papers. Van Buren, "The Artists and Their Works," 106. In 1920 or '21 Annetta Saint-Gaudens supposedly traveled to Trenton to study with Applegate, seeking "a more thorough knowledge of pottery." See "Professor Applegate, Noted Sculptor, Quits Art School After 14 Years," undated clip from unidentified Trenton newspaper, Applegate Papers; also Cassidy, 51.

[48] "Exhibits Sculpture," undated clip from unidentified Trenton newspaper, Applegate Papers. "The World of Art: The Architectural League," *The New York Times Book Review and Magazine*, April 3, 1921, 20. "Professor Applegate, Noted Sculptor, Quits Art School After 14 Years." "Applegate Voiced Protest Against Statue Immediately," *Santa Fe New Mexican*, Oct. 19, 1927, 2. Cassidy, 50. "Authority Upon Ceramics Here From School at Trenton," *Santa Fe New Mexican*, Aug. 27, 1921, 2. "Keramic" is a variation of ceramic commonly used in the 1800s and early 1900s (from the Greek κεπαμικοσ).

[49] Although the letter has not been found, its contents can be inferred from FGA to Gerald Cassidy and from Cassidy, 28.

[50] FGA to Gerald Cassidy.

[51] Clara Davidge Taylor to Mabel Dodge Luhan, June 16, 1919, Luhan Papers. Authors' correspondence with Oaklander. No record of the Taylors' visiting Santa Fe has been found.

[52] Cassidy, 28. Cassidy to Col. Ralph Twitchell, Aug. 30, 1920, Cassidy Family Papers, Box 14. A note on FGA to Cassidy states that the Cassidys sent the clay on April 30.

[53] "Urgently Need More Room for School of Art," *Trenton (N.J.) Sunday Advertiser*, Jan. 4, 1920, sec. 2, 7. "Professor Applegate, Noted Sculptor, Quits Art School After 14 Years." *Atlanta (Ill.) Argus*, July 18, 1919. Applegate sold off some of his Morrisville land to two individuals, each of whom paid only $1. The sales marked the first of many times that he sold land cheaply. The Applegates retained ownership of their home and its lot until 1925.

[54] "Professor Applegate, Noted Sculptor, Quits Art School After 14 Years." The vase featuring the two kneeling women is pictured in Cassidy, 28.

[55] Evans, *Art Pottery of the United States*, 409.

[56] "Professor Applegate, Noted Sculptor, Quits Art School After 14 Years."

[57] Cassidy, 28. *Atlanta (Ill.) Argus*, July 15, 1921. In November, after the Applegates had been in Santa Fe for several months, they received word that Clara Taylor had died under tragic circumstances. She apparently fell into a marsh near her brother's house on Long Island, and although the water was only a few inches deep, she got stuck in the mud, fainted, and then drowned. See "Bishop Potter's Daughter Drowns," *The New York Times*, Nov. 8, 1921, 9. Betty Applegate McClung told Gretchen Beall that her parents were extremely upset by Clara Taylor's death. They had received at least one very despondent letter from her and believed that she had taken her own life.

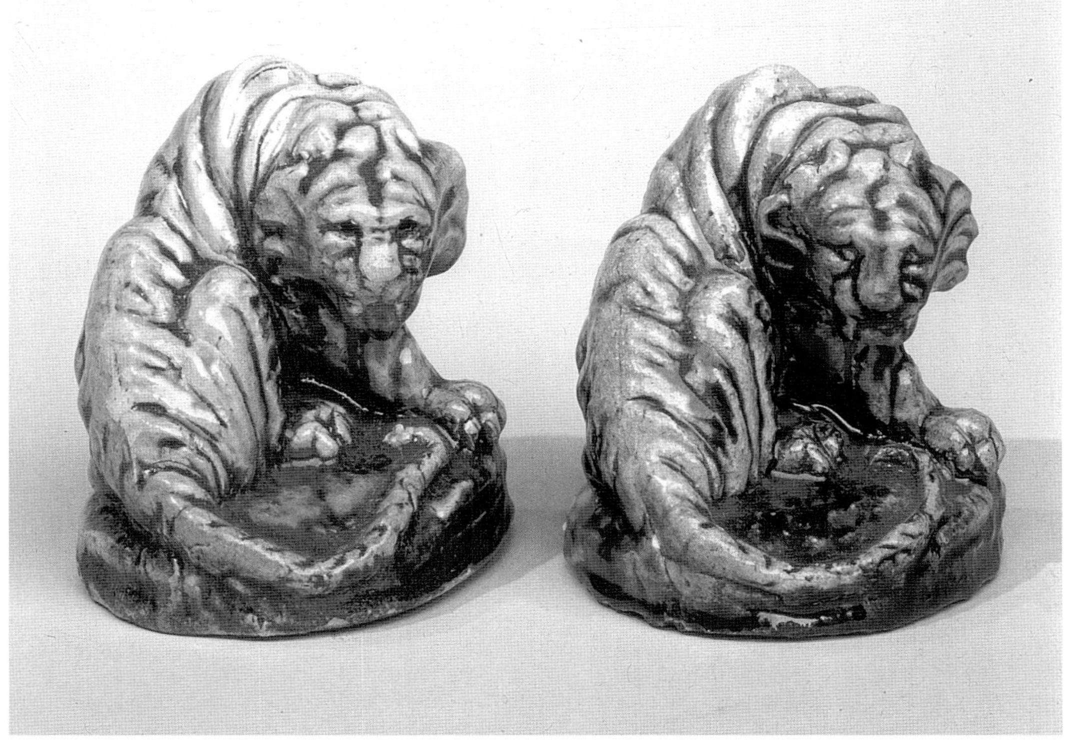

Two variations of *Tiger*, ceramic figures. Collection of Gerald Peters Gallery. Photograph courtesy of Gerald Peters Gallery, Santa Fe.

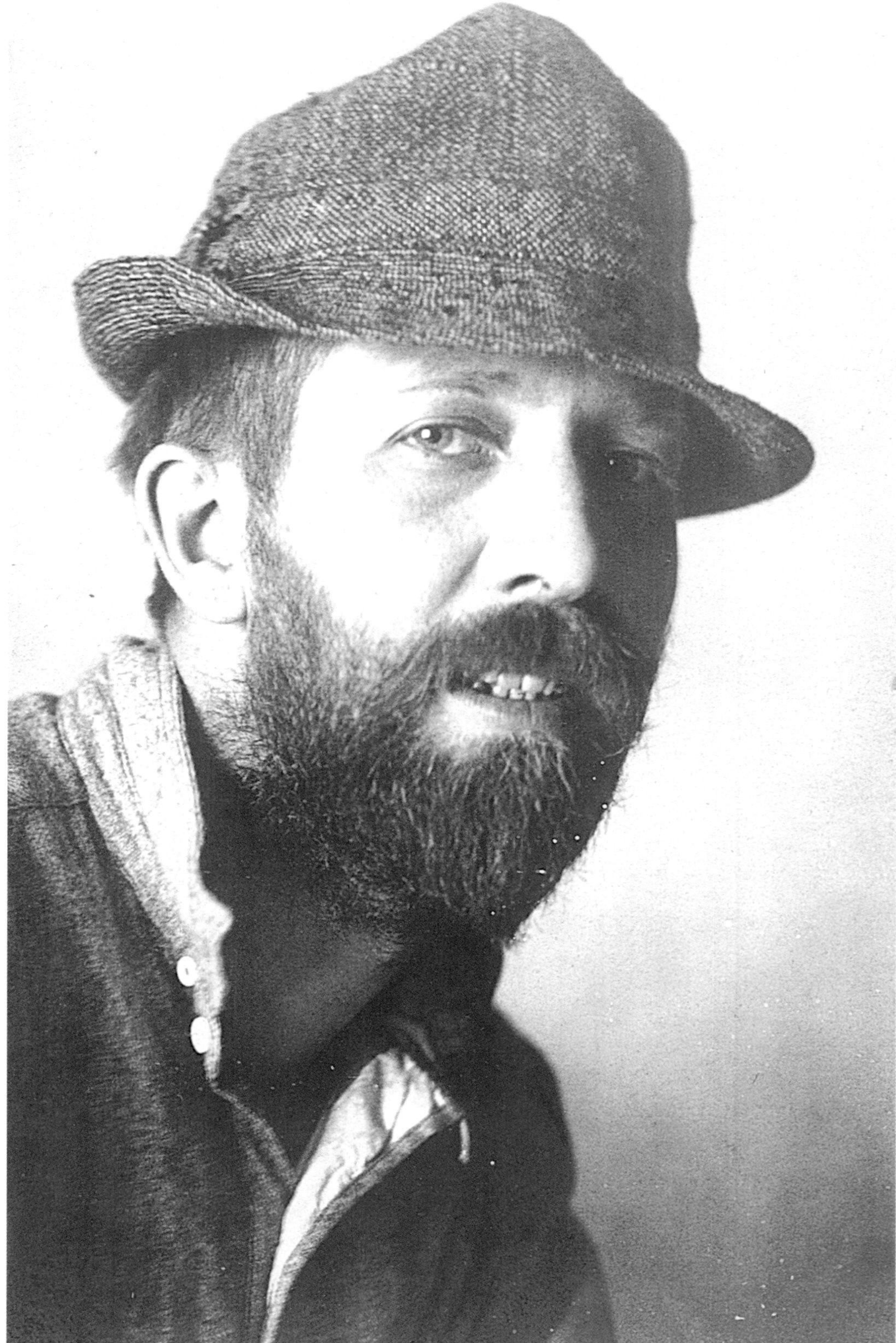

Frank Applegate. Photograph courtesy of the Applegate family.

4 The Wonder of Santa Fe

California's gorgeous climate and scenic beauty may have enticed other Easterners, but once Frank Applegate saw Santa Fe, the Golden State stood no chance. In Santa Fe he discovered a city that was ethnically diverse, aesthetically pleasing and, most importantly, welcoming to artistic individuals.

Applegate's decision to settle in Santa Fe produced dramatic changes in his life. In the first two years in New Mexico, he abandoned ceramics and a full-time teaching career, developed an interest in and started collecting Pueblo Indian and Spanish Colonial art, became an active supporter of Indian rights and tried his hand at woodcarving, painting, and building mud homes.

Frank, Alta, and 10-year-old Betty camped all the way from Illinois to the Southwest. Although the Applegates told the *Santa Fe New Mexican* that the trip was "delightful … in spite of the mud and rain," Betty remembered it as endless. It took a week to cross Kansas, much of it on dirt roads, and when the drive was not muddy and rainy, it was hot and dusty.[1]

In 1921 Santa Fe was a bustling small city of about 7,300. The capital of New Mexico had dirt roads, and burros still plodded down the streets bearing loads of firewood, including the piñon that perfumed the town all winter long. It would be several years before houses and businesses received numbered addresses. The lack of modern conveniences was one of the things that drew modern artists to Santa Fe, for the city served as an escape from an increasingly technological and mechanized society. Early on, Applegate expressed pleasure that the city was somewhat cut off from civilization, writing, "Since we've been here, we have left off taking all newspapers, magazines, etc., thinking it might be good for our souls."[2]

The family arrived in Santa Fe in time for the early September Fiesta. Then as now Santa Fe came alive historically and culturally during Fiesta, when the city celebrated its heritage with parades, dances, and pageantry. Pueblo dancers camped on the plaza, and performing groups sang and entertained. The first Fiesta was held in 1712 to commemorate Don Diego de Vargas' reconquest of the region in 1692-93, following the Pueblo Revolt of 1680; however, the event had been celebrated only sporadically until 1919, when Museum of New Mexico director Edgar Lee Hewett organized it anew.

The Fiesta celebration encapsulated the romance of the ancient city, which had been luring Easterners for many years. Santa Fe was the final stop on the Santa Fe Trail, a link with the Old West, and it had centuries of pre-settlement history behind it. The City of the Holy Faith was founded on the ruins of two ancient pueblos. Prehistoric artifacts were everywhere; as John Sloan, the New York painter who summered in Santa Fe for many years, said, "We dig down in our garden and we bring up pottery ages and ages old."[3] Santa Fe was surrounded by Indian pueblos and small Spanish villages populated by inhabitants whom the artists considered exotic and picturesque.

Equally important for the artists was the surrounding landscape. Shaped by ancient volcanos and wind, it was rough, unpredictable, and unlike anything in the East. The Sangre de Cristo Mountains rose to the east. To the west lay desert and mesas, with the Jémez Mountains off in the distance. North was the high country, where the Sangres climbed to join the rest of the Rocky Mountains. And above was the sky with its hard, brilliant light, a sky so big and blue that it seemed to reach to eternity. It was a landscape almost beyond description, and the responsibility for being true to it fell to the artists and writers.

The Southwest had been luring non-Hispanic white (later, "Anglo") artists since the first American exploration of the region.[4] Most of the early artists did not move there permanently but instead visited on painting trips and returned to their homes back East. Bert Phillips' and Ernest Blumenschein's visit to Taos in 1898 and Phillip's subsequent settlement there marked the beginning of the Southwest's first art colony.

"Year by year fewer and fewer artists feel the urge to journey Europeward," art critic Helen Appleton Read wrote in 1924.

> If they ... want a fiercer, grander, more exotic subject, they go West, preferably to the Southwest. ... Both nature and man have made a combination of paintable material that is hard to beat. For color and light, there are the fierce sun and gorgeous, unbelievable color of the desert; the pueblos have an architectural grandeur equal to any European ruin and are especially suited to present-day expression in that they follow distinct cubistic lines, while the Indian, if the artist is looking for types, offers a new beauty, a new character, more

stimulating than the much painted Italian fisherman or Brittany peasant.[5]

To a lesser extent, the artists also drew inspiration from the region's Spanish influence. Spaniards and their descendants had lived here since Don Juan de Oñate arrived in 1598, bringing Franciscan priests and farming and ranching families to settle what is today the northern part of the state. The mountainous landscape had kept parts of the area relatively isolated for centuries and helped to preserve medieval Spanish vernacular, lore, and institutions among the rural people. Residents of Old Mexico settled in northern New Mexico as well, and added "Mexican" culture to the melting pot.[6] New Mexico did not become a state until 1912, and the Americanization of the area was far from complete by 1920. Spanish was still spoken everywhere and used in governmental affairs, and pesos were common currency. The combination of cultures produced a region unlike any other in the United States.

Artists began to settle in Santa Fe in the first decade of the century. Painters Carlos Vierra, Paul Burlin, and Sheldon Parsons were among the first to make it their home. While the majority were painters, sculptors, composers, writers, and architects lived there as well.[7] The city's small size enabled artists to play a leading role in society, and the local newspaper, the *Santa Fe New Mexican*, regularly recorded their comings and goings, activities and antics.

Santa Fe's Museum of New Mexico opened in 1909, and the Museum of Fine Arts was dedicated in 1917 under the watchful eye of museum director Hewett. Robert Henri, founder of The Eight, worked there and helped to draw other artists to the city. The museum was unusual in that it contained studio space where artists could work free of charge. And on Henri's suggestion, Hewett adopted an open-door policy of exhibition, which allowed any artist in the state to show his work without having to go before a jury. The museum also brought in shows of national importance, sometimes featuring works by Pablo Picasso, Henri Matisse, and others on the cutting edge.[8] The museum and the School of American Research, which was established to study and preserve Pueblo Indian life, both had extensive collections of Native American art, and through them the artists quickly discovered the beautiful work being done by the nearby natives.

Santa Fe's cost of living was low, something starving artists found very attractive. Writer Elizabeth Shepley Sergeant recalled that during the 1920s, "one could rent two or three rooms in Santa Fe for $10 a month. The artists and writers of those days kept their horses in the dooryard, their butter in the well (if there was a well), and heated their small adobe rooms, hung with dusky saints … with piñon and cedar burned in small oval adobe fireplaces and air tight stoves."[9] The city also welcomed a solid tourist trade, due in part to artistic depictions of the region that found their way back East, and the tourists provided the artists with an ever-changing audience. Painter Gerald Cassidy, one of several who benefited from commissions for the Santa Fe Railroad, and his wife, writer Ina Sizer Cassidy, became seasonal residents of Santa Fe in 1912, and Cassidy and Vierra painted murals depicting New Mexico for San Diego's Panama-California Exposition in 1915. The Cassidy house on Canyon Road and the home of William Penhallow Henderson and his wife, poet and former *Poetry* magazine associate editor Alice Corbin Henderson, were among the first built in what would become Santa Fe's art district.

"I thought that I was coming to a desolate exile, and I found a new world of beauty," said Alice Corbin Henderson. Other writers of her acquaintance followed Henderson to Santa Fe, notably poet Witter Bynner, who purchased a home in 1922. Throughout the 1920s, writers of note spent seasons and sometimes years in Santa Fe, including poets Arthur Davison Ficke and John Gould Fletcher, folklorist B.A. Botkin, and writer Stanley Vestal, the latter two from the University of Oklahoma.[10] Paul Horgan, who wrote both fiction and non-fiction, lived there for a time. Poet, author, and essayist Mary Austin first came to Santa Fe in 1918 and returned repeatedly before buying land to settle there permanently in October 1923. Sinclair Lewis, Carl Sandburg, Vachel Lindsay, Edgar Lee Masters, and John Galsworthy visited, and D.H. Lawrence came down from Taos. Naturalist and author Ernest Thompson Seton was a friend of Austin's and a frequent visitor to the city, where he settled permanently in 1930. Willa Cather first came to Santa Fe in 1916 and returned in 1926, staying for a time in Austin's house.

Taos and Santa Fe also welcomed visiting artists such as George Bellows, Marsden Hartley, Stuart Davis, and Edward Hopper, who drew inspiration from the region but did not settle there. Others, such as John Sloan and Andrew Dasburg, preferred to live for part of the year in the City Different and the rest of the year back East.

The artists and writers came to Santa Fe in search of many things. Austin tried to explain to outsiders what New Mexico meant to them: "With an inert consciousness of having come at something fresher, we are nearer the original creative impulse than the schools have been able to take us. … This it seems, is the common denominator of the New Mexico interest. It has other and more explicit connotations for the individual according to his capacity. For one, it is new color relations; for another, a more robust sense of form, new rhythms in verse, new approaches to the story; to others, perhaps no more than a new source of unused material."[11]

Whatever Applegate was searching for, he found it in Santa Fe. The family had planned to stay in the city only long enough to visit several pueblos and for Applegate to investigate the supplies of the native clays and study the Indians' pottery methods, at which time they intended to continue on to Pasadena, California. Upon their arrival in Santa Fe, Gerald Cassidy invited the family to camp in his orchard, and within a week Frank had fallen under the city's spell.

"Applegate inquired for a house," recalled Ina Sizer Cassidy. "Thinking he wanted one to rent, Cassidy directed him to one, whereupon Applegate answered, 'I don't want to rent a house, I want to buy one.'"[12]

And so they stayed. It would be almost 10 years before they would visit California. It is not known how Alta reacted to this sudden change of plans, but from what relatives recall, she probably had come to expect such decisive action from her intractable husband.

By the second week of September, the Applegates had purchased a parcel of land on the Camino del Monte Sol. The "Road of the Sun Mountain" ran from Canyon Road up to Sun Mountain and the Sunmount Sanitorium, where convalescents with tuberculosis and other ailments came to get well. Francisco Romero y García sold the Applegates an 800-by-56-foot lot for 300 pesos.[13] The Applegates lived in their tent-camper on the property while Frank commenced building.

In October Ina Cassidy wrote of Applegate's renowned tile work, concluding, "Truly, Santa Fe is to be congratulated upon the acquisition of Mr. Applegate."[14] He soon fell in with other members of the art colony, most notably a group of largely unknown painters, all under 30, who had moved to Santa Fe during the previous three years. In 1921 these men–Will Shuster, Wladyslaw "Walter" Mruk, Willard Nash, Fremont Ellis, and Josef Bákos–formed a group for the purpose of exhibition called Los Cinco Pintores, or "the five painters."

The Cincos' first group exhibition was in November 1921. Their stated goal was "to take art to the people and … not to surrender to commercialism," and they planned to show in "mills, factories, school houses, and other places where people congregate but in which an exhibit will be a novelty." The latter goal went unrealized, for most of the shows were in galleries and at universities and museums. Their art was representational, not truly abstract (although it sometimes contained abstract qualities), but it was considered more advanced than that of other Santa Fe artists and seldom met with critical acclaim. "We were always hung under the stairs, or in some out-of-the-way alcove," Shuster recalled. Indeed, the Museum of Fine Arts designated one alcove "the Modern Wing."[15] Although all five men were considerably younger than Applegate, who was 40, they soon became friends.

From the beginning Applegate intended to preserve the atmosphere of "old Santa Fe" by allowing only Santa Fe–style (also called Pueblo Revival) structures, combining characteristics of Indian pueblos and Spanish Colonial architecture, to be constructed on his land. None of the Cinco Pintores owned his own home, and they were excited to learn that Applegate was building a Santa Fe–style house and studio. Applegate encouraged them to buy land from him and agreed to help finance the materials and help build the houses. How much each man paid Applegate is unclear. One source states the cost was $90 apiece. The land records show that each man paid between $600 and $750 for his parcel, but Applegate likely was including the cost of materials and labor in the price. As Ellis recalled it, Applegate "gave us all the empty land below his house, along the Camino. He bought the materials and hired two Spanish guys to help each of us. Applegate put it all down for us to pay later." Shuster contributed $200 from the sale of four paintings, and he also borrowed $1,000 from John Sloan to put toward his house (though perhaps only part of that went into the house). Shuster, Ellis, and Bákos did not pay Applegate for the land until February 1922, while Nash and Mruk did not buy land from him until August 1922.[16]

In late October the *Santa Fe New Mexican* reported that Ellis, Bákos, and Shuster were building their homes and studios on the Camino, with Nash to follow. None of them had experience in building with adobe bricks. If they had, they probably would have abandoned house-building efforts until the spring, rather than start construction with winter so near. "This was foolish," Bákos said, "but the Lord was with us."[17] Despite the fact that Applegate had studied architecture in college and had already built a house in Morrisville, Pennsylvania, and that Bákos was a skilled carpenter, the artists found adobe-building difficult. "Applegate … was the questionable expert on plumbing, and Shuster savvied electrical wiring," Shuster recalled. "What a bunch of ham builders we were!"[18]

The construction of adobe walls presented a unique problem for Shuster and Ellis, who were building their houses side by side. "Both were busily working away on adobe walls when 'Shus' noticed that Ellis' wall was slowly leaning off center. He hurried to warn Ellis and turned back to his own wall just in time to see it fall over, too. They did not know the primary rule that one must build a corner with the bricks, not just a wall in a straight line."[19]

Ellis remembered another mishap that occurred while building the roofs:

> I was up there [on my roof] with a hose and Shuster's inside [Ellis' house] and then I hear, "Hold it, hold it, hold it. It's leaking."

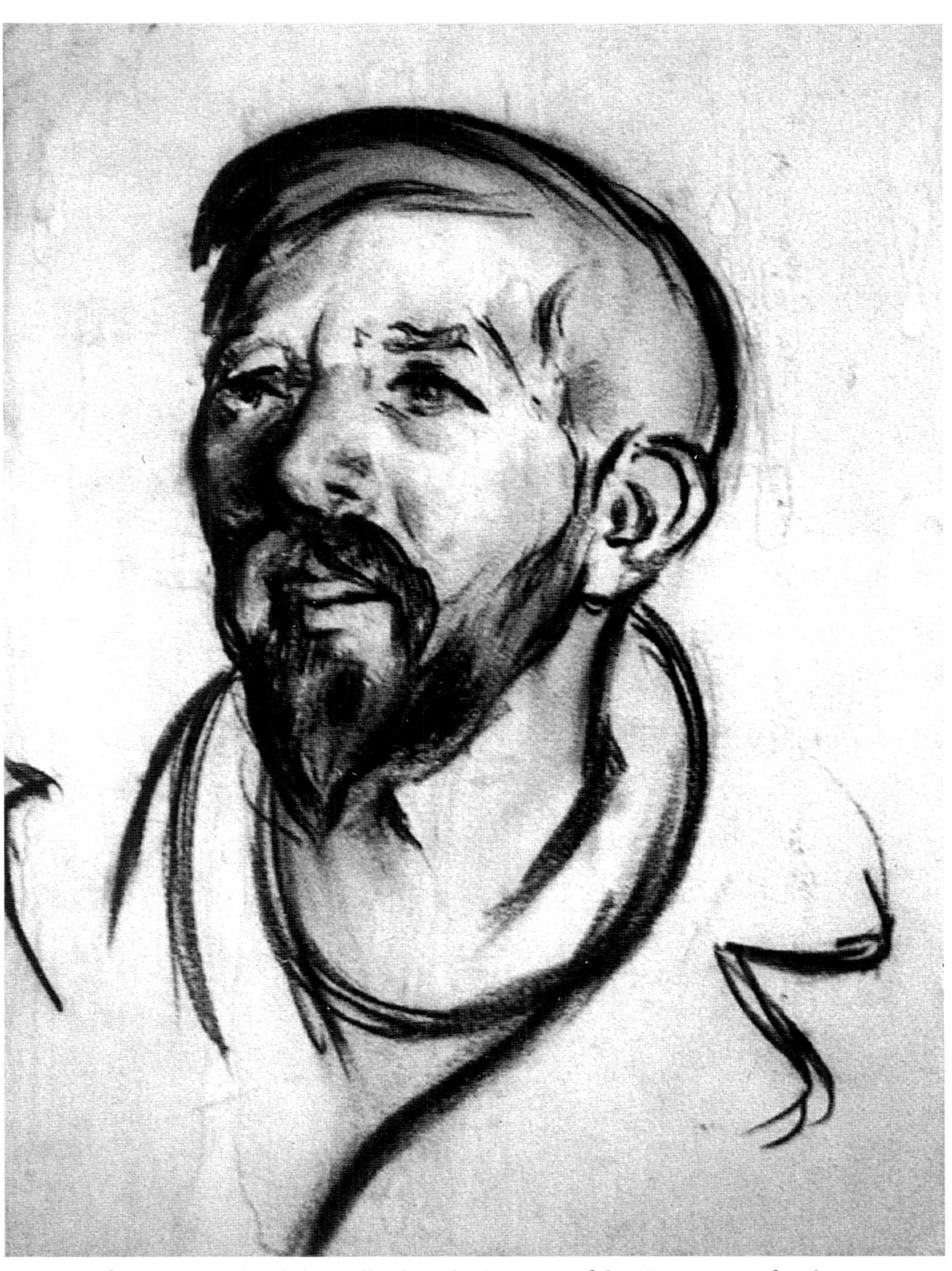

Señor Applegate, 1922, sketch by Willard Nash. Courtesy of the Hieronymus family.

CHAPTER 4:
THE
WONDER
OF
SANTA FE

[Shuster] said, "I don't think I'm going to have any leaks." So I went up there with the hose and he went inside, and "Hold it, hold it, hold it." His leaked just as bad as mine."[20]

Applegate did not complete all the work on his house by himself, for he reported, "I have the Mexicans do the building; they are very adept with adobe and cheap." The weather held out, and by December the houses were ready to live in. The Applegates' two-story dwelling was the first completed, followed closely by the Bákos home. The Shuster and Ellis abodes were ready to inhabit shortly after Christmas. Each house had its own distinctive artists' touches, including Bákos' handcarved furniture and frescos and Applegate's tiles. Applegate painted an exotic fresco in the dining room of the Bákos house and carved furniture for his own home (p. 129).[21]

Because Applegate often showed paintings with members of Los Cinco Pintores, and because he lived near them, many people believed he was a member of the group; Sloan even indicated that he thought so in a letter written to Shuster in 1923. However, the first time Applegate showed with the Cincos, publicity for the exhibition specified that it featured work by "Los Cinco Pintores and Frank Applegate," distinguishing him from the group. Applegate's temperament also differed from the younger men's. He was quiet and more or less a teetotaler, while they were known as rowdy partiers. Writer Willard "Spud" Johnson may have summed up the relationship best when he called Applegate "the step-father of the Cinco Pintores."[22]

Although the "Santa Fe style" is highly regarded today and is considered one of the few indigenous styles of architecture in the United States, few Santa Feans of the early 1920s appreciated it. The homes on the Camino were ridiculed, and the Cinco Pintores were commonly referred to as "the five nuts in their five adobe huts." A New York writer who called the style "Hopi" said it was "perfectly unadaptable to American life" and wondered "on what insane root the architects had dined."[23]

Applegate, however, was quite pleased with his home. "We live on a hill above Santa Fe about a mile from the Plaza, and look down over the town and the surrounding country for many miles," Applegate told Mary Mowbray-Clarke in May 1922. "We built us a mud house and have been living in it ever since. … We will probably build others later."[24] Applegate soon began buying up land along the Camino del Monte Sol and adjacent streets.

As soon as the family was settled, Applegate attended to his ostensible reason for coming to Santa Fe—to study the Indians' pottery methods. He made trips to the nearby pueblos to analyze the clays, meet the Indian potters, and learn their methods of firing. According to Ina Sizer Cassidy, he found the clay deposits "to be inadequate for the supply of any extensive pottery undertaking, and soon decided that no outsider had any moral right to come in and deplete the Indian's meagre supply. He felt there was no more than the Indians themselves needed, so he abandoned his idea of establishing a pottery and turned his attention to other forms of art."[25]

In retrospect this seems a rather drastic measure for someone who had devoted 15 years of his life to pottery and ceramics. Altruistic motives notwithstanding, perhaps Applegate had grown tired of working in the underappreciated field of ceramics. He had sketched his way around Europe, studied drawing at the Pennsylvania Academy of the Fine Arts and taught freehand drawing at the School of Industrial Arts, but he had never seriously applied his talent to media other than clay. New Mexico offered a new lifestyle, new experiences, and a new environment, so why not find a new way to explore it?

Implicit in his decision is the fact that Applegate must have arrived in the West with enough money to make building a pottery unnecessary. Yet, his switch to painting may have stemmed in part from concern over his financial future. Few sculptors were working in Santa Fe in the 1920s, and Applegate believed the dearth was related to tourists' disinterest in sculpted work. "It takes a little higher type of appreciation for good sculpture than for painting, for the appeal of color and other superficial elements is lacking. It is pure form that has to be reckoned with here," he noted in an essay in the mid-1920s. Applegate did not abandon ceramics entirely. He built a kiln for Ina Cassidy, who was also a sculptor, and he continued to produce ceramic pieces.[26]

Although it is as a painter that Applegate is remembered today, he did not take up the palette immediately. Instead he turned to another three-dimensional art form, woodcarving, producing not only furniture for his home but wooden sculptures. He spent most of the winter of 1921-22 making woodcarvings, and by April he had enough "interesting wood carvings in pure form" for a small show at the Museum of Fine Arts. By September 1922, however, he had begun to concentrate on painting, showing two paintings at that month's Fiesta exhibition.[27]

Along with his newfound interest in painting, Applegate developed an enthusiasm for the art of the Pueblo Indians and Hispanics. Many of Santa Fe's resident artists decorated their homes with Indian pottery and rugs and collected silver jewelry, and Applegate quickly became a collector, visiting pueblos to buy new pieces and excavating old ones. Although the art that came to be called "Spanish Colonial" was less popular at the time than Indian art, Applegate started collecting old religious woodcarvings and paintings, called santos, soon after he arrived in New Mexico.

The artists' interest in Indian and Spanish art stemmed not only from its beauty but from the fact that it was folk art, untaught and uninfluenced by machines. Many of the artists drawn to Santa Fe in the 1920s, like Applegate, desired to distance themselves from modern, industrialized society and find the "true" America. Their attitude has been characterized as "cultural primitivism," the belief that a simpler, less sophisticated lifestyle was a more desirable one.[28]

Some of Santa Fe's artists and writers were socialists, and many of them had socialist leanings. John Sloan formerly illustrated for the Socialist periodical *The Masses*, and his wife, Anna ("Dolly"), was active in the Socialist Party. Applegate's views would grow increasingly socialistic as he aged. There was talk of Bolshevism among Santa Fe's artistic ranks, and the year before Applegate arrived, the *Santa Fe New Mexican* printed an editorial urging that action be taken to prevent the Museum of Fine Arts from being "regarded as a center of anything remotely connected with Bolshevist ideas in art or otherwise." The art colony as a whole, several of whose members were veterans of the World War, declared itself insulted by the editorial, and called it a "smear on the painters who consider themselves modernists."[29]

Attitudes such as these undoubtedly spurred the artists and writers to become active in public affairs, and 1922 marked the beginning of Applegate's social and to a lesser extent political activism. What initiated this activity was the Bursum Bill. Named for New Mexico rancher and senator Holm O. Bursum, the bill "granted title to non-Indian settlers who had claims on Indian land if they could show continuous possession of that land for 10 years, with no compensation for the Indians."[30]

The battle over the Bursum Bill was one of the first major attempts by the artists, writers, and intellectuals to improve the Indians' quality of life. Since the first Anglo-American settlement of the West, government agencies had attempted to assimilate the Indians into mainstream American society by suppressing their traditional ways of life—for example, by forcing their children to attend boarding schools, by prohibiting their participation in religious dances, and by taking over land the Indians held sacred. The artists believed it was their duty and mission to preserve as much of Indian culture as possible, for who were the Indians if not the "true" Americans?

Led by poet Witter Bynner, art patron and writer Mabel Dodge Sterne (later Luhan) of Taos, writers Mary Austin and Alice Corbin Henderson, and John C. Collier, who in 1923 became executive secretary of the American

Indian Defense Association, the artists and writers rallied together to oppose the bill. They also met with all the tribal leaders to inform them of the bill's result if passed and helped organize the New Mexico Association on Indian Affairs to fight for Indian interests.[31]

As with many issues the artists would take up over the next decade, the sides drawn up in the Bursum Bill dispute were not clear-cut. Many of the same people who opposed the Bursum Bill later fought for the preservation of Hispanic villages, and the Hispanic landowners, including poor, rural ranchers, stood to benefit from the bill's passage, because it would give them clear title to the land on which they had ranches and farms. Additionally, some in the artists' circle were accused of having a vested interest in wanting the Indian bill defeated. Secretary of the Interior Albert Fall, who backed the Bursum Bill, spoke of "particular individuals who are now, under the cloak of protecting the Indians, engaged in misleading statements … some of them defamatory statements concerning officials of the Indian Bureau and of this department."[32]

The bill was defeated in 1923, due in part to a well-orchestrated publicity campaign led by Austin, Sterne (Luhan), and Collier. The "Protest of Artists and Writers Against the Bursum Indian Bill," an open letter that ran in publications nationwide, included such names as D.H. Lawrence, Harriet Monroe, Carl Sandburg, Zane Grey, and the majority of the Santa Fe and Taos artists and writers. The bill was attacked in *The New York Times, New York World, New York Tribune, Hartford Daily Times, Boston Transcript, Christian Science Monitor*, the *New Republic,* and *Sunset,* among other publications.[33]

By signing the protest Applegate turned another corner. He no longer merely observed and documented social ills, as he had in his letters from Europe and his sculptures of derelicts and laborers. Throughout the 1920s he and the other members of the artists' colony fought for Indian rights, the rights of Hispanics, historic preservation, and other causes that they believed threatened their adopted home and its native peoples. "You and your gang make noise that's heard," Sandburg told Alice Corbin Henderson in 1922. "I hand it to you as a healthy hell-raiser. You have located a nest of SOB's, and what will come of your noise about 'em there's no telling."[34] What came of their noise was sometimes good, sometimes misguided and sometimes more entertaining than useful. Applegate would always be more of a preservationist than a crusader, but in later years he found the voice to speak out against perceived injustice, as he and others sought to improve the lives of the Native Americans and rural Hispanics.

Endnotes

1 "Authority Upon Ceramics Here From School at Trenton," *Santa Fe New Mexican*, Aug. 27, 1921, 2. Beall written notes, Applegate Papers.
2 *Santa Fe New Mexican*, March 5, 1925. FGA to Mary Mowbray-Clarke, May 2, 1922, Mowbray-Clarke Papers, AAA, Reel D169A.
3 "Artists Headed for Santa Fe," *The New York Times*, reprinted in *El Palacio* 13 (1922), 169.
4 In *The Myth of Santa Fe: Creating A Modern Regional Tradition*, Chris Wilson dates the use of Anglo to denote Americans not of Pueblo or Spanish descent to the mid-1920s (p. 149).
5 Read, "Pueblos of Distinct Cubist Lines," *Brooklyn (N.Y.) Daily Eagle*, Oct. 26, 1924, reprinted in *Santa Fe New Mexican*, Oct. 30, 1924, 4.
6 Throughout this book, the word "Hispanic" is usually used to encompass descendants of the original families who came over from Spain to settle New Spain, "Mejicanos," or settlers who moved to what is now northern New Mexico from "Old" Mexico, and those of Indo-Hispanic (then called mestizo) descent (and none of these terms are mutually exclusive, since intermarriage had taken place since the days of the Aztecs). As seen in subsequent quotes, Applegate, Mary Austin, and others of the era usually referred to all people of Spanish descent as either "Spanish" or "native," but they sometimes used the term "Mexican" to distinguish those whose families arrived more recently from Old Mexico. For more on the racism inherent in the Anglos' choice of terms, and the history of the usage of such terminology, see Wilson, *The Myth of Santa Fe.*
7 Gibson, *Santa Fe and Taos Colonies,* 70.
8 Homer with Organ, *Robert Henri and His Circle,* 205. *Santa Fe New Mexican,* Dec. 19, 1923.
9 Sergeant, "The Santa Fe Group," in Weigle and Fiore, *Santa Fe and Taos: The Writer's Era,* 133.
10 Hawthorne, "Santa Fe Becomes the Eden of Authors," *The Literary Digest International Book Review* 4:12 (November 1926): 739. Gibson, 187.
11 Austin, "Indian Detour," *The Bookman* 68:6 (February 1929): 656.
12 Cassidy, "Art and Artists of New Mexico: Frank G. Applegate," *New Mexico Magazine* 12:6 (June 1934): 28.

13 Land records, Santa Fe County Courthouse. Believed to be about $1,500, based on the value of Mexican pesos at the time.

14 Cassidy, "Beginning of Greater Art Colony on Camino Monte Sol," *Santa Fe New Mexican*, Oct. 29, 1921, 2.

15 "Los Cinco Pintores," *El Palacio* 11:11 (Dec. 1, 1921): 139. Shuster interview with Sylvia Loomis, July 30, 1964, Shuster Papers, AAA, Reel 277, transcript, 4. Robertson, *Los Cinco Pintores*, 14.

16 "Los Cinco Pintores," *Artists of the Rockies and the Golden West*, Summer 1979, 66. Belshaw, *Camino del Monte Sol Architectural Historic Survey*, 42. Loughery, *John Sloan: Painter and Rebel*, 259. Land records, Santa Fe County Courthouse.

17 Cassidy, "Beginning of Greater Art Colony on Camino Monte Sol." "Los Cinco Pintores," *Artists of the Rockies and the Golden West*, 66.

18 Shuster, "Los Cinco Pintores Enlivened Art Colony," *Santa Fe New Mexican*, Sept. 23, 1951.

19 Robertson and Nestor, *Artists of the Canyons and Caminos*, 89-90. Betty Applegate McClung recalled this incident in an undated note to Gretchen Beall, Applegate Papers.

20 "Walls Tumbled, Roofs Leaked but Artists' Houses Still Stand," *Albuquerque (N.M.) Journal (North)*, Feb. 4, 1984, E-7.

21 FGA to Mary Mowbray-Clarke, May 2, 1922, Mowbray-Clarke Papers. *Santa Fe New Mexican*, Dec. 17, 1921. Ward, "Los Cinco Pintores," *Albuquerque (N.M.) Journal (North)*, Feb. 4, 1984, E-6.

22 Sloan to Shuster, Feb. 9, 1923, Shuster Papers, AAA. "Western Art Is on Exhibit, *(Norman) Oklahoma Daily*, Oct. 13, 1922, 1. Johnson, "Index to First Lines," *Laughing Horse* 12 (August 1925): 34.

23 Ward, E-6. Gerould, *The Aristocratic West*, 114.

24 FGA to Mary Mowbray-Clarke, May 2, 1922, Mowbray-Clarke Papers.

25 Cassidy, "Art and Artists of New Mexico: Frank G. Applegate," 49. Alice Clark Myers stated that Applegate had considered starting a ceramics school in New Mexico but found the clay resources unsuitable for high-temperature firing. See interview with Alice Clark Myers, October 7, 1967, Augusta Fink Papers, Box 1, Folder 30.

26 Applegate, "Tourists and Art," *Southwest Review* 12:1 (October 1926): 24-25. Cassidy, "Art and Artists of New Mexico: Frank G. Applegate," 50-51. Comfort and Comfort, eds., *This Is Santa Fe*, 112. According to Greenlee, "An Untitled Watercolor by Frank Applegate in the Colorado Collection at the University of Colorado, Boulder," 24, in an interview in 1987, Betty Applegate McClung said her father did not have a kiln in Santa Fe, but Ina Cassidy recalled one, and ceramic pieces believed to date to the Santa Fe years exist today. Of particular note is a portrait bust of a Native American that belongs to the Atlanta, Illinois, Public Library (p. 112).

27 FGA to Mary Mowbray-Clarke, May 22, 1922, Mowbray-Clarke Papers. "Applegate Carvings in Wood to Be Shown," *Santa Fe New Mexican*, April 8, 1922. "The Fiesta Art Exhibit," *El Palacio* 13:8 (Oct. 16, 1922): 99.

28 Gaither, "A Return to the Village: A Study of Santa Fe and Taos, New Mexico, As Cultural Centers, 1900-1934," (dissertation, University of Minnesota, 1957), 16-17.

29 Chauvenet, *Edgar L. Hewett and Friends*, 142.

30 Stark, *El Delirio: The Santa Fe World of Elizabeth White*, 50.

31 Kelly, *The Assault on Assimilation*, 217.

32 Forrest, *The Preservation of the Village*, 56-57. *Santa Fe New Mexican*, Jan. 23, 1923.

33 *Santa Fe New Mexican*, Dec. 6, 1922.

34 Blend, "Women Writers and the Desert: Mary Austin, Ina Sizer Cassidy, and Alice Corbin," (dissertation, University of New Mexico, July 1988), 373.

CHAPTER 4:
THE
WONDER
OF
SANTA FE

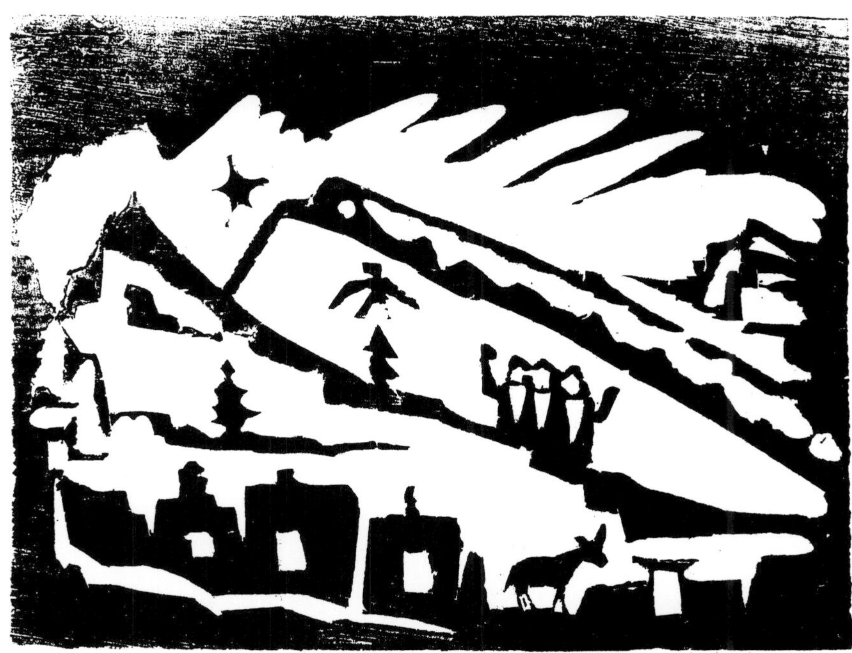

Mountain Side, woodblock print by Frank Applegate, which appeared in the August 1925 edition of *The Laughing Horse*.

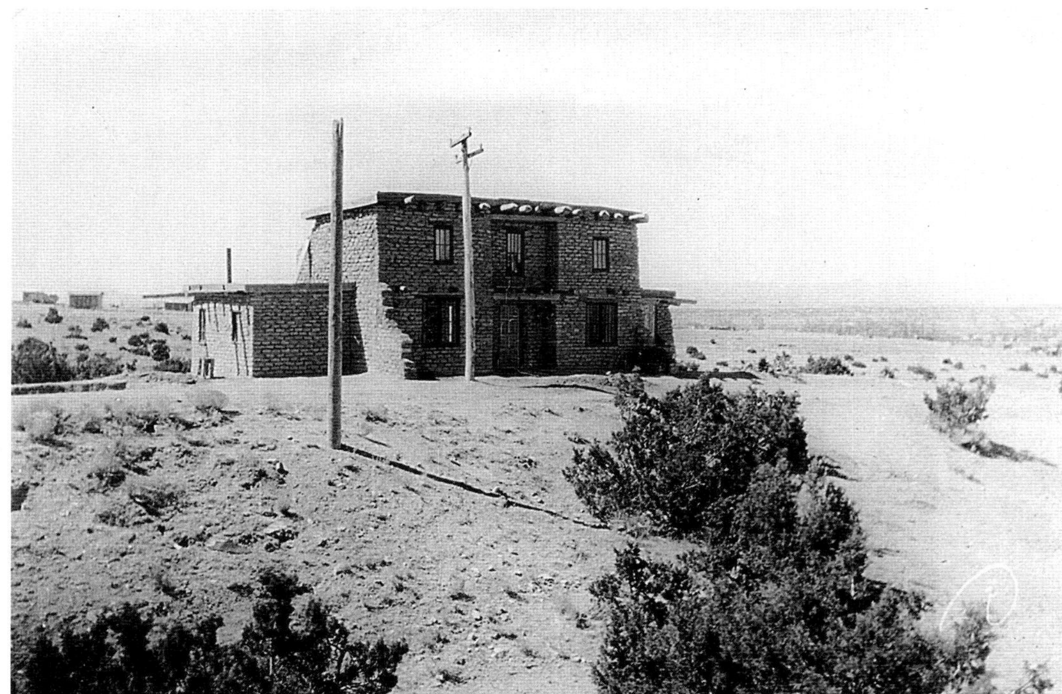

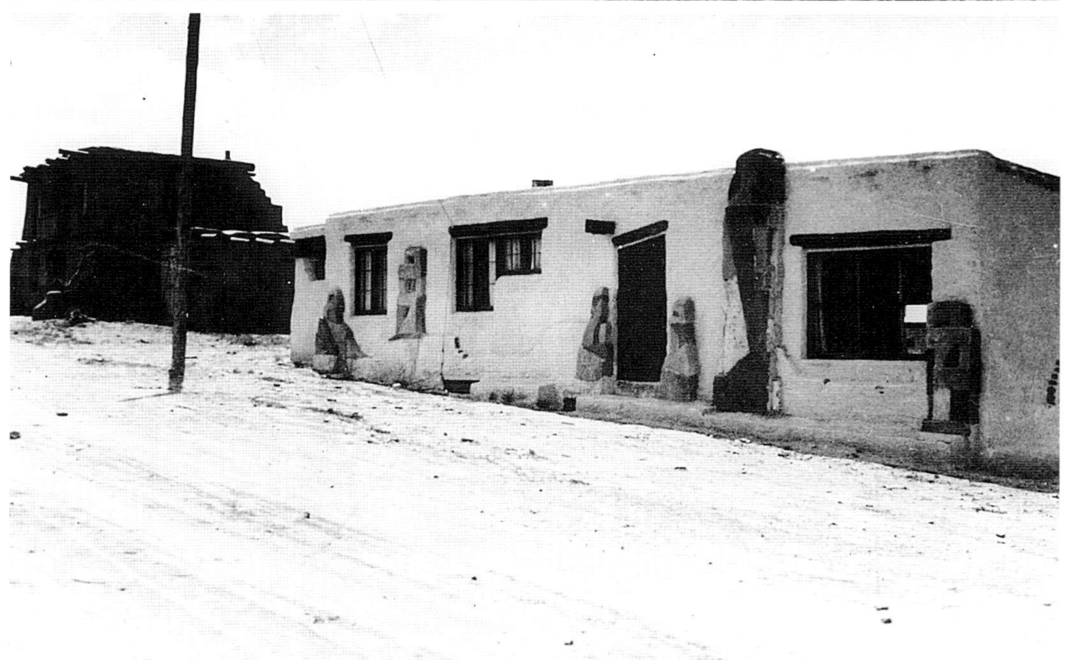

Top: Applegate's first house at 558 Camino del Monte Sol as it appeared in the early 1920s. Photograph courtesy of the Museum of New Mexico (neg. no. 7426). Bottom: The second dwelling Applegate constructed in Santa Fe was this building at 550 Camino del Monte Sol, shown here in 1923. Note the cubist sculptures on the front and the sloping lintel over the doorway. This building likely originally served as Applegate's studio; note its proximity to his first house, seen at left. Photograph by E.E. Nichols, courtesy of the Museum of New Mexico (neg. no. 178100).

5 The Sculptural Architect

The artistic community that gives present-day Santa Fe its reputation as a fine arts center lies scattered throughout the city in galleries, shops, studios, and museums. But the neighborhood that best captures the city's artistic soul–the creative, bohemian atmosphere that has drawn artists and art lovers there throughout this century–is the area southeast of the Plaza along Canyon Road and its intersecting streets. Here, galleries and shops filled with art and fine craft proliferate, and most of the buildings typify the Santa Fe style. Were it not for Frank Applegate, these quaint, charming streets would probably look very different. His architectural handi-work is evident not only in the houses he built but in the historically influenced design of many of the structures in the area.

From his first days in Santa Fe, Applegate acted with a sense of mission toward preserving the city's indigenously inspired beauty. He began purchasing land along and near the Camino del Monte Sol soon after his arrival. In the decade from 1921 to 1931, the Applegates bought dozens of pieces of land, usually small tracts of less than an acre. As landowners they had control over the style of the dwellings constructed, and they also could dictate stylistic guidelines before selling any land. In at least one instance they agreed to sell a parcel of land "subject to the restriction that one Santa Fe style residence only ... shall ever be erected on said land."[1]

Applegate was able to earn a small income from renting and selling houses and from selling land. According to a list of property valuation assessments published in May 1930, the Applegates owned a four-room residence with land, assessed at $2,630, a five-room residence with land, assessed at $3,415, which they reportedly rented out at $75 a month, and a six-room residence with land, assessed at $3,595.[2]

Applegate built houses in what today is called the Pueblo Revival or Santa Fe style, which combines the attributes of Indian pueblos with those of New Mexican missions. Common characteris-tics in the houses include buttresses, flat roofs, hand-hewn, randomly projecting vigas (wooden beams), hand-hewn corbels (brackets), exposed lintels, softly rounded corners, and thick, sloping adobe walls with a weighty, sculptural quality.[3] The style suited both Apple-gate's Arts and Crafts sensibilities, because it emphasized the handcrafted and incorporated local building materi-als, and his modernist sensibilities because the style used the materials openly in such a way as to reveal their character and structure.

During the decade he lived in Santa Fe, Applegate is known to have built four houses on and near the Camino del

Monte Sol, possibly to have built another, and to have extensively renovated one. He may have built others. His college architecture classes, including architectural modeling, and the experience of building the Morrisville, Pennsylvania, home no doubt helped him, as did his skill as a sculptor. Applegate wrote an essay in which he described his affection for adobe architecture and revealed modernist sentiments toward it. "The great charm of this style of building lies in its simplicity and plasticity and its local color, which derive naturally from the material of which it is built," he wrote. "At its best a building of this clay-like material is relieved of all non-essentials; and when it is planned with understanding of the medium, the fluid lines and plastic surfaces give it a character unapproachable in any other material." Although he employed local laborers to help with construction, he enjoyed working with adobe himself. "He was never happier than when in his old clothes laying up adobes," the *Santa Fe New Mexican* recalled after his death.[4]

Applegate's first house, a two-story dwelling at what is today 558 Camino del Monte Sol (p. 60), is considered one of the finest examples of Pueblo Revival architecture in the city. Constructed in 1921, it had a second-story balcony, corner buttresses, battered walls, and ax-cut vigas that projected random distances beyond the walls, as they would in a structure built by Pueblo Indians.[5]

The homes of Los Cinco Pintores—Fremont Ellis, Will Shuster, Walter Mruk, Josef Bákos, and Willard Nash—show Applegate's influence as well. "His background in modeling … enabled him to see clearly the sculptural possibilities of adobe," wrote researcher Michael Belshaw, who described the houses as "highly livable sculpture."[6] The fact that Applegate helped the younger men finance the work likely lent weight to his opinions concerning the houses' design.

While it is certain that Ellis, Shuster, Bákos, and Nash built homes on the Camino, whether Mruk built one is unclear. Mruk bought property from Applegate twice, in August 1922 and February 1924, and at least one of the purchases included a house. In November 1922, the *Santa Fe New Mexican*

reported that Applegate had decorated the chimney and façade of Mruk's new home "in abstract carved figures, which adds much distinction to it." It is unknown which house the newspaper refers to, and whether or not Mruk actually built the house himself. Several houses on the Camino, including those which today stand at 550 Camino del Monte Sol and 542 Camino del Monte Sol, have uniquely carved chimneys. It is known that Applegate built the first house, and he may also have designed the chimney at 542 Camino del Monte Sol, which was Shuster's first house.[7]

According to Maria Mathes, who researched the history of the house at 558 Camino del Monte Sol, Mruk "apparently knew himself well enough not to try to build an adobe house on the Camino." Based on the known chronology of events, it is most likely that Mruk did not buy Applegate's first house, at 558 Camino del Monte Sol, until February 1924. This house is sometimes called the Mruk house.[8]

In February 1923 Applegate began work on a building that included a very large studio (p. 60). This structure, at 550 Camino del Monte Sol, is "highly livable sculpture" at its finest. The adobe steps and shelves, zig-zags and curves, combine to produce a work of art removed from the stark and functional simplicity of pueblo dwellings. It is also notable for the sloping lintel over the front door. The caption for a photograph taken in 1923 describes this building as Applegate's studio, and Betty Applegate remembered having to sleep in it when guests took over the house. The sculpted chimney on this house resembles the one at Shuster's first house, and both chimneys are similar to cubist-inspired woodcarvings Applegate exhibited in 1923-24 (see Chapter 6).[9]

Applegate built other houses along the Camino, employing laborers who lived in the neighborhood and renting or selling the dwellings. He may have designed and built the house at 544 Camino del Monte Sol, which belonged to Andrew Dasburg. In 1924 he built a two-story New Mexico-mission-influenced home at 408 Camino del Monte Sol which he sold to architect Hugh Sener.[10]

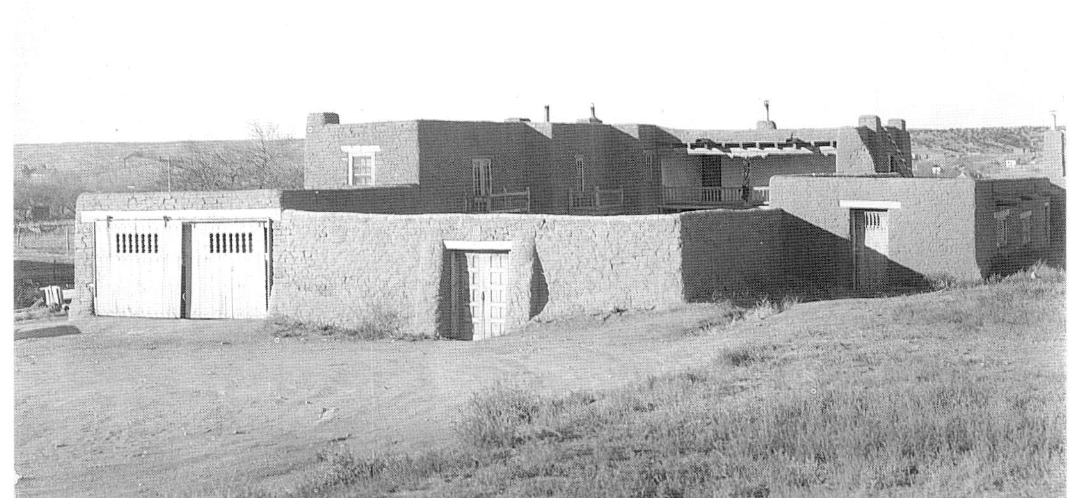

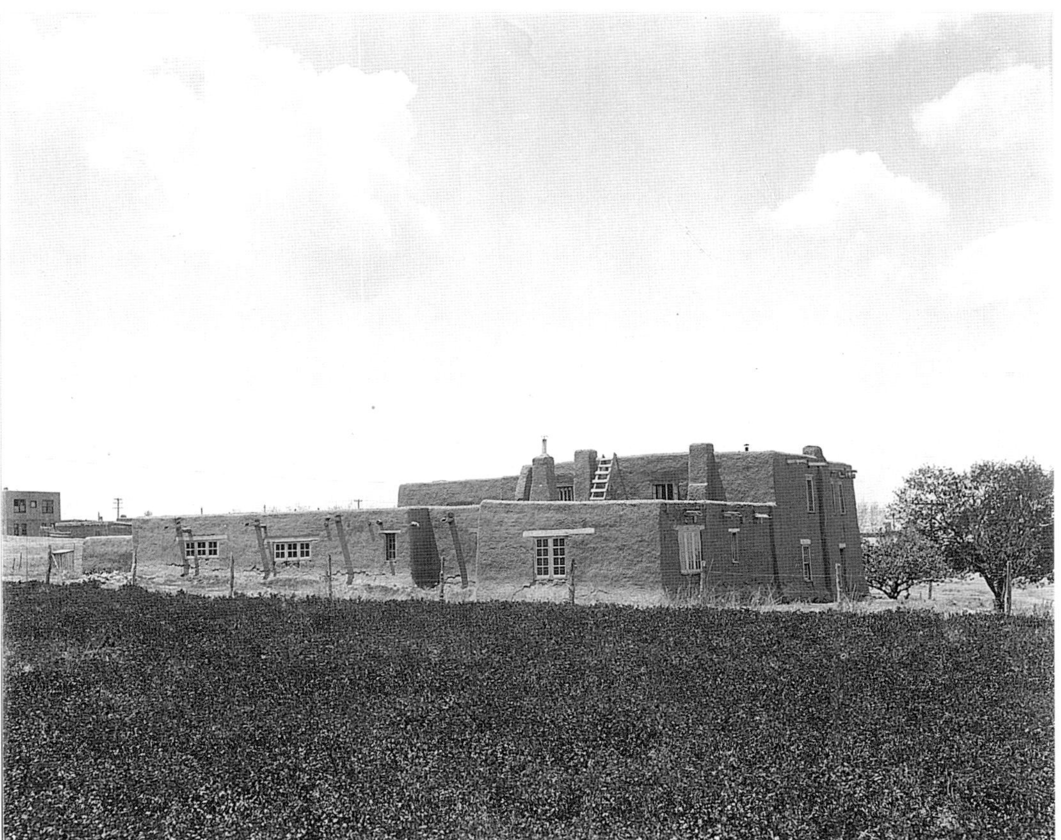

Top: The Applegates' home on El Caminito in Santa Fe, originally known as the de la Peña House. Photograph by Theo M. Fisher. Bottom: Another view of the de la Peña House. Published in *House & Garden*, August 1929. Applegate Papers.

That year the Applegates began negotiations to buy the de la Peña House and about three acres of surrounding property, which ran along the Camino but faced a side street, El Caminito. The de la Peña House was and remains one of the most historically and architecturally significant buildings in Santa Fe. Sergeant Francisco de la Peña, a Mexican Army soldier who had fought against Texans at the Alamo, purchased the house and land in 1845. The structure on the property at that time was an eighteenth century four-room house with a portal. When the Applegates bought it, the house had been occupied for more than 80 years by the de la Peña family, and two of de la Peña's daughters still lived there. The *Santa Fe New Mexican* called the property "perhaps the last large old Spanish hacienda available in the city." It took several years and a lawsuit for the sale to be finalized, but by March 1926 negotiations for the de la Peña House were completed.[11]

Applegate made major renovations on the house, eventually more than quadrupling its size, but retained much of the original structure. He designed it in a U-shape with his studio on the west side. He turned the original four rooms with their three-foot-thick adobe walls into living rooms and built a second story using the beams and portal from the ground floor. Recognizing that the porch lintel at the front entrance was unusual because its corbel brackets were part of the same log, he made a copy for the downstairs and moved the original lintel upstairs along with the first floor beams. He thickened the parapet over the porch to achieve a more massive effect. Details incorporated into the house included Spanish Colonial balconies taken from an old building, three old New Mexican trasteros (cupboards) built into the walls, squared, hand-hewn beams, and antique corbels. Applegate also preserved the elevated shepherd's bed that stood outside the house by enclosing and plastering it, making it part of the residence.[12]

The house was a showplace, filled with "a veritable treasure trove of santos and bultos and old native furniture." Its beauty and furnishings drew national attention as a superb example of Indian-Spanish architecture. *House and Garden* magazine published photographs of it in 1929, showing both the exterior and interior. One photo reveals rows of shelves lined with Native American pottery, while others show religious woodcarvings, a tin candelabrum, Spanish Colonial furniture, and Navajo rugs (see photographs throughout this book).[13]

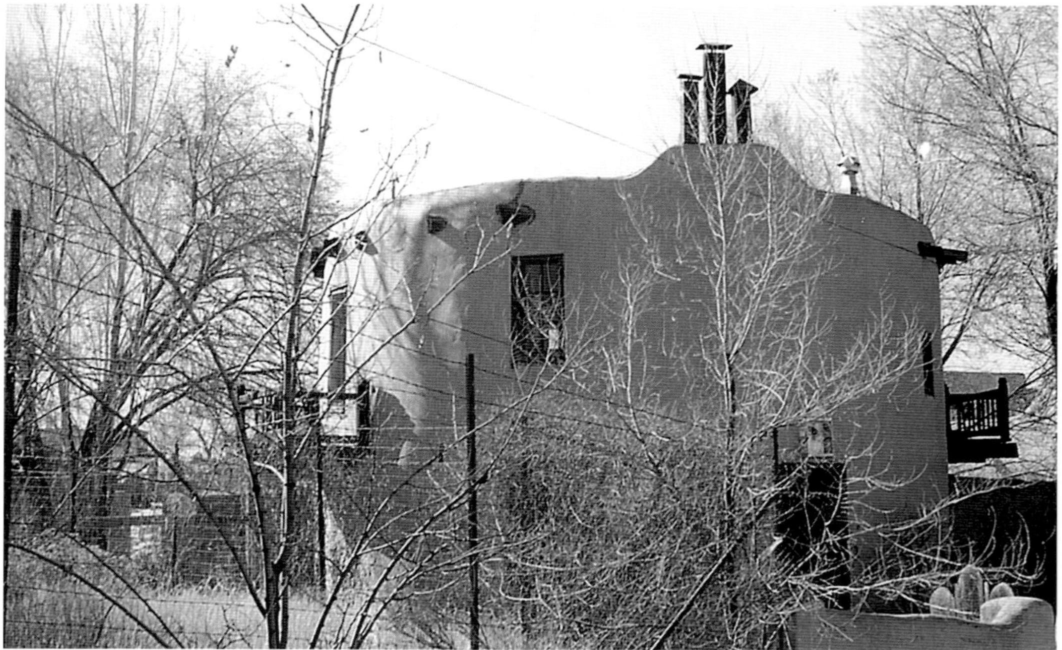

El Torreon, which Applegate built on El Caminito in 1930, as it appeared in 1965. Photograph courtesy of the Museum of New Mexico (neg. no. 74538).

The de la Peña House represented Applegate's crowning achievement, and he continued to work on it until his death. He also built another house, a rental property located across El Caminito from the de la Peña House, in 1930. Called "El Torreon," the dwelling was Santa Fe's only adobe "round house," designed to resemble a Spanish torreon, or defensive tower.[14]

Belshaw called the houses built by Applegate and those he helped to design "the finest distillation of Pueblo Revival architecture of the 1920s."[15] These houses, all of which stand today, and the other vintage homes on the Camino del Monte Sol, command prices of a half-million dollars or more. Few can afford to build or buy such homes today, with their thick adobe walls and detailed craftsmanship.

Although as a founding member of the Old Santa Fe Association Applegate later criticized dilutions of the Pueblo Revival style, the houses he built stretch traditional parameters. He revealed that it was possible to turn adobe into "livable sculpture," removed from the Pueblo and Spanish buildings that inspired it, while still maintaining the materials' and the style's natural integrity. When looking at how the Santa Fe style has evolved, one cannot help but recognize that Applegate left an enduring imprint on the city's architecture.

Endnotes

1 Applegates and DeHuffs to Ralph Drowne, Jan. 10, 1929, land records, Santa Fe County Court-house. Carlos Vierra made similar stipulations to people who bought land from him on Camino del Monte Sol; see Reeve, "The Making of an American Place: The Development of Santa Fe and Taos, N.M., as an American Cultural Center, 1898-1942," (dissertation, Texas A&M University, 1977), 190.

2 "Need for Accurate Appraisal Show on Camino and Acequia," *Santa Fe New Mexican*, May 6, 1930, 4. According to the land records, some of the sales involved only a token $1 fee, but this could have been a way to keep the sale prices private.

3 Belshaw, *Camino del Monte Sol Architectural Historic Survey*, 11-13, 27. Iowa, *Ageless Adobe*, 80.

4 Applegate, "New Mexico Backgrounds," *Southwest Review* 14:3 (Spring 1929): 356. "Frank Applegate Dies Suddenly at Home," *Santa Fe New Mexican*, Feb. 13, 1931, 5.

5 Belshaw, 33.

6 Belshaw, 33, 42.

7 Land records, Santa Fe County Courthouse. *Santa Fe New Mexican*, Nov. 13, 1922. Belshaw, 32.

8 Mathes, "The Walter Mruk House of Los Cinco Pintores," unpublished paper, n.d., 4. Land records, Santa Fe County Courthouse. Belshaw, 33. The Feb. 26, 1926, *New Mexican* reported that Mruk sold the house to Alta Applegate's mother, Agnes Chenoweth. The Applegates sold it to Helen Chauncey Bronson Hyde in 1928. No record of the sale from Chenoweth to the Applegates has been found.

9 *Santa Fe New Mexican*, Feb. 21, 1923. Belshaw, 32. The photo accompanied the article, "F.G. Applegate Has Five Canvases in Los Angeles Museum Exhibition," *Trenton (N.J.) State Gazette*, n.d., probably July 1923, Applegate Papers. Authors' interviews with Gretchen Beall. Will Shuster, who bought the house at 550 Camino del Monte Sol in 1937, maintained that Applegate had built it. See Dispenza and Turner, *Will Shuster: A Santa Fe Legend*, 93.

10 Belshaw, 27, 30. Regarding the Dasburg house, Belshaw states, "Records do not indicate who designed and built the house but style and property ownership suggest it was Applegate." Applegate sold the land to Dasburg in 1926; see land records, Santa Fe County Courthouse.

11 Historic Santa Fe Foundation, *Old Santa Fe Today*, 46, 47. *Santa Fe New Mexican*, April 3, 1926. Mary Austin to Ina Sizer Cassidy, March 18, 1926, Cassidy Family Papers, Box 1, Folder 2.

12 Drohojowska, "The Southwestern Aesthetic," *Architectural Digest*, June 1992, 108-110. Wilson, *The Myth of Santa Fe*, 245. Historic Santa Fe Foundation, *Old Santa Fe Today*, 47. Wilson calls the de la Peña House "Santa Fe's supreme fantasy restoration," for it took the Pueblo Revival style as far from a simple adobe as possible (at least, up to that time).

13 *Santa Fe New Mexican*, Sept. 15, 1926. "In the Pueblo Style of Santa Fe," *House and Garden* 55:9 (August 1929): 94-95. "Indian and Spanish in Santa Fe," *House and Garden* 55:4 (April 1929): 117.

14 "Coluzzi to Exhibit Frescoes in Applegate's Round Tower," *Santa Fe New Mexican*, May 31, 1930, 2. Will Shuster rented El Torreon in the late 1930s. Ralph Twitchell incorporated a torreon into his Santa Fe home; see Wilson, *The Myth of Santa Fe*, 138.

15 Belshaw, 43.

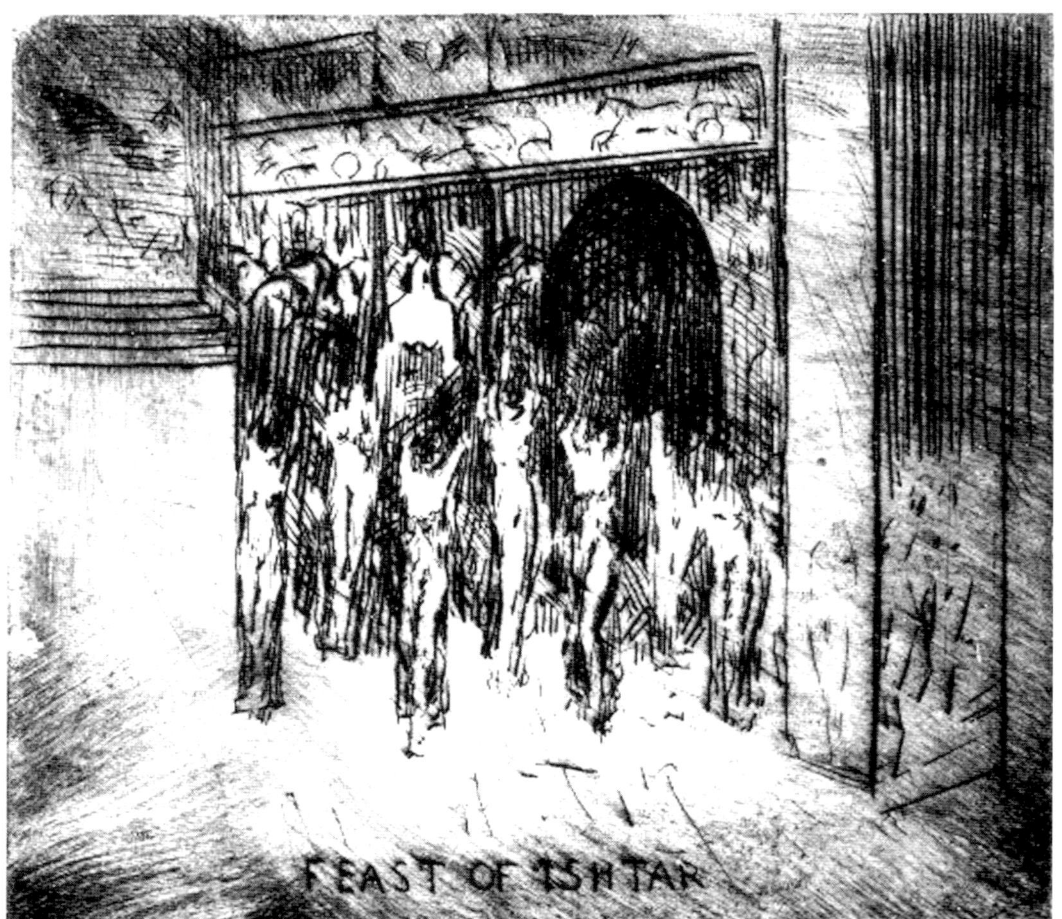

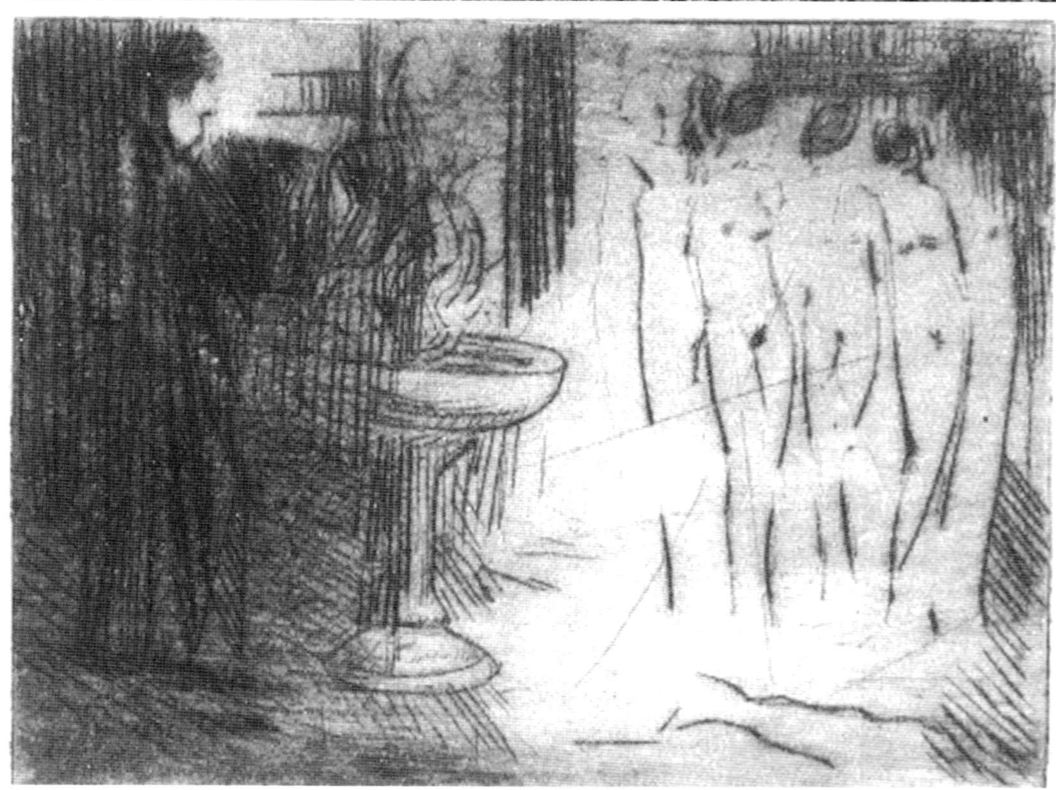

Top: *Feast of Ishtar,* etching. Bottom: *Ladies and the Washstand,* etching. Private collection.

6 The Southwestern Artist

Frank Applegate's career as a New Mexican painter garnered him high praise, considerably more than he had earned as a ceramicist. He exhibited his work more frequently than he had back East, due largely to the nurturing artistic atmosphere of Santa Fe and to the open door policy at the Museum of Fine Arts. Applegate's work was featured in several one-man shows during the 1920s, and although his attentions shifted away from art in the latter years of the decade, he displayed paintings at prestigious exhibitions until his death in 1931.

Several factors impede a discussion of Applegate's body of work. Despite the large number of paintings he created, very few of them are in public collections.[1] No records of sales have been found. Although a large collection of Applegate's watercolors exists, it is nearly impossible to date them, because he seldom gave them titles. Those watercolors listed in exhibition catalogs or mentioned in reviews are usually vaguely named, with titles such as "New Mexico Landscape." Nor can the watercolors be placed chronologically based on Applegate's documented travels, for he frequently revisited the sites where he painted. However, by matching some of the titles listed as appearing in exhibitions with known paintings, and by examining them, one can get a sense of their place in time. Additionally, Applegate's book *Native Tales of New Mexico* (see Chapter 13) contains five of his watercolors. All have titles, and four of them can be dated because they were exhibited.

One can also place most of Applegate's oil paintings chronologically. He painted only a handful of them and gave them titles, so the dates when they first were shown lend insight into their time of creation. Additionally, since the oils received a considerable amount of attention at exhibitions, contemporary critical evaluations survive.

Applegate's style constantly evolved during the decade he lived in Santa Fe, as he experimented with different forms, techniques, and media. He always tried new things, for he believed that art was as much about the process as about the finished product. As he told a reporter in reference to himself and several other Santa Fe modernists, "All of us are experimenting in a way, all hoping that we will never 'arrive,' as they say, and reach the stage where we may never change."[2] The need to navigate new artistic paths spurred him on throughout his career. While he devoted most of his talent and energy to painting, Applegate also tried his hand at etching, wood- or linoleum-block cuts, woodcarving, adobe-sculpting, and even religious art in the New Mexican Hispanic tradition. Still, it is as a painter that he is best known today.

Although the paintings of the Santa Fe modernists, including Applegate, displayed abstract qualities, the majority of paintings made in the early 1920s were representational. The artists painted what they saw; a mountain may not have looked to others as it looked to the artist, but the observer could still tell it was a mountain. While it would be several years before Raymond Jonson became New Mexico's first well-known abstractionist, Applegate and the other modernist artists examined and focused on the geometric elements in nature and emphasized them in their designs. More important than the realistic representation of objects or scenes was the artists' ability to convey their emotions toward those objects or scenes. "The artist's contribution is dependent not upon the locality but upon what he himself has individually to express," a contemporary critic wrote. Scholar Diane Greenlee, who studied an early Applegate watercolor, commented, "Rather than being a realistic representation of the scene, he alters the view to give the viewer a sense of the psychological and emotional impact the motif had upon him. ... The shapes and colors bear only minimal resemblance to the world the eye recognizes."[3] These traits are typical of modernist art.

Three of the Santa Fe artists whom Applegate first accompanied on sketching or painting trips were B.J.O. Nordfeldt, Andrew Dasburg, and Josef Bákos. Like Applegate, the three were modernists whose work in this period reflected the influence of Paul Cézanne. The post-impressionist French master served as a link from impressionism to modernism in general and cubism in particular, for Cézanne sought out the geometric forms in the natural world. In effect, he wanted to see, as the impressionists did, how scenes changed with the passage of time and the movement of the sun, and to convey what the eye saw while it was in the process of seeing, an idea upon which the cubists would expand. Unlike the impressionists, Cézanne used a limited palette of primarily blues and greens, and his works were solid and intransitive, not evanescent.

Greenlee surmised that Cézanne's influence on Applegate came second-hand, through Applegate's work with Nordfeldt and Dasburg, but Applegate's technique had little in common with that of the two painters.[4] Nordfeldt's style was unlike that of any Santa Fe artist, while paintings of the Hopi reservation made by Applegate and Dasburg show the vastly different approaches the men took to the same subject matter. Contemporary reviewers more often grouped Applegate's work stylistically with that of Los Cinco Pintores Bákos, Willard Nash, and Walter Mruk, but they showed a stronger, more enduring adherence to Cézanne than Applegate did, in part because his style changed considerably throughout his career.

In the mid-1920s a reporter writing on the Santa Fe art colony confronted Applegate with the following statement made by a critic about the city's "so-called Post-Impressionists": "All of these men have been more or less influenced by the flat technique, the crude and exaggerated forms of Cézanne." The critic said the work of Bákos, Nash, and Applegate was "very similar, especially in water-color: round clouds or a shaggy blue sky, and blocklike houses."

"I believe any of us whom you mention would prefer not to be referred to any so-called school of painting," Applegate replied. "We try to be very individual. ... I do not consider that I work in any way like the others. ... Cézanne is all well enough, but is no god to me, nor is he to Bákos or Nash. We are all three engaged in trying to paint in our own way as we see it."[5]

Just as Applegate appears to have adopted aspects of other's work into his own, it is likely he influenced their work as well. Since they often sketched and painted together and were each other's best audience, the relationships between the artists were mutually beneficial, with each one absorbing some of his colleagues' stylistic elements, expanding upon them, and in turn influencing others.

The 1922 Fiesta Art Exhibit marked Applegate's first exhibition as a professional painter. He showed two oil paintings, "Sculptured Rocks, Rito de los Frijoles" and "Corn Dance." "Sculptured

Rocks" (p. 131) is an abstract interpretation of a scene in Frijoles Canyon, a place where rocks echo with the souls of vanished Indian ancestors. The tall rocks are colored in a manner far removed from actual rocks–with reds, blues, oranges, yellows, and greens. It is difficult to look at them merely as rock forms, for they are also Indian women and children proceeding in a line, their robes, heads and featureless faces forming the rock shapes. The rocks stand in front of a canyon wall, fractured by deep blue lines–or are they Indians, passing by tree branches? In the foreground are whimsically colored, Marsden Hartleyesque bushes (possibly coincidental, since Hartley left New Mexico before Applegate arrived). The work is sculptural in feeling and somewhat heavy. It resembles a wooden sculpture Applegate showed a few years later, which he may already have completed by this time. A critic back East, upon seeing a photo of "Sculptured Rocks," called it a "remarkable composite example of all schools. Decidedly futuristic in character, yet the cubists will claim him as one of their own."[6]

"Sculptured Rocks" is representative of several of Applegate's earliest Southwestern paintings, which show the same sculptural quality and simplicity of form, the bold use of dark color and line, and the sense of rhythmic order. It is quite different from "Corn Dance," which he showed simultaneously. Also called "Santo Domingo Corn Dance" and "Corn Dance, Domingo," this oil (p. 134) depicts an Indian ceremony in an abstract manner. It is a lively, energetic composition, dominated by maize and companion hues. Action occurs on several planes, with dancers in a line, clowns climbing out of a kiva entrance and jumping off the roof of an adobe, and standing spectators jumbled together both under a green overhang at top and center and dwindling into the upper right-hand corner of the canvas. Two lines of dancers disappear off the canvas, as if their number were infinite. Women and girls watch from tiered walls at the upper and lower left, while at the lower right a group of people are set off by an adobe wall. The walls serve to draw the observer's eye toward the action taking place, especially the movement of the clowns, who are further set off by the curve of the roof on which they stand. Only the clowns have distinctive facial features, and only their bodies are sculpted and three-dimensional. The faces and bodies of the observers and dancers are simple, solid shapes. Here, as in all of Applegate's paintings of ceremonial dances, the pattern the dancers create is more important than the depiction of individuals. Distances are distorted and time compressed. The painting captures the entire lengthy spectacle at once by distorting the perspective and flattening the planes.[7]

In the book *Contested Terrain: Myth and Meanings in Southwest Art,* Sharyn R. Udall writes of a painting by Nordfeldt: "By means of his formal unifications in color, contour, and mass, he has linked the Pueblo's internally symbolic architecture to nature's forms. ... the dancers here represent nature as much as they signify culture."[8] Applegate responds in a similar way in "Corn Dance" and in other paintings of Indian ceremonies in which the land, the dancers, the pueblos are all one, spiritually linked.

Shortly after the Fiesta exhibit, Applegate joined with Los Cinco Pintores for a group showing of 30 paintings that traveled a circuit of Western museums during the fall. Applegate contributed six paintings to the traveling show, which opened at the University of Oklahoma in Norman. The school paper reported that students showed "unusual interest in the display as demonstrated by the many groups gathered at all hours in the exhibit room." The gallery visitors voted to select a painting for purchase by the School of Fine Arts, which was collecting items for a new museum. They chose Applegate's oil "Sculptured Rocks, Rito de los Frijoles," and he won $100.[9]

Applegate also exhibited an oil titled "Adobe Makers" at this time. The painting (p. 131) bears similarities to "Sculptured Rocks," with bright vivid blues, yellows, and reds, and boldly outlined figures composed of geometric shapes. Its subject matter harks back to his ceramic sculptures of laborers; however, these workers do not appear unduly pained by their efforts. They are rounded and solid, with a "salt of the earth" quality about them. The brightly colored brickmakers exude life as well as a sense of the exotic. With its coloring and rounded shapes, the painting is somewhat reminiscent of the exuberant works of Maurice Prendergast of The Eight and those of the Fauvists. The exhibition went on to Kansas, then to Oklahoma. Meanwhile a concurrent show by the Cincos and Applegate toured the Rocky Mountain region with a stop in Denver.[10]

By January 1923 Applegate reportedly had completed 15 canvases. As he told friends in Trenton, New Jersey, he had to exhibit so much he couldn't keep himself in pictures. He also produced some small terra cotta sculptures, several of which he sent to Trenton for an exhibit at his friend Henry MacGinnis' studio.[11]

Applegate exhibited several canvases in a show in January at the Museum of Fine Arts, including a second interpretation of Frijoles Canyon and a painting of Santa Fe Canyon. In April the museum devoted an alcove to his paintings, ceramics, and woodcarvings, with Bákos and Nordfeldt getting alcoves as well. *El Palacio*, the Museum of New Mexico's generally laudatory magazine, stated, "All of them [have] the modern viewpoint but each [is] highly individualistic in their treatment although there is a similarity to some extent in technique. It is strong, virile work that each of the three artists presents, some of it worthy to live as typical of the artistic achievements of the Southwest." These artists and other filled the galleries again in May, when Applegate's work was compared with that of Nicholas Roerich (who lived in Santa Fe for a time and inspired Los Cinco Pintores) and deemed, along with that of Bákos, Nordfeldt, and Gustave Baumann, to be "highly significant of the trend of modern art."[12]

Applegate experimented with printmaking around this time. Many of the other Santa Fe artists, including Nordfeldt, Dasburg, and Bákos, made block prints, and Baumann's reputation in the field was already well established. Willard "Spud" Johnson featured wood- and linoleum-block prints in his humor magazine *The Laughing Horse*, including

three by Applegate. "Old Chisholm Trail" (*Laughing Horse* 10 (May 1924): frontispiece) is a flat, cartoonish depiction of wiry, rangy cowboys who are having trouble getting their mounts going, with the subjects rendered in bold, simple lines. "Church at Rancho de Taos" (*Laughing Horse* 1:7 (1923): 14), his own take on that most depicted edifice, uses bold line and stark shapes to convey the impression of sunlight hitting the church's front and bathing its side in shadow. "Mountain Side" (*Laughing Horse* 12 (August 1925): 24) (p. 59) is a simple but powerful landscape, with adobes and a burro in the foreground, mountains flat against one another and a cloud-filled sky. The size of certain objects in the print is distorted—a bird is larger than a tree, the burro as big as a house. Rather than depicting a moment frozen in time, the image radiates energy.[13]

The artists living in Santa Fe in the early 1920s had limited contact with the better-known, more traditional ones residing in Taos. As Will Shuster recalled, "We had no connection with them … after all, it was four hours to Taos. … We didn't get out there very often." The Santa Fe artists, however, were well aware of the Taos Society of Artists and its frequent exhibitions around the country. By the spring of 1923 several Santa Fe artists had begun to discuss forming a society similar to the Taos Society for exhibition purposes. The discussion apparently resulted from the Taos Society's rejection of Bákos and William Penhallow Henderson for membership, and Bákos later stated, "Someone objected that I was being too modern."[14] Although several of the Taos Society's members, including Ernest Blumenschein and Victor Higgins, showed enthusiasm for the work of the Santa Fe modernists, the Taos Society collectively was known for its realist-traditional, academic-style paintings. In one of Applegate's first magazine articles, he discussed the difference between the two factions of artists at work in the Southwest, and attitudes toward them:

> The painters we have with us in
> the greatest numbers are the
> reproducers of romantic subjects.
> … The romantic painters make

very skillful illustrations and reproductions ... and win great local acclaim thereby. Their pictures are ubiquitous, filling hotel lobbies and museums and acclaimed by chambers of commerce and taxi drivers. ...

Creative art will scarcely be affected by the tourist's demands. ... To begin with, the creative artists are less in evidence than the illustrators. They are never urged to hang a picture in a Harvey hotel lobby. ... The "tripper" is unaware of their existence. Locally they have been called bolshevists, futurists, cubists, modernists, postimpressionists, and other mouth-filling and meaningless names. Now, they are a little more tolerated, if nothing more, and their pictures are sometimes looked at, although often blankly, scornfully, and without any understanding. The majority are very intolerant of any work of art they do not readily understand and their impulse is to reject it as unworthy of consideration.

He went on to explain that representational art can also be creative:

To the casual eye there often appears no difference between a creative work and a mere reproduction or illustration; that is, a seeming reproduction may have the essential quality that makes it a creative work of art. ... The strong creative artist usually avoids all the little tricks of technique, the choice of appealing and popular subjects and traditional "hokum." He is an individualist who develops his own technique and ways of working to suit his own purposes and any one is taking a liberty in trying to classify him with other artists simply because they happen to

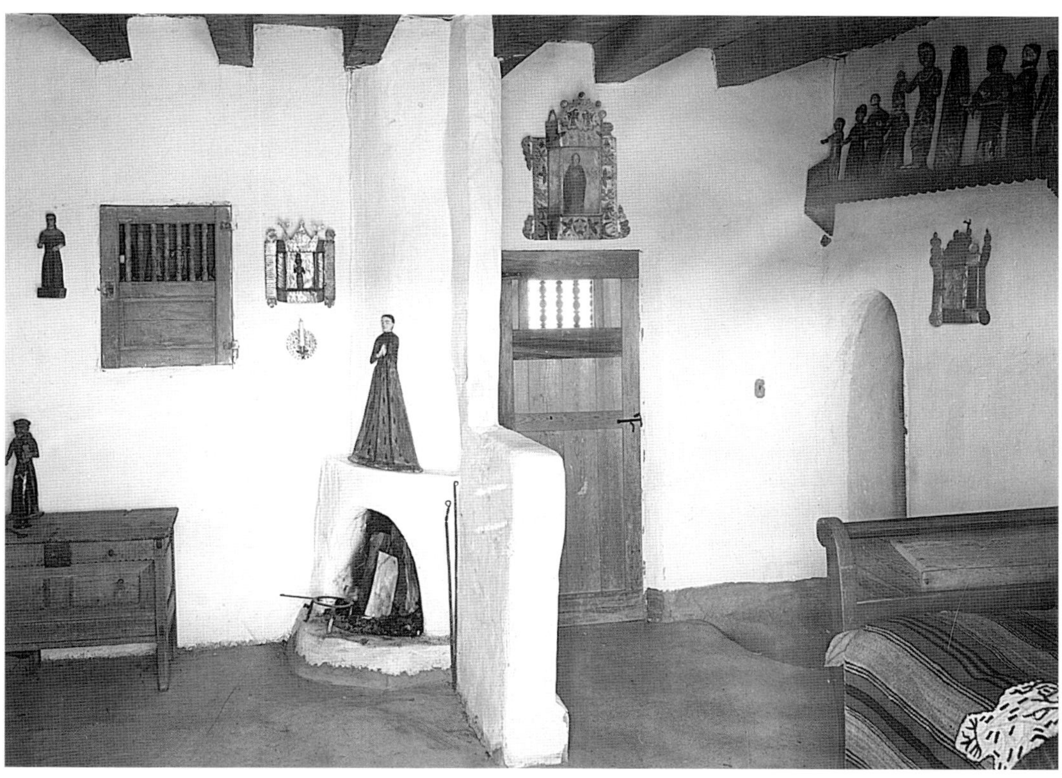

A room at the de la Peña House. Photograph by Ansel Adams (A113, dated August 21, 1930). Published in *Ladies Home Journal*, December 1930. Note in Frank Applegate's handwriting on the back of this photograph reads, "Spanish colonial fireplace with adobe wall shield to prevent drafts when door is opened. Small wall cupboard with spindle door. Old handmade Spanish colonial bed and chest. The chest was the most important piece of furniture in a N.M. Spanish Colonial house. Santos or carved wooden religious figures on the country shelf. Tin nichos containing figures; small tripod of iron; two iron spits for roasting meat; candle sconce; little arched doorway. Rare in adobe houses. This house is about 200 years old." Courtesy of the Center for Creative Photography and the Ansel Adams Publishing Rights Trust.

proceed in their work in a manner different from the conventional and traditional.

Applegate's concluding statement reveals how he saw himself: "The future of art in the Southwest as elsewhere rests with the rebellious ones, the non-conformists in art, the experimenters, the tireless seekers, the ones who cannot be moved by the scorn or the opinions of the crowd."[15]

It had come time for some of these "rebellious ones" to unite and reveal their work to the rest of the world. On June 6, 1923, Applegate, Bákos, Baumann, Blumenschein, Henderson, Higgins, Nordfeldt, and Walter Ufer met at Nordfeldt's studio and organized the New Mexico Painters. Blumenschein, Higgins, and Ufer were also members of the Taos Society, and they were the ones who had nominated Bákos and Henderson for membership in the exclusive Taos group.[16]

The society's lone position of authority was the office of secretary, which changed annually. Although under its bylaws the selection should have been made alphabetically, Blumenschein became the first secretary, probably because his name lent prestige, possibly because he was instrumental in forming the group. Applegate served as secretary for the 1924-25 season. The society's "Agreement" stated that it would hold an annual meeting in June, that each member must pay $10 annual dues, and that 5 percent of all sales made from its exhibitions would go to the society coffers.[17] In addition to exhibiting as the New Mexico Painters, the members also continued to show with other artists and individually.

The New Mexico Painters were a diverse group, and they painted in a variety of styles, but all were considered in the avant-garde. As a critic pointed out, "'New Mexico group' is to be liberally interpreted … since the subject matter is not confined to New Mexican themes but is more the common denominator of place which holds them together." In announcing the organization's formation the artists stated: "The name of the society may suggest that the object is to represent New Mexican landscape, Mexicans, Indians. While this is true in a way, these subjects are only the accidental urge to the creative artist. The real aim of the group is to produce beautiful original works of art that will give their exhibitions a high and dignified standard of excellence. The name itself is chosen … in that wider sense of the province of Nueva Mexico, which originally embraced most of the Southwest, and which to these painters means the blended elements of three civilizations." The *Taos Valley News* said the men represented "the progressive or radical conservative element in the art of to-day."[18]

Before sending their work out under the group name, the artists showed paintings individually as part of a summerlong exhibition of New Mexican art at the Los Angeles County Museum of Art. Applegate had five paintings in the show. One, "Telaya Mountain," (p. 137) is a bold, richly colored oil. The foothills in front are similar to the Hartleyesque bushes in "Sculptured Rocks," and the earth appears to be almost vibrating with emotion, with its vivid blend of browns, golds, and reds. Thick, dark, smudgy lines of deep green foliage separate the layers of the hills. Thick lines delineate the deep-green-and-blue mountain towering above, and heavy strokes of yellow set it off from the sky and clouds. It is a powerful, almost menacing landscape. The other paintings Applegate exhibited in Los Angeles were "Pueblo Indian Dance," "Adobe Makers," "Agua Fria," and "Koshare Santo Domingo." Most of the New Mexico Painters also had works in the 1923 Fiesta Art Exhibition, where Applegate showed "Navajos at Fiesta" and "Kivas at Walpi."[19]

The New Mexico Painters, meanwhile, arranged to show their paintings and other artwork at galleries around the country. Their exhibitions traveled circuits, one tour covering the Eastern and Midwestern galleries and museums, another going on display in the West. The society's terms stated that the galleries pay the packing and shipping costs, advertising, and catalog inserts, in exchange for a 25 percent commission on sales.[20]

The New Mexico Painters' first official show as a group was in October 1923 at New York's Montross Gallery, where Applegate had had success in his Trenton days. It featured 47 works on paper, including Baumann's prints and Nordfeldt's drypoint etchings, plus Applegate's ceramics and woodcarvings.[21] Other stops included the Casson Galleries in Boston, the Albright Art Gallery in Buffalo, the Toledo Museum of Art, and the Carson, Pirie, Scott & Co. gallery in Chicago.

In this first show Applegate exhibited the previously mentioned "Santo Domingo Corn Dance," plus the oils "Hopi Snake Dance," "Hopi Katcina Dance" and two watercolors. The two paintings of Hopiland are among Applegate's finest works. In "Hopi Snake Dance" (p. 133, bottom) the pueblo buildings loom like cliffs over the dance taking place, set off by a deep turquoise sky with white clouds. The colors of the buildings and earth range from deep yellow to deep green, while the ruddy-fleshed dancers are finely detailed, their costumes decorated in bright turquoise and white. Brown and yellow snakes capture the viewer's eye as they lie in bundles and dangle from the dancers' hands and mouths. Hundreds of spectators, rendered with spots of dark color, literally cover the roofs and crowd against adobe walls, lending the scene a sense of Cecil B. DeMille-like spectacle. No faces are visible, only masked, black-haired heads. The dancers and spectators are elements of the design, not animate beings. Unlike the collapsing perspective he employed in the painting "Corn Dance," the perspective here is realistically drawn, with objects in the foreground larger than those in the distance and figures balanced proportionately. As with many of Applegate's oils, the work is not abstract but modernist in its concentration on shapes, color, and the artist's impressions of the scene. The painting is not a realistic representation of what the eye sees but a scene as filtered through Applegate, conveying the majesty and mysteriousness of the ceremony.[22]

Applegate utilized the same palette and style in "Hopi Katcina Dance," (p. 136) which captures a segment of the dance at the pueblo at Walpi. The perspective is that of an observer sitting above the scene, and in the foreground, the corners of the buildings jut out from the edge of the frame. At left, a turquoise-colored ladder stretches out of a hole, at right, a naked child descends into another hole. Directly behind the roofs is a line of masked kachina dancers, their brightly colored, geometric masks as finely detailed as pieces of jewelry, with yellow rods protruding vertically from the masks. A row of women, whose orange sashes and white robes provide bright spots in the mostly subdued palette, stand in front of the dancers, their backs to the observer. Behind them, and taking up more than half of the canvas, is the pueblo itself, its softly geometric walls and chunky form echoing the region's rocky landscape. The deep gold of the walls is shaded with deep greens and blues, and the earth glows where the late-afternoon sun shines. A golden trail—a dirt path—seems to pour from the pueblo buildings like a waterfall, spilling into a stage for the dancers and further setting off their intricate costumes. Groups of Indian observers, their forms rendered by somberly colored geometric shapes, stand against the walls. At the top and upper right, bulky, cottony clouds surround the pueblo, and two pieces of bright blue sky peek in. The resulting canvas is moody and mysterious, yet Applegate finds things of beauty here— the magnificently sculpted pueblo as well as the line of dancers. One notes a vague similarity to the fantastic landscape paintings of Arthur B. Davies in the two oils. Both share a sense of "wondrous observer," of an artist confronting something mysterious and beautiful. A catalog listed "Santo Domingo Corn Dance" at $800, and "Hopi Katcina Dance" and "Hopi Snake Dance," at $500 apiece.[23]

Virgil Barker, reviewing the show at the Montross Gallery for the magazine *The Arts*, noted Applegate's background as a sculptor and said, "Perhaps this is why his work shows so welcome a freshness in handling hoary subject matter. Those Indian ceremonial dances have a superficial picturesqueness which has proved the mainstay of many a shallow piece of optical reporting; but on Applegate's canvases they seem more spirited and pictorially better organized than most previous renderings of them." The magazine also published a picture of "Santo Domingo Corn Dance." Barker's praise was among the many encomia Applegate would receive for his paintings of Indian dances. Art critics cited his ability to convey his inner reactions to the Indian ceremonies through the canvases and his dramatic use of color and composition.[24]

The Albright Art Gallery publication *Academy Notes* provides the only known photograph of Applegate's early woodcarvings. They have a sculptural, cubist quality, with figures made from a combination of shapes. A sharply angular and delicate carving of a man carrying a cross is especially striking. The other carvings pictured—one of an enrobed woman, the other two of indeterminate subject—are weighty and solid, resembling the rockwomen in Applegate's painting, "Sculptured Rocks." The photo also includes ceramic pieces, but whether they were made in New Mexico is unknown. They include two nudes, one standing and displaying her body in a classical pose, with a drape flowing over her right leg, the other seated with her hand on her chin and her right knee jutting out. Both are delicate and graceful, yet muscular. A third sculpture is of a Spanish dancer dressed in a flowing, striped skirt, caught in a sinuous modern dance. According to a letter sent by Ernest Blumenschein to Boston's Casson Galleries, the remaining terra cotta pieces included one of his tigers (p. 49), a "chocolate figure," a sculpture of trees, and a yellow pueblo building, while additional woodcarvings were of a fish and a man on horseback. Applegate asked $20 to $100 for his terra cotta pieces, and $20 to $50 for his woodcarvings, with "Spanish Dancer" at $100 and "Man Bearing Cross" at $40. Blumenschein noted, "Applegate gave no titles, simply wrote 'the prices are from $20 to $100.' Mr. Montross and I tried to adjust matters."[25] Applegate seemed to have cared so little about selling his work that he did not bother to price the individual pieces.

The New York Times reviewed the sculptures separately, calling them "abstractions definite in mood.":

> A horse and rider carved in wood and brightly painted, the most concrete of the group, hold their heads with conscious pride. An interplay of planes in two of the small wooden compositions, manipulated in a manner that a painter would juxtapose values, suggests the spirit and mystery of an altar. Another abstraction of darkly painted planes is unquestionably the spirit of an overburdened Christ. In the case of a quite sufficiently well modeled nude in terra cotta, realism only confuses, while in a glazed terra cotta tiger it seems to help the conception. One tiny little rhythmic dancing thing has drawn into its funny abstract being mystifying life impulse.[26]

The critic for the *Chicago Daily News,* no fan of modern art, compared the sculptures and woodcarvings to the work of Constantin Brancusi and wryly noted, "The managers of the exhibition are not to be blamed for not scurrying around to find cases to exhibit [the pieces]. … They would doubtless have been quite safe without being under lock and key."[27]

While some of their artwork traveled the circuit, the New Mexico Painters also held regular shows of current work at Santa Fe's Museum of Fine Arts. Often, the Taos and Santa Fe artists' paintings debuted there before being sent on tour. The shows at the museum rarely brought sales, for, as Alice Rossin (the Hendersons' daughter) recalled, "People in Santa Fe didn't buy art." The locals considered the modernists' work at best amusing, at worst, subversive. Their indifference to modernist art reached the point where the *Santa Fe New Mexican* felt compelled to print an editorial chiding the local populace for not attending art exhibits.[28]

Newspaper accounts of an exhibit held in February 1924, which featured six works by Applegate along with paintings by Bákos, Mruk, Dasburg, and Nordfeldt, illustrate both the typical Santa Fean's opinion of modern art and the artists' response to such opinions. The articles began with a review in the *Santa Fe New*

Mexican that said, "This modern stuff is the present day rage," and concluded, "There are no jokes in this exhibit. All of the pictures are painted by men who have learned to draw and who know how to mix colors."[29]

This review was followed by numerous letters that criticized the artists. The most amusing letter came from a writer calling himself "Cockatoo":

> Many conservatives seem to have been heard around the museum these days. … It must have been crowded with them. I have not heard them for the simple reason that I have not been there myself. I got as far as the door when I met a wild eyed person, perhaps a conservative, emerging. I inquired the trouble and he shouted, "They have just hung Nordfeldt, Bákos, and some more of their ilk."
>
> "Fine," I exclaimed joyously, "did they use good hempen rope?"
>
> "I did not say hanged, I said hung," he interrupted.
>
> "Mon Dieu," I exuded, terribly disappointed. "Do you mean to say the art lovers have again been insulted? What, I pray, are the attempts like?" For I had sworn never again to darken the doors of the museum when a modern show was on. "I can't tell you," he replied, "for when I see one of their pictures I go stone blind with rage."
>
> For myself I love the beautiful and lovely and sweet in art. I love to have the mirror held up to nature. Nature should be reflected in every brush stroke of the artist on canvas. I don't know much about nature, except real estate, but I do love to see painted pretty, soft fleecy clouds, cobalt sky, soft lavender in the far distances, soft blue on the mountains, and tender green in the fore ground. With, perhaps, somewhere in the picture, one of our romantic Indians giving one of his tribal dances before an adobe pueblo and a native driving burros of wood along the road. But you can't make those guys see it. They pretend to do a little creating and arranging on their own as though Nature were not already grand. …
>
> Do you know what I think? Those fellows are bolshevists. I think all those people who do not see things like the rest of us are trying to undermine the institutions of our country. They are spreading insidious propaganda of some sort. Perhaps Russia is in back of them. They are reflecting the views of Lenine [*sic*] and Trotsky. What I say is, "If they can't paint in the good old fashioned American way of our fore fathers they should not be allowed to paint at all."[30]

Willard "Spud" Johnson, editor of the *Laughing Horse*, weighed in with his opinion regarding the status of art in the city: "There are probably not more than twenty people in Santa Fe who ever care a hang what pictures are put on display in the galleries here. … Preferably [the others] would like 'pretty' things in the alcoves; but sometimes they are more pleased than disgusted with the 'crazy' ones–for the wilder the artists the more cause for Mr. Average Citizen to feel superior or at least complacent and smug."[31]

By the time the ruckus quieted down, nearly a month after it had started, it was apparent that the artists themselves had made up some of the letters, likely including the one from "Cockatoo." With tongues in cheek, they were attacking mainstream Santa Feans' attitudes toward them, using humor to defuse the underlying hostility.

By June 1924 five more artists had joined the New Mexico Painters–John Sloan, Randall Davey, Andrew Dasburg, Theodore Van Soelen, and Walter Mruk. The first three men already had substantial name recognition from their work in the East, and were known to favor the "radical experimental side" of art, so to include them could not have hurt publicity. Van Soelen, who attended the Pennsylvania Academy of the Fine Arts at about the same time as Applegate did, had moved to Santa Fe from Albuquerque in March 1922. Applegate helped Mruk get into the group; as Mruk wrote to Ufer, "I have talked over the proposition we discussed at Taos regarding my getting into the New Mexico Painters. Applegate will nominate me, Henderson, Nordfeldt, Joe [Bákos] will help, and with your support with Blum[enschein], I think the thing will go through." Applegate wrote to Ufer that he and Nordfeldt "felt very much honored to belong to the New Mexico painters and I know Joe Bákos feels the same way about it."[32]

Stops for the 1924 New Mexico Painters exhibition included the San Diego Museum, Los Angeles County Museum, the Fiesta Art Exhibition, Omaha, Nebraska, Kansas City, Missouri, Boston, Massachusetts, the Montross Gallery, and the Art Institute of Chicago. By the time the show reached the Montross Gallery in October, Applegate had contributed five oils (including the three from the previous year's exhibition) and 25 watercolors. "Montross may not have them all up, so I wish you'd ask him to let you see them all," he wrote Mary Mowbray-Clarke. "One of them, 'Wild Horses of Arizona,' Sully Lewis took with her exhibitions of modern painters last winter."[33]

The New Mexico Painters' exhibitions met with mixed critical response. *Arts and Decoration* called the painters "brilliant," while the critic for the *Chicago Daily News* compared their work unfavorably with that of the Taos Society, noting "Cézanne's brutal and spotty outlook on the world has taken root." The critic for the *Boston Herald* said, "What the artist fellows are after is not obscene, of course, to sophisticated Americans who have trotted Paris salons and galleries." But he speculated, more or less accurately, that the less sophisticated folk of New Mexico probably hated their work: "One wonders how long Bákos has lived among the plainsmen [*sic*] and escaped with his life. ... Somewhat similar apprehension might be felt for the lives of B.J.O. Nordfeldt and F.G. Applegate." He concluded by praising the exhibition overall. A critic in San Francisco called the artists "bad American painters doing the New Mexico landscape like a French landscape à la Cézanne, but doing it poorly."[34]

The reviews in *The New York Times* were generally but not entirely laudatory. One *Times* reviewer said, "Apparently the ceremonies and art of the New Mexican Indian cannot bear translation into another art or cannot bear translation by an alien people. By looking for local color, a vain effort ... they have found only confused exotic color." That reviewer went on to praise Applegate's "Wild Horses of Arizona," however, calling it "full of incident that is slowly revealed every moment a new animal appears." The *Times* printed a picture of Applegate's "Navajo Indians in Keams Canyon" in its magazine section. Although the painting's whereabouts are unknown, the magazine image reveals it to be a bold, striking landscape. Broadhatted Indians ride horses through the canyon (east of the Hopis' First Mesa) and through the center of the canvas, their backs to the viewer. The ruggedness of the canyon walls, whose heavy, jagged outlines and varied shading give them a sculptural quality, is offset by simple Indian figures and delicate yucca plants.[35]

The New Mexico Painters' tours were not great financial successes. Sidney C. Woodward at Boston's Casson Galleries, where the society exhibited in 1923 and 1924, did not take the show in 1925.[36] In an article in the *New York Sun* titled "Masterly Art Not Yet Fully Appreciated: The New Mexican Painters," published in December 1925, Henry McBride offered this insightful commentary:

> What happens when an artist thinks he has done wonders and the world remains cold? A tragedy, I suppose. When tragedies happen to whole groups of people, though, it is not so dire; it is not complete tragedy, it is something bearable. That thought enables one to look the display of the New Mexican painters' exhibition in the face. ... Their work is fairly good, I thought. Some of it is pretty good. But the whole city is not in a ferment over it. The Ferargil Galleries are by no means so crowded as the rooms of Scott & Fowles, where $80,000 worth of Maxfield Parrish paintings were sold shortly after the doors opened on the show. ...
>
> Why don't New Yorkers take more wholeheartedly to the work of the New Mexican painters? It certainly is a mystery. They swallow anything in the way of a Wild West movie. ... Perhaps it is that these painters do not dare to be as funny as the actors. One has to know one's subject very well before it is

possible to joke about it. ... These painters with German, Irish, Norwegian, Dutch and other names are comparatively new settlers in the State of New Mexico and feel they must take it seriously in order to be tolerated. ... To get along with their neighbors they must be solemn, even literal; to engage the attention of Boston or New York they must be slightly above their material; must deliver with a wink, as it were. ...

How reconcile two such opposites. Doubtless if the group as a group were to give up all thoughts of pleasing New York and were to buckle right down to the task of pleasing the Southwest we in the end might be more interested than we are at present. If all those princely ranch owners that we hear so much about were to compete violently for the productions of the Santa Fe school of art, so that the prices would rise to unheard of Maxfield Parrish heights, prohibitive to all save our own princes, we'd then have to notice them.[37]

McBride's commentary sums up the contemporary attitude toward the New Mexico Painters. Their work did not draw an overwhelming amount of interest or a great many sales. Still, the painters continued to show as a group for several more years.

By the mid-1920s, Applegate abandoned oils almost entirely to devote his skills to watercolors. He concentrated on landscapes but also painted town and street scenes, Indian ceremonies and rural Hispanic villages. Applegate's early watercolors are characterized by the use of dots for vegetation, serpentine strokes for hills, bold splashes of brushwork for the sky. Later, his paintings took on a somewhat Oriental feeling, with more delicate, calligraphic brushwork, possibly inspired by Japanese prints he owned. Several of Josef Bákos' paintings, including "Apache Canyon," show a minimalist touch similar to what Applegate used at this time.[38] The drawings featured on the map Applegate created for the inside covers of his book *Indian Stories From the Pueblos* (see Chapter 13) are in the delicate, Oriental-influenced style of some of his watercolors, indicating he may have continued painting in this manner as late as 1929.

In this period more than any other, Applegate's paintings show a relationship to some of Paul Cézanne's. Looking at Cézanne watercolors from the mid- to late 1880s, especially his depictions of Mont Sainte-Victoire, one notes delicate brushwork such as that which filled Applegate's landscapes. Another connection to Cézanne was Applegate's use of the color of the paper, an adobelike tan, as an element of the painting—for example, the adobe of a house, the dirt in a road or one shade of a cliff or mountain. Cézanne often left stretches of paper "open," both to indicate open space and to offset or balance color.[39] In his early and mid-period works, Applegate often employed the paper's lighter color to give the impression of light hitting the scene.

Applegate's landscapes are often awe-ful, as if he is humbled in the face of such grandeur. "The land chooses its own people," he once wrote. "Many artists come here expecting to remain and work but find the country so different from their former environment that they cannot adjust themselves and move on to greener pastures. The vastness and austerity of the land put them in a panic. To these artists ... it seems lonesome and forbidding."[40] Rather than shy away from the overwhelming landscape, Applegate embraced it and expressed its power. Many of his paintings feature a single mountain, darkly painted, looming above villages, foothills, or canyons. While other artists interpreted the sheltering quality of mountains, the dark colors Applegate used to depict them—frequently, they are the darkest objects in the paintings—gave them a threatening, brooding presence. But his mountains are also mighty and enduring, able to withstand the ravages of time.

Udall in *Contested Terrain* says the mountain symbolizes the "spiritual potency of nature." She adds, quoting Susan Sontag, "A landscape doesn't demand from the spectator his 'understanding,' his imputations of significance, his anxieties and sympathies; it demands, rather, his absence, it asks that he not add anything to it." Judging from

Applegate's quote above, he seems to have understood this. Udall also notes the significance of the color blue, which Applegate frequently used when painting mountains: "Blue held the power of profound meaning, enhancing the spiritual dimension of any form it entered." By incorporating blue, Applegate made the spirituality of the landscape evident without resorting to more obvious symbols.[41]

Applegate broke down the land into its geometric components, much as Cézanne did. One critic noted the connection, saying Applegate's work "traces a blood relationship to the Post-Impressionists," and described his landscapes as "reveal[ing] much of abstract quality … broken into planes which prevent monotony inherent in so many mountain pictures."[42]

Throughout his career, Applegate's palette stayed in the dark range, with blues and greens offset by blocks of fiery rust. He often went over the darker colors in his watercolors with a wash to lighten their intensity. Brief touches of bright paint, sparely applied, would draw the viewer's eye to some simply executed detail, such as a tree, the wheels of a wagon or a field. People, burros, and manmade objects were often a compilation of black geometric shapes, simply facets of the overall design. The resulting work is generally bold and direct, with an economical use of brushwork.

More than his oils, Applegate's watercolors borrow from the work of the Indian watercolor painters he knew and admired. Although his few watercolors of Indian ceremonies most obviously reveal the connection, his landscapes reflect it also in their ability to convey dimension while still appearing flat. Writer Mary Austin, referring to the Santa Fe modernists' "disentanglement from an over-Europeanized subjective foreground," noted that in Applegate's watercolors, "out of the apparently inextricable welter of landscape, a sky piercing peak, a wet gleam of arroyo and rearing cliff leap as freshly, as completely disentangled from the foreground as if it had just proceeded [*sic*] out of the in-knowing thought of the All-Father."[43]

Applegate often painted the same scene repeatedly. Critic Margaret Breuning of the *New York Evening Post* remarked on this, noting that each watercolor "seems to be the transcript of emotion that was awakened by some new angle of vision." She continued, "In each does the color and design seem to be conditioned by the particular aesthetic experience and to be quite free from formula or conventional procedure. There is nothing panoramic in these pictures of hills and rivers, canyon and town, rather the very heart of the scene is plucked out with bold directness before the essence of its peculiar quality can be vitiated with fussy procedure."[44]

Applegate regularly displayed his watercolors at the Museum of Fine Arts, at Fiesta exhibitions, and as part of other group shows in Santa Fe. One of the largest, in September 1925, was sponsored by John Curtis Underwood, a poet and art patron who offered a $500 prize to the artists who exhibited. It was Santa Fe's first-ever exhibit for prize money, and it was called "the finest group of oil paintings and water colors ever shown in Santa Fe." The winner, selected by Underwood, was Raymond Jonson (who sometimes joined Applegate on painting trips), though Applegate had been the rumored victor. "Applegate, Nash, and Bákos are 'good buys,'" Underwood told the *Santa Fe New Mexican.* "Nash is on his way, Applegate and Dasburg say so, and I believe it." Underwood bought one of Applegate's oil paintings, noting "the rich color in [the] fields." He later opened one of the city's first art galleries.[45]

Applegate also placed work in several prestigious large national shows. Will Shuster was appointed the Santa Fe representative for the Society of Independent Artists in 1924. He encouraged the local artists to join in the society's exhibitions, and Applegate contributed two oils, "Hopi Katcina Dance" and "Hopi Gift Ceremony," to the 1925 show at the Waldorf-Astoria in New York. Applegate was asked to submit six watercolors, all with generic titles indicating they were regional landscapes, to the 1925 Brooklyn Watercolor Exhibition, and he exhibited at two shows at the Pennsylvania Academy of the Fine Arts in 1925. The Society of Independent Artists show featured 1,180 works, the Brooklyn show about 600; nevertheless, several reviewers singled out Applegate's paintings for comment. One called his watercolors "fine specimens … very rich in coloring," another "authentic but heav[y] in color and in technique."[46]

Applegate became the secretary for the New Mexico Painters in 1925 and oversaw the installation of the show at New York's Ferargil Galleries in December 1925.[47] The interest in Southwestern works that had greeted the New Mexico Painters' first shows had died down, and the group exhibited at only a few galleries during the 1926 season. Meanwhile, Applegate took part in several shows as a member of "the Santa Fe Painters." This informal group, which included Andrew Dasburg, William Penhallow Henderson, Gustave Baumann, B.J.O. Nordfeldt, Sheldon Parsons, and Olive Rush, exhibited in Santa Fe, Roswell, Albuquerque, Wichita, and Chicago in 1925 and 1926. The emphasis was on smaller works "designed to attract the interest of people wishing to purchase art for their homes … at reasonable prices." In January 1926 Applegate exhibited two etchings at the Museum of Fine Arts. He also contributed four etchings by his old friend Arthur B. Davies to the show. All were described as "intangible and mystic."[48]

Despite the New Mexico Painters' quite limited success, the group proved somewhat galling to the Taos Society of Artists. The existence of two organizations of Southwestern artists caused confusion outside the Southwest, as evidenced by a story in the October 1925 *International Studio* that named Applegate and Nordfeldt as residents of the Taos colony. The Taos artists tried to distance themselves from most of the Santa Fe artists. During the artist-led fight to keep a summer cultural colony out of Santa Fe in the mid-1920s (see Chapter 9), the Taos Society even wrote to the chairwoman leading the fight in favor of the center and asked her "to please not 'class' them with the Santa Fe artists" because "they considered themselves real artists in Taos."[49]

The Taos Society disbanded in 1927. It "had outlived its usefulness, and maintaining it had become a burden." It is not known when the New Mexico Painters disbanded, nor if the members made a formal decision to do so, but their last show together was in 1927. Bákos, recalling the demise of the New Mexico Painters, said, "Baumann took over as secretary and he absolutely fell down on it. Then a few other things happened. Dasburg won a prize at the Carnegie, a dealer picked him up in New York; and the dealer thought he should withdraw, and so things like that happened and it finally dwindled out." Members of the group continued to show with one another and with other Santa Fe painters; for example, Bákos, Willard Nash, Dasburg, Nordfeldt, Raymond Jonson, and John Thompson of Denver exhibited together in 1927 and '28, calling themselves "Six Men." And in 1930 Applegate, Rush, Baumann, Nordfeldt, and Dasburg participated in a show as members of the "Santa Fe Society of Artists."[50]

Applegate's paintings continued to appear in major shows, including the annual exhibition of watercolors in the spring of 1927 at the Art Institute of Chicago, and the exhibition of contemporary American oil paintings in the fall of 1928 at Washington, D.C.'s Corcoran Gallery of Art. He showed four oils, including the early "Telaya Mountain," in an exhibition of Southwestern art at the California Palace of the Legion of Honor in San Francisco in late 1928.[51]

In November 1927 the Denver Art Museum hosted a one-man show of Applegate's watercolors. The museum invited him to participate because his paintings had drawn considerable interest during a New Mexico Painters exhibition earlier in the year (their last group show). The exhibit of 40 watercolors was hung at the Museum of Fine Arts in Santa Fe before going to Denver. It then traveled to the State Art Gallery in Norman, Oklahoma, which purchased the watercolor "Green Corn Dance, Santo Domingo, N.M." for the permanent collection.[52]

When examining this painting one should compare it to the watercolor "Santa [*sic*] Domingo," which was featured in Applegate's book *Native Tales of New Mexico* (see Chapter 13). The two share a resemblance that goes beyond the title, strongly suggesting the latter was painted in conjunction with the former.

The dominance of the land is all-important in "Santa Domingo" (p. 139). Five Indian men stand on and around a kiva while women in long skirts look on. To the right is an adobe wall, with sharp poles poking like barbed wire over the top and two robed women standing on it. To the left is a row of smaller, indistinct buildings. Dwarfing all are weighty tan hills and a vivid, dark blue mountain, which have a soft, textural quality. The color harmony gives the impression that the pueblo is a part of the land. The figures are tiny but important, especially one who stands alone, holding the ends of the ladder atop the kiva. The man calls others to a meeting inside the kiva—one of the Indians seems to be climbing inside, while another waits to enter. And the women observe. Although they are closer to the action than we are, they are still outsiders.

The ceremony taking place in "Green Corn Dance" (p. 139) may well be the one that is just getting under way in "Santa Domingo." For here is the ceremonial kiva with steps leading into it and two poles pointing out the top. Here is the adobe wall with pointed sticks atop it. The same two robed women stand on the wall, the other two women at lower left continue to look on near a group of buildings. The same forbidding blue mountain towers over all, the sensual foothills separating it from the pueblo.

It is as if a camera zoomed in on the kiva in "Santa Domingo," then zoomed out to capture more of the scene in "Green Corn Dance." The perspective is tilted slightly, putting the viewer at even more of a distance and flattening the foreground. The buildings, the earth and the groups of Indians are geometric forms, and the dancers are rendered in a two-dimensional manner similar to that of the San Ildefonso watercolorists (see Chapter 11). The dance, not the kiva, is the center of attention. The dancers proceed in a line angling down to the lower left corner of the canvas, while a group of Indians, perhaps children, look on. The mountain looming over the scene is even larger and more striking than in "Santa Domingo," its slopes

resembling huge, cloaked arms ready to envelop the hills and pueblo. Most remarkable are the delicately rendered, ephemeral koshare (clowns), who flit around the costumed dancers. In describing the koshare, a writer noted how they "shoot through every figure like a bright thread in tapestry, distinct from the pattern, but in perfect harmony with it," and that is precisely how Applegate presents them in this painting.[53]

While the style employed in the two paintings is similar, each shows minor variations in technique. For "Santa Domingo" Applegate used a manila paper that lends the scene a tannish-yellow tint. The colors are warmer, the sky nondescript.[54] For "Green Corn Dance" he used white paper to offset the rich color and left much of the canvas bare. There is less attempt to blend the colors; brush strokes are rough and deliberate and pencil marks can be seen in several places. Thick, light-black strokes delineate the frames of the adobes, outlining their geometric forms, and separate them from the foothills beyond. The gray-blue sky gives balance to the painting, playing off the blue and gray visible in the lower right corner.

The *Saturday Review of Literature* referred to "Santa Domingo" and the other watercolors that illustrated *Native Tales of New Mexico* as "full of bright sunlight … a robust blend of pious memories and contemporary color, uncommonly entertaining and with a truly convincing atmosphere of time and place."[55] Since these paintings appeared with titles in the book, it is possible to date several more of them.

"The Chimayó Valley" (p. 142), which Applegate exhibited in the spring of 1925, is somewhat busier than his spare later work. The lower three-fifths of the canvas features flattened, pastel-colored and brownish-gray cubist fields, while the top two-fifths is dominated by a richly colored blue mountain and brown hills. Despite the geometric quality, the angularity of Applegate's later watercolors is not in evidence. Instead he renders the land softly, with soft lines and foothills that are almost bushy. Tucked in the center of the canvas is a village of snug, happy-looking houses. The detail on trees and houses is rendered with tiny Oriental brushstrokes. The valley is sunny, with light captured by allowing the paper's natural off-white color to peek through. Yet in the background looms the somewhat menacing mountain and pearl-gray sky. One gets the impression of tranquility (rosy trees, the brightly colored doors of the houses) being only a moment away from something ominous (the mountain beyond, the gray sky). It is reminscent of the work of 19th century landscape artists such as Frederick Church and Albert Bierstadt who placed symbols of domesticity in the foreground and sublime mountains in the background.

"Lupita" (p. 145) is a portrait of two young Hispanics dressed in dark colors. It is remarkable for the emotions conveyed by the simply rendered faces and by Applegate's use of his trademark dark palette. As with his santos (see Chapter 12) and with the ceramic sculptures he made, Applegate proves here his ability to reveal emotion that is human and true. The picture has a sense of melancholy. The woman is robed in black with a bleak expression on her face. The man wears dark clothing and turns his face to the side, so that it is masked by his hat. Is this a modernist Hispanic counterpart to "American Gothic," Grant Wood's interpretation of rural life, which dates to the late 1920s?

In November 1927 Applegate exhibited two of the book's watercolors, both of which feature Hispanic village scenes. In "The Placita" the villagers—a man sitting in front of a house, a woman sitting in a doorway, a second woman leaving another house, and a burro, off to the side—are incidental, almost to the point of blending in with their background. All the figures are rendered loosely, with a few strokes, while heavier strokes define the village adobes and the mountains behind. The village takes up half of the canvas, the fields, mountains, and sky the other half. The work is enlivened by touches of color—a bright-blue wagon with pink wheels, apple-green fields, a woman's red shirt. The adobes insulate the villagers from the gray-blue, vaguely threatening mountains and gray sky that take up the upper third of the painting. Applegate placed the fields and the roofs of the adobes on the same plane, and the lines breaking up the fields run straight into the lines that create the mountains. Overall, the painting has a fine sense of balance, for everything flows together.

"The Land of Mañana" focuses in more tightly on a similar village, but here the villagers are more significant. Two women, one in a long, dark robe, the other in a shorter lavender dress, are baking bread in an horno, while a man sits in a doorway and another stands next to him. Both men wear large hats and do not show their faces. One woman's face is a blank oval, while the other is a vague profile. They are caught mid-action, and the woman in the dark robe, who stands dead center, appears to be coming directly toward the viewer. The walls of the adobe tower above everything else. Much of one wall, which faces the viewer and looms large in the work, is unpainted, giving the sense of natural light hitting the side of the building and also framing the dark-robed woman. There is a sense of religious ritual in her robed figure and in the way she carries her tray of loaves. The eye is next drawn to the horno, with its gaping black orifice, set off from the background by a slash of deep red. Sharp, gray fences and posts angle in, as if to surround the objects at center frame. A deep blue and gray sky peep in at the top of the canvas.

Stylistically, the two watercolors dating from 1927 are not much different from the one exhibited in 1925. Color usage is similar—the dark palette offset by bright spots of color, the use of the paper's natural hue to represent light hitting the image. The 1925 painting, "Chimayó Valley," does, however, have a softer quality, due in part to the use of dots, in an Oriental manner, to indicate vegetation. And the later works, especially "The Placita," show heavier strokes and a more angular composition overall.

Denver Art Museum art adviser Arnold Rönnebeck, a sculptor, printmaker, and frequent visitor to Santa Fe, was a great fan of Applegate's work and considered him "without a doubt among the important 'modernists.'"[56] (As Rönnebeck was a longtime friend of Marsden Hartley's, this was high praise indeed.) Reviewing the June 1927 New Mexico Painters' exhibit for Denver's *Rocky Mountain News*, he wrote,

> It is hard to believe that this over-sensitive colorist had been a potter up to only a few years ago, but at the same time this fact makes one think that he has not yet reached his climax as a painter. There are very few water-colorists like him in the country. His patternlike compositions, always exceedingly well-balanced and built up, are, in spite of the apparent abstractions, perfect portraits of the Santa Fe—or Navaho region. Often he leaves a great deal of the effect to the naked paper, and places which his brush has not touched at all become singularly expressive. A mountain may only be suggested by an outline, but it carries in it all the weight and bulk of the sometimes so sinister and brooding Sangre de Cristo or Jémez range. Somewhat heavier than his water-colors are Applegate's oil paintings (which may be due to the material), but they, too, are full of the highly imaginative and constructive feeling of the artist.[57]

Rönnebeck's review of Applegate's one-man exhibit was even more flattering. He compared Applegate's landscapes to descriptions of the New Mexican landscape found in Willa Cather's *Death Comes for the Archbishop*, which was at that time her latest novel:

> In the chapter, "The Vicar Apostolic," we read: "Across the level Father Latour could distinguish low brown shapes, like earthworks, lying at the base of wrinkled green mountains with bare tops—wavelike mountains, resembling billows beaten up from a flat sea by a heavy gale, and their green was of two colors—aspen and evergreen—not intermingled, but lying in solid areas of light and dark. … Below them, in the midst of that wavy ocean of sand, was a green thread of verdure and a running stream. This ribbon in the desert seemed no wider than a man could throw a stone—and it was greener than anything Latour had ever seen, even in his own greenest corner of the Old World. … Running water, clover fields, cottonwoods, acacias, little adobe houses with brilliant gardens, a boy driving a flock of white goats toward the stream—that was what the young bishop saw."

> And that is an amazingly congenial description of what we see in Applegate's water colors. Two artists gifted with high sensibility, but expressing themselves in different mediums, arrive at results so identical that Willa Cather's description of the country is at the same time a translation of Applegate's water colors into words. Those almost unbelievably green spots we see in his [watercolors]. There are the black-green patterns of evergreen—"not intermingled, but lying in solid areas of light and dark." There are the "little adobe houses with brilliant gardens" and their stoic, wooden inhabitants, awkward and motionless like the carved boultos [*sic*] and santos, piously beaming before candles and flowers in the white-washed rooms inside. And of course, there are always the "wave-like mountains," and always there are clouds.

Rönnebeck called Applegate's work "one of the outstanding contributions to the artistic tendencies of our time and of our country" and said, "It grows and will continue to grow out of his profound understanding and love for its very soil." He also noted that private collectors in Denver owned about a dozen of Applegate's watercolors.[58]

Applegate showed a landscape in the Fiesta exhibition of September 1927, and the Museum of Fine Arts devoted an alcove to 30 of his watercolors in October 1928. *El Palacio* called the paintings "virile impressions of Pueblo Land achieved with a paucity of line and color."[59] After this exhibition, his participation in shows began to taper off, and judging from museum records and press accounts, he showed locally only twice more before his death in 1931.

In the last years of his life, Applegate's interests broadened to such an extent that he was forced to devote less time to painting, but he never abandoned it entirely. In February 1929 he reported to Mary Austin that a high-ranking member of the Santo Domingo pueblo had asked him to paint portraits of him and his wife "for the benefit of his posterity." Although he had little experience with portraiture, Applegate was rather proud of receiving the request, since nearly every artist in town had tried to get the man to pose.[60]

The watercolors Applegate painted during his last years reveal a dramatic shift in technique and vision. The artist most responsible for this change was John Marin, who spent the summers of 1929 and 1930 in Taos, living in an adobe on Mabel Dodge Luhan's estate. Marin painted more than 100 watercolors during his residence in Taos, and his influence is apparent in the work of many New Mexican artists, including Ward Lockwood, Cady Wells, and Victor Higgins. Ansel Adams, who met Marin at Taos in the summer of 1930, wrote that the artists "are all acknowledging that Marin is doing things in water-color that put him at the top of American painters." Applegate's daughter, Betty McClung, remembered meeting Marin (and never failed to disparage him personally in later years). [61]

Marin's abstract technique lent itself beautifully to the New Mexico landscape. "Coming in closer to the landscape, Marin begins a search for abstract patterns in the mountains and the desert itself." wrote Sheldon Reich in *John Marin.*

> Dividing the composition diagonally, he manipulates the angular blue shapes of the mountains against the softer, warmer, and more complex patterns formed by the desert foliage. … The emotional content … is aided by the use of diagonal rather than horizontal divisions of space. …
>
> In a number of the Taos paintings, he tried to capture the sense of limitless space so characteristic of the Southwest. One way he attempted this was to show the mountains in the distance, leaving the desert bare between them and the viewer and thereby emphasizing a sense of vast emptiness. Another way was to place a large, solitary form midway between the stretch of desert and the distant mountains, a tree usually, to give a sense of scale to the picture and provide a reference point for measuring space.[62]

Marin recognized and extracted the landscape's geometric shapes and planes and telescoped certain elements, bringing the distant up close and vice-versa. He used line to frame his subjects and draw attention to the center of the canvas. Pencil and charcoal lines were obvious and deliberate. He frequently worked on a heavy white or off-white paper, to which watercolor paint adhered in varying degrees. Brushing the paper lightly allowed the white of the paper to come through, while a heavier stroke created dark, dramatic patches of color. It was a paper not for the faint of heart but for the decisive, because every stroke was vital. When Marin turned his gaze to Indian ceremonial dances, as in "Dance of the San Domingo Indians" and "Dance of the Pueblo Indians," he combined the flat style of the San Ildefonso watercolorists with geometric abstraction.

Applegate had been incorporating many of these techniques into his own work long before Marin arrived. Arnold Rönnebeck's review of his works in 1927, for example, noted Applegate's "patternlike compositions … well-balanced and built up," and said that Applegate often left "a great deal of the effect to the naked paper." But after seeing Marin's work, Applegate began to take his technique further. He adapted several of Marin's stylistic techniques to his own, and his painting became freer and farther removed from representational art. His strokes became broader and more vivid; a storm, for example, was now a heavy, diagonal slash of paint. Colors were much bolder than in his earlier watercolors, which, for all their richness, look positively faded compared to the later ones. He often placed the landscape in the center of the canvas, with balanced white space serving as a border or frame. He fractured images, enhancing the expressive nature of the work. He switched from adobe-colored papers to a heavily textured, vivid white paper from which the colors jump out. His landscapes became stark and minimalistic, capturing Nature's raw power in expressionistic strokes.[63]

One of the finest of Applegate's later watercolors is "Rain on Hopi Desert" (p. 147), which incorporates stylistic elements common to Applegate's work while strongly suggesting the influence of Marin. The painting is intensely dramatic as it captures the fierceness and suddenness of an Arizona rainstorm. A jagged black cloud emits a rainstorm over the land. The storm itself is a rainbow of washed color—yellow, blue, pink, and green, so translucent that one can see the edge of the land through it, as if looking through rain. Foothills and fields in the foreground are sharply cubist, with dark lines delineating their shapes. Vegetation is rendered by strokes of bright green, dots, and thin lines, while the greens, blues, and browns of the desert in the background are shadowed by the stormcloud's ominous gray and black. Marin's influence is apparent in the painting's fractured fields and angular lines, as well as in the way the image is framed by a border of white. The extensive amount of white canvas left showing, both around the image and within it, sets off the vivid colors. Many of the brushstrokes appear to have been applied quickly and deliberately, contributing to a sense of action taking place, yet this hurried quality belies the sense of concentrated order, the careful balance of sky and desert.[64]

"Santa Fe Evening" (p. 149) is a stark, expressionistic watercolor believed to be of the same period. Central to the composition are a wide-hatted man and a burro bearing wood. Two lines, indicating a street, frame them, angling away from the foreground. The pair stand against a background of stark white, their faces shadowed shapes. They appear alienated, framed in a triangular limbo.

Black is the predominant color in "Santa Fe Evening." Black lines frame the crowded, abstract buildings, black shapes compose their roofs, two black figures huddle together, black strokes surround the entire picture. Light aqua and sienna, green, brown, and a nearly black gray and blue-black complete the color scheme. The thick snow-white paper sets off the deep, disturbing color. The paint is at times applied heavily, at times brushed on lightly, so white escapes through it and the act of painting is made obvious. A wash covers some of the paint. Although white shows through at the top of the canvas, the bottom is crowded with paint, as if the scene were continuing on off the canvas. The overall effect is emotionally disturbing, menacing, claustrophobic.[65]

A similar menacing quality is evident in "Adobes at Night" (p. 155), believed to have been painted late in his career. The top half of the painting features a clump of adobe dwellings on a hill, set off by a stark bright wash of light (white paper tinted lightest rust by the thinnest of washes), giving the impression of light breaking through a cloud or lightning flashing in a storm. Rather than the angles of many of Applegate's later works, here he offers deep-hued watercolor paint applied so thickly and so wetly that the canvas appears soaked. It's as if the adobes were being washed away in a flood—the flood of darkness as night falls, perhaps. The vivid rust and orange adobe walls radiate intensity, while their windows and doorways are black, inscrutable. This is not the pastoral scene of "The Placita," this is something forbidding, mysterious, perhaps even haunted.[66]

Applegate sent his paintings to exhibitions right up to the time of his death in February 1931. He displayed a watercolor with the vague title "In New Mexico" in the Exhibition of Watercolors by American Artists at the Art Institute of Chicago in 1929. A year later, he was among the Taos and Santa Fe artists who contributed works for an exhibition at the Museum of Fine Arts in Houston, organized by Walter Ufer. This exhibit went on to the Brooks Memorial Art Gallery in Memphis in February 1931. At the time of his death, the Brooklyn Museum's International Biennial Water Color Exhibition featured four of his landscapes. Although the show had more than 800 paintings, one critic singled out Applegate for praise of his "well-considered mountain forms."[67]

No one knows in which direction Applegate would have taken his painting had he lived longer. He had mastered color, experimented with form and line, and was breaking free from the last restraints of representationalism. Perhaps he would have explored abstraction further, like Raymond Jonson and other New Mexican artists. Whatever his future may have held, the work Apple-

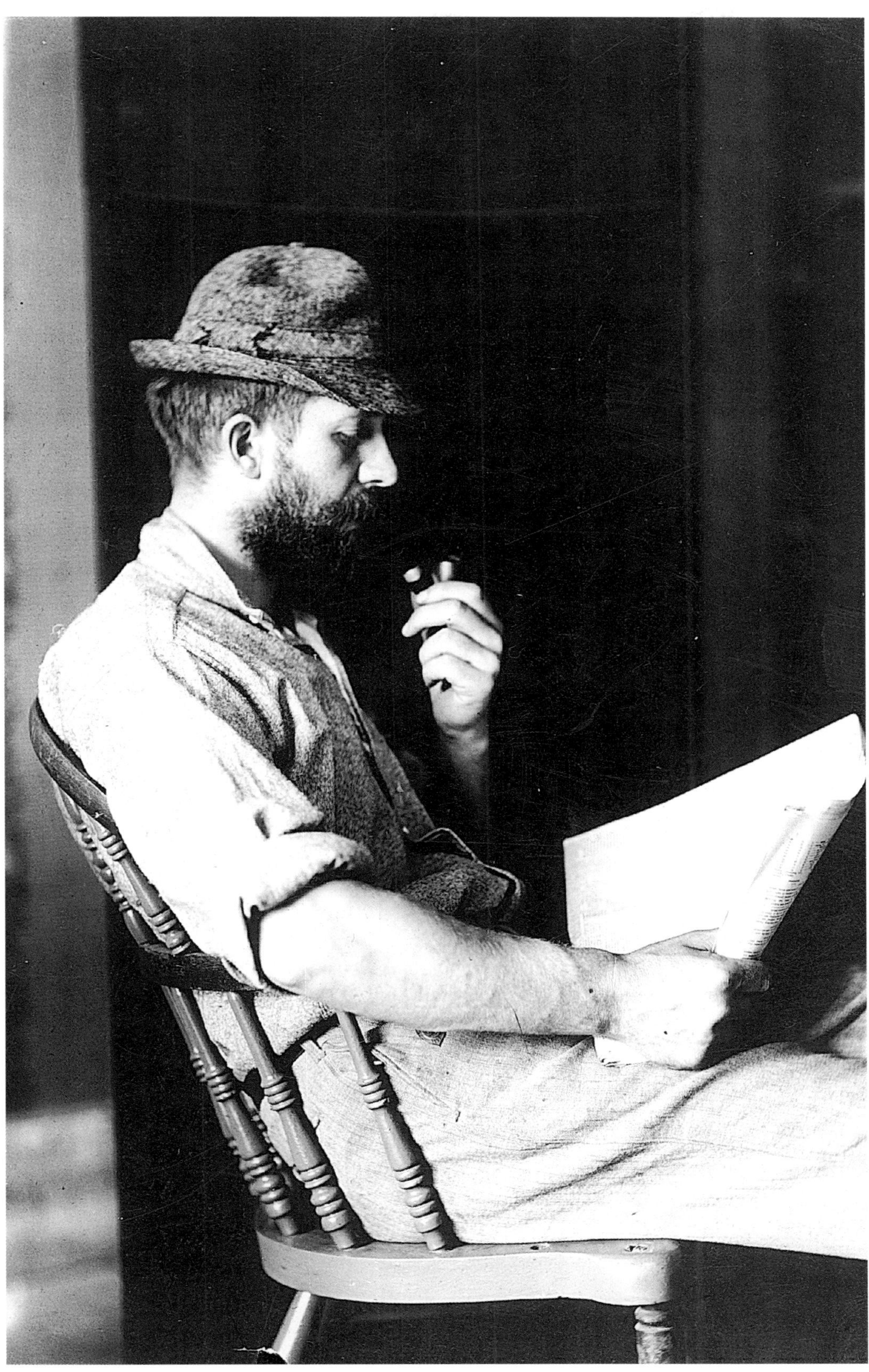

Frank Applegate in Morrisville, Pennsylvania, ca. mid-1910s. Photograph courtesy of the Applegate family.

gate left behind shows he achieved the goal he had spoken of in 1926. He never "arrived," never reached the stage where he refused to change. And he remained, until his death, a "tireless seeker," an artist who could never rest.

Endnotes

[1] One reason for this is that most of the paintings (and sculptures) were in private hands, away from Santa Fe, for decades. Applegate's daughter, Betty McClung, kept the artwork stored away until she sold most of it as part of the Applegate estate in the late 1980s. See the Epilogue.

[2] Murray, "Art in the Southwest," *Southwest Review* 11:4 (July 1926): 287.

[3] "F.G. Applegate Has Five Canvases in Los Angeles Museum Exhibition." *Trenton (N.J.) State Gazette,* n.d., probably July 1923, Applegate Papers. Greenlee, "An Untitled Watercolor by Frank Applegate in the Colorado Collection at the University of Colorado, Boulder" (Unpublished paper, University of Colorado, n.d.), 2.

[4] Greenlee, 8-9.

[5] Murray, 287.

[6] "The Fiesta Art Exhibit," *El Palacio* 13:8 (Oct. 16, 1922): 99-100. "Former Art School Faculty Member Wins Fame in West as Painter and Decorator," *Trenton (N.J.) State Gazette,* Jan. 15, 1923. The painting is in the collection of the Fred Jones Jr. Museum of Art, Norman, Okla. For an echo of "the rock form as woman," see Walter Mruk's "The Ghost of Carlsbad Caverns," made after his historic 1924 trip into the caverns with Will Shuster; pictured in Eldridge, et al., *Art in New Mexico,* 160.

[7] The painting described here is pictured in *Modernist Themes in New Mexico,* 4. The Museum of Fine Arts, Santa Fe, owns another Applegate oil of the Corn Dance.

[8] Udall, *Contested Terrain,* 24.

[9] *(Norman) Oklahoma Daily,* Oct. 19, 1922, 1. "School Gets New Paintings," *(Norman) Oklahoma Daily,* Oct. 26, 1922, 1. Purchase records, Fred Jones Jr. Museum of Art. Gwendolyn Meux, who studied with Applegate, worked in the University of Oklahoma art department; see Chapter 7.

[10] "Los Cinco Pintores," *El Palacio* 13:10 (Nov. 15, 1922): 131-132. "Adobe Makers" is in a private collection. Nothing is known of the other Applegate paintings in this exhibit—a watercolor titled "Mexican Ploughing" (although this may be the painting on p. 154) and two other paintings of unknown medium, "Glorieta" and "Monte Sol."

[11] "Former Art School Faculty Member Wins Fame in West as Painter and Decorator." Dowdell, "Art Instructors Hold an Exhibit," undated clip from unidentified newspaper, MacGinnis Papers, AAA, Reel 75.

[12] *Santa Fe New Mexican,* Jan. 6, 1923. "Three New Exhibits," *El Palacio* 14:8 (April 16, 1923): 123. "The Galleries in May," *El Palacio* 14:11 (June 1, 1923): 169-170. One of the canyon paintings is likely the oil pictured on p. 132.

[13] "Old Chisholm Trail" is pictured on p. 224 of Udall, *Spud Johnson and Laughing Horse.*

[14] Shuster interview with Sylvia Loomis, July 30, 1964, Shuster Papers, AAA, Reel 277, transcript, 5. Unsigned letter, May 26, 1923, Taos Society of Artists Papers, Exhibition Papers 1, Box 141. Bákos interview with Sylvia Loomis, April 15, 1965, Bákos Papers, transcript, 4.

[15] Applegate, "Tourists and Art," *Southwest Review* 12:1 (October 1926): 24-27.

[16] White, "The New Mexico Painters," *Southwest Art,* May 1986, 76, 79.

[17] White, 76, 78.

[18] Read, "Pueblos of Distinct Cubist Lines," *Brooklyn (N.Y.) Daily Eagle,* Oct. 26, 1924, reprinted in *Santa Fe New Mexican,* Oct. 30, 1924, 4. "'New Mexico Painters,' New Artists League," *Santa Fe New Mexican,* June 21, 1923. "The New Mexico Painters," reprinted in *El Palacio* 15:2 (July 16, 1923): 32. Note the perplexing contradiction in terms − "radical conservative."

[19] Los Angeles Museum Exposition Park, *Catalogue of an Exhibition of Paintings by Artists of New Mexico, June 6-Sept. 10, 1923.* "Fiesta Exhibition," *El Palacio* 15:6 (Sept. 15, 1923): 98. "Telaya Mountain" is also called "Landscape, Taos, N.M.," see *Modernist Themes in New Mexico,* 5. It is in the collection of the Gerald Peters Gallery, while the whereabouts of the other paintings mentioned in this paragraph (except for "Adobe Makers"; see above) are unknown.

[20] Ernest Blumenschein to Sidney Woodward, Aug. 14, 1923, Sidney C. Woodward Collection, AAA, Reel D194, 123.

[21] *New Mexico Painters,* catalog of the exhibition, Montross Gallery, private collection. See also White, 79.

[22] The "Hopi Snake Dance" discussed here is in the collection of the Gerald Peters Gallery. Another oil of the same title is in the collection of the Museum of Fine Arts, Santa Fe (p. 133).

[23] Albright Art Gallery, *The New Mexico Painters: Exhibition of Paintings, Prints, Pastels, Etchings.* "Hopi Katcina Dance" is also called "Hopi Niman Katcina Dance at Walpi" and "Katchina Dance at Walpi"; see *Modernist Themes in New Mexico,* 7. It was called "Hopi Masks (Niman Katchina Dance)" when it appeared in Erna Fergusson's *Dancing Gods.*

[24] Barker, "The Season Opens, *The Arts* 4 (October 1923): 213. For additional reviews praising his paintings of Indian ceremonies, see *Christian Science Monitor,* Oct. 6, 1923; "New Mexico Painters," *Boston Transcript,* Dec. 12, 1923; "New Group Joins New Mexico Artists," *American Art News,* Oct. 25, 1924, 1; "New Mexico Painters," *American Art News,* Oct. 13, 1923, 2; "New Mexico Painters in New York," *New York Evening Post,* reprinted in *El Palacio* 16:2 (Jan. 15, 1924): 31.

[25] Buffalo (N.Y.) Fine Arts Academy, "Collection of Works By New Mexico Painters, *Academy Notes* 19:1 (January-June 1924): 28. Blumenschein to Woodward, Dec. 18, 1923; Sidney C. Woodward Collection, AAA, Reel D194, 135. These woodcarvings quite possibly were the same ones he showed in April 1922; see Chapter 4.

[26] "A Modernist Sculptor," *The New York Times,* Oct. 21, 1923. Some of the ceramic pieces mentioned are in the collection of the Gerald Peters Gallery, and the Museum of Fine Arts, Santa Fe,

owns one of several tigers sculpted by Applegate, a gift from Alice Rossin, the Hendersons' daughter. If "Man on Horseback" was a bulto, it would indicate Applegate began making santos within three years of his arrival in Santa Fe. See Chapter 12.

[27] *Chicago Daily News*, Feb. 20, 1924, 10. The last recorded showing of sculpture by Applegate was at the Art Institute of Chicago in 1924. The pieces carried the generic titles "Figure in Wood," "Wood Sculpture," and "Small Sculpture." See Falk, ed., *The Annual Exhibition Record of the Art Institute of Chicago, 1888-1950*, 68. For another review of this show, see *Santa Fe New Mexican*, Feb. 25, 1924, 5.

[28] "Annual Report of the School of American Research," 1924, E. Boyd Collection, 194A. Nestor, "Viewpoint: An Interview with Alice Henderson Rossin," *El Palacio* 93:2 (Winter 1987): 18. "The Artists," *Santa Fe New Mexican*, June 21, 1928, 4.

[29] "Modernists Create Real Sensation with Exhibit," *Santa Fe New Mexican*, Feb. 12, 1924, 3.

[30] "Flaming Flamingo Flim-Flam Followed by Cocky Cockatoo, Too," *Santa Fe New Mexican*, Feb. 21, 1924, 5.

[31] Johnson, "Spud, Laffin Hoss Editor, Takes Brief Look at the Modernists," *Santa Fe New Mexican*, Feb. 13, 1924, 6.

[32] Read, 4. Mruk to Ufer, Jan. 7, 1923 (1924), Ufer Papers, as quoted in White, "The New Mexico Painters," in *The New Mexico Painters*, 9-10. Applegate to Ufer, Jan. 8, 1924, Ufer Papers, as quoted in White, "The New Mexico Painters," note 10, 106. Van Soelen and Applegate shared at least one common acquaintance in Philadelphia, painter Daniel Garber of New Hope, Pa., who once taught at the School of Industrial Arts. Whether Van Soelen and Applegate knew each other back East remains undetermined.

[33] "Los Angeles Museum's Western Painters Exhibition of the West," *El Palacio* 17:3 (Aug. 1, 1924): 57. FGA to Mowbray-Clarke, Oct. 24, 1924, Mowbray-Clarke Papers. The authors have been unable to track down this exhibition or the painting "Wild Horses of Arizona."

[34] Edgerton, *Arts and Decoration* 20 (December 1923): 15. *Chicago Daily News*, Feb. 20, 1924, 10. "New Mexico A La Cézanne," n.d., Bákos Papers. For additional critical reviews of the New Mexico Painters shows, see "Random Impressions in Current Exhibitions, *New York Herald Tribune*, Oct. 26, 1924, sec. 7-8, 18; Boyer, "Work of Santa Fe Painters Praised at San Diego," reprinted in *Santa Fe New Mexican*, June 28, 1924, 7; "In the World of Art," *Buffalo Evening News*, Jan. 12, 1924.

[35] "New Mexico Painters," *The New York Times*, Nov. 2, 1924, sec. 8, 3. *The New York Times*, Oct. 26, 1924, sec. 4, 13. For another critical review see "The New Mexico Painters," *The New York Times*, Dec. 13, 1923, sec. 9, 11.

[36] FGA to Woodward, Feb. 9, 1925, Sidney C. Woodward Collection.

[37] McBride, "Masterly Art Not Yet Fully Appreciated: The New Mexican Painters," *New York Sun*, Dec. 12, 1925, 9.

[38] *Selections from the Estate of Josef Gabryel Bákos*, plate 8; see also plates 12, 15.

[39] Adriani, *Cézanne Watercolors*, 67-68.

[40] Applegate, "Tourists and Art," 25.

[41] Udall, *Contested Terrain*, 9, 16, 18. Udall cites Wassily Kandinsky's landmark book *Concerning the Spiritual in Art* (1914) in her discussion of landscape painting. It is not known whether Applegate ever read this book, but Kandinsky's theories tie into the philosophy of Theosophy, which resembles the teachings of Gurdjieff, which Applegate studied in the late 1920s; see Chapter 7.

[42] "Work of Santa Fe Painters in Roswell Exhibition Gets Encomiums in the Press," reprinted from *Roswell (N.M.) Record* in *Santa Fe New Mexican*, Oct. 8, 1925, 5.

[43] Austin, "Indian Detour," *The Bookman* 68:6 (February 1929): 656.

[44] Breuning, "New Mexico Painters," *New York Evening Post Literary Review*, Sept. 25, 1926, 10. For additional reviews of Applegate's landscapes and street scenes, see "New Mexico Painters," *The New York Times*, Nov. 2, 1924, 8; "New Group Joins New Mexico Artists," *American Art News*, Oct. 25, 1924, 1; "The New Mexico Artists," *The New York Times*, Oct. 3, 1923, 14; "New Mexico Painters in Boston," reprinted in *El Palacio* 21:9 (Nov. 1, 1926): 247.

[45] Dunne, "Raymond Jonson Winner of Underwood $500 Art Prize," *Santa Fe New Mexican*, Sept. 15, 1925, 2. "Pioneer Gallery on Palace Avenue," *Santa Fe New Mexican*, Aug. 24, 1927, 6. Udall, *Modernist Painting in New Mexico*, 100. Underwood and Jonson were old friends at the time of the exhibition.

[46] Marlor, *Society of Independent Artists*, 22, 110. "Independent Group Shows 1,180 Works," *American Art News*, March 7, 1925, 3. FGA to Herbert B. Tschudy, March 21, 1925, "Paintings and Sculptures: Exhibitions, 1925 Watercolor Exhibition" file, Brooklyn Museum Archives. Brooklyn Museum, *Catalog of an Exhibition of Water Color Paintings . . .* , 1925. Pennsylvania Academy of the Fine Arts, *Catalog of the Twenty-Third Annual Philadelphia Water Color Exhibition*. Riis, "Brooklyn Museum Opens Gallery; Fine Exhibitions," *Brooklyn (N.Y.) Eagle*, n.d., Brooklyn Museum Archives. "Water Colors at Brooklyn Museum," *Christian Science Monitor*, May 6, 1925.

[47] These paintings were also exhibited in Columbus, Ohio, and Toronto; see *El Palacio* 19:12 (Dec. 15, 1925): 257. For a review of this show, see "Arthur Szyk Miniatures; The New Mexico Painters," *American Art News*, Dec. 12, 1925, 9.

[48] "Exhibit by Santa Fe Society Artists, *El Palacio* 19:1 (July 1, 1925): 19. "Work of Santa Fe Painters in Roswell Exhibition Gets Encomiums in the Press"; *Santa Fe New Mexican*, Feb. 22, 1926, 2. "Exhibits of Etchings and Prints," *El Palacio* 20:2 (Jan. 15, 1926): 51-52. An Applegate family member owns Applegate etchings, but it is not known what happened to the Davies pieces. Two other etchings by Applegate—one depicting the sanctuary of the church at Santa Cruz (p. 4), another, the church at Zia Pueblo—also survive. The etching of Zia Church is at the University of Colorado. It is quite possible that Applegate made these two etchings in 1929 to use as illustrations in the book on Spanish Colonial arts he was writing with Mary Austin. See Chapter 14.

[49] Comstock, "W. Langdon Kihn," *International Studio*, October 1925, reprinted in *El Palacio* 19:10

CHAPTER 6:
THE
SOUTHWESTERN
ARTIST

(Nov. 16, 1925): 214. H.S. Lutz to Paul A.F. Walter, May 20, 1926, Edgar Lee Hewett Papers, Box 31, Folder 1, 1926 Correspondence.

50 White, ed., *Taos Society of Artists*, 12. *Museum of Fine Arts (Houston) Bulletin*, 7:8 (November 1930). Bákos interview with Sylvia Loomis, April 15, 1965, Bákos Papers, transcript, 5. Udall, *Santa Fe Art Colony*, 16. A Blumenschein exhibition catalog for a Museum of Fine Arts exhibition in July 1928 listed him as still a member of the New Mexico Painters. See Taos Society of Artists Papers, Exhibition Papers II and Correspondence, 1925 and miscellaneous.

51 Falk, ed., *The Annual Exhibition Record of the Art Institute of Chicago, 1888-1950*, 68. *Eleventh Exhibition of Contemporary American Oil Paintings*, Corcoran Gallery of Art, Washington, D.C. *Catalog of the Southwest Exhibition, Nov. 1-Dec. 31, 1928*, California Palace of the Legion of Honor, San Francisco, Calif. The New Mexico Painters also exhibited at the Art Institute of Chicago prior to the watercolor exhibition; see White, "The New Mexico Painters," in *The New Mexico Painters*, 12.

52 Rönnebeck, "Applegate Exhibit at Denver," *El Palacio* 23:21 (Nov. 26, 1927): 540. According to purchase records, the school paid $50 for the painting. It is in the collection of the Fred Jones Jr. Museum of Art, Norman, Okla.

53 Fergusson, "Laughing Priests," *Theatre Arts Monthly* 17:8 (August 1933): 657.

54 The colors in the painting as it appears in *Native Tales of New Mexico* are much more yellow than those in the original painting, apparently due to a printing error.

55 "The Reader's Guide," *Saturday Review of Literature* 9:6 (Aug. 27, 1932): 70.

56 Rönnebeck, "Applegate Exhibit at Denver," 540.

57 Rönnebeck, "Santa Fe Painters and Their Art," *Rocky Mountain News*, June 19, 1927, drama section, 3. This article also indicates that Olive Rush had joined the New Mexico Painters.

58 Rönnebeck, "Applegate Exhibit at Denver," 542-543. The *Rocky Mountain News* featured Applegate's paintings in its pages at least twice. "Navajo Indians in Keams Canyon" ran on June 12, 1927. "The Mountains at Santa Fe" appeared on June 19, 1927. The whereabouts of both are unknown.

59 "October Art Exhibits," *El Palacio* 25:14-17 (Oct. 6-27, 1928): 267.

60 FGA to Austin, Feb. 5, 1929, Mary Austin Collection, Huntington Library. Whether or not Applegate completed the assignment is unknown.

61 Adams, *An Autobiography*, 46. Authors' interviews with Gretchen Beall.

62 Reich, *John Marin*, 184-185.

63 Rönnebeck, "Santa Fe Painters and Their Art." In an interview with Applegate's niece, Gretchen Beall, Betty Applegate McClung confirmed that the bold, stark watercolors rendered on white paper dated to Applegate's later years. As the illustrations in this book indicate, many of them have yellowed over time due to earlier adverse storage conditions.

64 Also called "Untitled, N.M. Landscape," see *Modernist Themes in New Mexico*, 6.

65 Applegate showed a painting of the same name in 1925, but the style of the "Santa Fe Evening" mentioned here is drastically different from his other works of that period, and it is believed he must have given the same title to more than one painting, which he did with many paintings. Private collection.

66 Private collection.

67 Falk, ed., 68. *Museum of Fine Arts Bulletin*, 7:8 (November 1930). "Works of Famous Artists to Be Seen at Brooks Gallery in February," *Memphis Press-Scimitar*, Jan. 30, 1931. Sherburne, "Brooklyn International Show," *Christian Science Monitor*, Jan. 24, 1931. Brooklyn Museum, *Catalog of an Exhibition of Water Color Paintings . . .*, 1931. Brooks Memorial Art Gallery, *An Exhibition of the Works of the Artists of Santa Fe and Taos*. According to a list from the Memphis show, Applegate's paintings were priced at $100-$150.

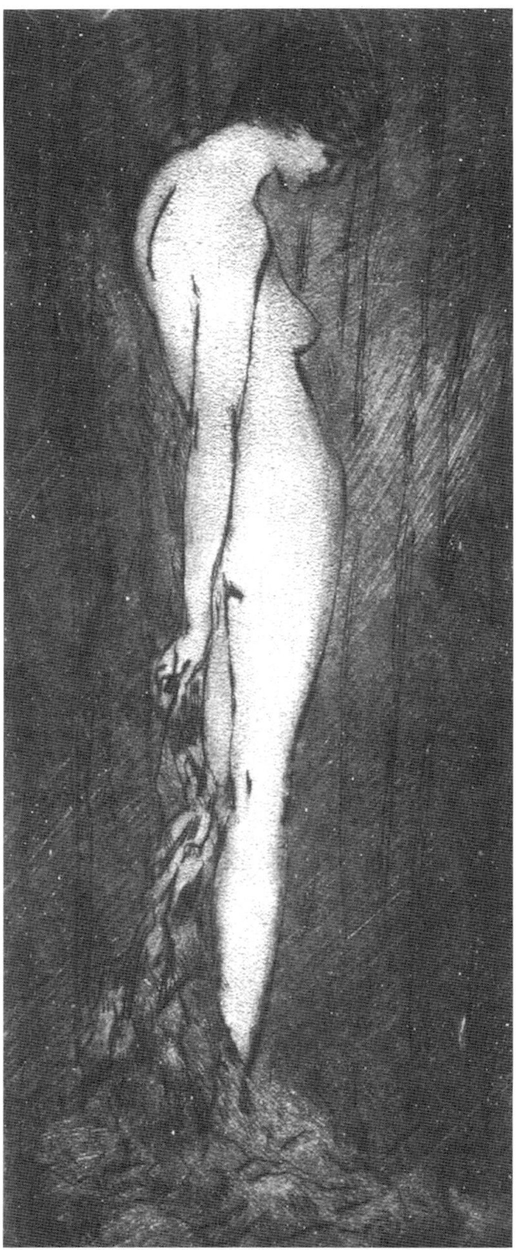

Standing female, etching. Private collection.

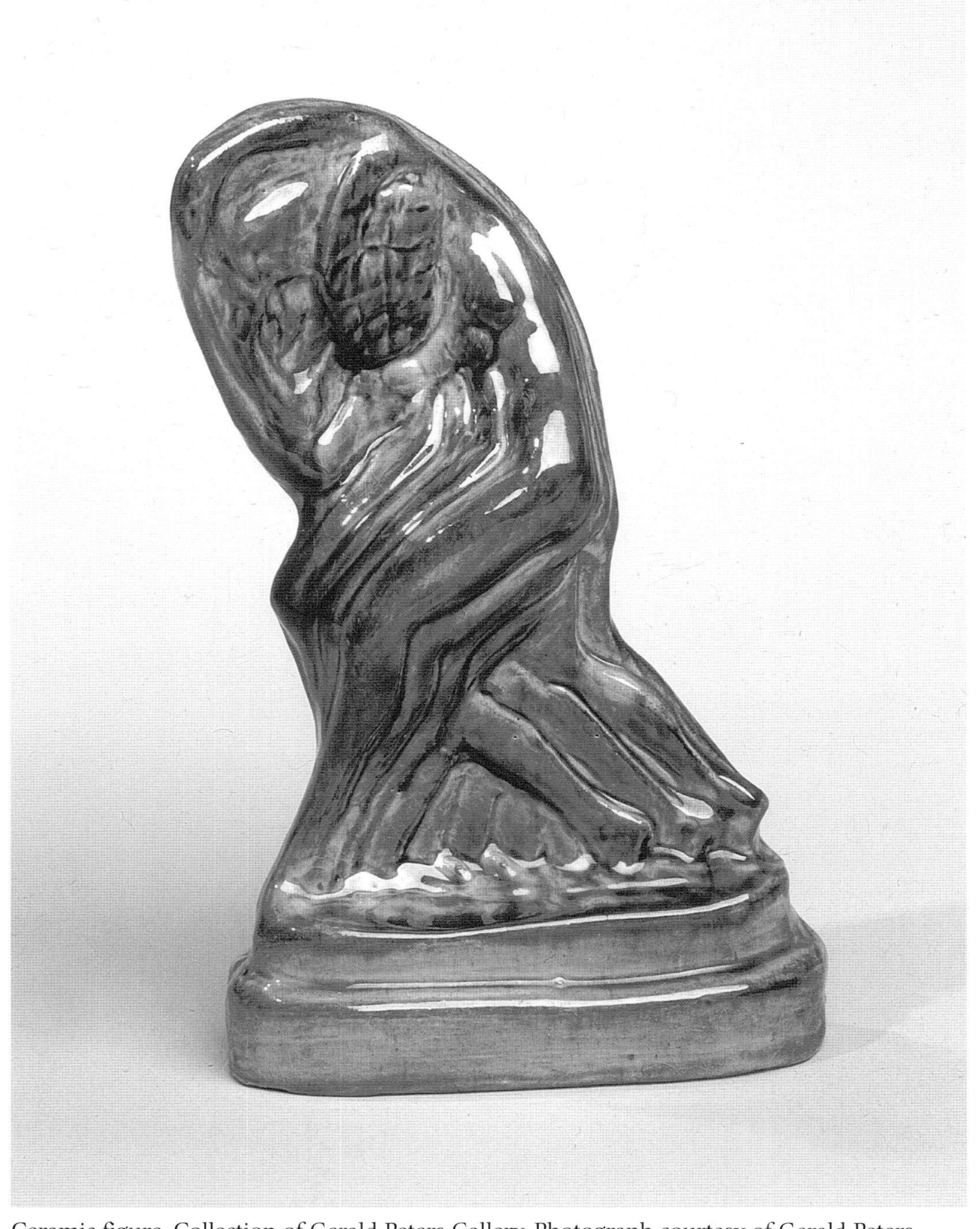

Ceramic figure. Collection of Gerald Peters Gallery. Photograph courtesy of Gerald Peters Gallery, Santa Fe.

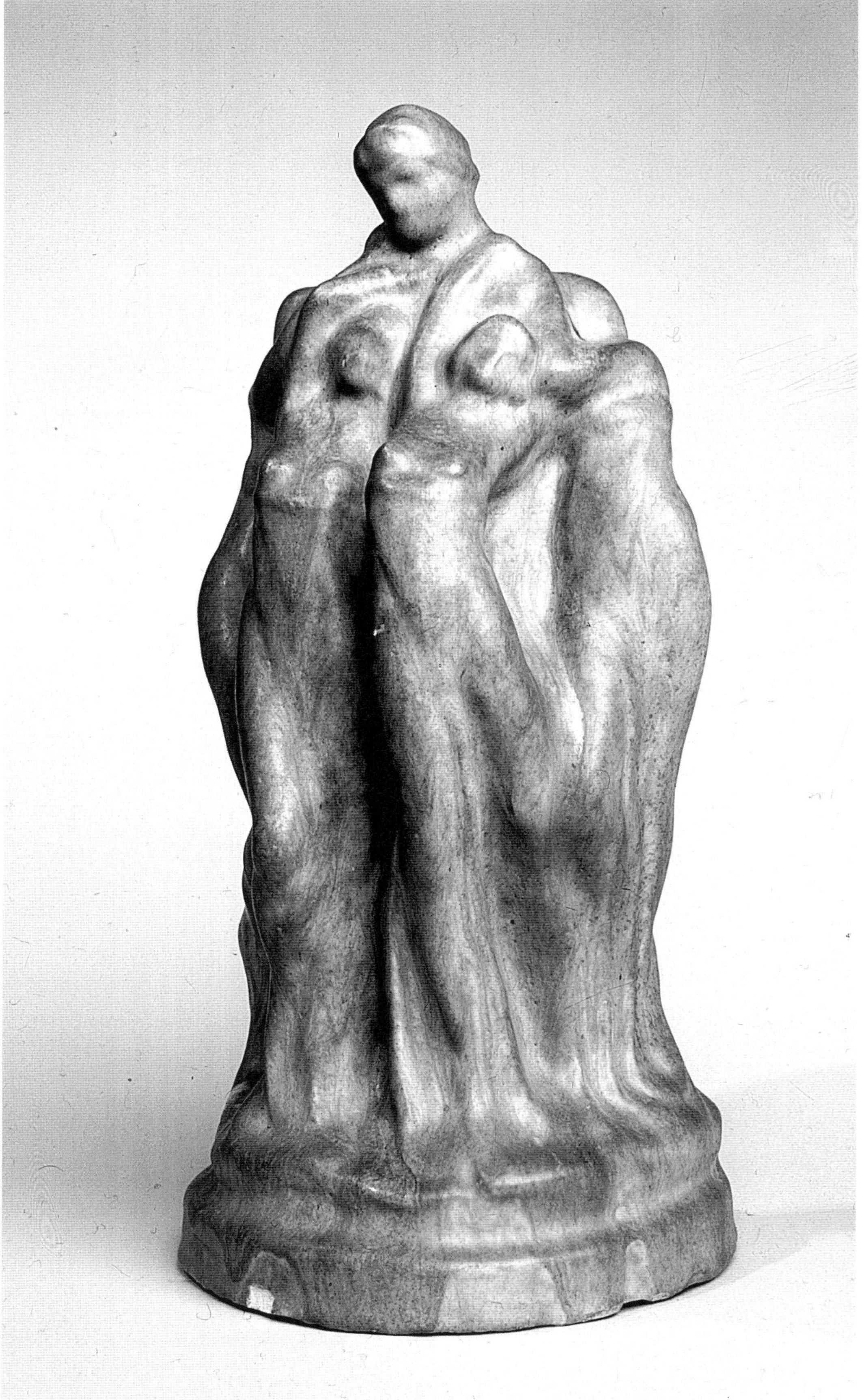

Ceramic figure. Collection of Gerald Peters Gallery. Photograph courtesy of Gerald Peters Gallery, Santa Fe.

7 Life among the Artists

The reputation of the Santa Fe art colony of the 1920s endures today not only for artistic reasons but because many of its members were colorful, unconventional personalities who questioned the status quo in both art and society. While the phrase "art colony" implies a group of like-minded artists gathering together deliberately and working in similar styles, Santa Fe's artistic community was different. Frank Applegate noted one distinct disparity among the visual artists soon after he arrived in Santa Fe, when he described the community as consisting of "about 20 painters … some of them moderns and some pot boilers painting romantic Indian subjects."[1] The painters could be distinguished further by their techniques. They employed styles ranging from the academic through urban realism, impressionism, and cubism, all the way to abstraction.

Mary Austin considered the term "art colony" inaccurate when applied to Santa Fe because she believed the artists' similarity lay solely in their choice of subject matter from the land and people around them. "There is … not anything that is ordinarily called a 'school' among the representatives of the various types of creative work going on," she wrote, "nor does the group at Santa Fe, as it is irritatingly described, constitute an 'artist colony.' Of the painters, no two came there for the same reasons, no two arrive at the same expression of what they find." The comments of a reporter from Oklahoma who visited Santa Fe in 1926 support Austin's assessment. "No one among them ever said, 'Come now, let us have a western Greenwich Village,'" she wrote. They "came because they loved it as 'A City Different'—not because they wanted to found a 'colony.'"[2]

Inaccurate connotation aside, the creative residents of Santa Fe were perceived as members of a colony for the simple reason that they frequently acted as a cohesive group. While the artists may have worked in dissimilar, distinctive styles, they lived and interacted as a homogeneous body. The contemporary press often referred to the supporters or opponents of a given cause as "the artists" when their ranks included not only artists but writers, anthropologists, archaeologists, and others. Although not all of Santa Fe's "intelligentsia" agreed on every topic and sometimes opposed each other on an issue, many of the individuals were bound together by shared beliefs in Indian rights, in the preservation and revival of traditional forms of art and architecture, and in progressive political and social movements. Novelist and historian Oliver LaFarge believed that from the mid-1920s to the early 1930s, the artists' colony "was the most influential single group in the city."[3]

By the time Applegate moved to Santa Fe, the art colony was already quite notorious among the established residents. Unlike other art colonies in which the artists kept to themselves, the Santa Fe artists were active in the community, whether the community wished them to be or not. Some of the artists had formed the Arts Club of Santa Fe in 1920 to serve as a "cultural clearing house," with branches devoted to music, art, and literature. The writers' section of the club, jokingly called the Genius Club and run by Austin, held group readings and wrote and produced plays. The Arts Club also organized artists' receptions and sponsored visiting speakers.[4]

The established residents considered the artists queer folk, for they dressed unconventionally, lived in "mud huts" and wanted to prevent Santa Fe from becoming a typical American city. According to Alice Rossin, daughter of Alice Corbin and William Penhallow Henderson, the townspeople saw the artists and writers as outsiders and invaders. "And they didn't approve of the fact that we wore the kind of clothes that we did—that we didn't get more formally dressed up. … We wore comfortable things for the dry and cold or dry and hot climate."[5] Applegate appreciated the region's casual lifestyle. Judging from photographs and relatives' recollections, his basic wardrobe consisted of heavy flannel shirts and workpants, but he sometimes sported turquoise jewelry and a bolo tie. He frequently went barefoot and often let his hair grow until it hung over his eyes.

An article written by the esteemed journalist William Allen White and reprinted in the *Santa Fe New Mexican* in 1922 lampooned the longtime residents' opinions of the "newcomers":

> These artists are a sad train to the devotees of the new Main Street idea [i.e., as espoused in the Sinclair Lewis novel *Main Street*]. The artists—painters, poets, potters, sculptors, singers, story writers, and sometimes gay dabblers in various arts—come sauntering into decent society, the women's clubs and men's civic organizations for instance, in negligee clothes. Sometimes these artists wear the 10-gallon hats and purple ties of the native or the silver buckles and belts of the Indian or the bright colors of the Spanish. The commercial nobility feels that these artists have no respect for money and place and power. It is a fearful pest to be inflicted upon a God-fearing community, to have a lot of carefree and untamed artists turned loose upon it. Imagine what would happen in any American town steeped in its own respectability if suddenly out of the sky a cloud of light-hearted people dropped who were more impressed with the clear air, the blue dome above the beautiful horizon and the joy of color and form in the landscape than with boosting the burg![6]

The animosity the "commercial nobility" felt toward the artists was sometimes obvious. For example, in 1924 City Council representatives proposed collecting a vocational tax of $5 a year from artists and writers. A meeting of the group at Joe Bákos' studio "was characterized by more amusement than indignation," the *Santa Fe New Mexican* reported. One artist "said he supposed they meant to tax art as a luxury—like automobiles—and he wondered where he would wear his license tag. It certainly couldn't be taxed on any income-basis, as far as Santa Fe sales are concerned, he said." Another artist suggested issuing a birth certificate for each painting or verse. A third pointed out, "the artists took $500 out of the town in sales in the past year, and spent $50,000," and suggested they be subsidized, as Lorenzo de Medici subsidized artists, rather than taxed.[7]

What Santa Fe's established residents found especially galling was that the artists and writers invariably put up a fight when confronted with something they thought was wrong. "They have revolted often and violently with words, oil paint, letters, pamphlets, and sometimes their fists to keep the village from becoming another Strawberry Point, Iowa," stated an editorial in the *Santa Fe New Mexican*. The majority of the townspeople were Republican and likely not pleased when the art colony came out in support of Progressive Party candidate Robert LaFollette in the 1924

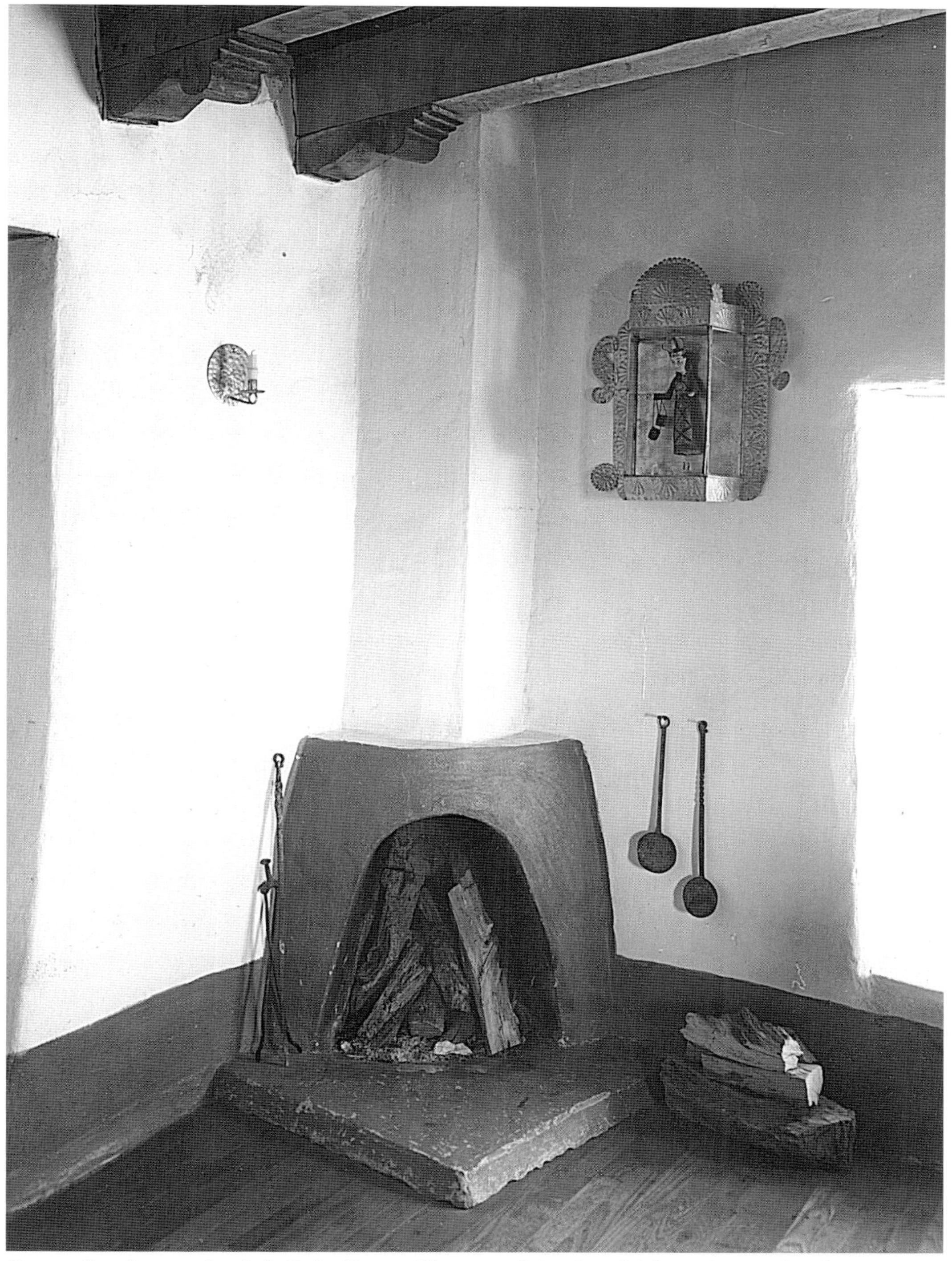

Corner fireplace at the de la Peña House. Photograph by Ansel Adams (A112, dated August 21, 1930). Published in *Ladies Home Journal*, December 1930. Note in Frank Applegate's handwriting on the back of this photograph reads, "Fireplace in pueblo style. 200 year old house in Santa Fe. Iron spoons, poker, spit, tin nicho containing old carved wooden saints of country, small candle sconce. The Spanish colonists lived for the first year (1598) in an Indian pueblo and in that time became well conditioned in Indian architecture. Interior of old Spanish colonial and Pueblo Indian houses have most features in common and the material is all the same." Courtesy of the Center for Creative Photography and the Ansel Adams Publishing Rights Trust.

presidential election. Using the slogan, "LaFollette, We Are Here," the artists and writers campaigned actively for "Fighting Bob," a supporter of Indian rights who had helped to defeat the Bursum Bill. With Witter Bynner in charge, they opened a headquarters on Palace Avenue, where "a busy aggregation of headquarters men, hammering on typewriters, or frantically mailing out LaFollette literature [was] visible, with the familiar red, green, purple, vermilion, crimson, and blue velveteen shirts much in evidence." They drafted a manifesto, sent to LaFollette and printed in the *Santa Fe New Mexican,* that called him "the first great humanitarian to run for the presidency in two generations [i.e., since Lincoln]."[8]

Despite local animus, no one could deny the collective influence of the artists and writers on Santa Fe's national standing. Their fame, eccentric reputations, and ability to get their work shown in major galleries and printed in major publications contributed significantly to the flood of tourists who visited the city each year. Santa Fe advertised itself as "the Mecca of Art." An official city map produced by the Chamber of Commerce had the homes of Los Cinco Pintores clearly marked, and the Camino del Monte Sol drew numerous curious visitors. The Studebaker Corporation even considered using John Sloan or other artists "tied up with the beauty of Santa Fe," in advertisements. By 1928 Santa Fe was being called "one of the five art centers of the United States."[9]

Not surprisingly, Santa Feans rarely bought the local artists' work. When an artist did sell a painting in Santa Fe, the price was often less than what he or she could get out East. Unless an artist had a wealthy patron, received commissions for portraits or public works, or had a second source of income, he was financially insecure. "There weren't art galleries in this town—I mean, selling galleries," recalled Alice Rossin. "Most people in Santa Fe came to the artist's studio to buy things." Applegate once wrote that some of the more sympathetic Santa Fe merchants "are beginning to acquire pictures, though, to tell the truth, most of them are taken in on long overdue bills." Will Shuster advertised his etch-ings "at low prices" in the *Santa Fe New Mexican,* and the Museum of Fine Arts held discount sales after exhibitions closed.[10]

Although an enduring myth holds that the Santa Fe artists and writers were upper-middle class, many of them struggled to pay their bills. Mary Austin and other writers had to subsidize their work by embarking on lecture tours. Many painters pursued other occupations on the side. Shuster produced ornamental ironwork, for example, and Bákos made furniture. He referred to this period, in hindsight, as "the years when artists had to work hard to pay for the luxury of painting."[11]

Teaching was another minor source of income. Applegate taught individual pupils, then in the summer of 1925 joined the faculty of the Chappell School of Art, a Denver-based school that ran a program in Santa Fe. He was among the lecturers at the school, along with Bákos, Andrew Dasburg, Walter Mruk, B.J.O. Nordfeldt, and Ernest Blumenschein.[12]

"In all the class work … the personal views of the instructors are minimized," *El Palacio* reported. "The sound underlying principles of art are unfolded, and students are taught to look for the elemental facts of form, light and shade and color, and to appreciate the historical development of the native arts of the Southwest. But in its course of 10 lectures by local artists the School provides an open forum for the discussion of all phases of art, from that of the prehistoric cliff dwellers and the primitive Spanish-American, down to the latest tendencies and problems of modern art." The summer sessions continued for three years. When the school canceled its 1928 season, *El Palacio* implied that an artistic rivalry had been the cause: no Chappell courses would be offered in Santa Fe "because of Denver's ambition to build up its own culture center."[13]

Painter and critic Cyril Kay-Scott filled the void by founding the Cyril Kay-Scott School of Painting in April 1928, and Applegate served on the faculty there, as well. Originally a summer school, its enrollment grew from an initial six students to more than 100 students from 14 states and one foreign country a year and four months later. In

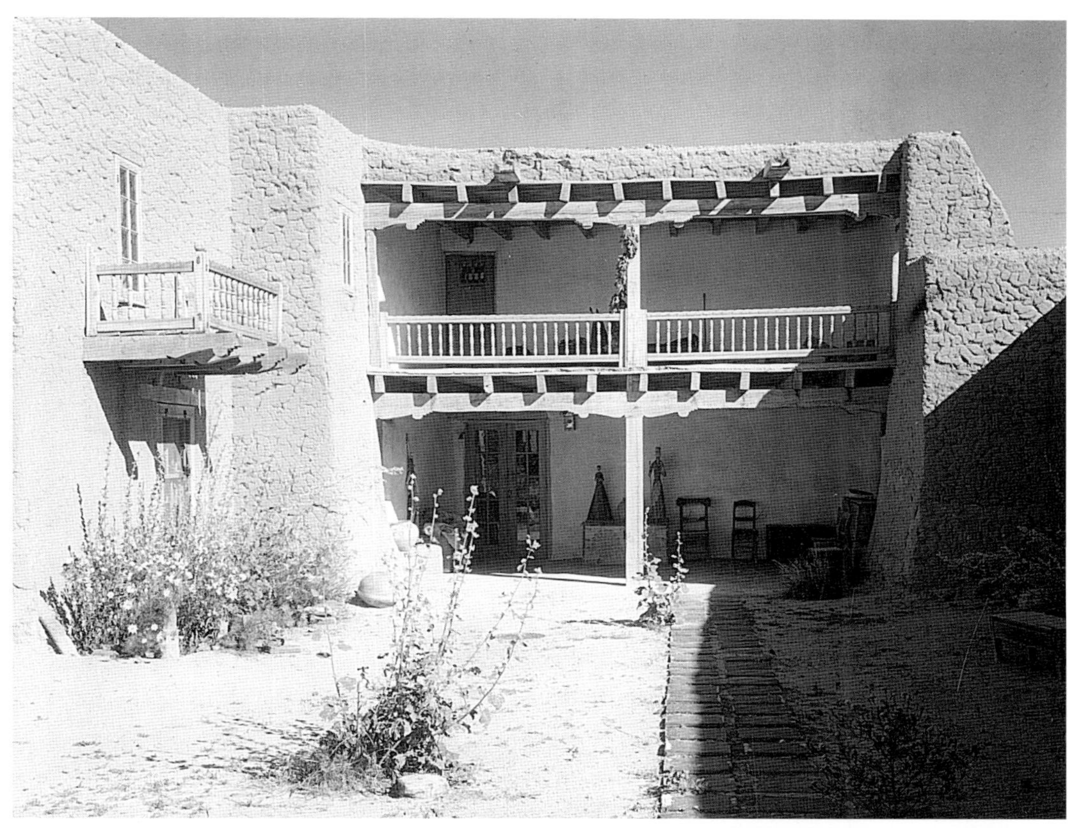

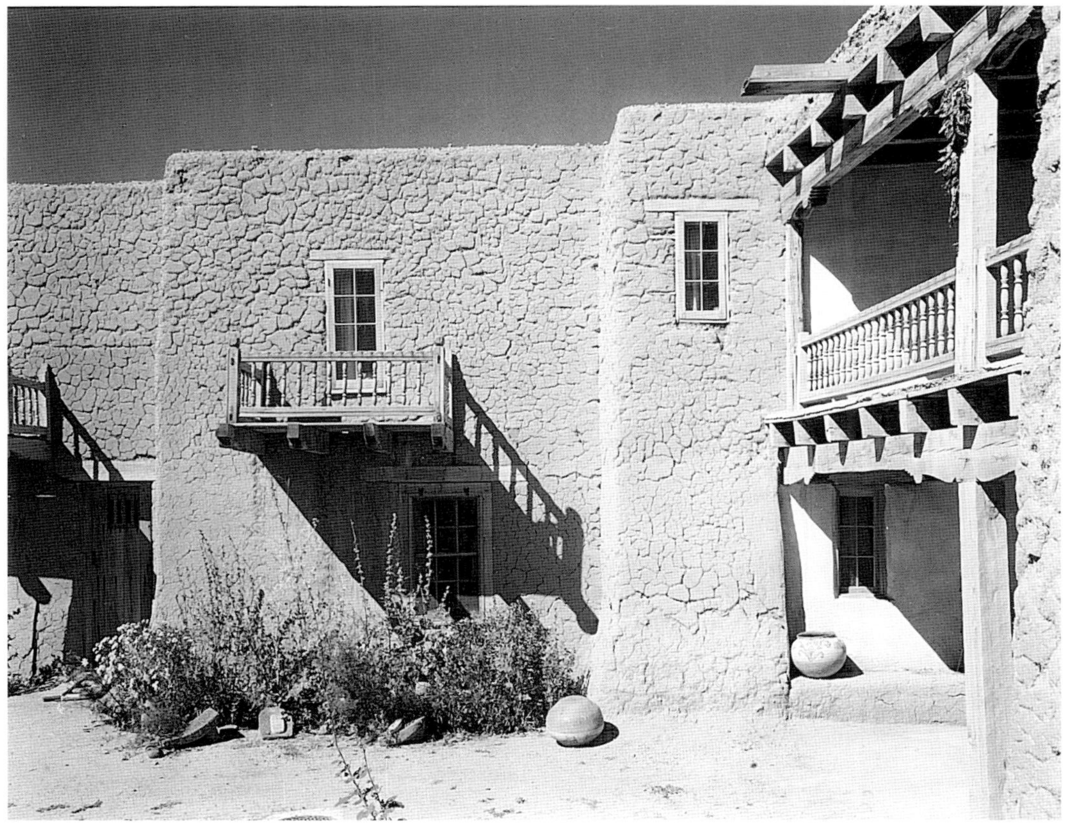

Top: The portal/patio at the de la Peña House (A116). Bottom: Another view of the portal/patio at the de la Peña House (A115). Photographs by Ansel Adams. Notes in Frank Applegate's handwriting on the back of these photographs indicate that this is an "old Spanish colonial ranch house that had been adapted to modern living condition without destroying character or spirit of the old." Courtesy of the Center for Creative Photography and the Ansel Adams Publishing Rights Trust.

August 1929 Kay-Scott's school evolved into the Santa Fe Art School, which offered classes year-round. Applegate both lectured there and served on the advisory board.[14]

Applegate apparently was able to support his family by teaching, selling Indian and Spanish Colonial art, being a landlord, and selling an occasional painting. It appears from some of his behavior–for example, selling some of his property for only a token fee, holding onto his Model T Ford for more than a decade, seldom bothering to price his work, amassing a huge native arts collection–that he had little interest in monetary gain. While other artists were hustling to make sales, Applegate was actually turning down offers to buy his paintings, claiming that he "preferred to have [them] go to a public gallery." He did little work in the lucrative genre of portraiture, and one can surmise from occasional remarks by him that "painting to order," whether on commission from a patron, a business or a government agency, was not an occupation he pursued. He was also known to be generous with what money he had. "He will be longest remembered by many an impecunious artist or writer for his helping hand, always given freely in aid of the ambitious or the struggling," the *Santa Fe New Mexican* said after his death.[15]

Yet in matters involving land, Applegate sometimes bullied people, including his friends. In 1925 property agreements between Applegate and the members of Los Cinco Pintores soured when he threatened the other painters with physical force if they did not sell a segment of the land back to him. The Cincos responded by erecting a fence, and the matter apparently was forgotten.[16] Similarly, in 1929 Applegate coerced John and Elizabeth DeHuff into selling him their share of a piece of land the Applegates and DeHuffs owned together so he could resell it.[17] Perhaps money did drive his actions to an extent, or perhaps his arrogance (to which Will Shuster referred when relating the Cincos incident and which family members recall) led him to pressure others.

Throughout the 1920s the artists and writers clashed with the other residents of Santa Fe over civic issues, most notably ones in which civic "improvements" threatened the preservation of "old Santa Fe." Eventually, however, they learned to work with the Chamber of Commerce and other civic organizations. They contributed their creativity to the city's amusements by participating in local theater and staging public dances. The artists hosted Pasatiempo, an irreverent, free-admission counterpart to Fiesta that featured concerts, singing, dancing, a children's animal show, and the "Hysterical Pageant," complete with humorous floats, outrageous costumes, and sly jabs at Santa Fe's movers and shakers. Applegate sometimes participated in the pageant. A highlight of Fiesta was, and remains, the burning of the giant puppet Zozobra, or "Old Man Gloom," which Shuster and Gustave Baumann created in 1926.[18]

Stories about the artists and writers have survived in part because they were detailed in the *Santa Fe New Mexican*. With the zeal common to small-town newspapers, the *New Mexican* routinely chronicled their antics and activities. Reporter Brian Boru "Bee Bee" Dunne, a friend to many of the artists, wrote about their exhibitions and social activities with equal enthusiasm. In breathless prose, Dunne described the inaugural ball given for Gov. James F. Hinkle at La Fonda, Santa Fe's finest hotel, in January 1923. The ballroom had been decorated under the direction of Applegate and Ina Sizer Cassidy: "The setting was unique as it was of surpassing beauty," Dunne wrote.

> A Spanish hotel with the lobby furnished like a palace of old Madrid; glass doors admitting the rays of a full moon; colorful bunting and oil paintings resplendent in the rays of myriads of artificial moons called electrics– these helped weave a spell over the visitor who stepped out of modern motor to join in the throng. It was Madrid at first–as one saw the tall-backed chairs, the rich upholstery, the polished carved tables of black walnut ... but ... one took a dozen steps and passed through Madrid– to Russia. The ballroom brought one to the mystic and weird

empire of the late Czar Nicky. ... It kept 2,000 people guessing and gasping.[19]

Prohibition moonshine flowed freely at many of the artists' social gatherings. Witter Bynner's almost daily "tea parties" sometimes featured tea but more often included spirits. The members of Los Cinco Pintores threw parties featuring Bákos' homebrewed beer and bootleg whiskey. Betty Applegate McClung remembered the "marvelous parties" sisters Elizabeth and Martha White threw at their home, "El Delirio." Painter Datus Myers and his wife, Alice Clark Myers, were known as great party-givers. Alice Rossin recalled that "the artists could put a party together between morning and evening."[20]

Looking back years later, Bynner remembered parties at the Henderson home. "We came on horseback then by day or at night on foot with lanterns, and would kick snow off our overshoes in the welcoming glow of the room with its corner adobe fireplace. Painters from nearby houses on the Camino would be there, Applegate, Bákos, Shuster, [Willard] Nash, sometimes Sloan and [Randall] Davey from streets farther away, often Indian painters like Awa Tsireh from the pueblos and occasionally a visiting writer, [Vachel] Lindsay with his chants, [Carl] Sandburg with his guitar, [Robert] Frost with his wit, [Charles] Lummis with a red bandanna round his gray temples ... ."[21]

The artists frequented Indian ceremonies together, and in June 1922 the Applegates traveled to San Juan Pueblo for a dance, as part of an entourage including Bákos, Bynner, painter Olive Rush, and Gwendolyn Meux, an instructor at the University of Oklahoma. Meux was acquainted with the Cinco Pintores and other Santa Fe artists. She became good friends with the Applegates, staying with them on several occasions, and at some point studied art with Frank. Also attending the dance was Alta Applegate's sister, Olive Chenoweth, a school principal who was visiting for the summer from Atlanta, Illinois.[22]

That July Chenoweth, Bákos, and Meux joined the Applegates on a camping-and-sketching trip to the Rito de los Frijoles ruins, also known as Bandelier National Monument. Chenoweth wrote a letter to the *Atlanta Argus* describing the trip:

> We left "Henry" [the Applegate Ford] on the top of the mesa and went down the trail five-eighths of a mile into the canyon below, then on a little more than half a mile up the canyon, just beyond Ceremonial Cave, where we spread our shelter. At night we slept on the ground rolled up in blankets. ... Our first afternoon proved a most thrilling one. Frank, Joe, and Gwen decided to go back to the mesa for some more supplies. While they were gone a shower came, so Alta and I stayed under the shelter. ... When the shower was over, I heard a rumbling noise on the mesa opposite. ...
>
> It occurred to us at the same moment that the sound was water coming down the canyon. We jumped up and ran to the stream just in time to see the water rushing down, its wall almost three feet high. We thought of the little rustic bridge down near Ceremonial Cave and hurried there, arriving just in time to see half of it swept along by the mad waters. In a moment Frank came running up on the other side. The noise was too much for a human voice, so he sat down on his pack and smoked his peace pipe, while we all watched the raging torrent. It wasn't long until the rest of the bridge went and Joe and Gwen came up. The boys dropped a big tree trunk across the turbulent stream. Frank was soon across and, giant-like, seized another still larger pine trunk which he succeeeded in laying close to the other.

The group spent five days at Frijoles Canyon, exploring the Anasazi ruins while the men sketched. They even slept in the Ceremonial Cave one night, 160 feet above the ground (with Olive choosing to sleep on the roof), an activity that was probably taboo even then. On the way back, they excavated pottery at ancient ruins. "We spent several hours at the prehistoric pueblo of Tsehirego and experienced the

CHAPTER 7:
LIFE AMONG
THE ARTISTS

discoverer's thrill more than once,"
Chenoweth reported.[23] Today, when the
federal government repatriates Native
American sacred artifacts, such actions
are illegal, but back then digging was a
popular pastime.

When painting sales were slow, it
helped to have a supply of game in the
larder, and Applegate hunted for deer,
squirrel, bear, and turkey. Will Shuster
was one of Applegate's hunting compan-
ions. The *Santa Fe New Mexican* reported in November 1924 that Shuster
and Applegate "left today by motor for
the mountains to study the color of wild
turkey feathers. They hope to see several
turkeys at close range and bring them
back as models for a painting of the
'Ideal Thanksgiving Dinner.'" They were
successful, bagging five large turkeys
between them for a neighborhood feast.
And, as the *New Mexican* reported, they
returned with a tale to tell:

> Applegate is some little wild
> turkey imitator. He gave the siren
> call with such fidelity that Shuster
> had to look around again and
> again to see whether he had a
> feather-throated companion. But it
> was merely Applegate, ceramics
> authority and wearer of the
> General Grant style of black beard.
> During the turkey hunt Applegate
> was crouched one afternoon
> behind a big log. He gave the
> turkey yell or call, all right, and
> "Shus" was near, gun in hand. The
> mountain lions heard the call.
> They, too, like turkey … it seems.
> And a lion got the surprise of his
> young life—so did Applegate—when
> the king of the forest crept up to
> the log which seemed to be
> emitting the turkey calls. The lion
> peered over the log, his paw raised
> to strike—and then he saw Apple-
> gate, of the black beard. The lion
> fell backwards, rolled down the
> canyon, boulders following with
> great rapidity, making a noise like
> Big Bertha storming Paris. Apple-
> gate can make a sound like a
> turkey—but the lions had never
> seen a bearded gobbler before. It
> was a shock.[24]

Another humorous incident involving the two men occurred in April 1925,
when Applegate came to Shuster's
defense in court. Shuster had been

ticketed for speeding up Canyon Road in
his Ford, known by all as the "Covered
Wagon" because of the large canopy that
made it useful for overnight camping.
Shuster fought the ticket, arguing that it
was "impossible to drive the 'Covered
Wagon' on a rough part of Canyon Road
24 miles an hour." He maintained that
"covered wagons are associated with
snail-like pace … they were the carriers
that crossed the plains so slowly that
they have been classed with turtles. Now,
when my covered bus comes out and
manages to hit up a clip of four miles
people say—'There it goes, look at it!'
And when it reaches a speed of ten
miles, people crane their necks and say
'My, how it is flying.'"

Applegate substantiated Shuster's
claim before the judge. "I have driven
Fords up Canyon Road for four years,
and I have known much about the pace
they travel," he said. "Shuster might have
come down Canyon Road at 24 miles an
hour but [was] certainly not going up at
that speed, without wrecking his car."[25]

What the *Santa Fe New Mexican*
failed to report, as Shuster later recalled,
was "that Buck Fletcher, our old cowpoke
traffic officer, totally ignored Frank
Applegate's passing me at the red school
house—he was clear up to Gormley's
street when Buck stopped me at
Delgado." The judge ruled against
Shuster but halved the fine to $5.[26]

Living on the Camino del Monte Sol
was like living in any neighborhood. The
days were filled with work, gossip, and
social affairs. One of Applegate's starkly
rendered, untitled watercolors depicts an
afternoon on the Camino (p. 154).
Residents play tennis, a painter works at
an easel, a curious burro stands to one
side, Shuster's "Covered Wagon" to
another. The telephone poles and wires
that gave the street the name Telephone
Road stretch across the scene, and the
bright blue Monte Sol hovers above. It's
an idyllic scene that captures a sense of
contentment in its minimalistic strokes.

Betty Applegate entered high school
in the fall of 1924. She was athletic and
fit in well with the other children in the
neighborhood, earning a reputation as
an outstanding horsewoman. "She rides
like an Amazon," Applegate boasted. "I
do not believe anyone in Santa Fe can

ride better." Mary Austin's niece, Mary Hunter, moved in with Austin in 1925, and she and Betty became great friends. Betty also socialized with the children of her parents' friends, including Alfred Dasburg and Dan Eastman (son of Ida Rauh Eastman, Dasburg's common-law wife), Deric Nusbaum (son of anthropologist Jesse Nusbaum), and Helen Blumenschein, whom she visited in Taos. Alfred Dasburg recalled that the young folks would often sleep outside, ride horses to school, hold track meets, and play polo. Betty often cared for his and

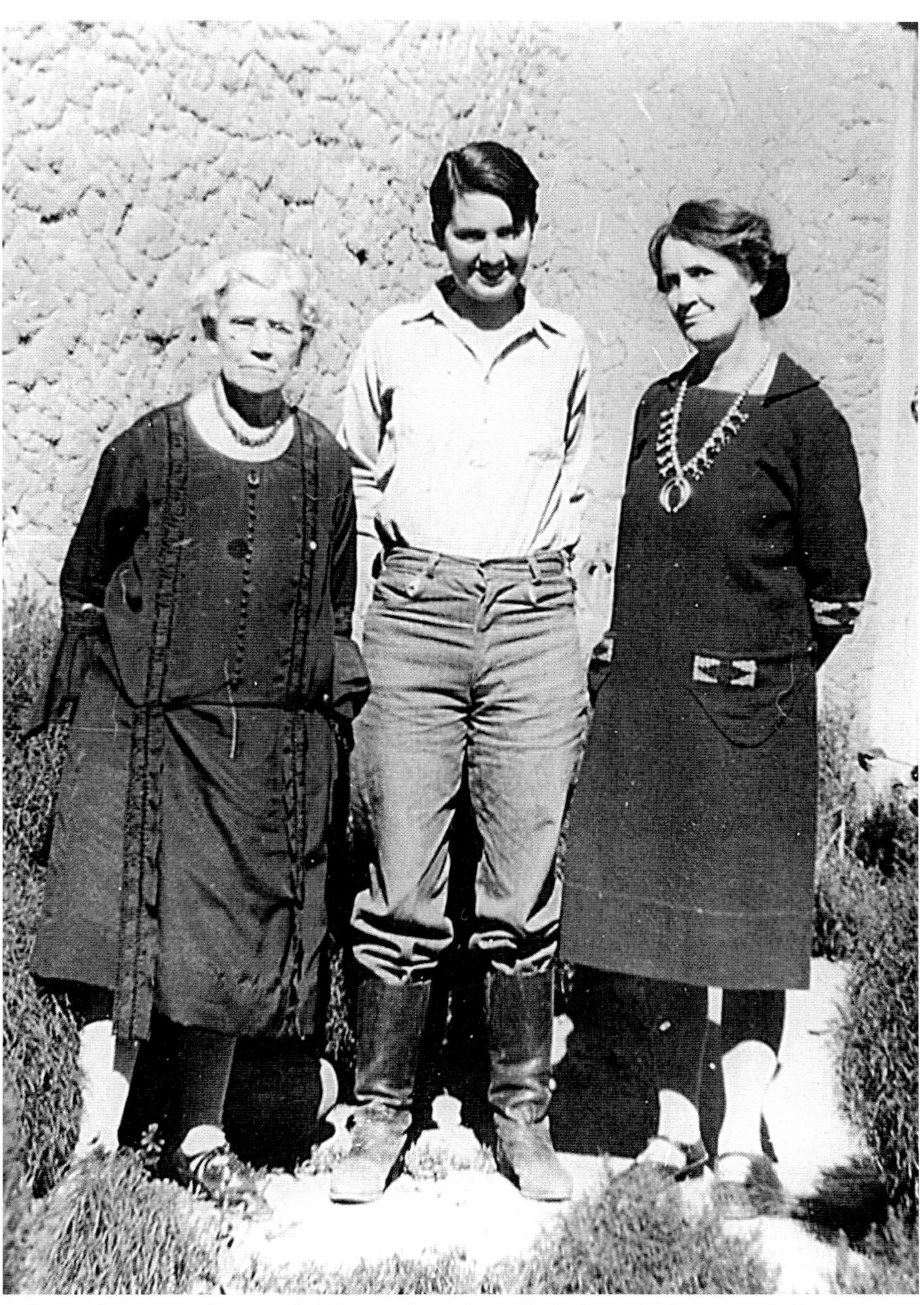

Left to right, Agnes Chenoweth (Alta Applegate's mother), Betty Applegate, and Alta Applegate in the mid- to late-1920s. Photograph courtesy of the Museum of New Mexico (neg. no. 13536).

Dan Eastman's horses, which shared a corral with hers. Tennis was also popular with the younger set. Frank, Alta, and Betty were all avid gardeners, an interest no doubt stemming from the family's Illinois roots, and Applegate's letters mentioned the bumper crops of vegetables and strawberries they grew in Santa Fe. [27]

The Applegates' social life broadened after they moved into the de la Peña House in 1926. The house was much larger than their previous residences, as Applegate continually expanded it, and the number of parties, organization meetings, and other social gatherings they hosted increased accordingly. One such party was in honor of a performance in Santa Fe by dancer Agnes DeMille, a school friend of Mary Hunter's. More than 50 people attended, including artists John Sloan, William Penhallow Henderson, Fremont Ellis, Gustave Baumann, Carlos Vierra, Andrew Dasburg, and Olive Rush, poet Arthur Davison Ficke, and former New Mexico territorial governor Herbert Hagerman. In her memoirs, DeMille remembered, "The poets said, pouring their cocktails … they thought the first number showed wit, the second none. The painters liked the color of my third dress. The Sunday school teacher wondered if I wouldn't come to a strawberry breakfast on Thursday. The Indians were convulsed. Why on the ends of the feet?"[28]

The Applegates frequently interacted with Chamber of Commerce secretary (and former head of the Santa Fe Indian School) John D. DeHuff and his wife, writer Elizabeth Willis DeHuff. John DeHuff's diary recounts dinners and parties they attended together, including ones for author Sinclair Lewis at Mary Austin's home in 1926 and with anthropologist Frederick Webb Hodge at the Applegates' in 1928. One night in March 1928, about 100 people attended a screening of filmmaker Robert Flaherty's 1926 documentary "Moana of the South Seas," with Flaherty in attendance, at the Applegate home.[29]

In 1930, when Betty was a college student, the *Santa Fe New Mexican* commented on a fad the Applegates' affairs exemplified, the "family party":

If all the people who are wondering what will become of the younger generation, could have been little mice in corners at this week's parties they would know … that they are growing up to be persons who have a perfectly grand time and really know how to do it in that good "old fashioned innocent" way that we've heard about for ever so long. These parties are really inspirations. They are the kind where a "feller" takes his mother and everybody enjoys his or herself. Family parties, i.e., mother, father, and daughter or son, have been the rage for some time. Mr. and Mrs. Frank Applegate and daughter, Betty, always entertain together. Miss Evaline Myers and her mother are charming hostesses. The J. Nusbaums and son Deric have taken up the family party idea.[30]

From outward appearances, the Applegates seemed content. Frank and Alta roamed the countryside in search of Indian and Spanish Colonial artifacts, coordinated activities for the Indian Arts Fund and Spanish Colonial Arts Society, and took long automobile trips together. In early 1929 they put more than 2,000 miles on their old Ford, traveling through the Southwest and "put[ting] up at camp cottages." In 1930 they drove to California, staying with Ansel and Virginia Adams at their San Francisco home in early February and meeting Adams' friend and patron Albert Bender.[31]

Although Alta and Frank appear to have been happy, life behind closed doors was not always that happy for Betty Applegate. Frank referred fondly to Betty in letters, but Betty, as an adult, said she felt very neglected by him. Applegate niece Gretchen Beall, who knew Betty well, said, "In all the years I knew her, she never had a kind word for her father." The family led a rather unsettled life, and as Betty recalled, they never knew how many friends would be at dinner or would be staying the night. Her cousins back in Illinois considered her quite spoiled, and recall how she kept to herself at family gatherings. [32]

The Applegates' trips to visit friends and family members in the Eastern United States numbered only a handful in the nearly 10 years they lived in Santa Fe. They drove back to the Cornish, New Hampshire, art colony, in the summer of 1924, then motored home to Atlanta, Illinois, where Frank recovered from a broken arm (the result of a losing battle with his Model T's crank, as family legend holds). Applegate was home again for the Christmas of 1925, as part of a trip in which he judged an art exhibition in St. Louis, attended to property-related matters in Morrisville, Pennsylvania, and spent time with his brother Alpheus in New Jersey. He visited at an unknown time en route to Washington, D.C., and again in 1928 to attend a party honoring his mother. His final meeting with the family took place in September 1930, when the Applegates attended his niece Dorothy Applegate's wedding. On the few occasions Applegate did see his conservative, agrarian relatives he struck them as quite bohemian. His dress and demeanor, common among the Santa Fe crowd, pegged him as an eccentric back home. Nevertheless, some of his relatives adored him. Donald Applegate recalled that he and his sister, Dorothy, were in awe of their Uncle Frank. "When I was about 5 or 6, Mama worried about whether we knew about religion and God, so she wanted to send Dot and me to Sunday school. I didn't want to go—I knew Uncle Frank! And I knew that he could do anything and probably do it better than God could!"[33]

The Applegates frequently welcomed relatives and friends from the East into their Santa Fe home. Mabel (Mrs. Winston) Churchill, painter and wife of the author, whom they had known at the Cornish art colony, visited in 1922. Neighborhood Playhouse co-founder Irene Lewisohn stayed with the Applegates in 1925 and joined the Indian Arts Fund. Frank's brother Archie and his wife, Edna, spent two weeks with Frank and Alta in 1928, at which time Frank jokingly made Archie a birthday cake out of plaster of Paris. Alta's widowed mother, Agnes Chenoweth, bought the Applegates' first house from Walter Mruk in 1926. She lived there until 1928, then moved into the de la Peña House

with the Applegates. Howard Kretz Coluzzi, the artist whom Applegate had befriended back East, settled in Santa Fe in 1925. When Applegate built the house on El Caminito known as "El Torreon," he hired Coluzzi to paint frescoes inside.[34]

Others whom Applegate had known in the East became seasonal residents of Santa Fe, including wealthy art patron Elizabeth Sage Hare, who eventually built a house on the Acequia Madre. Applegate also rented properties to temporary residents, one of whom was the Woodstock, New York, art colony painter Neil Ives, a student of Andrew Dasburg's.[35]

Bynner, the Harvard-educated poet, was another of Applegate's close friends, and Applegate was considered part of Bynner's "inner circle." A leader of Santa Fe's intellectual society, Bynner was the life of any party. "He told stories, made endless puns, drank and smoked constantly, did monologues, played old tunes on the piano, imitated his mother … or a toothless old aunt … recited limericks or poetry."[36] Bynner bought several of Applegate's paintings, wrote

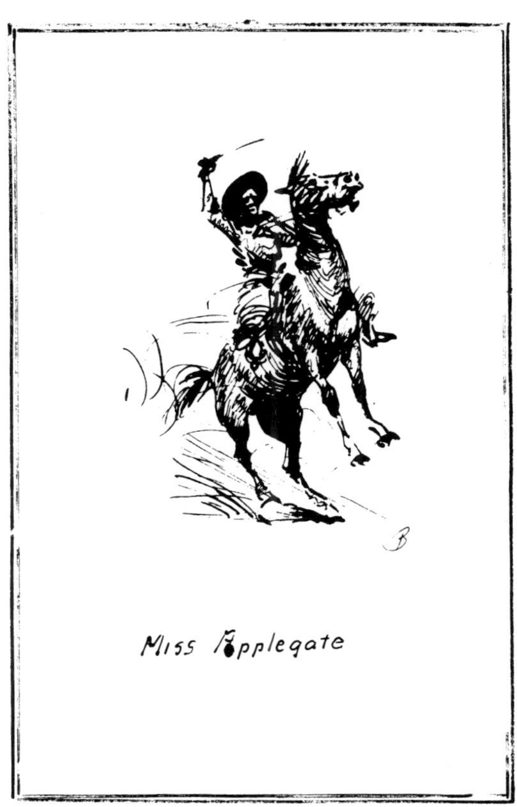

Pen and ink drawing of Betty Applegate, artist unknown. Applegate Papers.

the foreword to Applegate's first book, *Indian Stories From the Pueblos*, and, in the last few years of the decade, induced him to participate in a social activity that was new to him, community theater.

Dramatics had played an important part in Santa Fe's cultural life from the time Mary Austin organized the Santa Fe Community Theater in 1918. Given the flamboyant personalities among the local intelligentsia, their interest in performing is hardly surprising. Many of Santa Fe's seasonal and permanent residents had worked with theater groups in major cities around the country. Among them were Ida Rauh Eastman, a founder of the Provincetown Players; Bynner, whose plays had been produced in New York and San Francisco; and Lynn Riggs, whose best-known play, *Green Grow the Lilacs*, was the basis for the musical *Oklahoma!* The artists and writers served as actors, directors, playwrights, set designers, and publicists for local theater productions. "The city lacked a professional theater troupe, not to mention props, costumes and sets, and a spirit of camaraderie and community developed among the actors and crew as they relied on their imaginations and their own ingenuity to stage productions."[37]

Applegate's first role came in 1929 in Bynner's play *Cake, An Indulgence*, one of the most notorious productions ever presented in Santa Fe. *Cake* is the story of an emasculating woman, called The Lady, who searches for Heaven on Earth, dabbling in sex, religion, and cake along the way. It was quite controversial and much talked about, not least because, as everyone knew, Bynner had written the play to spoof his friend Mabel Dodge Luhan of Taos, wealthy art patron, author, and collector of artists and writers.

Although it had been produced twice in California, *Cake* had been rejected by New York producers, allegedly because they feared censorship for its racy dialogue and sexually oriented story line. Bynner exploited this fact for publicity purposes with the aid of the *Santa Fe New Mexican*, which proclaimed, "Santa Fe to see the play that Gotham feared," and covered the production more thoroughly than any New York paper ever covered Broadway. Many art colony members participated in the production. Raymond Jonson designed the stage set and lighting, and Cyril Kay-Scott, director of the Santa Fe Art School, had a leading role. Bynner himself directed. Alfred Dasburg played an angel, and John Sloan's wife, Dolly, made the costumes. Other colony members worked on sets and publicity.[38] Even *Laughing Horse* editor and Bynner's former secretary Willard "Spud" Johnson, whom Bynner accused Luhan of "stealing" by hiring and removing to Taos, had a role.

Applegate played the part of the Swami, described in the stage directions as "an elderly, long-haired swami, half of whose beard is black and the other half white" with "a thin, old body." The Swami tells the rapacious Lady, "Nothing is anyone's but solitude. And death"; but his solemn philosophy is tempered by the fact he wants to make love to the Lady and chases her around lasciviously. The production was "magnificently staged and costumed from local trunks and Oriental collections, the necessary properties challenged the imaginative ingenuity of the stage direction."[39]

The *Santa Fe New Mexican*, specifically editor and artists' crony E. Dana Johnson, made elaborate fun of *Cake*. The paper called it the "outstanding society event of the season" and noted that out-of-towners from Albuquerque, Taos, and Las Vegas were expected to be overnight guests during its two-day run.[40] The front-page banner headline on opening night, July 12, 1929, declared, "'Cake' Served at Rialto Theater Tonight and Tomorrow Night. Opens New Dramatic Era in U.S. and Europe."

Johnson had five "editors" review the play—the "city editor," "the editor," the "highbrow editor," the "telegraph editor," and the "society editor," all writing tongue in cheek. Humor aside, the reviews indicated the performances were better than the play. "As a spectacle of Santa Fe entertaining itself, it was worth going far to see," concluded "the editor." Years later, Johnson claimed Bynner had "never forgotten or forgiven the paper's treatment of *Cake*."[41]

Applegate's performance was well received, and he quickly became "the favorite" of Santa Fe's art colony actors.

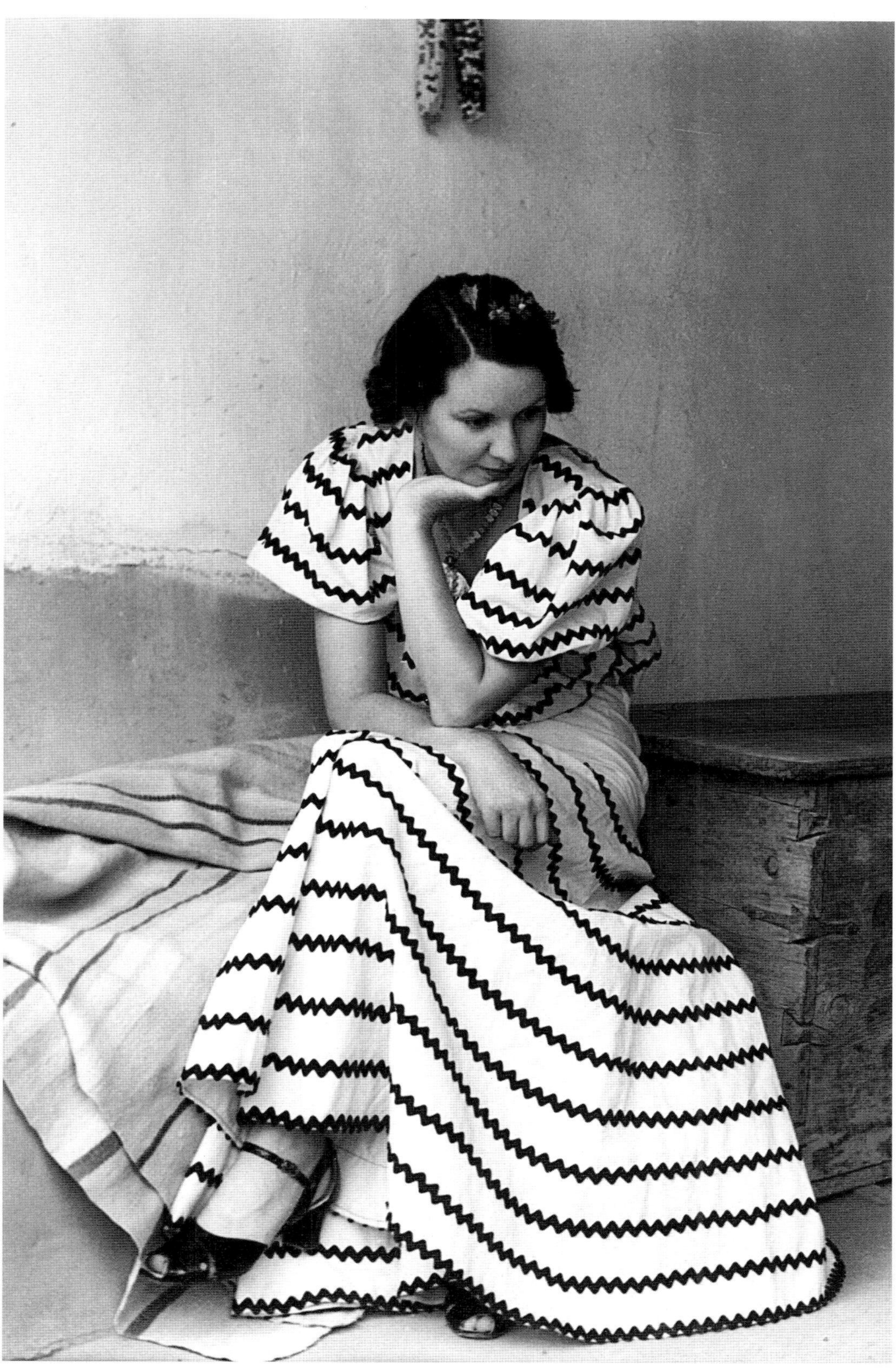

Betty Applegate in Fiesta costume in Santa Fe, ca. late 1920s. Photograph courtesy of the Applegate family.

CHAPTER 7:
LIFE AMONG
THE ARTISTS

In December 1929 he starred as Nat Jeffcote (described as "a tall thin gaunt domineering man of 60") in the Santa Fe Players' production of Stanley Houghton's *Hindle Wakes*. The play is about class differences and sexual double standards in Lancashire, England, and Applegate's character was a wealthy cotton manufacturer whose son becomes involved with a working-class girl. The cast also included writer Philip Stevenson and his wife, Gladys, actress Una Fairweather (*Cake*'s assistant director), and Raymond Jonson's wife, Vera. The *Santa Fe New Mexican*'s review said in part, "Whenever Miss Fairweather or Frank Applegate appeared there was no doubt about the lead. When they came on together it became very like one of those three-ball juggling acts with the lead passing back and forth faster than sight." The reviews doubtless were overly kind, but Applegate enjoyed acting. A year later, he had a bit part in the play *Captain Applejack,* which Stevenson directed.[42] Applegate would participate in local theater literally until the day he died.

Judging from letters Applegate's day-to-day life was fairly commonplace—a chicken-and-waffle dinner here, an Indian dance there, the occasional land purchase and exciting collectible find. But there was one aspect of Applegate's life that stands in contrast with the mundane: he followed a psycho-spiritual guru.

While present-day Santa Fe is a mecca for believers in New Age religions, a similar interest took hold of some in the local populace, including Applegate, in the 1920s, and it was due in part to a publication called *The New Age.* The magazine's former editor, an English philosopher and psychologist named Alfred R. Orage, had a group of disciples among Santa Fe's intelligentsia.

In the first two decades of the century, Orage used *The New Age* to develop the theory of "guild socialism," which others such as George Hobson expanded upon. Based on the belief that national guilds should control all means of production, guild socialism holds that workers in industry should govern the industries via self-governing organizations and that the community as a whole should own the industries. The concept ties into the Arts and Crafts movement and fits in with what Applegate and others in Santa Fe were trying to organize for the Indians and rural Hispanics. With the founding of the National Guilds League in 1915, the guild socialist movement assumed organized form. The Bolshevik Revolution and the postwar economic situation effectively killed the movement in Britain, and Orage's teachings evolved into something more spiritual.[43]

Anyone with even a token awareness of consciousness-raising will find Orage's jargon somewhat familiar. His teachings were based on the theories of George Gurdjieff, who ran the Institute for the Harmonious Development of Man near Fontainebleau, France. Gurdjieff believed that "by certain spiritual and physical exercises, the artificial and mechanical personality could be stripped bare, the true personality discovered, and the way opened to a new kind of awareness through which lay access to genuine humanity and the higher wisdom. ... This doctrine was wrapped in a cocoon of cabalistic, numerological, gymnosophistical jargon about the fourth dimension and the true ratio of zero to infinity."[44]

Orage resigned the editorship of *The New Age* in 1923 and moved to New York to raise money for Gurdjieff's institute.[45] According to his disciple Carl Zigrosser, he focused his lectures on "the harmonious development of man's three faculties or centers—the moving (or instinctive), the emotional, and the intellectual. Only a man with a fully developed 'I' can be called truly integrated and fully responsible." In order for the individual to find his "essence," he needed to strip away "impressions from his environment and education" as well as "inherent biases."

"Such insights as these," wrote Zigrosser, " ... eventually brought me to a realization of the utter mechanicality of man ... the extent of man's capacity for illusion about himself and his inner workings."[46]

Orage was a mesmerizing speaker, whose "hazel stare was one of the most effective things about him." He "could hold an audience ... by an extraordinary

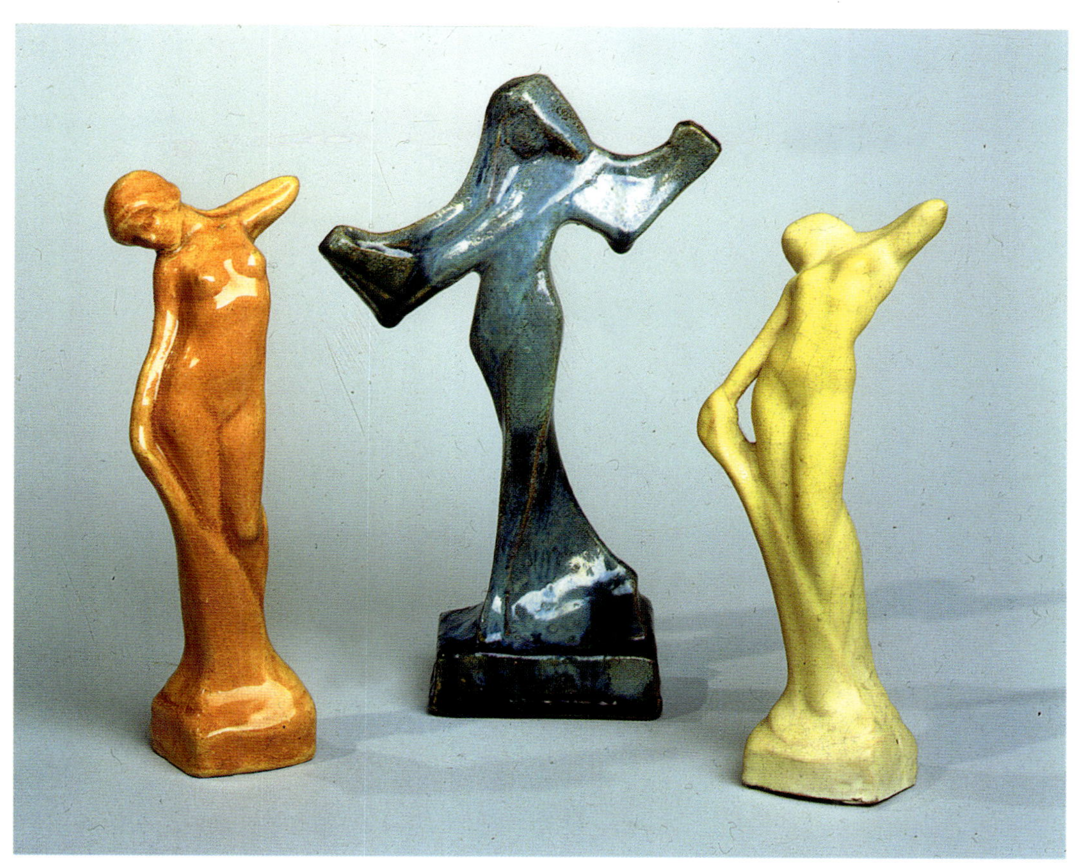

Ceramic figures. Collection of Gerald Peters Gallery. Photograph courtesy of Gerald Peters Gallery, Santa Fe. Figure on left exhibited in 1924.

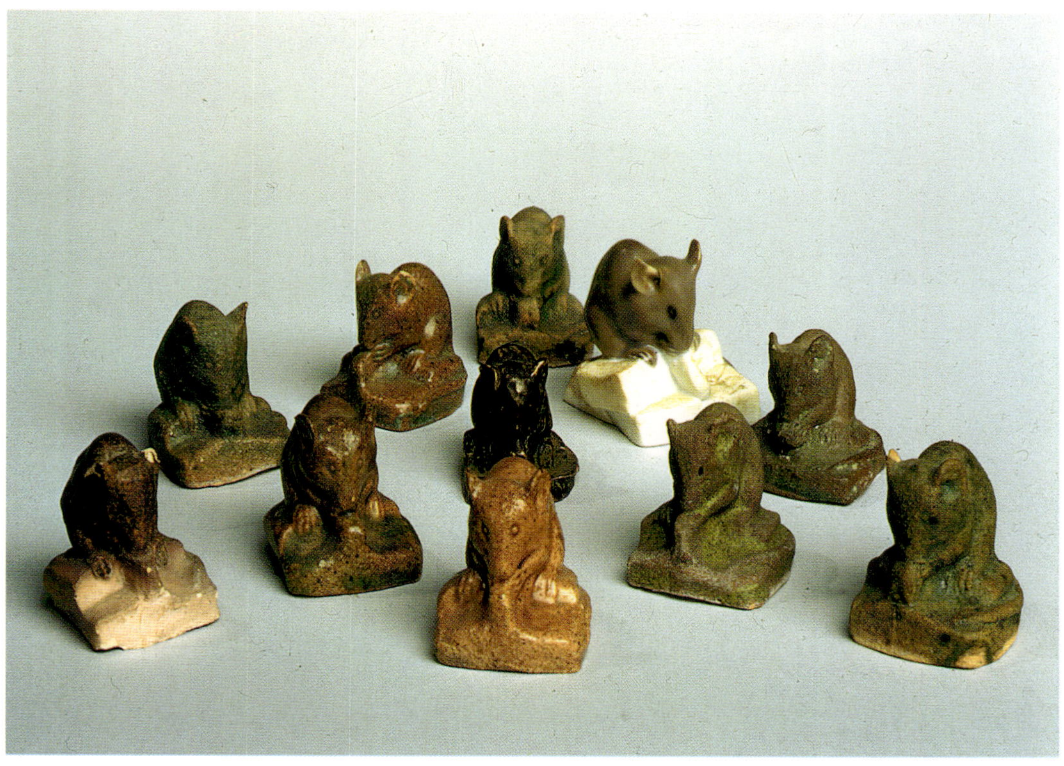

Ceramic mice. Collection of Gerald Peters Gallery. Photograph courtesy of Gerald Peters Gallery, Santa Fe.

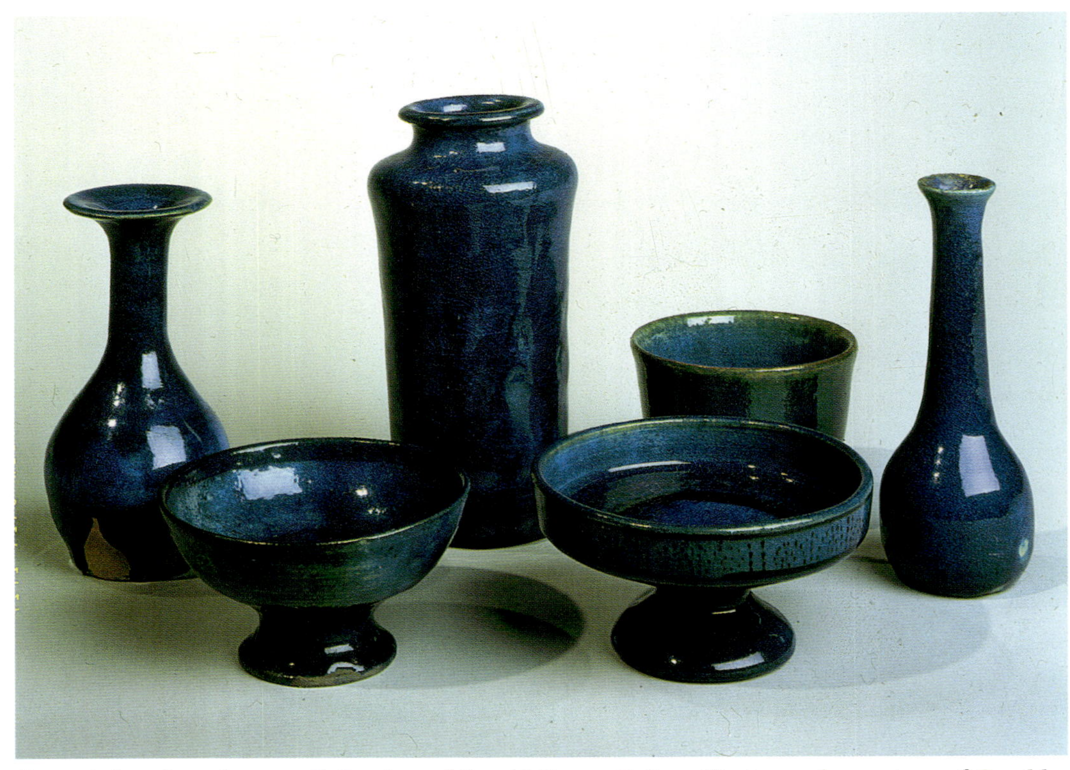

Ceramic bowls and vases. Collection of Gerald Peters Gallery. Photograph courtesy of Gerald Peters Gallery, Santa Fe.

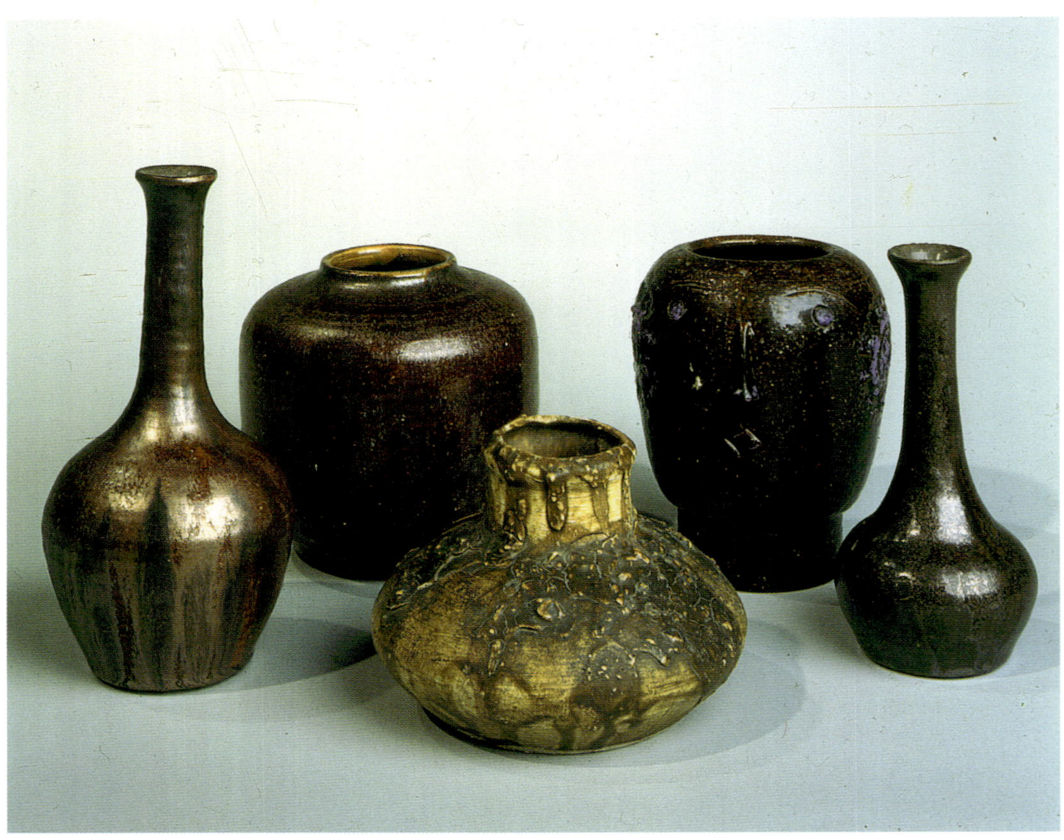

Ceramic vases. Collection of Gerald Peters Gallery. Photograph courtesy of Gerald Peters Gallery, Santa Fe. Exhibited in 1921.

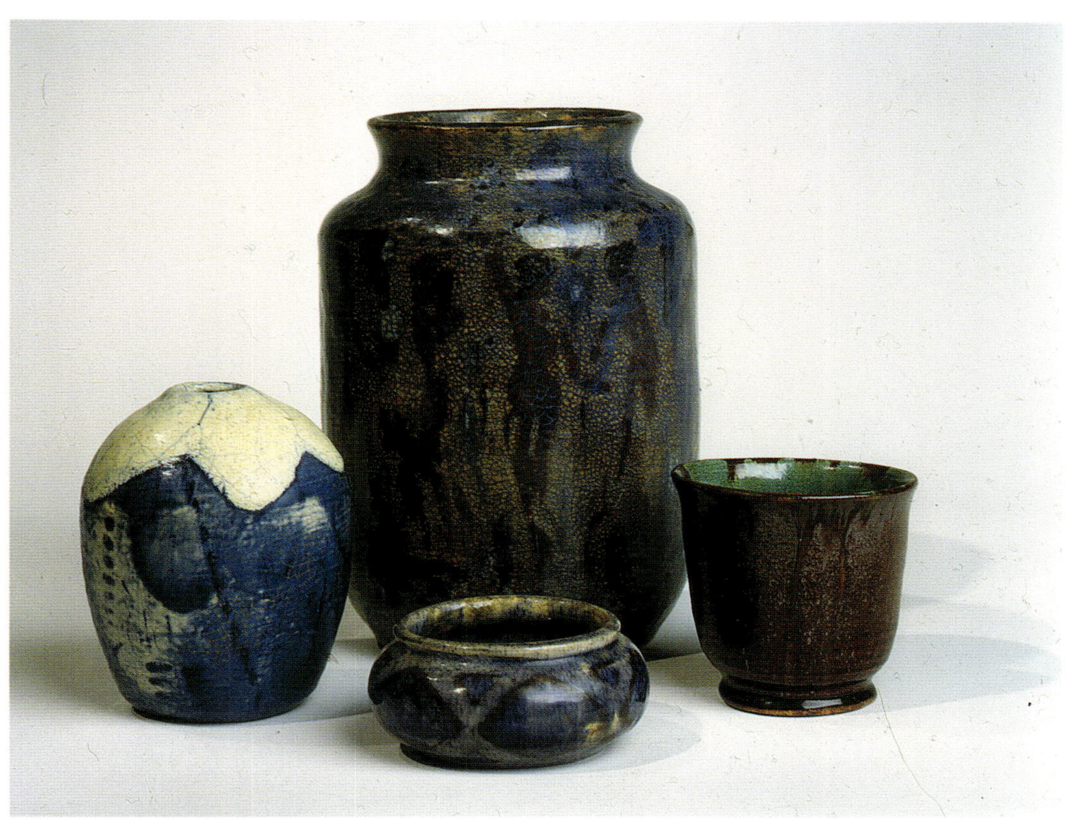

Ceramic bowls and vases. Collection of Gerald Peters Gallery. Photograph courtesy of Gerald Peters Gallery, Santa Fe.

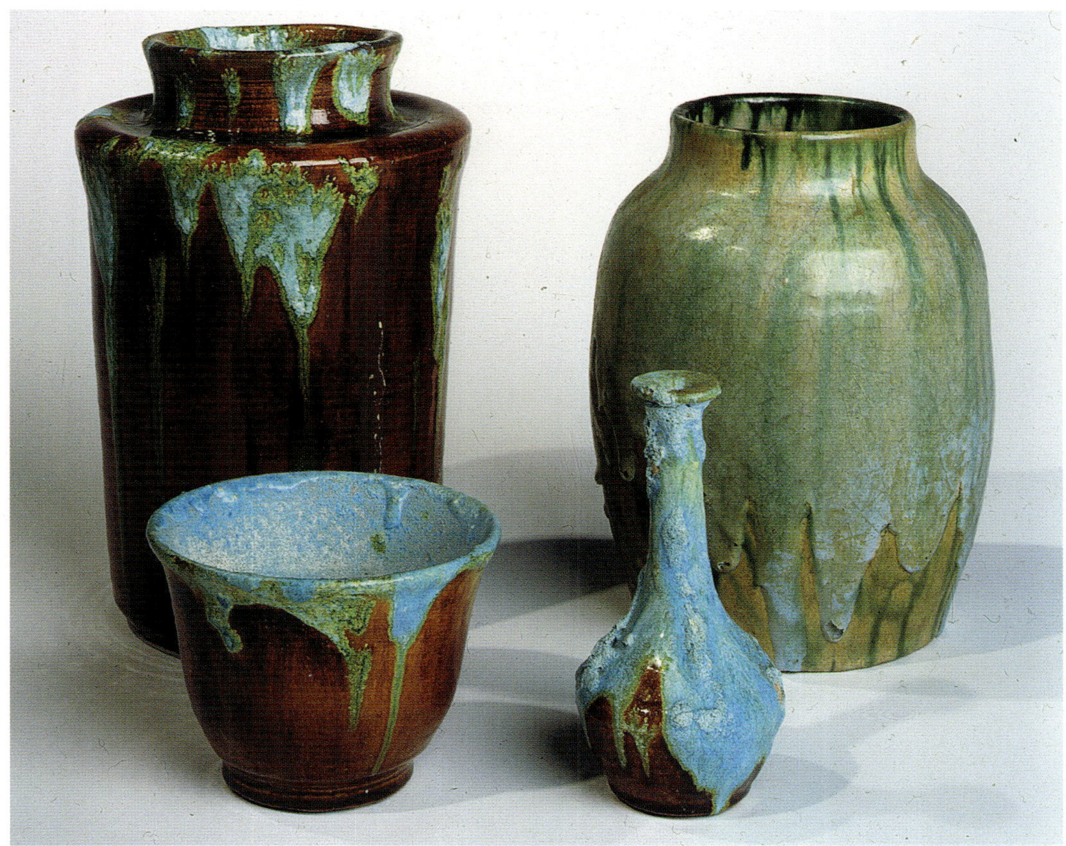

Ceramic bowls and vases. Collection of Gerald Peters Gallery. Photograph courtesy of Gerald Peters Gallery, Santa Fe.

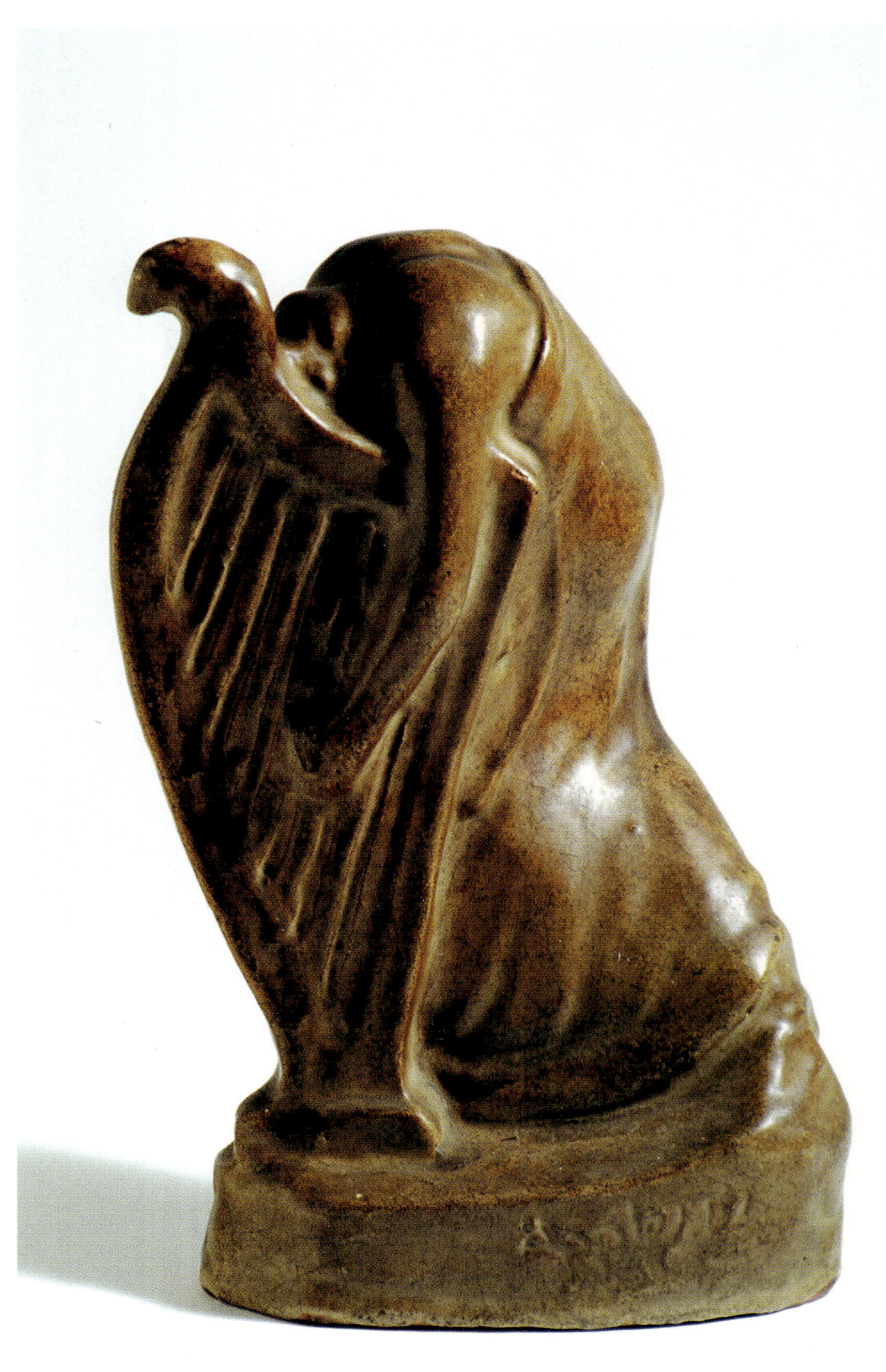

Woman Playing Harp, ceramic figure. Private collection. Made in 1916 as a wedding present for Ruth Applegate and Howard Hieronymus.

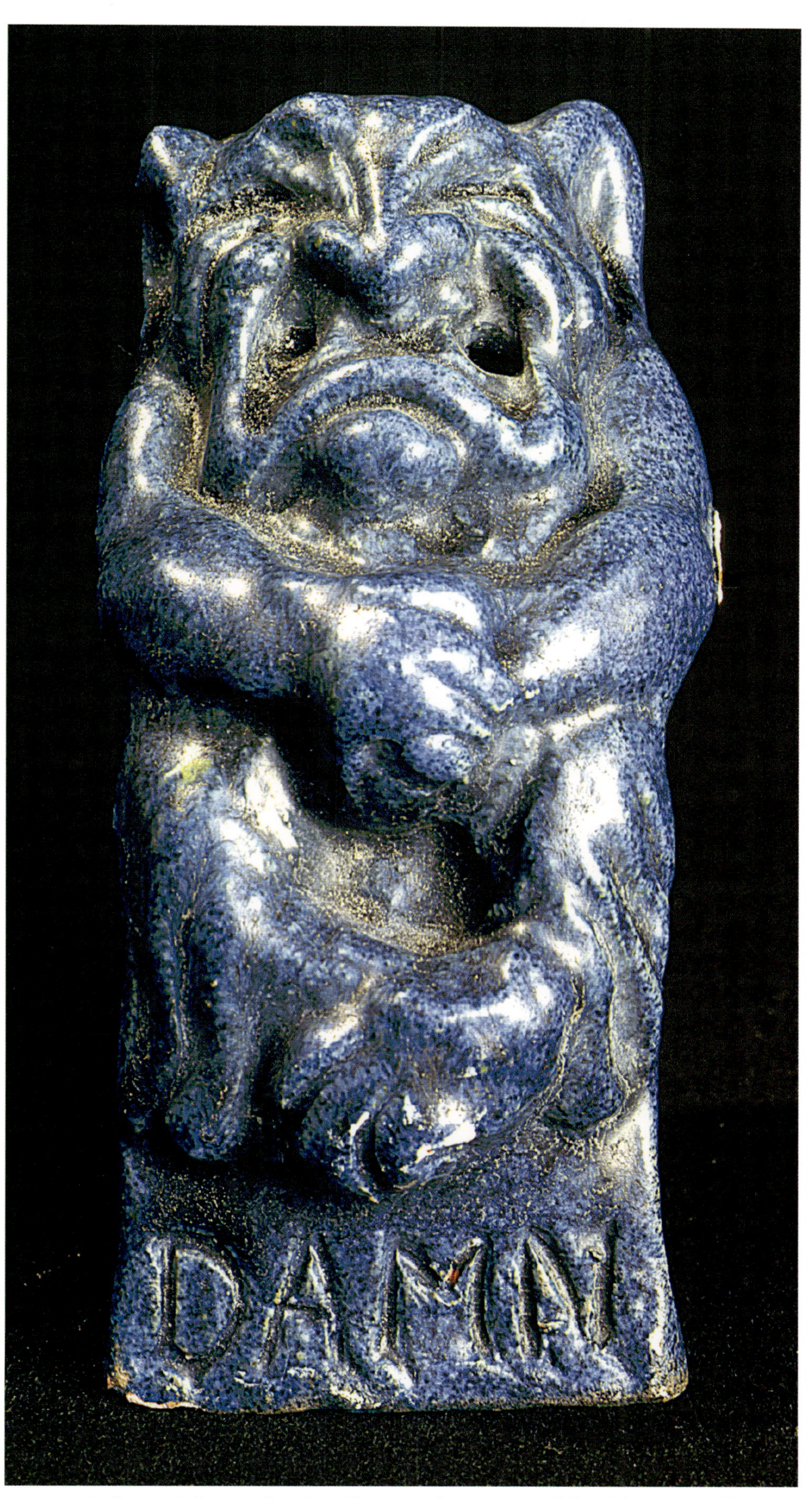

Damn, ceramic figure. Private collection. Photograph courtesy of Gerald Peters Gallery, Santa Fe. First exhibited in 1915.

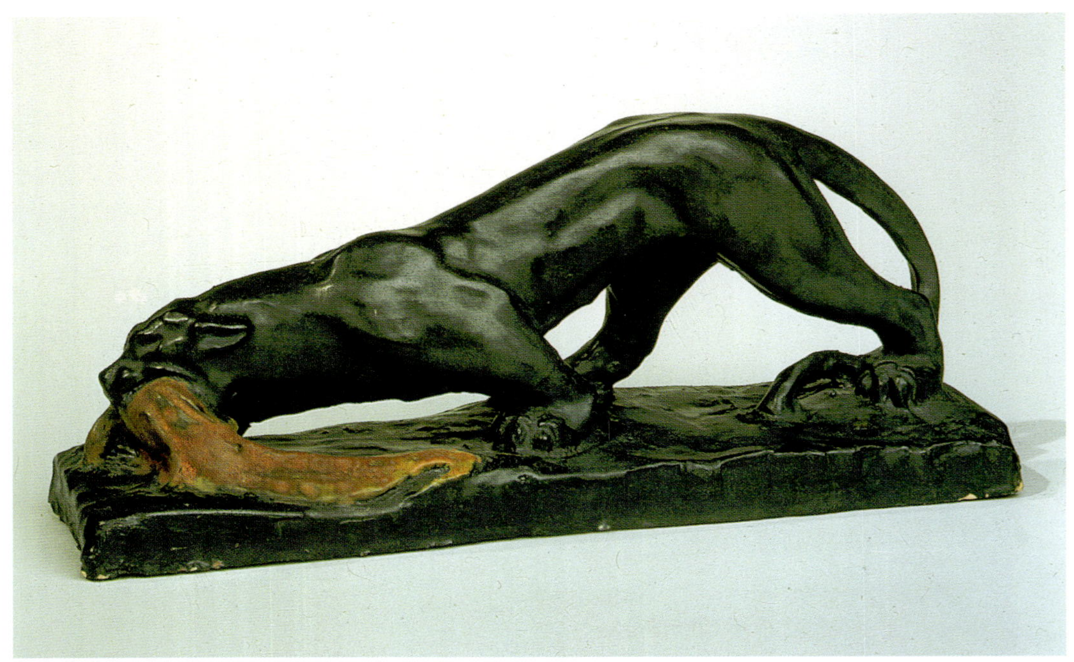

Panther with Prey, ceramic figure. Collection of Gerald Peters Gallery. Photograph courtesy of Gerald Peters Gallery, Santa Fe. Exhibited in 1916.

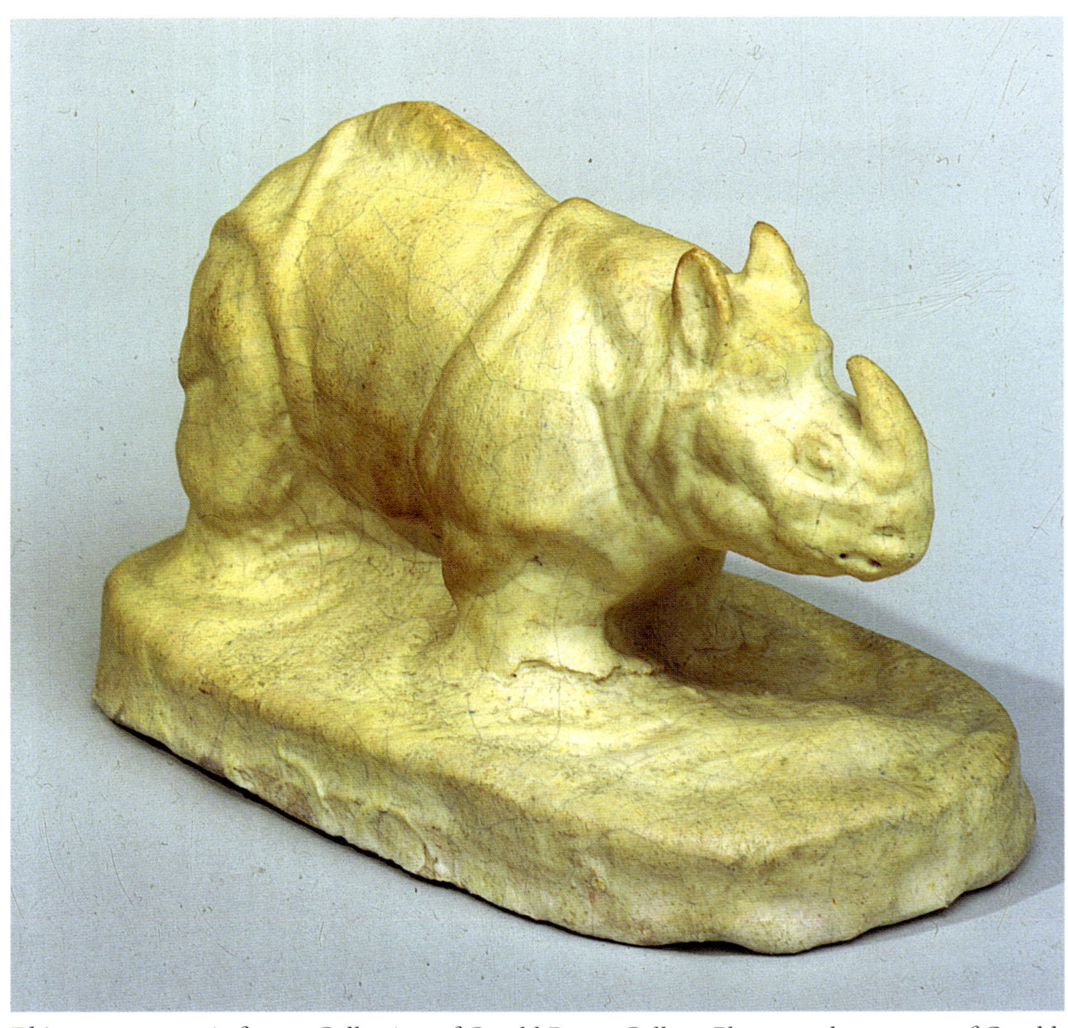

Rhinoceros, ceramic figure. Collection of Gerald Peters Gallery. Photograph courtesy of Gerald Peters Gallery, Santa Fe. First exhibited in 1915.

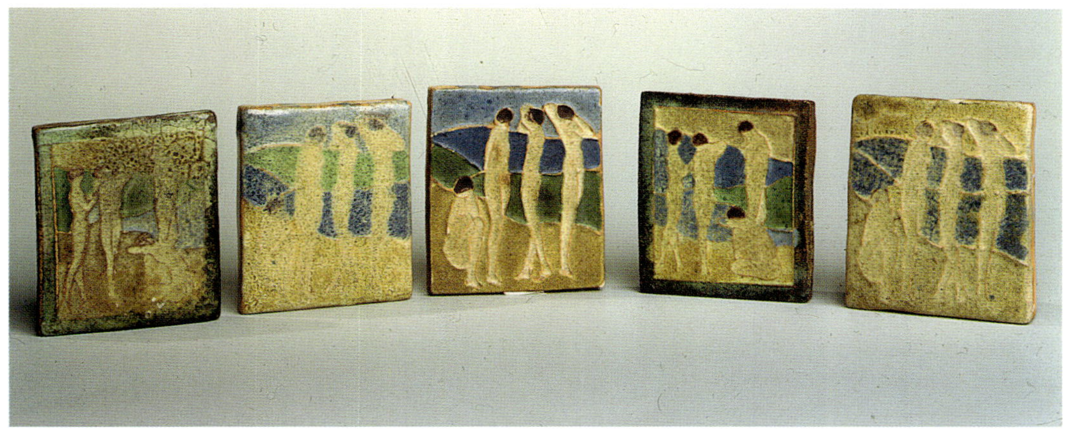

Ceramic tiles. Collection of Gerald Peters Gallery. Photograph courtesy of Gerald Peters Gallery, Santa Fe.

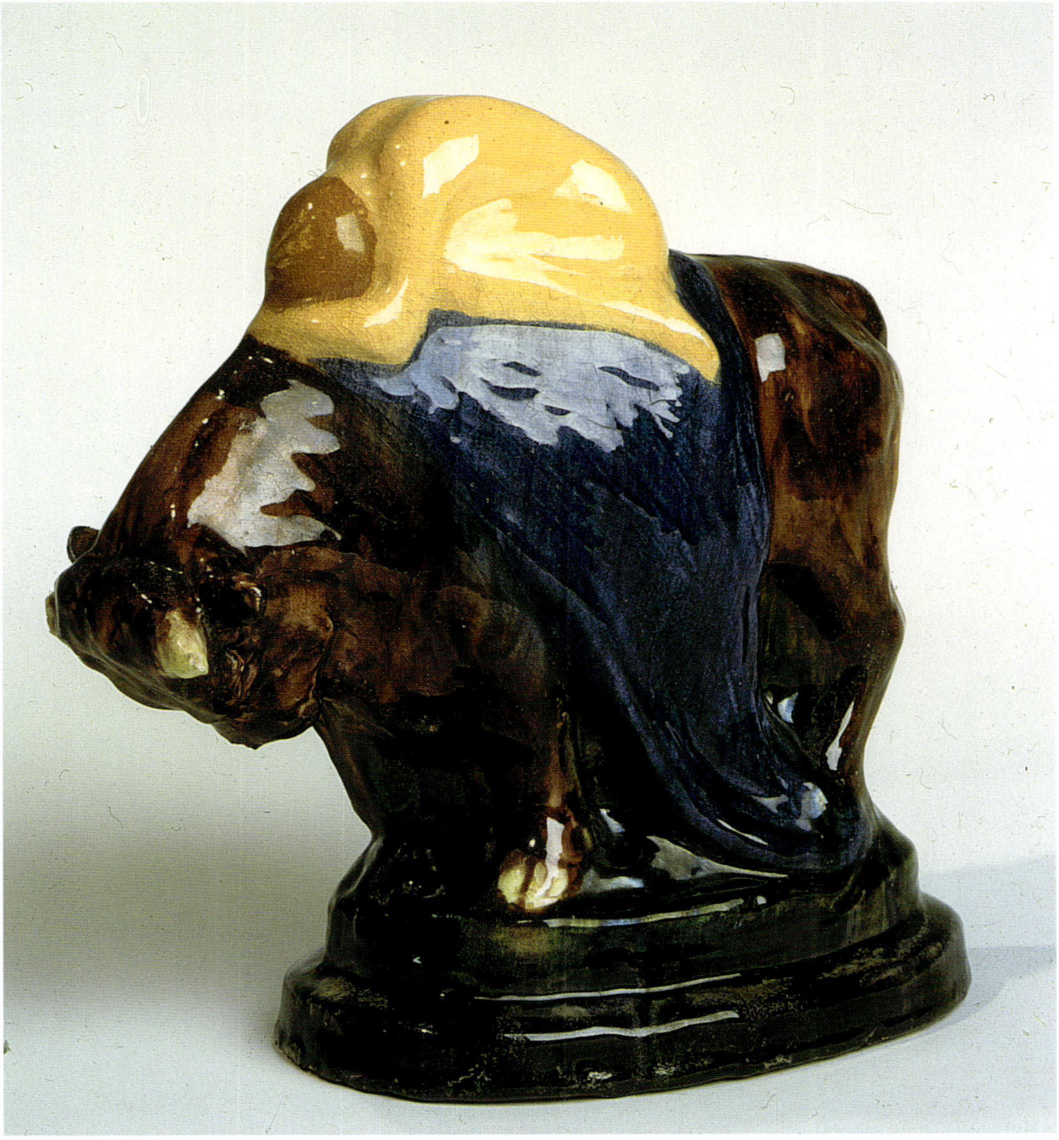

Woman Riding Bull (*Europa*), ceramic figure. Collection of Gerald Peters Gallery. Photograph courtesy of Gerald Peters Gallery, Santa Fe.

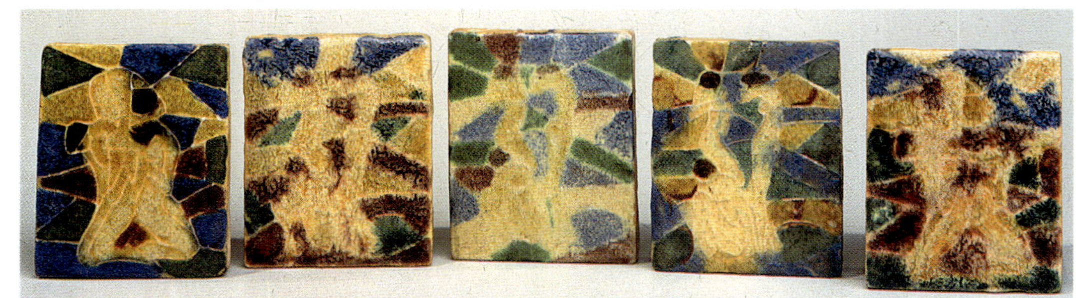

Ceramic tiles. Collection of Gerald Peters Gallery. Photograph courtesy of Gerald Peters Gallery, Santa Fe.

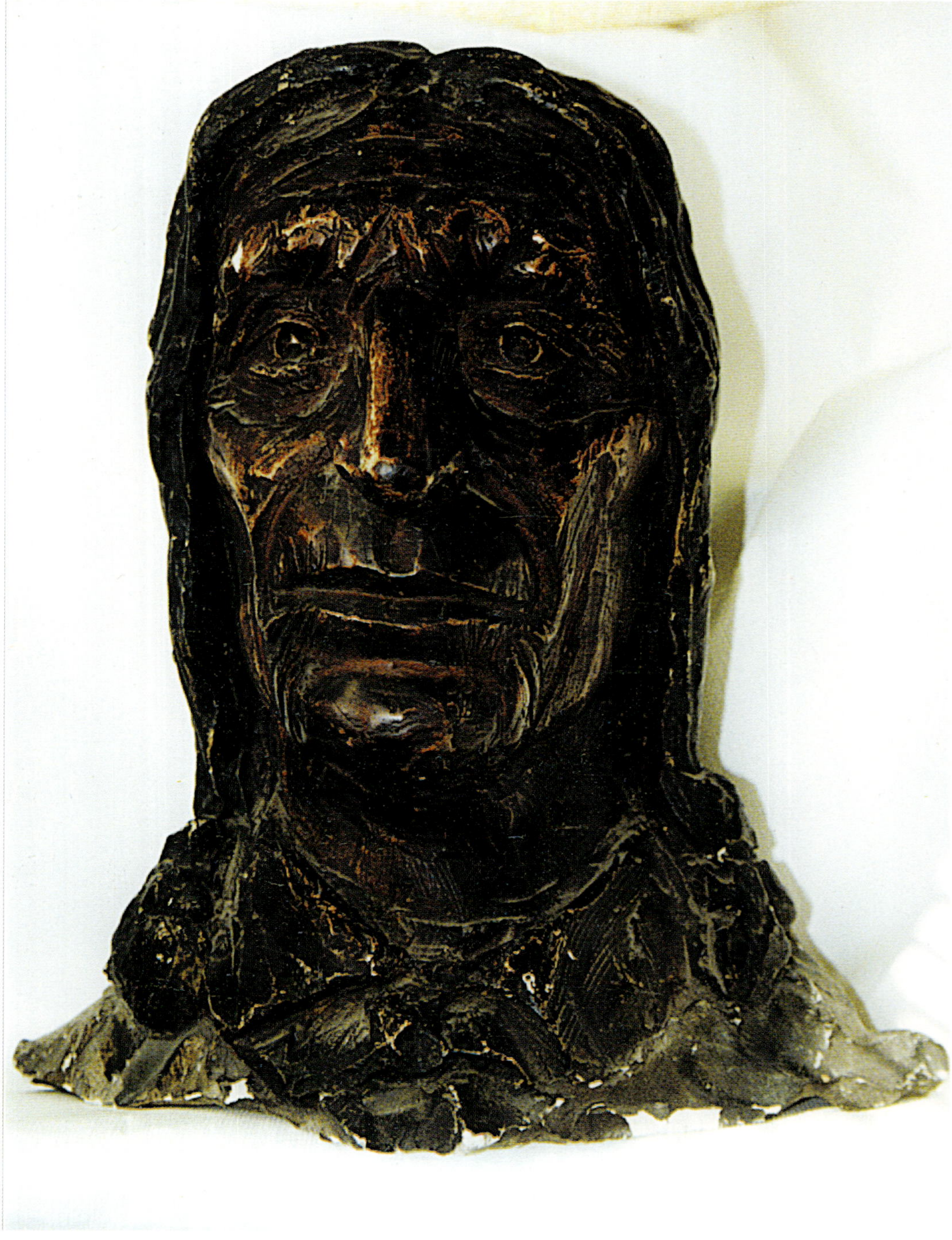

Indian, ceramic bust. Atlanta Public Library, Atlanta, Illinois.

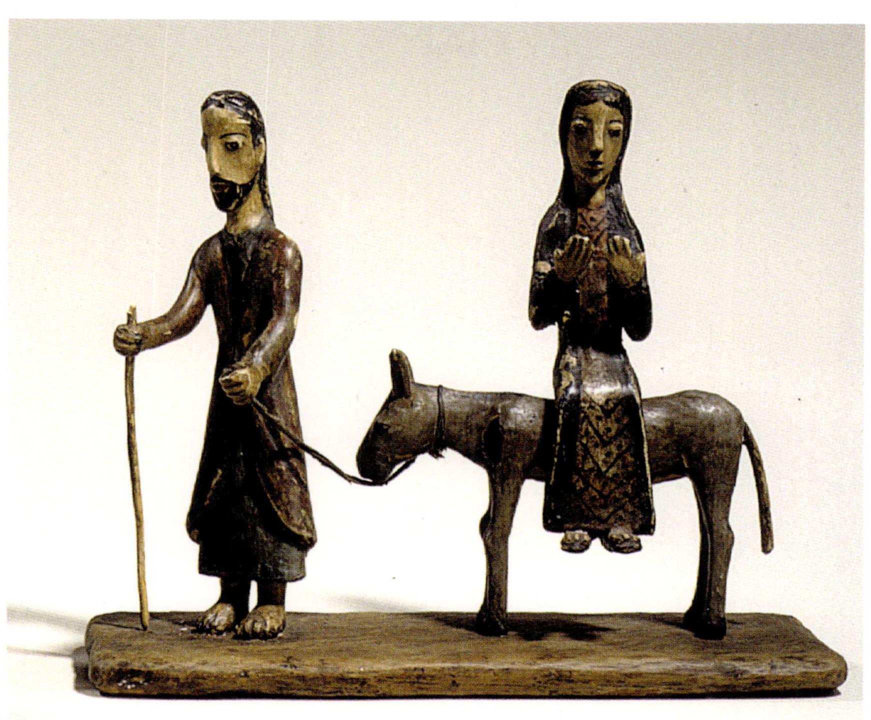

Flight into Egypt/La Huida a Egipto, bulto, attributed to Frank Applegate. Private collection. Photograph courtesy of Sotheby's.

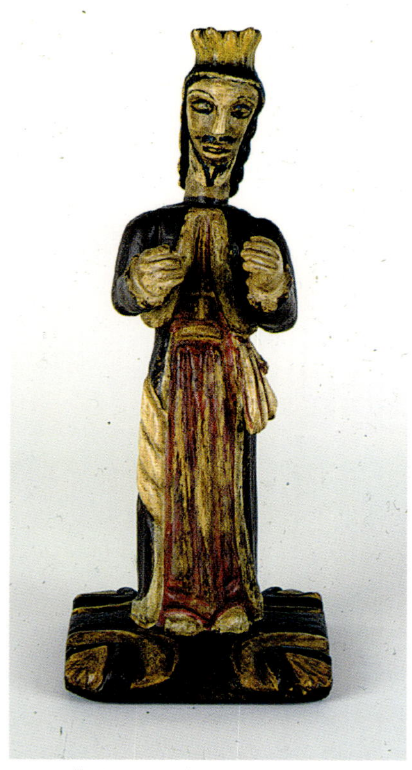

Saint Joseph/San José, bulto, attributed to Frank Applegate. Collection of Eugene Coombs. Photograph courtesy of Móntez Gallery, Santa Fe.

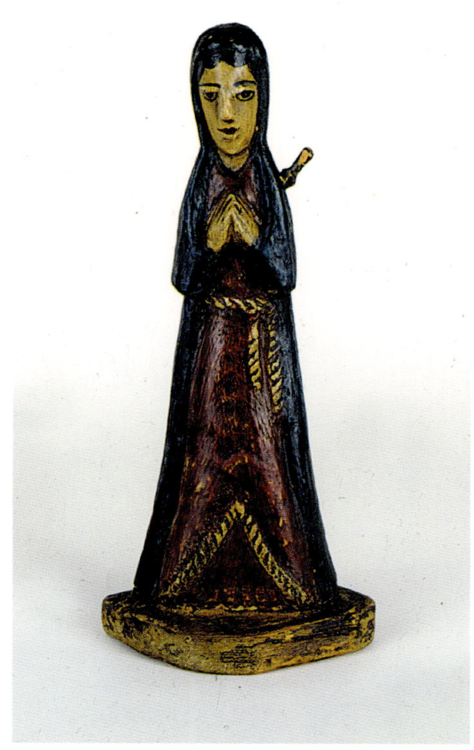

Our Lady of Sorrows/Nuestra Señora de los Dolores, bulto, attributed to Frank Applegate. Collection of Rey Móntez. Photograph courtesy of Móntez Gallery, Santa Fe.

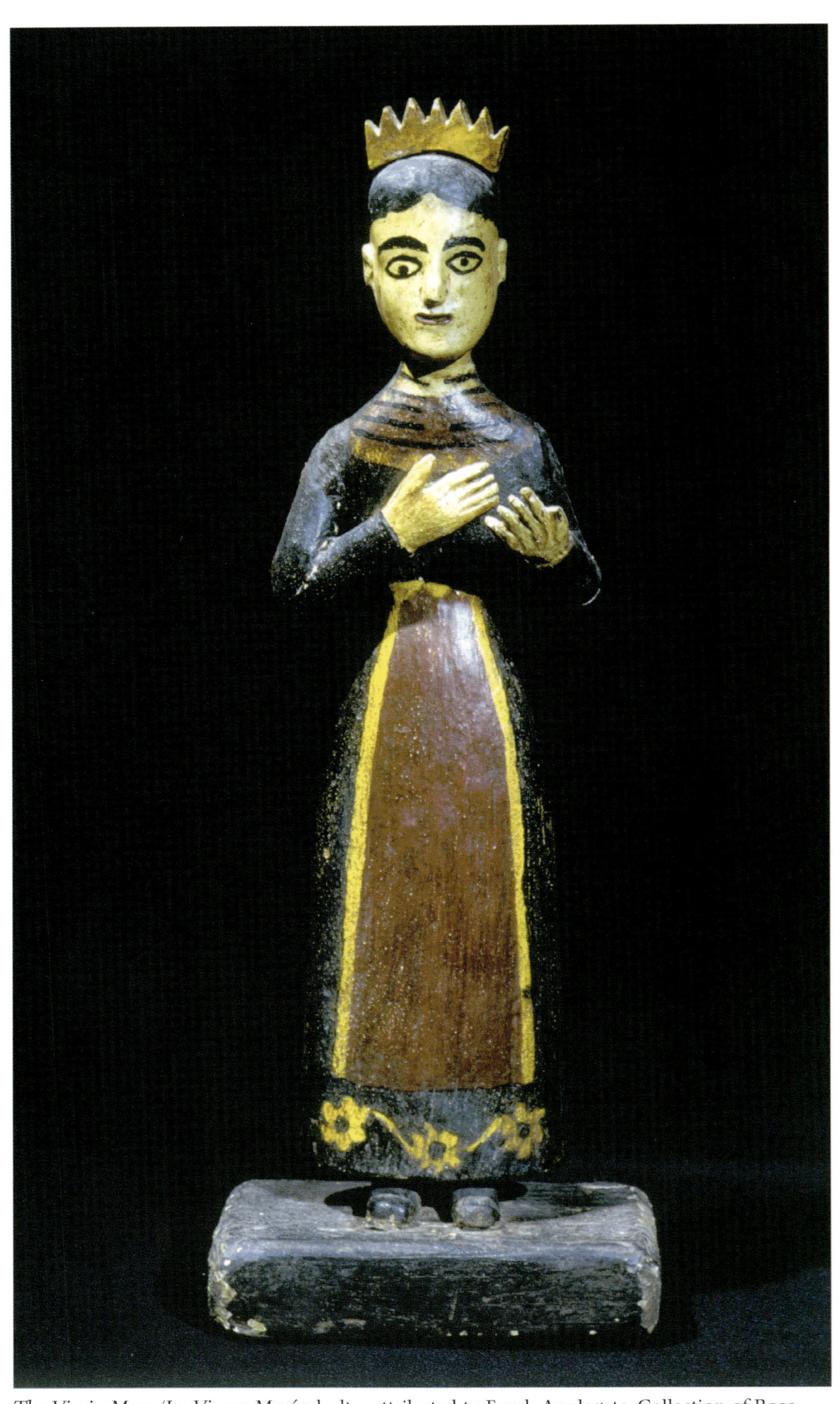

The Virgin Mary/La Virgen María, bulto, attributed to Frank Applegate. Collection of Rose Gibbs. Photograph courtesy of Gerald Peters Gallery, Santa Fe.

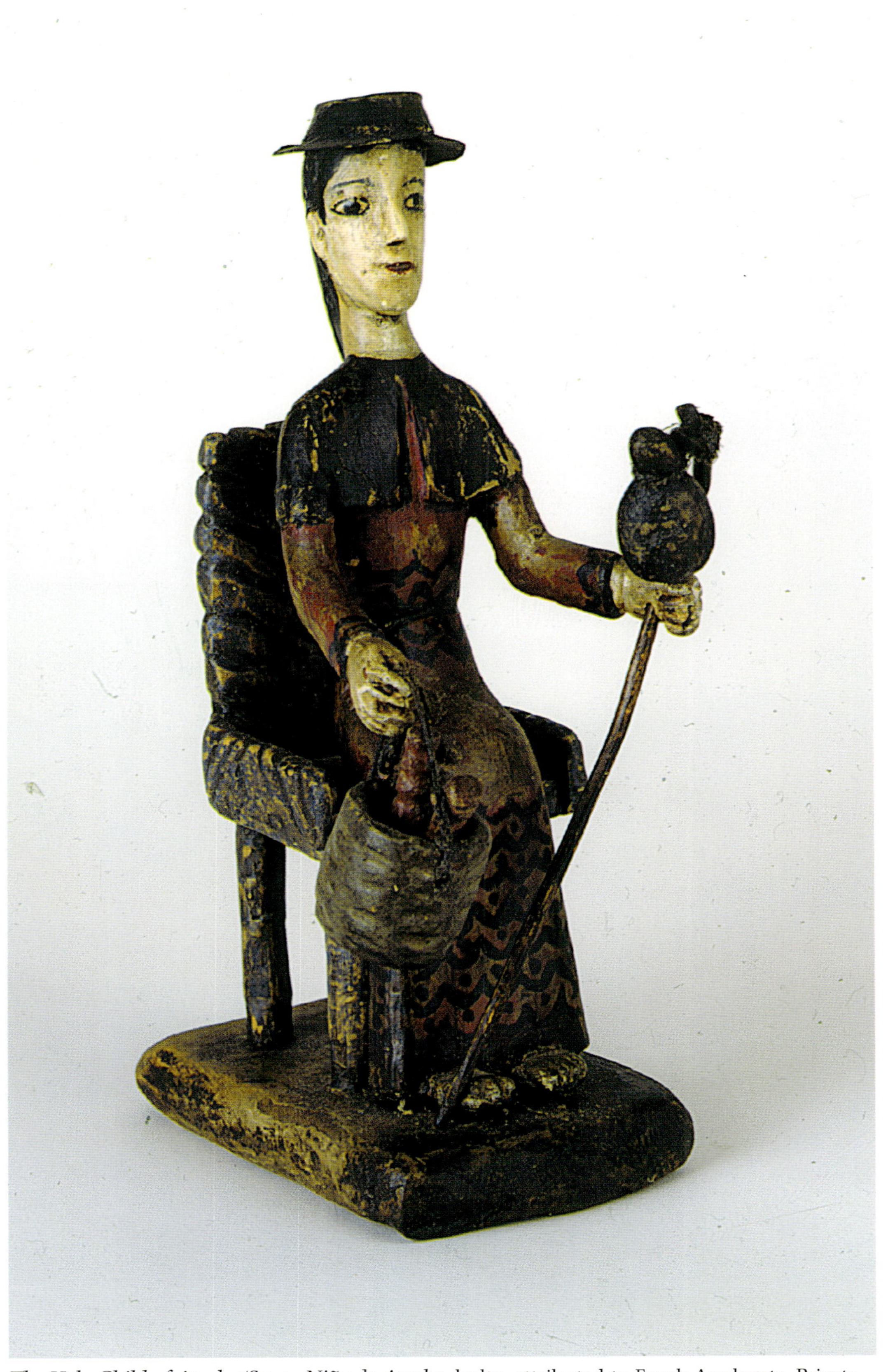

The Holy Child of Atocha/Santo Niño de Atocha, bulto, attributed to Frank Applegate. Private collection. Photograph courtesy of Móntez Gallery, Santa Fe.

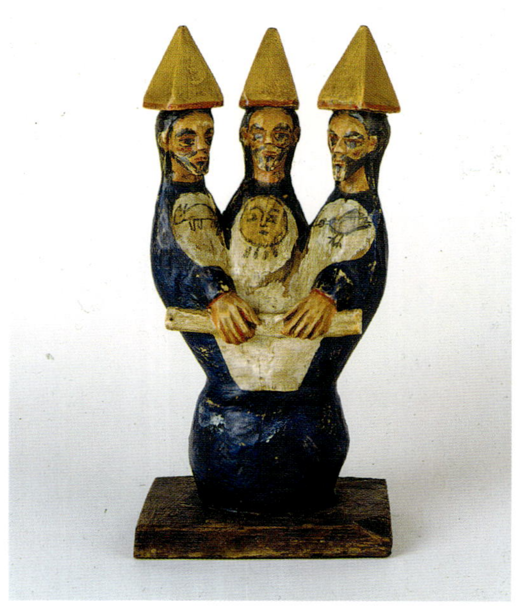

The Holy Trinity/La Santísima Trinidad,
bulto, attributed to Frank Applegate. Collection of Larry Ballard. Photograph courtesy of Móntez Gallery, Santa Fe.

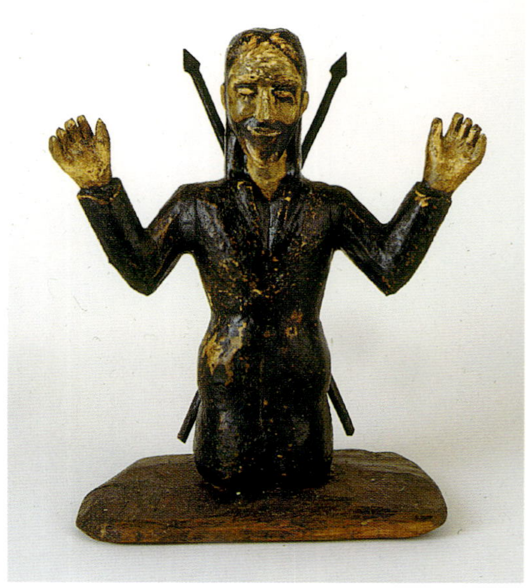

Saint Philip of Jesus/San Felipe de Jesús,
bulto, attributed to Frank Applegate. Private collection. Photograph courtesy of Móntez Gallery, Santa Fe.

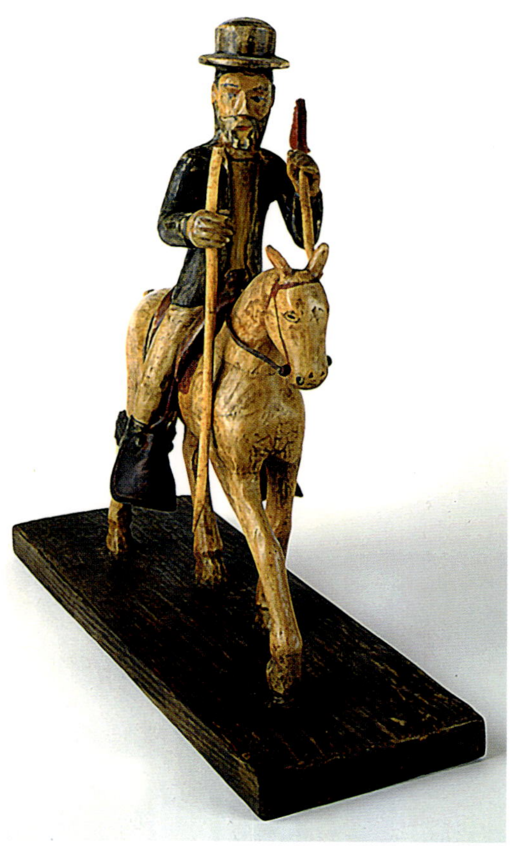

Saint James the Greater/Santiago, bulto, attributed to Frank Applegate. Collection of Larry Ballard. Photograph courtesy of Móntez Gallery, Santa Fe. Possibly exhibited in 1923.

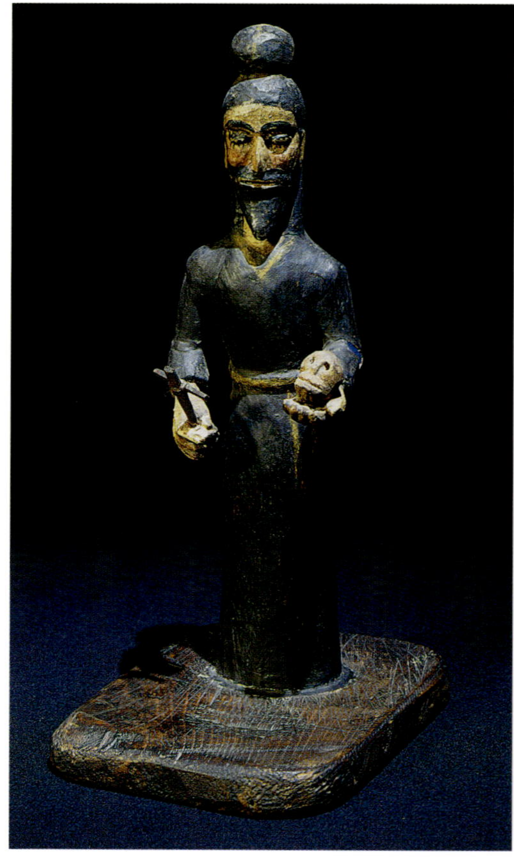

Saint Francis of Assisi/San Francisco de Asís, bulto, attributed to Frank Applegate. Collection of Fred and Kelly Birner. Photograph courtesy of Gerald Peters Gallery, Santa Fe.

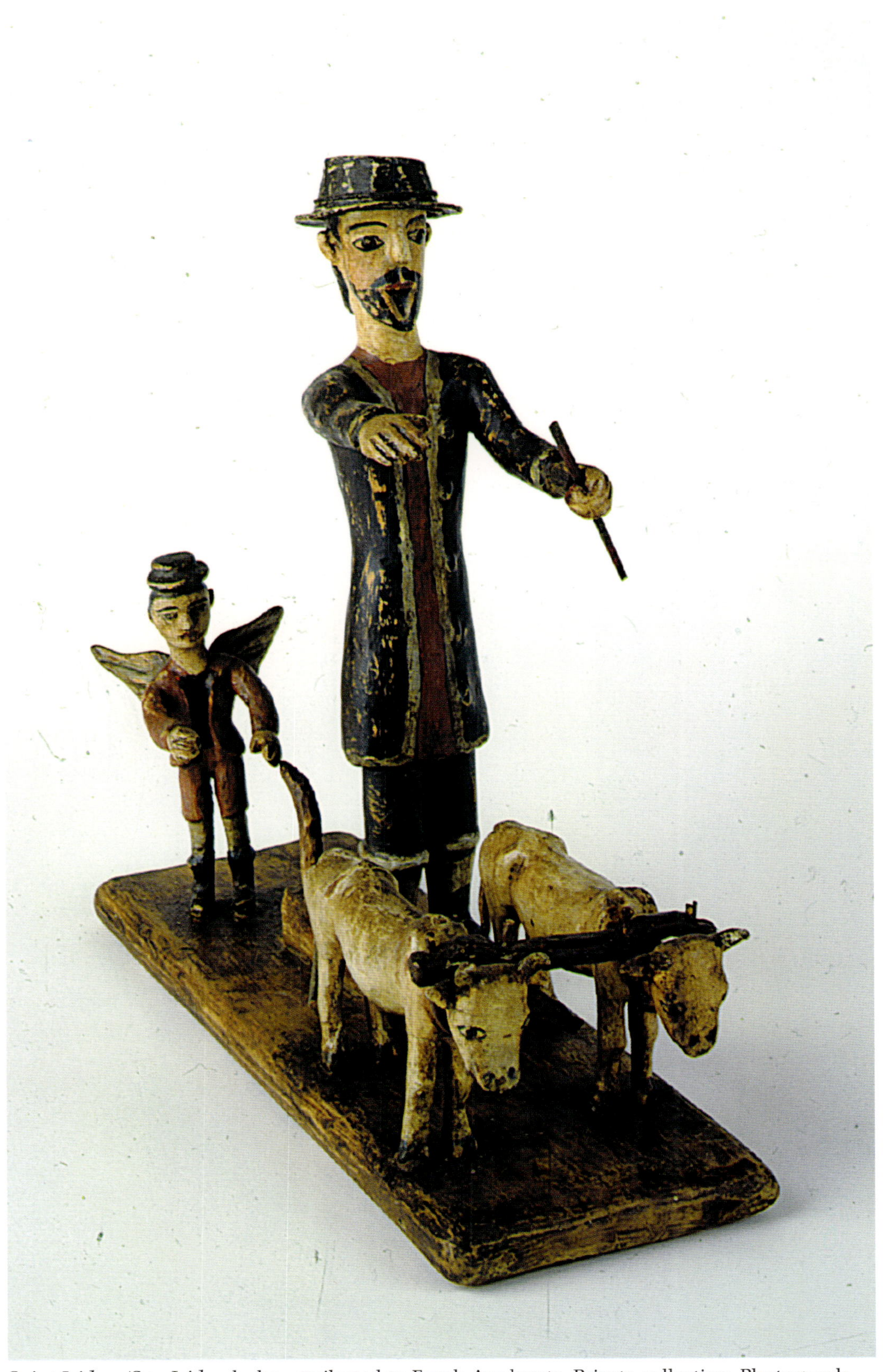

Saint Isidore/San Isidro, bulto, attributed to Frank Applegate. Private collection. Photograph courtesy of Móntez Gallery, Santa Fe.

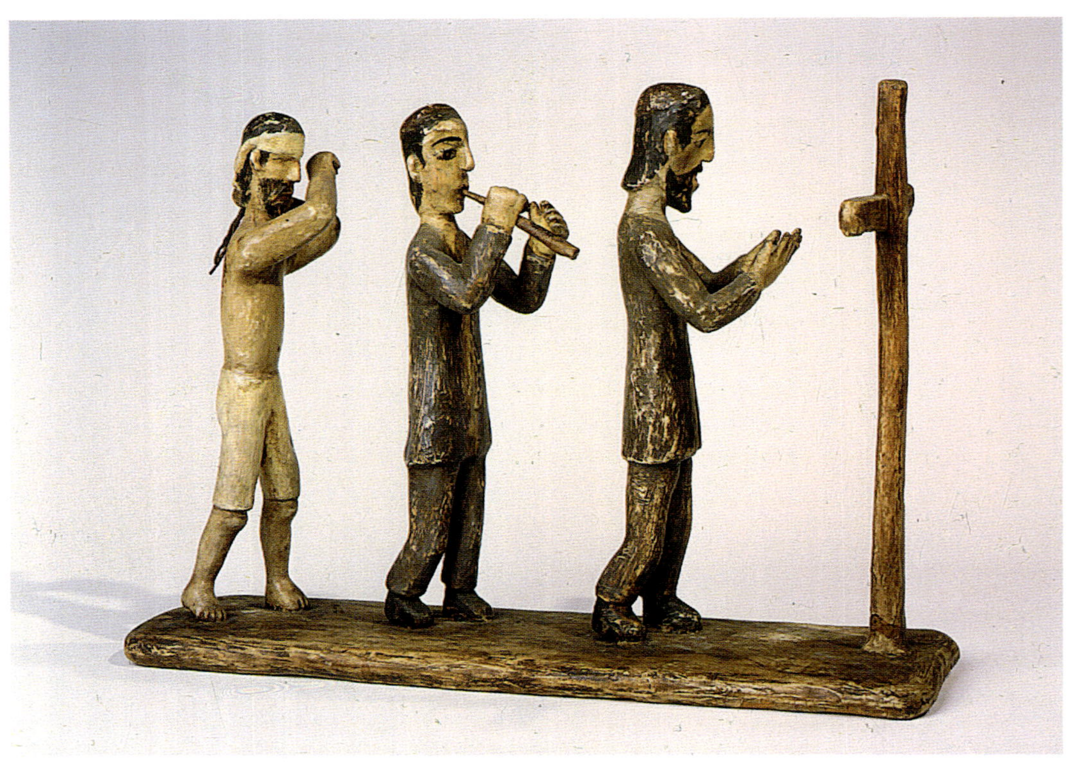

Penitente Procession, bulto, attributed to Frank Applegate. Collection of Barbe Awalt and Paul Rhetts. Photograph courtesy of Gerald Peters Gallery, Santa Fe.

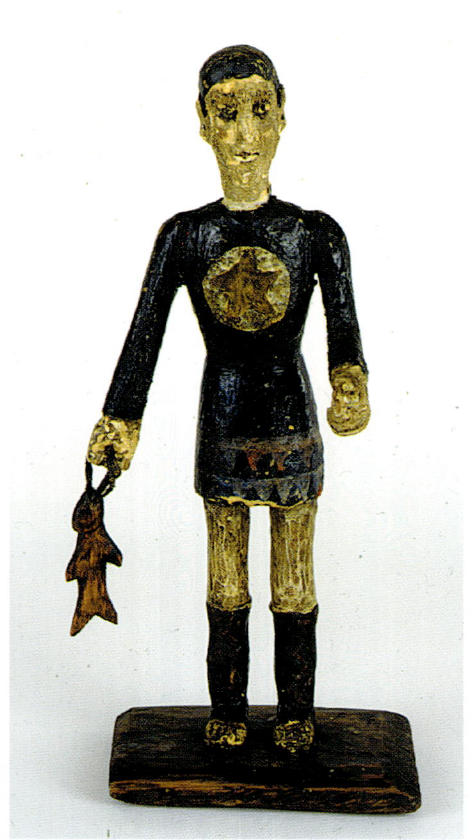

Saint Raphael the Archangel/San Rafael Arcangel, bulto, attributed to Frank Applegate. Private collection. Photograph courtesy of Móntez Gallery, Santa Fe.

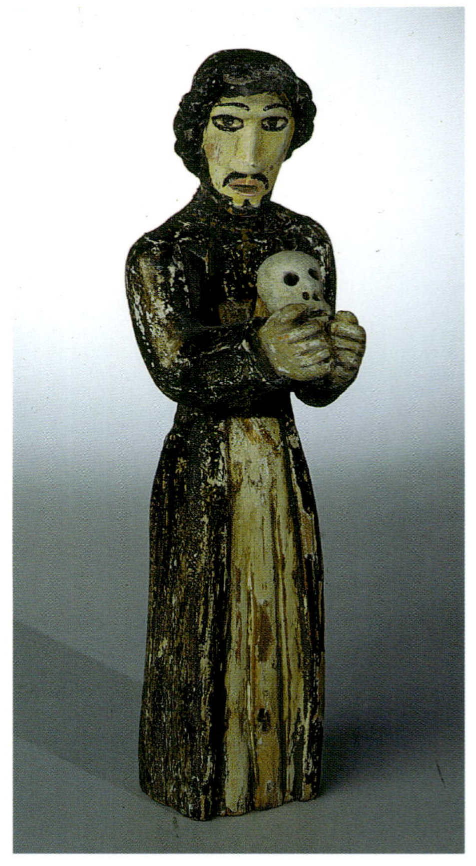

Saint Francis of Assisi/San Francisco de Asís, bulto, attributed to Frank Applegate. Collection of Rey Móntez. Photograph courtesy of Gerald Peters Gallery, Santa Fe.

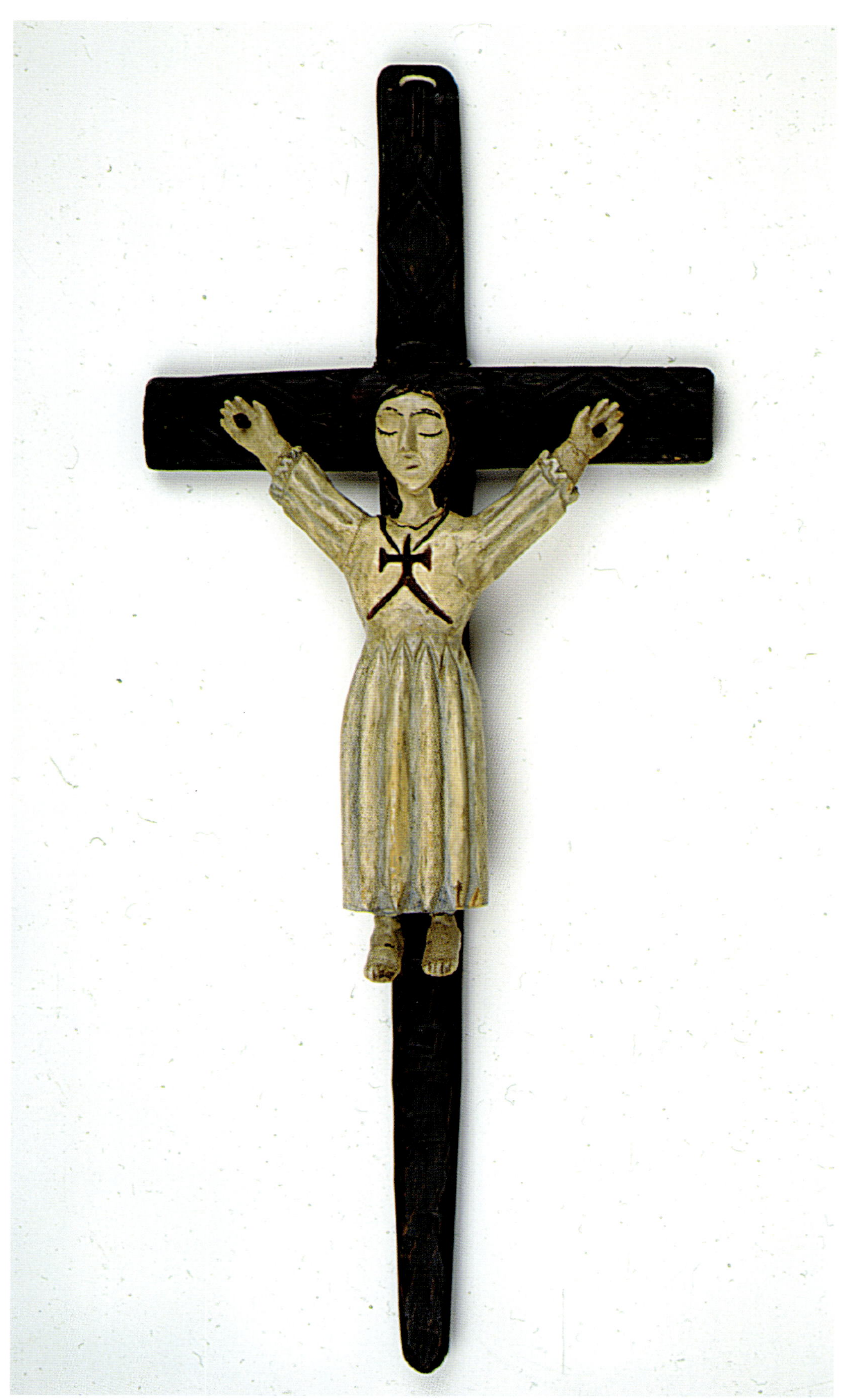

Saint Liberata/Santa Librada, bulto, attributed to Frank Applegate. Collection of Nancy Briggs. Photograph courtesy of Móntez Gallery, Santa Fe.

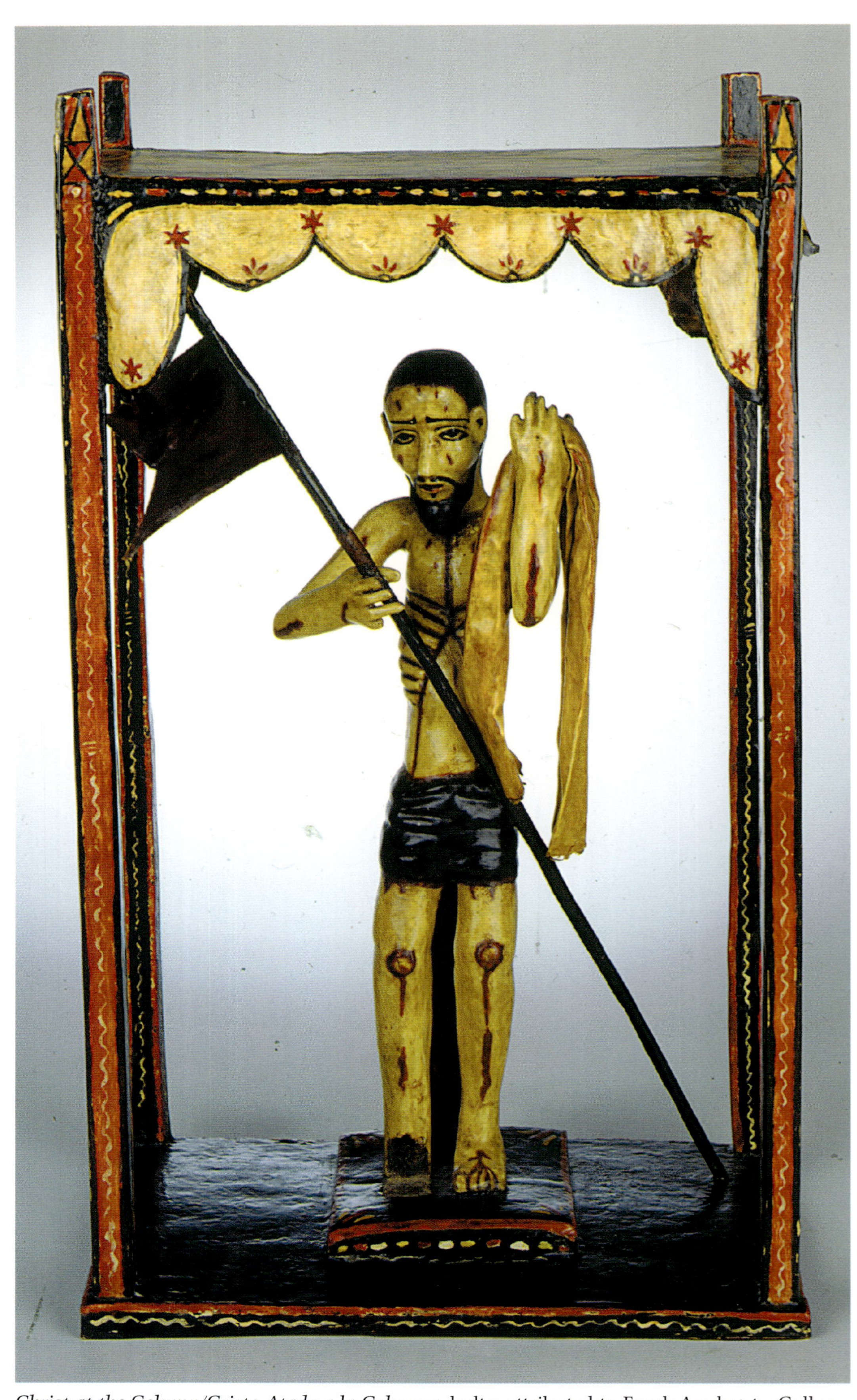

Christ at the Column/Cristo Atado a la Columna, bulto, attributed to Frank Applegate. Collection of Chuck and Jan Rosenak. Photograph courtesy of Gerald Peters Gallery, Santa Fe.

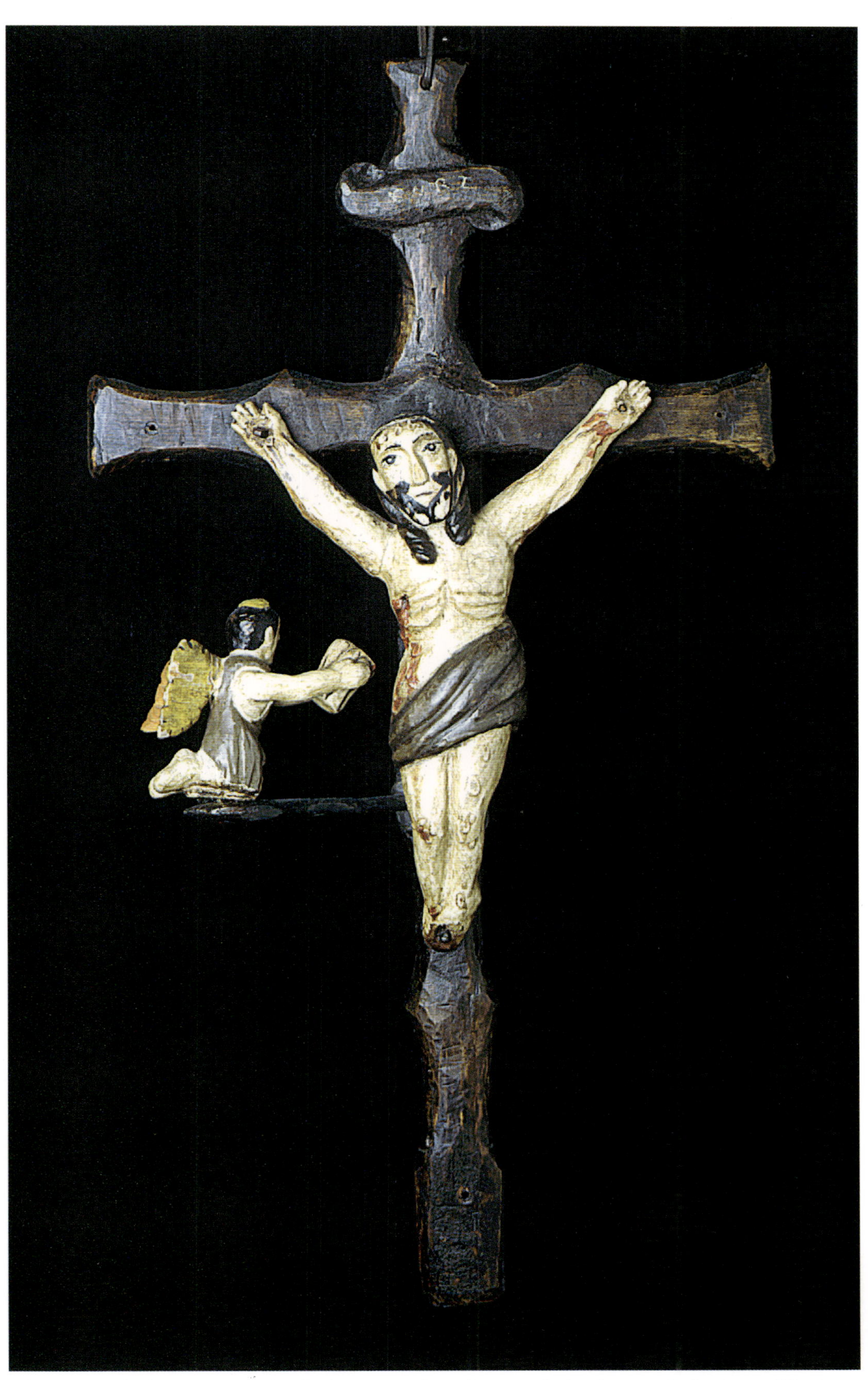

Christ Crucified/Cristo Crucificado, bulto, attributed to Frank Applegate. Collection of Daria Labinsky and Stan Hieronymus. Photograph courtesy of Gerald Peters Gallery, Santa Fe.

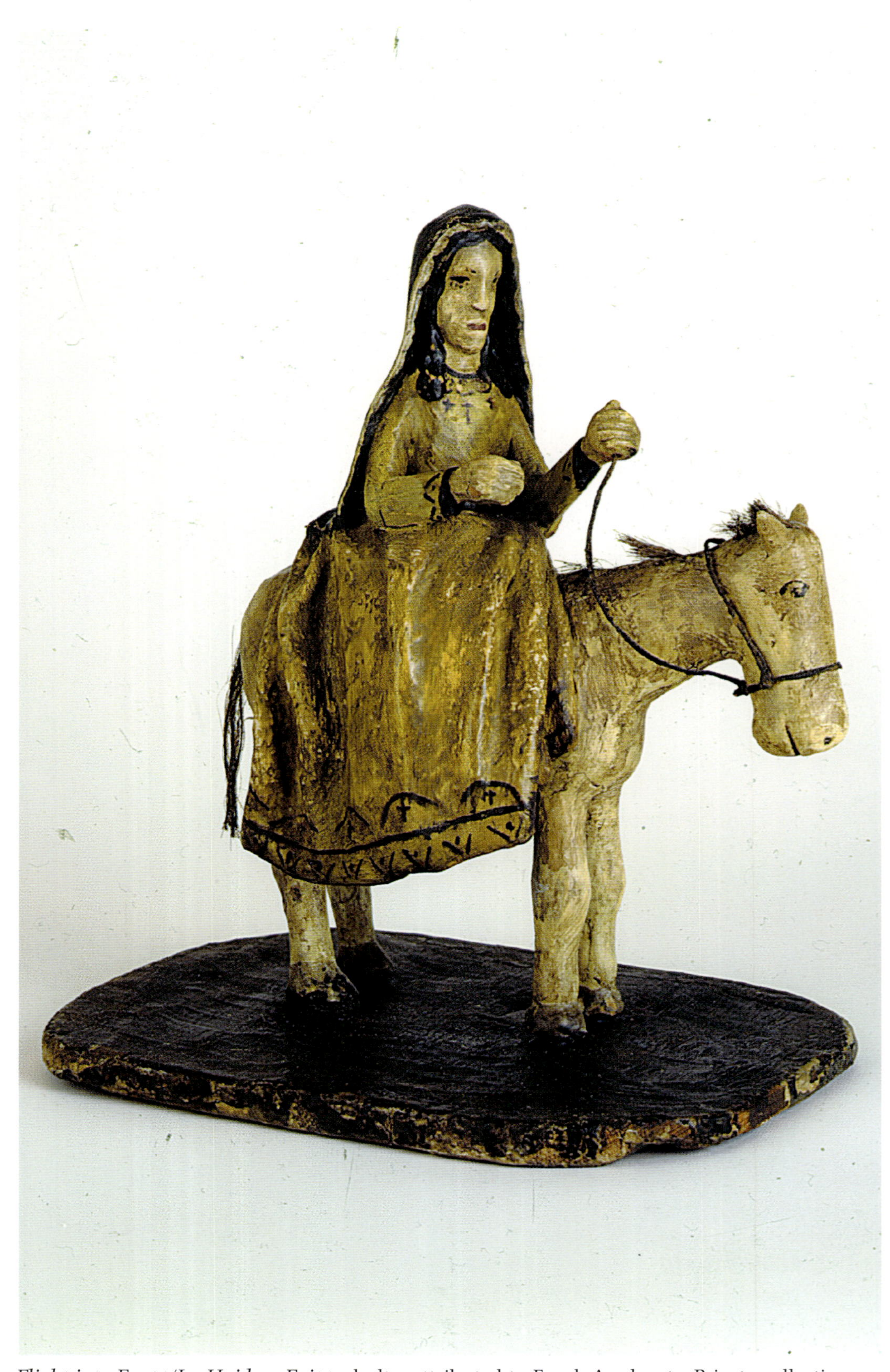

Flight into Egypt/La Huida a Egipto, bulto, attributed to Frank Applegate. Private collection.
Photograph courtesy of Móntez Gallery, Santa Fe.

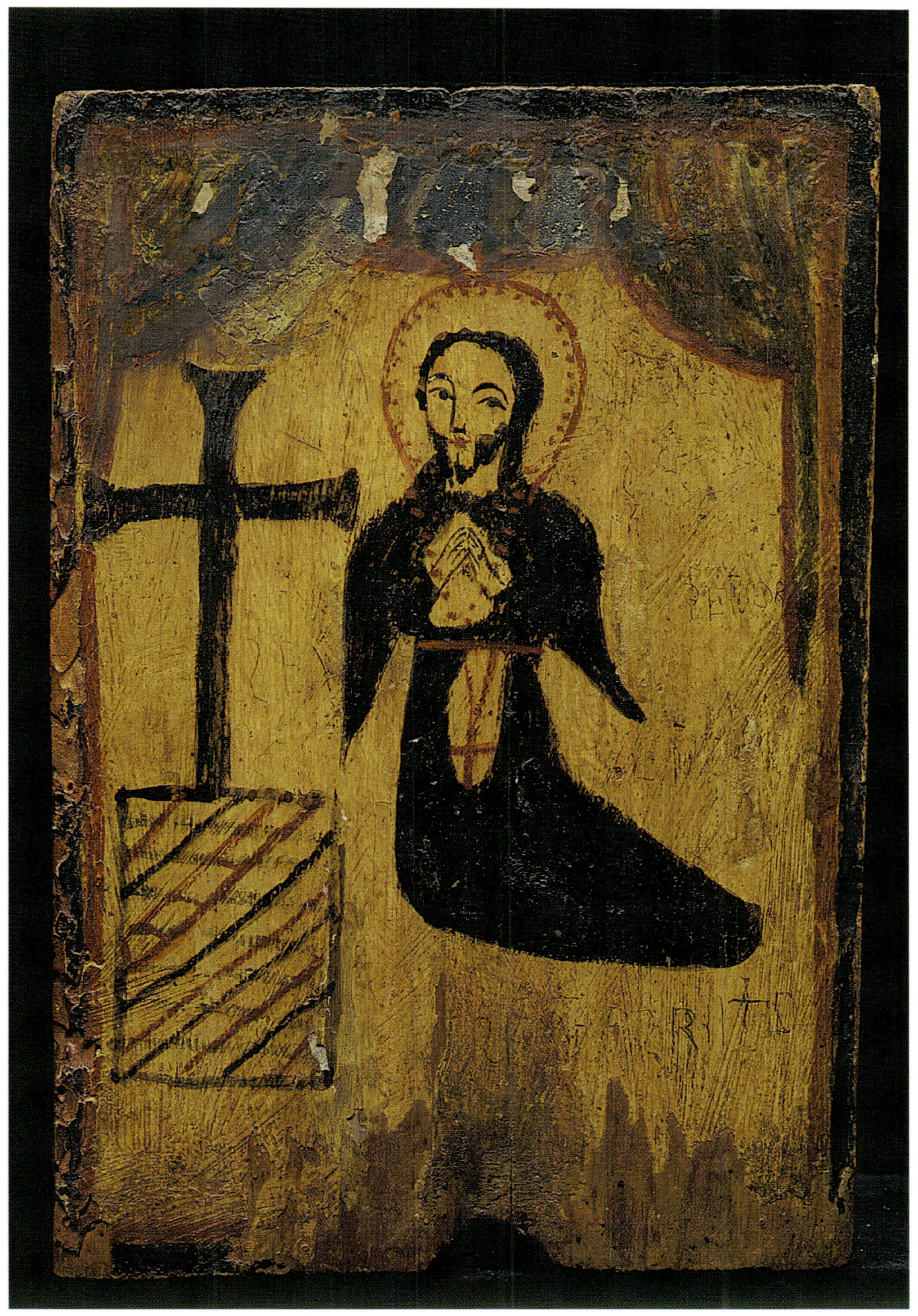

Saint Cajetan/San Calletano, retablo, attributed to Frank Applegate. Collection of Spanish Colonial Arts Society Museum. Photograph courtesy of Gerald Peters Gallery, Santa Fe.

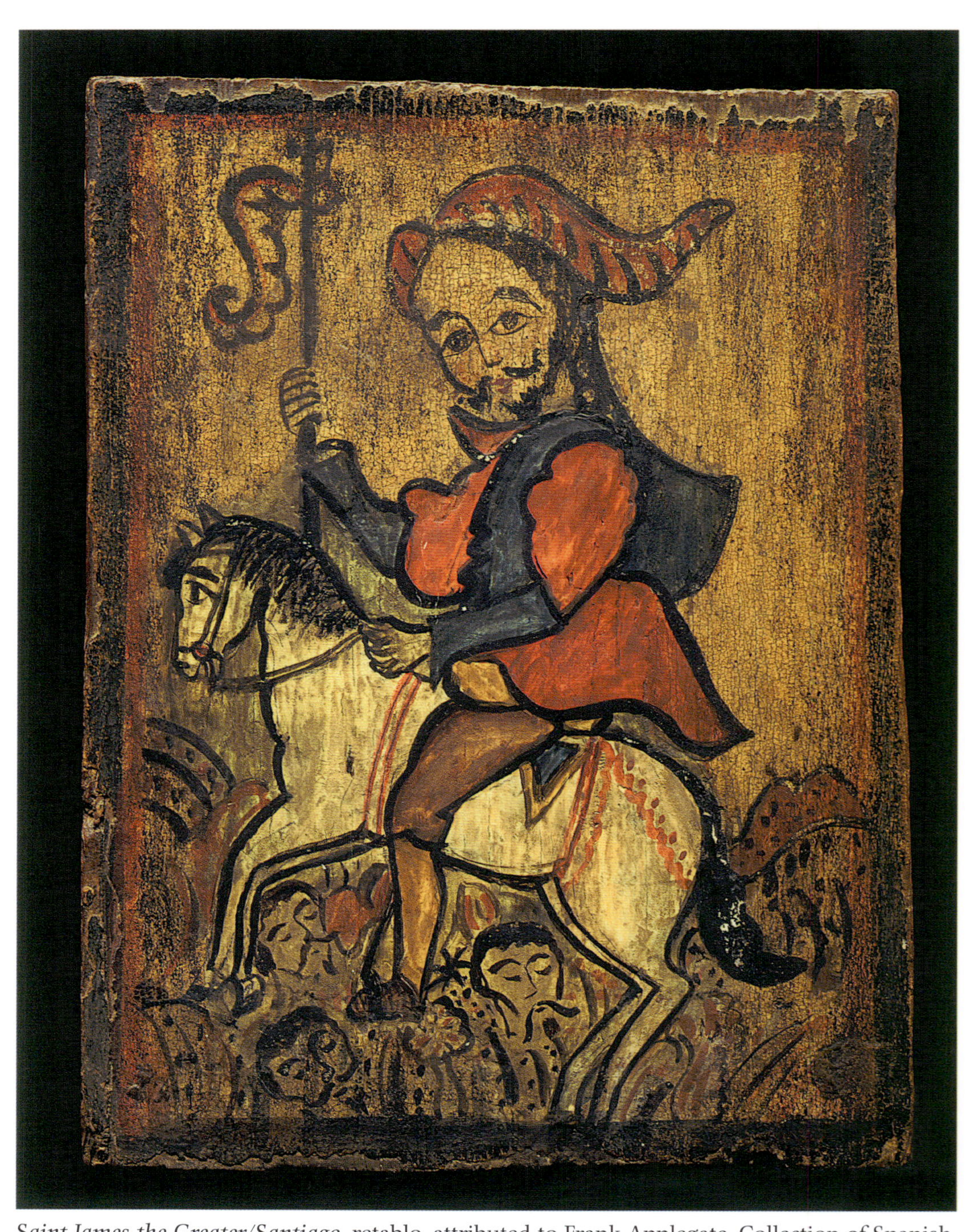

Saint James the Greater/Santiago, retablo, attributed to Frank Applegate. Collection of Spanish Colonial Arts Society Museum. Photograph courtesy of Gerald Peters Gallery, Santa Fe.

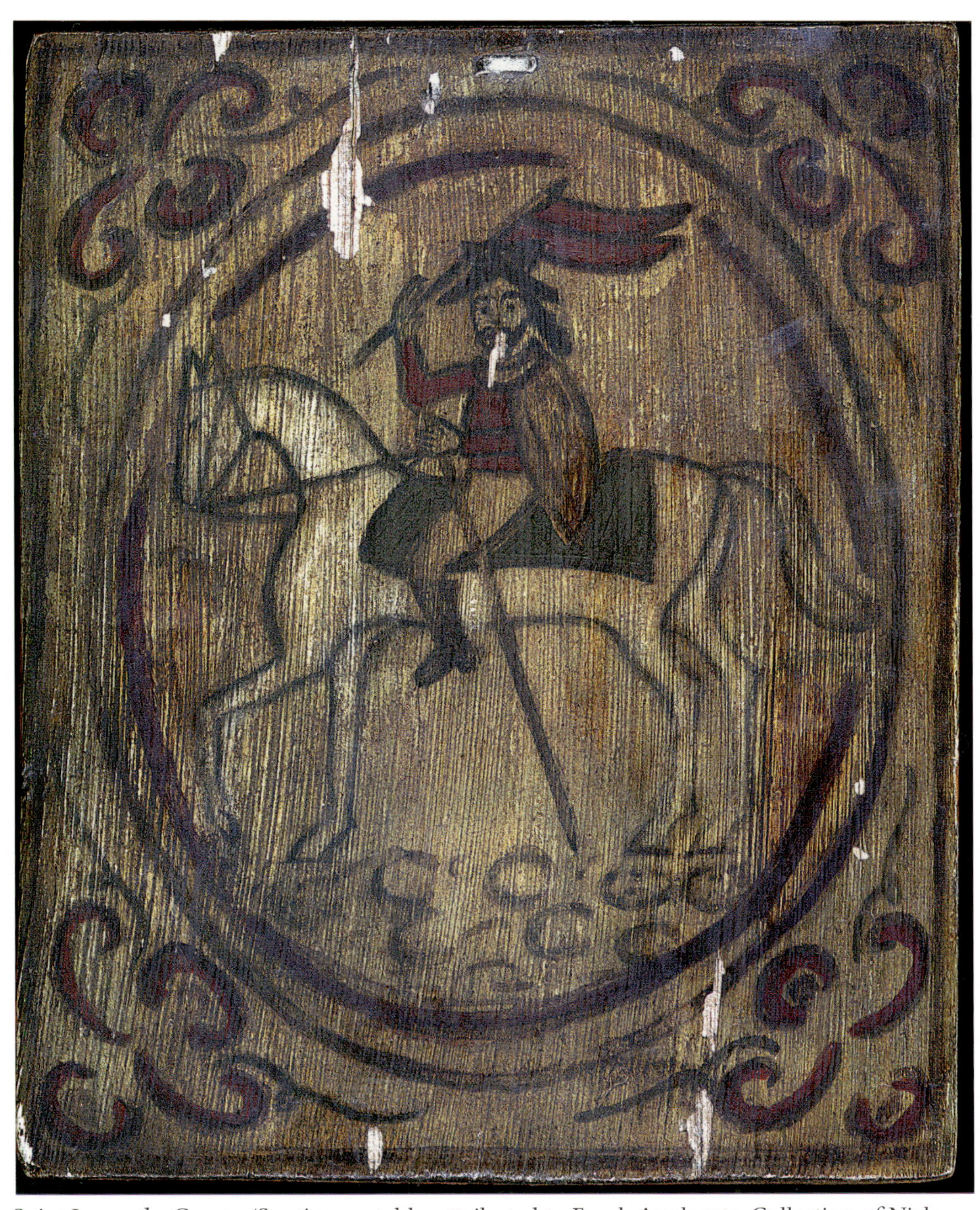

Saint James the Greater/Santiago, retablo, attributed to Frank Applegate. Collection of Nick Herrera. Photograph courtesy of Gerald Peters Gallery, Santa Fe.

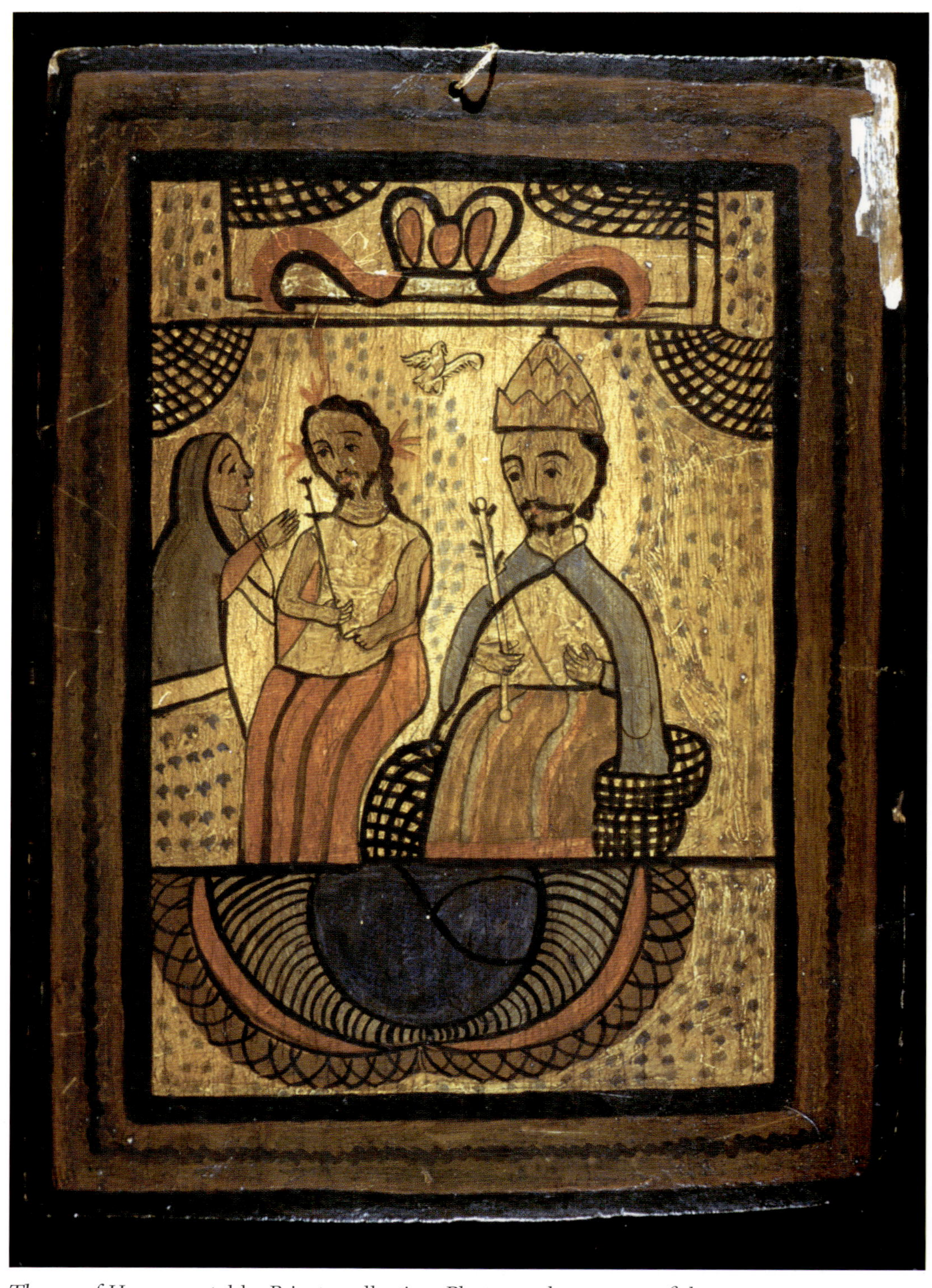

Throne of Heaven, retablo. Private collection. Photograph courtesy of the owner.

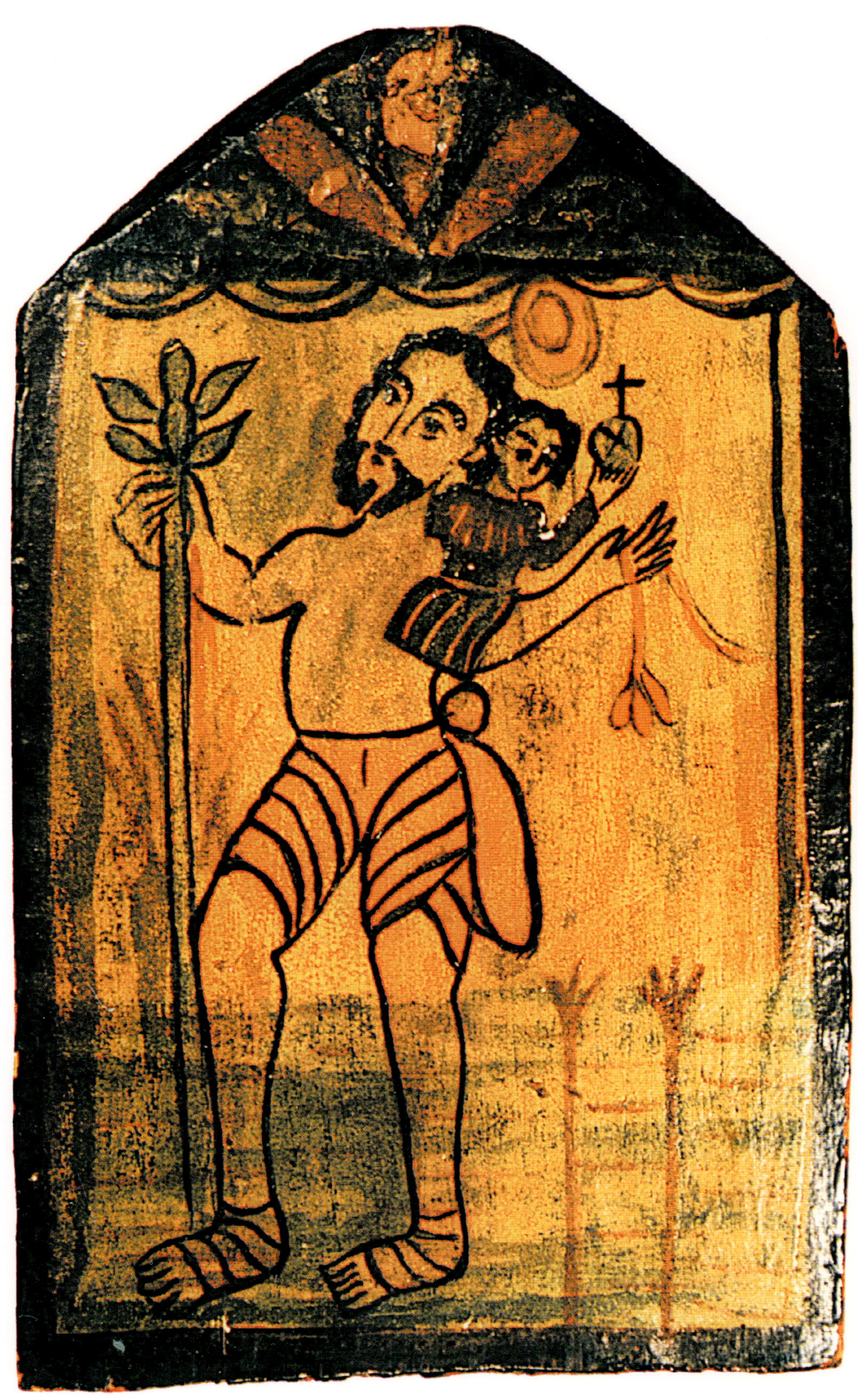

Saint Christopher/San Cristóbal, retablo. The Regis University Collection of New Mexico and Colorado Santos. Photograph courtesy of Paul Rhetts. Painted by Applegate as a gift to Mary Austin in 1928.

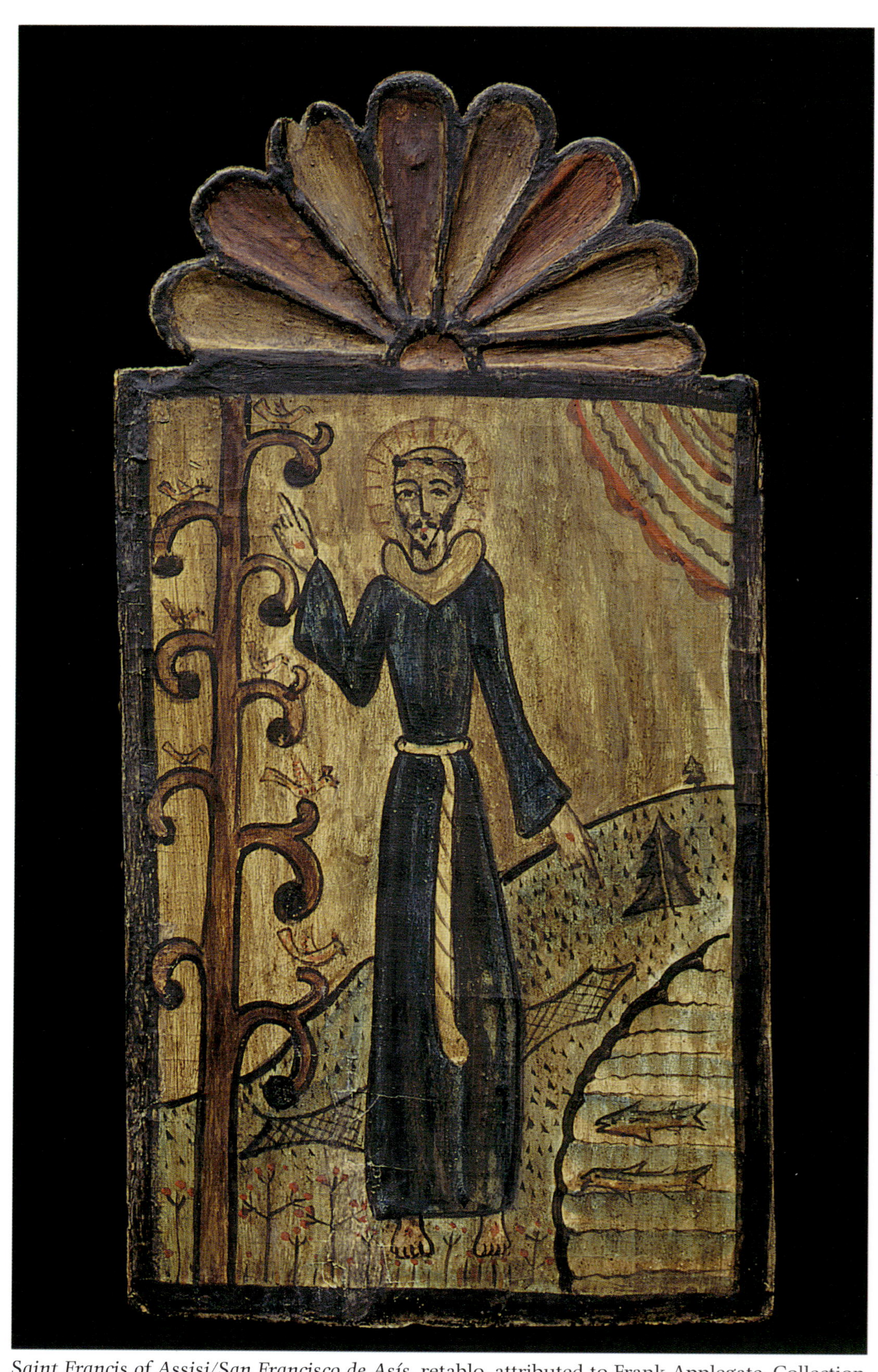

Saint Francis of Assisi/San Francisco de Asís, retablo, attributed to Frank Applegate. Collection of Spanish Colonial Arts Society Museum. Photograph courtesy of Gerald Peters Gallery, Santa Fe.

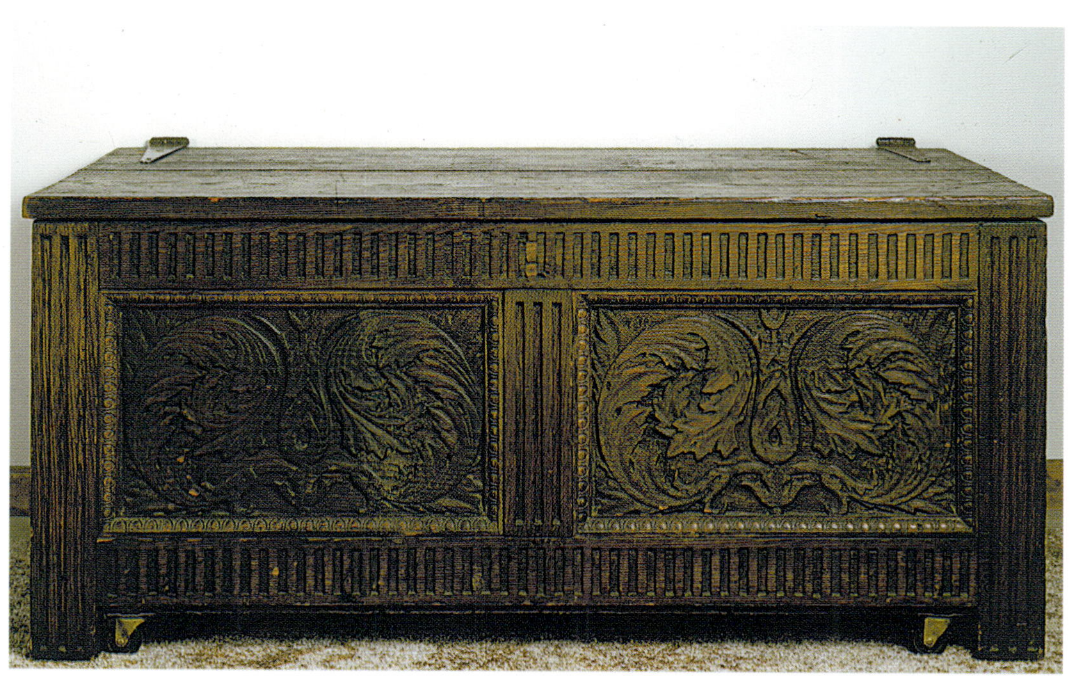

Carved wooden chest. Private collection. Photograph courtesy of the owner.

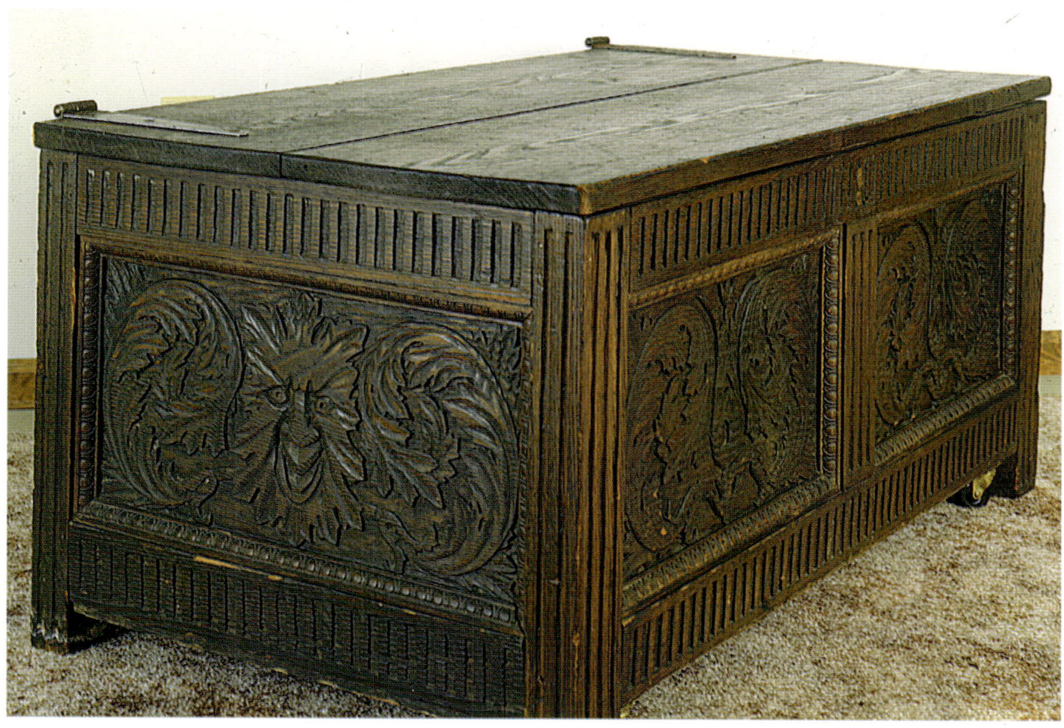

Carved wooden chest. Private collection. Photograph courtesy of the owner.

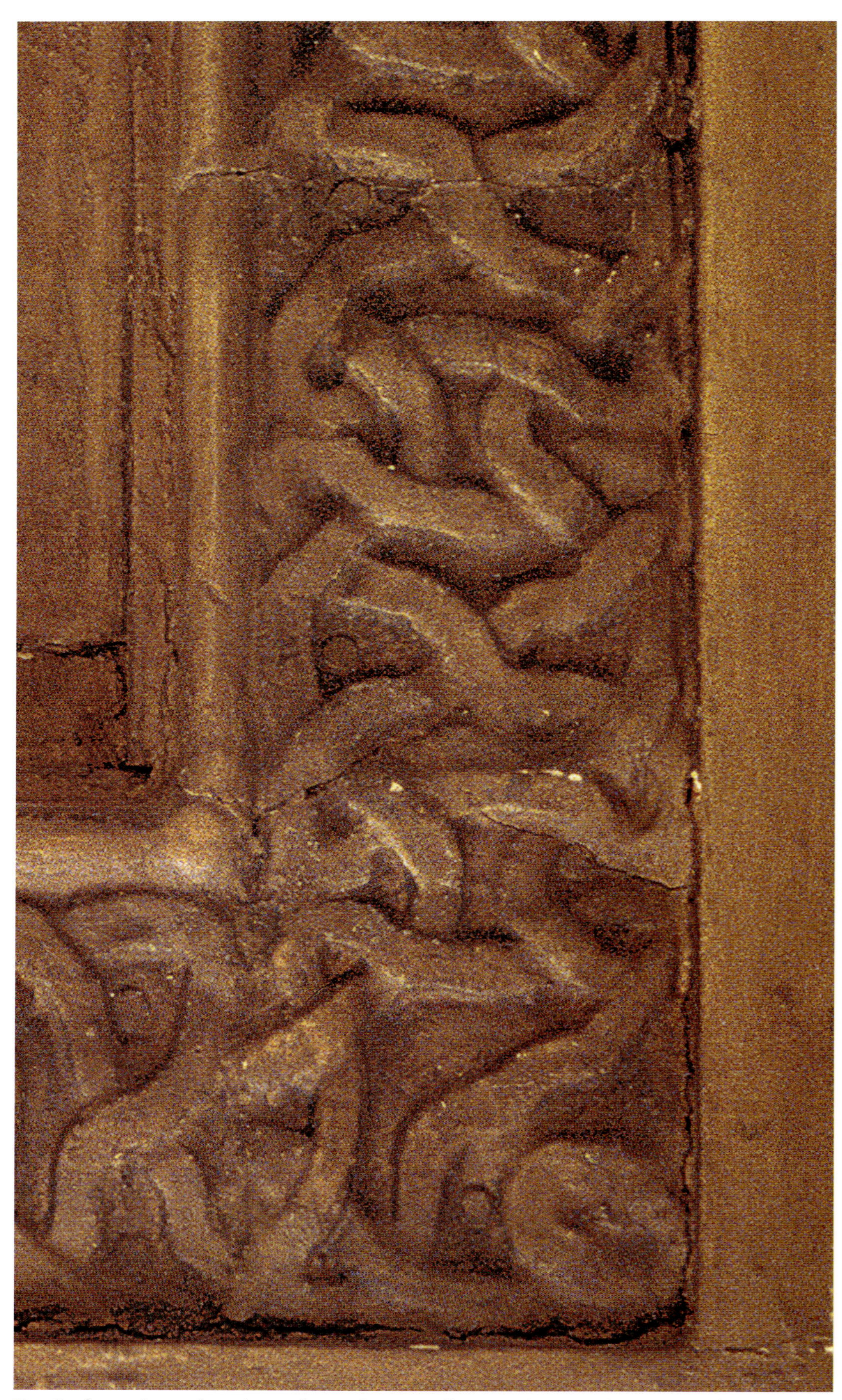

Detail of carved wooden picture frame. Private collection. Photograph courtesy of the owner.

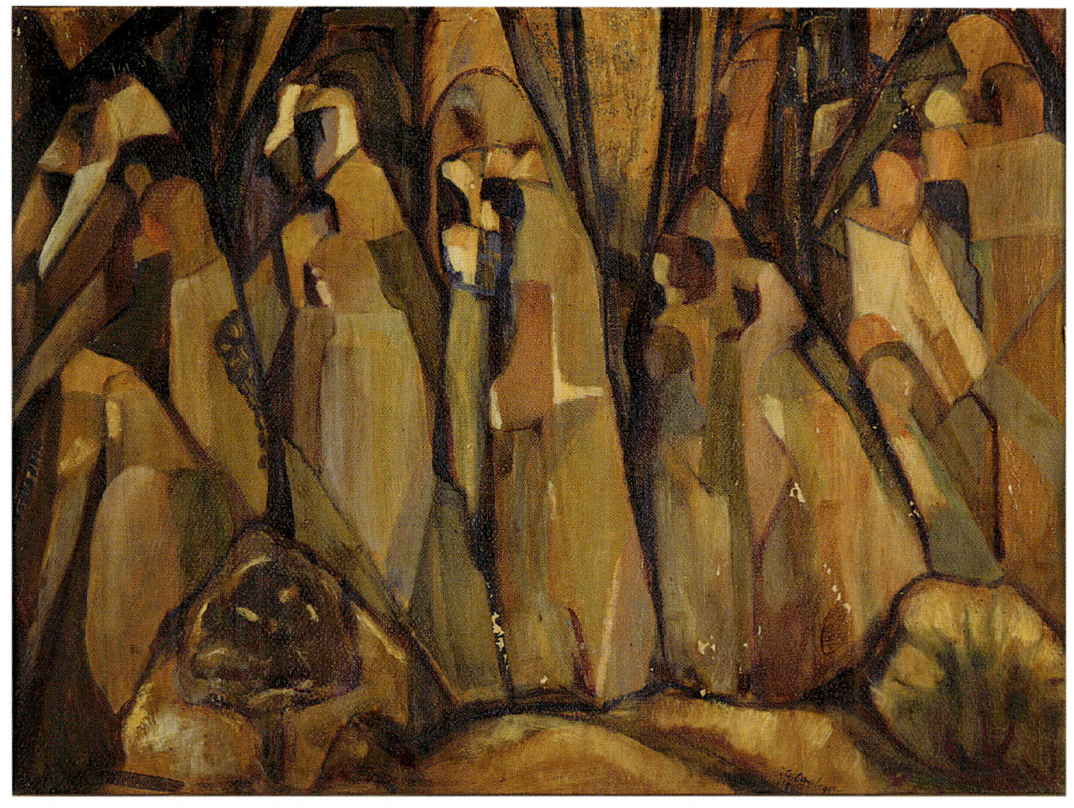

Sculptured Rocks, Rito de los Frijoles, oil on canvas, 23" by 29". Collection of Fred Jones, Jr. Museum of Art, the University of Oklahoma. Photograph by Konrad Eek. First exhibited in 1922.

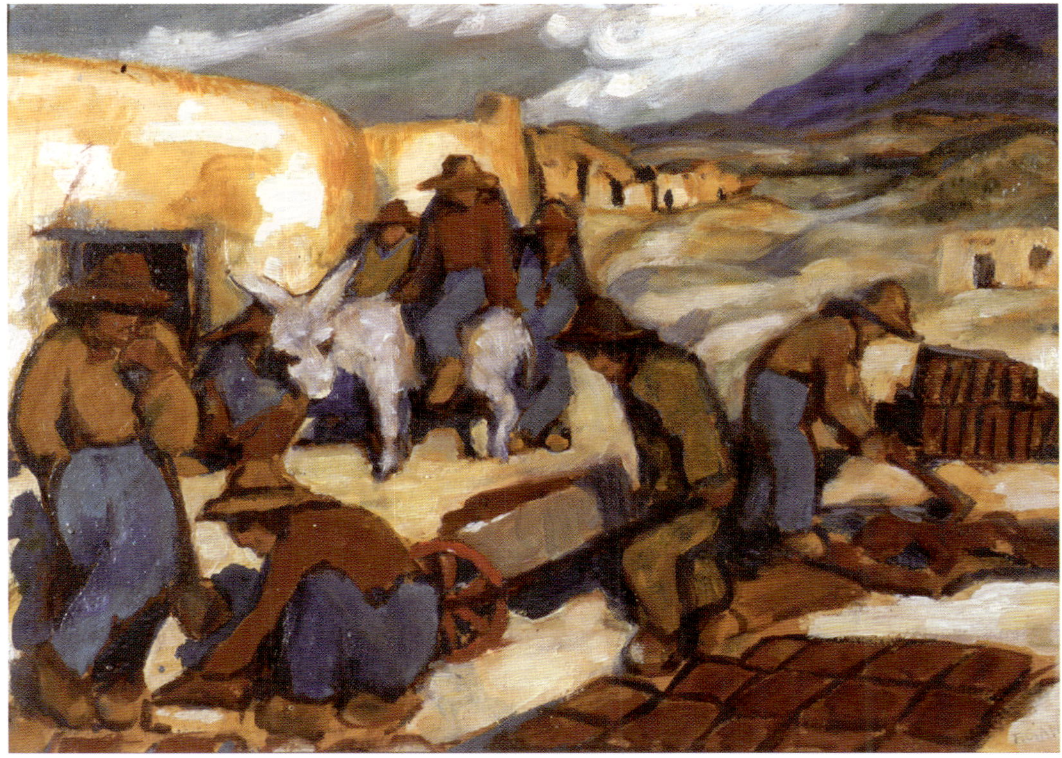

Adobe Makers, oil on canvas, 11 ½" by 17 ¾". Private collection. First exhibited in 1922.

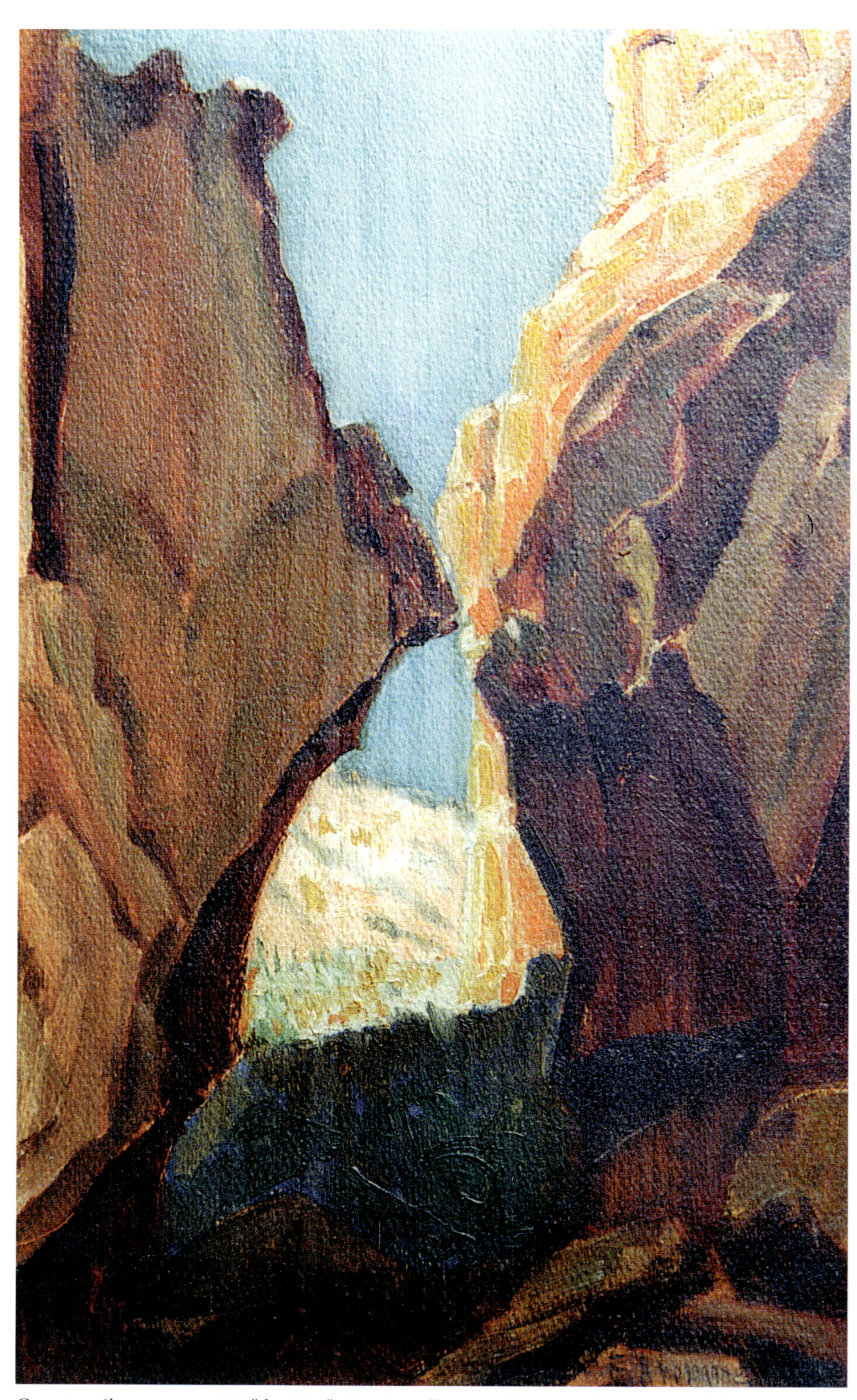

Canyon, oil on canvas, 17 ½" by 11 ¼". Private collection. Photograph courtesy of the owner.

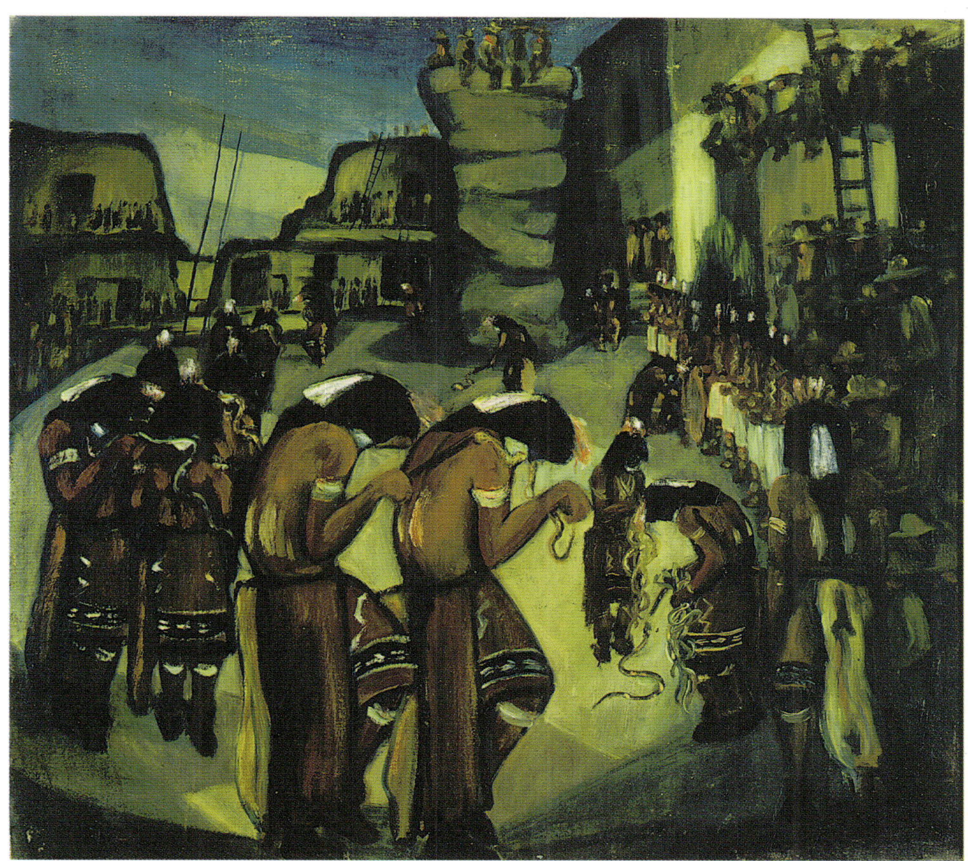

Hopi Snake Dance, oil on canvas, 24" by 27". Photograph courtesy of Museum of Fine Arts, Museum of New Mexico.

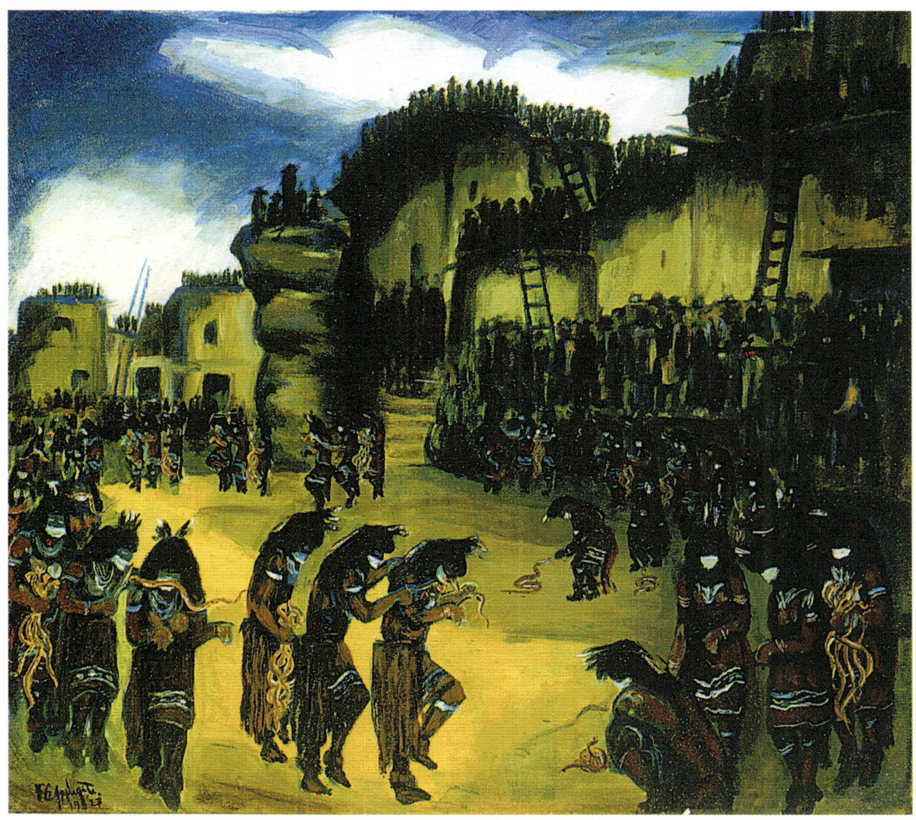

Hopi Snake Dance, oil on canvas, 23½" by 26½". Private collection. Photograph courtesy of Gerald Peters Gallery, Santa Fe. First exhibited in 1923.

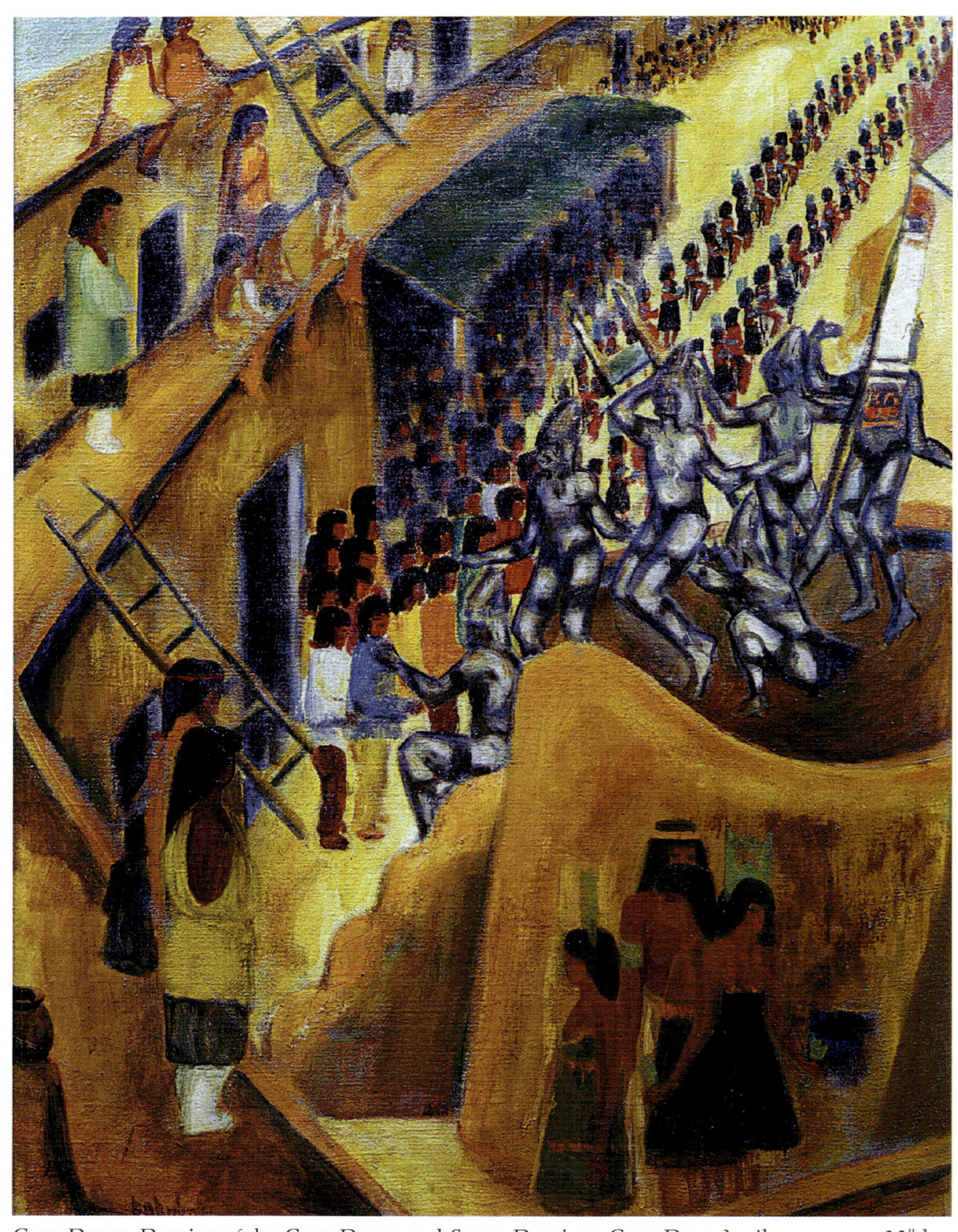

Corn Dance, Domingo (aka *Corn Dance* and *Santo Domingo Corn Dance*), oil on canvas, 32" by 24½". Private Collection. Photograph courtesy of Gerald Peters Gallery, Santa Fe. Published in *Modernist Themes in New Mexico: Works by Early Modernist Painters*. First exhibited in 1922.

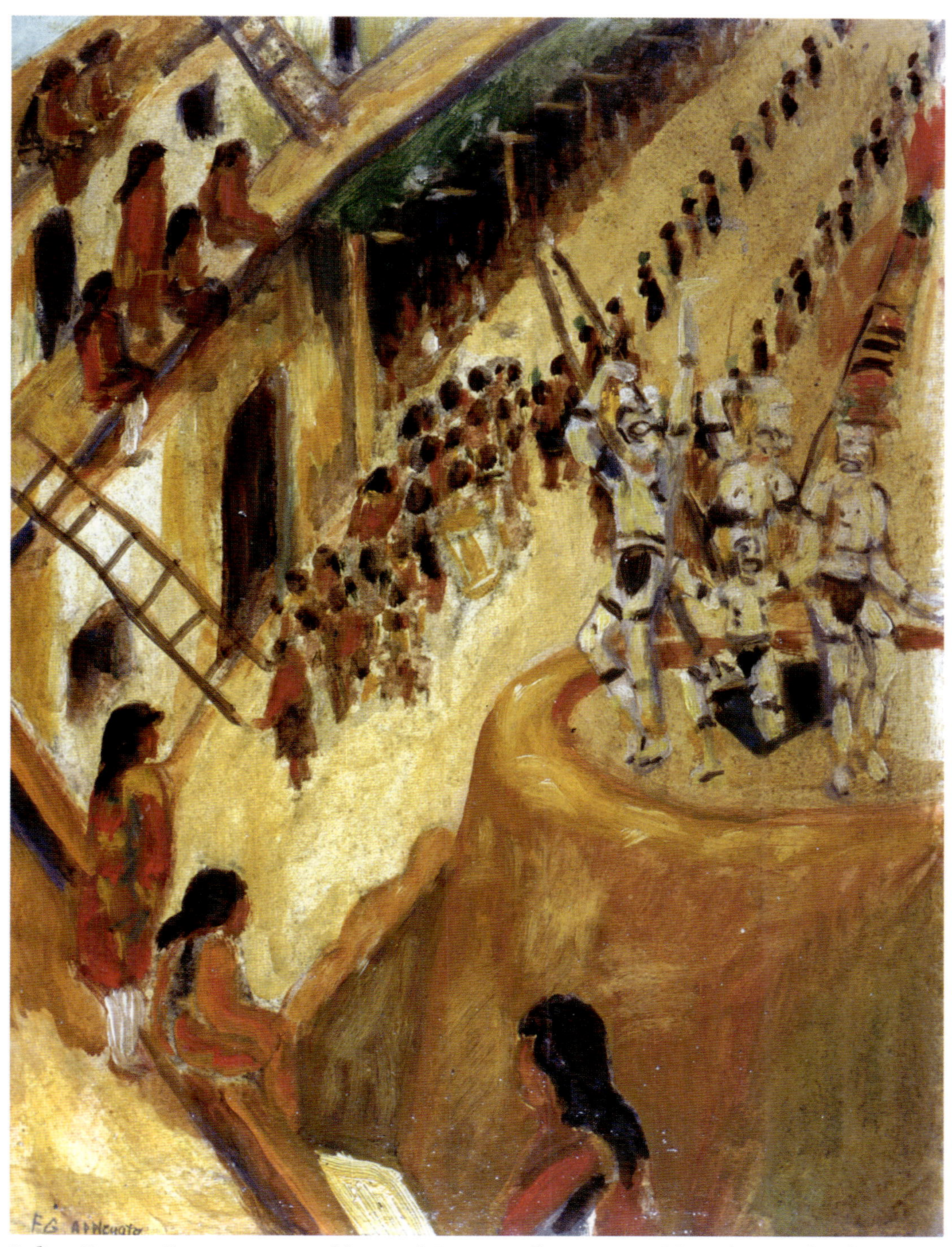

Indian Dance, oil on canvas, 13½" by 10½". Private collection. Possibly a "first draft" of *Corn Dance*.

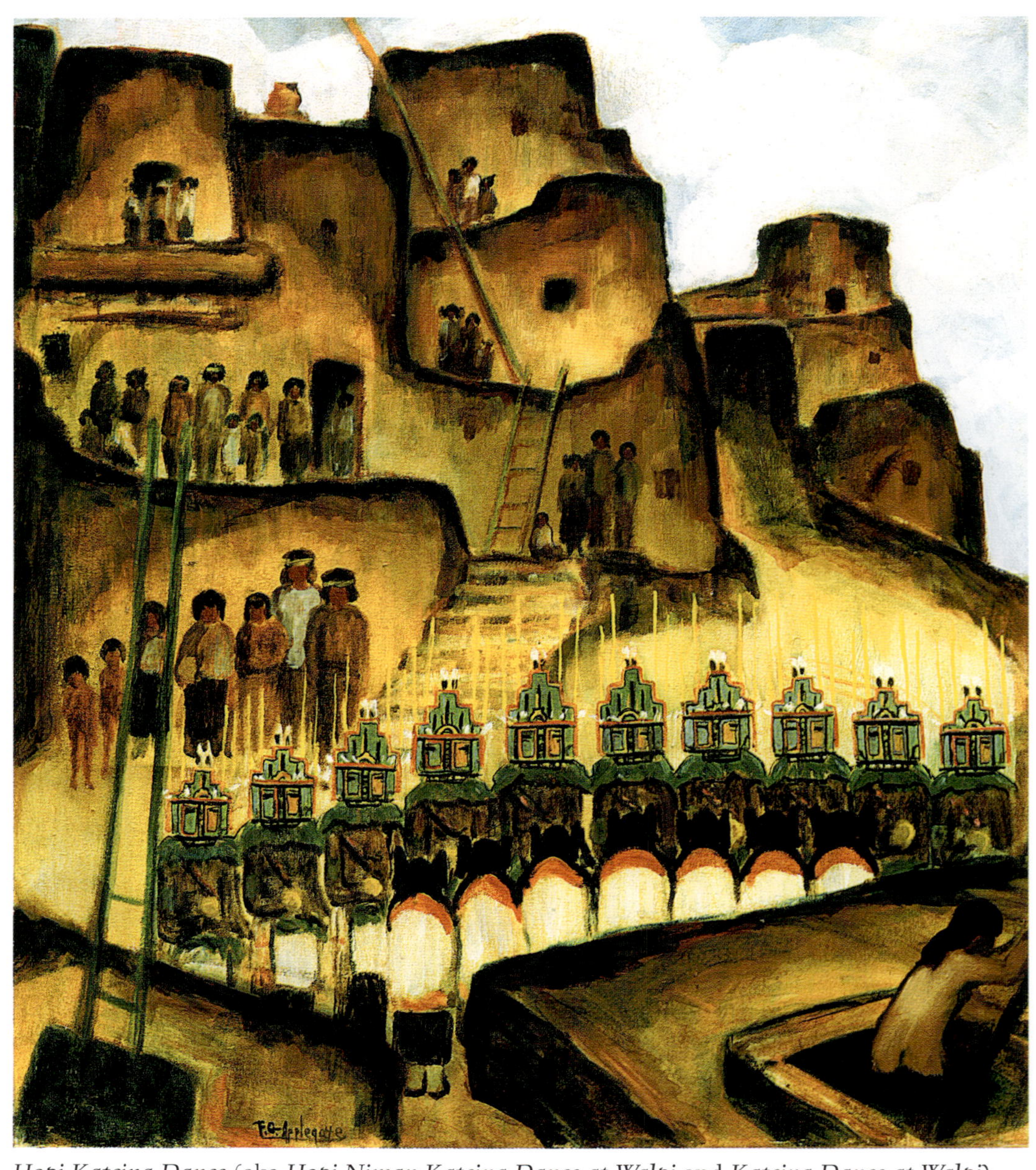

Hopi Katcina Dance (aka *Hopi Niman Katcina Dance at Walpi* and *Katcina Dance at Walpi*), oil on canvas, 27" by 24". Private collection. Photograph courtesy of Gerald Peters Gallery, Santa Fe. First exhibited in 1923.

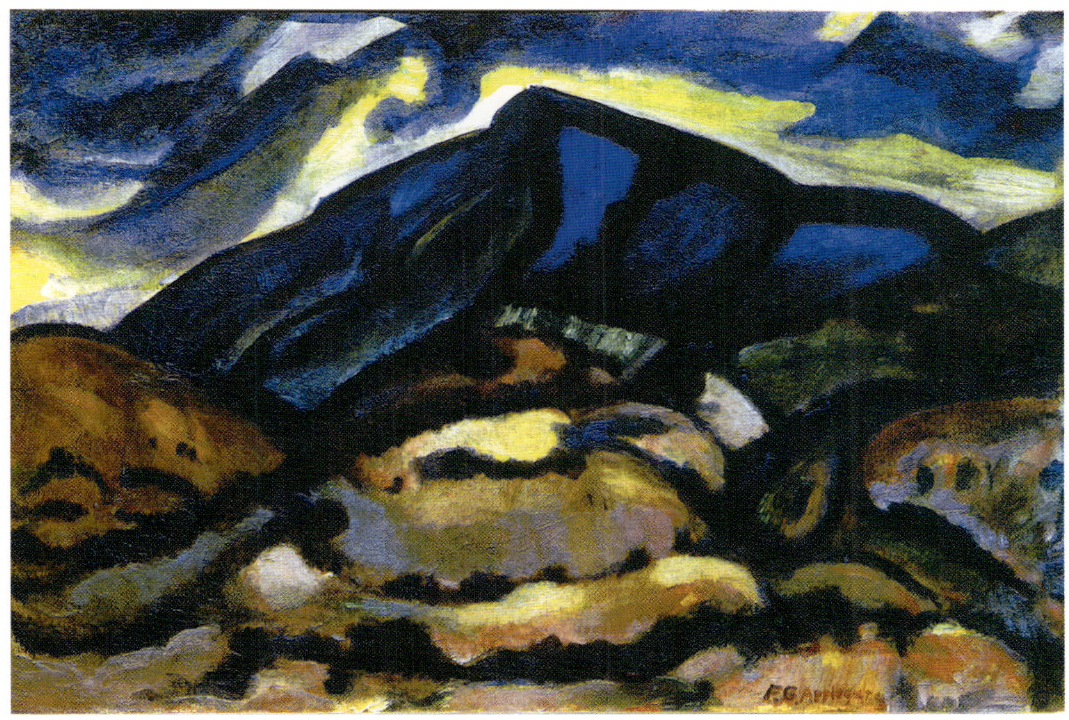

Telaya Mountain (aka *Landscape, Taos, N.M.*), oil on canvas, 20" by 30". Private collection. Photograph courtesy of Gerald Peters Gallery, Santa Fe. First exhibited in 1923.

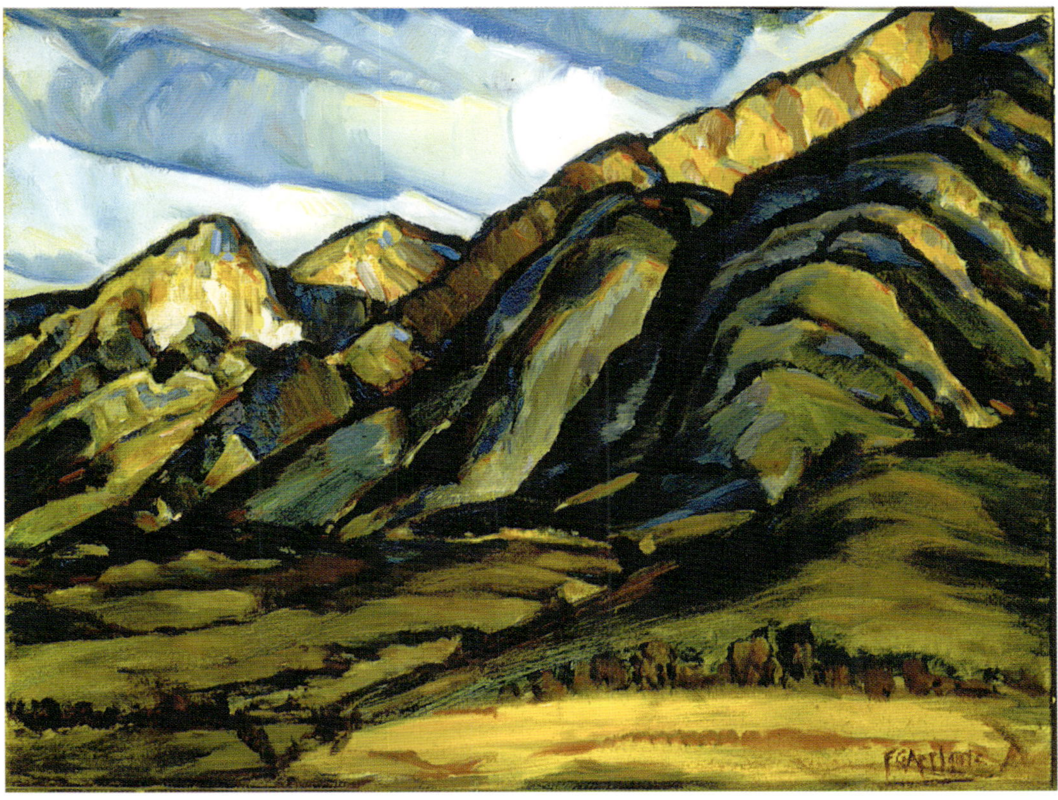

Taos Mountain Landscape, oil on canvas, 18" by 24". Private collection. Photograph courtesy of Gerald Peters Gallery, Santa Fe.

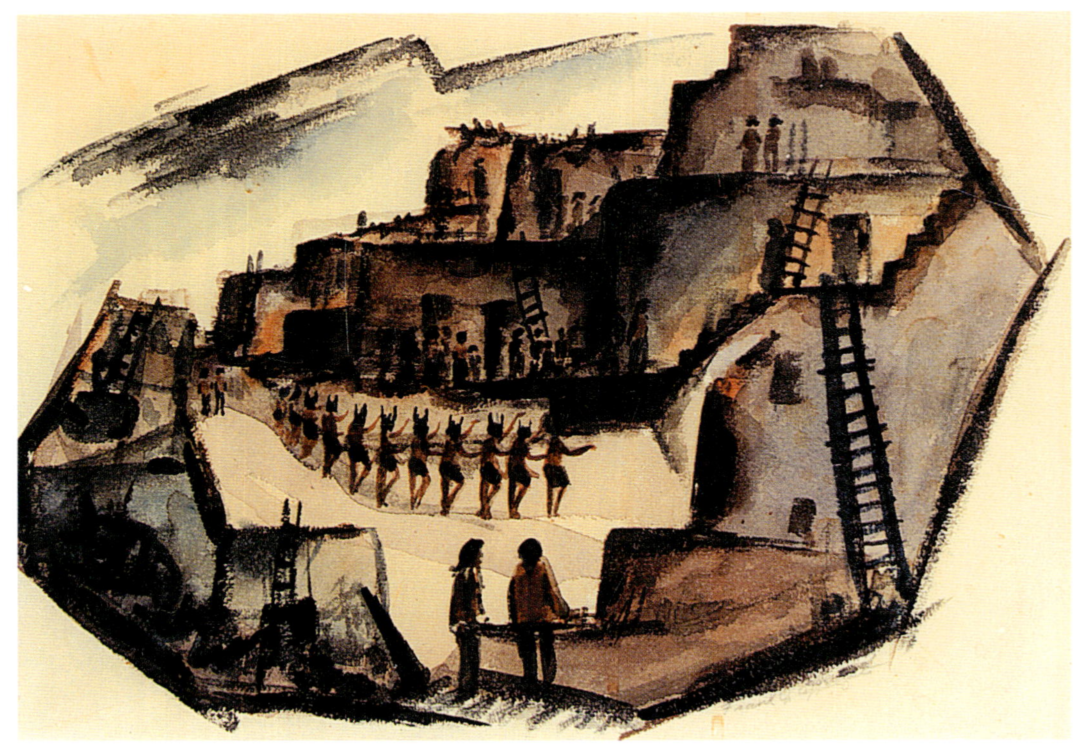

Hopi Antelope Dance, watercolor, 11½" by 16¾". Private collection. Photograph courtesy of Gerald Peters Gallery, Santa Fe.

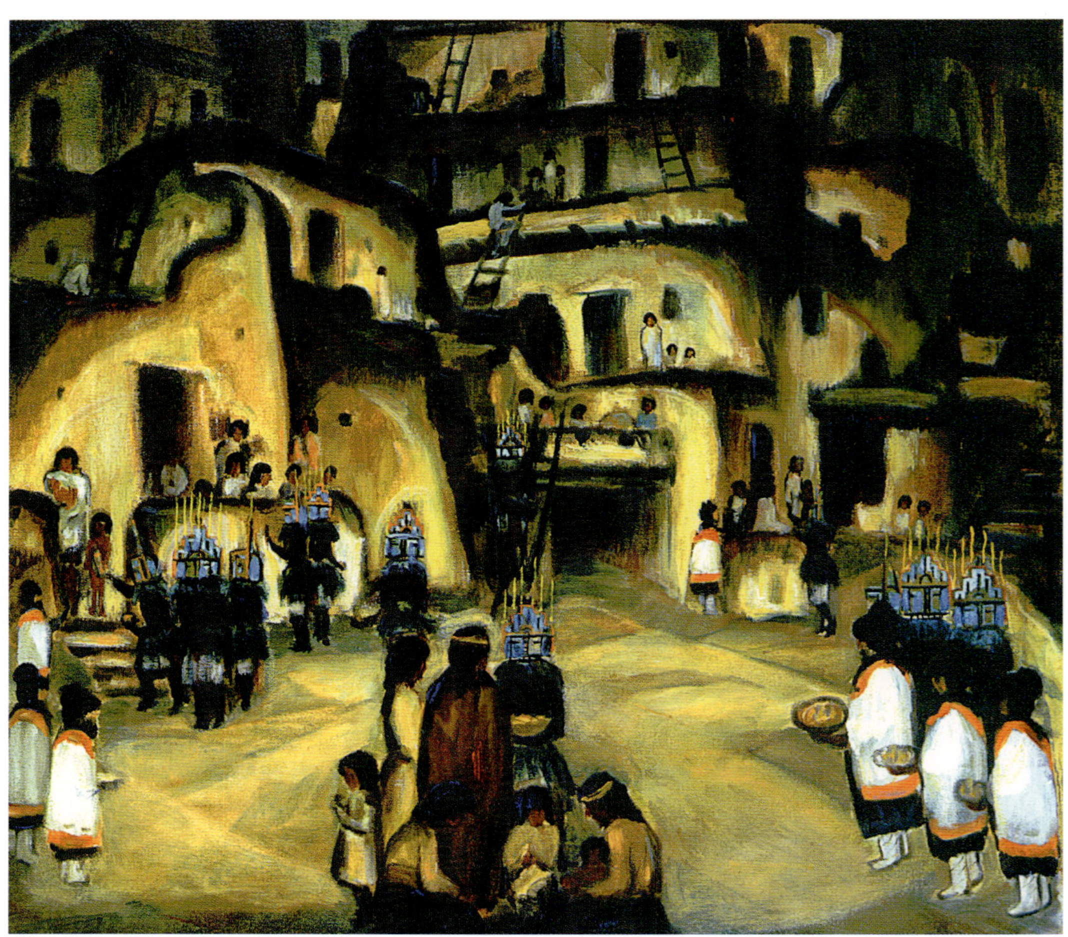

Untitled (probably *Hopi Gift Ceremony*, ca. 1925), oil on canvas, 24" by 27". Private collection. Photograph courtesy of Gerald Peters Gallery, Santa Fe.

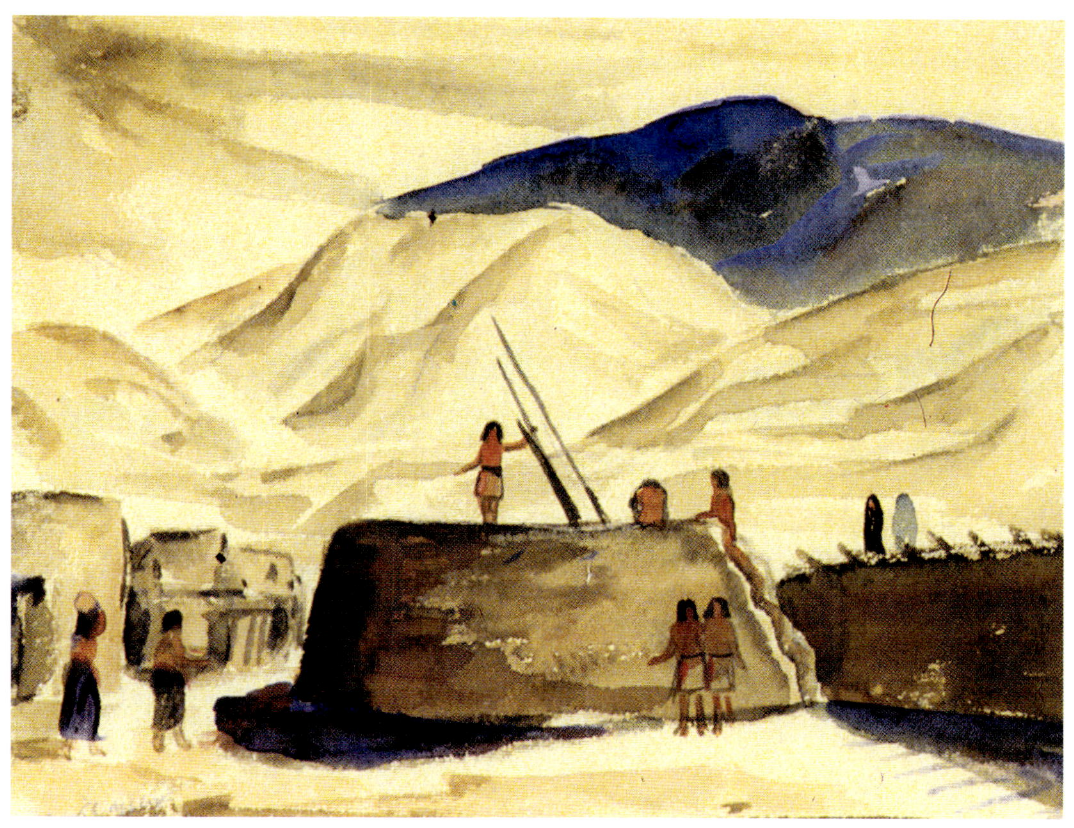

Santa Domingo, watercolor, 8⅜" by 11". Private collection. Photograph courtesy of the owner. In *Native Tales of New Mexico*, published in 1931.

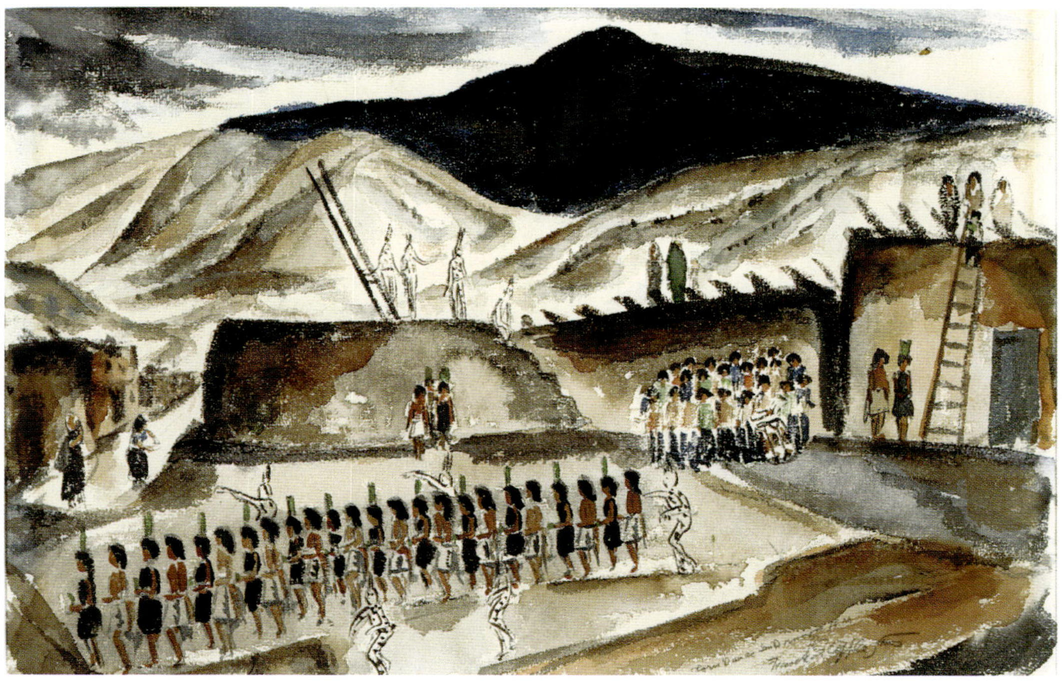

Green Corn Dance, watercolor, 19½" by 25½". Collection of Fred Jones, Jr. Museum of Art, the University of Oklahoma. Photograph by Konrad Eek. Exhibited in 1927.

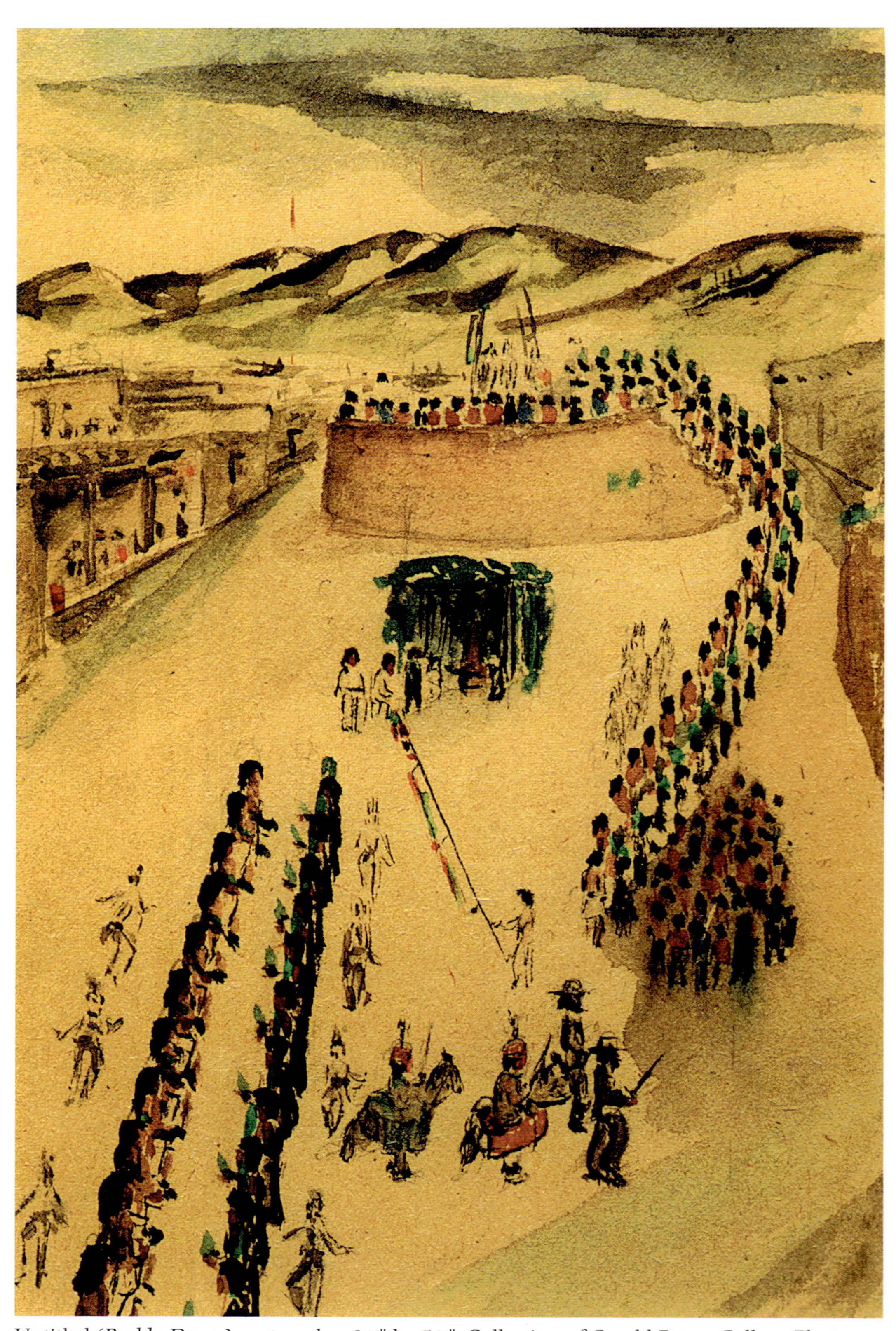

Untitled (*Pueblo Dance*), watercolor, 8½" by 5¾". Collection of Gerald Peters Gallery. Photograph courtesy of Gerald Peters Gallery, Santa Fe.

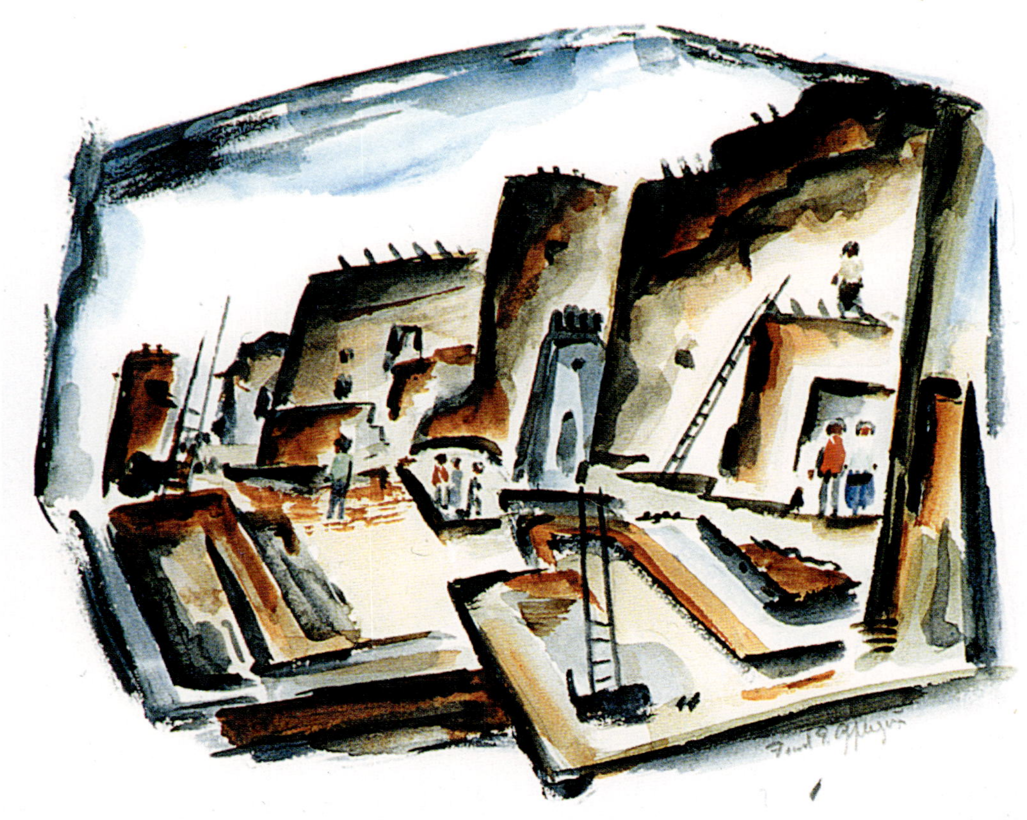

Walpi, Hopi Village, watercolor, 7 ½" by 9". Private collection. Photograph courtesy of Gerald Peters Gallery, Santa Fe.

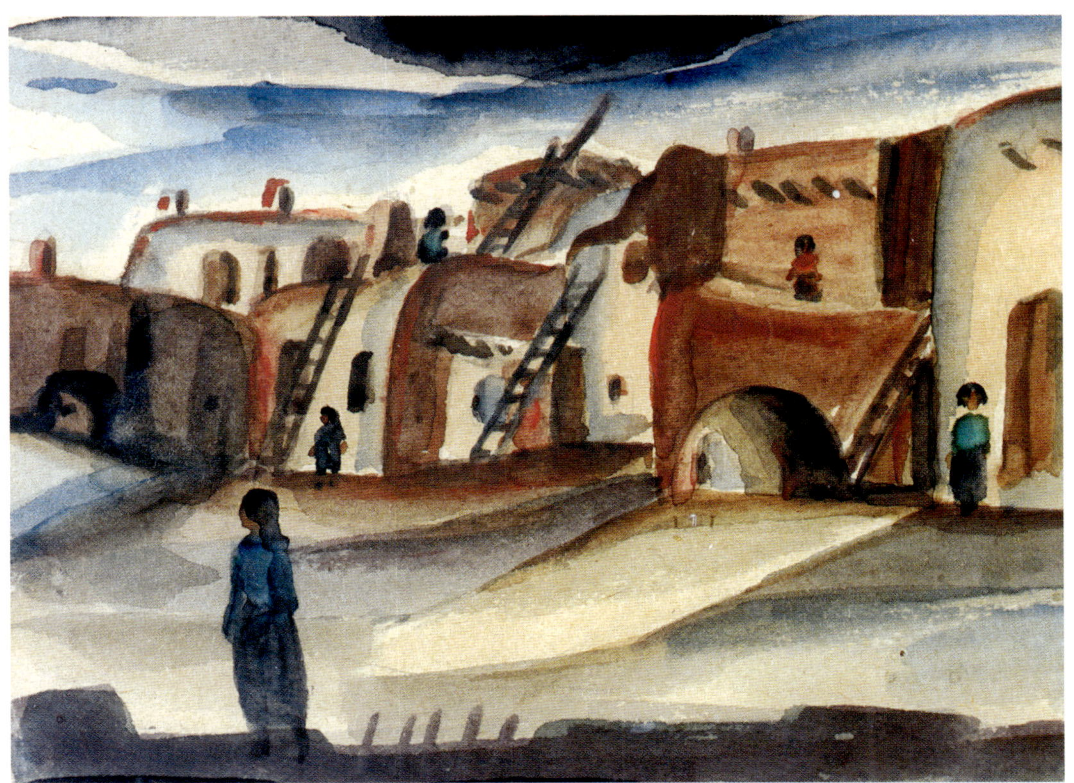

Indian Pueblo, watercolor. 5 ⅝" by 8 ⅜". Private collection. Photograph courtesy of the owner.

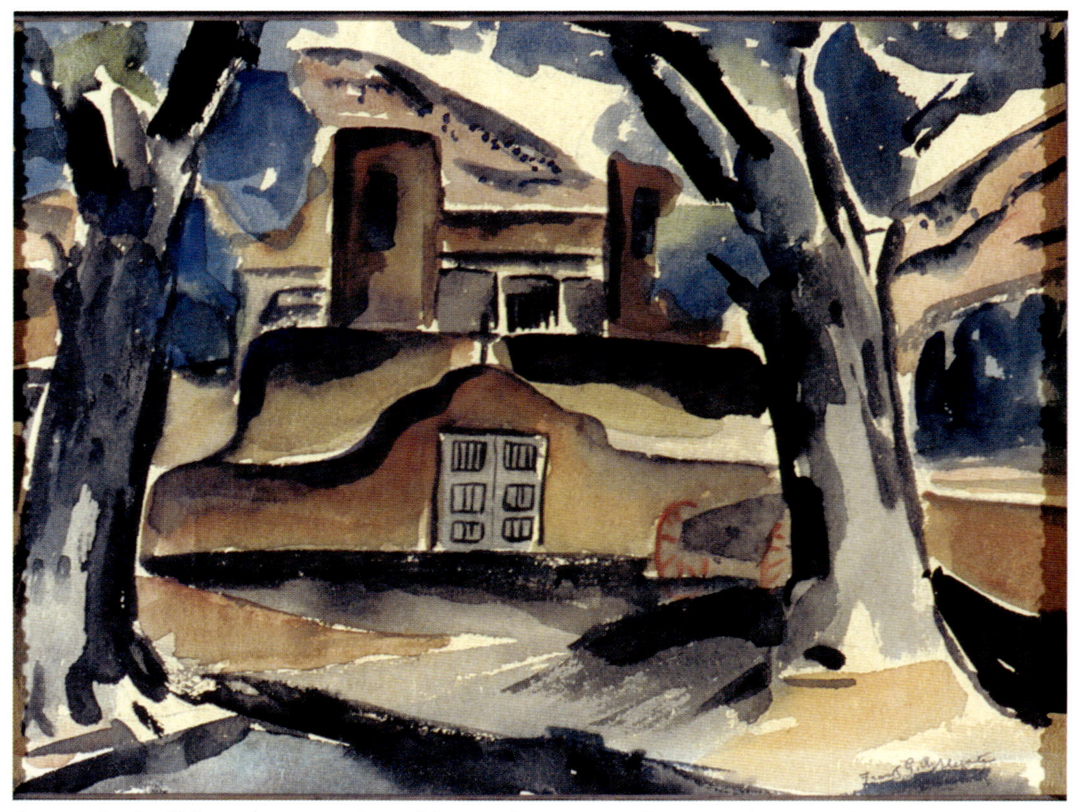

Santuario de Chimayó, watercolor, 8" by 11½". Private collection. Photograph courtesy of the owner.

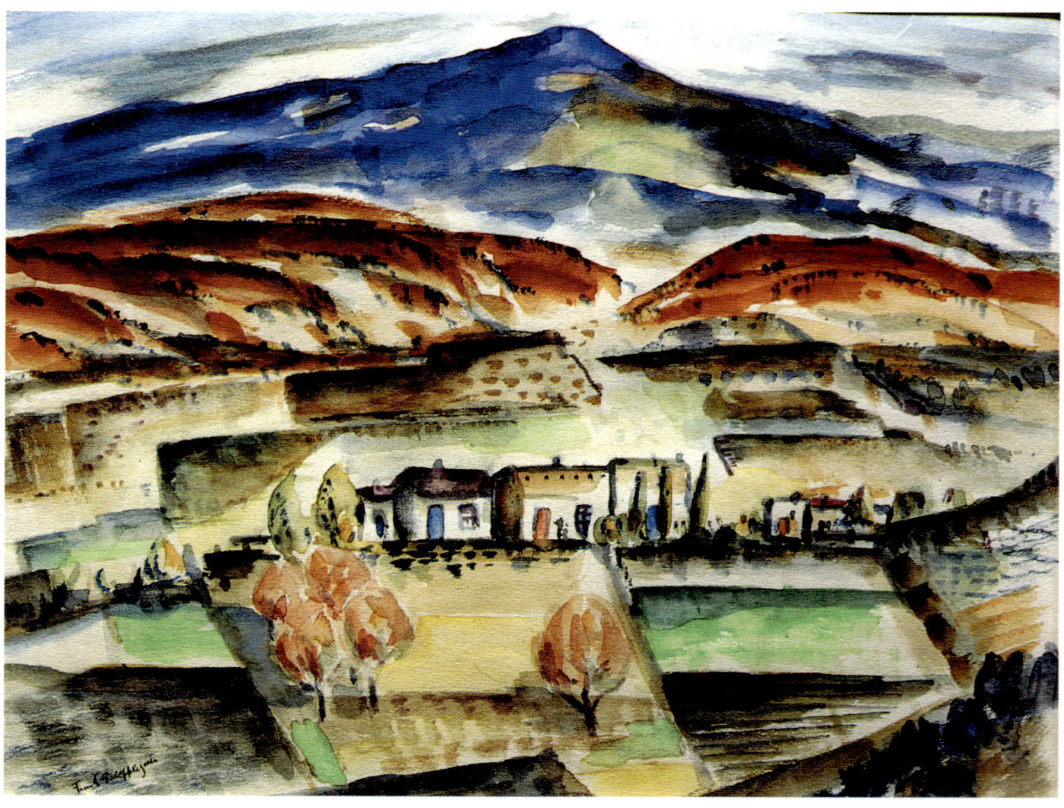

Chimayó Valley, watercolor, 8¾" by 11¾". Private collection. Photograph courtesy of Gerald Peters Gallery, Santa Fe. First exhibited in 1925.

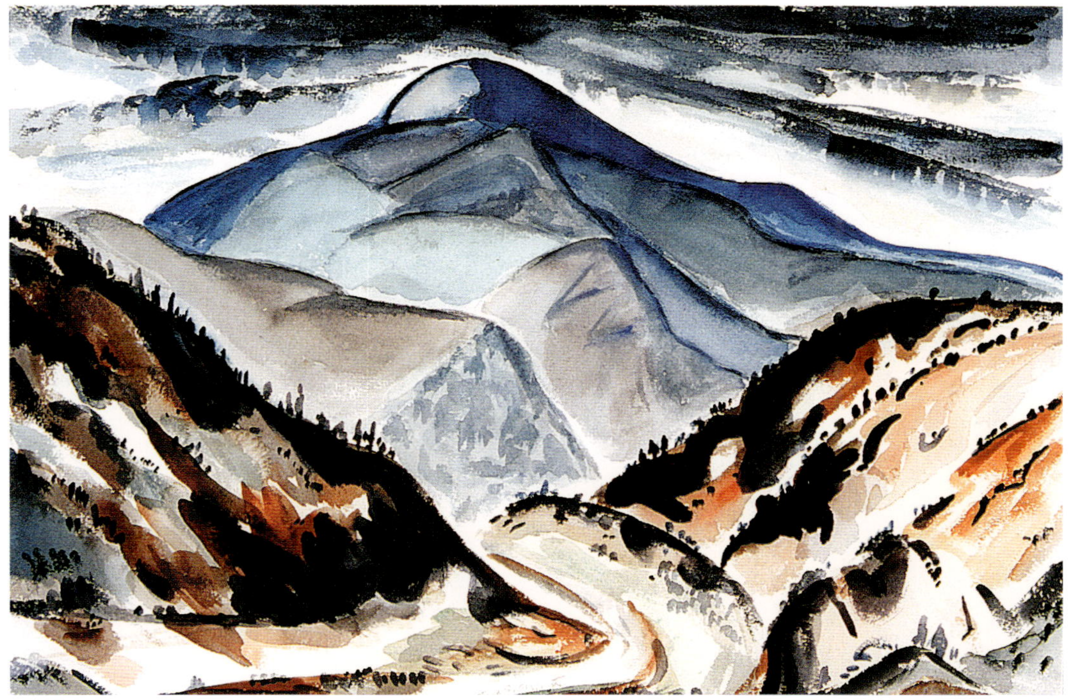

Untitled, watercolor, 11¾" by 17¾". Collection of Brimmer and Stephanie Sherman. Photograph courtesy of Gerald Peters Gallery, Santa Fe.

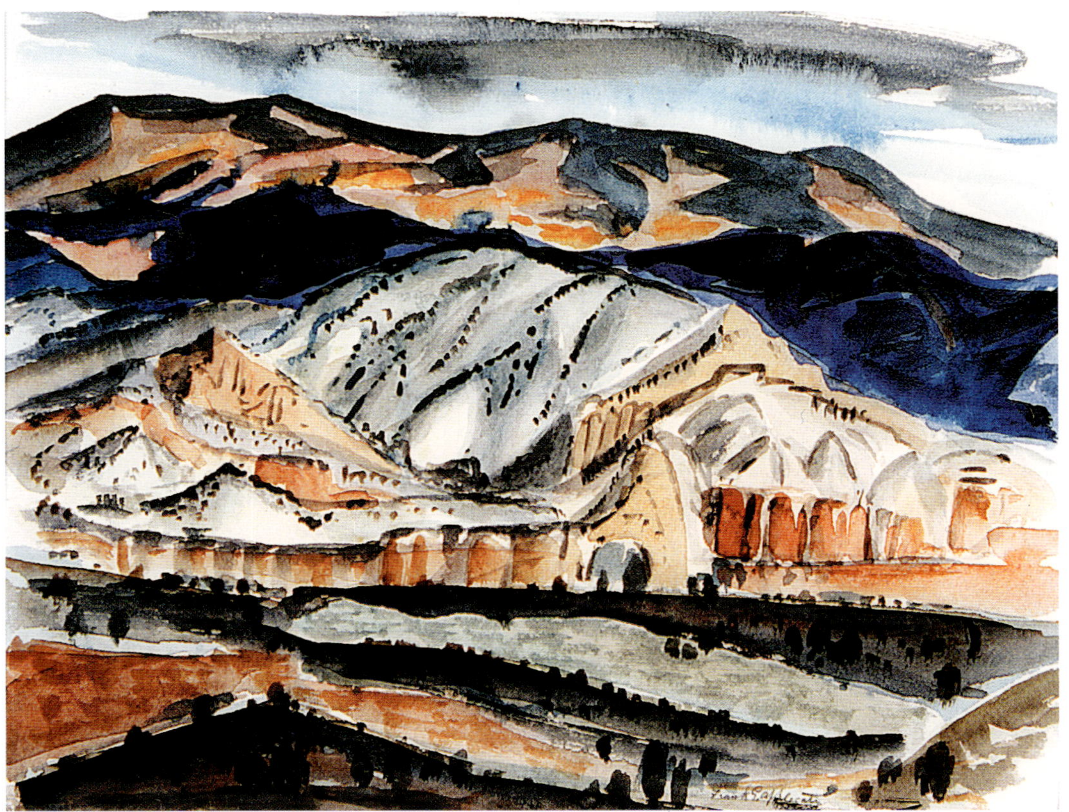

Camino de Chimayó, watercolor, 8½" by 11½". Private collection. Photograph courtesy of Gerald Peters Gallery, Santa Fe.

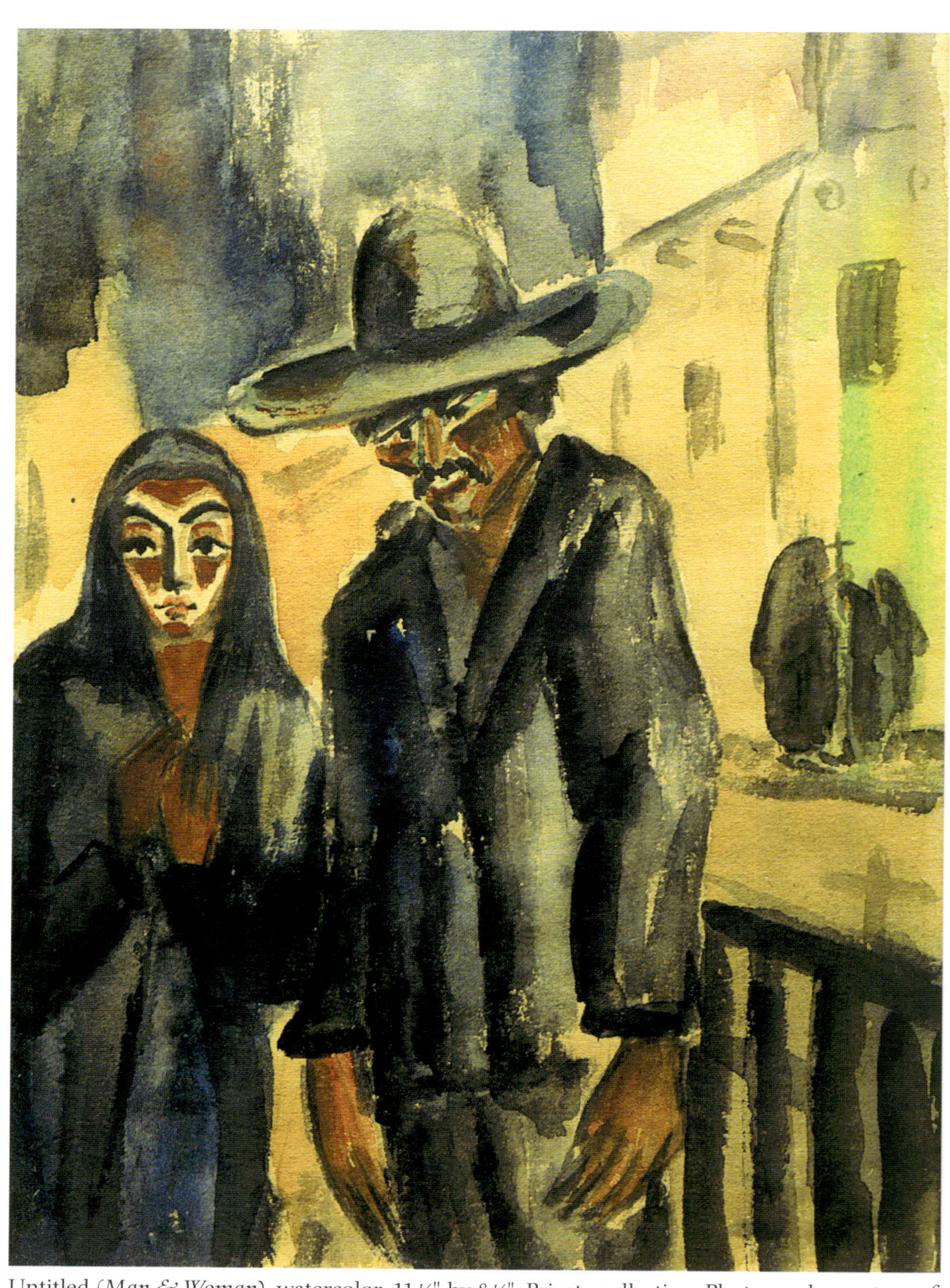

Untitled (*Man & Woman*), watercolor, 11½" by 8½". Private collection. Photograph courtesy of Gerald Peters Gallery, Santa Fe.

144

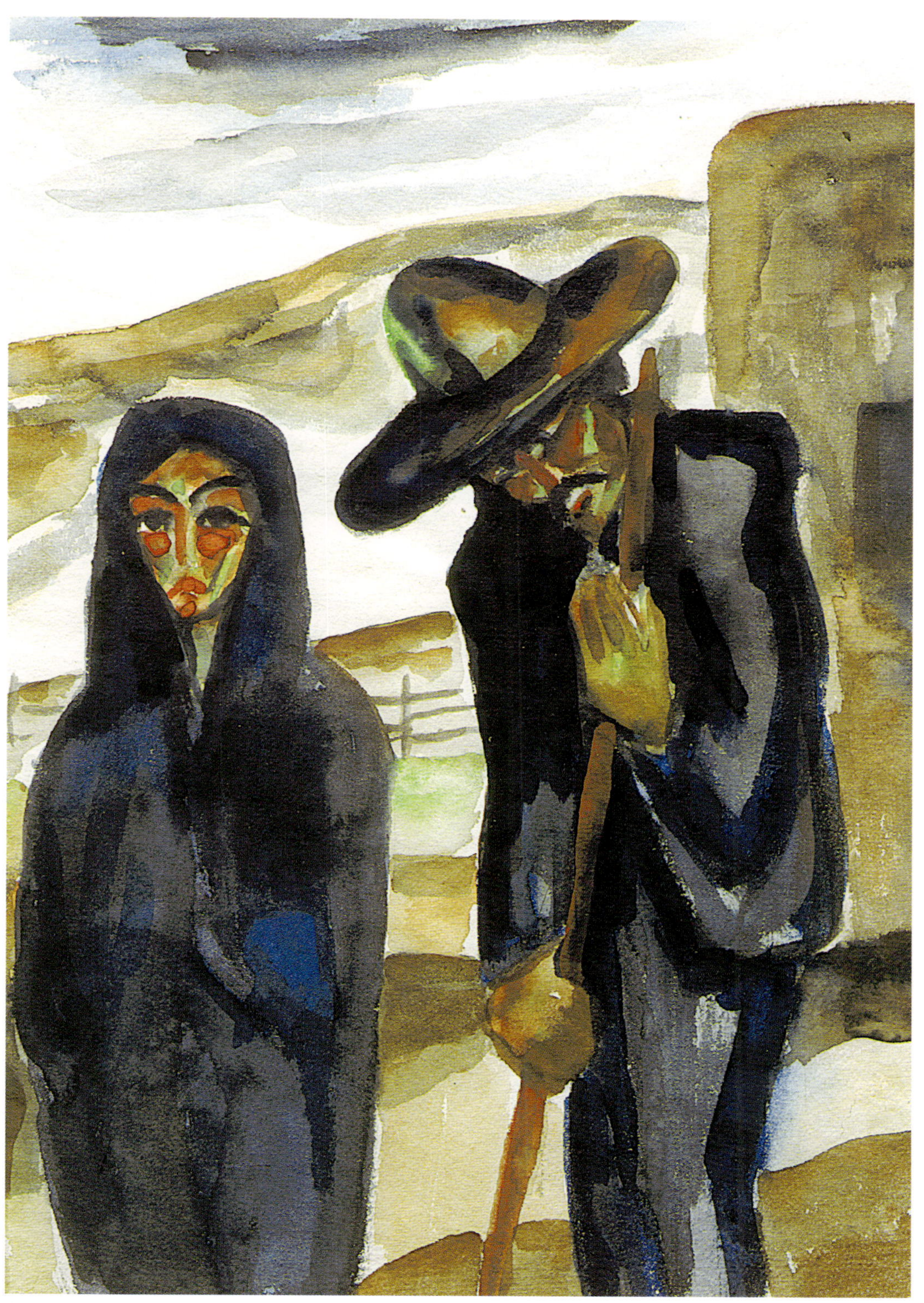

Lupita, watercolor, 13¾" by 9¾". Private collection. Photograph courtesy of Gerald Peters Gallery, Santa Fe. In *Native Tales of New Mexico*, published in 1931.

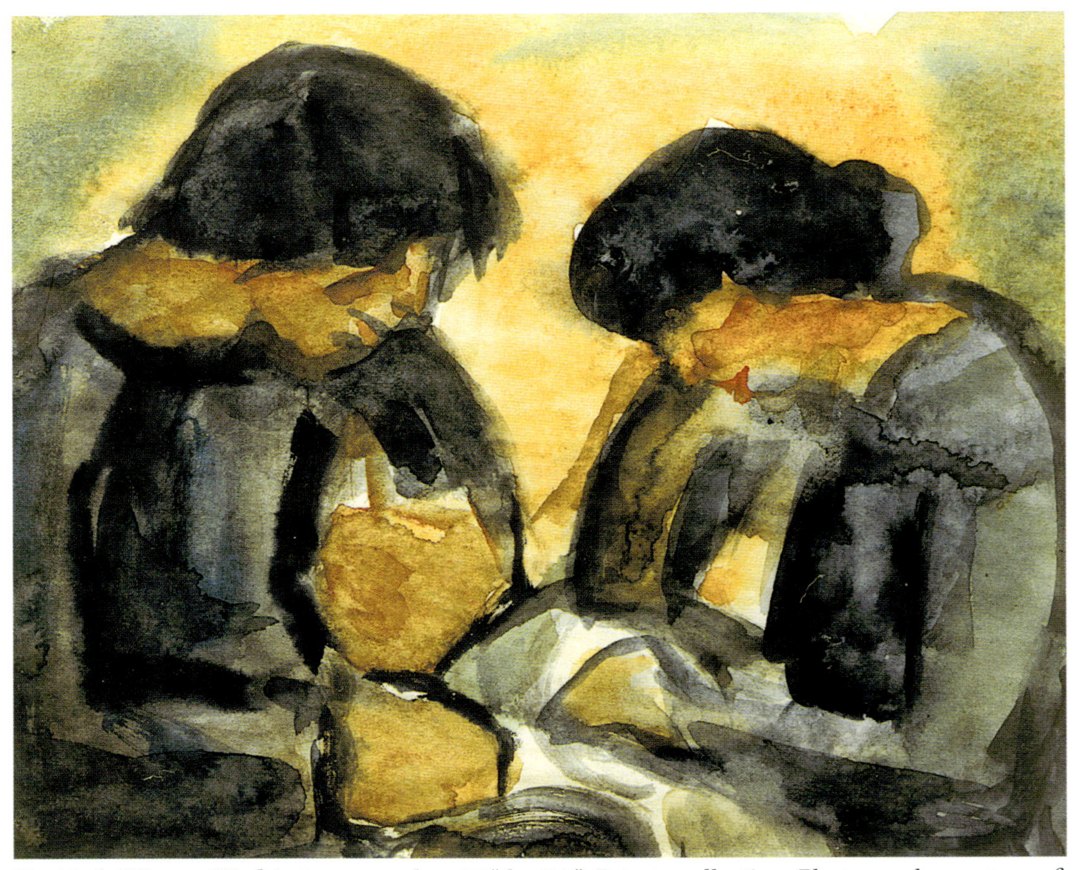

Untitled (*Women Working*), watercolor, 6¼" by 5½". Private collection. Photograph courtesy of Gerald Peters Gallery, Santa Fe.

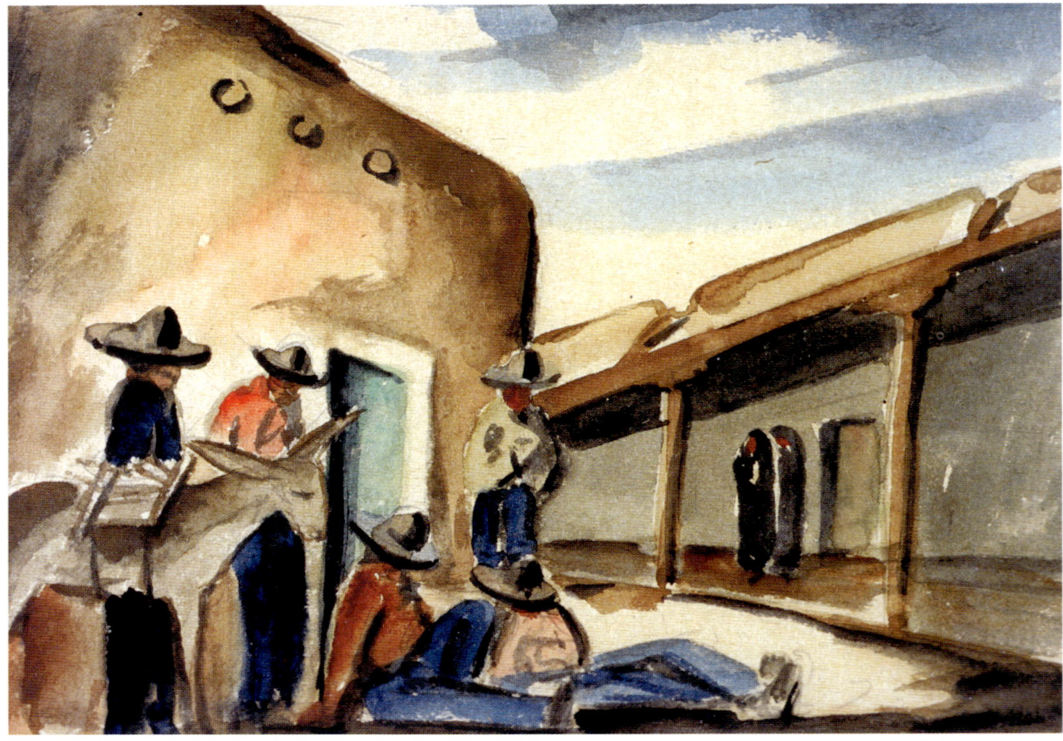

Hispanic Scene, watercolor, 5⅝" by 8⅜". Private collection. Photograph courtesy of the owner.

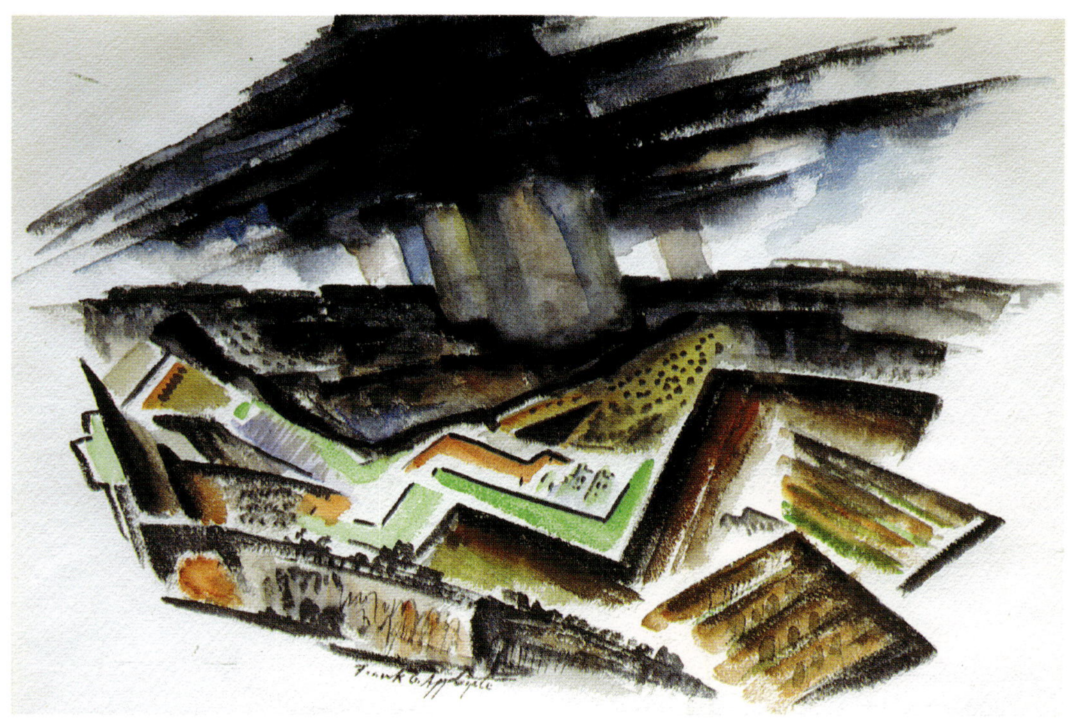

Rain on Hopi Desert, watercolor, 11" by 17". Private collection. Photograph courtesy of Gerald Peters Gallery, Santa Fe. Published in *Modernist Themes in New Mexico: Works by Early Modernist Painters.*

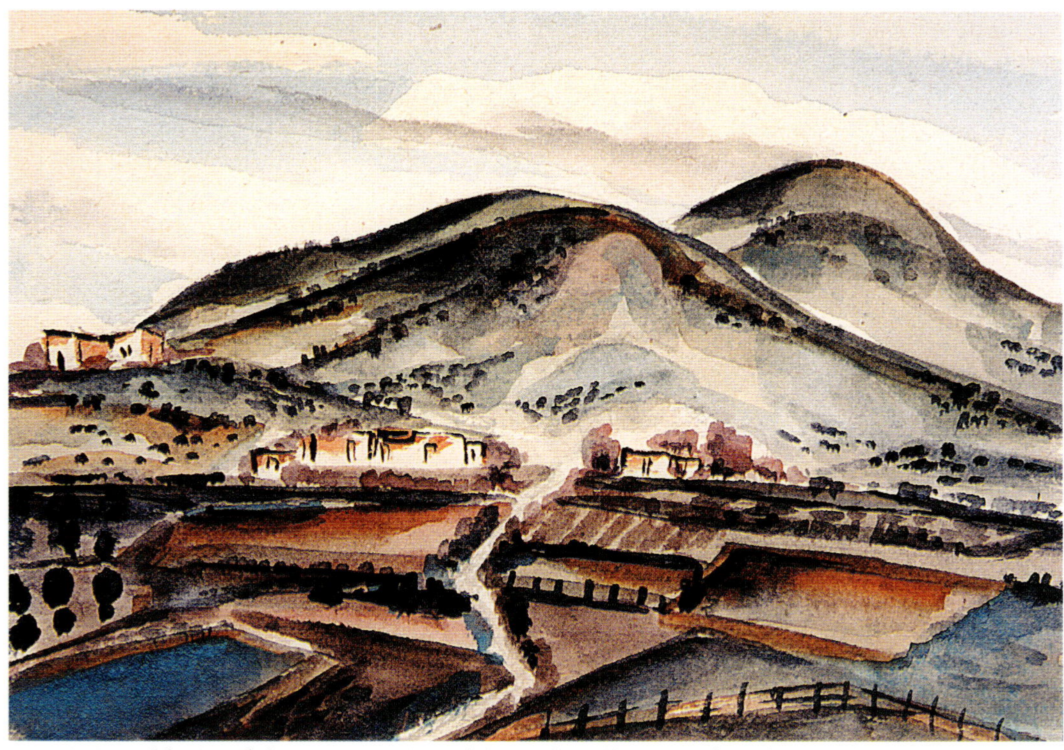

Untitled (*Fields & Adobes*), watercolor, 6" by 8¾". Collection of Herbert and Margaret Pickworth. Photograph courtesy of Gerald Peters Gallery, Santa Fe.

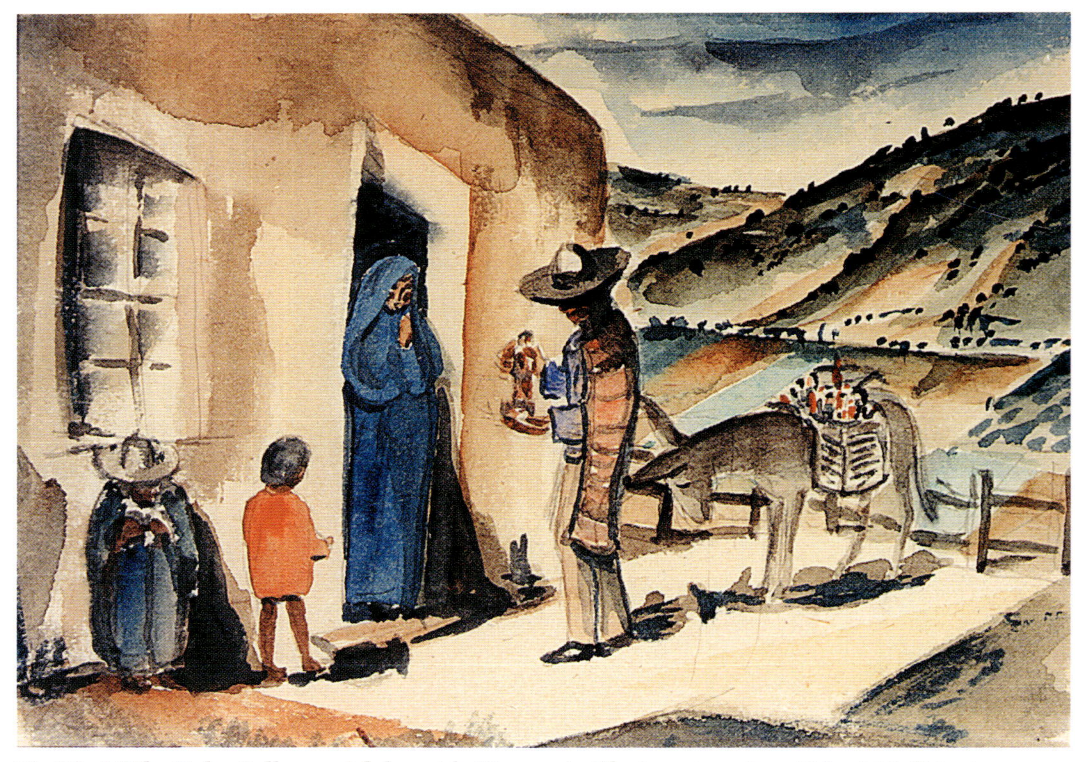

Untitled (*The Bulto Seller* or *Adobe with Woman in Blue*), watercolor, 6" by 8 ¾". Private collection. Photograph courtesy of Gerald Peters Gallery, Santa Fe.

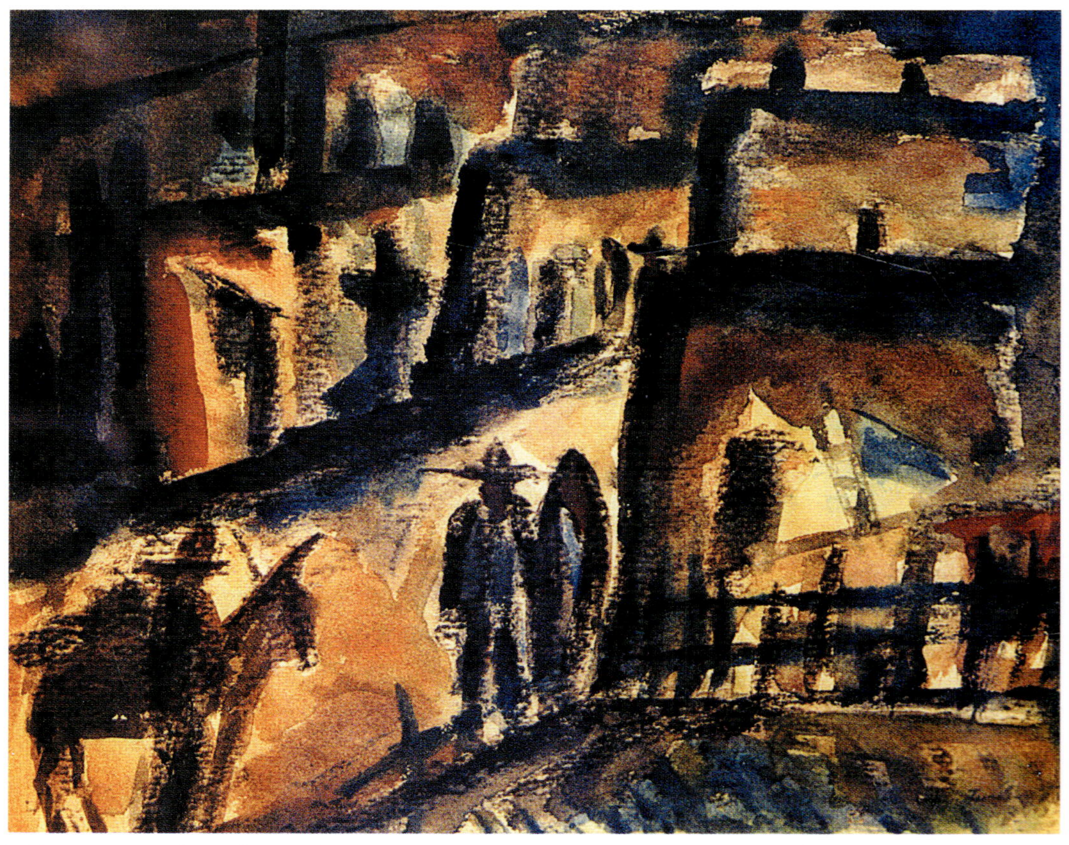

Village, watercolor, 8" by 10". Private collection. Photograph courtesy of the owner.

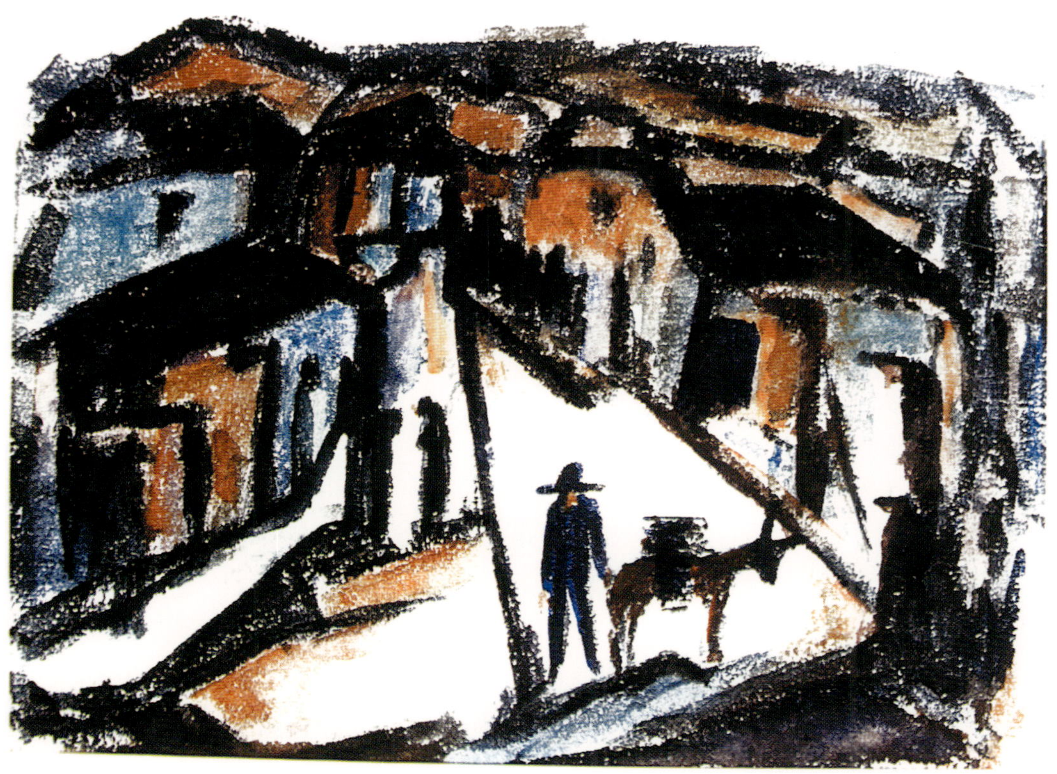

Santa Fe Evening, watercolor, 9 ¼" by 12 ¾". Private collection. Photograph courtesy of Gerald Peters Gallery, Santa Fe.

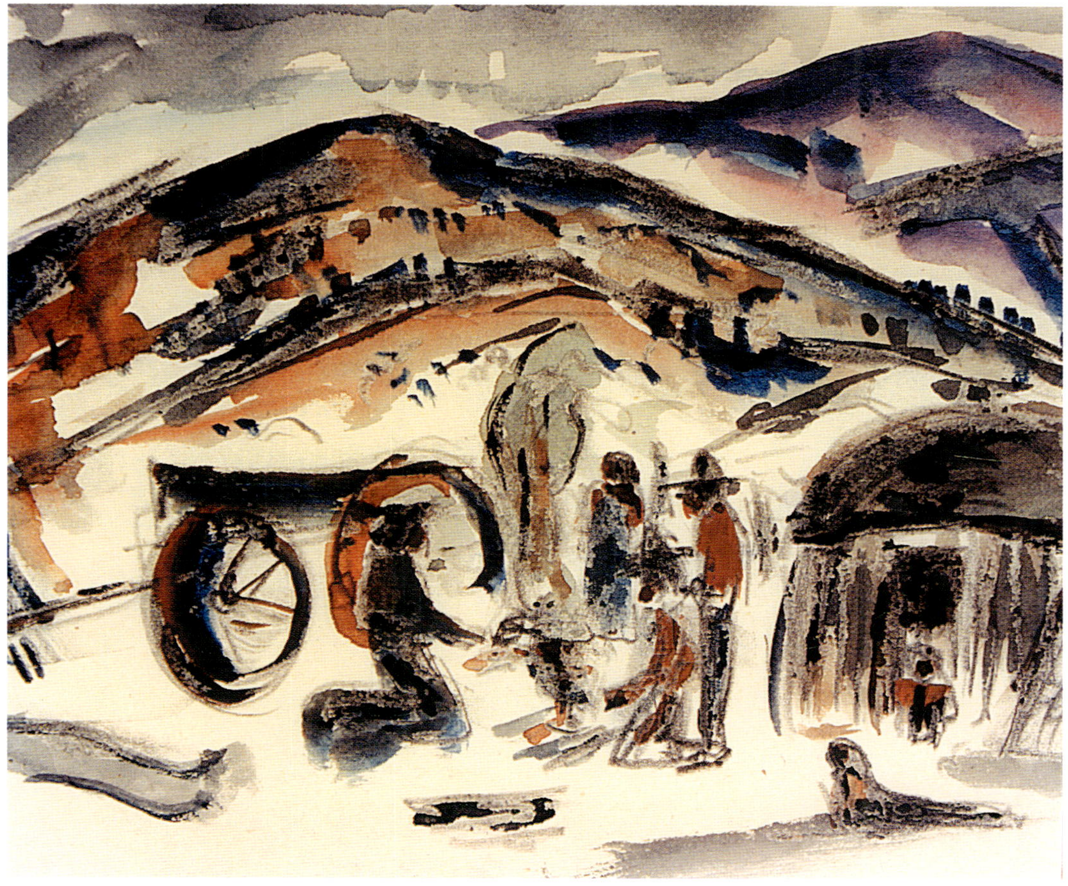

Untitled, watercolor, 6 ¾" by 8 ¼". Collection of Gerald Peters Gallery. Photograph courtesy of Gerald Peters Gallery, Santa Fe.

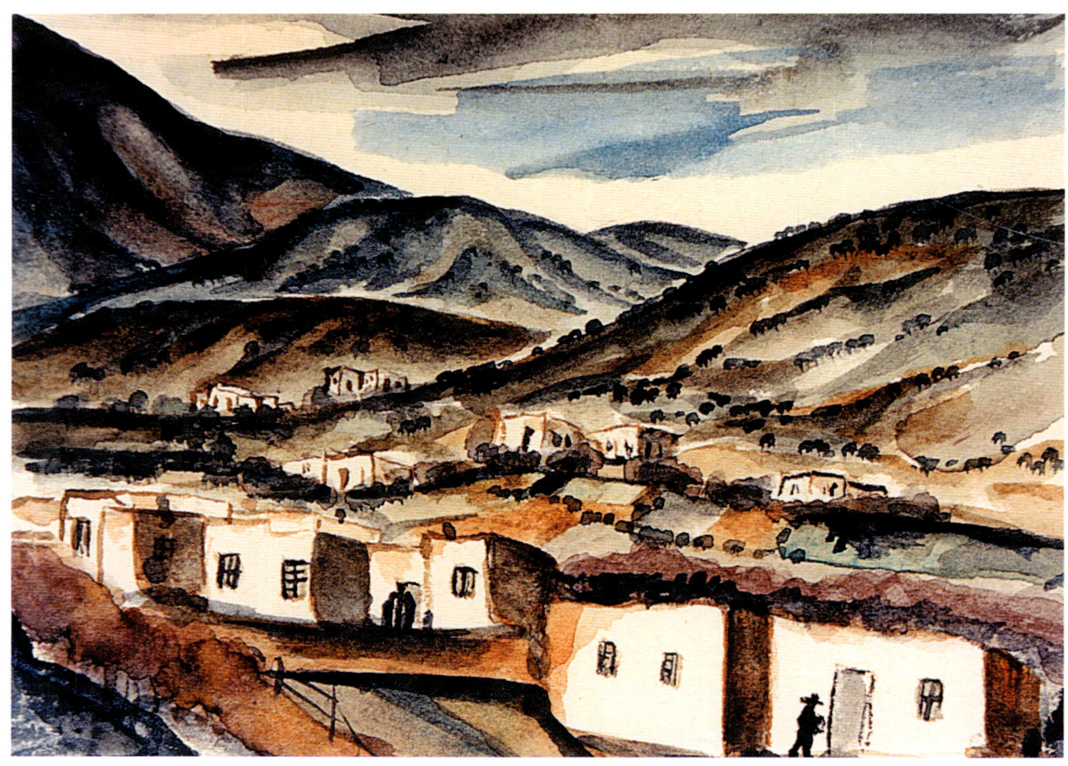

Untitled (*Adobe Landscape*), watercolor, 6" by 8¾". Private collection. Photograph courtesy of Gerald Peters Gallery, Santa Fe.

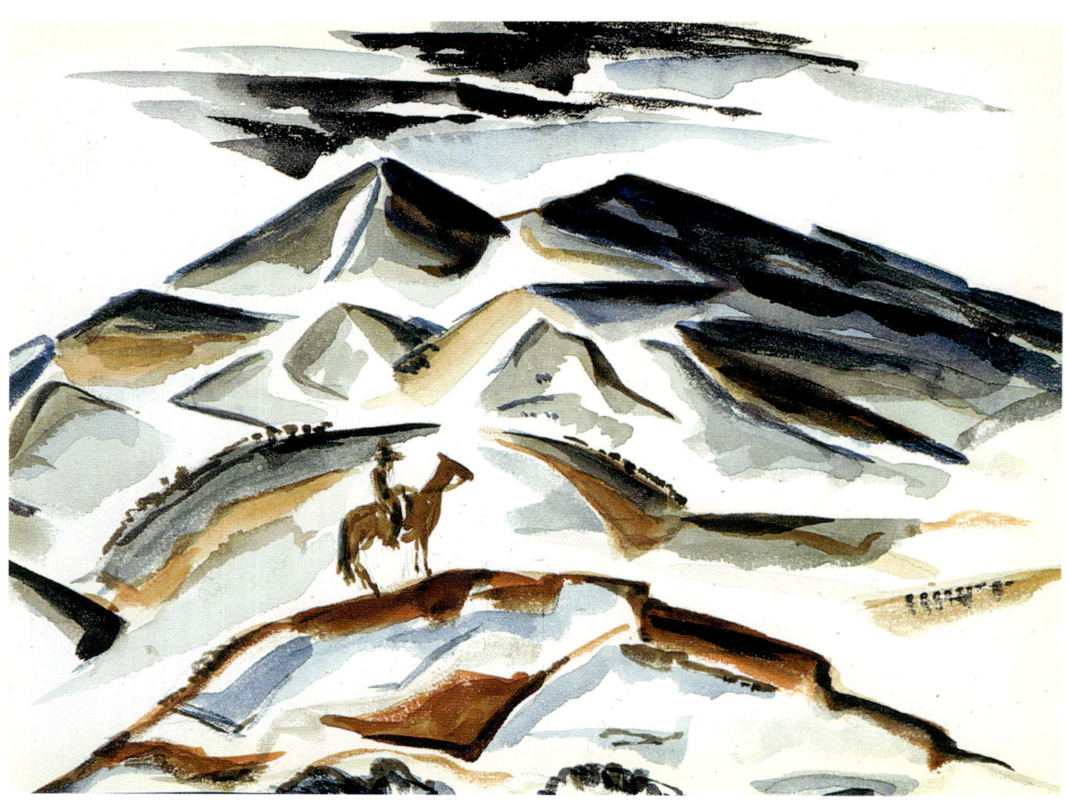

El Navajo, watercolor, approximately 8" by 10". Private collection. Photograph courtesy of the owner.

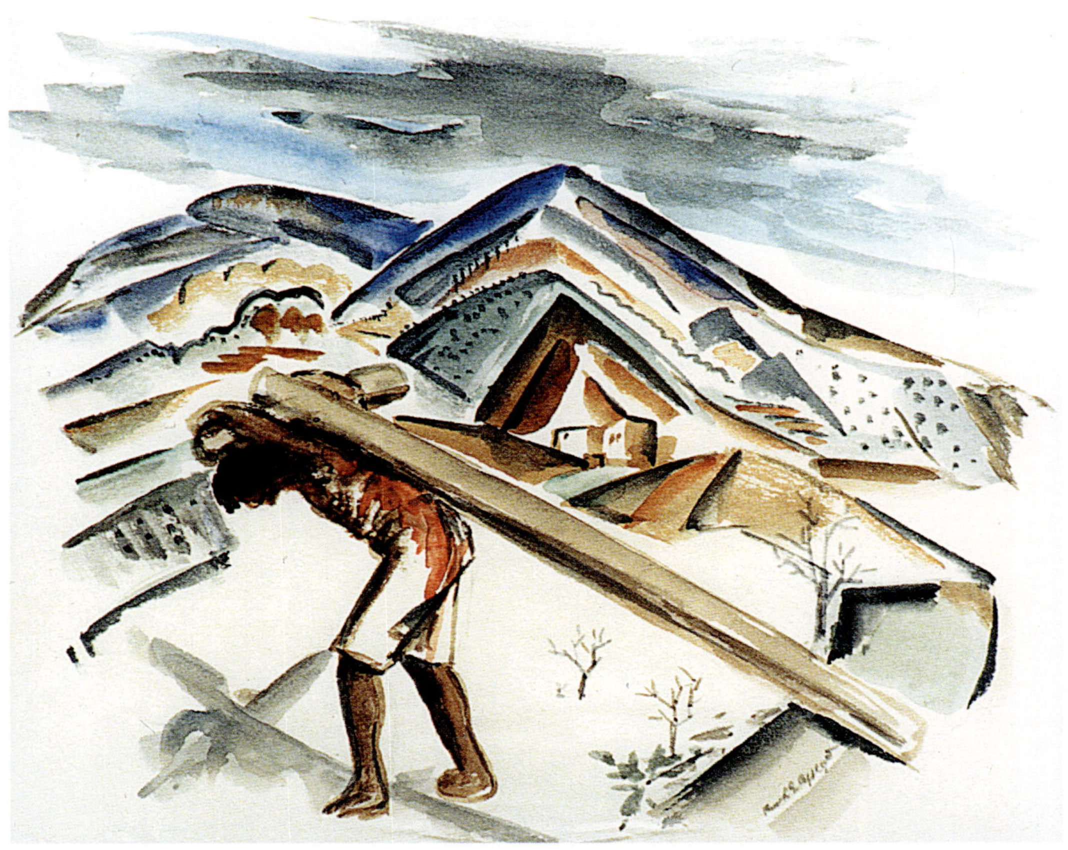

Untitled (*Penitente/Cross*), watercolor, 8 ¾" by 11 ½". Private collection. Photograph courtesy of Gerald Peters Gallery, Santa Fe.

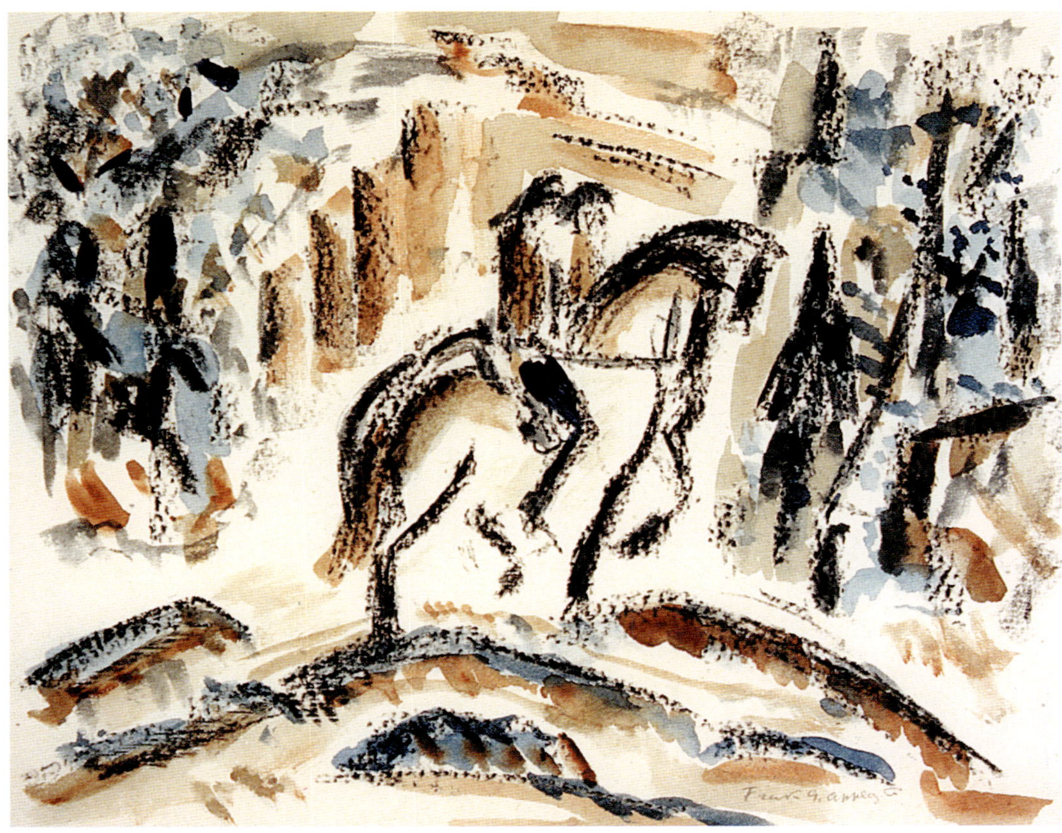

Two Horsemen, watercolor, 8" by 10 ½". Private collection. Photograph courtesy of Gerald Peters Gallery, Santa Fe.

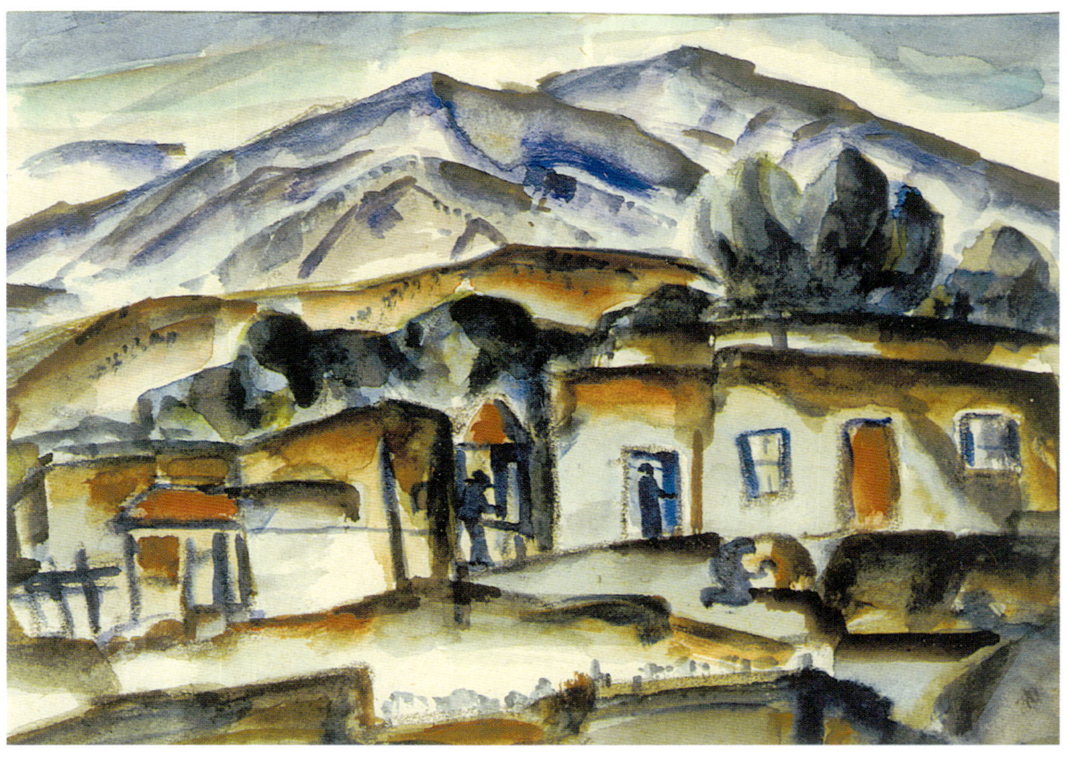

Untitled, watercolor, size unknown. Private collection. Photograph courtesy of the owner.

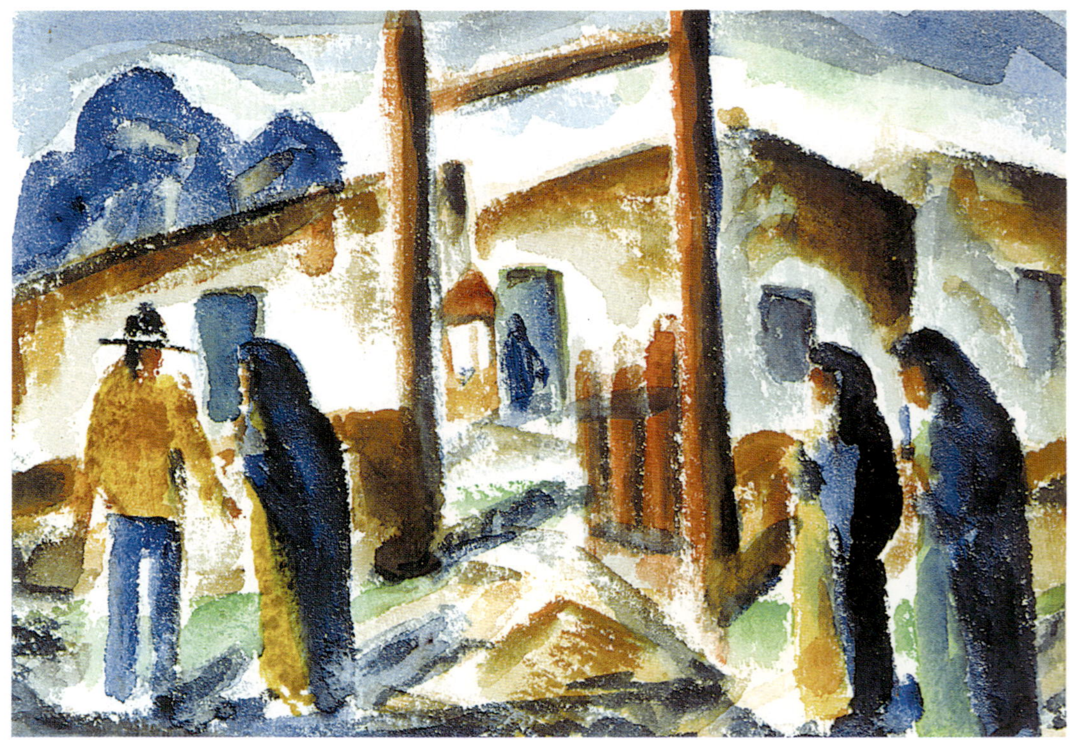

Untitled, watercolor, size unknown. Private collection. Photograph courtesy of the owner.

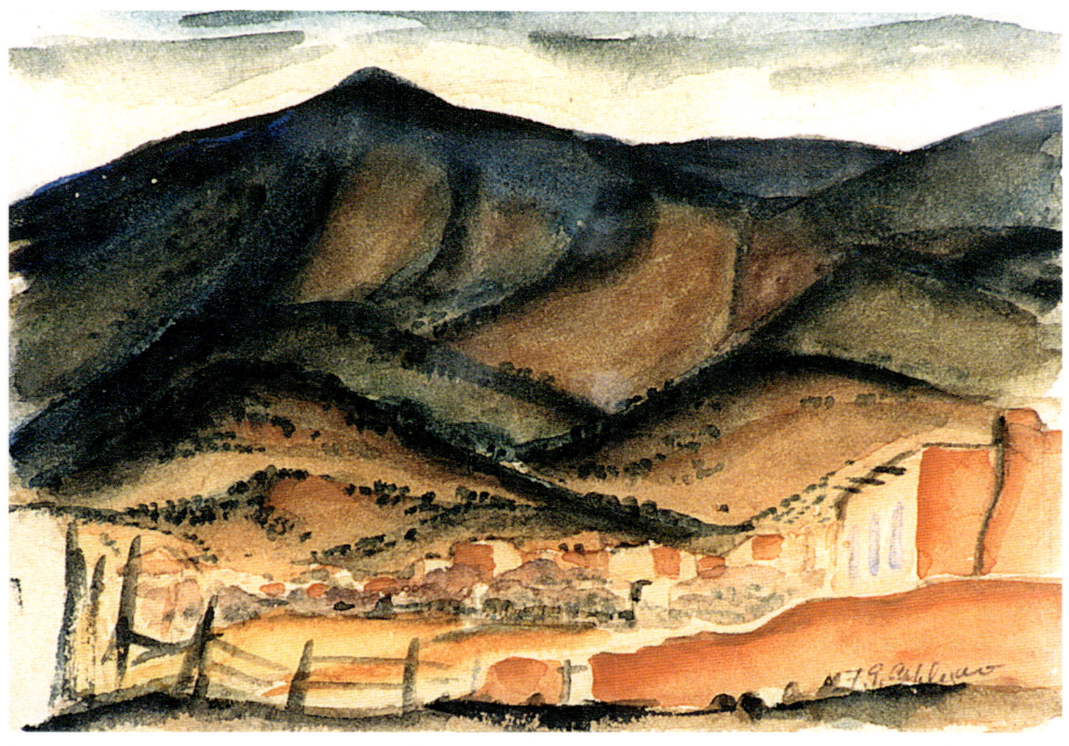

Los Lomas, watercolor, 5¾" by 8½". Private collection. Photograph courtesy of Gerald Peters Gallery, Santa Fe.

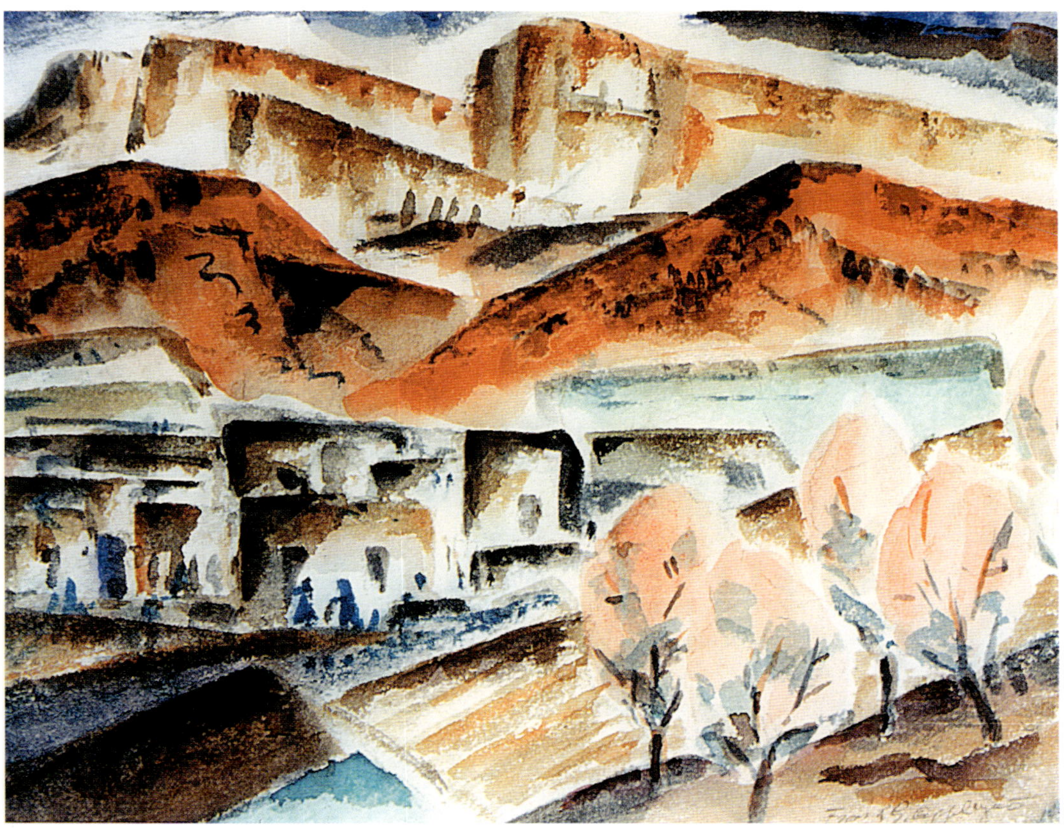

Untitled (*Village/Orchard*), watercolor, 6¼" by 8¼". Private collection. Photograph courtesy of Gerald Peters Gallery, Santa Fe.

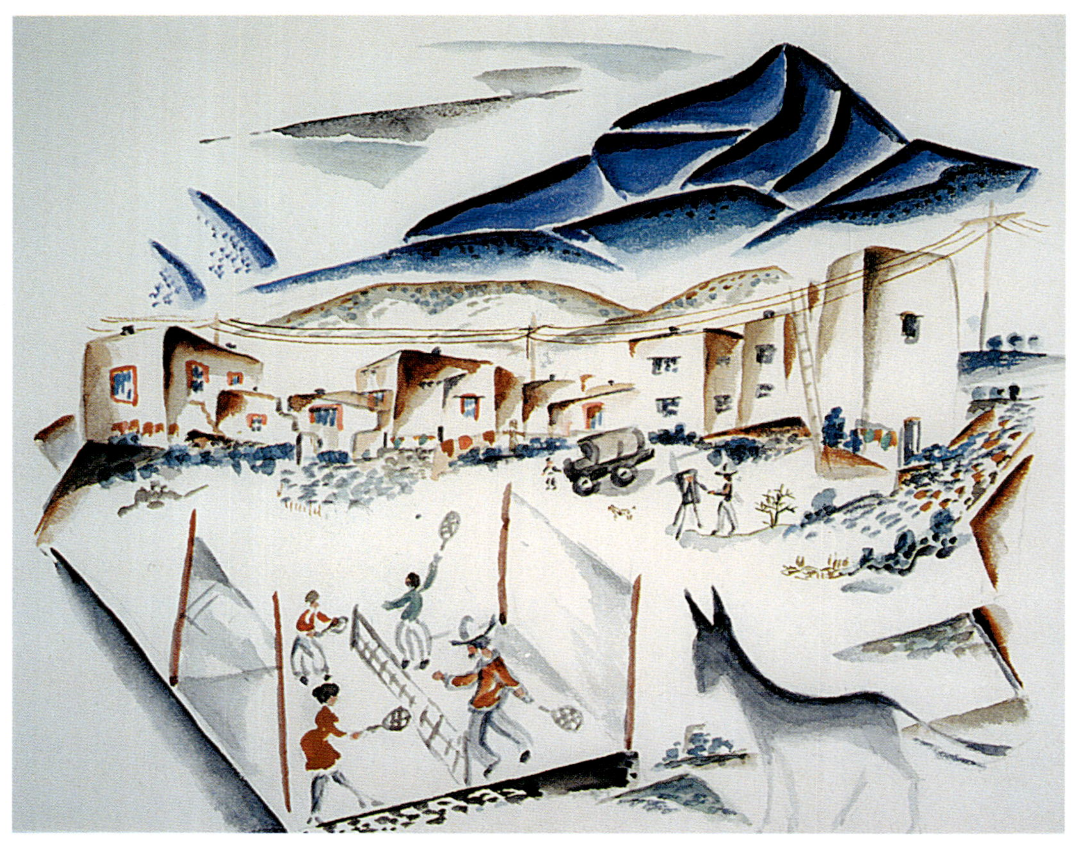

Untitled (*El Camino del Monte Sol*), watercolor, 8½" by 11½". Private collection. Photograph courtesy of Gerald Peters Gallery, Santa Fe.

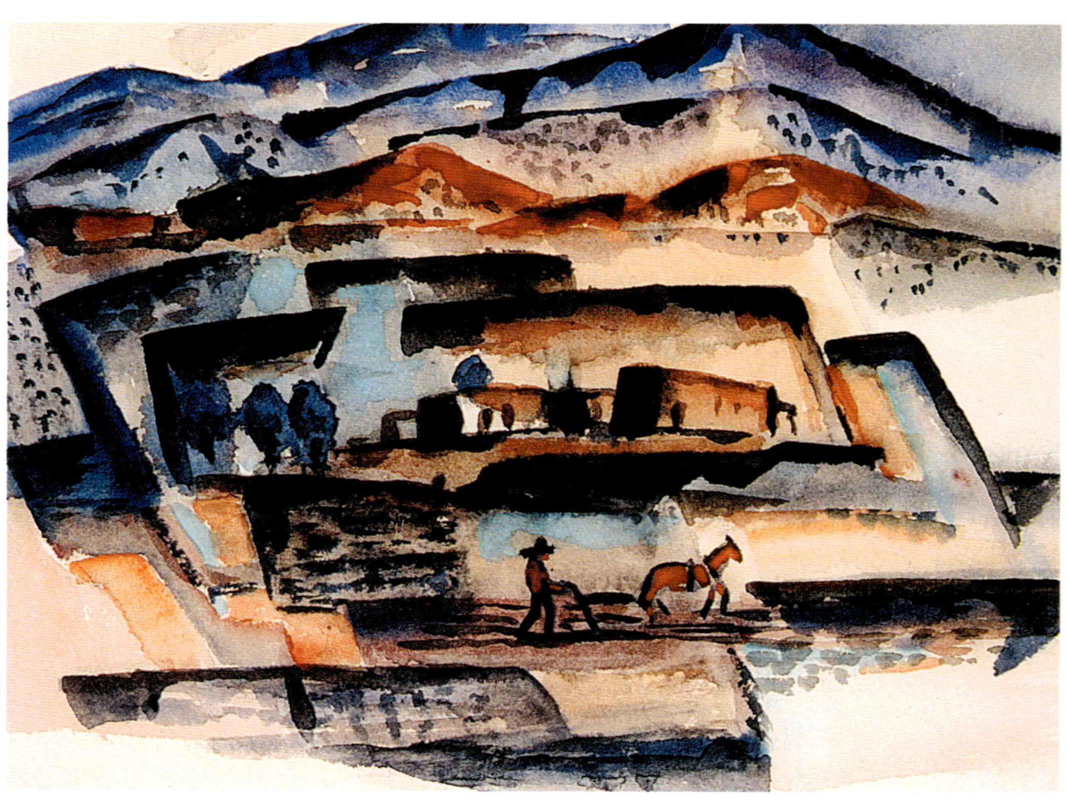

Man Plowing Fields, watercolor, 8" by 10¾". Private collection. Photograph courtesy of Gerald Peters Gallery, Santa Fe.

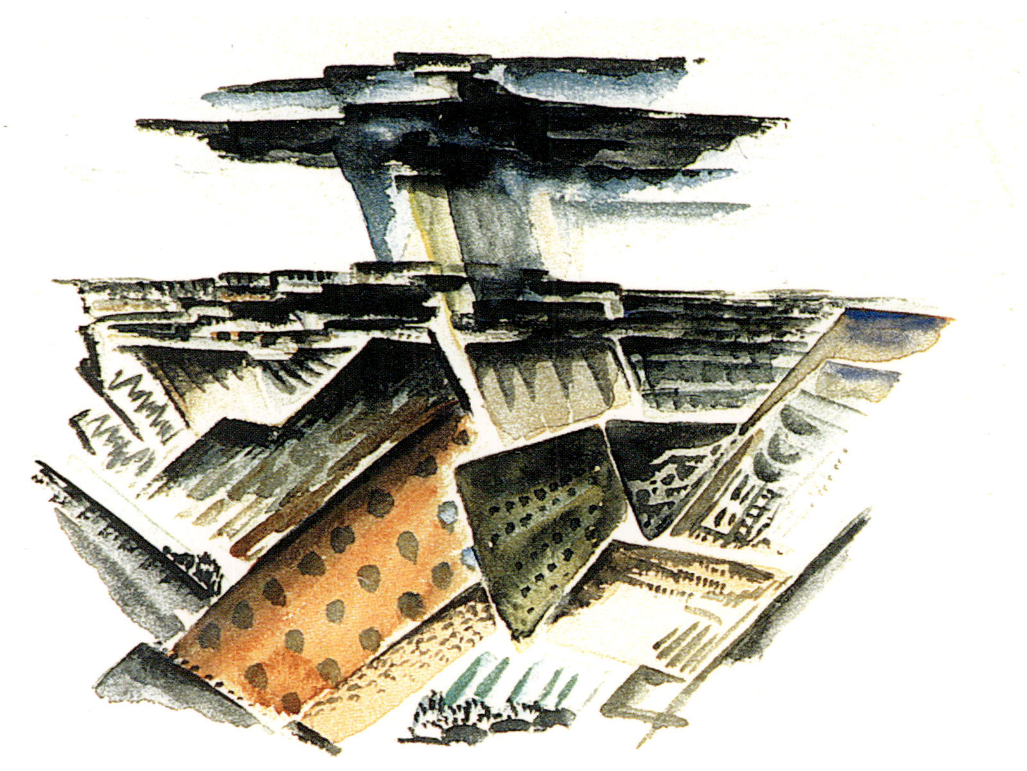

Rainstorm in Valley, watercolor, 8½" by 11". Private collection. Photograph courtesy of Gerald Peters Gallery, Santa Fe.

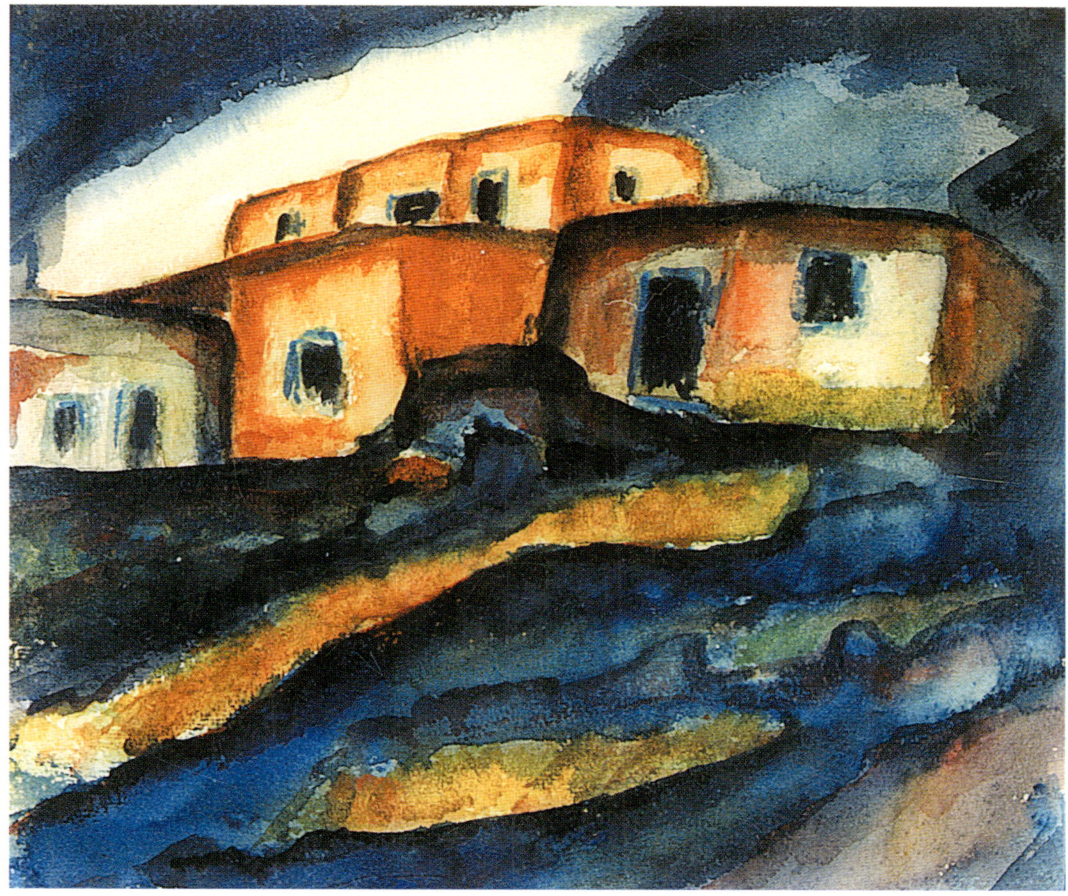

Adobes at Night, watercolor, 9¼" by 11¼". Private collection. Photograph courtesy of Gerald Peters Gallery, Santa Fe.

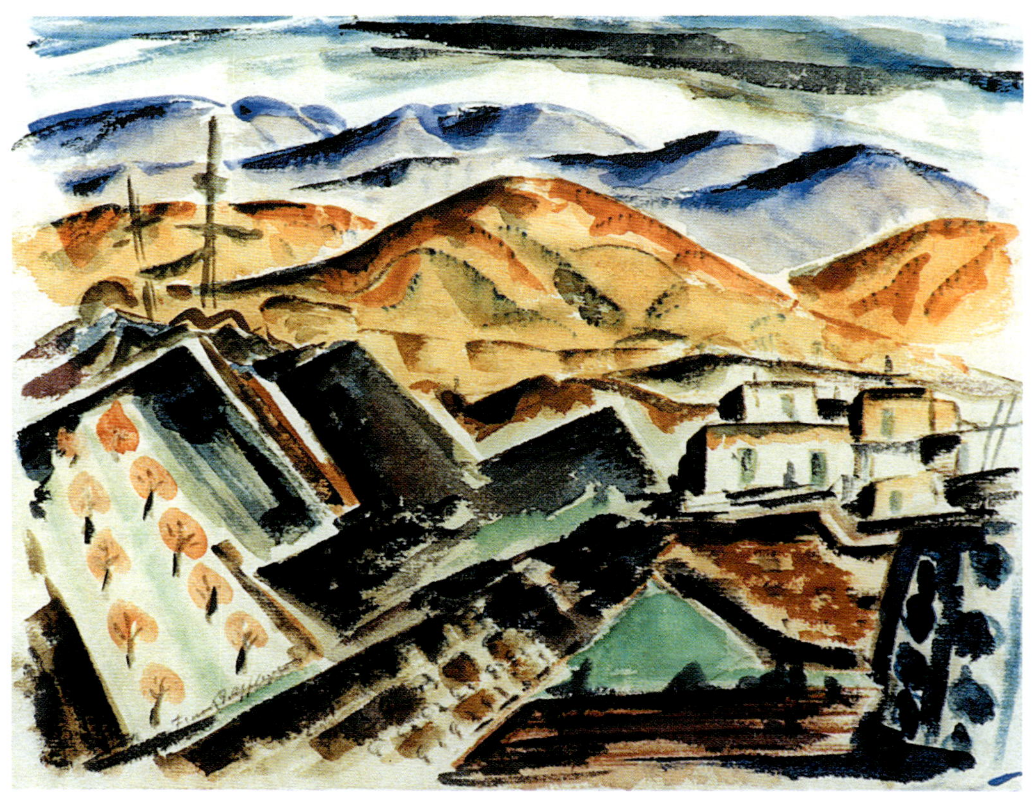

Red Trees, watercolor, 8¾" by 11½". Private collection. Photograph courtesy of Gerald Peters Gallery, Santa Fe.

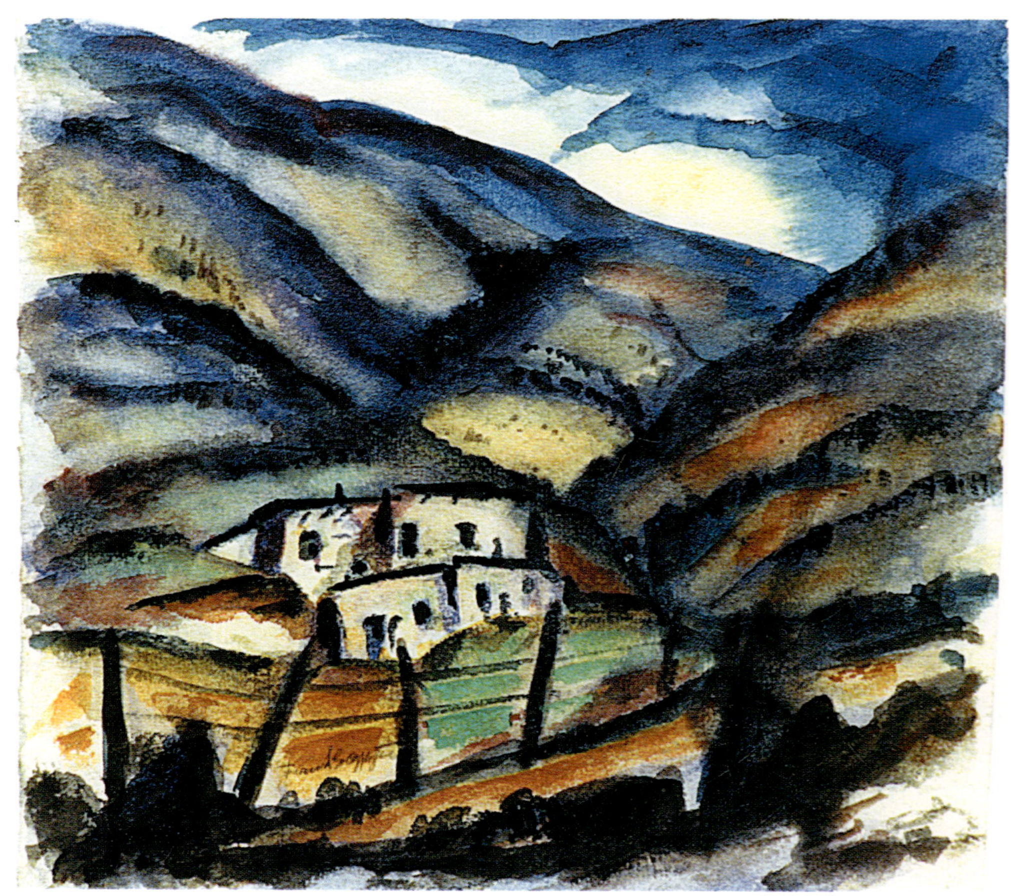

Houses Behind Fence, watercolor, 8½" by 9¼". Private collection. Photograph courtesy of Gerald Peters Gallery, Santa Fe.

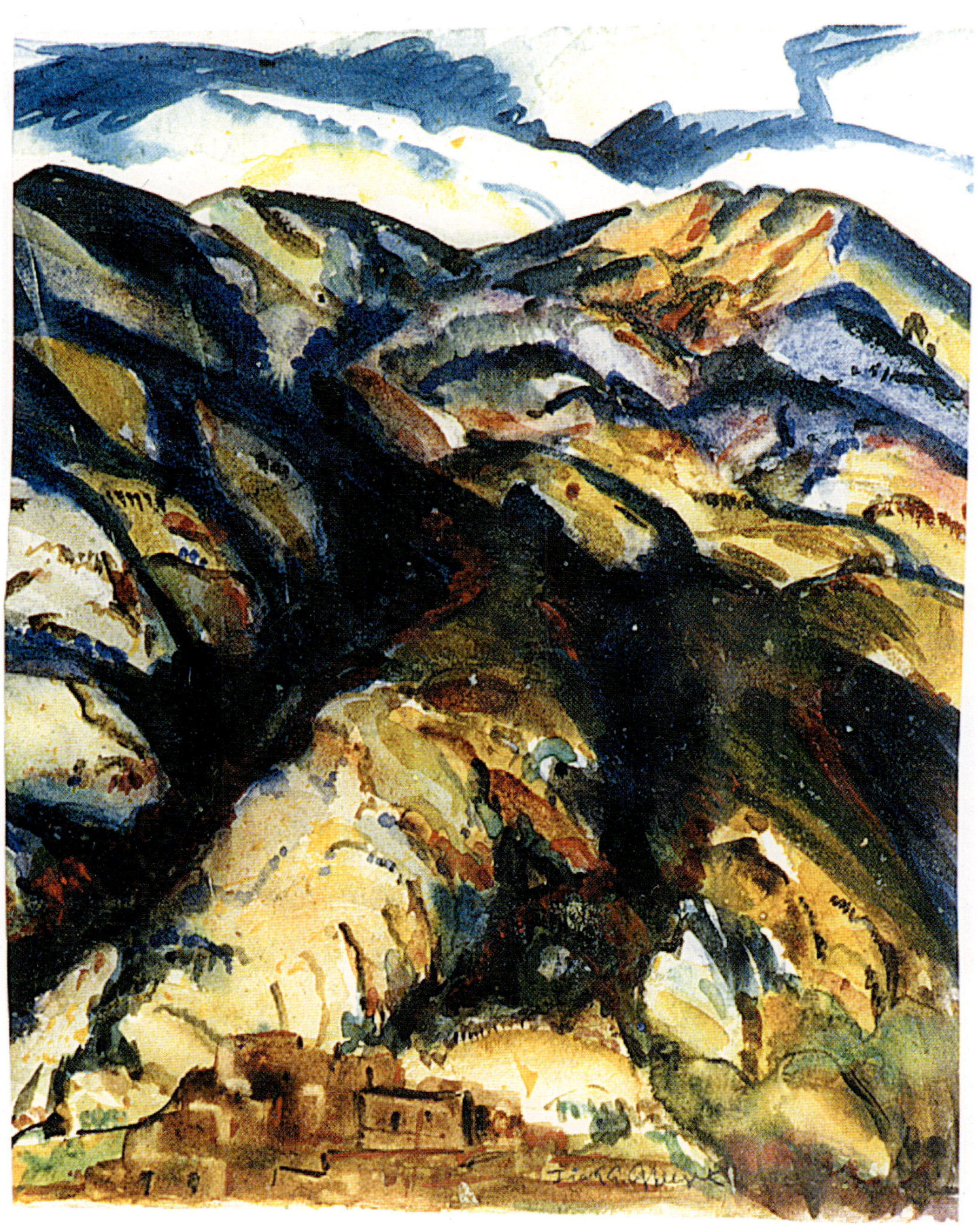

Village in Valley, watercolor, 11" by 9¼". Private collection. Photograph courtesy of Gerald Peters Gallery, Santa Fe.

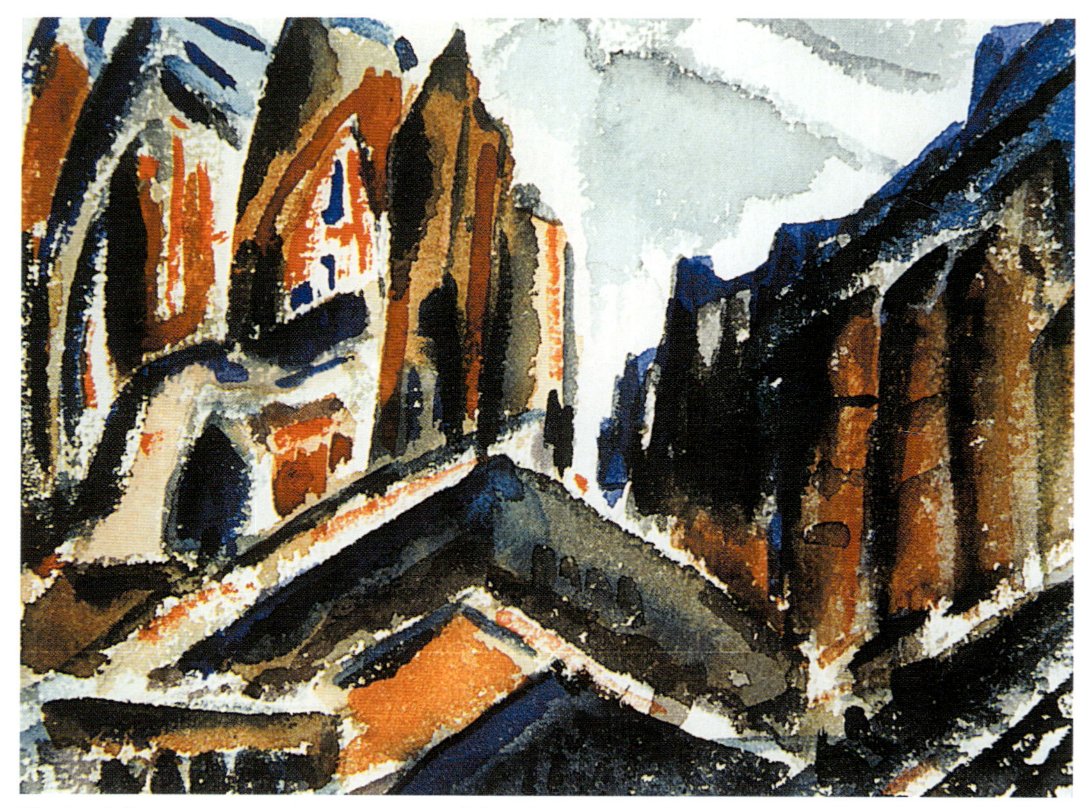

Untitled (*Mountainscape*), watercolor, 5" by 7". Private collection. Photograph courtesy of Gerald Peters Gallery, Santa Fe.

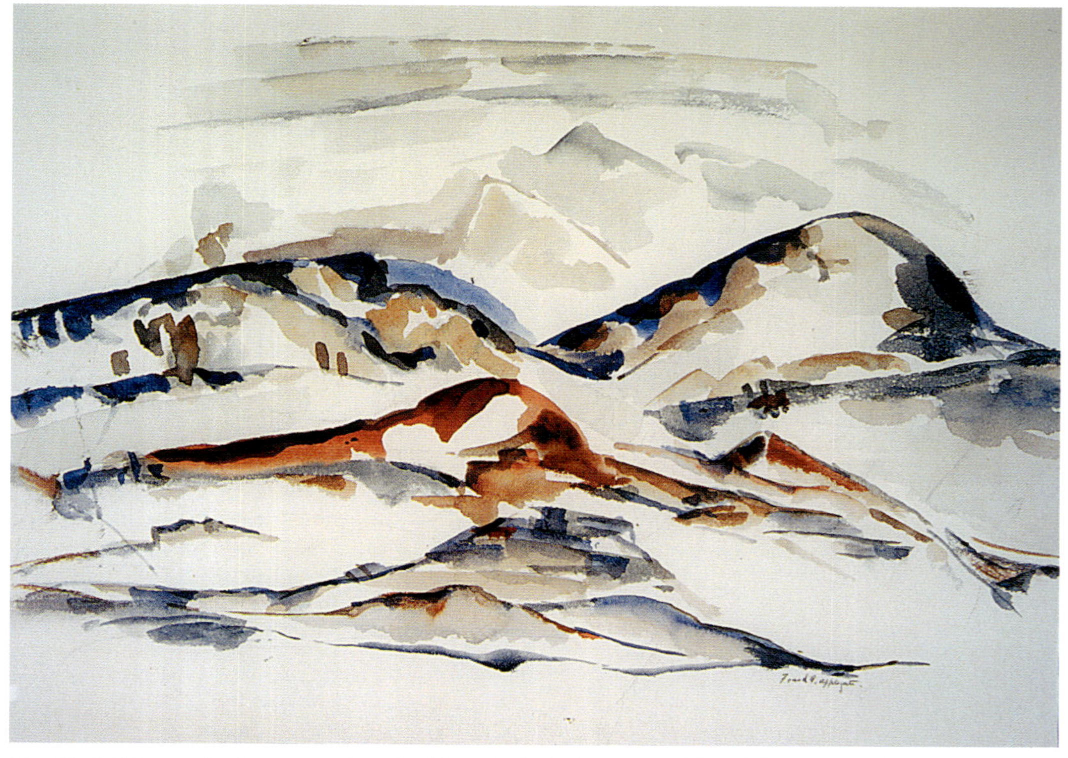

Untitled (*Mountains*), watercolor, 9½" by 13½". Collection of Gerald Peters Gallery. Photograph courtesy of Gerald Peters Gallery, Santa Fe.

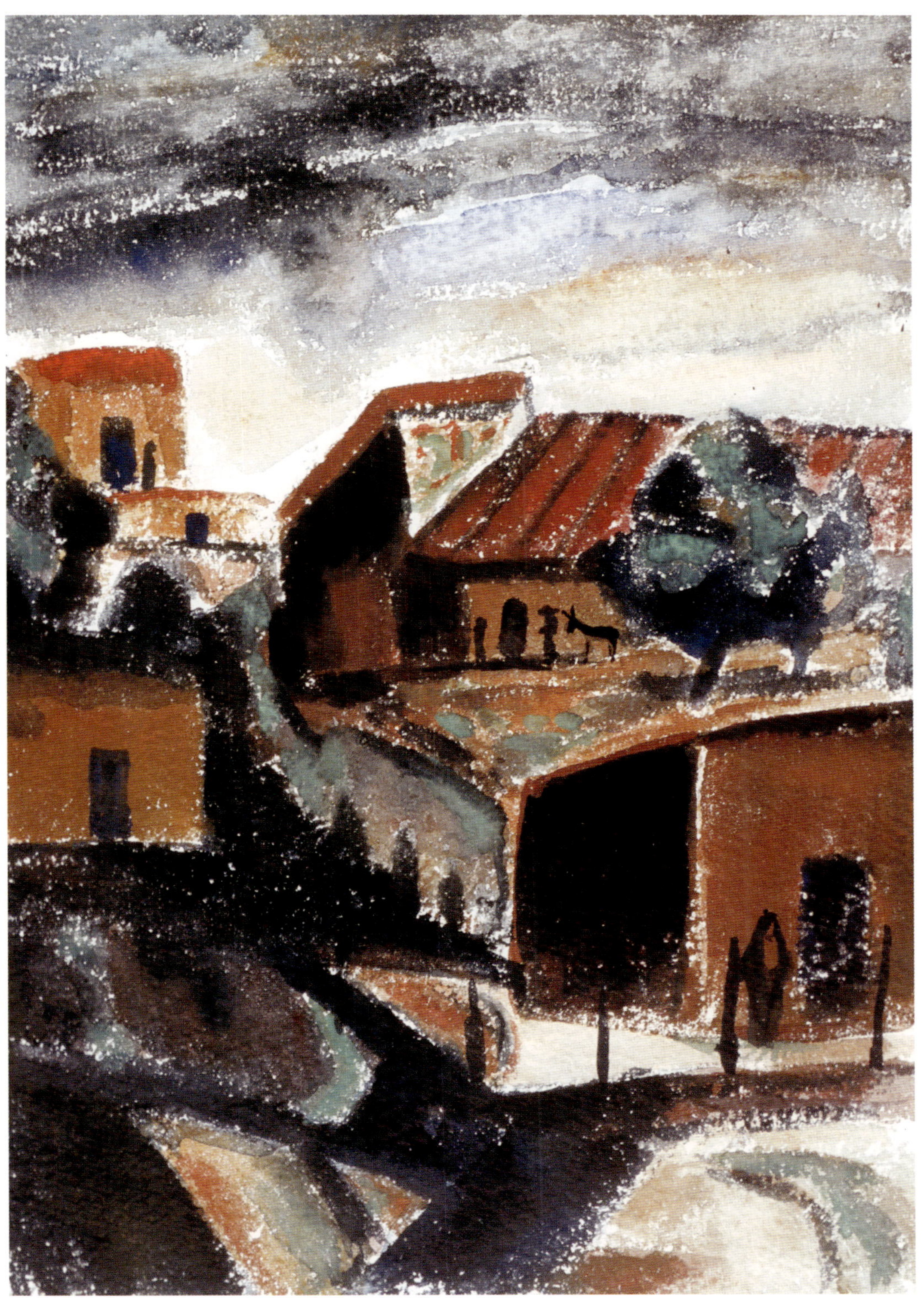

Street Scene, watercolor, 13" by 9½". Private collection. Photograph courtesy of the owner.

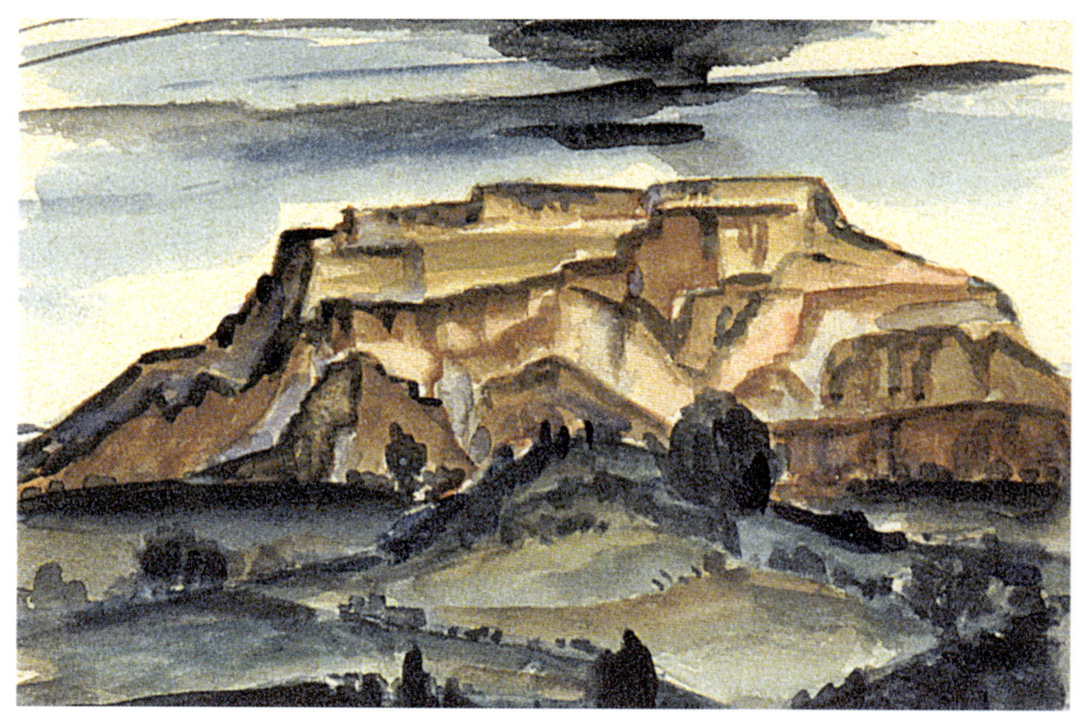

Untitled, watercolor, 5½" by 8½". Private collection. Photograph courtesy of the owner.

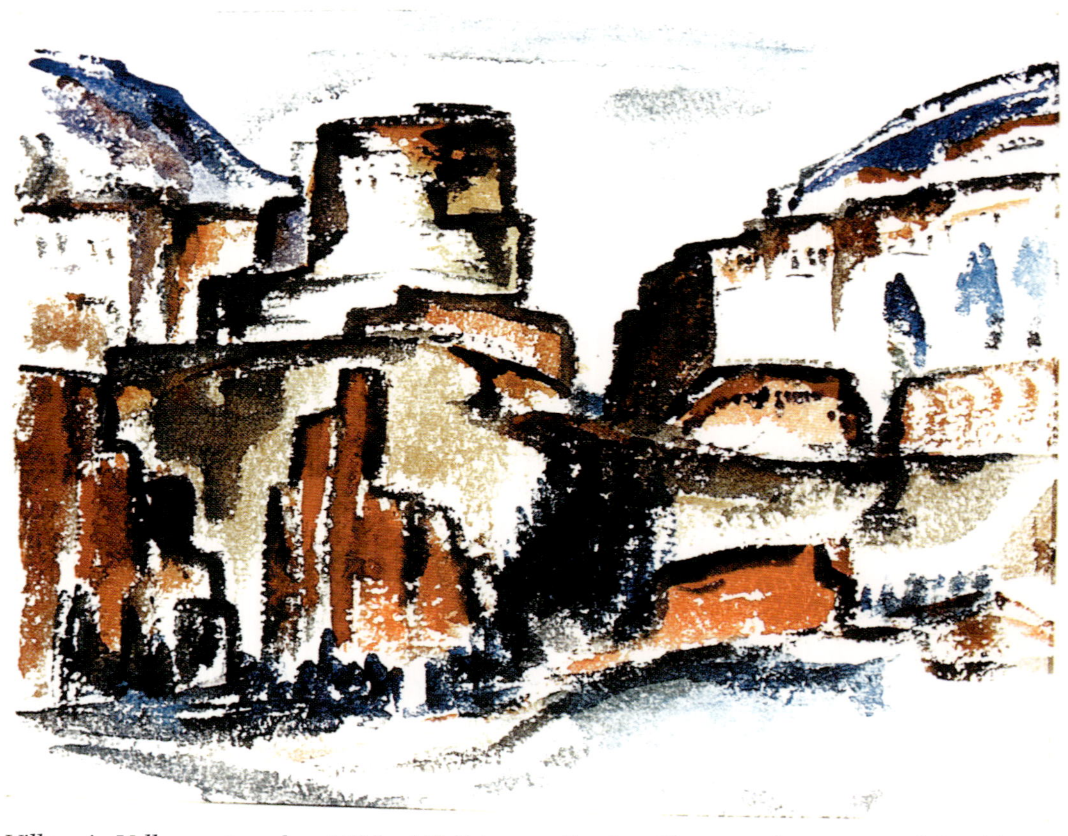

Village in Valley, watercolor, 9½" by 12". Private collection. Photograph courtesy of Gerald Peters Gallery, Santa Fe.

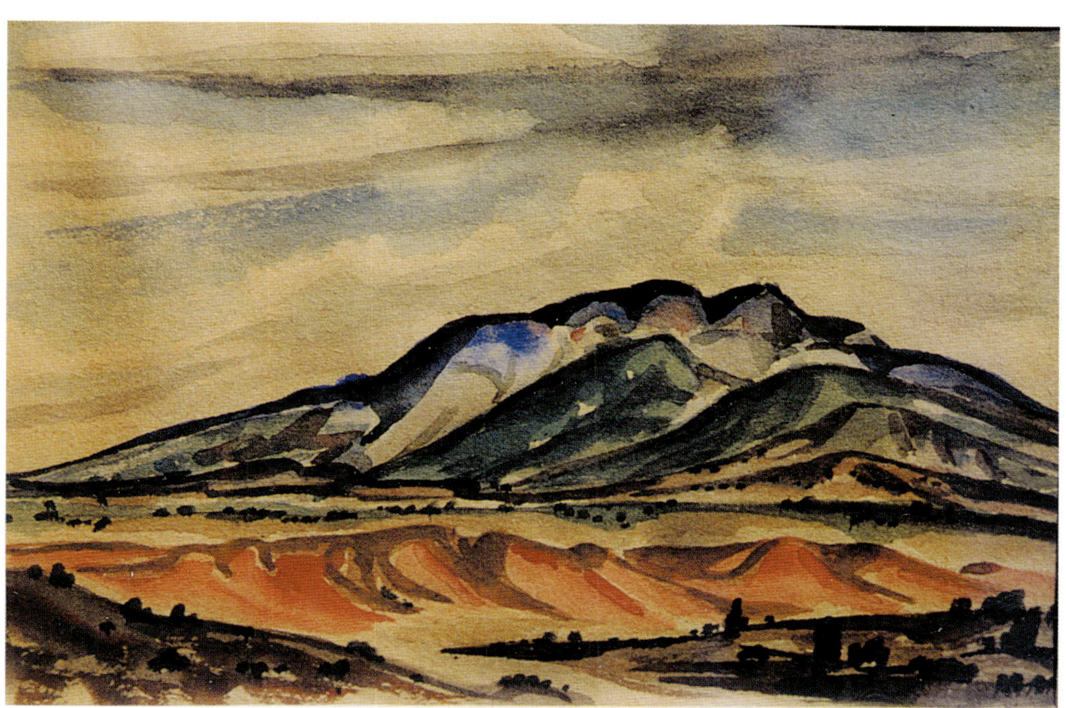

Mountain, watercolor, 5" by 8". Private collection. Photograph courtesy of the owner.

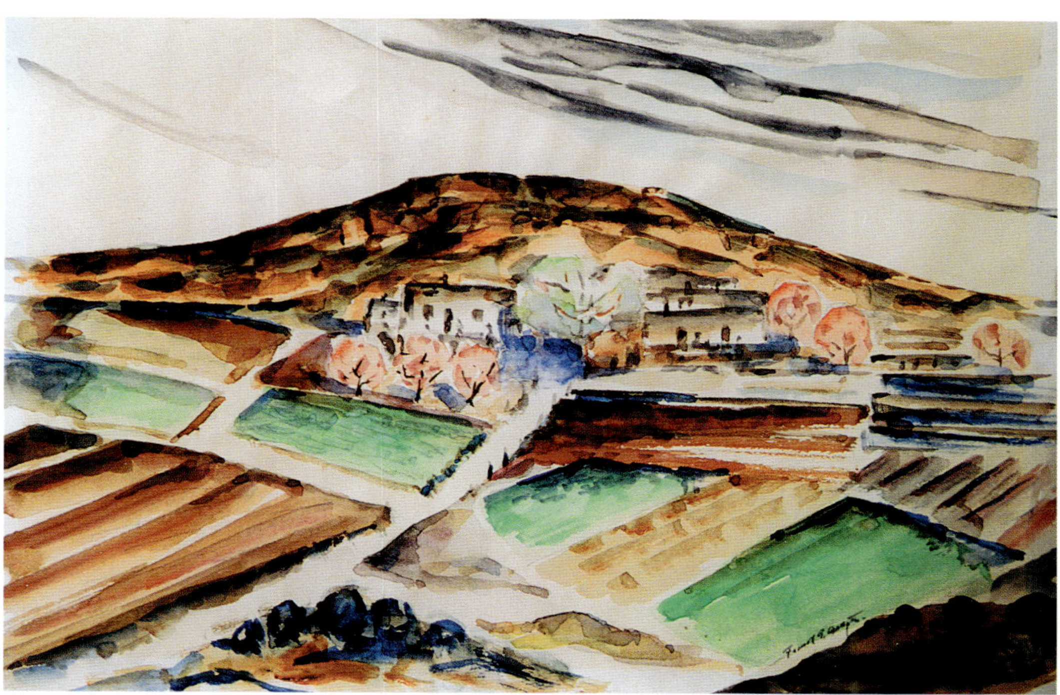

Fields, watercolor, 8½" by 11". Private collection. Photograph courtesy of the owner.

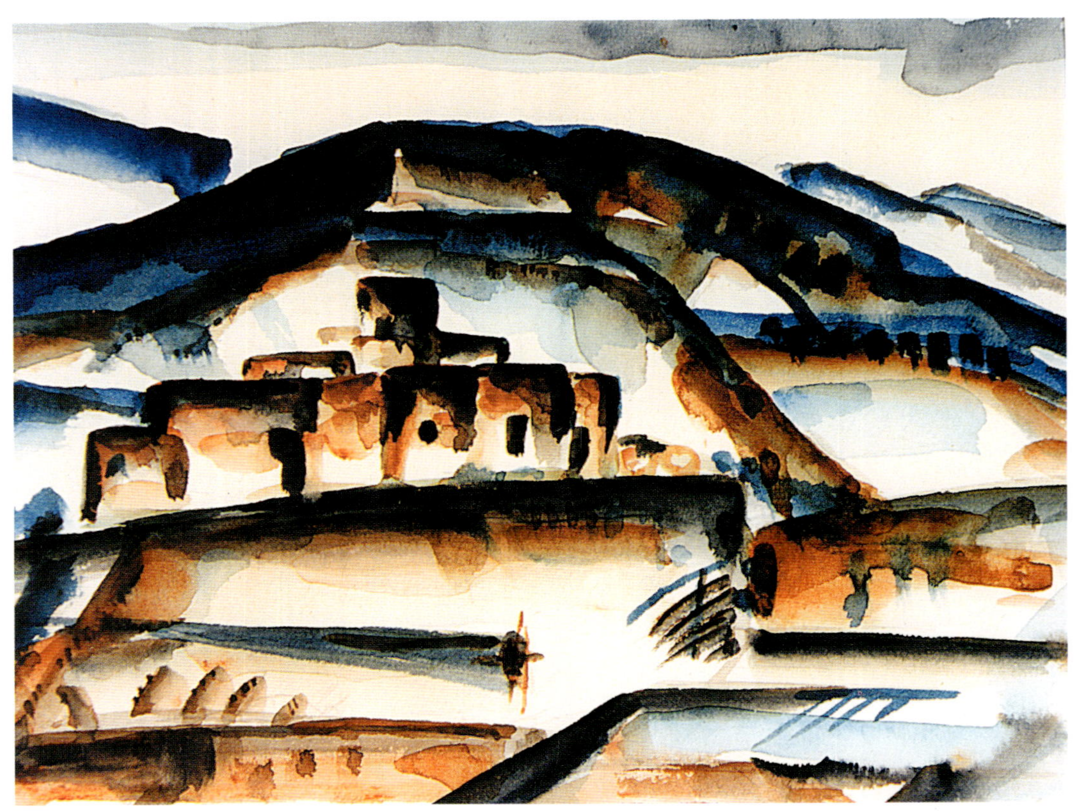

Untitled (*Village Blue/Brown*), watercolor, 6" by 8 ¾". University of New Mexico Fine Art Museum Collection. Photograph courtesy of Gerald Peters Gallery, Santa Fe.

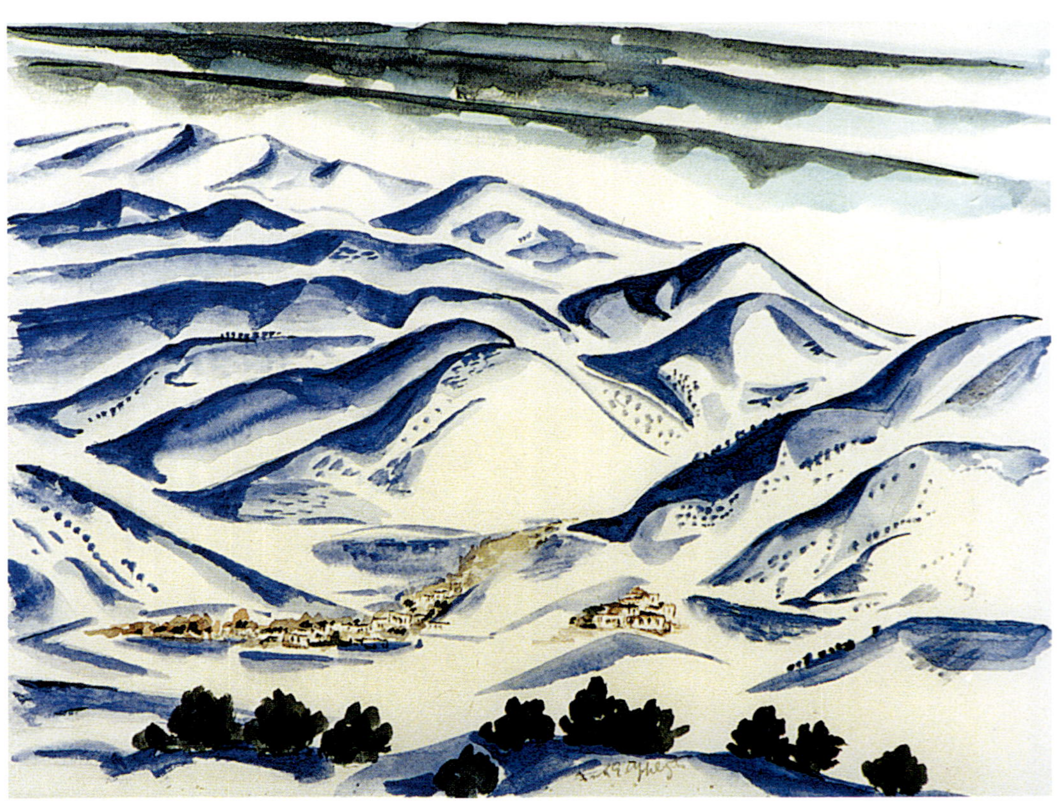

Across the Rio Grande, watercolor, 8 ¼" by 11 ½". Private collection. Photograph courtesy of Gerald Peters Gallery, Santa Fe.

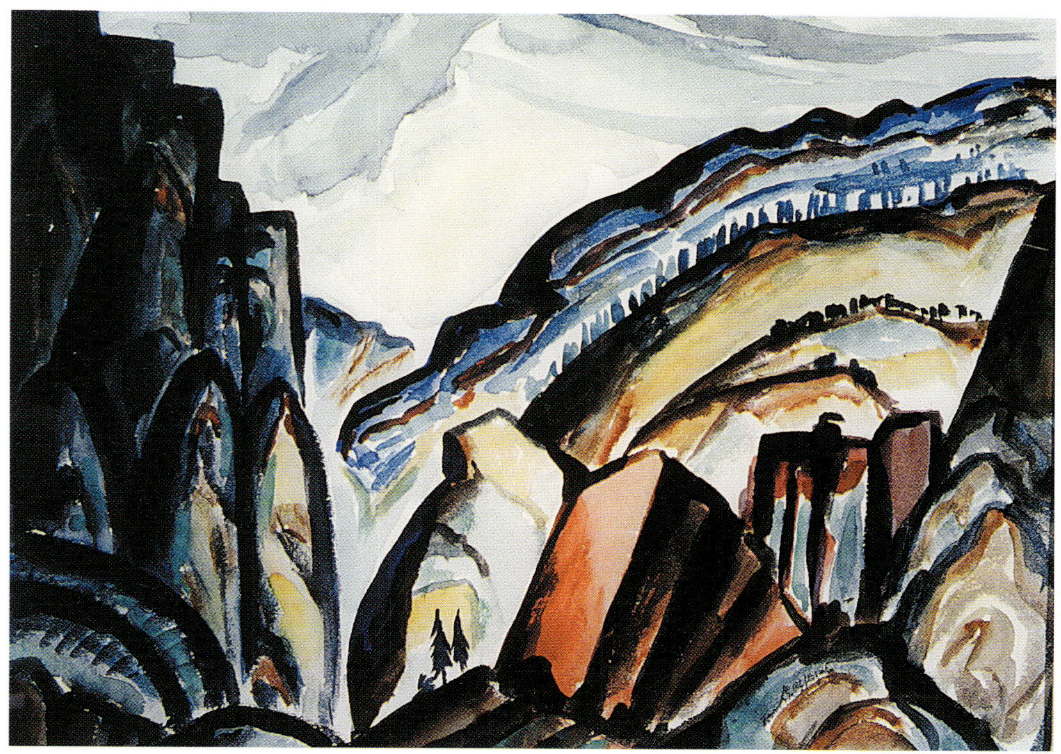

Untitled, watercolor, 9¾" by 13¾". Private collection. Photograph courtesy of Gerald Peters Gallery, Santa Fe.

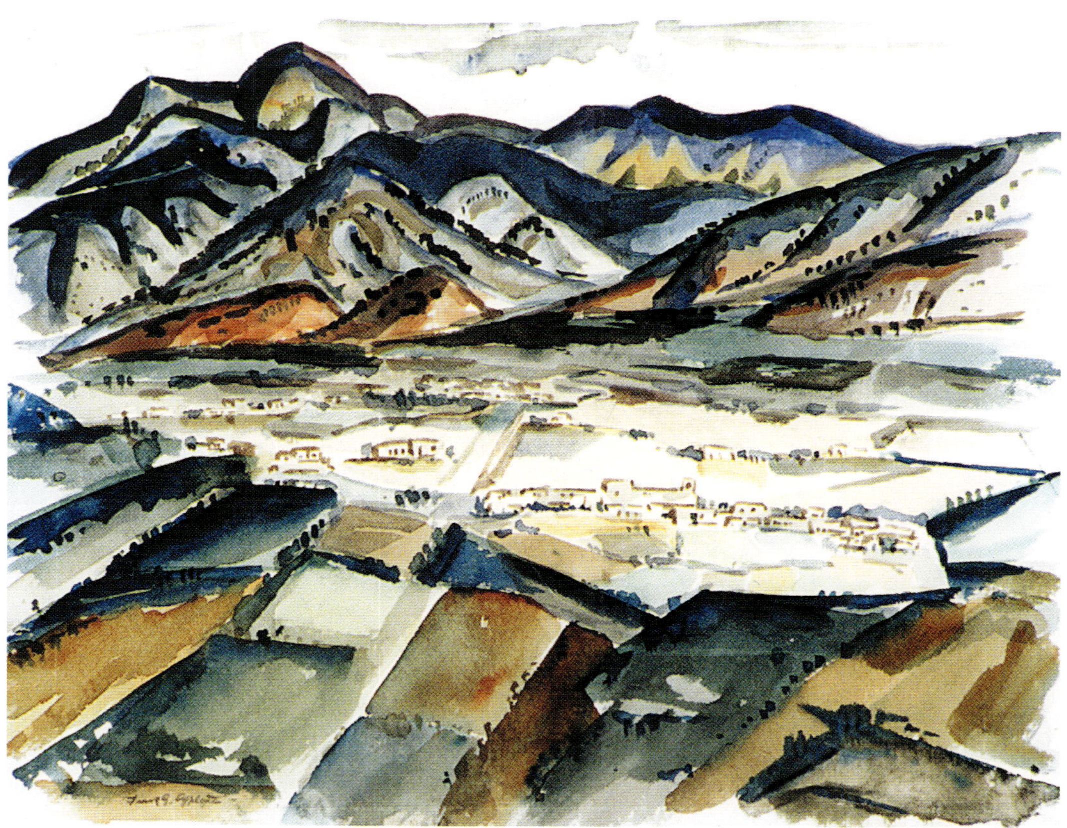

Navajo Country, N.M., watercolor, 8½" by 11½". Private collection. Photograph courtesy of Gerald Peters Gallery, Santa Fe.

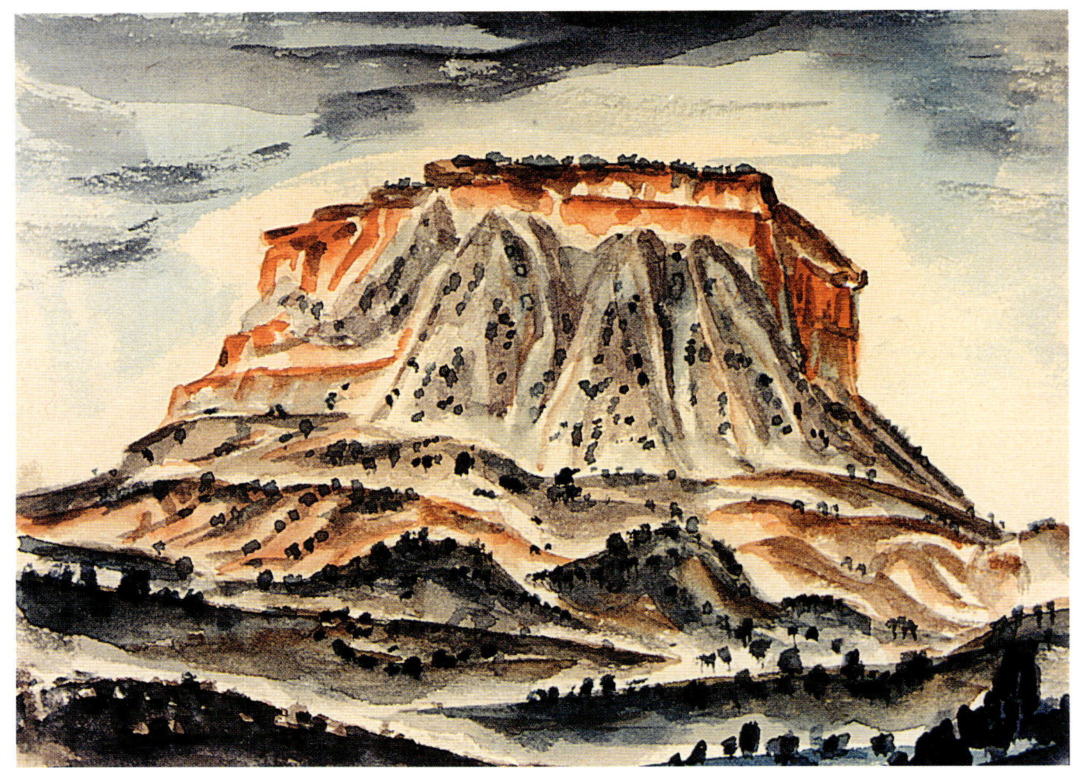

Untitled (*Mesa*), watercolor, 6" by 8¾". Private collection. Photograph courtesy of Gerald Peters Gallery, Santa Fe.

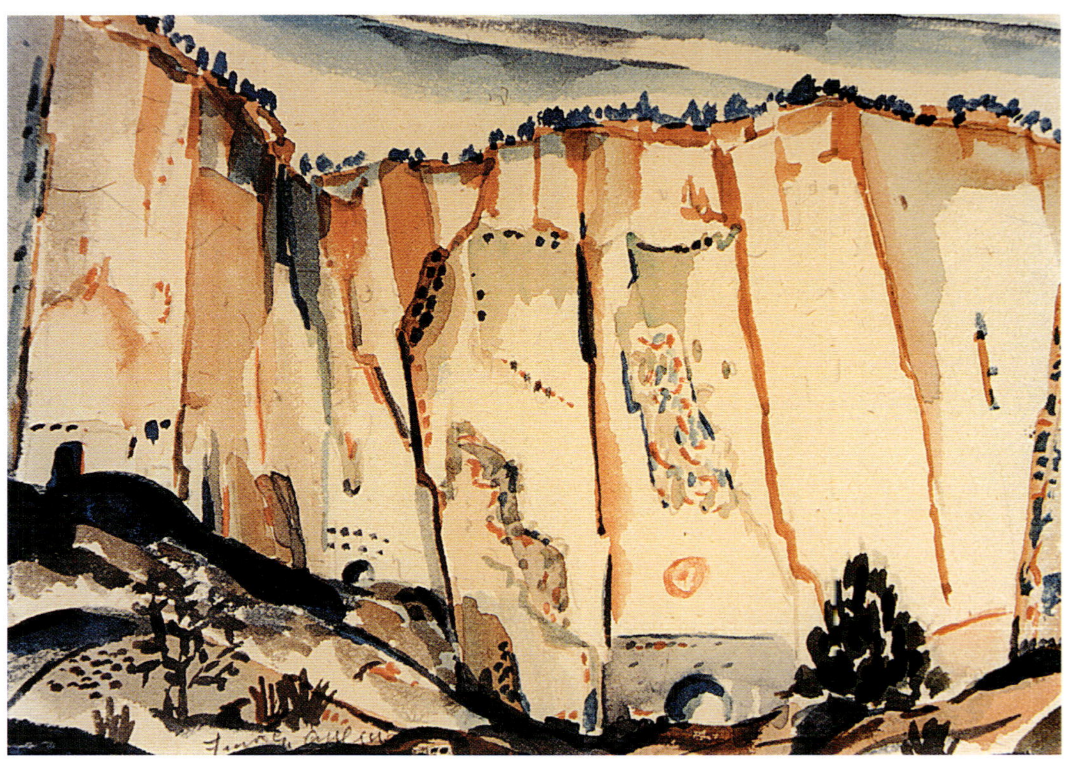

Untitled (*Cliff Dwelling*), watercolor, 5½" by 8¼". Private collection. Photograph courtesy of Gerald Peters Gallery, Santa Fe.

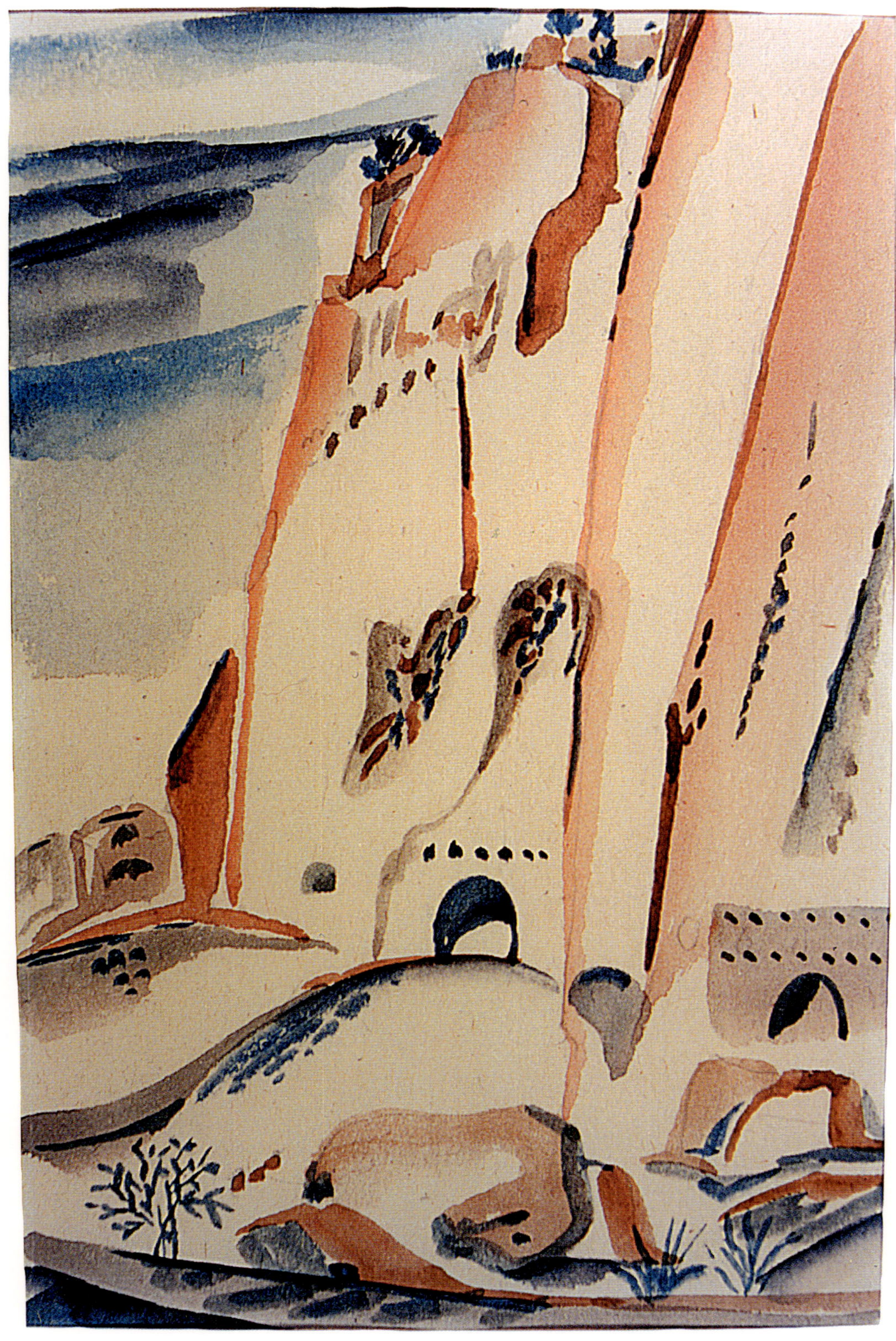

Untitled (*Cliff Dwelling*), watercolor, 8½" by 5¾". Private collection. Photograph courtesy of Gerald Peters Gallery, Santa Fe.

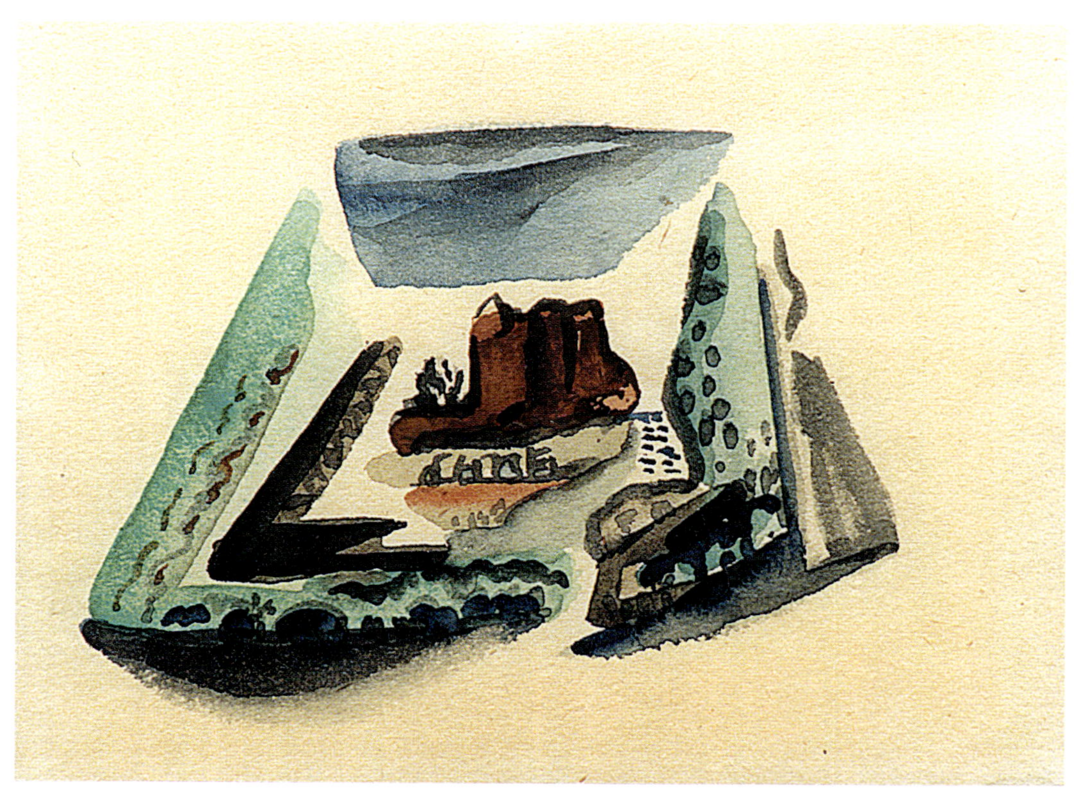

Untitled (*Landscape*), watercolor, 5¾" by 8⅜". The Karotkin Collection. Photograph courtesy of Gerald Peters Gallery, Santa Fe.

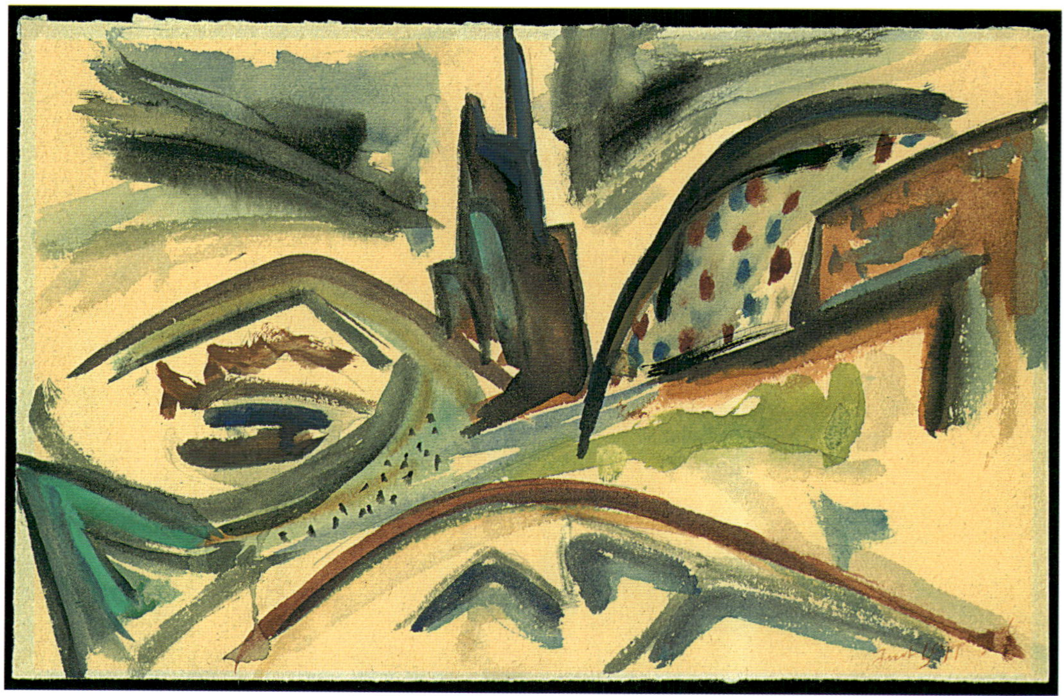

Northern New Mexico Landscape, watercolor, 6½" by 10½". Collection of Ken and Becky Phillips. Photograph courtesy of the owners.

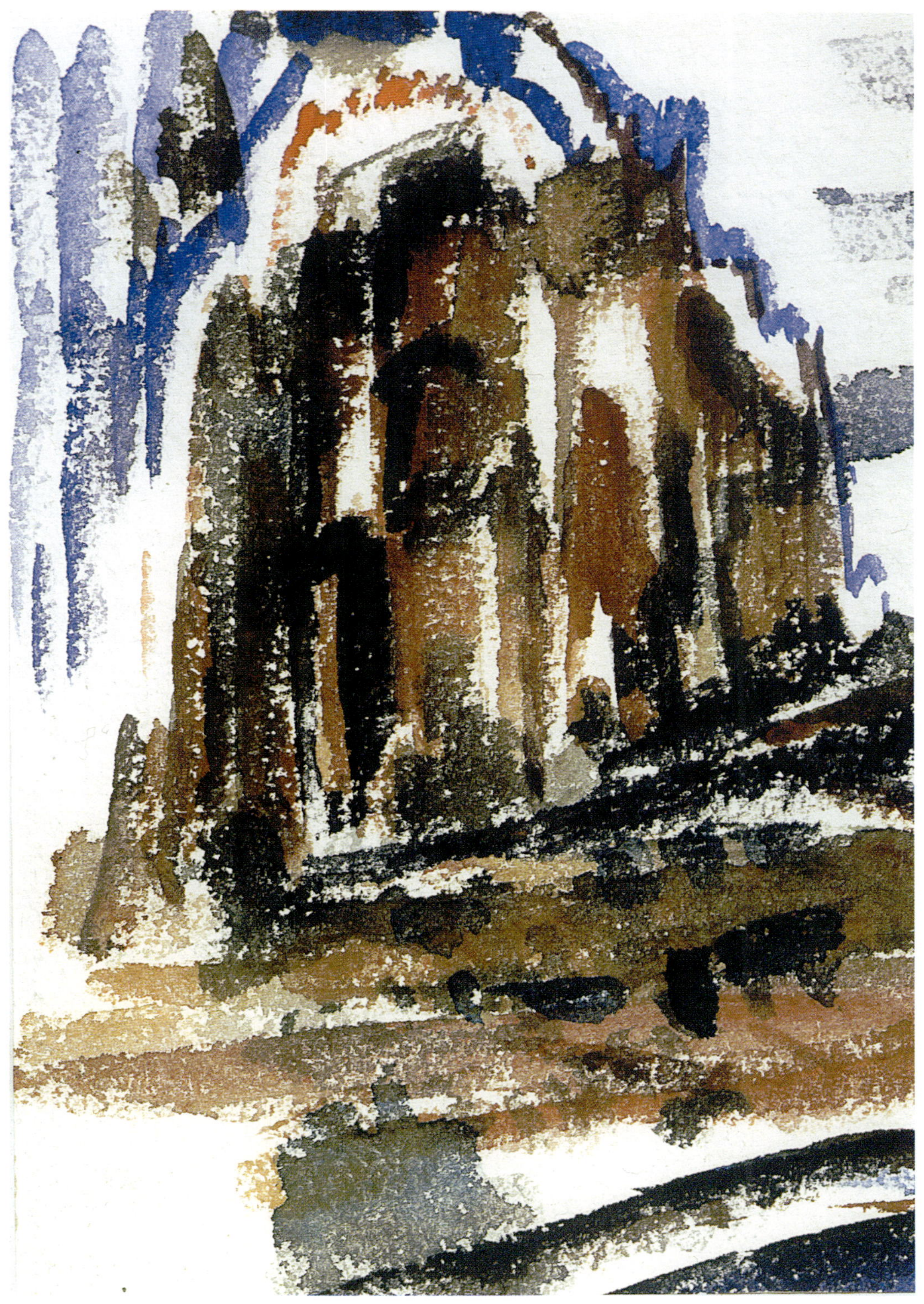

Untitled, watercolor, 7¾ " by 5½". Collection of Daria Labinsky and Stan Hieronymus.
Photograph courtesy of Gerald Peters Gallery, Santa Fe.

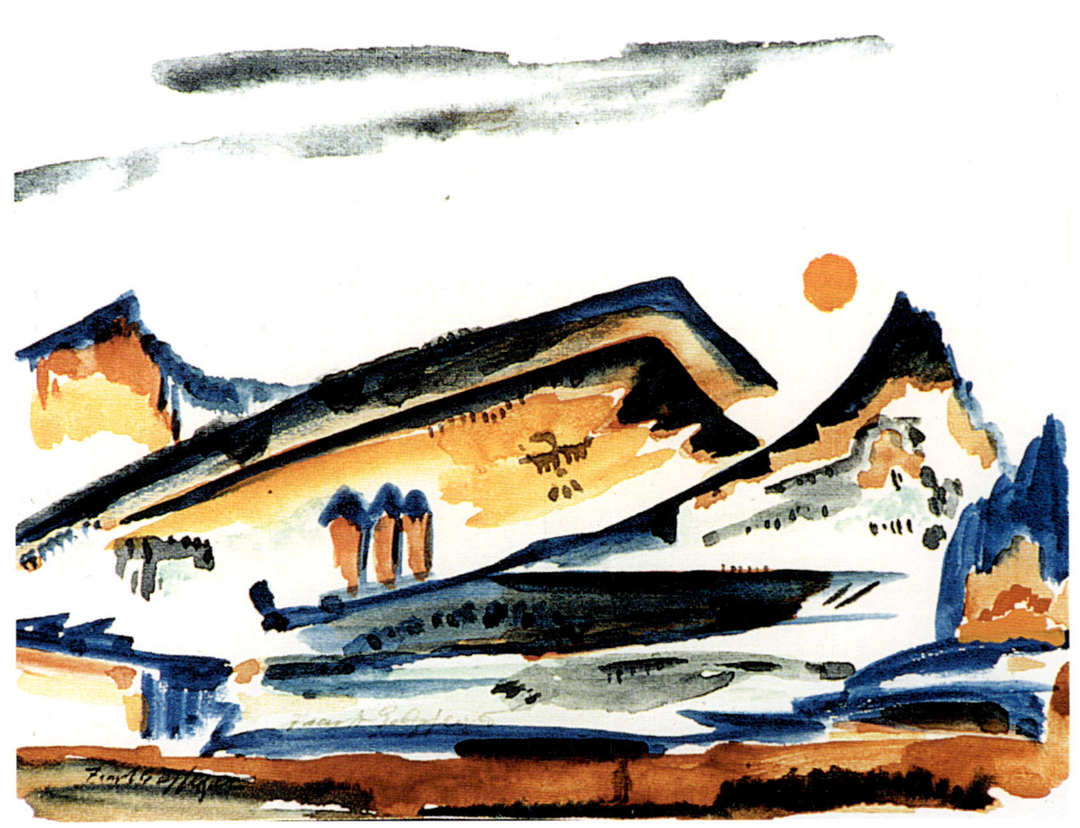

Sunrise Hopi Country, watercolor, 4¾" by 6¼". Private collection. Photograph courtesy of Gerald Peters Gallery, Santa Fe.

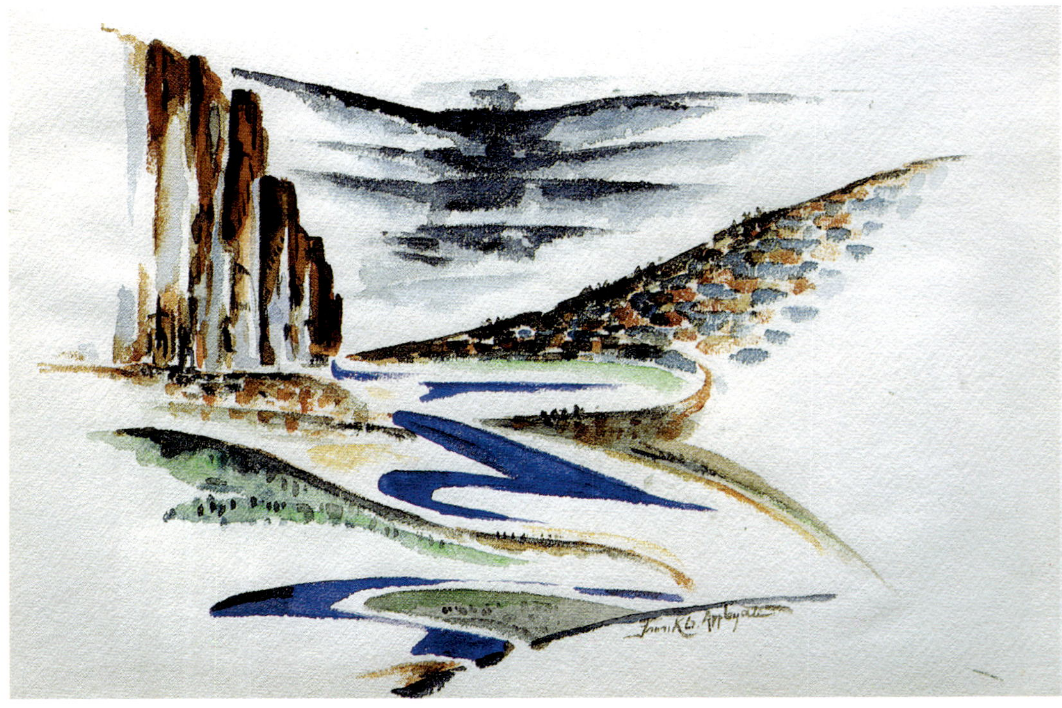

Untitled (*River in Canyon*), watercolor, 11¼" by 17". Private collection. Photograph courtesy of Gerald Peters Gallery, Santa Fe.

warmth and selflessness that seemed to flow from him even when his utterances verged on nonsense." Orage toured the United States in 1928 and gave fund-raising lectures. Ansel Adams met him in San Francisco and discussed with Orage the belief that ideas and moods could be communicated through music.[47]

In July the tour brought Orage to Santa Fe on Zigrosser's suggestion. Waiting there was another devoted follower, the progressive thinker Elizabeth Sage Hare, who had studied under Orage and taught his precepts in New York for a number of years. Hare paved the way for Orage's visit, writing to Zigrosser in June, "I have a little group going and hope I can keep Orage here long enough [to] do a little work with them. There is good material, and we meet each Wednesday evening. I can't do more than teach a little of the method, and this has been difficult enough. ... We have had five Wednesdays and no one has dropped out yet."[48]

"We have a small group here organized by Orage ... and we meet once a week at my house," Applegate told Zigrosser that December.[49] The group also met at the home of the Hendersons. Witter Bynner attended one of the "philosophy evenings" there and wrote a scathing denunciation of Orage's teachings and his disciples in a letter to his friend and fellow poet, Arthur Davison Ficke. "He is a highly polished and first-class con man," Bynner wrote:

> If you but rephrase one of his statements in starker language than his own, but with absolute accuracy, he flatly denies having made it and tries to twist you into a quandary with one of his questions. In spite of my misbehavior, Alice invited me to a later session in which he spoke on literature to practising [sic] writers and one or two of the devoutest disciples, the latter including, by the way, [architect] Johnny Meam [sic] ... & Bert Hagerman.

> As far as this discussion went it was logical and reasonable, and gave me a chance, to a certain degree, of speaking with him rather than against him. He mentioned that literature is only important in so far as the writer succeeds in conveying what he wants to the group he intends to reach. ... Mary Austin challenged him repeatedly but without too much heat, saying that once upon a time she had easily reached a large *Ladies Home Journal* audience, but that now only dire need of the 1,200 dollars she had received for a recent article had led her to return to that large audience. She said that she would rather debauch herself by writing for such audiences. She would sell her body but that she wouldn't get as much for it. We all agreed. ...

> The man cancels his own statement. Yet he does it so suavely that most of his audience listens with awe. ... Apart from his charlatanism, and even with it, he is a charming and witty fellow. It was the spectacle of the roomful and the general abasement of human intelligence that was so sickening. Imagine the Hendersons, for instance—Alice, plump cheeks shining with admiration and reverence, Willie actually reduced to obeisant silence, Johnny M with the expression of a landed trout, Betty Hare embalmed in her own virtue ... etc. etc.[50]

It is not known what if anything Applegate gained from studying the Orage "method." Although he appears to have been a very practical, down-to-earth person, it is not entirely surprising that the search for one's "true self" might appeal to him. The 1920s was the decade of Sigmund Freud, when psychoanalysis first trickled down from the universities into the popular culture. His close friend Mary Austin was profoundly influenced by mysticism, and her belief in the "I-Mary," her own personal approach to self-awareness, guided many of her actions. Recall also Applegate's friendships with John Mowbray-Clarke and Clara Davidge Taylor, two confirmed mystics, back East. No doubt Applegate also wondered about the subconscious, and, having lived with Indians, whose every action was based on the spiritual, he was probably receptive to the idea that physical actions could have spiritual value. As a modernist artist, he likely pondered the spiritual aspects of art.[51]

In September 1928 Orage wrote to Alice Corbin Henderson: "I'm delighted to know that the meetings not only continue but intend to after Betty's departure. … I hope you will remember me to all my friends of the group. Attaining self-consciousness is a hell of a job, tell them; and there's no let up on it and very few pickings. But a hundred times a day I am reminded that the effort is always being repaid." They were still corresponding in 1930, at which time Orage recommended the still-active group contact a woman who taught "harmonious physical development"—gymnastics, rhythms, dance, pantomine—"as a means to keeping the body structure in organic alignment and equilibrium."[52] The New Age had indeed arrived.

As the Roaring Twenties whimpered to a close the Great Depression and its severe economic hardships began to be felt from the streets of Berlin to the Dust Bowl of Oklahoma. For many New Mexicans the Depression seemed merely to be more of the same. New Mexico's economy suffered greatly in the early 1920s, when a national postwar depression produced a severe drop in agricultural prices and caused 47 percent of the state's banks to fail. The second half of the 1920s produced only minimal growth.[53] Still, Santa Fe and Taos' relative isolation protected their economies somewhat, for they were self-sufficient small towns where one still could live fairly cheaply despite rising property costs.

The Depression apparently had little effect on Applegate's fortunes. The Applegates could afford to keep Betty in college. She enrolled at Baker University in Baldwin City, Kansas, in 1928, transferred to Michigan State University for a year (living with Frank's brother Professor Albert Applegate and his family), and finished up at the University of New Mexico, graduating in 1932. Gardening and hunting helped ensure the Applegates' pantry remained stocked, and by the time Santa Fe felt the Depression's worst tremors, Applegate was dead. He was not around to see the effects, both positive and negative, that the Depression would have on the artistic community of Santa Fe.

Endnotes

1 FGA to Mary Mowbray-Clarke, May 2, 1922, Mowbray-Clarke Papers, AAA, Reel D169A.

2 Austin, "Indian Detour," *The Bookman* 68:6 (February 1929): 653. "Santa Fe Has Unique Place in Literature," *(Oklahoma City) Daily Oklahoman*, July 18, 1926.

3 *Santa Fe: The Autobiography of a Southwestern Town*, 287.

4 Udall, *Santa Fe Art Colony*, 15.

5 Nestor, "Viewpoint: An Interview with Alice Henderson Rossin," *El Palacio* 93:2 (Winter 1987): 18.

6 *Santa Fe New Mexican*, Sept. 25, 1922, 2.

7 "Might Tax Scenery As Well As Artists, Say Santa Feans," *Santa Fe New Mexican*, Jan. 12, 1924.

8 *Santa Fe New Mexican*, Sept. 4, 1942. "Art, Literary Colony Opens LaFollette Headquarters," *Santa Fe New Mexican*, Oct. 28, 1924, 7. For a photo of the LaFollette campaigners, Applegate included, see "People and Places," *New Mexico Magazine*, August 1967, 34.

9 "Might Tax Scenery As Well As Artists." Santa Fe and Vicinity Map, compiled by the Chamber of Commerce, 1925. J.H. Sheldon to Museum of New Mexico, Aug. 30, 1926, Edgar Lee Hewett Papers, Box 31, Folder 2, 1926 Correspondence. *Dallas Morning News*, Oct. 21, 1928.

10 Nestor, 18. Applegate, "Tourists and Art," *Southwest Review* 12:1 (October 1926): 23. "Will Shuster Busts Loose on Advertising," *Santa Fe New Mexican*, Dec. 14, 1925, 3. *Santa Fe New Mexican*, Sept. 19, 1925.

11 "Los Cinco Pintores," *Artists of the Rockies and the Golden West*, Summer 1979, 69.

12 "Chappell School of Art," *El Palacio* 18:9 (May 1, 1925): 211.

13 "The Chappell School of Art," *El Palacio* 19:4 (Aug. 15, 1925): 64-65. "Not Coming to Santa Fe," *El Palacio* 24:20-21 (May 19-26, 1928): 409. Udall, *Santa Fe Art Colony*, 18. Applegate's former pupil Paul St. Gaudens and his mother, Annetta, taught at the Chappell School in Denver from 1927 to about 1929. See Melrose, "Famed St. Gaudens Family Left Its Mark on Denver," *Rocky Mountain News*, Nov. 26, 2000.

14 "Santa Fe Art School Launched," *Santa Fe New Mexican*, Sept. 5, 1929, 5.

15 "Former Art School Faculty Member Wins Fame in West As Painter and Decorator," *Trenton (N.J.) State Gazette*, Jan. 15, 1923. "Frank Applegate Dies Suddenly at Home," *Santa Fe New Mexican*, Feb. 13, 1931, 5.

16 Will Shuster to John and Dolly Sloan, Dec. 4, 1925, Shuster to Sloans, Feb. 17, 1926, Shuster Papers, Box 8, Section 11A, Museum of New Mexico Fine Arts Museum. In 1927 Shuster took out a loan to pay off mortgages he owed to John Sloan and Applegate. See Sloan to Shuster, March 28, 1927, same collection.

17 Elizabeth DeHuff to "Mother and Dad," Jan. 11, 1929, DeHuff Papers, MSS 99, Box 10, Correspondence, Folder 26. She states in the letter that while the sale enabled them to pay off a mortgage, they could have gotten more for the land had they sold it to an outside party. Applegate noted that Elizabeth DeHuff was also upset that he had bought some land she herself wanted to buy

"some time when she made a lot of money writing"; see FGA to Mary Austin, Feb. 5, 1929, Mary Austin Collection, Huntington Library.

18 *Santa Fe New Mexican*, Oct. 23, 1926, 3. "Hysterical Pageant to Eclipse Past Efforts," *Santa Fe New Mexican*, July 28, 1928. Wilson, *The Myth of Santa Fe*, 212-213.

19 Dunne, "Inaugural Ball Breaks All Records for Gor[g]eousness," *Santa Fe New Mexican*, Jan. 3, 1923, 1.

20 Nestor, 19. Undated note from Betty Applegate McClung to Gretchen Beall, Applegate Papers. Applegate knew Alice Clark Myers at the University of Illinois, where she was a year ahead of him; see interview with Alice Clark Myers, October 7, 1967, Augusta Fink Papers, Box 1, Folder 30. In 1905 she became the third woman in the United States to graduate college with a degree in architecture. Thanks to the Myerses' daughter, Evaline Foley, for sharing her recollections with the authors.

21 Bynner, "Alice and I," in *The Works of Witter Bynner: Prose Pieces*, 133-134.

22 "Artists at San Juan Dance," *El Palacio* 13:2 (July 15, 1922): 23. Greenlee, "An Untitled Watercolor by Frank Applegate in the Colorado Collection at the University of Colorado, Boulder," (Unpublished paper, University of Colorado, n.d.), 1. *Atlanta (Ill.) Argus*, June 9, 1922. Meux bought two of Applegate's watercolors, which are now in the collection of the University of Colorado.

23 *Santa Fe New Mexican*, July 29, 1922. Chenoweth, "A Visit to the Cliff Dwellings," *Atlanta (Ill.) Argus*, Aug. 11, 1922.

24 *Santa Fe New Mexican*, Nov. 19, 1924. "Applegate, Disguised As Turkey, Fools a Lion; Mutual Surprise," *Santa Fe New Mexican*, Nov. 25, 1924, 5.

25 "Shuster Fined for Speeding in 'Covered Wagon,'" *Santa Fe New Mexican*, April 24, 1925, 3.

26 "The Santa Fe Scene," article from unidentified newspaper, Dec. 19, 1959, Shuster Papers, AAA, Reel 171. "Shuster Fined for Speeding in 'Covered Wagon.'"

27 FGA to Mary Mowbray-Clarke, Oct. 3, 1925, Mowbray-Clarke Papers. Robertson and Nestor, *Artists of the Canyons and Caminos*, 99-100. FGA to Mary Austin, July 18, 1926, Mary Austin Collection, Huntington Library. Undated note from McClung to Beall, Applegate Papers.

28 "Miss Mary Hunter Gives Brilliant Party for DeMilles of Hollywood," *Santa Fe New Mexican*, July 16, 1927, 8. DeMille, *Dance to the Piper*, 112-113.

29 John DeHuff diary entries, Jan. 31, 1926, Sept. 4, 1928, March 31, 1928, DeHuff Papers, MSS 99, Box 5, Diaries 8-9. Flaherty lived on Camino del Monte Sol in 1928; see Belshaw, *Camino del Monte Sol Architectural Historic Survey*, 31.

30 *Santa Fe New Mexican*, n.d., 1930, Applegate Papers.

31 *Santa Fe New Mexican*, July 31, 1929. FGA to Austin, Feb. 6, 1930, Feb. 19, 1930, Mary Austin Collection, Huntington Library. For more on the relationship between Adams and Applegate, see Chapter 14.

32 Authors' interviews with Gretchen Beall. Beall suggests that Betty's unpleasant recollections of her father may have stemmed from the fact that she was an adolescent when he died and was never able to develop an adult relationship with him.

33 *Atlanta (Ill.) Argus*, Aug. 29, 1924, Sept. 19, 1924, Dec. 25, 1925, Sept. 12, 1930. Morse, "Memories of Uncle Frank," 2, Applegate Papers. "Notable Family Reunion," *Atlanta (Ill.) Argus*, Sept. 14, 1928, 4. Phone conversation between Donald Applegate and Gretchen Beall, 1986 (transcribed by Beall and in Applegate Papers). As evidence of yet another skill acquired by Applegate, he crafted tin sconces for Dorothy's wedding. See Morse to Gretchen Beall, Oct. 14, 1987, Applegate Papers.

34 FGA to Mary Mowbray-Clarke, May 22, 1922, Oct. 3, 1925, Mowbray-Clarke Papers. FGA to Austin, Feb. 2, 1928. Morse, 3. *Santa Fe New Mexican*, Feb. 26, 1926, 2. "Coluzzi to Exhibit Frescoes in Applegate's Round Tower," *Santa Fe New Mexican*, May 31, 1930, 2.

35 *Santa Fe New Mexico*, Jan. 6, 1926, 6.

36 Gish, *Paul Horgan*, 15. Wilbur, general ed., *Works of Witter Bynner: Selected Poems*, lix.

37 Cassidy, "Art and Artists of New Mexico: The Little Theater in Santa Fe," *New Mexico Magazine* 16:10 (October 1938): 25.

38 Gibson, 97-98. "Cast Is Picked for 'Cake,'" *Santa Fe New Mexican*, June 22, 1929, 5. "'Cake' to Be Outstanding Society Event of the Season," *Santa Fe New Mexican*, June 29, 1929, 5.

39 Smith, ed., *Cake, An Indulgence*, in *The Works of Witter Bynner: Light Verse and Satires*, 175, 180, 188. Cassidy, "Art and Artists of New Mexico: The Little Theater in Santa Fe," 25.

40 *Santa Fe New Mexican*, June 29, 1929.

41 "How Witter Bynner's 'Cake' Tastes to the Staff," *Santa Fe New Mexican*, July 13, 1929. Bynner to Arthur Davison Ficke, Dec. 4, 1936, in Kraft, ed., *The Works of Witter Bynner: Selected Letters*, 151.

42 Gibson, 95. Houghton, *Hindle Wakes*, 26-27. "Hindle Wakes Departure for Santa Fe Players," *Santa Fe New Mexican*, Dec. 14, 1929, 2. *Captain Applejack* program, Norman McGee Collection, Folder 4.

43 Carswell, *Lives and Letters*, 146.

44 Carswell, 172. Coincidentally (or perhaps not), one of Orage's first New York lectures took place in the Sunwise Turn, the bookshop and gallery on 44th Street that was co-owned by Mary Mowbray-Clarke, the Applegates' old friend. Orage married Sunwise Turn co-owner Jessie Dwight in 1927. See Carswell, 211.

45 Martin, *'The New Age' Under Orage*, 289. Carswell, 212. Mabel Dodge Luhan developed an interest in Gurdjieff's work in the mid-1920s, and poet and essayist Jean Toomer lectured on Gurdjieff in Santa Fe in 1926.

46 Zigrosser, *My Own Shall Come to Me*, 162. Zigrosser, who managed New York's Weyhe Gallery at the time, visited Santa Fe and Taos in late 1928 and purchased several of Applegate's watercolors, as well as some of the santos he collected. See Zigrosser, *A World of Art and Museums*, 94; also FGA to Zigrosser, Dec. 6, 1928, Zigrosser Papers.

47 Carswell, 272. Newhall, *Ansel Adams, The Eloquent Light*, 54.

48 Hare to Zigrosser, June 9, 1928, Zigrosser Papers, MS 6, Box 18, Folder 669.

[49] FGA to Zigrosser, Dec. 6, 1928, Zigrosser Papers.
[50] Bynner to Ficke, July 26, 1928, Bynner Papers. bMS Am 1891.1 (371). By permission of the Houghton Library, Harvard University. Reprinted with permission from the Witter Bynner Foundation for Poetry. Ficke was a friend of Applegate's; see Austin to Ficke, May 4, 1929, Mary Austin Papers, Center for Southwest Research, MSS 31 BC, Box 1, Folder 5. Ficke donated 18 Applegate watercolors to the Museum of Fine Arts, Santa Fe; see the Museum's *Handbook of the Collections*. Ansel Adams also attended this meeting. See interview with Ansel and Virginia Adams, April 4, 1973, Augusta Fink Papers, Box 1, Folder 29.
[51] Will Shuster stated that Alta Applegate was a medium; but no other evidence has been found to support this claim. See interview with Shuster, August 1967, Augusta Fink Papers, Box 1, Folder 30.
[52] Orage to Henderson, Sept. 12, 1928, April 20, 1930, Alice Corbin Henderson Collection.
[53] Popejoy, "Analysis of the Causes of Bank Failures in New Mexico, 1920-25," *University of New Mexico Bulletin* 1:1 (Oct. 1, 1931) 10, 19.

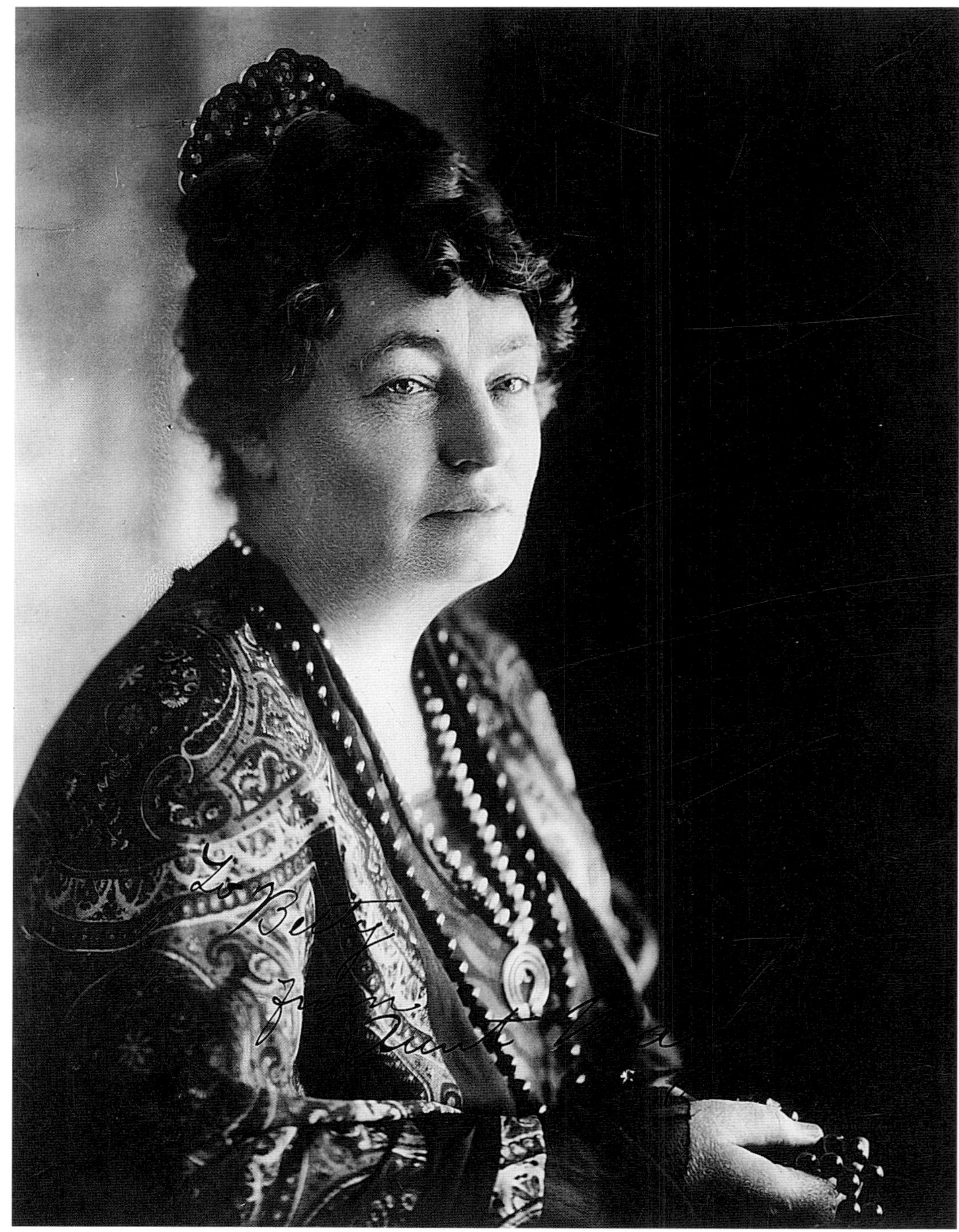

Mary Austin. Photograph inscribed "To Betty from Aunt Mary." Photograph courtesy of the Applegate family.

8 Frank and Mary

Frank Applegate's closest friend in Santa Fe was his neighbor Mary Hunter Austin, a writer whose interests went far beyond the printed word. Austin was an intellectual in a time when intellectual women were still considered freakish by many people. She wrote about rural folks and rural themes but spent much of her life in cities, preferring the intellectual stimulation they offered. Austin was nationally and even internationally renowned, and tourists would come by her home to gawk at her until she put up a wall for privacy. She was a spiritualist who prophetically foresaw many of the environmental problems that affect the Western United States today.

It may have seemed odd to some people that Applegate and Austin were such good friends. Applegate was described as "an easygoing, kindhearted man blessed with a gift for friendship," while Austin was derisively labeled "God's Mother-in-Law," said to have "an air of infallibility and an imperious outlook," and sometimes would withdraw from her friends for no apparent reason. She was 13 years older than Applegate. Yet they shared similar backgrounds, both having been raised in small towns in central Illinois. For all Austin's arrogance and imposing presence, she was still at heart a Midwestern woman, generous to her friends, who loved to cook, garden, tell stories, and gossip. Of her friendship with Applegate,

Austin wrote, "There was a sympathy between us which had its root in a common derivation from rural Illinois and a not too unlike past. Through incidents of our common youth and the shared pioneer history we began to know each other."[1]

Despite frequent poor health, Austin was passionately, feverishly driven to her work, writing books, articles, poetry, and plays, traveling the international lecture circuit, helping to further Indian and Hispanic arts and fighting for numerous causes. She took on adversaries "with the rhapsodic faith characteristic of converts," as Witter Bynner said. She felt a "strong sense of mission to guard the Southwest's natural-social milieu from the juggernaut of Anglo-American progress."[2] She believed in preserving the Indian and Spanish cultures for their ability to deepen and enrich American culture. And when she fought her various battles, Applegate was often at her side, figuratively if not always literally. She fueled his nascent social activism, his support of causes in which she, too, believed. Together they tried to prevent the technological advances of the 20th century from irrevocably changing Santa Fe and the native peoples of northern New Mexico.

Austin believed she and Applegate shared a common appreciation for the New Mexican life. "He drew freely on my greater factual intimacy with that life, and I was helped in my interpretations of it by the communality of our approach," she wrote. Austin also appreciated Applegate's "quick intelligent help … his inimitable faculty of comradeship." Frank's common sense often tempered Mary's hyperbole, for he encouraged her to see things rationally rather than emotionally. Alta Applegate recalled that Austin frequently tried to start quarrels with Frank, but he would refuse to rise to the bait.[3]

Austin began visiting Santa Fe in 1918, and in 1923 she rented one of Applegate's houses on the Camino and started making plans to settle in the city permanently. She chose architect John Gaw Meem to design and build her Pueblo Revival home. Austin bought a lot on the east side of the Camino del Monte Sol in October 1923, but Meem did not complete the house until the fall of 1925. Applegate served as an "adviser" on the building of the home, and Betty Applegate McClung recalled that he often ridiculed the house as it was being built. (Applegate apparently did not agree with the house's design.) Nevertheless, Applegate hand-hewed some of the beams and corbels in Austin's home, which she named "Casa Querida" – Beloved House.[4]

Casa Querida was the site of frequent community gatherings and visits by well-known writers and artists whom Austin had met in New York, California, and England. There she hosted the meetings of the Genius Club, described as "a salon for Santa Fe's literary set," and she seriously considered building a kiva, a Pueblo Indian ceremonial room, for the club in her back yard.[5]

"Her friends were legion and bound to her 'with hoops of steel,'" proclaimed the *Santa Fe New Mexican* upon her death. The Applegates were probably flattered that someone as famous as she was their friend and neighbor. It is clear from letters between Austin and the Applegates that they were proud of her and her work. "A kinder neighbor I have never known," recalled Alta Applegate after Austin's death. "I wish I could write so that I might tell the reading public of the kind, sweet, generous, sympathetic side of her wonderful character." Austin, in turn, felt very close to Alta, who reminded Austin of her deceased sister, Jennie, "in appearance and in the quality of lovableness."[6]

Since she traveled frequently on lectures, for health reasons, and to muster support for various causes, Austin rented out her home and relied on Applegate to watch over it and make sure the garden was tended. His letters apprised her of events in Santa Fe, including the latest gossip. Applegate also handled various practical matters for Austin, such as paying her property taxes and gardener's fees, trying to sell her car and straightening out financial matters. When she suggested constructing a kiva in her back yard, he pointed out just how much it would cost. Austin even had Applegate witness the bequest of her brain to a brain researcher after her death.[7]

The strong friendship between Austin and Applegate caused speculation that they were romantically involved. But throughout her life, Austin had shared friendly intimacy with many men, often married, because they were experts in fields that interested her. They included Jack London, H.G. Wells, Lincoln Steffens, Herbert Hoover, Sinclair Lewis, Charles Lummis, philanthropist Albert Bender, and photographer Ansel Adams. The men, in turn, appreciated her intellectual capacity, her quick mind, her love of a good argument and other qualities that distinguished her from traditional females. "Mary's egotism was enormous, pathetic really, but she had a great mind and a great imagination," recalled longtime friend John Collier. To Austin, Applegate was "all that a brother could be to me and more than either of my brothers ever were."[8]

Austin saw herself in the role of universal mentor, although, as her old friend Ina Sizer Cassidy pointed out, "whether this role is prompted by the spirit of generosity, a desire to share her knowledge, a subconscious prompting of her old 'teacher' habit, or an exposition of egotism, one is never sure." She had many loyal friends, and after Applegate, her closest male companion in Santa Fe was Witter Bynner, who loved to argue with her, sometimes ridiculed her, but also adored her. He was among the guests at a surprise party for her 57th birthday in September 1925, along with Gustave and Jane Baumann, Andrew Dasburg and Ida Rauh Eastman, Gerald and Ina Cassidy, and Will and Helen Shuster. Applegate presented her with a carved wooden lamb, and Shuster gave her a watercolor.[9]

Austin was a hard-working writer, but accuracy was not one of her strong points. When writing articles, she rarely cited references to support her arguments. She "seemed to work more through intuition than through factual knowledge." She wrote from her mind, her heart, and her observations and considered herself not only a writer but an anthropologist and ethnographer as well. "She commonly discovered a subject of engaging interest, developed a viewpoint on it, then presumed to speak on the subject as an expert." Austin's ego, her sense of self, was her most dominant personality trait. Throughout her life she often claimed full credit for achievements for which many people fought, such as Indian reform. "She had an arrogant assumption that the Southwestern field was primarily hers, an insistence upon her position as the oracle and interpreter of Indian and Spanish culture."[10]

Her arrogance often extended to the same people she fought for, the Indians and Hispanics, and she sometimes affected a racist superiority, at least by today's standards. Bynner recalled, "a Santo Domingo Indian confided, with an indulgent smile, as to Mary Austin: 'She tells us what we believe—and we always say yes.'" When her house was under construction, she wrote a friend, "I am trying … to get a house built in Santa Fe, in Santa Fe style, with Santa Fe workmen, which means that I must be continually on the watch."[11]

Austin relied on the Applegates, especially Alta and Betty, to come to her aid during her frequent illnesses. She once told a friend "she did not know how she would have endured her illness had it not been for the kindness of her friends in Santa Fe, especially the Applegates." In September 1925 Ina Sizer Cassidy wrote to Austin's niece, Mary Hunter, "For the past two weeks now, Mrs. Applegate has given up everything else to look after your aunt. … She told me yesterday that she couldn't do it much longer." Yet until her death, Alta and Betty continued to take care of Austin whenever serious illness struck.[12]

Austin and Applegate's commitment to one another grew stronger as the years passed. Although Austin occasionally criticized Applegate to others, they were comrades in the best sense of the word—workers united in support of shared causes. Upon completing an article about Applegate after his death, Austin told an editor, "Enclosed you will find the article about Frank Applegate and his work, which of course is also my work."[13]

So close were they that Austin claimed to have had a premonition of Applegate's untimely death. In the last few months of 1930, she was preparing for a series of lectures she would present in the East. Ever the mystic, she recalled, "Always I have been gifted—or plagued—by a kind of fore-knowing, which makes me vaguely aware of the future progress of events, and along in the Fall of 1930 I began to be distressed with the presentiment that something was to intervene in [a book on Spanish Colonial art, which she and Applegate were writing; see Chapter 14]. So I insisted on Frank's committing [to paper] all that he had learned about the technique of the Spanish arts. I did not imagine that anything would happen to Frank, who was apparently so hale and strong; I thought it much more likely that it would happen to me." The sense of foreboding was so strong, Austin wrote, "that when he drove me to the train for my usual trip East, I bantered him to kiss me good by, thinking it would be a comfort to him to recall it if anything did happen."[14]

It was Austin who was left to remember that kiss. Before that time, however, she and Frank had battles to fight, causes to support, and change to oppose, together.

CHAPTER 8:
FRANK
AND
MARY

Endnotes

[1] Fink, *I-Mary*, 226. Gibson, *Santa Fe and Taos Colonies*, 199, 205. Blend, "Women Writers and the Desert: Mary Austin, Ina Sizer Cassidy and Alice Corbin" (dissertation, University of New Mexico, July 1988), 249. Austin, "Frank Applegate," *New Mexico Quarterly* 2:3 (August 1932): 213.

[2] Bynner, "Indian Drumbeat in the Southwest," in *Works of Witter Bynner, Prose Pieces*, 248. Gibson, 213.

[3] Austin, "Frank Applegate," 213, 217. Ina Sizer Cassidy's notes about Mary Austin, 1933-34, Cassidy Family Papers, Carton 5, June 2, 1934.

[4] Austin, "Frank Applegate," 213. *Santa Fe New Mexican*, Oct. 29, 1923, 6; Nov. 11, 1925, 6. Authors' interviews with Gretchen Beall. Greenlee, "An Untitled Watercolor by Frank Applegate in the Colorado Collection at the University of Colorado, Boulder" (Unpublished paper, University of Colorado), 26.

[5] Blend, 162.

[6] "Mary Austin," *Santa Fe New Mexican*, Aug. 14, 1934, 4. Doyle, *Mary Austin, Woman of Genius*, 275. Austin, *Earth Horizon*, 357.

[7] FGA to Austin, June 27, 1926, Feb. 5, 1929, Feb. 6, 1929, Feb. 20, 1929, Mary Austin Collection, Huntington Library. Stineman, *Mary Austin, Song of a Maverick*, 133. Austin's body, including her brain, was cremated after her death in 1934.

[8] Stineman, 201. Collier, *From Every Zenith*, 155. Austin to Alta Applegate, Feb. 15, 1931, Applegate Papers.

[9] Cassidy, "I-Mary and Me: The Chronicle of a Friendship," *New Mexico Quarterly* 9:4 (November 1939): 205. "Artists and Writers Give Mary Austin Surprise Birthday Party," *Santa Fe New Mexican*, Sept. 12, 1925, 5.

[10] Sergeant, "Mary Austin: A Portrait," *Saturday Review of Literature* 9:8 (Sept. 8, 1934): 96. Gibson, 210. Stineman, 172-173. Fergusson, in Houghland, ed., *Mary Austin: A Memorial*, 25.

[11] Bynner, 248. Austin to Ruth Kelsey Dihl, June 16, 1925, Dihl Papers, Box 360, Folder 2.

[12] Doyle, 270. Cassidy to Hunter, Sept. 15, 1925, Cassidy Family Papers, Box 14. Quoted by permission of The Bancroft Library, owners of the Cassidy Family Papers, [ca. 1897-1965]. BANC MSS 67/1 p. Betty also served as Austin's driver during the summer of 1929; see Austin to Mabel Dodge Luhan, Aug. 10 (n.d., 1929), Luhan Papers.

[13] Austin to T.M. Pearce, July 5, 1932, Pearce Papers, Folder 15, Box 30. Pearce was then editor of the *New Mexico Quarterly;* see Chapter 14 for more on him.

[14] Austin, "Frank Applegate," 216-217.

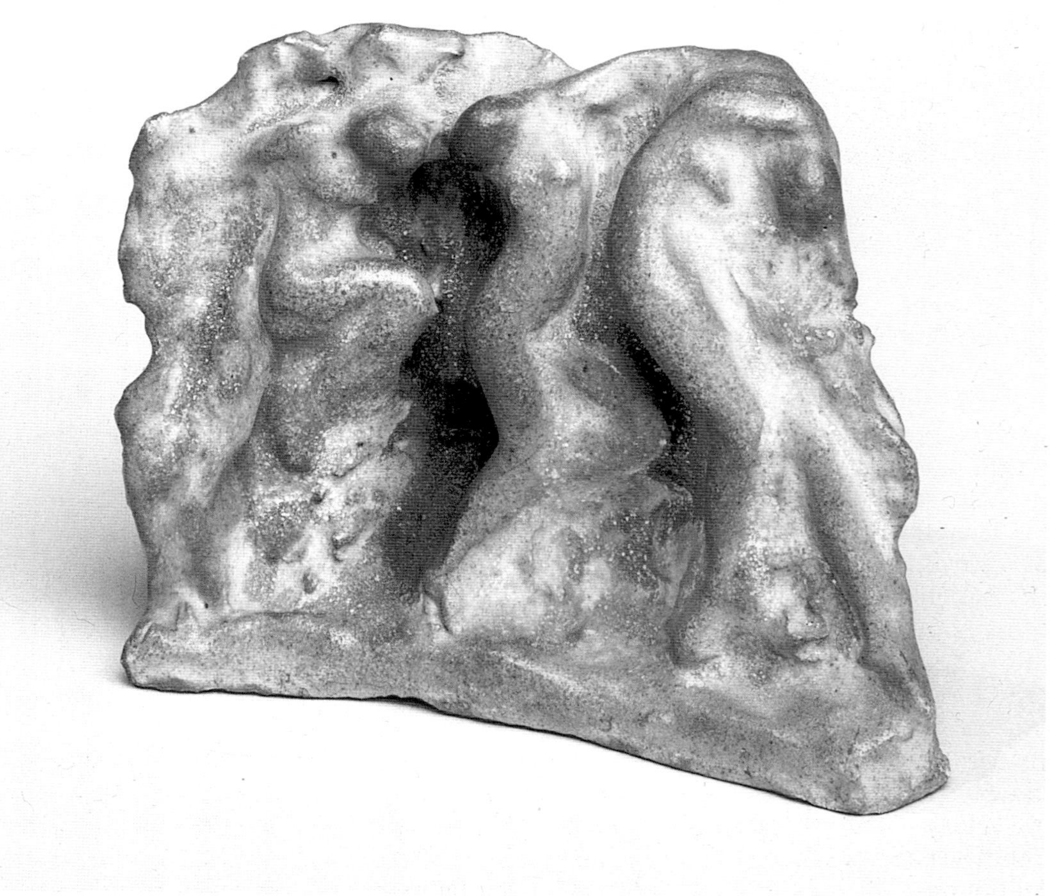

Ceramic figure. Collection of Gerald Peters Gallery. Photograph courtesy of Gerald Peters Gallery, Santa Fe.

9 The Chautauqua and Old Santa Fe

Mary Austin was not one to give credit where it was due if she stood to gain from accepting the credit herself. There is, however, at least one crusade for which she rightfully should receive most of the credit, the battle over "the Chautauqua." The conflict has become an entertaining footnote in Santa Fe's colorful history, but its significance stretches far beyond the facts surrounding it.

The episode started out mildly enough. In October 1925 the General Federation of Women's Clubs, led by its Texas branch, proposed establishing a cultural center in Santa Fe. The local Kiwanis Club and several members of the Chamber of Commerce supported the project. The federation selected a site for the center in the foothills east of Sunmount Sanitorium, and the City Council agreed to donate the land.[1]

What the federation proposed was a far cry from the old-fashioned "tent city" Chautauquas that Mary Austin and Frank Applegate had known during their Midwestern childhoods, with their famous orators and educational lectures. This was to be a summer college, a pan-American university, teaching music, art, history, anthropology, ethnology, and archaelogy with an emphasis on the Southwest and past and present Indian civilization.

"One condition laid down was that it was not to be a Tent City, nor anything temporary; that it would be a permanent establishment, consisting of buildings in the style of architecture prevailing in the locality where built," wrote School of American Research director Edgar Lee Hewett.[2] Hewett was one of the cultural center's first and strongest supporters, and he committed the School of American Research's prestige and facilities to it.

At first, Hewett reported, the proposed center had more or less "the undivided support of the community." Suddenly, there arose what he termed "a wave of opposition … of obscure origin." Much of the opposition came from the artists and writers and their friends. Applegate, Austin, the Hendersons and other residents of the Camino del Monte Sol and Sunmount Sanitorium had a vested interest in not having a cultural center constructed near their houses, and as a major landowner, Applegate had a substantial financial investment at stake. "Landowners on the south side of the city … saw its future in low-density residential planning and did not want the clustered housing the cultural center might bring." Their aversion, however, was more than merely an early example of the "not in my back yard" syndrome. These old outsiders had no intention of letting new outsiders come in and change their city. As Ruth Laughlin, a writer who was part of the Santa Fe colony, recalled, "These people had discovered an Old World charm and tranquility in Santa Fe and were determined to preserve it. ... They were individualists who argued violently with each other but united against too much change in their adopted home."[3]

Austin's opposition to the cultural center was based in part on her past experiences living in Monterey and Carmel, California artists' havens that she believed had been ruined by "cultural colonies." "In each case she said the project was impermanent, resulted in construction of flimsy buildings, ... brought little money in the community and created an atmosphere which in Monterey resulted in the disappearance of all the old processions, religious observances, and customs which made Monterey 25 years ago very similar to Old Santa Fe."[4]

Austin and other writers and artists brought the debate to national attention. Austin published several articles in national periodicals decrying the "Chautauqua" and spoke out against it in speeches before civic clubs and other community groups across the Southwest. The articles brought results. *The New York Times* and *Hartford Courant* published editorials against the cultural center, and influential people from around the country wrote to the leaders of Santa Fe opposing the plan. Austin also had hundreds of letters printed and sent to the leaders of every women's club in the federation, in which she advised the women to stay away from Santa Fe.[5]

Although it is commonly believed today that the fight over the cultural center was a case of the artists and other intelligentsia battling the business community, that view is not entirely accurate. Some artists, in fact, supported the center, and in any case, Hewett considered the artists and literary people "a negligible factor" in the debate. Cultural center opponent James A. Massie wrote, "The opposition includes large institutions which have heavy investments here, taxpayers, property owners, large realty interests, educators, the daily newspaper ... business and professional men, artists, writers, architects, and the Spanish-American organizations. The objectors represent a property invest-

ment here of over $2 million, the bulk of the solid residential growth of Santa Fe in recent years, and some have lived here for more than a generation."[6]

A member of the Santa Fe Women's Club, however, reported "only about 8 percent of the signers [to a petition opposing the center] are members of the Chamber of Commerce ... so you can see what little representation the real business of Santa Fe has in the protest. Such is a price paid by a community for having so-called 'creative minds' in its midst."[7]

Proponents of the center at first welcomed the debate, believing any publicity was good publicity that would help them when it came time to start raising funds. But reactions soon turned bitter. The *Santa Fe New Mexican*, led by editor E. Dana Johnson, came out against the center and was accused of biased reporting. Paul A.F. Walter, cultural center supporter, School of American Research associate, and president of the Historical Society of New Mexico, told Hewett that the paper "garbled, misquoted, lied, and willfully distorted"; that Johnson had "sworn to defeat the project" because of a perceived slight from a cultural center supporter; and that the opponents were "a vicious minority that controls the only adequate avenue [of] publicity of the town." The opponents were accused of having ulterior motives, and Walter told a fellow supporter, "Our local squabbles ... have been given nationwide publicity through the avenues which are open to several of the people who are making capital for themselves out of opposing our proposition." Attorney Francis C. Wilson was accused of secretly "furnishing the leadership and brains to the gang" in order to protect his land holdings near Sunmount from the unwelcome neighbor.[8]

The Chamber of Commerce as a body supported the cultural center, and the Federation of Women's Clubs voted in April 1926 to stick with their selection of Santa Fe for the center, incorporating the name "the Cultural Center of the Southwest." Public meetings on the subject were characterized by heated, emotional discussions. Austin presided on a "throne," a bootblack stand that allowed her to tower over those in attendance. Walter reported that "some of the merchants have been threatened with loss of trade by supporters of the other side and are afraid to come out and take a stand." The battle even spurred Witter Bynner to run (unsuccessfully) as the Democratic candidate for the state legislature.[9]

On April 23, 1926, between 60 and 75 cultural colony opponents met at Sunmount Sanitorium to draw up a petition to present to the City Council and to request that a public meeting be called within a week. Those who signed the petition included most of the artists and writers, along with several dozen other Santa Feans. That same meeting marked the formation of the Old Santa Fe Association. In a press statement the association stated its reasons for opposing the cultural center. Rather than play on emotions, it made reasoned arguments:

> The sudden introduction of several thousand persons from other states, intent on their own methods of development and accustomed to newer surroundings, can only be a body-blow to the town's normal life and growth. The incorporation of a new "cultural colony" inside America's most seasoned town is an obvious and deplorable incongruity. The primitive type of architecture to which Santa Fe owes much of its beauty and distinction, is no longer inexpensive, and would necessitate a greater outlay than most people can afford for a three-months-in-the-year residence. On the other hand, if three or more thousand newcomers in a town of eight thousand inhabitants erect houses of the standard modern style, common to summer resorts, Santa Fe could hardly survive as the "city different." In the economic life of the town, the proposed summer camp colony could only bring confusion and detriment; temporarily swollen business with succeeding depression, an influx of outside merchants, concessionaires and others. The presence for a period of many months each year of a large number of surplus houses, would seriously damage rental values in the city.[10]

Massie was named association president, *New Mexican* editor E. Dana Johnson, secretary. Applegate was appointed to one of the Old Santa Fe Association's two committees, the membership committee, while others serving on committees included John Gaw Meem, Alice Corbin Henderson, Francis Wilson, Drs. Harry and Frank Mera, and Carlos Vierra.[11]

Late in 1926 the Federation of Women's Clubs withdrew its support for Santa Fe as the cultural center site. Local supporters continued to fight for it into 1927 but finally abandoned their efforts. Austin convinced Elizabeth Bacon, the president of the Southwestern Chautauqua in Dallas, to establish a Chautauqua at Las Vegas, New Mexico.[12] It opened in the summer of 1927, and Austin spoke there.

Some of the center's supporters continued to hold hard feelings toward the opponents (that is, the artists) for many years. Those who had never supported them in the first place now had another reason not to. However, the fight did not cause the severe split several historians have claimed it did. Many of those who fought on opposite sides of the cultural center debate later united to fight for various preservationist causes, joined civic organizations together, and served on the same boards. For example, in 1929 the Kiwanis, Rotary, and Lions clubs, Chamber of Commerce, and Women's Board of Trade all endorsed the creation of the Santa Fe Art School.[13] Chamber of Commerce member John DeHuff interacted socially with the artists and became the treasurer for the Spanish Colonial Arts Society, which Applegate and Austin founded. And Edgar Lee Hewett and Paul A.F. Walter worked with Applegate and others in historic preservation efforts.

The victory left the artists and writers feeling a sense of power. They had won once again. Sometime-resident writer Stanley Vestal went so far as to claim, "The world has learned to listen when the artists of this enlightened group lift up their voices in praise or protest." By 1929 Witter Bynner was proclaiming, "We are no longer outsiders. We are insiders. We belong here. … The people who were born here have shown us ... that there is a reason for our belonging here."[14]

The cultural center's legacy, the Old Santa Fe Association, set goals "to preserve and maintain the ancient landmarks, historic structures, and traditions of Old Santa Fe, to guide its growth and development in such a way as to sacrifice as little as possible of that unique charm, born of age, tradition and environment which are the priceless assets and heritage of Old Santa Fe." In an article published in the *New Republic*, Austin said the establishment of the Old Santa Fe Association "placed the artist on the same footing as a business man ... came near to the unprecedented heresy of assuming that an artist *is* a business man." A list of artists, their property and income, revealed "many of them ... were as 'solid' citizens as though they had been members of the Chamber of Commerce."[15]

The Old Santa Fe Association held meetings to discuss the meaning of "Santa Fe style," defining the phrase and setting up guidelines for builders, architects, and architectural restorers. Painter Carlos Vierra was in charge of compiling the guidelines into a pamphlet. Vierra, one of the first artists to settle in Santa Fe, fought to preserve the old architecture long before it became the vogue. He helped design the Museum of Fine Arts, and built one of the city's first Pueblo Revival homes. Vierra was one of a group that first discussed setting up such style guidelines in 1912, along with Sylvanus G. Morley, Kenneth Chapman, Frank and Harry Mera, and Bronson Cutting.

Vierra and artist Sheldon Parsons also took photographs of the best existing old Santa Fe-style houses and collected and exhibited old photos to show examples of the original architecture. "There is at present nothing to help a prospective builder who wishes to use the Santa Fe style," the *Santa Fe New Mexican* said. "It is believed that such a handbook, giving him the fundamentals, will go far toward preventing copying of glaring errors, and monstrosities."[16] A chief concern was that the mission-style architecture common to Southern California not flourish in Santa Fe.

Applegate later discussed certain "glaring errors" of adobe architecture in an essay. "It is easy to distort the fluid lines into humps and waves and all sorts of unpleasant excrescences; and when unsympathetic materials such as brick, hollow tile, and cement are substituted for adobe the chances for ugly and nasty effects are greatly increased," he wrote. "The same mistaken and shortsighted enterprise that gives the average town or city in the Southwest such uniform commonplaceness [has] almost ruined the ancient royal city. ... The old and typical arcades were torn down around the historic plaza; ugly and typically American false fronts were run up before the stores; and homes were built of wood and brick in the style of America's worst period of architecture."[17] It was the goal of the Old Santa Fe Association to prevent such architectural decay from destroying the city further.

From the viewpoint of Santa Fe's ruling class, the association's goals were somewhat radical. Adobe buildings were still considered little more than "mud huts," California bungalows and red-brick houses being the popular styles. The members of the Old Santa Fe Association, however, were not alone in their appreciation of what they called "Santa Fe style." A journalist from Los Angeles writing in 1926 noted, "While the town itself is pleasantly laid out, the streets are—with one exception—strictly modern, with barely a trace to denote the hoary age of the town." The exception referred to was the Camino del Monte Sol, which he called "both unique and interesting."[18]

According to the *Santa Fe New Mexican*, the Old Santa Fe Association's efforts succeeded from the start:

> "We want one of these, now, what you call it, Santa Fe style houses," is becoming a common statement on the part of intending builders or renters ... instead of having to argue people into the community architectural style, newcomers are demanding it. ... And if anyone is pessimistic about the success of the crusade to stamp the Indian-Spanish character upon Santa Fe building, he needs only get in his flivver and drive meditatively hither and yon. Literally hundreds

of thousands of dollars is being expended on new homes a la Santa Fe. Twenty-thousand dollar adobe residences are not rare among those now being completed.[19]

By August 1930 the paper was reporting, "This architectural type, needless to say, is no longer to be called a 'fad.' Millions of dollars have been put into it in Santa Fe. Millionaire business men have adopted it and it has been adapted to all kinds of building purposes, public and private."[20]

The *New Mexican* also pointed out another benefit of building in the Santa Fe style: a simple exterior could hide a luxurious interior, keeping property taxes low. Although the exteriors may have been crude "because of the desire of the owner to adhere to the antique and artistic atmosphere," the newspaper stated, the result, nevertheless, was "unrevealed improvement values," while "in other cases the general exterior aspect of a property leaves an exaggerated idea of its real value."[21]

The advocacy of Pueblo Revival architecture was not the first time the efforts of Applegate and the other artists and writers proved to be financially sound as well as aesthetically pleasing. Many of their actions have been remembered as whimsical, altruistic, or just plain contrary, but in actuality most of them were pragmatic. The battle over the Chautauqua, the founding of preservation organizations, the formation of the New Mexico Painters—all had an economic rationale behind them, at least to some extent. While the artists and writers may have loved beauty, practicality and the bottom line were never far from their minds.

Endnotes

[1] Chauvenet, *Edgar L. Hewett and Friends*, 175-176.

[2] Hewett to Percy Jackson, May 22, 1926, Edgar Lee Hewett Papers, Box 31, Folder 1, 1926 Correspondence.

[3] Ibid. Chauvenet, 184. Laughlin, "Santa Fe in the Twenties," *New Mexico Quarterly Review* 19 (Spring 1949): 64.

[4] "Opposition to Club Cultural Colony Holds Meeting and Petitions the City Council," *Santa Fe New Mexican*, April 24, 1926, 6.

[5] Paul A.F. Walter to Hewett, May 9, 1926, Hewett Papers, Box 31, Folder 1, 1926 Correspondence.

[6] Hewett to Walter, May 8, 1926, Hewett Papers, Box 31, Folder 1, 1926 Correspondence. James A. Massie to Ina Sizer Cassidy, May 14, 1926, Cassidy Family Papers, Box 8. Quoted by permission of The Bancroft Library, owners of the Cassidy Family Papers, [ca. 1897-1965]. BANC MSS 67/1 p.

[7] Santa Fe Women's Club to Mrs. W.C. Martin, May 5, 1926, Hewett Papers, Box 31, Folder 1, 1926 Correspondence.

[8] Walter to M. Hobson, Nov. 25, 1926, Hewett Papers, Box 31, Folder 2, 1926 Correspondence. Walter to Hewett, April 28, 1926, May 5, 1926, Hewett Papers, Box 31, Folder 1, 1926 Correspondence. Walter to Martin, Jan. 6, 1927, Hewett Papers, Box 31, Folder 1, 1927 Correspondence.

[9] "Cultural Center of the Southwest," *El Palacio* 20: 9 (May 1, 1926): 171. "Mary Austin Dies; Funeral Thursday," *Santa Fe New Mexican*, Aug. 14, 1934, 3. Walter to Hewett, May 9, 1926, Oct. 25, 1926, Hewett Papers, Box 31, Folder 2, 1926 Correspondence.

[10] "Opposition to Club Cultural Colony Holds Meeting." "Old Santa Fe Association States Reasons," *Santa Fe New Mexican*, May 10, 1926, 6.

[11] "Opposition to Club Cultural Colony Holds Meeting."

[12] Gibson, *Santa Fe and Taos Colonies*, 258. Austin to Elizabeth Willis DeHuff, Jan. 1, 1927, Pearce Papers, MSS 255, Box 3, Folder 14.

[13] "Santa Fe Art School Launched," *Santa Fe New Mexican*, Sept. 5, 1929, 5.

[14] Vestal, review of *Indian Stories From the Pueblos*, *Folk-Say* 1930, 424. Bynner, "It's Our Fiesta," *Santa Fe New Mexican*, Sept. 6, 1929, 5.

[15] Meem, "Preface," in Historic Santa Fe Foundation, *Old Santa Fe Today*, 5. Austin, "The Town That Doesn't Want a Chautauqua," *New Republic* 47:605 (July 7, 1926): 196.

[16] *Santa Fe New Mexican*, May 24, 1926.

[17] Applegate, "New Mexico Backgrounds." *Southwest Review* 14:3 (Spring 1929): 356-357.

[18] "Mr. Grouch's Liver Very Bad; Hates Santa Fe Almost As Much As Katherine F. Gerould Does," *Santa Fe New Mexican*, June 26, 1926.

[19] "Encouraging," *Santa Fe New Mexican*, Sept. 15, 1926, 4.

[20] "The New Theater," *Santa Fe New Mexican*, Aug. 1, 1930, 4.

[21] "Need for Accurate Appraisal Show on Camino and Acequia," *Santa Fe New Mexican*, May 6, 1930, 1.

CHAPTER 9:
THE CHAUTAUQUA
AND
OLD SANTA FE

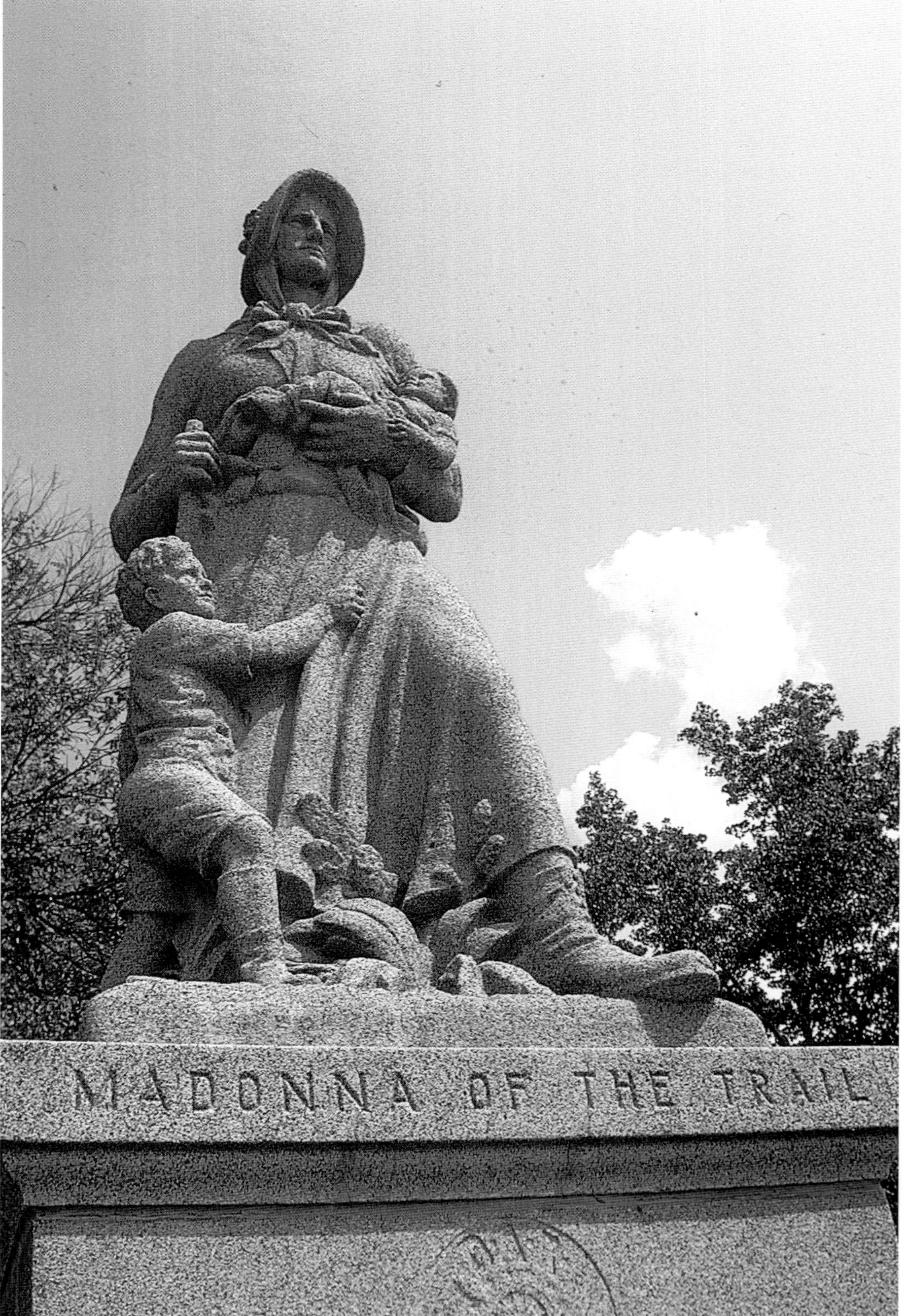

Madonna of the Trail statue. Photograph courtesy of the authors.

10 Applegate the Activist

The battle over the cultural center and the organization of the Old Santa Fe Association marked a turning point in Frank Applegate's life. From that time on, he began to speak out when an issue captured his attention. No longer was he merely a participant in battles led by others; now, he was the one leading the battles. Mary Austin no doubt encouraged him to take an active interest in certain matters, but in some cases Applegate led the way.

The seeds of activism were sown even before Applegate moved to Santa Fe. By the time he arrived there, he already had become a bit of a "crank," as far as middle-class society was concerned. His early career as a ceramicist carried with it a belief in the value of working with one's hands, and he brought long-held views about the evils of mechanized society with him to New Mexico. In an essay he vented his spleen concerning the homogenization of the United States and the spoiling of native cultures, stating, "The old Mexican life here is being spoilt rapidly by Fords, cheap lithographs, jazz, etc." He railed against the increasing influx of automobiles and wrote essays attacking the mistreatment of Indians. The image of Applegate as an easygoing fellow, the man of "kindly humor" that has survived in the accounts of those who knew him, was not entirely true. His niece Dorothy Morse acknowledged this fact, referring to him as a "gentle giant" but also recalling "if really angered, his anger could be colossal." While his obituary in the *Santa Fe New Mexican* was glowing in its praise, it also pegged him as "at times blunt and outspoken."[1] This bluntness could offend people, as clearly shown in accounts of an event known as the "Madonna of the Trail" controversy.

As with the battle over the cultural center, the details surrounding the "Madonna of the Trail" fight have been distorted over time. The most common version of the story holds that Applegate and Austin stuck their noses where they had no business being, and as a result of their interference, "Santa Fe lost a $10,000 statue."[2] In that light the controversy appears to be another example of artists deciding what was best for Santa Fe, and other Santa Feans be hanged. Although this line of criticism bears weight, contemporary accounts of the controversy, which warranted dozens of column inches in the *Santa Fe New Mexican*, put the matter in a somewhat different light.

In the mid-1920s the National Old Trails Road Association and the Daughters of the American Revolution decided to place identical statues of a pioneer woman and her children, named "The Madonna of the Trail" and also called "The Pioneer Woman," in a dozen states along the route of the National Old Trails Memorial Highway, to mark routes used to settle the West. At a meeting held in Albuquerque on October 3, 1927, Santa Fe tentatively was selected as New Mexico's site. For reasons subsequently to be made clear, however, after a meeting in Santa Fe on October 4, Albuquerque won (or as some might have it, lost) out over Santa Fe. An editorial in the October 5 *Santa Fe New Mexican* congratulated Albuquerque on "landing" the statue, and noted that Albuquerque "is less sufficiently provided with historical markers than Santa Fe." The editorial stance of the newspaper, which strongly supported the historic preservation efforts of the Old Santa Fe Association, was that Santa Fe had no need for and no interest in the statue: "Santa Fe's best bet is to keep Old Santa Fe, a living memorial to the past."[3]

There the matter would have rested, had not someone–most likely a supporter of Santa Fe's bid for the "Pioneer Woman"–thought "the real story" needed to be told. An Associated Press account appeared in the *New Mexican* on October 12. Two days later Chamber of Commerce secretary John DeHuff, who attended the meeting as the chamber's representative, gave the following account in the form of a letter to the editor. His chronicle of events expanded upon and encompassed the Associated Press article.

According to DeHuff, Mrs. Francis C. Wilson, wife of Applegate's attorney and friend and past regent of the state D.A.R., represented the city of Santa Fe at the Albuquerque meeting and was eager to have the monument located in Santa Fe. Mrs. Wilson invited several committee members to come to Santa Fe on October 4 to meet with "a number of people … thinking, of course, that their presence would add to Santa Fe's chances for landing the monument." Among the Santa Feans invited to meet with the committee were Applegate and Austin.

"It had never once occurred to me, and I feel sure that it had never occurred to Mrs. Wilson or any other supporter of Santa Fe's claim, that any one living here would, or could object to the location of the monument in Santa Fe," DeHuff wrote.

Mr. Applegate soon got up and began with an uncomplimentary reference to the Santa Fe chamber of commerce, stating that this was another case of where the chamber of commerce was attempting to put something over on the Santa Fe public without letting the public know anything about it [that is, as it did with the cultural center]. Mrs. Wilson interrupted him immediately and said: 'Now, don't start anything along that line, Mr. Applegate, it has nothing to do with this case,' etc. Mr. Applegate then made a statement to the effect that he had canvassed all the artists and writers in Santa Fe and that none of them wanted the monument here, that it was not artistic, and Santa Fe did not want something unloaded on it that it didn't want. Mrs. Austin made a few remarks, the tenor of which was that the so-called Pioneer Woman monument did not represent the real pioneers of this region at all, that the real pioneers were the Spanish people, and that they had not been consulted and were not represented at all. She further stated that she felt that the Old Santa Fe Society [*sic*] should have been consulted before the matter was given a public hearing and that she felt that nobody had had any chance to know what was on the boards, or words to that effect. Mrs. [Trigg] Moss [a member of the D.A.R. committee] was infuriated with the tenor of Mr. Applegate's remarks and asked him to leave the room and to make an apology. He left the room.

The committee subsequently voted 5-2 in favor of Albuquerque.

"About two weeks ago," DeHuff continued, "I learned that whatever city got this monument would be expected to stand an expense of from one thousand to fifteen hundred dollars for freighting it from St. Louis, setting it up, etc. That complicated matters a good deal, for I did not feel that we could very well go before the Santa Fe public at this time and make a drive for funds for this purpose. However, both Mrs. Wilson and I felt that if we could be given time the necessary amount could be raised in some way or another. So that point was not raised in the committee's deliberations."[4]

In a second letter to the editor, chamber president James C. McConvery took Applegate and Austin to task:

> Like any other citizen, Mr. Applegate is entitled to his opinion, but a decent respect for the opinions of others is always wise. In this case two persons, invited as a courtesy to help present Santa Fe's claims as the appropriate site for this statue, came under that assumption and without first privately stating their objections to Santa Fe members of the committee, went into the meeting and assumed to decide for the community in a manner needlessly offensive to a guest of the city and her national organization. ... As the matter had been given full publicity in the local press, the proper medium, and no objection had been heard from any quarter, it was naturally assumed that none existed. ... Tastes differ as to the statue, but many persons of discrimination have approved it. ... I object seriously to the assumption of any individual or group that he or she or they are authorized to take a matter of this kind out of the hands of the citizens in general, represented by the Chamber, and tell Santa Fe what she must or must not do. I especially object when such persons do not come into the community organization on a basis with everyone else and do their share of the work and carry their share of the burden.[5]

An editorial that ran on the same day criticized the statue, designed by August Leimbach of St. Louis, from an aesthetic standpoint for being "too much reminiscent of a tigress defending her young, and ... over-masculine." "After all," it continued, "the pioneer mothers were womanly, in addition to being courageous; this interpretation seems to us to have robbed the subject of grace through over-emphasis of intrepidity. However, the sentiment and the motive behind this enterprise are beyond praise." The editorial went on to censure the way the matter had been handled: "The *New Mexican* was never in favor of starting a drive for funds for this statue, but quite in favor of thanking the D.A.R. for its offer and giving it requested information about the appropriateness of Santa Fe. Also, if anyone had cared to bring up a discussion of its merits, quite possibly Santa Fe could have politely broken it to the lady that we would not bid for it. Everything would have been lovely and happy. It was most ill-advised, if we may put it gently, for anyone to sit in by special invitation and then slap the lady and the Chamber of Commerce in the face."[6]

Applegate and Austin replied to the charges leveled against them at considerable length. Austin claimed the accounts printed in the newspaper presented the matter "in a light calculated to create in the community, and out of it, a complete misunderstanding of the situation."

"I was invited by phone to attend a meeting 'and discuss the memorial statue offered by the D.A.R.,'" Austin wrote.

> I had not previously seen any reference to the matter in the local press. ... I attempted when the visiting committee turned up, to ascertain something of the project but was put off in a patronizing and wholly uncalled for manner. ... I was somewhat irritated by the attitude of the group who wished to bestow the monument upon us, particularly because when I asked what artists had seen and approved the monument, I was informed that "you will have to rely upon us for that." Not only is the monument indifferent art, but as a descendant of a long line of Pioneer Mothers myself, I felt that the monument did not represent them truly. ... Moreover I meant all that I have been reported as saying, that the Pioneers of New Mexico are not the Pioneers of the D.A.R.; that they should have been consulted and that I considered it profoundly discourteous for the D.A.R. to think of setting up one of their monuments in the city of Santa Fe without the widely expressed approbation of the New Mexican pioneers. As for the chamber of commerce ... I felt that their own presentation of Santa Fe's claims to the monument

indicated a profound doubt on their part of the propriety of accepting it. Particularly as they professed themselves later in ignorance of the fact that a considerable sum of money would have to be raised and now admit that they had decided not to raise the money.

According to Austin, the chamber had formulated no plan to raise the more than $1,000 it would cost to bring the statue from St. Louis. This jibes with the comments cited previously–from DeHuff, that he "did not feel that we could very well go before the Santa Fe public at this time and make a drive for funds for this purpose"; and from the editorial, that "the *Santa Fe New Mexican* was never in favor of starting a drive for funds for this statue."

Austin denied that she used "any discourtesy in speaking," at the meeting, although she admitted having felt it warranted. She then got to the crux of the matter–the state of affairs between the writers and artists and the governing civic bodies.

> Mr. McConvery has really put his finger on the source of the difficulty between the chamber of commerce and that portion of the community whose standards are larger than mere local sentiment. Mr. DeHuff says that it "never occurred" to him that anyone would oppose the monument, and Mr. McConvery has himself stated that he had assumed what I would say without taking the trouble to find out in advance. Matters which have to do with art and culture are matters of professional concern with a considerable portion of the community, whose professional standing, their personal integrity, and incomes depend upon their public attitude on just such things as have come up during the past two years between the chamber of commerce and the creative workers of the community. And in every case trouble seems to have arisen over the failure of the chamber of commerce to ascertain the facts and invite the proper publicity.

Now there is one way to obviate this recurring stupidity, a way which has already been taken in other communities having large numbers of creative citizens, which works out to the advantage of both. It is for the mayor to create an advisory committee of people who specialize in art and culture and education, with whom he may privately consult when any matter comes up calling for public decisions in these departments.[7]

Not only did the artists and writers want to have a say in civic affairs, but they wanted to do so in a quasi-official capacity. Such a suggestion no doubt infuriated longtime Santa Feans, coming from a woman who had lived permanently in Santa Fe for just over two years.

Next, Applegate related his version of the "Madonna of the Trail" tale. While Austin had responded to the critics with passion and the unswerving belief in her own infallibility, Applegate argued his points like an attorney, step by step, and made it clear that his complaints were based on both aesthetic and practical reasons. First, he contended that by the time of the meeting with the D.A.R. members, the issue was "past history," since the chamber already had decided not to pay for it. He also stated that, when asked whether he would support a fund-raiser for the monument, "I replied that I would be willing to give ten dollars toward a fund to keep the statue away from Santa Fe and that if the statue was wanted here I had better not be asked to the meeting."

"Thus," he stated, "I gave fair warning. In attending this meeting I did not know that I would be expected to keep silent and only supply local color and acquiesce in everything said. I was under the impression that I was asked in my capacity as a professional artist and was therefore privileged to give my professional opinion on the merits of the proposed statue, somewhat as a lawyer might be asked to pass on a questionable point of law." He continued:

> I had seen some cuts of this statue and was adversely impressed by it and raised the question of whether Santa Fe, as a whole, wanted the statue unloaded on it in this

manner, that the Old Santa Fe Association, to my knowledge, had not been consulted and that I had spoken to a number of artists and writers and that none of them cared for the statue. I said further that if a single artist in Santa Fe was found who approved of the statue I would withdraw all further protest. Mrs. Moss interrupted me at this point and said artists had nothing to do with the statue, that it was between the D.A.R. and the chamber of commerce. I replied that the chamber of commerce had previously tried to give Santa Fe a Chautauqua. … I was again interrupted and asked not to bring that up.

Applegate claimed Austin had spoken "in a manner to which no one could possibly take exception" and that he himself had acted with decorum:

I said that I had no quarrel with the D.A.R., but what I did object to was the inartistic quality of this particular statue. I said I did not consider it a work of art. It was at this point that Mrs. Moss lost her temper … and said I was excused from the meeting. I thanked her very kindly in my most suave and courteous manner and departed bearing no rancor whatsoever. Moss, her anger overcoming her … tossed it to Albuquerque.

That was the end of the affair as far as I was concerned. I gave my most professional opinion on the merits of the statue and if it was not appreciated it was through no fault of mine and if I was the cause of the statue's being turned to Albuquerque, then I can only stand in amazement that one lone individual in a city of eight thousand people was able to accomplish such a feat.

Applegate then cited credentials to support his opposition to the statue, noting that while at the University of Illinois he "did considerable work in the cement laboratories," and citing his tenure as a sculptor and teacher in the East, during which time he "went thoroughly into the processes of reproducing sculpture both in terra cotta and artificial stone. …"

"I happen to know the costs and processes of reproducing sculpture in concrete, or to use a coined word, artificial stone," he stated.

The intrinsic value of the material in a concrete statue eight or ten feet high should not amount to more than twenty-five dollars. A caster and a helper can easily make such a cast in one day. The initial cost of making the original and the molds is the greatest expense. But once the mold is made the statues can be turned out at little expense and as near alike as cement blocks. Now, the twelve statues for the twelve states were to be all alike and of concrete. Had each city where they were to be placed paid fifteen hundred dollars that would have amounted to a total of eighteen thousand dollars, which should go a long way toward paying the total cost of the monuments, so that Santa Fe could hardly have boasted of a ten thousand dollar statue had they gotten this one. … Concrete is a very good material for sidewalks, paving, cellar walls, foundations, and many other useful purposes but is hardly considered suitable for sculpture. … Considering the number of people who have stopped me on the street or called me on the telephone to tell me of their pleasure that the statue was going to Albuquerque, I think it would have been difficult to raise fifteen hundred dollars to bring it here.

An ensuing statement illuminates Applegate's philosophy on artists and art: "I am not blaming the artist too much. He does the regular and expected thing, usually with a committee making numerous suggestions and demands. He follows the demands or loses the commission. … Sculpturesque qualities are lost sight of, and the monument becomes a meretricious and sentimental illustration in concrete, rather than a monumental work of art with sculptural qualities. The only consolation the artist has in such a case is to work with his tongue in his cheek." Applegate obviously had very little interest in competing for public commissions.

Chapter 10:
Applegate
the Activist

Applegate criticized the monument's "unsculptural and badly proportioned details and accessories," and studying the statue, it is easy to agree with his assessment. The "Pioneer Woman" is ungainly and awkwardly posed, and the *Santa Fe New Mexican* rightly called it "over-masculine"–the woman looks like a man in drag. Applegate added that he had "heard on good authority" that Moss "compelled the artist to make changes according to her ideas, and that the figure of the child purports to be a portrait of her own child." He concluded:

> Had I known what I know now, I need not have become so excited over the statue's coming to Santa Fe, for now I understand that it was merely a gallant gesture that the chamber of commerce was making to the D.A.R. when it presented Santa Fe's claims for the statue, and that the members had no intention of raising fifteen hundred dollars, in which case the statue would have gone elsewhere by default. How much simpler it would have been had this been explained beforehand, and the linen washed in the basement, as it were.
>
> Sincerity to a cause can always be gauged by the sacrifices one is willing to make on its behalf. Had the members of the chamber of commerce been as sincere in their efforts to get the statue here as mine were in keeping it out and had each contributed ten dollars toward getting it here as I was willing to do to keep it out, one lone bandit could not have robbed Santa Fe of it.[8]

Thus, Applegate contended, he and Austin had been made public scapegoats for a decision the chamber of commerce had made before the two of them became involved in the issue. And there the matter ended. No further mention of the controversy appeared in the press, and "The Madonna of the Trail" stands in Albuquerque to this day.

The debate over the "Madonna of the Trail" monument is interesting for several reasons beyond the insights it offers into Applegate's personality. Like the battle over the cultural center, the affair serves as an example of what the artists were up against as they tried to keep Santa Fe "the City Different," and not let it become another Strawberry Point, Iowa. Or, looking at it another way, it exemplifies what civic bodies had to endure from the artists and writers who questioned their every move.

Secondly, the incident indicates that members of the Old Santa Fe Association believed their input into civic affairs was vital, and that they should be consulted in matters regarding Santa Fe's public art. Austin's statements carried a veiled threat, that if the artists and writers were not consulted, someone, in this case the members of the chamber of commerce, would be sorry, for the art colonists would continue to make trouble at every turn. With the Old Santa Fe Association receiving broad-based support from Santa Feans from many walks of life, including chamber members and newspaper editors, the artists and writers' opinions could carry considerable clout.

Additionally, in *The Myth of Santa Fe: Creating a Modern Regional Tradition*, Chris Wilson interprets the incident as indicative of efforts to keep Anglo-American history out of the Santa Fe story. "This controversy crystallized the emerging consensus that overt Anglo-American manifestations had no place in Santa Fe's public identity," he wrote.[9] Such efforts continue to the present day.

As a result of the monument fracas, Applegate joined the Santa Fe Chamber of Commerce in early 1928, along with his good friend Gerald Cassidy. "We thought then we could have something to say whenever we pleased if we were not pleased at things proposed," he explained. *Santa Fe New Mexican* editor E. Dana Johnson may have goaded him into it, for an editorial printed during the fight over the statue stated: "The Chamber is quite well equipped and fitted to be a proper spokesman for Santa Fe. Everyone should join it. It ill becomes those unwilling to do so to indulge in hasty or ill-considered criticism of the people who are willing to do the work."[10] The comments of chamber president McConvery about certain individuals not doing "their share of the work" in the community may also have had an effect.

Applegate's chamber membership hardly meant that he had switched allegiances and decided to side with the city on civic matters. He continued to speak out on affairs of importance to him. As the owner of substantial property in and around the Camino del Monte Sol, Applegate took a proprietary interest in the neighborhood, and in the late 1920s he locked horns with the city over a plan to widen the Acequia Madre. Acequia Madre, or "mother ditch," is the ancient irrigation canal that supplies Santa Fe with much of its water and also the name of the street that runs along the ditch, intersects the Camino del Monte Sol and abuts what was Applegate's property. In November 1927 the city proposed to widen the Acequia to 40 feet, a decision reached after several years of debate on the subject. In May 1927 the Old Santa Fe Association had recommended the widening not exceed 30 feet. Conveniently, Applegate was a member of the committee that made that recommendation.

Applegate, labeled "heavy property owner near the intersection of the two thoroughfares" by the *Santa Fe New Mexican*, pointed out that the "60-foot-wide" Acequia would open into the 20-foot-wide Camino, which could not be widened without tearing down houses. He offered to donate enough land to the city for a 30-foot-wide street. As residents of the area today can attest, the city's plans were not carried out. In January 1928, however, Applegate sold a few small pieces of his land along the Acequia Madre to the city for a token fee.[11]

Applegate did not win all of his skirmishes with the city. In July 1930, as spokesman for the Old Santa Fe Association, he attacked the proposed "new theater" going up on lower San Francisco Street. "Since viewing the projection for the façade of the proposed theatre to be built on one of Santa Fe's oldest streets, I feel that I would entirely forfeit my integrity, both as an artist and as a citizen of Santa Fe, if I did not register a

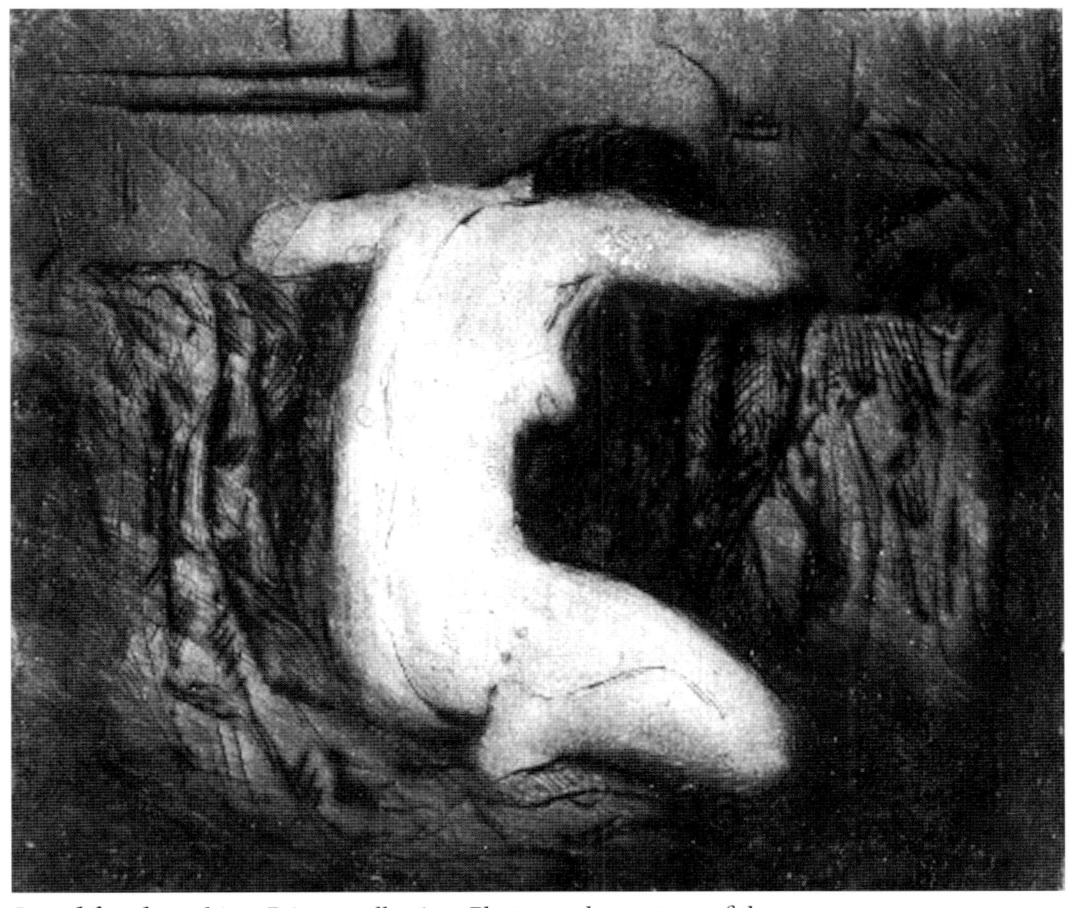

Seated female, etching. Private collection. Photograph courtesy of the owner.

protest against the erection of this Hollywood affair in our ancient city," he stated. "Were this a building designed for private use one could merely point to it as a very bad example of constructive vandalism, and ignore it the balance of the time, but since it is to be a building that can function only by soliciting the patronage of the public I consider that it is entirely within my prerogatives to openly state my reaction to it." He accused the builder of wanting to include "as many styles of architecture as possible with the exception of that of Santa Fe."[12] Despite having the support of the *New Mexican,* he lost the battle, for the Lensic Theater, which stands today, contains both Moorish and art deco elements.

Several issues that Applegate supported stemmed from his love of the land and his and Alta's enduring fervor for automobile travel. In the fall of 1930 he called on the New Mexico Highway Department to set up roadside campsites, precursors to today's rest areas or waysides. "I am particularly impressed with the need of such places on the road to Chama," Applegate said. "I took a trip up there recently and with a world of magnificent country all around you, you have to travel miles and miles to find a place where you can get off the road. At the very least there should be frequent parking places where one can stop without being in the traffic."[13]

The *New Mexican* took up the fight, commenting, "It is a regrettable fact that in the once wild, spacious and unfenced reaches of New Mexico they are now fencing in the highways so that for instance one has to travel nearly all the way to Las Vegas after leaving Pecos, to find a place to drive the car off the road, enjoy the scenery or eat lunch in the out of doors. A few years ago one could drive off into the timber and camp almost anywhere. … This is in line with the general sentiment that the highway department of New Mexico should begin regarding the road as something more than a mere railroad track to get the traveler from one town to the next."[14]

The desire for roadside campsites complemented another aspect of highway beautification that Applegate supported, billboard regulation. Billboards

had irritated him since the early 1900s, when he saw the Quaker Oats man staring down at him from a sign in Germany. He succeeded in organizing a local anti-billboard organization and fought for passage of a state House bill that prohibited billboards within 300 feet of a highway intersection and gave owners 60 days to remove signboards found offensive.

The anti-billboard movement started in the East in the mid-1920s and was part of a nationwide "America Beautiful" campaign. Organizations across the country, including the National Committee for the Restriction of Outdoor Advertising and the General Federation of Women's Clubs (former Chautauqua supporters), were outspoken opponents of outdoor advertising. By July 1928 30 states had placed restrictions on advertising along state highways.[15] The citizens of New Mexico were fortunate in that much of the state's land, including national forests and national parkland, belonged to the federal government, which already prohibited billboards on its land. Opponents of outdoor advertising, however, wanted more regulation.

Applegate published an article in the *Santa Fe New Mexican* titled, "Why Solicit Tourist and Then Hide Scenery with a Billboard?" in which he proposed banning them entirely from the city. "It would be one of the best things the Chamber of Commerce of Santa Fe ever did, give the city invaluable advertising and at the same time arouse the envy of our neighbors," he wrote. "In talking with fellow members of the Chamber of Commerce I have yet to find one who views billboards as anything but a nuisance when placed along our highways."[16]

In 1929 the U.S. Bureau of Public Roads named the auto industry as the most offensive of outdoor advertisers. Applegate petitioned his fellow Santa Feans to threaten a boycott of Ford automobiles: "A large number of us here in Santa Fe who operate a certain make of car are writing to the advertising manager of the factory making the car and telling him that, though we like our present car, yet that in the future we prefer to buy cars that are not advertised on billboards—and we mean this. We do not like to drive our cars for pleasure and then be humiliated and the scenery spoiled for us by billboards advertising the car we are driving."[17]

In some cases the billboards were not only ugly but dangerous as well. The *New Mexican* reported that 200-foot signboards near Arroyo Hondo formed a traffic hazard and were a menace to the public safety. "These signboards have been put up … in defiance of a well-known and increasingly public senti-ment against the defacing of the land-scape and depreciation of property values with commercial ugliness," the paper stated. In February 1930 the New Mexico Highway Commission placed restrictions on highway advertising.[18]

Billboard opponents from across the nation appeared before Congress seeking federal regulation of outdoor advertising, and Applegate allegedly was among them. Although no official record has been found, family members recalled his appearance because he briefly visited them in Atlanta, Illinois. Niece Dorothy Applegate Morse remembered "how distinguished he looked … going from Santa Fe to Washington to plead to a congressional committee to ban bill boards on highways, especially scenic ones. His goatee was neatly trimmed, hair in place, shoes shined and he was wearing English tweeds even to his hat."[19]

While the automobile gave millions of Americans the freedom to roam the country, automobile touring also contrib-uted to unwelcome changes in Santa Fe. Reporting in 1928 on the increase in tourism, the *New Mexican* noted that gasoline sales in Santa Fe had risen 183 percent in three years, and the number of auto licenses had increased 20 per-cent. The city's population swelled 54 percent between 1920 and 1930, with the 1930 Census putting it at 11,176, and the increase was due in large part to tourists' glowing accounts of the city.[20]

Despite efforts to preserve the "new world of beauty" that the Applegates and others had come to love, the City Differ-ent changed much in the nearly 10 years Applegate resided there. He and others did what they could, but Santa Fe was a city destined for change, in large part *because* of the romantic, unconventional reputation that made it unique. A place

that drew tourists like a magnet, a city with a climate and lifestyle of national renown, could not stay unspoiled for long.

Endnotes

[1] Essay on santos, Mowbray-Clarke Papers, AAA, Reel D169A. *Santa Fe New Mexican*, Aug. 7, 1924. See Chapter 11 for essay on Indians. Morse, "Memories of Uncle Frank," 4, Applegate Papers. "Frank Applegate Dies Suddenly at Home," Feb. 13, 1931, 1, 5.
[2] "Artists Object, Statue Is Forfeited; Mrs. Austin, Applegate Protest," *Santa Fe New Mexican*, Oct. 12, 1927, 5.
[3] "Memorials," *Santa Fe New Mexican*, Oct. 5, 1927, 4. In attendance at both meetings was one "Judge Truman of Kansas City," president of the National Old Trails Road Association, who would go on to greater things. See Harry S Truman to Bess Truman, Oct. 3, 1927, in Ferrell, ed., *Dear Bess*, 333.
[4] "Chamber of Commerce Gives Version of Statue Episode," *Santa Fe New Mexican*, Oct. 14, 1927, 5.
[5] "A Statement by President McConvery of Chamber," *Santa Fe New Mexican*, Oct. 14, 1927, 5.
[6] "That Statue," *Santa Fe New Mexican*, Oct. 14, 1927, 4.
[7] "Mary Austin Asked for Her Opinion on Statue and Gave It; Mrs. Moss Discourteous," *Santa Fe New Mexican*, Oct. 18, 1927, 3.
[8] "Applegate Voiced Protest Against Statue Immediately," *Santa Fe New Mexican*, Oct. 19, 1927, 2.
[9] Wilson, *The Myth of Santa Fe*, 315.
[10] FGA to Austin, Jan. 19, 1928, Mary Austin Collection, Huntington Library. "That Statue."
[11] *Santa Fe New Mexican*, Nov. 22, 1927, Nov. 23, 1927. Land records, Santa Fe County Courthouse.
[12] "Petition Will Ask Salmon to Use Santa Fe Style," *Santa Fe New Mexican*, July 30, 1930, 1.
[13] "Oregon, Washington Provide Camp Sites by the Roadsides," *Santa Fe New Mexican*, Oct. 16, 1930, 4.
[14] Ibid.
[15] *The New York Times*, April 29, 1928, sec. 10, 11; July 16, 1928, 24.
[16] *Santa Fe New Mexican*, July 31, 1929, 2.
[17] *The New York Times*, April 29, 1929. "Why Solicit Tourist and Then Hide Scenery with a Billboard?"
[18] "Signboards on Lamy Road Violate All Regula-tions," *Santa Fe New Mexican*, March 20, 1929, 3. *The New York Times*, Feb. 23, 1930, sec. 3, 4.
[19] Morse, 2.
[20] *Santa Fe New Mexican*, Oct. 20, 1928, 3, Jan. 13, 1931.

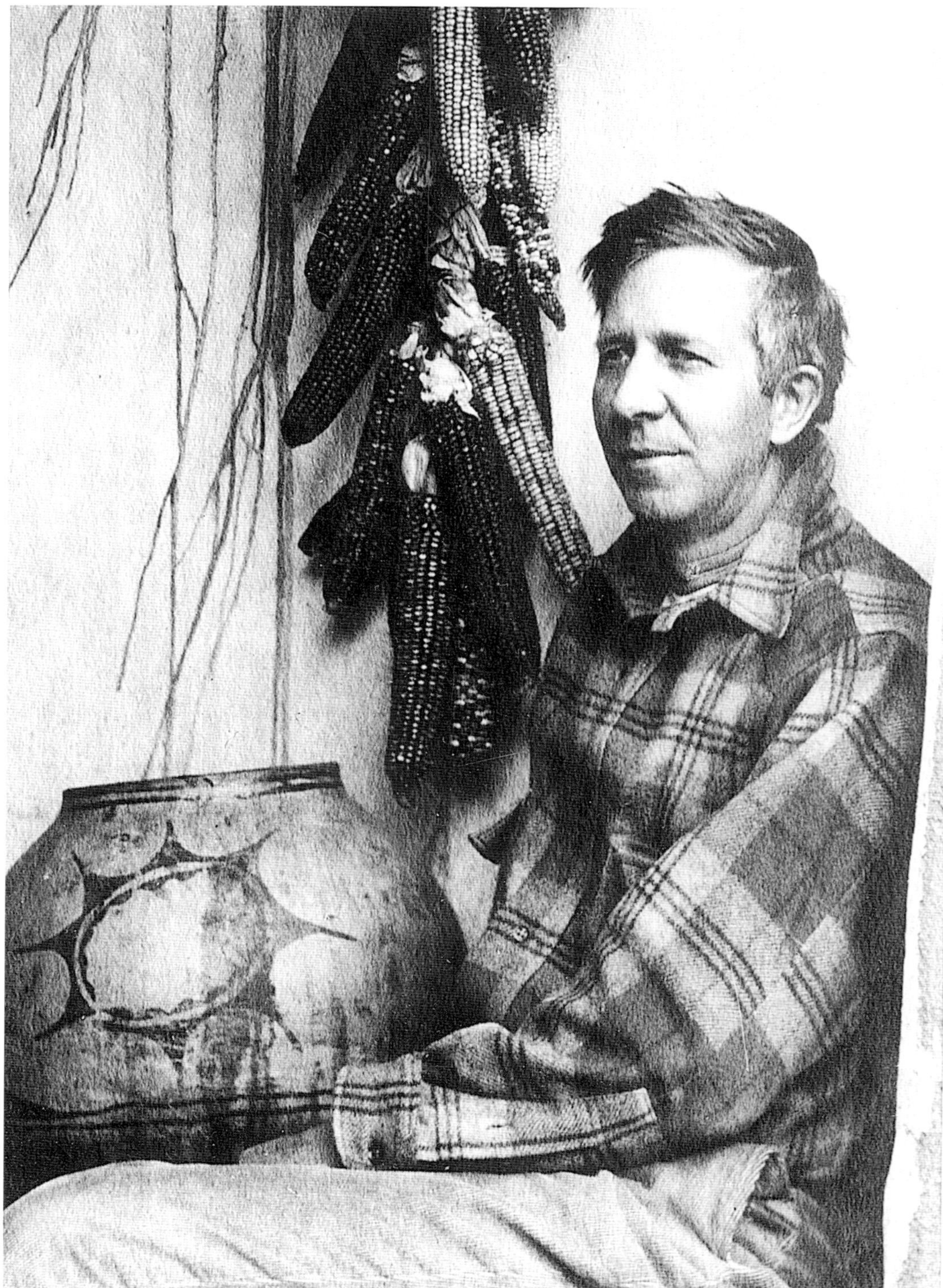

Frank Applegate by Ansel Adams, ca. late 1920s. Courtesy of the Center for Creative Photography and the Ansel Adams Publishing Rights Trust.

11 The Artists and the Indians

The relationship between the artists and writers who lived in New Mexico in the 1920s and the Native Americans who inhabited the nearby pueblos was multifaceted. The artists first approached the Indians as subjects for their paintings, with the representational painters treating them as romantic emblems of a simpler time and the modernist painters looking at them both for stylistic inspiration and as sources of design elements. The artists then became the Indians' defenders against egregious American policies. They attacked the Bursum Bill and other legislation that sought to deny Indians' land rights and prohibited ceremonial dances. The Indians and the artists also shared a business relationship, with artists acting as dealers in Indian art objects. Additionally some of the artists and writers became friends with members of Pueblo tribes, sharing in their social gatherings and inviting them to their own.

From his first years in New Mexico, Frank Applegate's relationship with the Indians encompassed all these aspects, and even a few more. He also served as a teacher of ceramic arts, helping the Hopis improve the quality of their pottery, and he became a chronicler of Indian legends and lore in his books of folktales.

In the summer of 1923 Frank and Alta sent Betty to stay with the family in Illinois and took a long trip to Arizona, during which they visited the Zunis, Navajos, and Hopis. En route, they stopped in Gallup, New Mexico, to see the Navajo houseblessing at the Santa Fe Railroad's El Navajo hotel. "For a Navajo to bless the opening of a white man's dwelling with the same rites attached to the dedication of his own hogan, is so unusual as to make it of more than a passing interest," Applegate wrote in a letter. "On the walls of the new lobby have been placed reproductions of the oldest authentic sacred paintings of this nomadic race. Enough cannot be said of the decorative character of these paintings—of their structural composition, their beauty of line, and mass of color. They rank with the best decorative art of any people. They are reminiscent of Assyria and Egypt, of Greece and Japan." As the letter indicates, Applegate already was captivated by Indian art and had begun to collect it.[1]

Frank and Alta spent five months on the Hopi reservation, living in Polacca, at the foot of the mesa on which stands the Hopi village of Walpi. Applegate studied the pottery of the First Mesa Hopis during this first visit. By 1920 an increase in the manufacture of First Mesa pottery had adversely affected its quality. The growing tourist demand and the policies of certain pottery dealers had led to the production of many cheap and shoddy wares, thick, underfired, carelessly decorated pieces with paint that came off. [2]

Applegate related an account of his time with the Hopis in a letter to F.H. Douglas of the Denver Art Museum in 1930. He noted that he went there "at the instigation of one of the Indian Commissioners."

> At that time ... the Hopi pottery had reached such a state that they could sell little of it for two reasons. It broke so easily and the black which they used in painting their designs rubbed off if touched. I had a class of about 40 women. ... I confined my work entirely to technical problems and left designs, shapes, etc. entirely to the women. ... First I analised [sic] all the clays (about a dozen) that were to be found in the vicinity and selected the one most suitable for use, and then altered the black until it would not rub off when fired. Since that time Hopi pottery has come up until now it has become a great economic asset to the Hopis.

Applegate proceeded to give a detailed history of the Hopis and their pottery and discussed their materials, techniques, and designs. He noted that the women historically mixed iron oxide with red clay to produce a dark brown paint.

> In making their new style of pottery the women needed a blacker paint, so they mixed the iron oxide with the boiled down juice of a variety of mustard. This gave a rich black, but unfortunately one that rubbed off easily when fired. (I helped them overcome their difficulty by having them mix a small amount of silicate of soda—waterglass—with their paint, which vitrified the color just enough to set it without, however, altering its richness.

Applegate also found that the clay they were using would not fire hard:

> For some reason they had abandoned or lost the old strata of clay from which Hopi pottery had formerly been made and were using a clay that could be fired only at a heat that was beyond their methods. In fact it was almost

a pure alumina oxide. By tests I found them suitable clay deposits which solved the difficulty. I made about 500 tests of fusibility and practical firing points of the different clays, of which there were about a dozen. ... I got them to use a different clay that fired hard at a low temperature. [3]

Applegate discussed his results at a meeting of the New Mexico Association on Indian Affairs, which counted many artists and writers among its members, in November 1923. "Mr. Applegate went into pueblos and gave the Indians there, whose pottery had degenerated in tensile strength and density, a practical object lesson in the better use of clays and manufacturing methods," the *Santa Fe New Mexican* reported. "A bunch of Indians [tried] in vain to break with their hands a bowl Applegate made out of clay he located on the mesas, of a kind formerly used but which the Hopi had lost track of. The Indians, it is said, were much pleased when he rolled the bowl violently across the street without its breaking." The newspaper later reported that the Hopis were enthusiastically "using the old clays which enabled their forefathers to make better wares" and were pleased with "the results of their pottery making since Applegate spent some days out there, pointing out the neglected better clays which they should be using." According to Betty Applegate McClung, the Hopis initiated Frank and Alta into their tribe. During the stay with the Hopis, Applegate also excavated ruins at Sikyatki and Sichomovi, including the ancient burial mounds. [4]

While Applegate maintained that he devoted his attention to technical problems, he is credited with introducing the tall vaselike pottery shape, which became very popular with both the potters and the public. These vases ranged in height from seven or eight inches to three feet tall, and the taller ones were often used as umbrella stands. "Nothing expresses more succinctly an awareness of vernacular Art Nouveau and early Art Deco tall ceramic vases—a staple in dry-goods stores across the country at this time— than the cylindrical Hopi version, a hand-raised ceramic vase in traditional buff-colored clay and with striking, symbolically balanced designs."[5]

The introduction of the vase marks the first time Applegate is reputed to have convinced Native Americans to change their artwork to make it more marketable to the Anglo public, and he would persuade Hispanic artisans to do the same. While he meant well, some art historians and anthropologists later criticized such interference, saying it weakened the original art by accelerating design changes, rather than letting the artists introduce new styles slowly and on their own terms, if at all.

The Applegates are known to have stayed with the Hopis on three other occasions, and they likely visited at other times as well. In February 1925 painter Andrew Dasburg accompanied Alta and Frank to Arizona, and the three spent a month with the Hopis and Navajos. Frank and Alta returned to the reservations that summer with Josef Bákos and again in the summer of 1927. Unlike the Pueblos living along the Rio Grande, the Hopis were open to sharing information about their religious rituals with outsiders.[6] After the 1927 trip Applegate relayed a mysterious Navajo legend, a story that foreshadowed his later folktales, in the *Santa Fe New Mexican*:

> A vast palace or city of stone, hidden away in a secret oasis encircled by impassable badlands, gorges, red rock walls and pinnacles, lies at the end of a mysterious road which takes form out of the trackless waste west of Tohatchi on the Navajo reservation. In this secret Forbidden City are all the luxuries known to the white man and many others: gardens and temples and what not, according to the glittering legend which seems to have more or less currency out in Navajoland. "Believe it or not," said Frank Applegate ... compadre of the Hopi and the Navajo, who used to live in Hopiland. "This isn't my tale—I'm merely telling you what I have heard. It comes from more than one source. ... In midsummer, so it is said, the Navajos drive their cattle and sheep out that road for some purpose which has never been made clear. It is declared that no white man with one exception has ever been allowed to travel this road, and that he was not seen again. Whether this Navajo [palace] has radio and bathrooms and grand opera and jazz, I couldn't say. It is generally described as a 'stone palace,' I believe. The theory that the Navajos have some such civic or religious center entirely concealed isn't so incredible, when you know something about the roughness of some of the Navajo country."[7]

Little else is known about Applegate's extended stays with the Hopis and Navajos, but he provided some insight into the visits in his folktales, most of which were published in the books *Indian Stories From the Pueblos* and *Native Tales of New Mexico* (see Chapter 13). In one story he mentioned having spent an evening with a man named Supela, during which Supela "was pointing out prehistoric pueblo ruins of the Hopis and telling me tales of their peregrinations previous to their settling on their present inaccessible, rocky mesa." Together, they watched a bohana (white man) kill a snake, showing no concern for its significance to the Hopis. In another tale he noted that he spent time with a man named Percy, with whom he "had many long talks about the 'long time ago' of the Hopis." A third recounted tales shared by a group of Hopi women while making pottery, another found Applegate sitting atop a kiva at Walpi with a Hopi friend named Morning Cloud.[8] He met one Navajo friend, Nah Gee, "at Tom's Trading Post in Polacca."

"After Nah Gee had caused Gargantuan helpings of mutton stew to disappear and had bedded his family down for the night," Applegate wrote, "he came over to my camp fire and sat down for a smoke. I contributed some bottles of soda pop, of which Navajos are inordinately fond." Nah Gee, Applegate discovered, had been forcibly taken to boarding school and eventually studied at the infamous Indian school in Carlisle, Pennsylvania.[9]

Applegate found Indian ceremonies and rituals fascinating. He often expressed fear that they would die out, and with good reason. The Committee on Indian Affairs of the YWCA fought to ban the dances, which it considered immoral, pagan rituals that impeded the assimilation of the natives into American society. In the early 1920s Commissioner of Indian Affairs Charles Burke banned Indian ceremonial dances, and only pressure from the artists, writers, and other Indian supporters forced Burke to relax his order.[10]

The Applegates made numerous trips to the northern New Mexico pueblos, sometimes taking Betty out of school for a few days so she could attend a special dance. "We have many friends among the Indians here and visit them on their pueblos," Applegate wrote. "They let us know when they are going to have a particularly nice ceremony. When they are treated as they should be, they are wonderful."[11]

According to writer Mary Austin, the Indians frequently invited the artists to special dances unlike those they produced for the tourists. The ceremonies often took place over several days, requiring overnight stays at the pueblos. Indians occasionally stayed with the Applegates in Santa Fe, much to young Betty's chagrin. She remembered that they just sat, silently, for long periods of time, and she thought they were unclean, but her parents were unsympathetic to Betty's complaints.[12]

The San Ildefonso Pueblo was a favorite destination, and the Applegates became friends with the pueblo's renowned watercolor artists, including Awa-Tsireh (Alfonso Roybal) and Julián Martínez. Their work was already well-known by the time the Applegates moved to Santa Fe in 1921. Awa-Tsireh had been painting with watercolors for several years and already had exhibited in New York by the time Applegate met him.[13] Although Martínez was an outstanding watercolorist, he is best known for his design work on the black-on-black pottery of his famous wife, María.

Alta wrote a letter about a visit they paid to the pueblo in early 1922. "Mr. Cassidy came and invited us to go with them out to San Ildefonso, to see the Deer and Buffalo dance. ... Betty begged

so to be taken that I let her miss school." Alta described the ceremony, which started at sunrise:

> This ceremony is a prayer for plenty of game, which is represented by Indian dancers. Some represented buffalo, some mountain sheep and some deer; there were just two who represented antlers. They dress to look as near like animals as possible, big horns of the animals are always used. They carry sticks about a foot long and so go on all fours through most of the dance. It was quite impressive to see them come down the hillside over a well-worn path. ... We followed them to the plaza, where they danced and then went to the kiva for certain services. We were cold by that time and Mrs. C[assidy] took us to Marie and Julian's home. They are two of the finest pottery makers around here. ... We visited the governor, and such a welcome he gave us. After Mass the Indians danced again and all day repeated the dance.

Later, they drove to San Juan Pueblo. The Applegates had begun collecting Indian artifacts by this time, for Alta mentioned that they purchased four pairs of the carved sticks used in the basket dance and later sold three of the pairs.[14]

With his modernist's eye Applegate saw Indian ceremonial dances as kaleidoscopic presentations. "About the only way I can convey information, or an impression, to your mind is to recall the tin toy one held to their eye as a youngster and turned in the hand watching the triangles and blocks of colored glass tumble and move. Magnified, that is an Indian ceremony," he wrote.[15] He rarely passed up a special dance and was still attending them a week before he died.

The Hopi Snake Dance, the most frequently described and depicted of all the Indian ceremonies, intrigued Applegate deeply. It amazed him that the Hopis could be bitten repeatedly by the snakes, yet show no ill effects. "Applegate believes the secret of the Hopi immunity from poison in the snake dance is the fact that the Indian takes the greatest care in handling the snakes, however careless it appears, and that very seldom is any dancer bitten," reported the *Santa Fe New Mexican*. "The emetic taken after the dance, he thinks, is merely a purification medicine, concocted from stewed beetles, and has no relation to snake bite."[16]

In a letter to the *Atlanta Argus* Applegate gave a carefully observant, dryly humorous description of the Hopi Snake Dance. More than any other of his letters, this one foreshadowed the often amusing folktales he later compiled in books. He began by explaining the legend behind the snake dance, how the snakes are actually brothers to the Hopis, and how they have the ears of the underground gods. He continued:

> At this time the snakes are shown the very greatest honor and consideration. Seven days previous to the event, the Snake Priests start hunting the snakes. They go painted and stript except for a necessary and carry a snake bag, a pouch of sacred corn meal, a charming feather, and a digging stick. The first day they go north, the second west, the third south, and the fourth east. When they find a snake they first charm him with the feather, then sprinkle sacred corn meal on his head, pick him up quickly, and put him in the bag. If they see by a snake's trail in the sand that he is at home, they dig him out with their sticks. When they bring the snakes home, they take them to their underground lodge room, called a Kiva, where they entertain them for two days, telling them what should be told the underground gods. On the seventh day they give the snakes a bath in Hopi holy water. Then they all, the Indians and the snakes, proceed to the open plaza of the village, where a grand ball is held in honor of the visiting brothers. The snakes not being equipped for dancing, the Indian holds his partner in his mouth and dances with him or her that way. The Indians are dressed and painted as follows: Eagle feathers in hair; eagle wing at back of head; face painted very black to nose, rest of face painted startling white; body black and red to suit the occasion. Large strands of turquoise around neck; girdle of real deer skin; skin

of red fox trailing behind; tortoise-shell rattle fastened to knee; the snake dressed "au natural [*sic*]."

Applegate then described the dance in detail, using allusions the home folks could relate to:

> ... all dance around the plaza to the music of the Antelope Chiefs ... when they come to "swing them to the right" they all drop their partners and choose new ones till all the visitors have been danced with. There are no wall flowers at this dance. ... When all the snakes have been danced with they are all brought to the middle of the plaza and dumped in a heap by the gatherer-up and sacred meal dumped over them. Then each Indian gathers up as many as he can carry and runs down the side of the mesa, out to the fields, where the snakes are turned loose, unharmed, to take their message, of what nice hospitable people the Hopi are, and what they need, to the underground gods. ... As proof that the Snake Dance Ceremony is highly efficient, it has been raining much since. Therefore, I would like to recommend this method to the farmers of Illinois, for raising good crops, with the farm adviser as the main medicine snake chief.

He concluded, "When one sees the first dancer come out, carrying a four-foot rattler, squirming in his mouth, it gives him a real thrill."[17]

The Applegates traveled to the pueblos not only to attend ceremonies but to collect Indian art objects. Many Santa Feans were avid collectors of Indian art, and Applegate was among the most avid. While the first collectors had appreciated the art from an anthropological stance, for what it taught them about the Indians, the artists and writers primarily looked at the art for its aesthetic value. Applegate, who was always interested in how things were made, approached the art from both viewpoints. His Arts and Crafts sensibilities appreciated both the utilitarian nature of many Indian art objects and the artistic ability evident in the works. He developed a reputation as "the trader with whom they most willingly deal, whose reputation for fair prices and good judgment is wide spread."[18]

Some of the artists and their friends amassed so much Indian artwork (and Spanish Colonial art) that they began selling it to the public. In April 1924 Andrew Dasburg, John Evans (Mabel Dodge Luhan's son), B.J.O. Nordfeldt, Witter Bynner, Wladyslaw "Walter" Mruk, William Penhallow Henderson, and Fremont Ellis founded the Spanish & Indian Trading Company, first in Santa Fe's Prince Plaza, then just north of La Fonda. Although Applegate's name is not on the incorporation papers, he may have been some sort of informal partner in the business, for he wrote in January 1925 of "the Spanish & Indian Trading Co. store here which Dasburg, Witter Bynner, Nordfeldt, John Evans ... and I have here." Each partner put up $500, and sales were more than $27,000 in the first year. The shop, Applegate said, had "a very big stock of rare things of Southwestern and Spanish origin exclusively, such as rare pottery, silver work, blankets, baskets, paintings, carved & painted chests, old Mexico native furniture, and all sorts of rare things too numerous to mention." During their stay with the Hopis in February 1925, Applegate and Dasburg collected artifacts and bought items for the store. Applegate reported acquiring "fine baskets, katchinas, pottery, silver, rugs, and several rare things" at this time.[19]

The shop also sold new Indian artwork, including pottery, jewelry, and watercolors, and sponsored tours to the pueblos, cliff dwellings, and ruins. Santa Fe's second Indian and Spanish Colonial art shop, the Old Santa Fe Trading Post, opened in 1927. Owners James Seligman and Richard Day recruited "experts" Applegate, Dasburg, and Bynner to collect items to sell for the store, including old blankets, santos, pottery, silver work, chests, silver-ornamented leather, Indian beadwork, antique oil paintings, and ceremonial items. The dealers and collectors helped accelerate the revival in Indian crafts, which ultimately made it possible for Indians "to have more dignity and independence than at any time before in their dealings with Whites." The money the Indians earned also increased their financial empowerment, enabling them to buy additional farmland.[20]

At the same time these collectors were dealing in Indian arts and crafts, they were becoming alarmed that some of the finest pieces were falling into the hands of tourists (as opposed to serious local collectors). Correspondingly, supporters of the Indians became increasingly concerned about the way Indians were being educated in government-run boarding schools. The schools' goals were to assimilate the students into white society, teach them marketable skills, and "transform 'lazy savages' into useful citizens." The Indian Bureau banned the teaching of tribal arts and crafts in all of its schools until 1930.[21]

In the fall of 1923 supporters of Indian art in Santa Fe formed the Indian Pottery Fund, an organization with two purposes: One, to acquire the best examples of Indian art, to prevent it from being carted away by "outsiders"; two, to use these fine examples to educate modern Indians about the work of their ancestors so that the ancient designs and methods would live on.[22]

Applegate was one of the first members of the Indian Pottery Fund, also called the Pueblo Pottery Fund, along with Austin, Dasburg, Nordfeldt, writer Elizabeth Shepley Sergeant, Dr. Harry P. Mera, and Kenneth Chapman. Mera, the county health officer, and Chapman, a painter, were experts on Indian pottery who worked for the Museum of New Mexico. The group's members focused on historic "post-Spanish" Pueblo pottery, rather than prehistoric pottery. "Old historic Pueblo pottery is very rare and scarce," Applegate wrote, "much more so than the prehistoric, for they buried much prehistoric pottery with the dead and all that is necessary is to dig it up again, while the old Pueblo pottery is broken and never made that way again."[23]

The nucleus of the collection came from donations from the members' private caches. The first pieces contributed to the Pueblo Pottery Fund were displayed at the Museum of New Mexico in December 1923. As the collection grew, it was moved to the museum basement. Unfortunately, the fund did not have the support of Museum and School of American Research director Edgar Lee Hewett, who "had little interest in post-Conquest materials." Nor did Hewett approve of the amount of time Mera and Chapman spent on Indian Pottery Fund work rather than museum work. Although the School of American Research officially praised the Indian Pottery Fund's efforts, Hewett considered it the school's competitor, and he eventually forced the fund to move its collection out of the museum.[24]

The pottery fund was incorporated as the Indian Arts Fund in September 1925, with Applegate, Dasburg, Chapman, Mera, and attorney Francis C. Wilson listed as incorporators. The Indian Arts Fund's stated goal was "to revive the Arts & Crafts of the Indians by giving them free access to the choicest specimens of their tribal handiwork. To educate the people of the United States as to the value of America's only surviving indigenous art." At the time of incorporation Chapman estimated the group had amassed a collection of pottery worth between $3,000 and $5,000.[25] Also at this time the fund expanded the collection to include hide paintings, weavings, jewelry, and other forms of artwork.

The group purchased outstanding examples of contemporary work as well as old pieces. Mera and Chapman were the driving forces behind the fund for many years, and Applegate served on the board of trustees until his death. Chapman's writings in *El Palacio* and national art magazines helped popularize Pueblo pottery, and he eventually became one of the country's foremost experts on the subject.

The Indian Arts Fund's trustees included notables and experts from around the United States. Among them were Herbert J. Hagerman, former territorial governor of New Mexico; wealthy collector Elizabeth Sage Hare; anthropologist Frederick Webb Hodge of the Southwest Museum and Museum of the American Indian; archaeologist Alfred Kidder; Taos writer and collector Mabel Dodge Luhan; Neighborhood Playhouse founder Irene Lewisohn; James H. McMillan, who ran the Spanish & Indian Trading Company; dealer James Seligman; Margaret McKittrick,

CHAPTER 11:
THE ARTISTS
AND
THE INDIANS

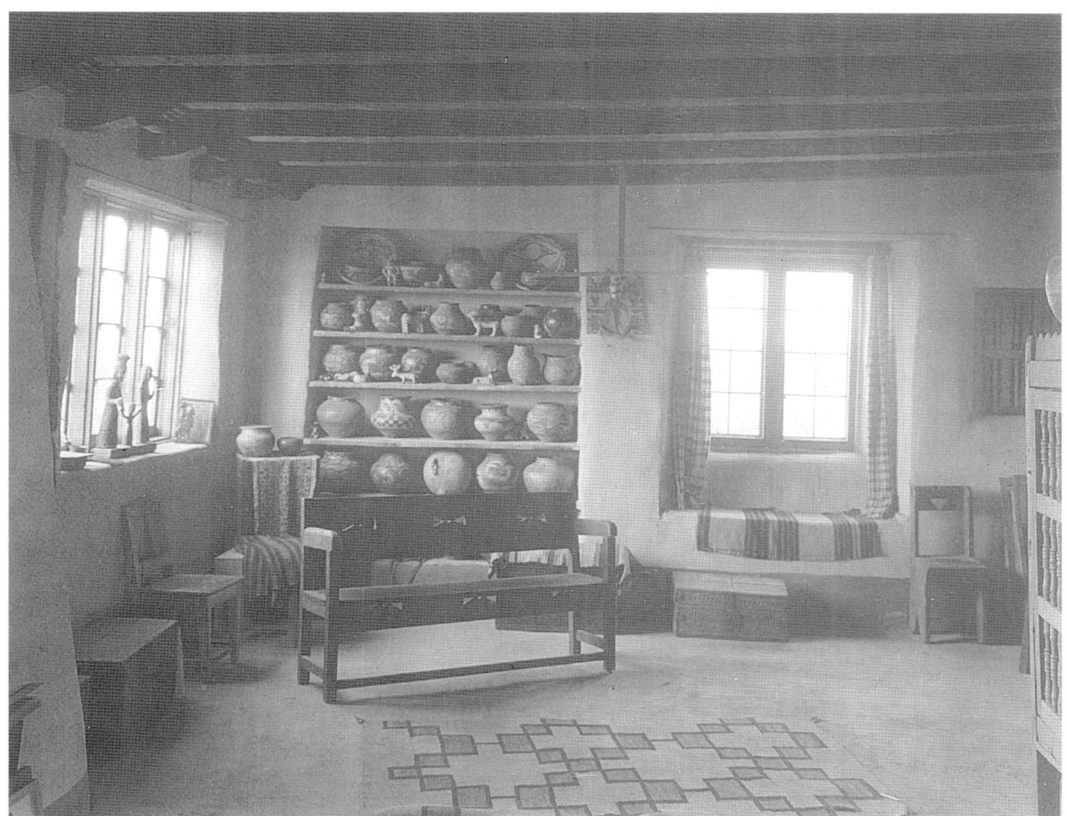

The sitting room at the de la Peña House with numerous Native American pots on the built-in shelving. Published in *House & Garden*, August 1929. Applegate Papers.

199

chairman of the New Mexico Association on Indian Affairs; archaeologist Sylvanus G. Morley; and Martha and Elizabeth White, wealthy patrons of the arts who lived in Santa Fe and owned a gallery of American Indian art in New York City. Many of these people had connections to Santa Fe, although living elsewhere, and were avid collectors. It was no accident that the two most prominent dealers in Indian art in Santa Fe, McMillan and Seligman, were on the board of trustees, while Herman Schweizer, who collected Indian art for the Fred Harvey hotel chain, gave the organization right of first refusal on pieces.[26] By working with the dealers and by bargaining with the Indians themselves, the Indian Arts Fund was able to purchase outstanding pieces at fair prices.

Many of the items Applegate had unearthed during excavations at ancient ruins became part of the collection, as did pieces he had bought from San Ildefonso, Hopi, and other villages. Some of his first donations were artifacts he had dug up or bought at Sikyatki and Sichomovi in the summer of 1923, and he and Dasburg donated and sold pieces they had excavated and bought in Arizona in February 1925. The Indian Arts Fund also purchased some of Applegate's private collection with contributors' funds, either directly from him or through the Spanish & Indian Trading Company. The list of items he contributed or sold—Zía water jar, Santo Domingo bowl, Cochití seed jar, Santa Ana storage jar, Santa Clara water jar, Ácoma water jar, San Felipe cooking jar, Zuni food bowl, Hopi water jar, Picurís storage jar, etc.—reveal the range of his interests. One purchase record shows he received $20 for an early Ácoma jar and $35 for a large Zuni jar.[27]

Frank and Alta loved to hunt for Indian and Spanish Colonial artifacts, and Applegate's letters frequently mentioned his latest "find." In an article for the *New Mexico Highway Journal,* he noted, "It seems that no sooner does a person become a resident of New Mexico [than] the collecting bug bites him. From thenceforth, he will rise in the middle of the night to buy an old rug, a santo, bulto, chest, bed, wagon wheel, or almost anything else which had a his-

toric Indian or Spanish significance." He obviously spoke from experience, for that magazine stated, "His huge home ... is a veritable treasure house of Navajo rugs, santos, bultos, Spanish chests, Spanish furniture, Hopi rugs, saltillo rugs, bayeta rugs, pottery from a dozen pueblos, ceremonial costumes and articles, and so on."[28]

Applegate studied the origins of Indian artwork and wrote two articles on the subject, as he later would write about Spanish Colonial art. He sought assistance from Frederick Webb Hodge of the Southwest Museum in researching the Anasazi of the Basketmaker and Early Pueblo periods.[29]

Like most of his fellow collectors, Applegate seems not to have realized or cared that some of the pieces he collected were part of sacred Indian rituals, and although they may have been purchased honestly from one tribe member, others did not wish them sold. A theme of the Arts and Crafts movement, as scholar J.J. Brody stated, was that "religious or ritual art of any tradition was admired for a combination of its formal qualities and a generic 'spirituality.'" The collectors of Indian (and Spanish Colonial) art appreciated it secularly and for its part in a holistically spiritual society while ignoring its specific religious meanings. Fred Kabotie, the famous Hopi watercolor artist, reported seeing two sacred "Corn Maiden" masks with tablitas (carved and painted wooden tablets) in the Museum of New Mexico's basement while employed there in the mid-1920s. They "could only have been the legendary Hopi Shalako Mana, or maidens," he wrote. "I asked where they'd come from, and was told that they belonged to a couple named Applegate, artists, who had bought them from a Hopi policeman. ... My grandfather explained that the ceremony hadn't been performed for at least 75 years. ... I only hope that some day, somehow, we'll get back those beautiful Shalako masks."[30]

The Indian Arts Fund was not alone in receiving Indian artifacts from Applegate. In the fall of 1927 he sold the Denver Art Museum "a number of rare specimens of Pueblo pottery and old Indian ceremonial objects of great artistic

and historical value." The Applegate
Collection, as it was called, contained 12
Hopi ceremonial items and 10 pieces of
pottery.

"Perhaps the greatest treasure in the
Applegate collection is the complete
costume, including mask, tablita, and
rattle of a Niman Katchina, used by the
Hopi Indians to celebrate the 'Going
home' of the Katchinas or spirits of the
old people," *El Palacio* reported. "Only
this summer, and only after great difficulties has Applegate been able to secure
the costume."[31]

Soliciting money was one of the
Indian Arts Fund's main tasks. "The
operation [was] a model of simplicity:
dun everybody everywhere for money;
spend the money the moment a worthwhile article came into the market."
Contributions to the fund came from
around the United States, often in
increments of $5 and $10. The group
held meetings in Santa Fe to educate
residents on their efforts and encourage
donations. Philanthropist John D.
Rockefeller, Jr. viewed the fund's collection in 1924 and was greatly interested.
He returned in 1926, contributed $2,500
to the Indian Arts Fund, and donated
items from his own collection.[32]
Rockefeller later would make a much
more generous contribution.

In addition to collecting and fund
raising, the Indian Arts Fund worked to
fulfill its second goal, the education of
Indians. The *Indian Arts Fund Bulletin*
reported, "Photographs of many of the
most distinguished jars have been
supplied to the Indians of the various
pueblos (particularly those where the art
has almost died out) and by personal
encouragement this activity has meant in
at least one pueblo the revival of the art
where it had become completely ex-
tinct—forgotten over a period of many
years—and in others a betterment of
design and the return to older, more
sound traditions."[33]

Members reported that the Indians
were enthusiastically receiving their
assistance. "Potters in the northern
pueblos are deeply appreciative of the
loan of drawings of designs on old
pieces, which they copy perfectly," the
Santa Fe New Mexican reported. "We
can't teach the Pueblo how to make

pottery," Applegate was quoted as saying.
"He knows how; but we can aid him
substantially in materials and in leading
him back to the old designs."[34]

The preservation of old methods and
ancient styles was important to the
Anglos who supported Indian art. One
way they encouraged a commitment to
traditional styles was by coordinating the
Southwest Indian Fair and Industrial
Arts and Crafts Exhibition, commonly
called the Indian Fair, which took place
annually during Fiesta starting in 1922.
Many of the artists helped organize it,
judged it, and donated and raised prize
money. Applegate often judged the
Indian pottery.

"The fair ... is the most remarkably
complete, varied and beautiful collection
of the products of the Indian's skill ever
assembled in the country—a genius for
decoration unequaled by any nation of
people, inherent and inherited," declared
an editorial in the *New Mexican*. "This
art is one of the world's great treasures.
... It is with satisfaction that we observe
this great movement is starting along the
right lines, eliminating carefully all that
which is not truly Indian and fostering
and encouraging that which is the real
thing."[35]

The first Indian Fairs emphasized
what the Indians were doing to revive
the ancient tribal arts. In order for an
Indian's artwork to be considered for a
prize, it had to reflect the ancient artwork. Nothing innovative would be
considered. Critics today point out that
this prevented the Indians from creating
art on their own terms. "The facts that
the rugs, pots, and silverwork were well-
made handicrafts, that they had the
approval of major arbiters of advanced
taste, that they were made by Indians,
were not enough to give them legiti-
macy; they had to have some sort of
antiquarian credentials."[36]

The 1927 Indian Fair was the first for
which the Indian artists were asked to
sign their work. "At most pueblos other
than San Ildefonso, potters found this
generally unacceptable, feeling that 'our
own people know who made the pots,'
and, moreover, 'the old timers never
would have thought to sign.'" But the
Anglo artists believed signed art had
greater monetary value, and many of the

Indians complied. The 1927 fair brought in $2,077, of which $1,223.30 went to the Indians. María Martínez, the great San Ildefonso potter, took home $98.50 from pottery sales, more than any other artist. "In addition to a variety of special awards, first and second prizes were given the best baskets, large pots, beadwork, costumes, group exhibits, agricultural products, bow and arrow contests, and other competitions." The fair also included exhibits from pueblo day schools. Prizes for the 1928 Southwest Indian Fair were offered in 53 categories, including six exclusively for school exhibits. A note on the bottom of the premium list read, "The admission to the Fair is free to Indians wearing something characteristically Indian."[37]

Applegate served on the Fair Committee from 1927 to 1930. During that time, the committee selected all pieces for exhibition and sale; the Indians had no say in the matter. Committee members used donations to purchase the best examples of pottery before the event, to assure they would be displayed. The Fair Committee took charge of selling the artwork and paid the artists when the fair was over.[38]

Market factors played a large part in the Anglos' efforts to encourage a return to old techniques and styles. They knew or thought they knew what would sell, and they believed the Indians stood only to benefit from increased sales. The parameters did stretch over time, however, and grew to include such objects as candy boxes, ashtrays, bookends, and candlesticks. And potters such as María Martínez became innovators, creating totally new designs and experimenting with different methods of firing. "Anthropologists and amateur committees realize that mere imitation even of one's own ancestral art is stultifying and that if Indian native art is to survive it must be a growing thing."[39]

By September 1927 the Indian Arts Fund's collection of historic handiwork had increased to such an extent that it was called "doubtless the finest collection of Pueblo pottery of the historic period in existence," and its pottery collection alone numbered 790 pieces. The organization created a department of textiles, with a nucleus of 12 outstanding examples of weaving, and collected a few choice specimens of early Navajo silverwork. Applegate was elected to the executive committee (for what would be a life term) and continued to serve on the board of trustees.[40]

At that time the Indian Arts Fund announced it would focus on teaching arts and crafts in the government schools. The New Mexico Association on Indian Affairs asked that the group "prepare material to be placed in the Pueblo day schools for the purpose of encouraging the Indian children to appreciate and study the art of their own pueblo." Kenneth Chapman arranged for colored photographs to be put on permanent exhibit in the day schools, starting with those at Tesuque, Cochití, and Zuni pueblos. The association also had Chapman photograph the entire collection so that photos could be sent to places where the artifacts could not.[41]

Chapman gave the Association on Indian Affairs a progress report a year later. "These exhibits have stimulated the interest and pride of Pueblo children in their own ancestral art and serve as models for design in class work," he said. "They also promote contacts between teachers and the adult craft workers who come to the school houses to study the exhibits." Indian Arts Fund members had made field trips to ten pueblos, Chapman said, and crafts workers had responded positively to the encouragement given for excellent work. He concluded, "The work of the past year has given additional proof of the soundness of the arts and crafts committee's program: that of furthering the self-respect of the Indians by helping them to help themselves."[42]

The need for the Indian Arts Fund collection to have its own home became clear early in its existence. In September 1925 Chapman stated, "We cannot consistently make the museum our depository while assuring donors that their contributions will remain in Santa Fe." At a meeting that November the group passed a resolution establishing a building fund, to be compiled by "setting aside 10 percent of all cash contributions and income not set aside by donors for a specific purpose."[43] By July 1926 the organization had raised $500 for the building from local contributors, and a site had been chosen.

In September 1927 the trustees of the Indian Arts Fund incorporated the Laboratory of Anthropology and began to make serious plans to turn their dream of a museum into reality. The *Indian Arts Fund Bulletin* of October 1928 stated the organization's desire for a museum unlike any other. "Strange as it may seem," wrote Willard "Spud" Johnson in his introduction to the bulletin, "this is the first time any museum or archaeological society has attempted to acquire and preserve such a record for such a purpose. Museums all over the country have heterogeneous collections of value and interest; many even have representative objects of the various periods. But this is the first attempt to actually bring together for a people, their history, written in fibre and in clay rather than in words." Johnson bemoaned the fact that the collection was stored in the basement of the museum, "where no one other than Indian Arts Fund members could have access to it." The proposed building was to be a research facility for Indians who wished to study the arts of their ancestors and would include a lab for the analysis of materials used to make the historic artwork.[44]

Although most donations to the Indian Arts Fund were in increments of $5 and $10 or were pieces of art, the fund received a windfall in 1928. John D. Rockefeller, Jr. donated $200,000 for the erection and equipping of buildings and promised an additional $70,000 for the budget, paid over five years, which would include contributions from other sources that he would match. Rockefeller's generosity toward the Laboratory of Anthropology continued for nearly 20 years.

The building site, 75 acres near Sunmount Sanitorium, was donated by Martha and Elizabeth White and Francis Wilson.[45] The lab's board included trustees from around the country, many of whom served on the Indian Arts Fund board.

The Lab of Anthropology's stated purpose was to be "anthropological research, public education, graduate instruction in the field and welfare of the native races of the Southwest." Its goal was to unite the work being conducted by already existing organizations, including the Historical Society of New Mexico, the Indian Arts Fund, and the Society for the Revival of Spanish Colonial Arts (see Chapter 12). The lab's organizers cited the Indian Arts Fund's successful fund raising as indicative of what the new institution would be able to do.[46]

In an essay Applegate wrote that the lab would "be primarily for the use of the Indian and only secondarily for the benefit of the white student who may wish to study Indian art in its own locale." It would be "for the betterment and continuance of Indian art ... readily accessible to the Indians themselves" and not for "the uncomprehending curiosity of the white man."

"It is high time this collection was made, for many of the pueblos are rapidly being denuded of their fine old examples of art by tourists and traders," he said. "This museum is especially necessary now because the government causes a wide gap in the Indian's education by keeping him in boarding school away from the pueblo during his formative years, when he would naturally be learning his native arts and crafts and ways of making a living at home."[47]

The trustees of the Indian Arts Fund pledged their full support of the Lab of Anthropology and agreed to place its collection under the custody of the museum and lab for a period of three years, upon the erection of a suitable building.[48] The fund continued to expand its collection, which was enlarged to embrace the best examples of native textiles, bone and wood carvings, metal art, paintings, and jewelry. By 1929 the pottery collection numbered more than 1,000. That year the fund spent $2,500 to purchase the Chief White Antelope blanket, considered one of the finest Navajo blankets in existence.

The Indian Arts Fund lost its storage facilities at the Museum of New Mexico before the Laboratory of Anthropology was completed. Hewett requested that the fund remove its collection from the museum basement by November 1929. That "started the futile hegira of hundreds of irreplaceable objects from first one basement to another and another." In January 1931 Applegate noted, "The first unit of the laboratory is nearing completion and we hope to move the collection to it soon." The Lab of Anthropology opened later that year.[49]

Applegate remained an active member of the Indian Arts Fund right up to his death in February 1931, and he donated a Hopi carrying basket and a Picurís clay baking slab during the last meeting he attended, two weeks before he died. By January 1931 the Indian Arts Fund collection included 1,564 pieces of pottery, 110 blankets, 59 textiles other than blankets, 84 baskets, and 60 pieces of silver.[50]

In retrospect, the work of Indian Arts Fund has primarily received praise because the group set things aside exclusively for the Indians rather than for the benefit of museum visitors. The fund "has done what state or federal officialdom could never achieve: a collection of Indian art of exquisite taste and authenticity, completely on Indian terms. There is no white man's 'presentation and orientation' here."[51] Critics, however, point out that none of the fund members were Indians; the selection of the "best examples of Indian art" was all in the hands of whites.

When modern historians examine the actions of the Anglo artists, writers, scientists, and other intellectuals with regard to the Indians, they find much to criticize. The relationship was a complicated one and has been the subject of debate for decades. First and foremost, the whites saw the Indians as fellow artists. The Anglo artists believed Indian pottery, painting, weaving, and basketmaking had value as fine art and was not, as was more commonly believed, merely folk craft or ethnographic curiosity, and they sought to help the Indians improve the quality of their work. Applegate did so with the Hopi potters, for example, and William Penhallow Henderson advised the San Ildefonso watercolor artists. "Although Henderson did not attempt to influence the painting style and technique of his Indian artist friends, he did offer them advice on technical matters such as which tempera paints to buy, showing them the best kinds, ones that would not

fade." The artists and writers saw Pueblo painting as "real" art that belonged in an art museum.[52]

Awa-Tsireh, Julián Martínez, and the other San Ildefonso painters in turn served as artistic influences on the modernist artists, as did the designers of Pueblo pottery. The artists appreciated the Indian works' symbolism and inherently abstract qualities. Some of Henderson's works, such as the murals for the Santa Fe Railroad ticket office, show their influence. Likewise, many of Applegate's paintings of Indian ceremonies, such as "Green Corn Dance" and "Santo Domingo Corn Dance" (see Chapter 6), reflect the flat, symbolic watercolors painted by the men of San Ildefonso. One critic noted the resemblance, saying that Applegate's paintings of ceremonial dances "suggest flat Indian wall paintings and decorations on pottery."[53] John Marin, who spent the summers of 1929 and 1930 in New Mexico, was strongly influenced by the Indian watercolor style, as is evident in his interpretations of Pueblo Indian dances. Indian art eventually contributed to the shift from realism to expressionism, and later, to abstract modern art.

Critics have condemned the Anglo artists for frequently referring to the Indians as "primitives," and to their art as "naive," indicating they considered the work instinctive rather than learned and therefore attached less value to it. But not all of the artists and writers shared the belief that the art was solely instinctive. "The Pueblo Indians have been using water-colors for centuries ... and the talents of the Pueblo artists is based upon a centuries-old tradition and technique," wrote Alice Corbin Henderson. John Sloan was so captivated by the Indian watercolors that he arranged to have them shown at the Society of Independent Artists Exhibition in New York in 1921, and the SIA declared, "these Indian paintings are the greatest art produced in America." Efforts such as these introduced a large audience to the art and "helped to bring artists forth from the obscurity that had been caused by stupid, sometimes apparently vicious, policy at the hands of government agents."[54]

As stated previously, the Anglo artists of the early 1900s also have been condemned for encouraging the Indians to make their art more marketable to whites. While it is true they did this, they were following a path that began long before they arrived on the scene. Non-native influences had been incorporated into Indian art since the first conquistadores traveled in the region. After the Spanish reconquest following the Pueblo Revolt, the Pueblo Indians "abandoned mineral glaze-paint decoration in favor of vegetal and mineral coloring that did not melt during firing—the matte-paint technique." In ceramic wares the Spanish imported into Mexico from Europe, the Pueblo Indians saw the "clarity, complexity, and control over pottery design" that the matte-paint technique afforded.[55]

By the time the Santa Fe art colony was in full form, the Pueblo Indians and Navajos had been dependent upon the tourist trade for income for decades, however unfortunate some might consider the fact. The arrival of the railroad in New Mexico accelerated changes in the shapes, styles, and design elements. The first traders to sell Indian wares encouraged them to weave a certain blanket pattern, make pottery curios, and otherwise turn their art into a marketable commodity.[56] One may look at the traders' efforts as motivated by profit, but it is hard to argue that Applegate and other artists had significant mercenary intentions. Their desire stemmed as much from a social-humanist outlook. They thought the Indians possessed a means to escape poverty,

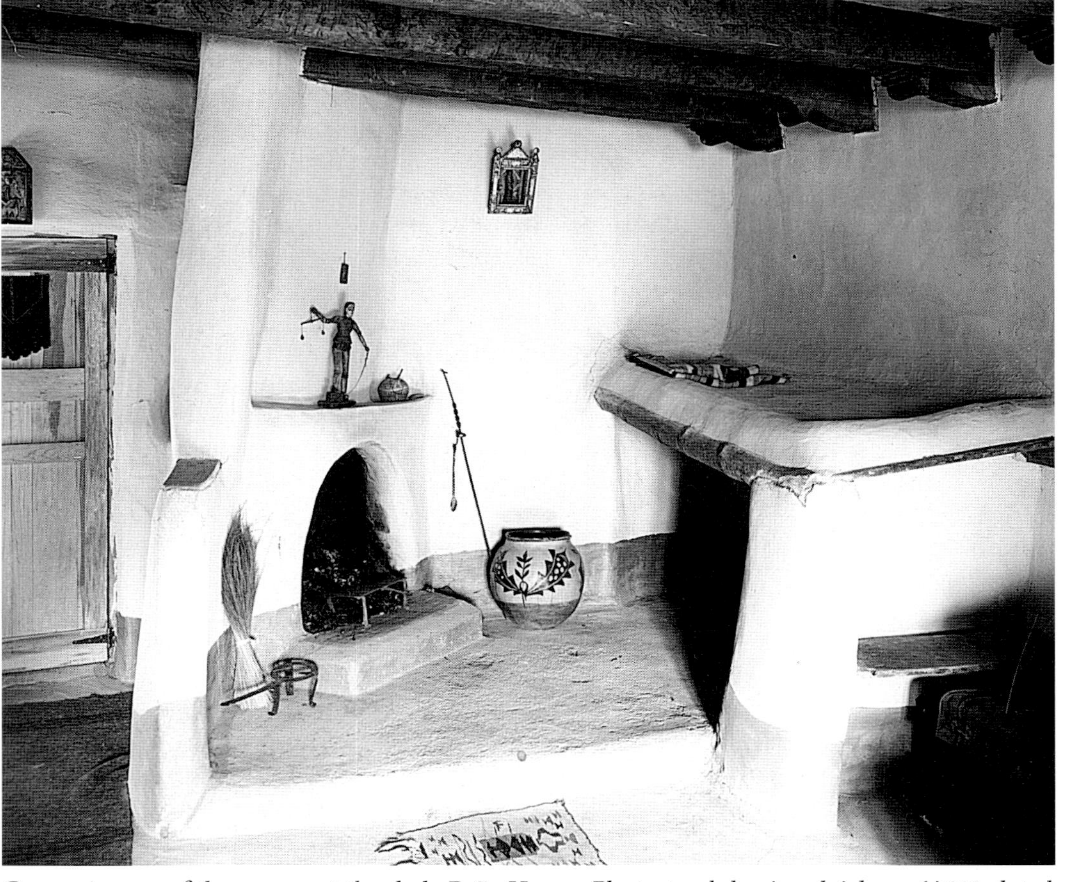

Corner in one of the rooms at the de la Peña House. Photograph by Ansel Adams (A111, dated August 21, 1930). Published in *Ladies Home Journal*, December 1930. Note in Frank Applegate's handwriting on the back of this photograph reads, "old home in Santa Fe with fireplace and adobe. Home about 200 years old of ranch type standing on outer edge of city. The affair in the corner is an old adobe bed. The children were placed on blankets. There are few of these old beds left in New Mexico. Most of them having been torn out to make way for more modern beds." Courtesy of the Center for Creative Photography and the Ansel Adams Publishing Rights Trust.

and they wanted to help them attain that goal. Additionally, the members of the artists colony were among the first to recognize the value of preserving the authentic, unadulterated examples of Native American art.

Archaeologists such as Edgar Lee Hewett helped to reverse the trend toward commercialization of Indian art. Hewett's excavation at Puye in 1907 and the Frijoles Canyon ruins beginning in 1909 uncovered prehistoric pottery, and Hewett realized that the prehistoric artifacts could be used to reintroduce modern-day Indians to lost forms of art, such as lost patterns and glazes. In addition Hewett saw the painting and clay work of San Ildefonso artists such as Ta-e (Crescencio Martínez) and María and Julián Martínez and encouraged them to teach it to others. The School of American Research analyzed the Pueblo Indians' potterymaking methods and taught them how to make stronger wares.[57]

The Anglos encouraged, and some-times prodded, Native American artists to work within restrictive parameters. The trademark features of Pueblo Indian watercolors derived from fragments of prehistoric murals found in Frijoles Canyon. "White preconceptions of what Indian art should look like conformed to these. It was assumed that Indian paint-ing should have strong outlines within which flat colors were confined, no specific backgrounds, and should be planar—and so, among the Rio Grande Pueblos, it developed. That the White influences were unconsciously spread through selective buying seems prob-able."[58]

Coupled with the Anglos' desire to preserve ancient art forms was their interest in preserving the Pueblo culture. Some historians have censured the artists and writers for encouraging the Indians to retain their primitive ways instead of helping them to learn a trade or modernize their pueblos. Rather than encourage the Indians to work in, say, factories, their Anglo supporters "argued that the Indians would be far better off making beads out of turquoise, doing shell work, and generally having 'things to do during the winter months.' Pre-sumably agriculture would occupy them

during the summer." The artists and writers "chose to dictate an idyllic way of life that pushed the Indians back into the past and denied them access to an industrial future."[59] Given that the alternative appeared to be cultural extinction at the hands of government agencies, it is hardly surprising that the Anglos believed the Pueblo Indians would be better off maintaining their traditional lifestyle. Of course, the Anglos would have done a greater service had they given the Indians more of a say in matters that affected them.

The artists also have been criticized for romanticizing Indian life in their paintings. By portraying the Indians in their true poverty, the argument follows, they may have contributed to the im-provement of Indian life. It is true, many of the artists filtered Pueblo culture "through a screen of discontent, of longing for a simpler, more fundamental way of life." Perhaps, as art historian Van Deren Coke has suggested, "the Indians seemed too self-sufficient and alien in culture for this kind of involvement." In any case the paintings of Indians by Applegate, John Sloan, Andrew Dasburg, and others in the modern vein were a far cry from the romantic images created by Taos artists such as W. Herbert Dunton and Joseph Henry Sharp. The modern depictions of Indian dances, with their dark palettes and muscular strength, were considered quite radical—unroman-tic, decidedly realistic, and, as far as public opinion was concerned, unattrac-tive. "The Indians are not as pretty as the old ones used to be," lamented one art critic, reviewing a show by the New Mexico Painters.[60]

The artists helped the Indians improve their lives through means other than art. They sold their own paintings to raise money to feed them and fought to protect Pueblo lands. During one drought year, they hosted plays at the museum, auctioned off cartoons and gave benefit dances to purchase hay for the Indians' livestock and milk for their children. They spoke out against the performances of sacred Indian ceremo-nies as entertainment during the Fiesta, Santa Fe's largest and most popular annual event, and in favor of letting the Indians retain their religious rituals.

They set up the Indian Arts Fund for the express purpose of educating future generations of Indian artists and helped them sell artwork at the Indian Fair, in local shops, at the White sisters' Ishauu Gallery in New York, and elsewhere. When Alice Corbin Henderson and Mary Austin traveled on lecture tours, they brought along San Ildefonso watercolors to sell, and they organized shows of Indian paintings in Chicago and New York.[61]

The artists and other intellectuals acted in large part out of a sense of collective guilt over the actions of their Anglo predecessors and the American government. "If it were possible for the government to return the city of Santa Fe and its environs to the descendants of the peoples who lived, loved and labored here for the last three or four centuries and at the same time remove all Anglos and forbid them ever again entering, Santa Fe would be one of the most attractive communities in America; an International Monument," Will Shuster once wrote. "It is bad enough that we Anglos have imposed our clumsy hands on the lives of these peoples slowly but dominatingly over a period of sixty or seventy years. ... Slowly we have wrested from them the simple beautiful things that were theirs and impressed upon them that standardized and specialized existence which breeds in our great cities and like wind blown germs spreads and infects virgin country."[62]

Applegate, too, felt a sense of guilt, as he indicated in a piece written shortly before his death in 1931. In it he recalled the first time he was incited to anger by government actions toward the Indians. Specifically, he was outraged that the Indian Bureau could forcibly remove children from the pueblos and place them in boarding schools.

"I was invited by some of the people of Zia to come to a grand thanksgiving ceremony and dance they were to give at the pueblo," he wrote.

> I arrived at the pueblo but I was surprised to find it silent. ... As I walked across one of the deserted plazas that should have been crowded with happy smiling people, a woman or two with small babies and a very old man came out to greet me. Their faces looked sad and worried and after greeting them I asked them what the matter could be and where was everybody. One of the women answered that a girl of the pueblo was lost and could not be found. ... I stayed about the pueblo for a while, trying to make helpful suggestions. ...
>
> The next afternoon I returned to hear what news there might be of the missing child. In the plaza of Zia I found everybody I had seen the day before, and instead of sorrow and anxiety, I saw that they were all deeply stirred by anger. Strangely some of that anger seemed to be directed toward me, and from several who had been my good friends I received hard and resentful looks. Finding one who seemed calmer, I asked him what news there was of the missing child, or if they had found her. "Yes," he said, but seemed not inclined to say anything further. "Where," I asked him. "Indian School," he said. ...
>
> I had heard of things like this, but I had never before realized them as facts. For the first time I understood something of the deep and hopeless resentment of the Indians, frustrated in every normal instinct and helpless before the violation of their most human feelings. For I knew as well as they did how completely in finding the child in school they had lost her. She would be kept there either until they sent her home infected with tuberculosis to die, or after seven or eight years ... they let her return to her Indian home with a smattering of American education and so utterly spoiled for pueblo life, that the best she could hope for was to be a servant in some white family, or take to prostitution as an alternative to the aimless ineffectual life with a husband of her own tribe, himself made incompetent as an Indian by an education which could not make him white.
>
> I did not say much to the men of Zia. What I had to say was said elsewhere, and in company with scores of other white people who

had also seen these things, and what we did together was not entirely without effect. If you go to Zia now you will see there a day school in the village, where the children can get what is important to them to know of white learning, without being separated from their parents. ... Until this happened I was never rid of a shamed feeling of guilt for what occurred at the time the little girl was lost, and it is only since that time that I began to feel the same freedom and welcome at Zia.[63]

As well-intentioned as the actions of the artists and writers may have been, many of them operated under the belief that they knew what was best for the Indians. As J.J. Brody wrote, "Even the most sensible, humanistic, and scientifically objective of the Whites seemed unable to avoid (or even recognize) attitudes that can be described only as paternal and racist."[64]

It cannot be said that Applegate stood apart from Brody's assessment, for he was a product of his age. What is known is that many of the Indians respected him and spoke warmly of Alta. The Applegates in turn welcomed Indian friends into their home, as did many of the artists and writers. The Native Americans appreciated Applegate's humor and his storytelling abilities, and he was called "a favorite of several of the Indian governors." The Applegates spent months living with Indians and visited them frequently. They told him the legends of their tribes, which he would later retell and compile in book form. Applegate considered the Indians' art great art, and his paintings were obviously influenced by the Indian watercolors he saw. A high-ranking Santo Domingo Indian asked Applegate to paint portraits of him and his wife. And, when Applegate died, the Zias gave him a ceremonial Indian burial.[65]

If there was a single underlying principle that guided the artists and writers in their actions regarding the Pueblo Indians, it was the belief that self-empowerment was essential to the Indians' survival. The Anglos' goal was to persuade the Indians to continue to produce art, for they believed that once continuous production was assured, a market system would enable the Indians to realize a sustaining profit. The creation of the Indian Arts and Crafts Board in 1935 helped achieve this goal. The board, a U.S. Department of the Interior commission authorized by Congress at the behest of John C. Collier, sponsored art classes and exhibitions, set up craft guilds, and established quality and authentification standards. "Of all economic programs sponsored by the government for Indians, the craft guilds were probably the most successful," Brody wrote. "They increased the income of individual Indians and tribes, were wholly owned and mostly operated by the communities."[66]

Even without the guilds, the sale of Indian crafts enabled some of the Indians to escape poverty. As historian Lonn Taylor reported: "Figures gathered in 1933 showed that 20 people at San Ildefonso were making pottery; they made 1,800 pots that year and sold them for $9,900. The next largest source of income was farming, at which 22 people earned $2,548. ... The per family income at San Ildefonso was in 1933 $762, compared to $290 at neighboring Nambé pueblo, which did not have a pottery industry." Unfortunately, something the artists and writers had not foreseen was that the social structure of the pueblos also changed, because new wealth created jealousy and competition.[67]

Applegate's work with the Indian Arts Fund and the Indian Fair paralleled his efforts with New Mexico's other population of pre-American inhabitants, the Hispanics. He would encourage their artists, collect their artifacts, educate their children, and coordinate a market for their fine crafts just as he had the Indians'. He would become the country's foremost expert on Spanish Colonial art, as his research into the subject came to dominate all other aspects of his life.

Endnotes

1 "F.G. Applegate Has Five Canvases in Los Angeles Museum Exhibition." *Trenton (N.J.) State Gazette,* n.d., probably July 1923, Applegate Papers.

2 Sikorski, *Modern Hopi Pottery,* 22.

3 FGA to F.H. Douglas, Dec. 12, 1930. F.H. Douglas Papers, Denver Art Museum, Department of Native Arts. While Applegate states in the letter that he stayed with the Hopis in 1922, other evidence indicates it was in 1923.

4 "Indian Arts and Crafts Are Discussed by Association," *Santa Fe New Mexican,* Nov. 27, 1923, 5. *Santa Fe New Mexican,* May 6, 1924. Authors' interviews with Gretchen Beall. Indian Arts Fund Records, 1-Pottery 1-401, Indian Arts Fund Papers.

5 Bartlett, "A History of Hopi Pottery," in Frederick, ed., *Hopi and Hopi-Tewa Pottery,* 13. Coe, "Native American Craft," in Kardon, ed., *Revivals! Diverse Traditions,* 68.

6 FGA to Mary Mowbray-Clarke, Jan. 9, 1925, Mowbray-Clarke Papers, AAA, Reel D169A. *Atlanta (Ill.) Argus,* May 29, 1925. *Santa Fe New Mexican,* Aug. 15, 1927, 8. White, "The New Mexico Painters," in *The New Mexico Painters,* 12. Brody, *Pueblo Indian Painting: Tradition and Modernism in New Mexico, 1900-1930,* 123. Dasburg hoped to sell some of his santos and use the proceeds to stay in Polacca for a year; see Dasburg to Mabel Dodge Luhan, March 5 (n.d., 1925), Luhan Papers.

7 "Stone Palace of the Navajos," *Santa Fe New Mexican,* Feb. 8, 1927, 4.

8 "The Snake Priest's Trousers," 33, "A Hopi Quarrel," 52, "Turtle Shells," 109, "Parrot Feathers," 163, all *Indian Stories From the Pueblos.* Fergusson in *Dancing Gods* calls Harry Shupela "the chief Snake Priest at Walpi" (p. 148).

9 "Navajo Nieces," *Native Tales of New Mexico,* 228, 229. Applegate states that "Nah Gee" is a pseudonym.

10 Dunn, *American Indian Painting of the Southwest and Plains,* 221.

11 FGA to Mary Mowbray-Clarke, May 2, 1922, Mowbray-Clarke Papers.

12 Austin, "Indian Detour," *The Bookman* 68:6 (February 1929): 656. Authors' interviews with Gretchen Beall.

13 Elizabeth Willis DeHuff maintained that Applegate, Carlos Vierra, and Alice Corbin Henderson purchased Awa-Tsireh's first paintings; however, she implies that this occurred in 1919, before Applegate arrived in New Mexico. See Elizabeth DeHuff to Mrs. Kramer, n.d., DeHuff Papers, Box 10, Folder 31.

14 "From New Mexico," *Atlanta (Ill.) Argus,* Feb. 10, 1922, 2.

15 "F.G. Applegate Has Five Canvases in Los Angeles Museum Exhibition."

16 "Stone Palace of the Navajos."

17 Applegate, "Home Coming Day Among the Hopi Indians," *Atlanta (Ill.) Argus,* Sept. 14, 1923.

18 Mary Austin to Alfred V. Kidder, Feb. 18, 1929, A.V. Kidder Correspondence, #89-LA2.026.

19 Nestor, *The Native Market of the Spanish New Mexican Craftsmen,* 5. FGA to Mary Mowbray-Clarke, Jan. 9, 1925, April 12, 1925, Mowbray-Clarke Papers. Coke, *Andrew Dasburg,* 65. Other documents verify Applegate's interest in the store; see Zigrosser to Dasburg, Jan. 13, 1926, Zigrosser Papers, MS Coll. 6, Box 9, Folder 369; "Mrs. Applegate Dies in Denver," *Santa Fe New Mexican,* July 31, 1944, 1.

20 "Old Santa Fe Trading Post Is Name of the Latest Curio Store to Open," *Santa Fe New Mexican,* July 23, 1927, 4. Brody, *Indian Painters and White Patrons,* 72, 88.

21 Garmhausen, *History of Indian Arts Education in Santa Fe,* 22, 30.

22 Dunn, 229. This group apparently evolved from a similar one created by Kenneth Chapman, Elizabeth Shepley Sergeant, Wesley Bradfield, and H.P. Mera in 1922.

23 FGA to Mary Mowbray-Clarke, April 12, 1925, Mowbray-Clarke Papers.

24 Chapman, "The Pottery of Santo Domingo Pueblo," in *Memoirs of the Laboratory of Anthropology, Vol. 1,* xiii. *Santa Fe New Mexican,* Dec. 11, 1923, 2. Amon Carter Museum of Western Art, *Quiet Triumph,* 14. Chapman to Hodge, Sept. 15, 1926, Frederick Webb Hodge Manuscript Collection, MS.7.MAI.1.121. Courtesy of the Southwest Museum. Chauvenet, *Edgar L. Hewett and Friends,* 200.

25 "Articles of Incorporation of Indian Arts Fund," Indian Arts Fund Collection. Dunn, 229. Batkin, *Pottery of the Pueblos of New Mexico,* 32.

26 Amon Carter Museum of Western Art, 12.

27 Indian Arts Fund Records, 1-Pottery, 1-401. Purchasing Committee report, Sept. 10, 1927, Indian Arts Fund Papers.

28 Applegate, "If You Buy Antiques," 34, "An All Star Sales Force," 31, both *New Mexico Highway Journal* 7 (April 1929). Courtesy of *New Mexico Magazine.*

29 Applegate to Hodge, Nov. 27, 1929, Frederick Webb Hodge Manuscript Collection.

30 Brody, *Pueblo Indian Painting,* 34. Kabotie with Bill Belknap, *Fred Kabotie: Hopi Indian Artist,* 42. In contrast, a Hopi in *Hopi Indians of Old Oraibi* tells author Mischa Titiev that the Hopis did not feel sentimental about ceremonial items (20). These items were collected during the Applegates' February 1925 trip and donated and sold to the IAF that year. See the Epilogue for an account of the repatriation of items Applegate collected.

31 Rönnebeck, "Applegate Exhibit at Denver," *El Palacio* 23:21 (Nov. 26, 1927): 543-544. Authors' correspondence with Denver Art Museum Library. Applegate received $810 for the materials; see Denver Art Museum to FGA, Sept. 27, 1927, and Oct. 7, 1927, Douglas Papers. Three years later Applegate was still negotiating with the museum over payment for several Indian pots. See FGA to Douglas, Dec. 8, 1930, Douglas Papers.

32 Amon Carter Museum of Western Art, 10, 12. *Santa Fe New Mexican,* July 1, 1924. Garmhausen, 33.

33 *Indian Arts Fund Bulletin,* No. 1, 1925, 3.

34 "Indians Eagerly Welcome Aid in Ancient Crafts," *Santa Fe New Mexican,* May 6, 1924, 2.

35 *Santa Fe New Mexican,* Sept. 6, 1922.

36 Brody, *Indian Painters,* 71.

37 Bernstein, "From Indian Fair to Indian Market," *El Palacio* 98:3 (Summer 1993): 18, 47.

38 Bernstein, 18.

39 "Old Art in New Forms," *New Mexico Association on Indian Affairs Bulletin* 8:1-2, reprinted from *New Mexico Magazine.*

CHAPTER 11:
THE ARTISTS
AND
THE INDIANS

[40] "Indian Arts Fund to Aid Young Indians to Learn Old Stuff," *Santa Fe New Mexican*, Sept. 10, 1927, 2.

[41] "Indian Arts Fund to Aid Young Indians to Learn Old Stuff." "Indians Eager to Equal Work of Ancestors," *Santa Fe New Mexican*, Jan. 17, 1929, 7.

[42] "Indians Eager to Equal Work of Ancestors."

[43] Chapman to Hodge, Sept. 15, 1925, Frederick Webb Hodge Manuscript Collection. Indian Arts Fund Chronology, Nov. 6, 1925, Bruce Ellis Collection, Box 390, Folder 6.

[44] *Indian Arts Fund Bulletin*, October 1928, 5. *Santa Fe New Mexican*, Oct. 24, 1928, 4.

[45] "Rockefeller Gives $270,000 to Anthropology Laboratory in Santa Fe," *Santa Fe New Mexican*, Dec. 31, 1928, 1. Most likely, the land deeded to the lab was the same land Wilson fought to protect during the debate over the cultural center (see Chapter 9). A letter from Rockefeller to Applegate is in the Applegate Papers.

[46] "Rockefeller Gives $270,000 to Anthropology Laboratory in Santa Fe," 7.

[47] Applegate, "New Mexico Backgrounds," *Southwest Review* 14:3 (Spring 1929): 355.

[48] Laboratory of Anthropology Correspondence, Lab Inc. 1920s, Box 2, handwritten statement.

[49] Amon Carter Museum of Western Art, 14. Applegate to Hodge, Jan. 18, 1931, Frederick Webb Hodge Manuscript Collection. Chauvenet, 200.

[50] Executive Committee minutes, Indian Arts Fund Chronology, Jan. 26, 1931, Bruce Ellis Collection, Box 390, Folder 6.

[51] Amon Carter Museum of Western Art, 5.

[52] Adkins, "William Penhallow Henderson and Southwestern Indian Art," *El Palacio* 93:2 (Winter 1987): 23. Brody, *Pueblo Indian Painting*, 152.

[53] Adkins, 2. Read, "Pueblos of Distinct Cubist Lines," *Brooklyn (N.Y.) Daily Eagle*, reprinted in *Santa Fe New Mexican*, Oct. 30, 1924, 4.

[54] Henderson, "An Indian Goya Who Amazes Artists," *Literary Digest*, Oct. 17, 1925, 46. Dunn, 224, 227.

[55] Frank, "From Settler to Citizen: Economic Development and Cultural Change in Late Colonial New Mexico, 1850-1920," dissertation, University of California, Berkeley, 1992, 266-267.

[56] Frank, 267. Brody, *Indian Painters*, 61, 62.

[57] Cahill, "America Has Its 'Primitives,' " *International Studio* 75 (March 1922): 127-128. Taylor, "Arts and Crafts in the Santa Fe Style," paper presented at the Winterthur Conference on the Decorative Arts, Wilmington, Del., 1990, 7-15.

[58] Brody, *Indian Painters*, 14.

[59] Stineman, *Mary Austin, Song of a Maverick*, 176, 178.

[60] Truettner, "The Art of Pueblo Life," in Eldridge, et al., *Art in New Mexico*, 63. Coke, *Taos and Santa Fe, the Artists' Environment*, 108. *Chicago Daily News*, Feb. 20, 1924.

[61] Robertson, *Los Cinco Pintores*, 9. "Artists to Hold Auction for Benefit of Pueblo Indians," *Santa Fe New Mexican*, Feb. 8, 1923. Brody, *Pueblo Indian Painting*, 104. Seymour, *When the Rainbow Touches Down*, 22.

[62] Shuster to Walter F. Dantzscher, The Gilliams Service, July 3, 1926, Shuster Papers, AAA, Reel 169.

[63] Applegate, "The Lost Child of Zia," in *Native Tales of New Mexico*, 198-202. An examination of manuscript copies of this story in the Applegate Papers indicate that Mary Austin contributed significantly to this part of the tale. The "lost child" bears similarity to the character Slim Girl in Oliver LaFarge's *Laughing Boy*, published in 1929.

[64] Brody, *Indian Painters*, 90.

[65] Mowat, "The Artist in the Southwest," *El Palacio* 20:10 (May 15, 1926): 196. *Santa Fe New Mexican*, Feb. 18, 1931, 2.

[66] Philp, *John Collier's Crusade for Indian Reform*, 185. Brody, *Indian Painters*, 72.

[67] Taylor, "Arts and Crafts in the Santa Fe Style," 20-22.

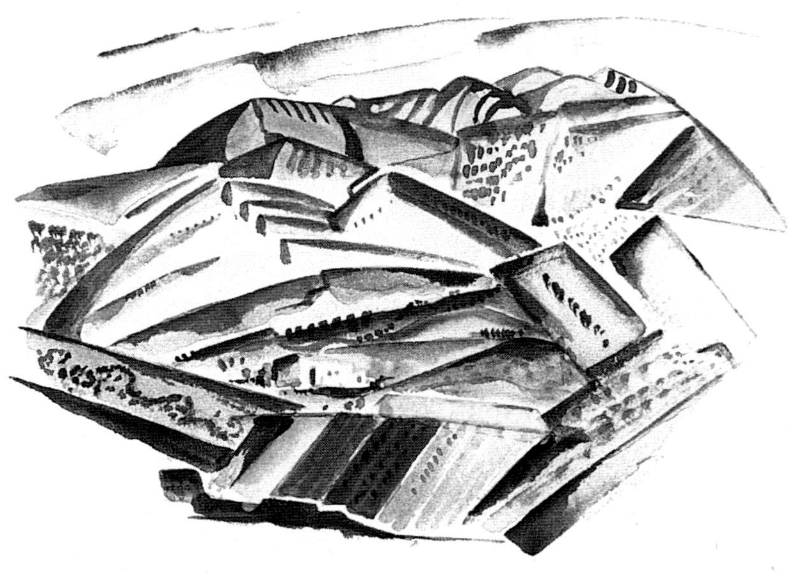

Farm & House in Valley, watercolor, 8" by 10¾". Private collection. Photograph courtesy of Gerald Peters Gallery, Santa Fe.

12 Spanish Colonial Revival

Frank Applegate was as fascinated with New Mexicans of Spanish descent and their arts and craftwork as he was with the Pueblo Indians. Santa Fe was unlike anywhere else he had lived, in part because Spanish culture was on an equal footing with American culture in the city. Governmental and business affairs were transacted in both Spanish and English, and citizens of Spanish descent held high offices. The Hispanics and Anglos lived side by side; indeed, many of Applegate's neighbors were Hispanic.

When he arrived in New Mexico, the Hispanic residents of the small villages surrounding Santa Fe lived in a manner similar to that of their ancestors, subsisting primarily by farming and raising livestock. Most of what they needed to survive—food, clothing, houses, furnishings—they grew, raised, or made themselves. For this reason and because they lived in mountainous terrain, the rural villagers were still somewhat isolated from Anglo civilization in the 1920s.

Many of the villagers were descended from Spanish settlers who came to northern New Mexico from the southern part of New Spain, now known as Mexico, during the Spanish colonial period, 1598 to 1821. The furnishings and devotional objects those colonists brought with them eventually needed to be replenished, and their descendants began to make the pieces themselves. As traditions such as woodcarving, embroidery, tinwork, weaving, pottery, and furniture-making were passed down from generation to generation, the descendants evolved into artisans of great skill. Their fine arts and crafts, including weaving, woodcarving, embroidery, and tinware, came to be called Spanish Colonial art.

To an extent the Anglo artists and writers romanticized the Hispanics as they did the Indians. The Spanish culture "gave to those modern explorers a sense of artistic heritage which they could not find in any other place in their homeland." The artists and writers "waxed romantic about the superiority of their simple, nonmaterial neighbors who wanted, and needed, nothing more than what the earth provided."[1] This romanticization manifested itself in the Anglo artists' interest in religious and other handmade art.

Applegate became enamored of Spanish Colonial art soon after his arrival in New Mexico. He developed a deep, abiding interest in the dramatic religious icons, or santos—a word that encompasses handcarved wooden statues of saints, or bultos; depictions of Christ on the cross, called crucifijos; religious paintings on wood, known as retablos; and religious paintings on hide.

Many of the artists and writers collected the religious art and used it to decorate their homes, but Applegate was

211

drawn to it with a singular passion. "Every few dollars ahead were spent for things which interested him, and thus the collection grew," Alta Applegate recalled. Art experts of the time considered santos folk craft rather than fine art, and thus attached little value to them. Just as the work of cubist artists in France spurred an interest in African art, it took the modernist artists' arrival in New Mexico to stir Anglo enthusiasm for Spanish Colonial art. "Even the first painters who came into the [Rio Grande] valley scorned [santos] as beneath their notice, but they belonged to the Academic school who see nothing in the primitive where even they see it, except something savage and uncivilized," Applegate wrote. "It is usually only the more modern painters who will drift in here who show any real appreciation for them."[2]

"Before Applegate's advent the exotic santos and bultos to be found in every native home, were regarded by collectors and dealers alike as mere curios," wrote Ina Sizer Cassidy. "His discerning eye and knowledge of aesthetic values recognized them for what they really were, rare and valuable examples of primitive art."[3]

The artists' attraction to Spanish Colonial art was "part of a universal revaluation of popular and primitive arts … proclaimed as the most original American folk art. Their ingenuous qualities which happily ignored academic conventions immediately appealed to the newly emerging aesthetic of the 1920s." Applegate's interest in the religious art was due in part to this realization. "To me they are the only really primitive paintings ever done in America," he wrote, referring to retablos. "They are very beautiful and interesting. The only thing that amazes me is that they have not been exploited long ago." He and other artists and writers found a spiritual force in the emotional intensity of the works, a force that contrasted sharply with their largely Protestant backgrounds. "Here was an abundance of emotion made visible in vivid ritual, and here was a powerful metaphor for creativity held before artists who had left genteel traditions in the East and Europe to create an art of spiritual strength."[4]

Additionally, the artistic style of the santeros, the makers of this religious art, meshed with the modernists' own. Bold color, thickly applied paint, strong, heavy line, abstract shapes, and a two-dimensional quality were evident in many retablos. However, the santeros' style was a throwback to the pre-Renaissance, medieval art of their Spanish ancestors, while the modernist painters operated at the other end of the spectrum, having studied and rejected the artistic conventions of the Renaissance.[5]

Scholar Charles Briggs suggests another reason for the interest of the Anglo artists: "a fascination that did not emanate solely from [the santos'] status as 'primitives' or 'antiques' but appears to have been enhanced by the animism that was supposedly associated with their veneration."[6] Unfamiliar with Catholicism, the artists possibly misunderstood the Hispanics' "worship" of the religious figures. Applegate, for one, tried to understand and explain the meanings behind Hispanic and Indian religious ritual and symbolism and wrote about his interpretations.

Applegate also studied the processes behind the artwork—the types of organic paints and wood used, the reason they were coated with gesso, or calcinated gypsum (so the paint would adhere), the tools needed, the iconography. With careful examination he eventually became quite knowledgeable; he could date many items, recognize which saints were depicted and determine a piece's relative rarity. Mary Austin, who dated her interest in Spanish Colonial art to 1918 and who discussed her admiration of it in the book *The Land of Journey's Ending*, recalled that her and Applegate's "first conference on the subject had to do with a carved figure of Our Lady of Innocence, which I had recently secured from a morada at Abiquiú, which had been repainted with crude colors of house paint, which Frank undertook to show me how to remove, thus uncovering the delicate workmanship underneath."[7]

Alta Applegate was almost as passionate about Spanish Colonial art as her husband was, and together they scoured the countryside in search of items for their collection. "It was great fun to go

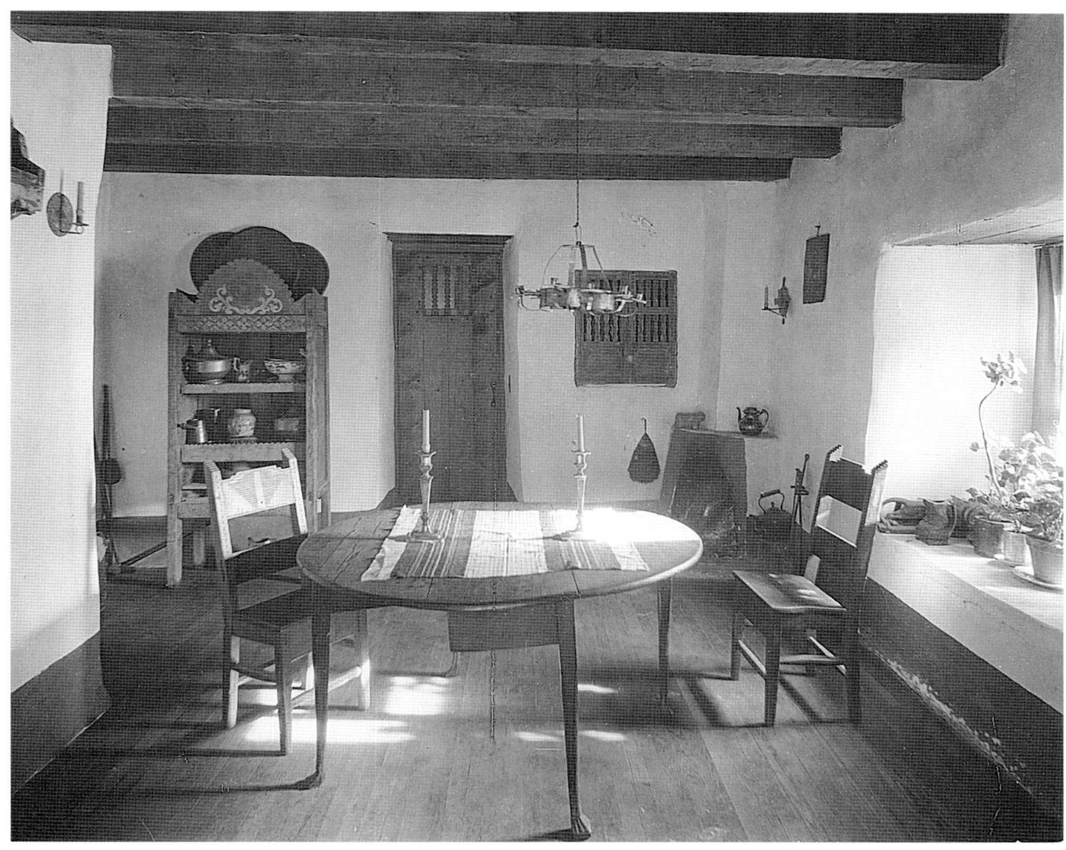

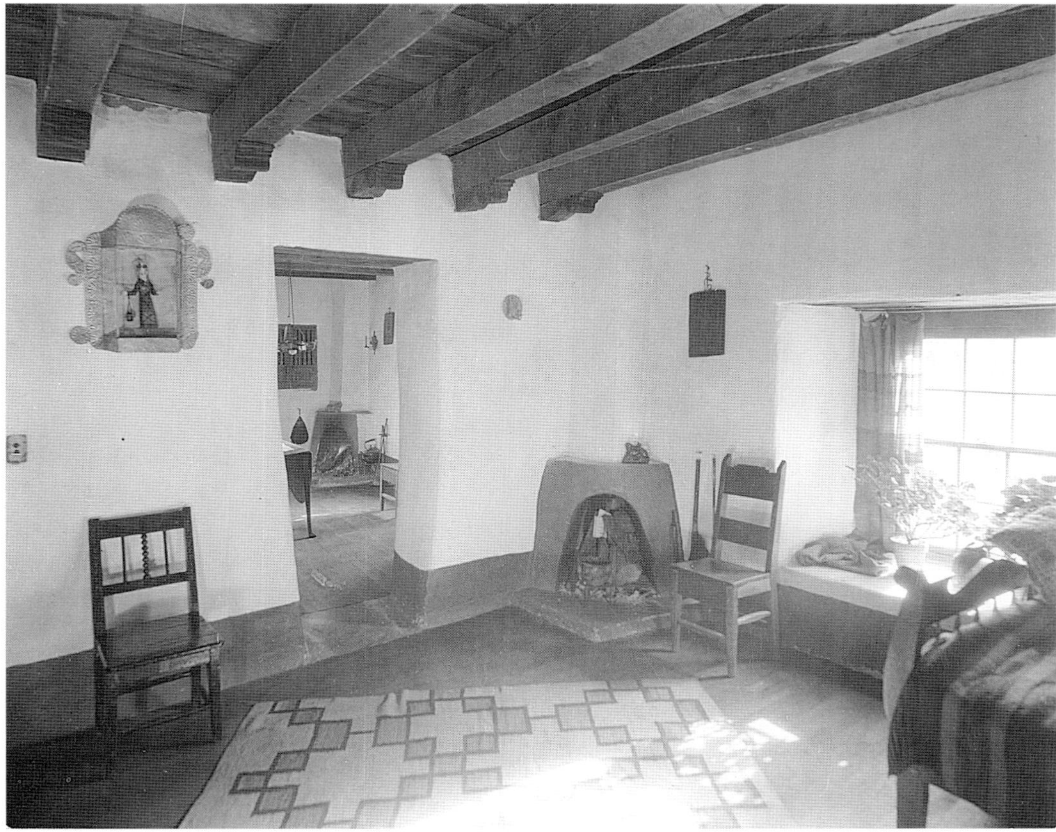

Top: Interior view of the dining room at the de la Peña House. Published in *House & Garden*, April 1929. Bottom: Interior of one of the bedrooms at the de la Peña House. Applegate Papers.

for the day on such a hunt, getting acquainted with the pleasant Spanish people in the small towns, seeing them in their homes, and learning their interests," she recalled. "Many of our loveliest trips and best times were had on these hunting expeditions–some of our most enjoyable of our Spanish friends discovered." She took charge of cataloguing the items in the ever-expanding collection.[8]

The collection grew beyond the santos to include gesso-painted dowry chests, carved trasteros, or cupboards, spindle cabinets, woven blankets, and altar screens or reredos–large structures of columns, niches, and panels that were painted like retablos. Applegate also purchased a few 19th century hide paintings, which were extremely rare, since the church hierarchy came to believe that a religious subject was desecrated when painted on animal skin. As with his collection of Indian art, Applegate soon amassed many more items than he could display. By January 1925 he estimated that he had nearly 200 bultos and retablos, in addition to the other items.[9]

With the establishment of the Spanish & Indian Trading Company in 1924, Applegate became a dealer in Spanish Colonial art, along with Andrew Dasburg, B.J.O. Nordfeldt, and other avid collectors. Applegate developed a rapport with the Hispanics as he had with the Indians, and they knew him as "Señor Frank." Austin wrote, "I have had curio dealers, who make a handsome profit on the sale of works executed by the native [here, Spanish] before the advent of Americans, complain to me that the said natives would rather sell their work to Frank Applegate than to the dealers, 'even when we pay a higher price for it.' This is actually the case. ... The natives [sell] to Frank Applegate ... because they [recognize] in him an appreciation not only of the artistry in their work, but of its human significance."[10]

Historians later criticized Applegate and other collectors for buying up the art. Scholar Suzanne Forrest surmised that they reasoned, "like Lord Elgin with the Parthenon marbles, that it was a form of cultural preservation," and said the Hispanic and Indian villagers "often parted reluctantly with their family icons and heirlooms out of economic necessity." Applegate, however, believed that many of the Hispanics had little interest in the old pieces and that santeros made religious art for profit as well as devotion. "A santero usually had his shop in or near his home and on the edge of a town," he wrote. "He would paint a number of Santos Retablos, then load them on his burro and go from house to house selling his wares. For an ordinary Santo Retablo he received a sheep or a bushel of wheat; for a very special one he might obtain a cow or a horse."[11]

By the 1920s, even those who lived in relatively isolated villages had ready access to mass-produced religious icons and furnishings, which had begun to reach northern New Mexico back in 1821, when the Santa Fe Trail opened. For decades the villagers had been replacing their old wooden artifacts with mass-produced, factory-made items. Alta Applegate recalled that they "found many rare handmade articles discarded in old store rooms no longer used. These articles were often replaced by new factory made pieces–in our minds, the latter couldn't compare to the charming old things. Occasionally, a fine old chest was being used in a barn for feed."[12]

In the fall of 1924 Applegate decided to sell some of his personal collection of retablos in order to buy better examples of them. He contacted Mary Mowbray-Clarke in New York City, and she agreed to display them at her Sunwise Turn gallery and sell them on a commission basis. That November Applegate shipped Mowbray-Clarke 38 pieces, including "three French colored prints framed in old Mexico metal composed of tin, silver, and lead, and also one painting from old Mexico on silver and tin metal ... for [comparison] and historical reasons." Prices ranged from $32 to $180, and Applegate added, "I priced them as low as I could allowing you 25 percent commission." He continued:

> I have been wild about these paintings ever since I've been in New Mexico and have collected all I could afford to and really more than I could afford. As you sell them, if you do, I wish you would forward [the] check immediately

for it so I can invest in others. … I made the selection as carefully as I could to get as interesting and varied a collection as possible. These are all very old and if you will notice are nearly all made on adzed boards made by splitting up logs before saws were introduced. To me, these are the rarest and most interesting primitive [*sic*] specimens of American art and no one had seemed to appreciate [them] till I and Dasburg & Nordfeldt came.[13]

The New York papers were not sure how to approach the works, and quoted extensively from an essay Applegate wrote to accompany the exhibit, which explained how the pieces were made. *The New York Times* cited the pieces' "profoundly interesting character" and said, "the pictures are small and selected to represent different painters and subjects, and there is as much variety as in any small modern exhibition. The subjects are religious Saints and Madonnas, some of the types severe with a Byzantine regularity of drapery and gesture; others are tender and realistic, one or two, not the best, show traces of humor. The color in all is restrained and strong and the design bold with a marked Spanish character."[14]

J.B. Neumann's Print Room in New York City exhibited 14 of the retablos beginning in April 1925, along with santos from the collection of Mabel Dodge Luhan, who wrote a foreword for the show catalog. The *Times*, reviewing the show for the second time, said, "These santos … came out of a need as great as the need for homes and furniture and clothes. … They are not the work of artists but a people's necessity. … This is not sophisticated naivete, artifice fostered, but the very best these pioneers could do, and as such they have the beauty of almost terrible intensity, an unquestioning faith that can still through these images perform miracles."[15]

The santos did not sell particularly well in New York, and Applegate told Mary Mowbray-Clarke that she could reduce the prices by 50 percent. "That will bring them on a level and in some places lower than Santa Fe prices," he wrote. "But I'd like to sell a few more."

The market for santos was stronger in Santa Fe. "People are beginning to collect them and the prices are much better for them," Applegate wrote. "A few years ago they were only considered curiosities by tourists. Now they have taken their place as primative [*sic*] art."[16]

Applegate's comments notwithstanding, Spanish Colonial art never became as popular as Indian art. For one thing, Indian artwork had been on the market much longer than Spanish Colonial art and was more familiar to collectors. Indian art had a national audience, while interest in Spanish Colonial art was mostly limited to the Southwest and Southern California. It was not until 1943, when the Museum of Modern Art launched the exhibition, "Religious Folk Art of the Southwest," that Spanish Colonial art would begin to receive its due. Additionally, many of the santos illustrated a most severe aspect of Catholicism, redemption through suffering, and as such they featured holy figures bearing crowns of thorns, wounds dripping blood, and tortured expressions—the "terrible intensity" the *Times* critic noted. Such dramatic imagery was hardly what the average collector was looking for in the way of decoration. Still, the Neumann Print Room continued to show Applegate's santos for several years, and New York's Weyhe Gallery also exhibited them.[17]

In the fall of 1925 Applegate wrote that the santos "are getting very rare and scarce here and in the store we sell them up to $300 each now." Applegate, Austin and other Santa Fe collectors saw that the supply was dwindling. The making of religious pieces had nearly died out by the time the Applegates arrived in New Mexico. The opening of the Santa Fe Trail in 1821 increased the distribution of commercial prints, and by the 1860s even remote villagers clamored for mass-produced lithographs. This demand contributed to the decline in production of wooden retablos. The coming of the railroad in the 1880s enabled traders to transport plaster statues of saints to the West. In the ensuing decades bultos continued to be made, in part because they were needed for religious processions, but their production had declined dramatically by the early 1920s.[18]

The near-demise of the Spanish crafts distressed Applegate, and he lambasted the forces behind their extinction, "the American traders and exploiters who by their superior aggressiveness forced their machine-made civilization on them." "Now cheap colored lithographs are taking place of the old gesso or wood paintings," he wrote. "Cheap cotton goods are replacing their wonderful weaving, and tin and paper covered houses their old dirt and adobe houses with cactus growing on them. The American public schools have shown the younger generation how much superior a colored crayon drawing of an Easter egg is to the primitive art of their forefathers."[19]

Applegate and Austin began to encourage modern-day woodcarvers to continue their ancestors' traditions. According to Austin, Applegate's interest developed naturally. "In collecting old pieces, Frank had often recourse to native workmen for repairs, and by this means we came to realize that the capacity for handcraft, of a fine and satisfying quality … had not completely disintegrated," she wrote. Soon after his arrival in New Mexico, he and Austin, "began to have conversations about beginning a craft revival movement in New Mexico. … Both envisioned this revival as one in which Anglo-American patrons would provide artistic guidance and market accessibility and Hispanic craftsmen would provide the manual skills and reap the monetary benefits."[20]

Their efforts to encourage the talents of contemporary Hispanic (and Indian) artists arose at a time when people around the country were making similar attempts with other cultural groups whose work was endangered by industrialization and cultural homogenization.[21] Such efforts can also be seen as a reaction (though perhaps not a conscious one) to a widespread interest in American Colonial crafts, furnishings, architecture, and art. During the colonial revival, which started in the late 19th century and continued well into the 20th, the public clamored for authentic and reproduced colonial furniture, colonial-style homes, and colonial decorative arts. The revival carried with it a pro-Anglo bias (for who were the colonial craftspeople if not English subjects?) and championed the quality of English-influenced work above that of native and immigrant cultures.

Applegate's familiarity with the English and American Arts and Crafts movements and with craft revival movements in the East contributed to his appreciation of the craftsmanship evident in Spanish Colonial art and to his belief in the importance of encouraging artists to develop their talents. As a proponent of Arts and Crafts and as a man who loved to work with his hands, Applegate felt a kinship with all craftspeople, be they woodcarvers, makers of Indian pottery, or his fellow Santa Fe artists. "He was never happier than when … chatting with craftsmen about their work," the *New Mexican* stated.[22]

One of the "native workmen" who helped Applegate repair santos, and one of the first woodcarvers he encouraged, was a carpenter and farmer named José Dolores López of the small town of Córdova. Applegate met López through Lorin Brown, a young man who taught school in Córdova and befriended members of the artists colony. Each year during Holy Week Brown opened the four-room adobe where he and his mother lived to artists and writers who traveled to Córdova to witness the rituals of the Penitentes.[23]

La Fraternidad Piadosa de Nuestro Padre Jesús Nazareno (the Pious Fraternity of Our Father Jesus the Nazarene), commonly called the Penitente brotherhood, is a lay religious society that began in the late 18th century. The mysterious holy order, the subject of numerous works by the artists and writers, was best known for its penitential Holy Week ceremonies, which centered on a reenactment of Christ's passion. During the ceremonies, the Penitentes would perform self-flagellation and sometimes crucifixions, using ropes rather than nails.

Among those who annually attended the ceremonies were Austin and the Applegates, the members of Los Cinco Pintores, and Aileen Nusbaum, wife of Museum of New Mexico anthropologist and collector Jesse Nusbaum. The group would gather at Brown's house on Holy

Thursday. Although the major event was the observation of the Penitentes' processions, much of the visit was spent conversing and roasting apples and piñon nuts over an open fire.[24] In his book *Echoes of the Flute*, Brown, writing under the name Lorenzo de Córdova, remembered those visits:

> There was always a couple who chose to sit out on the stoop, wrapped in a blanket. They served as our listening post, reporting any faint sound of pito [flute] or alabado [hymn narrating the passion] carried by the night air. … As soon as "Here they come!" was sounded, a point of interception was discussed. If the procession was coming from the morada [Penitentes' meeting place] to the church, there was a point of vantage which took us over a mud roof. … We had to climb up one ladder and down the next to a lane which gave on the trail followed by the Brethren on the way to church. This spot afforded a good bird's-eye view of the ramp-like ascent to the front door of the morada, a brief interval in which one could count the number of devotees in the dancing light of the shielded lanterns.
>
> Knowing that we had plenty of time, we did not hurry up and down the ladders. Cutting across the village square, we stationed ourselves close to the eastern Puerta de la Plaza, a narrow passage leading to the front of the church.
>
> Here, if there had been any crossbearers, the maderos [wooden beams] would be leaned against the wall of the churchyard. … An unusually long time brought an excited volley of conjectures. El Santo Madero, who carried it? Was it Pedro or was it Canuto? … Surmises and denials passed back and forth in subdued whispers.

The Penitentes would be on their knees, traveling the path, "getting lashed. … As if hypnotized, we watched them finally reach the church door. … About 45 minutes later, we watched the group's exit from the church. … Visibly impressed, we returned home in subdued silence, listening as the rumbling of the trailing crosses and the shrill of the pito grew fainter and fainter."[25]

The group occasionally saw a daylight procession by the Penitentes. "Córdova was dominated by an old Calvario [replica of Calvary] on the crest of the grade leading to Truchas," Brown wrote. "It was visited faithfully at least once each year by fulfillers of vows. When this happened, we were afforded a rare sight of somberly garbed acompañadores and white-drawered flagellants with their black hoods limned against the sky and the imposing background of the Sangre de Cristo Mountains."[26]

Many of Brown's Holy Week guests also visited during fishing and hunting season. Over the years, they were introduced to other villagers, and Brown frequently served as a translator during the visits for those who needed one. No doubt these visits fueled Applegate's enthusiasm for Spanish Colonial art. In the 19th century, Córdova was the home of some of the finest santeros, and much of their work had survived.

"We always had to visit Tia Lupe [Guadalupe Martínez], the well-known santera [here, keeper of the santos] of the village church with its carved pulpit and rare collection of retablos and bultos," Brown wrote. "It took time to appreciate the carving and colors of these draped and clothed images. Robes had to be lifted and black bunting pulled aside to disclose the beautiful craftsmanship beneath."[27]

José Dolores López, whom Brown introduced to Applegate, was a member of the Penitente morada. "It was his voice that proclaimed to the visitor from outside, as they waited in the church for the service of the Tinieblas, the high ideals of his Order. … It was he who sang the seemingly interminable verses of the alabado." It is possible that López revealed to Applegate some of the secrets of the Penitentes. After Applegate's death, Betty Applegate wrote that her father was "one of the few Americans who have ever been taken completely into their confidence."[28]

Applegate was impressed with López's skill as a woodcarver, and by 1922, he had persuaded López to market his work at the Santa Fe Fiesta. Applegate introduced López to Austin, "who became very much interested in the man and his philosophy," and to others in the group.[29] Through them, other Santa Feans learned of López's fine carving work, and he began to develop a clientele of buyers.

During most of the 1920s López made furniture and carved animals, but in the late 1920s or early 1930s he began carving religious images. He made most of his sales during the Fiesta and received orders there for future work. His carved picture frames and screen doors were very popular with Santa Feans, and he created several doors for Austin's home. "His carved figures of birds, animals of every kind, and other interesting articles became the vogue, bringing an unending stream of visitors and buyers to his door." Elizabeth Sage Hare, herself a passionate collector of Spanish Colonial art, wrote of López: "If you went to Córdova in the spring there was always much to see–the whole winter's output; but in the fall there would be little left but the small animals cut while López was at his summer's work in the fields. ... He had a great feeling for animals. He carved pigs, dogs, squirrels, beavers, a whole orchestra of cats, and many birds in every conceivable form of flight ... all were delicate, humorous, or robust according to the creature's essential quality, with the artist's own gift added to emphasize it."[30] Many other members of the López family became woodcarvers as well.

Although the relationship between López and Applegate was businesslike, the two men were also friends. The Applegates would visit the López family in Córdova a few times a year. In letters López frequently referred to Applegate as "my dear friend" or "brother," to himself as "your brother," and to Alta as "mother" or "sister." Both men were born storytellers. López was said to have "tales with a moral to suit any occasion" and was known as a "chistero," or joker. Visitors to the López home were "received with the courtliest of manners, not affected but genuine, with an ease and grace which charmed and made for him many friends who delighted to return to visit with this unusual personality."[31]

Another woodcarver whom Applegate befriended and encouraged was Celso Gallegos of Agua Fria. Gallegos has come to be seen as a link between the 19th and 20th century santeros, for in the 1920s he was the only prominent Hispanic woodcarver to concentrate on religious figures rather than secular pieces. Gallegos did not copy the polychrome santos of his ancestors but "drew upon his lively imagination and made use of natural textures."[32]

"He sat in his little shed, carving figures and praying while he carved ... for him the carving of santos was a religious action, and when they were finished, he would give them to his friends." Only rarely did Gallegos apply paint, and then only a small amount. After meeting Applegate and other art colony members, Gallegos also began to make secular pieces, including whimsical animal figures such as chess-playing horses and a dodo. He was also a talented embroiderer.[33]

Applegate repaired old santos and apparently made new ones himself (pp. 113-128). Although it is not known when he began making santos, a review of the woodcarvings he showed with the New Mexico Painters in 1923 mentions several religious wood sculptures, including a brightly painted horse and rider, which may have been Santiago (St. James). Author Thomas J. Steele, S.J., believes Applegate was New Mexico's first Protestant and first Anglo saint-maker. Steele classifies Applegate as a "romantic revival" santero–one who creates santos for historical, economic, and/or artistic reasons–rather than a true folk santero.[34]

Applegate painted retablos on hand-adzed pine boards, and he carved and painted bultos. His skill as a woodcarver, evident in the woodcarvings and furniture he created in the early 1920s, is apparent in the delicate construction of the bultos as well. Crosses are carefully chip-carved, legs of animals gracefully turned, a tiny angel's wings intricately notched. The faces of his holy figures differ from one another but wear Hispanic features. Unlike his other wooden sculptures and paintings on canvas, Applegate's santos were traditional and imitative, "modernist" only in the respect that the old santeros' works reflected design elements adopted by modernist artists, such as bold line and vivid color. He sought to emulate the 19th century santeros—perhaps to help himself understand the processes behind their work, perhaps to ingratiate himself with Gallegos and other santeros, or perhaps because he saw it as another artistic challenge to be met. In any event he was proud enough of his religious artwork to present a retablo to Austin on her 60th birthday (p. 127). One can only wonder how his fundamentalist-preacher father would have reacted upon seeing Applegate's dramatic depictions of Catholic sacred images. [35]

The rural artisans proved successful at selling their wares during the annual Fiesta's Spanish Fair, and Applegate, Austin, and other fans of Spanish Colonial art decided they could further aid the craftspeople by creating an organization similar to the Indian Arts Fund. Late in 1924 or early in 1925 they established the Society for the Revival of Spanish Colonial Arts. The society's goals were much like those of the Indian Arts Fund—to raise money to purchase the finest examples of Spanish Colonial art, to encourage contemporary artisans to continue in the paths of their ancestors, and to educate people about the importance of the art. The society also worked to preserve historic buildings and collected Spanish Colonial drama and folklore.[36]

Scholars have criticized the use of the term "Spanish Colonial," claiming it was meant to distinguish the work of Hispanics who carried on the traditions of Old Spain from those who had emigrated from Mexico comparatively recently and whose work showed Mexican and Pueblo influences. Both Applegate and Austin acknowledged early on, however, that the ancient artwork was not the product of pureblood Spaniards. At the outset Applegate stated that it was made "by the mixed descendants of the Spanish conquistadores." Austin indicated that she considered both the recent Mexican immigrants and the mestizos (Indo-Hispanics, people with Indian and Spanish blood) superior artisans, writing in an essay, "What everybody knows about Indians, what Frank Applegate wrote of the hand-craftiness of the descendants of Spanish pioneers, is proof enough that the Spanish speaking peon derives from both lines of his descent the capacity to make things requiring a high degree of artisan skill, and to make them beautifully and well."[37]

The term Spanish Colonial art is misleading for another reason, however: Much of the work called Spanish Colonial was made in the post-Colonial period, after 1821. Austin claimed to have coined the phrase "Spanish Colonial art," and later mentioned in a letter that Applegate was adamant the word "colonial" be included in the phrase, although she indicated he preferred the term "New Mexican Colonial Arts."[38]

From the start, the Society for the Revival of Spanish Colonial Arts was closely linked with the Indian Arts Fund, and the groups shared several common members. In an Annual Report of the School of American Research, the Indian Arts Fund was referred to as the Indian and Spanish Crafts Fund. That name also appeared on letterheads Kenneth Chapman was using in September 1925.[39] Apparently, Indian Arts Fund members eventually decided two distinct organizations were needed.

Austin was named director of the society, and Applegate was placed in charge of arts and crafts. Other members included Elizabeth Sage Hare; James McMillan of the Spanish & Indian Trading Company; James L. Seligman of the Old Santa Fe Trading Post; architect John Gaw Meem; Herman Schweizer, who collected artifacts for the Fred Harvey Company; and Mrs. Elon (Blanche Ferry) Hooker of New York, a wealthy friend of Austin's who supplied financial backing. In 1927 Alta Applegate served as the group's secretary. One way in which the Society for the Revival of Spanish Colonial Arts differed from the Indian Arts Fund is that it included Hispanics (although not *rural* ones, the people whom the society was trying to help) among its members. Members of the Otero family joined early on, and later, J.M. Ramírez and Benigno Muñiz oversaw the Spanish Market.[40]

Austin spent considerable time and effort raising funds for the society. She solicited money from Santa Fe- and Taos-colony writers and artists, from towns-people, and from audience members at her lectures back East. Mary Cabot Wheelwright, who later founded the Wheelwright Museum of Indian Art, was a generous donor.[41]

At the 1926 Fiesta the society introduced a competition in traditional arts as part of the Spanish Fair. It "broadcast a list of examples of such crafts as might be profitable to revive and [offered] prizes for new work that conformed most exactly to the old models."[42] Austin and Applegate were among the organizers, and Applegate chaired the awards committee, which recruited Hispanics in the nearby small towns to spread the word. The committee awarded prizes in the categories of carved figure, woven rug, knitted bedspread, hooked rug, tin box, tin candlesticks, patchwork pillow top, bead work, crochet work, drawn work, braided rag rug, and woven rag rug.

The competition was open only to Spanish-speaking New Mexicans. An awards description stated, "All articles must be genuine Spanish Colonial. That is they must be of the kind and style in use in Spanish Colonial times. They must not be new American materials or designs. In awarding prizes, credit will be given for faithfulness to the ancient patterns and materials. It is the object of this competition to reawaken an interest in and an appreciation of the work of the pioneer settlers of the Southwest."[43]

"The original plan was to finance the prizes from funds generously contributed by outsiders who are interested in community arts," the *Santa Fe New Mexican* reported. "But people of Santa Fe, equally generous and more directly concerned, wished to participate personally, by offering prizes for articles in which they were particularly interested." The prizes ranged from $2-$25, and Celso Gallegos, the woodcarver from Agua Fria, won $15 for a carved figure. Several prizes were not awarded due to a lack of entrants: The competition was announced in June, and the *New Mexican* noted, "long before the publication of the list [of prizes to be awarded] many of the men who might have been interested had already left their homes for the summer's work in mountain pastures, wheat fields, wood camps, and mines."[44]

Many items sold well. Austin recalled that Gallegos earned a total of $60. "Frank took it to him in round silver dollars, and the old man was so overcome that he wept and tried to kiss Frank, which in view of Frank's great length of limb, was not easily managed."[45]

When it came to Spanish Colonial art, Austin and Applegate shared a belief that "enlightened patrons were indispensible in rekindling the dying embers of 'native' art" and that they and their friends were those patrons. After all, who knew the aesthetic preferences of Anglo-American culture better than Anglo artists? "Our unskilled Spanish speaking labor could … become skilled by the proper sort of teaching … they could become specialized technicians of high capacity," Austin wrote. Obviously, "the proper sort of teaching" could only be that which she approved and organized. Applegate echoed this paternalistic sentiment in a letter, in which he noted, "the natives really have a great deal of pride and it is more a matter of directing that pride. I have noticed that the praise of an Anglo for their things goes a long way with them." As an example, he mentioned José Dolores López. "He is swelling with pride in his work and is even outdoing himself because of our praise, for it is the first real appreciation he ever received for the things he has always loved to do, and even his children, cousins and neighbors are becoming proud of him and his children are helping him and trying to do things on their own."[46]

Critics today attack the belief that Anglo praise and encouragement was essential to the success of these artists. "At a time when overt Anglo-American racism against both Hispanos and Indians was marked, the Anglo-American members of this movement were among the more sensitive and well-intentioned of the newcomers," wrote Charles Briggs in *The Woodcarvers of Cordova, N.M.: Social Dimensions of an Artistic "Revival."* "Nevertheless, the 'revival' involved a classically patronizing formula—the appropriation of control over an ethnic resource primarily by members of a superordinate society. Accordingly, the patrons attempted to direct the evolution of the art according to a set of principles that emanated from the concerns of their cultural milieu, rather than from those of the Hispano artists."[47]

This and other criticisms are similar to those leveled against the artists' work with the Indians. For example, the Anglos also have been censured for trying to maintain the historic traditions of the art. "Their goal was the isolation of purely 'traditional,' 'colonial,' or 'Spanish' crafts from syncretic innovations," Briggs wrote. "The patrons defined the category of 'traditional' Hispano art and determined which works conformed to this definition on the basis of their own historical assessment and aesthetic judgment rather than upon the Hispano artists' understanding of their heritage."[48]

"While this purist approach had the value of preserving knowledge of traditional forms and techniques, it also put a damper on innovation and kept much work at the level of reproduction of existing pieces," wrote art historian William Wroth.[49] By the end of the 1920s the revivalists came to realize this, and some of them began to encourage individuality of expression.

Not only did the Anglo patrons hold Hispanic artists to strict standards with regard to Spanish Colonial art reproduction, they also suggested ways to make the contemporary art more marketable to Anglos. They encouraged the woodcarvers to carve useful items, such as screen doors and lazy susans, and to leave them unpainted. When, at the end of the decade, López began carving bultos, Applegate suggested he produce less-dramatic representations of the saints and refrain from painting them. "López's polychrome technique proved to be rather too gaudy for the Santa Fe market ... and it was suggested that he leave his work unpainted," Briggs wrote. "Although López did sell a few pieces of polychromed furniture in Santa Fe, he largely heeded the patrons' advice and concentrated instead on chip-carving and incised designs."[50]

The artists and writers undoubtedly believed they were acting altruistically. They saw their goals as empowerment through art and increased self-esteem. "Austin and Applegate were motivated from the beginning by a desire to improve the economic conditions of Hispanic New Mexicans, convinced that by doing so they were also making a statement concerning American values and helping to turn them in more humanistic directions." Therefore, it is hardly surprising that the artists and writers encouraged the artisans to make things that would sell. In the case of José Dolores López, their instincts proved accurate. "The family prospered, acquiring more land and better implements until they were considered quite wealthy. ... Don José and his family accumulated money for which they really had no use." The sales he made during and after the annual Fiesta proved quite profitable. "A hobby which had before yielded José a dollar or two ... now became a source of the cash which was becoming increasingly important."[51]

An editorial in *The New York Times* praised the efforts of Austin and the others: "One of the finest things about the new order is the breaking down of racial antagonism. It is, of course, a useful movement which gives to poor farmers, wood-cutters, sheepherders, and their families employment of an enjoyable and profitable nature. ... [They] are beginning to realize that they are supplied with tools, materials, and a market, not because they are in need of help but because their artist friends want the rest of the country to share in the beauty New Mexico alone can contribute."[52]

As with their support of the Indians, the Anglos' actions stemmed in part from a sense of collective guilt over the Americanization of the Hispanics. "What I am trying to do," Austin wrote, "is to restore to the Spanish people the opportunity which they once made and we Americans stupidly destroyed." The Society for the Revival of Spanish Colonial Arts attempted to rectify the situation but made it clear that it was not a charitable organization. It aimed "at giving advice and instruction to those workers who [want] to fill in their spare moments with handiwork, but it is prepared in any case where genuine talent is found to furnish tools and materials where these are lacking."[53]

In addition to encouraging Hispanic artisans to take up the ancient crafts, the Society for the Revival of Spanish Colonial Arts actively worked to preserve Spanish Colonial art. As with Indian art, Applegate worried that fine pieces were being removed from their native habitat by tourists. Unfortunately, the Anglos' interest in Spanish art inflated its price, and curio dealers began hiring Spanish-speaking people to scour the northern New Mexican communities for artwork. They solicited householders for santos and would enter churches and carry off religious objects.[54] Most of the priests in the small towns showed little interest in preserving the old artwork or architecture.

In articles and lectures Applegate explained unique aspects of Spanish Colonial art and defended it to those who lacked appreciation for it. He theorized that the work produced by the early New Mexicans was the most authentic Spanish art, because the Renaissance had brought influential foreign artists to Spain. "Thus one may better study the folk arts of 16th and 17th century Spain in New Mexico than in Spain, for the survivals are freer of foreign influence and represent more the ideals and achievements of the people than of the few hired artisans, who gilded the period in the mother country," he stated. He elaborated on this idea in a lecture: "In Spain, the objects made of more valuable materials were preserved, and these were the objects which the foreign artists were brought in to make. … Here, the folk art continued as a pure stream, uninfluenced by sophisticated tastes." He also acknowledged the influence of the New Mexican settlers' isolation on their art, writing, "Even in the best colonial times, a year was required for the official supply train to make a round trip from Mexico to Santa Fe. The result was that the things the colonists made for themselves, became, as time went on, actually more primitive in form, being largely influenced by limitations of tools and materials and by the arts and crafts of the Indians among whom they settled."[55]

El Palacio reported on a lecture given by Applegate, an overview of Spanish Colonial arts that included nuggets of information which later would appear in his and Austin's manuscript on the subject (see Chapter 14). His research indicated that the most common piece of furniture was the chest, which came to New Mexico by way of Old Mexico and sometimes had a Chinese influence, for "many Chinese chests found their way through Mexico into New Mexico." Few woodcarvers made chairs, he said, because people sat on the floor or on chests. He considered shelves and cupboards among the most beautifully carved items, and found Moorish influences in tables, saddles, and floor cushions, but never in art of a religious nature, because it was considered pagan.

"The religious art reflects the Byzantine traits, and the strong tendency to symbolize, which came from the Byzantine," he stated. Applegate's research and obsessive collecting had enabled him to distinguish the work of a number of different santeros by style, although very few could be identified by name. He noted that the santeros, like religious artists in other countries, "often copied types from the people they knew."

Applegate contended that the pottery and weaving of the Pueblo Indians had long made the colonists' adoption of these crafts unnecessary. "Weaving was held back for a century because the early Pueblos wove well in cotton," he said. "When weaving was taken up by the Spanish colonials, they had forgotten their own designs and copied those of the Navajos. They were retaught the weaving art by master craftsmen, sent from Mexico as instructors by the viceroy of New Spain about the year 1800. These instructors brought with them the Mexican designs, which at the time, were introduced into the art of New Mexico."[56]

Applegate also studied the speech of the rural Hispanics and the impact of English and Indian languages upon it. "Many Spanish words used here have been obsolete in Spain for 300 years," he wrote. "Spanish tunes played here have been forgotten in Spain for hundreds of years; many miracles and mystery plays are still given by the folk here that were common in Spain long ago." His research into the subject led Mary Austin, herself a student of Hispanic songs and drama, to say of him, "there has been no more careful student of folk speech in the Southwest."[57] His study of dialect would prove useful in later years when he compiled Hispanic folktales in the book *Native Tales of New Mexico*.

By the end of the decade *El Palacio* was referring to Applegate as "the leading authority" on the topic of Spanish Colonial arts. "His study … has been made more valuable and rich because of his previous studies of the colonial arts of New England," the magazine stated. "It has taken him not only to the out-of-the-way corners of New Mexico, but also into Mexico and Spain, to trace the origins of the arts which flourished in the early periods of New Mexico. … Mr. Applegate … has found colonial arts as they existed in early New Mexico even superior to the first handicrafts of the eastern states."[58]

There is no other evidence of Applegate's studying New England folk art, nor of his traveling to Mexico or Spain to conduct such research. It is possible, however, that he investigated New England folk art during his summers in New Hampshire (especially the summer of 1924, by which time he had begun collecting Spanish Colonial art) and may indeed have visited Mexico, as many Santa Feans did. And he may have had the opportunity to view Spanish arts and crafts while visiting Spain in the early 1900s.

Applegate's expertise on the Spanish Colonial arts brought him substantial recognition, and he was asked to write a piece on the subject for the magazine *The Survey*. Editor Paul Kellogg, in assigning the article, told him, "if you can write on them just as you talk them it will be splendid. … We are planning to give up a section of the issue to the Spanish Americans in New Mexico. Culturally speaking, it will be the high spot of our number, and your article should prove one of the most revealing of them all. … We want the evolution of the thing; want it concrete; want it interpretive not only of the arts but the people. And there is no one who could do it like you." The article traced the origins of the arts and the Hispanics' efforts to preserve their Spanish heritage through craft.[59]

Unfortunately, articles by Applegate and accounts of his lectures mention no sources of information. Although a few anthropologists and authors, most notably Charles F. Lummis and Austin, had studied the Spanish settlers, and although the Catholic Church owned centuries of archival records, research into the history of Spanish Colonial arts was still quite new. Most of the information was undoubtedly a product of firsthand examination and observation, and it is likely fellow collectors, members of the Historical Society of New Mexico and Hispanic Society of New Mexico, and other students of the work contributed as well.

During the 1926 Fiesta the Society for the Revival of Spanish Colonial Arts organized an exhibit in the Museum of Fine Arts, which included tin shrines and sconces, native rugs, carved crucifixes, santos, chests and cupboards, painted doors, a large tin candelabrum, and drawn work. Santa Feans were encouraged to add anything they might have at home to the display as well, likely so the society members could see what was out there behind closed doors.[60] The society had begun acquiring pieces of Spanish Colonial art for its collection. Members purchased items through dealers, directly from Hispanic householders, and from churches, and relied heavily on Applegate's expertise.

The collection's first home was the basement of the Museum of New Mexico, and pieces later were exhibited in the rooms of the historical society in the Museum of New Mexico's Palace of the Governors. Among the finest pieces the society acquired were the altar and colateral (multi-paneled altar screen) from the church at Llano Quemado, near Taos. Applegate purchased it from the church building committee, which was replacing it with a screen made of milled lumber by the village carpenter. According to Austin, "Frank was notified that it was for sale, and went up immediately, arriving a little in advance of the curio dealers, and secured it for $500." The historical society used it as a focus for the Old Palace's "ecclesiastic room," where it was installed in 1929, and Applegate wrote the descriptive label for it.[61]

The Society for the Revival of Spanish Colonial Arts also worked for the preservation of buildings, relying on architect John Gaw Meem to inform them of what needed to be done. Meem learned "that homes and churches in the mountain villages were being stripped of hand-carved doors, and household patron saints were being sold right out of their niches," and the society attempted to prevent such actions. The society raised money for the restoration of the mission church bell tower at Ácoma and repair of the mission-church interior at Trampas. It was aided in its restoration attempts by grants from the Society for the Preservation and Restoration of the New Mexican Mission Churches and by the Fred Harvey Company.[62]

The society also took an interest in the Spanish-American Normal School at El Rito. The school had been established in 1909 to train Spanish-speaking teachers for northern New Mexico schools. By 1925 it also offered vocational education courses in weaving and woodworking. Applegate and Austin served on the school's board of directors, and Austin said they were "asked to co-operate with [the school] in reintroducing these arts into their manual training department." The society supplied the school with "examples of good old blanket designs [and] photographs of other good models of furniture and woodcraft," and the Anglo artists helped compile a collection of colored drawings for the rug and blanket makers.[63]

The Society for the Revival of Spanish Colonial Arts expanded the 1927 Spanish Fair competition categories to include blanket weaving, handmade furniture, figure carving, tinwork, braided and hooked rugs, and crochet. Member Nina Otero-Warren organized an exhibition of work by students from the El Rito school for the fair, and the Fiesta also featured an exhibition of ancient Spanish Colonial artwork. The 1928 Spanish Fair included prizes of $5 to $20 in the various categories. José Dolores López took four first prizes in the furniture division, and Celso

Gallegos won $10 for a woodcarving. Alta Applegate oversaw the exhibit and sales that year, assisted by her husband and Elizabeth Sage Hare. The exhibitors received a total of $700 in sales and prize money. Alta also took charge of the 1929 Fiesta exhibition, which was set in two rooms of the Old Palace and drew exhibitors from as far north as Taos and as far south as Albuquerque. The 1929 fair raised more than $800 for the artisans.[64]

By the late 1920s the Applegates' personal collection of both Spanish and Native American art and antiquities had reached museum proportions. The *Santa Fe New Mexican* noted in April 1927 that they owned between 700 and 800 santos. At a lecture Applegate gave on santos, "he showed several specimens of Santos, one from Italy, one from Old Mexico, and three or four from New Mexico to illustrate the work of different artists," the *New Mexican* reported. "The earliest one in Mr. Applegate's collection is dated 1732."[65]

Applegate decided to sell off a substantial part of his collection of Spanish Colonial art, along with some of his Indian art and artifacts, in 1928. The buyer was Alice Bemis Taylor of Colorado Springs, Colorado, a frequent visitor to Santa Fe, who had learned of the collection from Meem. Taylor purchased the pieces in several lots during 1928 and 1929. Included in the sale were more than 160 retablos, more than 130 bultos, a painting on canvas of the Virgin of Guadalupe, two reredos, a painting on buffalo hide purchased from an old church at Pecos, and six tin nichos (wall niches). Applegate's collection "planted the seed for the Taylor Museum's remarkable collection of the religious folk art of New Mexico." The museum eventually became part of the Colorado Springs Fine Arts Center, which Meem designed. Taylor also purchased santos from the Spanish & Indian Trading Company and the Old Santa Fe Trading Post.[66]

The Native American items included a Pueblo dance wand and knee rattle, a Hopi tablita headdress, a Zuni turquoise drill, an Apache carrying basket, a Jémez ceramic plaque, a Hopi hide painting, and several items of clothing. A partial list in the Taylor papers indicates prices of the Native American items ranged from $6 for a Hopi ceremonial rattle to $150 for a snake dancer's costume and for each of several buffalo hide Indian masks. The Native American pieces alone brought Applegate just over $3,000.[67]

Applegate's decision to sell the items to an out-of-state collector no doubt angered some of his friends and fellow admirers of Spanish Colonial art. Unfortunately, the Society for the Revival of Spanish Colonial Arts did not have the money to make such a purchase, nor, apparently, were any wealthy Santa Feans sufficiently interested. The reason behind the decision is not known. The Applegates do not appear to have been financially strapped at the time, for Frank continued to make land deals, rent houses, and donate items to the Indian Arts Fund and other groups. By early 1928 they employed a part-time housekeeper. Perhaps Applegate wanted only to receive a fair price and sell to someone who would appreciate the pieces and provide a suitable home. Perhaps he preferred the thrill of the hunt to owning the pieces, and the cash earned from the sale allowed him to continue to buy what he pleased. In any event, if the April 1927 report in the *Santa Fe New Mexican* was accurate, Applegate sold Taylor less than half of his collection at this time, so he still had many items to give away or sell. He joined the Historical Society of New Mexico in 1928, and the society's ledger reports donations of a retablo of Santa Ana on wood in January 1929 and an altar painting from an old church at Taos, 7 feet by 8 feet, representing eight saints, in November 1929.[68]

Applegate continued efforts to ensure that the ancient arts and crafts would remain in the public eye. He worked with the historical society to set up a permanent display of Spanish Colonial arts, then valued at $1,000, in the Palace of the Governors. He also recommended which items the Spanish arts society should purchase for its collection. He was especially proud of the acquisition of two hide paintings which had been in the ruins of the church at San Ildefonso and belonged to the head of a local auto wrecking com-pany. One was of the Crucifixion, while the other featured three friars acting out chapters in religious history. The paintings were placed on exhibit at the museum in 1931. *El Palacio* also noted that "through [Applegate's] kindness, many interesting exhibits have been loaned the State Museum."[69]

One of the Society for the Revival of Spanish Colonial Arts' most celebrated preservation efforts began in February 1929, when Applegate sent Mary Austin, who was lecturing at Yale University, an article from the *Santa Fe New Mexican* stating the Santuario de Chimayó was in the process of being sold by descendants of the builder.[70] Bultos and other items belonging to the church had already been sold to dealer James McMillan. Catholics today consider the Santuario de Nuestro Señor de Esquipulas at El Potrero de Chimayó, located 25 rugged miles north of Santa Fe, one of the most holy and important shrines in the United States. Since its construction, a communal effort led by Bernardo Abeyta in 1815-16, pilgrims have traveled to the sanctuary to worship and seek blessings from a source of dirt believed to have curative powers.

Austin fired off a letter to the *New Mexican* denouncing the proposed sale. Many residents of Chimayó were also justifiably angry, and some of them made the trip to Santa Fe, found McMillan, and retrieved the bultos and a large chest.[71] Although the sale of the sanctuary fell through, Applegate and Austin wanted to make certain it could not happen in the future. Acting on behalf of the Society for the Revival of Spanish Colonial Arts (for which Applegate was then serving as treasurer), they began to search for a way to preserve the Santuario. Nearly daily correspondence ensued between the two, with Applegate acting as Austin's eyes and ears in New Mexico. Based on past experiences, Applegate considered the Santuario to be "unsafe as long as it is in native hands."

"They are likely at any time to go on a restoring jamboree and ruin it," he told Austin, "as they almost did when they put on wooden towers and [a] tin roof a few years ago." Nor did he trust the local clergy. "The priest at Santa Cruz [just south of Chimayó] sold the two old church bells from the Santa Cruz church to a carpenter," he wrote. "So you see he is not to be trusted with antiquities further than you can throw a cat."

"A Catholic society (incorporated to preserve mission churches and the antiquities inside them) is very badly needed for this section," he stated, "as enough missions have already been vandalized by the unsympathetic and ignorant priests." He thought the Santuario belonged under the control of the Roman Catholic archbishop, with a guarantee that it never be altered or changed when repaired. Although the Society for the Preservation and Restoration of the New Mexican Mission Churches already existed, Applegate believed a "Catholic society," led by the powerful archbishop, would carry more weight with priests than a secular one.[72]

Other concerned citizens soon rallied to the cause. Among the first to join was John Gaw Meem, who belonged to the mission church restoration society. The society had been working for years to get the titles to the Santuario and its land from their owners. It had the support of Archbishop Albert T. Daeger, who joined in the negotiations along with several other interested parties. Because they all feared publicity would cause the owners to raise their asking prices, the negotiations were conducted outside the public eye.[73]

Meanwhile, Applegate had discovered that the priest who said Mass at Córdova had told workmen to replace an old door at the Córdova church. "The old solid panel door was lower than his head and he had to stoop a little to go through it," Applegate told Austin. "He only visits the church once a month to say Mass. They were getting ready to tear out the door and wanted to sell it to me for enough to buy a new kitchen door. ... I told them not to touch it for a week, anyway. ... Also the priest is after them to put on a tin roof." Applegate informed Meem of the door's impending demise, Meem contacted Archbishop Daeger, and Daeger blocked the proposed replacement.[74]

Austin soon found an anonymous benefactor, known only as a Yale graduate and Catholic, to contribute $5,000 to purchase the Santuario de Chimayó. But the owners, the Chávez family, raised their price to $6,000, and negotiations continued through the spring and summer before the donor agreed to contribute the extra money. Additionally, before the sale could be finalized, both the Society for the Preservation and Restoration of the New Mexican Mission Churches, which was to oversee the physical aspects of the Santuario, and the Society for the Revival of Spanish Colonial Arts, on whose behalf Austin had received the donation, had to incorporate as non-profit organizations.[75]

On October 15, 1929, Applegate, Meem and Austin attended the ceremony transferring title from the owner to the Roman Catholic Church. The agreement stipulated that "no changes or repairs could be made in the chapel without the consent of the society." Austin later recalled feeling very close to Applegate at the signing—once again, their partnership had produced positive results.[76]

That same day the Society for the Revival of Spanish Colonial Arts was incorporated as the Spanish Colonial Arts Society, although both names were used interchangeably until at least 1931. Its goals, as stated in the incorporation papers (of which Applegate was among the signatories), were the encouragement, promotion, preservation, and revival of Spanish Colonial art; the education of the public through lectures, articles, and exhibitions; the education of those of Spanish descent through schools and classes; the collecting of superior examples of Spanish Colonial art; and the finding of a suitable facility to house the collection.[77]

The Spanish Colonial Arts Society elected officers on November 25. Austin was elected chairman, Applegate, vice-chairman, Datus Myers, secretary, John DeHuff, treasurer. The board of trustees included many Indian Arts Fund and Society for the Revival of Spanish Colonial Arts members. Applegate was appointed curator of the collection. The Society for the Revival of Spanish Colonial Arts' funds, totaling $1,017.33, were turned over to the Spanish Colonial Arts Society in December 1929. A substantial portion of the money was directed toward "research and prizes related to

New Mexican Spanish folk drama." Austin had a special interest in this subject area, and she lectured on the topic at universities and outlined plans to set up a traditional Spanish street theater in Santa Fe.[78]

One of the society's first acts, a natural outgrowth of the annual Spanish Fair, was to open a shop where modern-day artisans could sell their wares. Applegate outlined the basic concept in a letter to Austin:

> I found people in Cordova very much interested in doing things for the Fiesta and now several of them are carving and doing other things. I think the society can soon open a shop in the old Sena Plaza that would pay. I think all the people in Cordova would soon be carving and making furniture if there was a good sale. They are improving very much and with the smallest direction would do wonderful things. … I'm sure that in a short time, a shop to sell exclusively New Spanish Col[onial] things would pay—carving, furni-ture, blankets, rugs, tinwork, carpets, and all the other things they made.
>
> More and more interest is being shown by the natives in handcrafts. We have had several letters recently from them in different parts of the state asking particulars and where they can sell their things. So next thing we will have to have a shop exclusively for them with a competent person to handle it and direct them in their work until they are well under way. I can easily see we can't depend on the curio stores to do them justice. They are more interested in pushing curios and antiques at a very large profit. So we must make up our minds to a shop of our own. … I know also we can get the material as fast as we are willing to pay for it and in that way we can dictate designs and materials, etc. Workers and artists among natives are only waiting for instruction and help.[79]

CHAPTER 12:
SPANISH
COLONIAL
REVIVAL

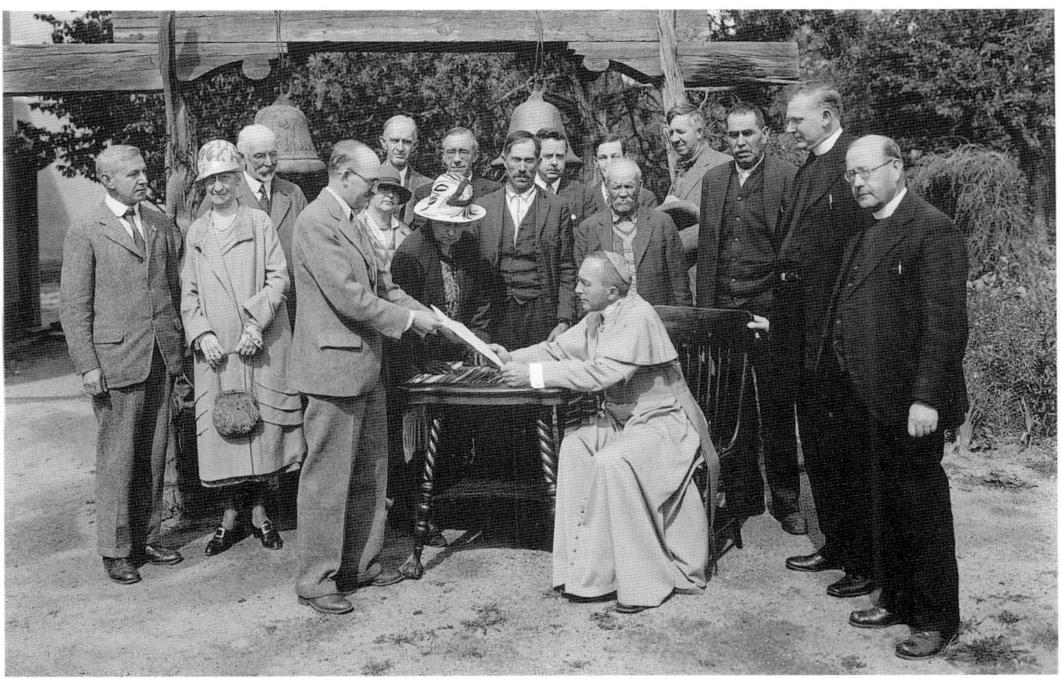

The transfer of the deed of El Santuario de Chimayó on October 15, 1929. In the foreground, John Gaw Meem presents the deed to Archbishop Albert T. Daeger. In the background, from left to right, are Paul A.F. Walter, Mrs. John Robinson, Dr. Francis Proctor, Alice Corbin Henderson, E. Dana Johnson, Mary Austin, Gustave Baumann, Marcos Chávez, Daniel T. Kelly, Judge Charles Fahy, José Chávez, Frank Applegate, Victor Ortega, Bishop Espalage, and Father Salvatore Gene. Photograph courtesy of the Center for Southwest Research, General Library, University of New Mexico (neg. no. 000-558-0005).

Apparently this idea was not new to Frank. He and Alta may have discussed a similar plan, relating to the Indians, as far back as 1922, when Alta stated in a letter:

> Another old Indian woman was making a squaw dress. Her embroidery was done beautifully, but these women have no opportunity to get good colors. If I only could I'd buy good embroidery wools and give them to these women to work with. Why in the world people with money can't ever see ways like this to use it, instead of eternally endowing something, I can't see. It's so plain, some of the needs of these struggling people.[80]

The Spanish Arts Shop, which opened on Sena Plaza in May 1930 at a rent of $50 a month, was unique in its exclusive inventory of Spanish New Mexican crafts, both ancient and new. The shop supplied the materials to the craftsmen and women in the northern New Mexico villages, then bought the finished crafts from them and sold them at a small markup at the store. The shop also worked with and sold pieces made by students at the El Rito Normal School, the Taos Pueblo school, and other rural schools that taught the old methods of handiwork, and Applegate served as a judge in the school competitions. The store sold items through mail order to individuals and a few galleries around the country, notably the Indian Trading Post in Chicago. Local sales were largely to tourists. By late in the summer of 1930, the shop was reported to be "brimming with blankets, carvings, embroideries, furniture, and many other things." Applegate reported in July that the weavers Preston and Helen Cramp McCrossen, who ran the shop, were "selling more … and things are going all right there. We keep getting a little nicer things all the time."[81]

The Spanish Arts Shop was beautifully laid out to resemble the rooms of a house. Customers could walk into a viga-and-latilla-ceilinged living room, complete with kiva fireplace, chairs, desks, tables, cupboards, and chests. Chimayó weavings decorated the walls, floor, and tables, as did handmade accessories, tin light fixtures, ornamental candlesticks, bultos, and retablos. A second room was furnished as a bedroom.[82]

The furniture craftsmen made reproductions of older Spanish Colonial pieces. Some of the items offered for sale were reproductions of pieces Applegate owned, including a large, elaborately carved trastero (a copy of which could be had for $20) and a table with hand-lathed rungs.[83]

A field worker acted as a liaison between the craftspeople and the Spanish Colonial Arts Society. His duties included corresponding and meeting with the artisans and buying supplies for them. The position was paid for by donations from Cyrus McCormick, Jr., of the farm equipment and newspaper publishing family, who owned a home at Nambé, north of Santa Fe. Through Austin's influence McCormick began making a monthly donation of $175 in January 1930, stipulating that "the account is to be in favor of the Field Worker in the Spanish Arts, who is yet to be appointed, [and] will cover salary, transportation, and other necessary incidentals to the work." McCormick further stated that Applegate was to be in charge of hiring the field worker. He also made donations to the dramatic fund. His charity continued through December 1931.[84]

Applegate served as the society's unpaid field worker until May 1930, when Preston McCrossen took over the position at a salary of $75 a month. By that time the society had about $1,500 in its treasury and $650 in the field work fund. Applegate continued to handle some of the field workers' duties. He tracked down and corresponded with a supplier of weaving materials in Massachusetts, supplied the Chimayó weavers with yarn, and paid them for their work. He also obtained crewels and linens for women embroiderers, and Nellie G. Dunton collected old designs from which the women could work. Alta Applegate also worked with the artisans, particularly the women.[85]

Applegate had a thorough understanding of weaving, as revealed in "If You Buy Antiques," an "as told to" article that appeared under his byline in the April 1929 issue of the *New Mexico*

Highway Journal. The story offered advice on buying Southwestern blankets and indicates that he had learned how to date blankets, how to distinguish between authentic pieces and cheap copies, about the history of Navajo and Chimayó weaving, the composition of dyes used, and how patterns varied with the maker. This information undoubtedly proved useful in working with the weavers for the shop, whose rugs sold for $3.50 to $10 apiece.[86]

The arts society encouraged the production of crafts based on old designs, since a stated goal was to preserve historic arts and keep out inauthentic influences, especially those derived from mass-produced objects. (Of course, the stipulation did not pertain to the modern items the craftsmen made, such as screen doors and lazy susans, which were more accurately described as improved versions of mass-produced items.) By the time the Spanish Arts Shop opened, however, society members had come to realize that to insist on reproduction was folly. "It is nearly impossible to persuade [a Spanish descendant] today to copy an old piece exactly as it is given to him," Applegate wrote. "He can never understand why he must not make alterations more to his own mind. Nor will a native craftsman make any two pieces exactly alike." Applegate initially may have found this attitude exasperating, but eventually he came to accept it. According to William Wroth, "A laissez-faire position, adopted by artist Andrew Dasburg and to some extent, Frank Applegate, welcomed innovation, with the attitude that the artists' work be allowed to sink or swim on its own."[87]

José Dolores López was a frequent contributor to the shop, and his sons George and Ricardo made items as well. "Economically, the López family prospered with José's careful and constant *labor*, or farm work, the cash brought home by his sons from seasonal employment … along with the sales from carvings." Among the items he made were furnishings such as tables, chests, and cupboards, and decorative, whimsical pieces, including carved animals and trees. Applegate encouraged López to make the small, decorative items, be-cause they were easier to sell than larger pieces. But López also enjoyed making them. "Like the toy-makers of Old Mexico [he seems] to derive great joy from inventing things to amuse the child—of six or sixty," an article noted. Spanish Arts Shop records show that López received 45 cents for a carved bird, $3 for a shelf, and $18-$20 for a large piece such as a trastero or chest.[88]

López's letters to Applegate illustrate the distance (literally and figuratively) between Santa Fe and Córdova at the time. In one, he expressed concern about shipping the delicate pieces through the mail and indicated he had no time to deliver them by hand. Another note reports a journey down to the Spanish Arts Shop to see Applegate, at which time he hand-delivered some carved flowers. "If there is demand for them, let me know so I can continue making [them] for the Fiestas, if possible," López wrote. Other letters indicate López's pieces were in such demand that he had trouble completing orders when farmwork was heavy.[89]

It was at Applegate's suggestion that López began the woodcarving for which he is best remembered, that of religious figures. One source indicates he started making them in the late 1920s, while another dates Applegate's inducement to 1930. He would carve them out of white pine or the roots of the cottonwood tree, and like Celso Gallegos, López left the bultos bare, rather than cover them with gesso and paints in the manner of the early santeros.[90] This runs contrary to what Applegate was preaching in all other areas of Spanish Colonial arts, and what he himself was doing as a folk santero, namely, re-creating old pieces. Applegate's change of heart is further indication that he no longer was insisting on authentic reproduction and may well have been market based. The unpainted bultos had a look more in keeping with modern tastes, and Applegate likely believed they would sell better—none of that morbid Catholic blood and suffering. (Recall that he had relatively little success selling the old santos he consigned to New York galleries in the mid-1920s.)

López's first bulto, which took a prize at a Fiesta competition, was of San Miguel. It stood about two-and-a-half-feet high and carried a flaming sword. He made dozens of bultos, reinterpreting San Miguel, creating magnificent halos for Nuestra Señora de la Luz, casting Adam and Eve out of a Garden of Eden complete with hidden snake in the Tree of Life. How much influence Applegate had on López's artistic style, beyond what has been mentioned previously, is unknown. Art historians consider his work entirely original, and the López family maintained that José Dolores drew his inspiration almost entirely from his own mind, with minimal help from old church santos or pictures and descriptions in religious books. His nephew, Federico Córdova, recalled, "Once I asked my Uncle José Dolores, and this is true, 'How do you make your carvings, Uncle?' And he replied, 'At night I go to bed, but I keep thinking, and thoughts come into my head.' He got ideas for carvings such as the Adam and Eve tempted in Paradise that he made. These ideas came to him through reading some books that he had."[91]

López's singular style merged the abstract concepts of the times (of which he likely was ignorant) with the traditional iconography of the santeros who preceded him. His saints wear flattened faces with wonderfully expressive features. Their bodies are made of simple shapes, with limbs carved separately and carefully attached to convey the intended attitudes. The pieces are removed from realism and bear little resemblance to the works of previous santeros. Evident in all is an intricate, ornamental filigree work that illustrates the painstaking care he put into his efforts. Eventually, López's santos influenced generations of religious woodcarvers, not least the talented members of his own family, and major museums purchased his carvings.

Some modern-day historians criticize the members of the Spanish Colonial Arts Society for commercializing the work of the santeros by crassly marketing santos as mere art objects, ignoring their religious significance. It is debatable whether the santeros would agree with such criticism. Santeros had been selling their work for years, often traveling to different towns and making pieces to order, receiving payment in cash or goods.[92] However, selling religious paintings and carvings to fellow Hispanic Catholics who appreciate them for religious reasons is not the same as selling them to Anglo collectors.

López was a very religious man and a caretaker of the santos in his church, but he did not consider his own figures religious in themselves. López "used to refer jokingly to his carvings as 'monos' [monkeys, humorous things]. He admitted that he was not producing religious items. … José did not feel that the products of his knife were santos." His son, George, explained, "These are palos, just blocks of wood, until they are blessed." Nevertheless, many of López's neighbors considered selling to outsiders sacrilegeous.[93]

Celso Gallegos, the woodcarver of Agua Fria, made santos as an act of devotion but sold them in the Spanish Arts Shop, receiving $3.50 to $6.50 apiece. Although his opinions on selling the santos is unknown, he enjoyed winning prizes for them, as noted earlier. By 1931 Gallegos' work was considered "fairly well known, not only in New Mexico but in California and in the East," and his carvings had been exhibited in Chicago.[94]

One cannot overlook the economic reasons behind the establishment of the Spanish Colonial Arts Society and the Spanish Arts Shop. The artisans were not only preserving their culture, they were attempting to improve their economic well-being. "For the Hispanic, the option of working as a creative artist was clearly superior to entering the ranks of the urban poor and becoming dependent upon the homogenized mass culture of Anglo-America."[95]

The 1930 Spanish Fair included prizes for cookery for the first and only time. The dishes had to be made of cornmeal, beans, or chile. The fair realized sales of $535.15. Of that $481.64 went to consignors, $53.51 to the Spanish Colonial Arts Society. Although the fair was considered a success, Applegate expressed the hope that the Spanish Arts Shop would succeed as a year-round market, thus eliminating the need for an annual Spanish Fair.[96]

Austin reported in October 1931 that "we have been extremely successful, everything considered, with the shop. The natives have responded very well to the opportunity to produce. ... Under ordinary circumstances the shop would have been self-supporting by this time; as it is, we think we can carry it on with a little help until times improve, by which time it will be permanently established on a self-sustaining basis."[97] Such success, however, was not forthcoming.

In theory the concept behind the Spanish Arts Shop sounded logical, if paternalistic: Give the workers the means to improve their lives, and show them how to do so. It meshed perfectly with the themes of self-empowerment and the tenets of the Arts and Crafts movement that Applegate and others espoused. In reality, however, the concept was naive, and the store was ultimately a failure. Several factors contributed to its demise. The craftspeople often could not meet the deadlines set by the Spanish Colonial Arts Society members, for they had to fit weaving, woodcarving, and metalwork into their full-time schedules as farmers, herders, raisers of families, bakers, etc. Additionally, the McCrossens proved inept at handling the mail-order end of the business. Numerous letters to them report pieces received in irreparable condition—mirrors smashed, lazy susans broken, frames bent, always as a result of poor packaging. López's qualms about sending items through the mail proved correct.[98]

Despite Applegate's optimistic predictions to the contrary, the public showed relatively little interest in Spanish handicrafts. The demand was not nearly as strong as that for Indian arts, as evidenced by the items' comparatively low prices, and customers sometimes complained because pieces did not fit in with their furnishings or were otherwise unsatisfactory. One letter expressed a client's disappointment in a table he had received: "The picture made it look quite imposing, but the real piece is undernourished looking." Another spoke of the unsuitability of some handwoven fabric for seat cushions, and said, "I do wish they would leave out those greens ... they spoil the combination."[99]

Very few galleries wanted to consign the work. Frederick Rummelle, an interior decorator in Carmel, California, considered taking on some pieces of furniture, but "Rummelle felt that the pine furniture was unsaleable due to the high cost of crating and shipping, which added 67 percent to its cost in Santa Fe, and to its lack of antique finish." Despite limited success during the first few years, the Spanish Arts Shop frequently could not pay its rent or its suppliers. Eventually, market factors, including the high prices paid to furniture makers ($40 for a chest, $15 for a table, $5-$20 for a chair), and the increasing impact of a depressed economy forced the Spanish Arts Shop to shut its doors. It closed in October 1933, although Applegate was not alive to witness its demise.[100]

As a social reformer Applegate considered the Spanish Colonial Arts Society's efforts a success because they raised the artisans' self-esteem. "It is pathetic to see the renewal of happiness and self-respect in the older workers on finding their handicrafts, so long despised, welcomed and appreciated," he wrote. "Both Celso Gallegos and José Dolores López, our most popular woodcarvers, will reduce their prices when sales slow down, rather than be deprived of the pleasure of making new pieces. It is true that although these people have lived with the Americans for two generations, many of them never took any part in current social events until they began, a few years ago, to come forward to help the American artists in some of their undertakings. They associate the revival of their own arts—and truly—with the arrival in New Mexico of poets and painters. Sometimes the old men can be seen at the yearly Spanish Fair on De Vargas, beaming ecstatically, with tears in their eyes, at the exhibition of arts and crafts they had feared were lost forever."[101]

William Wroth wrote of the Hispanic crafts revival,

> On the one hand, the revival can be seen as a colossal and expensive failure. Huge sums of money were spent on projects, with little result. The world was bent on its inevitable course toward further mechanization of human life;

handcrafts no longer had a vital role to play, as their demise during World War II demonstrated. The market created was both artificial and limited: The government-generated market was artificial because it depended on massive amounts of federal funds; the private market was limited to the wealthiest sector of the Anglo-American population.

On the other hand, the revival planted a seed. A large number of Hispanic men and women learned a craft. It gave them pleasure to make things with their hands, not only to sell but also to furnish their own homes. … This skill gave Hispanics an option for employment and proved a hedge against both economic hardship and rapid assimilation. They had the option to be artists, not merely cogs in the great American economic machine.[102]

Applegate and the other founders of the Spanish Arts Shop did not realize the success they had hoped for. They were, however, successful in encouraging a renewed interest in Hispanic art and craft among the craftspeople themselves. The seeds planted by the 1920s revival of the art of rural Hispanics continue fruitful to this day in the work of modern New Mexican artists through whom the ancient traditions live on.

Endnotes

[1] Forrest, *The Preservation of the Village*, 49-50.
[2] Alta Applegate to T.M. Pearce, May 2, 1940, Pearce Papers, MSS 255, Box 30, Folder 15. Essay, Mowbray-Clarke Papers, AAA, Reel D169A.
[3] Cassidy, "Art and Artists of New Mexico: Frank G. Applegate," *New Mexico Magazine* 12:6 (June 1934): 28.
[4] Wroth, *Christian Images in Hispanic New Mexico*, ix. FGA to Mary Mowbray-Clarke, Oct. 24, 1924, Mowbray-Clarke Papers. Schimmel, "The Hispanic Southwest," in Eldridge, et al., *Art in New Mexico*, 143.
[5] Steele, *Santos and Saints*, 34-36.
[6] Briggs, *The Wood Carvers of Cordova, N.M.*, 5.
[7] Austin, "Frank Applegate," *New Mexico Quarterly* 2:3 (August 1932): 213.
[8] Alta Applegate to Pearce, May 2, 1940, Pearce Papers. "Mrs. Applegate Dies in Denver," *Santa Fe New Mexican*, July 31, 1944, 1. A report on a lecture Applegate gave for the Art League of New Mexico, which ran in the Jan. 14, 1931, edition of the *Albuquerque Journal*, said the Applegates had several thousand photographs of Spanish Colonial art, but no evidence of them has been found.
[9] FGA to Mary Mowbray-Clarke, Jan. 9, 1925, Mowbray-Clarke Papers.
[10] Applegate, "Spanish Colonial Arts," *The Survey* 66:3 (May 1, 1931): 156. Austin, "Mexicans and New Mexico," *The Survey* 66:3 (May 1, 1931): 189.
[11] Forrest, 49. Applegate, "Spanish Arts and Crafts" (probably the text for a lecture), DeHuff Papers, MSS 99, Box 7, Folder 15.
[12] Alta Applegate to Pearce, May 2, 1940, Pearce Papers.
[13] FGA to Mary Mowbray-Clarke, Nov. 6, 1924, Mowbray-Clarke Papers.
[14] Essay, Mowbray-Clarke Papers. "The World of Art," *The New York Times Magazine*, Dec. 14, 1924, 9.
[15] "Art: Exhibition of the Week," *The New York Times*, April 26, 1925, sec. 8, 11. The *Times* refers to the gallery as the Newman Gallery and Applegate spelled it that way in letters; the correct name is listed in the catalog in the Mabel Dodge Luhan Papers. Luhan had exhibited santos in New York as early as 1919.
[16] FGA to Mary Mowbray-Clarke, April 12, 1925, Mowbray-Clarke Papers.
[17] Mather, ed., *Colonial Frontiers*, 98. FGA to Austin, Jan. 11, 1928, Mary Austin Collection, Huntington Library. Schimmel, in Eldridge, et al., 113. Andrew Dasburg to Carl Zigrosser, Feb. 4, 1926, Zigrosser to Dasburg, Jan. 13, 1926, Zigrosser Papers, MS 6, Folder 369.
[18] FGA to Mary Mowbray-Clarke, Oct. 3, 1925, Mowbray-Clarke Papers. Frank, *New Kingdom of the Saints*, 33-34.
[19] Essay, Mowbray-Clarke Papers.
[20] Austin, "Frank Applegate," 214. Taylor and Bokides, *New Mexican Furniture*, 226.
[21] Kardon, "Within Our Shores: Diverse Craft Revivals and Survivals," in Kardon, ed., *Revivals! Diverse Traditions*, 24.
[22] Taylor and Bokides, 226. "Frank Applegate Dies Suddenly at Home," *Santa Fe New Mexican*, Feb. 13, 1931, 5.
[23] Lorenzo de Cordova [Brown], *Echoes of the Flute*, 6.
[24] Brown, Briggs, and Weigle, *Hispano Folklife of New Mexico*, 17.
[25] Lorenzo de Cordova [Brown], 7-8.
[26] Lorenzo de Cordova [Brown], 11.
[27] Lorenzo de Cordova [Brown], 9-10.
[28] Brown, et al., 210. Applegate, Betty, "Los Hermanos Penitentes," *Southwest Review* 17:1 (October 1931): 100. Tinieblas: the darkening of the sun and moon at Christ's death.
[29] Steele, 135. Brown to Charles Briggs, Dec. 11, 1972, E. Boyd Collection, Correspondence, 8A.
[30] Brown, et al., 209. Hare, "The Wood Carver of Cordova," *Travel* 81:1 (May 1943): 21.
[31] Spanish Colonial Arts Society Records. Brown, et al., 206-207. Briggs, "The Role of *Mexicano* Artists and the Anglo Elite in the Emergence of a Contemporary Folk Art," in Vlach, ed., *Folk Art and Art Worlds*, 216.
[32] Boyd, "Celso Gallegos," *El Palacio* 60:5 (May 1953): 215.
[33] Stevens, "Celso Gallegos," *Santa Fe New Mexican*, Jan. 13, 1974, 6. Briggs, *Wood Carvers of Cordova*,

203. Boyd, "Celso Gallegos," 215. "Celso Gallegos, Fabricador de los Santos de Bulto," *El Pasatiempo* (supplement to the *Santa Fe New Mexican*), Sept. 5, 1931, 6.

34 "A Modernist Sculptor," *The New York Times*, Oct. 21, 1923, reprinted in *El Palacio* 15:9 (Nov. 1, 1923) 150. Steele, 125-127. A bulto of Santiago was one of more than a dozen Applegate bultos the Móntez Gallery in Santa Fe offered for sale beginning in 1994.

35 Sept. 9, 1928. The retablo of San Cristóbal is in the collection of Regis University, Denver. As of this writing, santos attributed to Applegate continue to be discovered. How many he made is unknown; he never wrote about them, and surviving family members did not know he made them until informed so by the authors. Spanish Colonial art expert E. Boyd knew of his work, either as a restorer of old santos or a maker of new ones, to the point where she could distinguish an "Applegate smell," on certain pieces. See Boyd, *Saints and Saint Makers of New Mexico* (1946; revised edition, 1998), 53-54. The authors do not believe Applegate intended to deceive anyone with his religious artwork, for there is no indication he ever tried to pass it off as anything other than his own.

Several experts on santos, including Father Steele, have conjectured that Alta Applegate may have painted retablos, because her initials (A.B.A.) appear on several retablos attributed to Applegate, including one in a private collection and two in the Spanish Colonial Arts Society Collection. Alta is not known to have been a painter, and these retablos resemble the San Cristóbal Frank Applegate is believed to have made. Perhaps someone may have initialed them to indicate her ownership of them.

36 "Spanish-Colonial Arts Society Commences 5th Year of Activity," *Santa Fe New Mexican*, Dec. 19, 1928, 5. A group of Santa Feans, including Kenneth Chapman, had founded the Society for the Preservation of Spanish Antiquities in New Mexico in 1913, but that organization was short-lived.

37 FGA to Mary Mowbray-Clarke, Oct. 24, 1924, Mowbray-Clarke Papers. Austin, "Mexicans and New Mexico," 187.

38 Wroth, "The Hispanic Craft Revival in New Mexico," in Kardon, ed., *Revivals! Diverse Traditions*, 85-86. Austin, "Frank Applegate," 214. Austin to Helen McCrossen, April 25, 1931, Shop Correspondence, 1931, Spanish Colonial Arts Society Papers.

39 Report in E. Boyd Collection. Chapman to Hodge, Sept. 15, 1925, Frederick Webb Hodge Manuscript Collection, MS.7.MAI.1.121. Courtesy of the Southwest Museum.

40 Austin, "Frank Applegate," 214. Austin to Gerald Cassidy, Feb. 27, 1927, Mary Austin Papers, Center for Southwest Research, MSS 31 BC, Box 1, Folder 3. Weigle, "The First Twenty-Five Years of the Spanish Colonial Arts Society," in Weigle, ed., et al., *Hispanic Arts and Ethnohistory in the Southwest*, 183-184.

41 Shop Correspondence 1931, Folder 2, March 12, 1931, Spanish Colonial Arts Society Papers. Weigle in Weigle, ed., et al., 184.

42 "Spanish-Colonial Arts Society Commences 5th Year of Activity."

43 "Spanish Arts, Crafts Awards Are Announced by Committee," *Santa Fe New Mexican*, June 2, 1926, 2.

44 "Fifteen Prizes Awarded for Spanish Colonial Arts," *Santa Fe New Mexican*, Aug. 11, 1926, 4.

45 Austin, "Frank Applegate," 214.

46 Briggs, *Wood Carvers of Cordova*, 46. Austin, "Mexicans and New Mexico," 187. FGA to Austin, March 1, 1929, Mary Austin Collection, Huntington Library.

47 Briggs, *Wood Carvers of Cordova*, 50.

48 Briggs, *Wood Carvers of Cordova*, 46-47.

49 Wroth, "Hispanic Southwestern Craft Traditions in the Twentieth Century," in Wroth, ed., *Hispanic Crafts of the Southwest*, 5.

50 Briggs, *Wood Carvers of Cordova*, 53.

51 Forrest, 70. Brown, et al., 209. Briggs, "What Is a Modern Santo?" *El Palacio* 79:4 (March 1974): 42.

52 "Colonial Arts of New Mexico," *The New York Times*, Oct. 22, 1928, 24.

53 Gibson, *Santa Fe and Taos Colonies*, 211-212. "Spanish-Colonial Arts Society Commences 5th Year of Activity."

54 Briggs, "The Role of *Mexicano* Artists," 217. Gibson, 170.

55 "Spanish Colonial Arts," *El Palacio* 29:21 (Dec. 5, 1930): 330. "Folk Arts Pure in New Mexico, Frank Applegate Tells Audience," *Santa Fe New Mexican*, Nov. 26, 1930, 5. Applegate, "Spanish Colonial Arts," 157.

56 "Spanish Colonial Arts," *El Palacio* 29:21 (Dec. 5, 1930): 329-332. Some of Applegate's findings have since been discredited; for example, Charles M. Carrillo's research has shown that rural Hispanics did make pottery; see *Hispanic New Mexican Pottery: Evidence of Craft Specialization, 1790-1890* (Albuquerque: LPD Press, 1998).

57 "The World of Art." Austin, "New Mexico Spanish," *Saturday Review of Literature* 7:49 (June 27, 1931): 930. Perhaps Austin was not aware of Aurelio Espinosa, a pioneering scholar of New Mexican folklore and language.

58 "Spanish Colonial Arts," *El Palacio* 29:21 (Dec. 5, 1930): 329.

59 Paul Kellogg to FGA, Sept. 3, 1929, Cassidy Family Papers. Quoted by permission of The Bancroft Library, owners of the Cassidy Family Papers, [ca. 1897-1965]. BANC MSS 67/1 p. Applegate, "Spanish Colonial Arts," 156-157. Originally the article was to feature photographs by Ansel Adams; see FGA to Adams, Sept. 7, 1929, transcription in Augusta Fink Papers, Box 1, Folder 36.

60 "Spanish Colonial Arts Exhibition Is Unique," *Santa Fe New Mexican*, Aug. 4, 1926, 2.

61 Cash, *Santos: Enduring Images of Northern New Mexico Village Churches*, 100. Austin, "Frank Applegate," 215. "Description of Santos in Society's Collection," Spanish Colonial Arts Society Papers. It stands today in the Palace of the Governors.

62 Chauvenet, *John Gaw Meem: Pioneer in Historic Preservation*, 67. Gibson, 171.

63 Taylor and Bokides, 230. Stineman, *Mary Austin, Song of a Maverick*, 243. Austin, "Frank Applegate," 216. "Spanish-Colonial Arts Society Commences 5th Year of Activity." The society apparently

planned to sponsor branches in other towns, for Austin told Gerald Cassidy that Las Vegas, N.M., was to be the first local chapter; see Austin to Cassidy, Feb. 27, 1927, Mary Austin Papers, Center for Southwest Research, MSS 31 BC, Box 1, Folder 3.

[64] *Santa Fe New Mexican*, Aug. 15, 1927, 8. "Beautiful Workmanship by the Spanish Colonials," *Santa Fe New Mexican*, Sept. 1, 1928, 2. "Spanish Colonial Arts Exhibition Most Successful," *Santa Fe New Mexican*, Sept. 3, 1929, 2.

[65] "New Mexico Santos to Become Priceless, Declares Applegate," *Santa Fe New Mexican*, April 2, 1927, 2.

[66] Batkin, "The Taylor Museum: A Tribute to Folk Culture," in *Colorado Springs Fine Arts Center: A History and Selections From the Permanent Collection*, 44. Taylor Collection list, Colorado Springs Fine Arts Center Archives. Wroth, *Christian Images in Hispanic New Mexico*, 50, 55, 73-74. One of the altar screens was painted by Rafael Aragon and is reputed to be from the Santa Cruz Valley. The other is in the style of the Quill Pen Santero. It had belonged to a women's Penitente chapter near Chamita and was later moved to a morada near Hernandez, where Applegate purchased it. See Cash, *Santos*, 101, 123.

[67] Taylor Collection list, Colorado Springs Fine Arts Center Archives. The list includes a price for only one Spanish Colonial piece, a retablo of San Gerónimo at $35.

[68] FGA to Austin, Jan. 19, 1928, Mary Austin Collection, Huntington Library. Museum of New Mexico History Bureau Collection, Box 380, Item 7.

[69] "Artes Nativos de Nuevo Mexico," *El Pasatiempo* (supplement to the *Santa Fe New Mexican*), Sept. 5, 1931, 4. "Loan Exhibit: Two Santos Placed on Exhibit in Museum, Loaned by Colonial Arts Society," *El Palacio* 30:19-20 (May 20, 1931): 252. "Historical Society Lecture," *El Palacio* 29: 17-20 (Oct. 15, 1930): 325.

[70] FGA to Austin, n.d., probably Feb. 9, 1929, Mary Austin Collection, Huntington Library.

[71] FGA to Austin, Feb. 20, 1929, Mary Austin Collection, Huntington Library. "Chimayo People Protest Against Dismantling of Miracle Chapel," *Santa Fe New Mexican*, Feb. 11, 1929, 5.

[72] FGA to Austin, Feb. 20, 1929, Feb. 22, 1929, March 1, 1929, Mary Austin Collection, Huntington Library. AU 1003, 1005, 1007.

[73] Meem to George Parmalee Day, Sept. 12, 1929, Meem Archives/Correspondence, Box 2, File E. FGA to Austin, Feb. 22, 1929.

[74] FGA to Austin, Feb. 22, 1929. Meem to the Rev. Father Salvador [sic], March 7, 1929, Meem to Daeger, March 13, 1929, Meem Archives/Correspondence, Box 2, File E.

[75] Austin to Meem, March 20, 1929, Meem Archives/Correspondence, Box 2, File E. Meem to Day, Sept. 12, 1929, Day to Meem, Oct. 7, 1929, Meem to Day, Oct. 15, 1929, Meem Archives/Correspondence, Box 2, File E. Meem to Austin, March 13, 1929, Meem Archives/Correspondence, Box 2, File E.

[76] Meem to Day, Oct. 15, 1929. Austin, "Frank Applegate," 215.

[77] Spanish Colonial Arts Society Papers, 1929 Folder.

[78] Spanish Colonial Arts Society Papers, 1929 Folder. Weigle in Weigle, ed., et al., 186.

[79] FGA to Austin, Feb. 22, 1929.

[80] "From New Mexico," *Atlanta (Ill.) Argus*, Feb. 10, 1922, 2.

[81] Nestor, *The Native Market of the Spanish New Mexican Craftsmen*, 9. Spanish Colonial Arts Society Minutes, May 19, 1930, Miscellaneous Minutes, Reports and Expenses, 1930-34; Ernest Lyckman to Helen McCrossen, Nov. 26, 1930, Adelina Otero-Warren to Helen McCrossen, Nov. 10, 1930, Spanish Colonial Arts Society Correspondence, Craftspeople; John V. Conway to FGA, May 14, n.d., Circa 1931 Miscellaneous Lists; all Spanish Colonial Arts Society Papers. Gibson, 172. FGA to Austin, July 16, 1930, Mary Austin Collection, Huntington Library.

[82] Description of Spanish Arts Shop based on photo in *El Pasatiempo*, Sept. 5, 1931, 6, reprinted in Pierce and Weigle, eds., *Spanish New Mexico: The Spanish Colonial Arts Society Collection*, vol. 2, 15.

[83] "Muebles Tipicos para la Casa y el Jardin," *El Pasatiempo* (supplement to *Santa Fe New Mexican*), Sept. 5, 1931, 8. Photograph, Applegate Papers.

[84] Austin *per* McCormick to DeHuff, Jan. 17, 1930, Spanish Colonial Arts Society Papers. Weigle in Weigle, ed., et al., 192.

[85] Spanish Colonial Arts Society Minutes, May 19, 1930, Miscellaneous Minutes, Reports and Expenses, 1930-34; Paul Bernat to FGA, June 1, 1930, Spanish Colonial Arts Society Correspondence; Spanish Colonial Arts Society Minutes, May 19, 1930, Miscellaneous Minutes, Reports and Expenses, 1930-34; Paulita Peña to Alta Applegate, Sept. 6, 1930, Spanish Colonial Arts Society Correspondence, Craftspeople; all Spanish Colonial Arts Society Papers. Austin to Mrs. Meredith (Elizabeth Sage) Hare, Oct. 2, 1931, Applegate Papers. Dunton took over management of the Spanish Arts Shop in December 1931.

[86] Applegate, "If You Buy Antiques" *New Mexico Highway Journal* 7 (April 1929): 34. Courtesy of *New Mexico Magazine*. "Spanish-Colonial Arts Society Commences 5th Year of Activity."

[87] Applegate, "Spanish Colonial Arts," 157. Wroth, "The Hispanic Craft Revival in New Mexico," 86.

[88] Briggs, "What Is a Modern Santo?" 43. McCrossen, "Native Crafts in New Mexico," *School Arts Magazine* 30:7 (March 1931): 458. Shop Reports, Inventories, Craftspeople, Spanish Fair 1931-34, Jan. 5, 1932, Spanish Colonial Arts Society 1930-34 Miscellaneous Minutes, Spanish Colonial Arts Society Papers.

[89] Spanish Colonial Arts Society Correspondence, Feb. 10, 1930, and n.d., Spanish Colonial Arts Society Papers. The quoted note is in English, however, since all of López's other correspondence is in Spanish, it can be assumed that someone, possibly a Spanish Colonial Arts Society or López family member, translated it.

[90] Hare, 21, 32. Briggs, *Wood Carvers of Cordova*, 53. Steele, 135. It is believed Celso Gallegos began making santos before Applegate arrived in New Mexico, so the fact that Gallegos made unpainted bultos cannot be attributed to Applegate.

[91] Hare, 21. Briggs, *Wood Carvers of Cordova*, 190.

[92] Cash, *Santos*, 17.
[93] Briggs, *Wood Carvers of Cordova*, 37; "What Is a Modern Santo?" 46; "The Role of *Mexicano* Artists," 218.
[94] Shop Records, Spanish Colonial Arts Society Papers. McCrossen, 458.
[95] Wroth, "The Hispanic Craft Revival in New Mexico," 86-87.
[96] "The Spanish Colonial Arts Society," *El Palacio* 29:3 (Sept. 2, 1930): 105-106. Spanish Colonial Arts Society 1930-31 Ledger, 59; Spanish Colonial Arts Society Minutes, May 19, 1930, Miscellaneous Minutes, Reports and Expenses, 1930-34, Spanish Colonial Arts Society Papers.
[97] Austin to Hare, Oct. 2, 1931, Applegate Papers.
[98] Spanish Arts Shop Records, Spanish Colonial Arts Society Papers.

[99] Ishauu Co. (Elizabeth White's shop) to Helen McCrossen, July 8, 1931, Shop Correspondence 1931; Elizabeth Sage Hare to Helen McCrossen, Nov. 13, 1931, Shop Correspondence 1931, Spanish Colonial Arts Society Papers.
[100] Taylor, "Arts and Crafts in the Santa Fe Style," paper presented at the Winterthur Conference on the Decorative Arts, Wilmington, Del., 1990, 32, 33. Shop Correspondence, Spanish Colonial Arts Society Papers.
[101] Applegate, "Spanish Colonial Arts," 157.
[102] Wroth, "The Hispanic Craft Revival in New Mexico," 93. For more on the "government-generated market" see the Epilogue.

CHAPTER **12:**
SPANISH
COLONIAL
REVIVAL

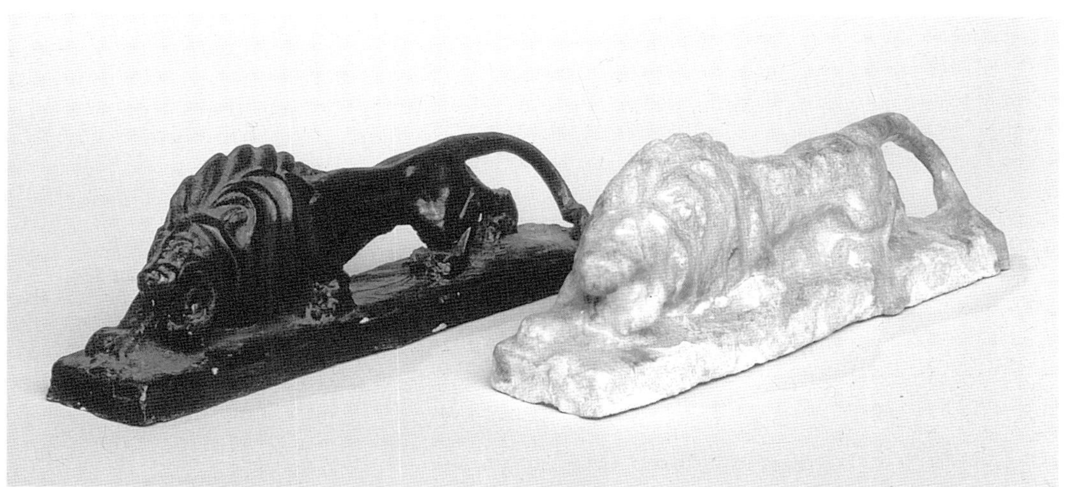

Two variations of *Wounded Lion Charging*, ceramic figures. Collection of Gerald Peters Gallery. Photograph courtesy of Gerald Peters Gallery, Santa Fe. First exhibited in 1915.

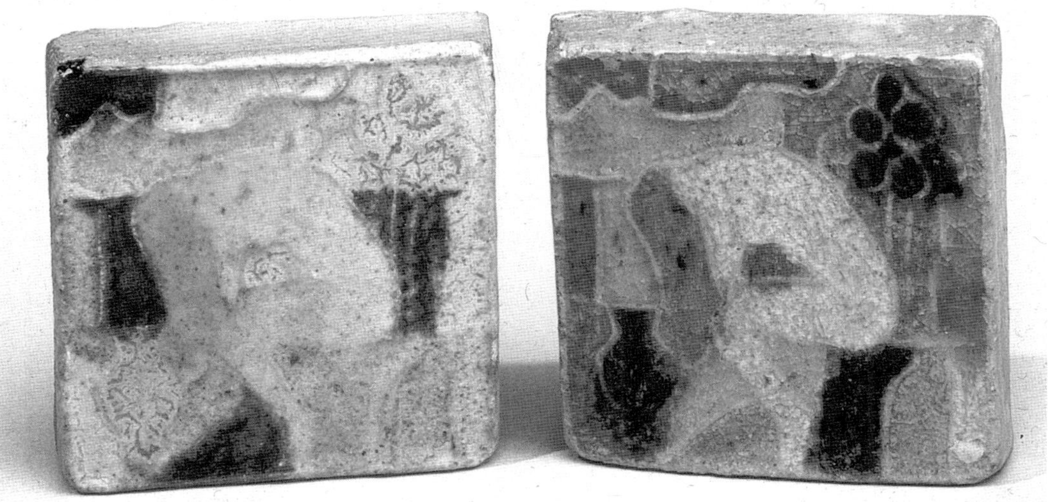

Ceramic tiles. Collection of Gerald Peters Gallery. Photograph courtesy of Gerald Peters Gallery, Santa Fe.

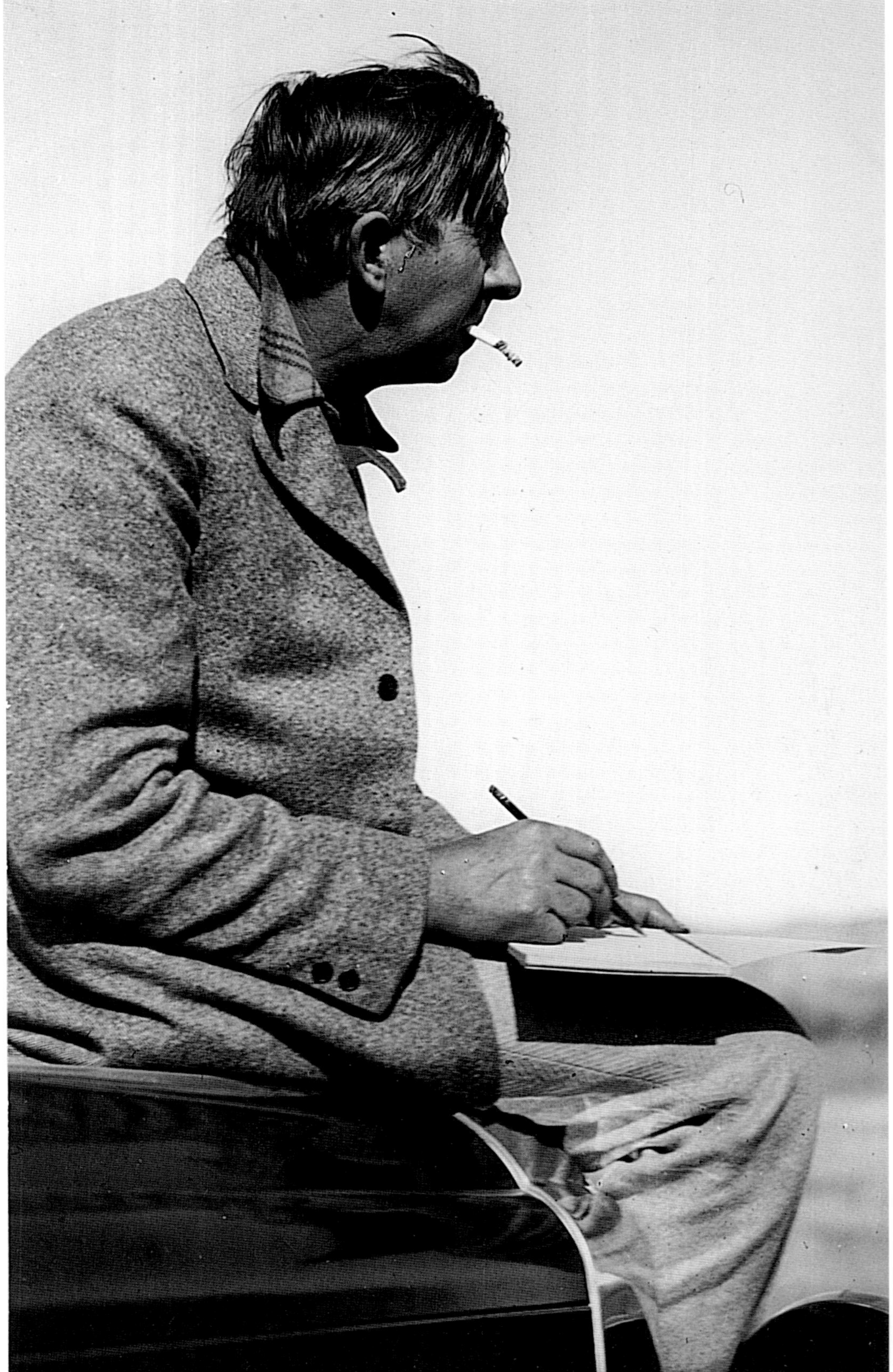

Frank Applegate by Ansel Adams, ca. late 1920s. Courtesy of the Center for Creative Photography and the Ansel Adams Publishing Rights Trust.

13 From Brush to Pen: Applegate the Writer

In 1977, when the Rio Grande Press reprinted Frank Applegate's *Indian Stories From the Pueblos*, publisher Robert B. McCoy called it "a great book to read, by a great writer who also was a painter of magnificent talent."[1] Such praise seems unwarranted for a man who did not begin writing professionally until age 45 and practiced the vocation for only a few years. Yet, like many writers, Applegate had been subconsciously preparing to become a writer for his entire life. His life experiences and studies were the sources from which he drew inspiration as an author and essayist, and when he finally put pen to paper, he had a wealth of information stored inside, ready to be released.

Applegate's interest in writing was a link to his father, whose newspaper correspondence had entertained the residents of Logan County, Illinois. It was the elder Applegate who saw that the letters Frank wrote home from Europe in 1906 were published in the *Atlanta Argus* and *Lincoln Daily Courier*. Frank proved a skilled storyteller from the start, and over the next 20 years he contributed amusing anecdotal letters to those newspapers.

It was not until the late 1920s, however, that Applegate devoted serious effort to writing. Mary Austin encouraged him to become a writer and took the credit when he proved adept. Austin also convinced him to join the Genius Club, the informal writers' salon that met at her home in Santa Fe. "I got Frank writing because I had so many requests for articles about things in New Mexico and the Southwest which I couldn't write myself and none of the Geniuses would qualify for," she told a mutual friend. "He has done some very good work."[2]

Applegate's body of published work was slim, comprising a few magazine articles, a book review and several dozen folktales. The magazine essays are straightforward examples of explanatory journalism, written in an authoritative, strongly opinionated voice. His first published essay, "Tourists and Art," appeared in the October 1926 issue of *Southwest Review*. It discusses the two factions of artists at work in the Southwest—the "creative artists" and the "reproducers of romantic subjects" (see Chapter 6).[3]

Applegate discussed art further in "New Mexico Backgrounds," which also appeared in *Southwest Review*. This essay focused not on Anglo artists but on native ones, comparing Pueblo art with Spanish Colonial art. He reiterated his strong opinions regarding the deleterious effect of the Spanish conquest and mass culture on native peoples. "The art of the Pueblo Indian shows an undisturbed cultural development through long ages, as though it were finished and the last word had been said," he wrote. "The Spanish colonial art, while it was executed by people of a supposedly higher civilization, seems in contrast both culturally and technically primitive and unfinished. Pueblo Indian art is in fact the product of centuries of seclusion; but the development of Spanish colonial art was rudely interrupted by the invasion of Nordic Americans with their machine-made, monotonous mass culture."

Applegate went on to explain the basics of Pueblo pottery, basketry, silverwork, weaving, watercolor, and architecture, meanwhile criticizing "militant, proselyting missionaries"; the government, for sending Indians to boarding schools; the first "predatory" American settlers, for showing "the utmost contempt for the cultural arts of the native Spanish colonials"; and the contemporary "pseudo-cultured," for spoiling "the simplicity of [the] Spanish colonial background."[4]

What is striking about "New Mexico Backgrounds" is that it could have been penned by Austin. The words are as angry and harsh, the opinions as strong as Austin's are in many of her writings. Applegate continued in this vein in a folkloric essay he contributed to *Southwest Review* called "Sandía the Tragic."[5] The article relates the history of the Sandía Indians, whom Applegate claimed "had the most tragic and unfortunate history of all the pueblos in New Mexico." He chronicled how Coronado's arrival in 1540 led to years of Spanish tyranny, and how attempts by missionaries to convert the Indians to Christianity resulted in the Sandías' exodus to Hopiland. "Indian gods are often local and are supposed to have their abodes in places near the homes of their worshippers," he explained. "Out there in the Hopi desert the gods of the Sandías were impotent."

Applegate outlined the Sandías' return to their home on the Rio Grande, about 10 miles north of Albuquerque, and their reluctant acceptance of Christianity. The muddling of the three religions—Christian, Sandía, and Hopi—led to their ostracism from other tribes until their numbers dwindled almost to extinction. "They grow vines and make a good deal of wine which they drink," Applegate wrote, "and thus forget some

of the troubles or, as some would say, add to their plight. Year by year they grow fewer and fewer. There are now less than seventy of them left to inhabit what remains of their crumbling pueblo." Applegate offered no solutions to the Sandías' problems, merely presenting them in the hopes of fostering understanding.[6]

Applegate was the "author" of an "as told to" article by Tom Howard which appeared in the April 1929 issue of the *New Mexico Highway Journal*. Titled "If You Buy Antiques," it offered advice on buying Southwestern antiquities, specifically Navajo and Chimayó weavings. The article includes a humorous anecdote, similar in style and tone to those that populate Applegate's later folktales. He described the tale as "within the writer's knowledge as a fact":

A sad-faced Navajo was standing on the platform wrapped in the grimy folds of a Pendleton blanket for which he had paid not more than five dollars probably as many years before. Its degree of decrepitude and filth was almost beyond imagination.

The Limited pulled into the station. On the observation platform was a typical "dude" in golf panties. He vaulted the rail and ran up to the Indian.

"Thirty dollars?" he hollered, yanking at the blanket.

Astounded, the Indian shook his head.

"Forty?" shot back the would-be purchaser.

Before he could get any further protest he thrust four ten-dollar bills in Poor Lo's hand and snatched the blanket away, racing back into the car. A minute or so later a delighted "dude" danced around the back platform for the edification of a group of young ladies. He was wrapped in the grimy—and probably verminridden—Pendleton.

"It's a real Indian blanket," he proclaimed. "I know, because I bought it of[f] that Indian over there."

While the train became a speck in the distance, John Indian gazed after the brass railed platform. Then he looked at the four tens in his hands.

"Damn fool," he grinned and walked to the nearest store where a brand new Pendleton was bought for $7.95.[7]

Applegate had little sympathy for fools, dudes included. The article tells of another Indian from Isleta Pueblo, "who every year makes all the dances at the various pueblos selling glass beads he purchases at the 5 and 10."[8] As far as Applegate was concerned, Indians had every right to hoodwink ill-prepared Anglos.

Through Austin's intervention Applegate received an assignment from the *New York Herald Tribune* to review the book *Desert Drums* by Leo Crane. The book details the plight of the Pueblo Indians and efforts by the Indian Bureau, well-meaning do-gooders, and politicians to "help" them. One of the reformers Crane took to task was Austin herself, which did not sit well with Applegate. His review was mixed, and it gave him the opportunity to attack some of his favorite targets. He called the Indian Bureau "an ineffective and unenlightened government bureau entangled in its own red tape in Washington, and headed by a political spoils appointee." He outlined the Bursum Bill affair and foresaw upcoming Pueblo land battles. He criticized Crane for supporting the forced relocation of Indian children to boarding schools, writing, "Leo Crane's favorites among the Pueblos appear to be Laguna and Isleta: Pueblos that have practically given up all Indian arts and culture and that are now living very much as do their mestizo Spanish-American neighbors. To such a condition does the practice of kidnaping Indian children and sending them away from the pueblo finally bring the Indians. Away from the pueblo the children have no chance to learn the ancient arts and ways of Indian life. Instead of becoming cultured in the Indians' traditional ways of living, they sink to the lower strata of our society and perform our most menial tasks indifferently and without interest."[9]

Applegate's final article, "Spanish Colonial Arts," ran posthumously in the magazine *The Survey*. The article offered a basic introduction to Spanish Colonial art and included information that he had covered in lectures. It also outlined the topics addressed in his most ambitious writing project, the manuscript on Spanish Colonial arts that he and Mary Austin had begun in 1928 (see Chapter 14).[10]

Although Applegate's factual essays are well written and interesting, they reveal little of the creative talent displayed in his folktales, most of which were collected in the books *Indian Stories From the Pueblos* and *Native Tales of New Mexico*. These vividly descriptive stories about the lives and legends of Indians and rural Hispanics were less a product of his imagination than they were a recounting of tales heard and events witnessed, told sometimes with humor, sometimes with grim concern.

Although it is not known when Applegate began to write down some of the stories he had gathered over the years, by February 1929 he reached an agreement with the J.B. Lippincott Company to publish a collection of the tales. The book deal came together with the aid of Walter Lippincott Goodwin, Jr., eldest son of Applegate's friend Elizabeth Sage Hare. "I write another Indian story now and then," Applegate told Austin that month. "I have promised to let Lippincott's print them in book form and they are going to illustrate them with Indian paintings printed in color. Mrs. Hare's oldest son is with Lippincott's … and he is very anxious to oversee the printing of the book and get it out in very fine form. Mrs. Hare is extremely pleased herself with the stories." A week later, he told Austin that he had completed about 20 stories.[11]

By undertaking this project Applegate was participating in a movement that harked back to the Brothers Grimm and Walt Whitman and was very much in vogue in the 1920s, the interest in folktales as literature and the folk rhythm in literature. No longer were such tales passed down only orally, or appreciated solely for their didacticism or amusement. *Folk-Say: A Regional Miscellany*, an annual journal of folk literature that published several of Applegate's stories, labeled this movement "the New Regionalism," a return to the Regionalism that was at its height in the 1870s and 1880s. The magazine held that "the future of American literature lay in the hands of those writers who … would find their materials and methods in their own regional culture–a culture, that is, with its roots in oral tradition. … It is developing a new feeling for locality … it is bringing to native materials the maturity of sensitive, civilized minds, supplementing first-hand acquisition with research and sympathy, getting beneath mere physical sensations to causes and meanings." Obviously, the "New Regionalism" reflected the ideas that had first drawn artists and writers to the Southwest–the desire for fresh American material from which to create innately American art; the escape from modern, industrialized culture; and the appreciation of native cultures. As Austin, who had trod this path long before him, later wrote, Applegate "foresaw … the fusion of all tales, however colored by descent, in a pattern which will declare itself as Native to the country, the scene, the experience that shaped it."[12]

Applegate's motive for writing the book was historical as well as literary. In a letter to J. Frank Dobie, the cowboy scribe of Texas, he expressed a sentiment about Dobie's stories that is shared by all collectors of folktales: "I am glad it has been done … before too much of the source has been wiped out. In 20 years I fear much of it could not have been found out and written about." He also suggested to author-conservationist Arthur Carhart that he interview old miners "before everything is buried with them." By collecting these tales Applegate was engaging in yet another form of cultural preservation, the principle that had become his guiding star. "He wrote not for a ready fiction market, but to record what he had learned of the history of pueblos and individuals."[13]

Indian Stories From the Pueblos was released late in the summer of 1929.[14] It contained 18 short tales, both narrations of familiar legends and never-before-told firsthand accounts. The inside front and back covers featured a map of the Pueblo region, illustrated by Applegate and with place names written in his hand. In the preface he explained a bit about Pueblo religion and made it clear that he in no way considered himself an expert on the subject:

> Only the cacique or high priest of a pueblo has a complete understanding of the religious beliefs of his village, and he imparts this knowledge only to his acolytes, one of whom is to succeed him when he dies. The majority of the Pueblo Indians thus have little knowledge of the inner meaning of their religion and the ceremonies they perform. No white person has yet adequately explained Pueblo Indian religious beliefs, although many have described well certain phases of their beliefs and rituals.[15]

Thus, Applegate revealed another motive for writing the stories: to promote understanding of the Indian culture by discussing aspects of it that whites may find curious, such as religious rituals and symbolism, and explaining their significance.

Witter Bynner wrote the glowing foreword to *Indian Stories*, in which he likened the tales to fairy stories: "One who knows Pueblo Indians catches their true accent on page after page of Mr. Applegate's homely and vivid record. Bare as the style is, it exerts a spell like the bareness of Indians in one of their apparently simple dance-rhythms." Bynner mentioned Applegate's "intimate and sympathetic life among the Pueblos" and noted he was "a familiar in the Tewa villages around his home town, Santa Fe." He concluded, "Months at a time he has lived in Hopi villages, lived the Hopi life, felt Hopi feelings, studied and revived Hopi art among the native pottery-makers, painted Hopi persons and ceremonies, and listened meantime to such stories as he has caught for us in this volume. He has caught them as patiently, as gently, as surely, as I have seen an Indian pick up in gifted hands a live woodpecker from a tree-trunk or a live trout from a stream."[16]

Indian Stories From the Pueblos opens with "Ancestral Eagles," and the first paragraph alerts the reader to Applegate's critical, progressive opinions.

For "Ancestral Eagles" is the story of Tabo Salukama, a Hopi Indian who, Applegate tells us, was sent to an Indian boarding school where "he had had it impressed upon him that Indians were savages and that their religious practices and ceremonies were the result of low and base superstitions. He was also taught that the middle-class American culture was the flower of highest civilization, and that all Americans were one hundred per cent pure in their ideals, religious beliefs, and practices. Likewise he was taught that the Indian Bureau and its agents were always solicitous for the welfare of the Indians and always stood ready to help them in any emergency."[17]

Naturally, Tabo learns a thing or two. When a Navajo steals an eaglet that is needed for a ceremony, Tabo seeks assistance from the Indian Bureau and the president of the United States. He, and indirectly the reader, eventually comes to realize that the Hopi ways are best, and "white man's nonsense" is of little use to Indians on the reservation.

As in Applegate's essays, the prose style in the folktales is explanatory, with the stories presented in a straightforward manner. Just as Applegate kept his brushwork to a minimum in many of his paintings, so he used words sparingly and with care. Applegate narrated many of the tales himself and frequently indicated that he was repeating what others told him or remembering incidents he observed. Often his narration framed a tale, as he let the Indians tell the stories themselves. The effect is to draw the reader into the scene as if the reader, like Applegate, was sitting there listening.

As noted previously, Applegate had a talent for languages, enough so that he traveled around Europe with relative ease as a young man. Although he likely had some command of Hopi and Tewa (the latter spoken in the six pueblos north of Santa Fe) many of the Indians he met could speak English. While the story "Turtle Shells" concludes with the sentence, "The Hopi woman told this story in English so that the bohana (white) visitor could understand it," it is the only story so noted. Additionally, when Applegate used an Indian narrator to tell a tale, he related the narration in the awkward English of the speaker, indicating that he had heard it told in this manner. Some of the older Indians spoke Spanish, for he noted in "The Hopi Famine": "I absent-mindedly greeted this old Indian in Spanish, as I often did the older Indians among the Spanish-speaking people of the Rio Grande valley." Applegate stated that the old man told him his life story in Spanish, and he translated it into English, further evidence that Applegate's command of Spanish must have been excellent. [18]

Applegate offered several tales about the Hopis to illustrate the differences between Hopi and Anglo humor. In "The Snake Priest's Trousers" he noted that the Indians considered the fact that someone stole the trousers of the great snake chief Supela a matter of extreme gravity. Another such story is the fictionalized account of an incident that took place in the early months of 1925, when Santa Fe artists Carlos Vierra and Henry Balink went to Hopi country to paint. Applegate, who was living with the Hopis at Polacca that winter, wrote a letter to the *Santa Fe New Mexican* about the event:

> I should like to correct a rumor that may have reached Santa Fe to the effect that two painters of that place, Henry Balink and Carlos Vierra, have had the D.T.'s since coming here to Hopi to paint Indians. It all started when they very carelessly rented a little house here among the sand dunes at Polacca, below the Walpi mesa. This little house happens to be the summer home of the Walpi snake priest, Hal Supala [*sic*], better known to the Hopi as Little Grey Fox Pretty Walking.
>
> On the evening of their arrival the two artists built a big cozy fire, to cook their evening mulligan and warm themselves thoroughly. After supper they were sitting, enjoying themselves, replete with Navaho mutton and non-intoxicating Polacca natural soda water, when Henry gave a blood curdling yell and jumped for a rafter overhead, while Carlos followed with another yell and hopped to the top of the stove and thence grabbed

himself a rafter, both yelling "snakes" so that they were heard clear to Walpi.

Harry Supala, provident snake chief that he is, had been anticipating next summer's snake dance at Walpi, and here and there had been collecting rattlers and parking them in his summer house to hibernate against the time they'd be needed next summer. The heat which the artists provided led the snakes to believe summer and dancing time had arrived, and the first inkling that Henry had that anything was amiss was when he got a bird's eye view of a snake's head rising insinuatingly between his knees.

The Hopi, hearing the yells and commotion came running from all parts and were amazed to see two bolcanas [*sic*] holding rafters and dancing in the air. The English word "snakes," which they heard over and over, meant nothing to them; their favorite word for that reptile being "chua." But finally Little Grey Fox Pretty Walking suspected what might be the cause, though perfectly astonished at the effect, and with his sacred corn meal and feather palio [palo?] charmed his little brethren of the desert and carried them away in a flour sack.

But Henry and Carlos' hair still fails to properly succumb to any amount of combing, and they still jump if they see an innocent piece of string or rope lying around.[19]

In "The Artists and the Snakes," as presented in *Indian Stories*, Applegate gave the two artists the names Heinrich Bollensch and Carlos Verencia. He elaborated on the newspaper account, fleshing out the details and adding descriptive color. And as he sometimes did when quoting Indians, Applegate wrote Heinrich's dialogue in dialect, so that he is quoted as saying, "Der is schnakes in der home, Carlos. Look once by der rat holes in der corner ver I tink it is yet pumple pees vot sing."[20] (Apparently Vierra had no accent, for he is quoted in plain English.)

Applegate indicated that Anglos found the incident amusing but Hopis did not: "They only saw that their sacred snakes had been jeopardized and thought that these men were more in sympathy with the culture of the Hopis than were the general run of the white people they had known and had considerately suspended themselves from the rafters to avoid stepping on and injuring the sacred snakes."[21]

Revered reptiles were just one aspect of Indian religion discussed in the tales. Spanish missionaries, and the influence of Christianity on the Indians, are the subject of several ironic or tragic stories. In "San Juan de los Caballeros," for example, the Indians pray to a statue of Jesus to end a drought, and the ensuing deluge results in starvation and death. "The Holy Water" tells of wrongful acts committed in the name of religion upon the Indians of Nambé and relates the Nambé version of the Pueblo Rebellion of 1680, when the Indians overthrew the Spanish colonial government. Other tales concern the arrival of Spanish settlers, Indian enslavement, and Indian battles with Spanish soldiers. A well-known legend is related in "The Turk of Pecos," the story of Francisco Coronado's fruitless search for the cities of gold. "Estevan the Magnificent" is a version of a story found in both Spanish and Indian lore about a Moor who rose to great power among the Indians but whose pride led to a violent death.[22]

"Ago Po," on the other hand, pokes fun at whites, specifically a white journalist who takes at face value everything a joking San Ildefonso Indian—"the koshare, the fun-maker of the pueblo"—tells her. To the "keen, wily" Ago Po, the journalist is a sucker: "Often in the past he had secured a great deal of amusement from such as she; and when he had seen her alight in the plaza he had marked her as his own. ... he knew the nature of his victim and how to impart the proper thrill." The story apparently was based on an actual event, for Applegate noted the journalist presented her findings to Kenneth Chapman at the Museum of New Mexico, who informed her that Ago Po "was the greatest joker and farceur among all the Indians he knew."[23]

Many stories use humor to teach readers about Indian ways. "The Little Fish of San Juan" explains why the San Juan Indians will not eat fish. "Cochití Ancient Hunting Dance" discusses the significance of that rarely performed ceremony, which the Applegates attended in March 1929.[24] Some tales illustrate the cliche "Deep down, we're all alike" by showing similarities of behavior and traits common to humankind. These include "Hopi Quarrel," a tale of a domestic dispute, and "A Hopi Affair," a classic story of matchmaking.[25]

Indian Stories From the Pueblos was illustrated with seven watercolors, some of which (probably all, but several are unsigned) were painted by the skilled artists of the San Ildefonso Pueblo. Awa-Tsireh, the pueblo's most famous painter, contributed "Indian Game Animals," "The Skunks," and "Dog Dance." From Po-ca-no (Julián Martínez, by then already renowned for his pottery designs) came "Green Corn Dance," and Oqwa Pi painted "Spring Planting Dancers." Two paintings, "Cochití Ancient Hunting Dance" and "The Mountain Lion Pursuing a Deer," are unsigned but may be the work of the aforementioned artists since they share common characteristics.[26]

The plates were printed in color and hand-tipped into position, and the brilliant, vibrant works leap from the pages.[27] They are symbolic and flat, with no background or foreground and no attempt to render three dimensions. The artists used formalized patterns and paid minute attention to detail. The works are carefully balanced and rhythmic, with the rhythm enhanced by the repetition of figures. Not a line is out of place. Both animals and people are captured in stylized mid-action, frozen in a timeless tableau. In "Indian Game Animals," for example, several deer alight at a run, a bear displays a just-killed deer, and an elk poses in midstep.

Applegate added notes to the paintings explaining the symbols used, the significance of the dances, the meanings behind the dancers' costumes, and other pertinent information. He had collected and studied Indian watercolors extensively. In an essay (unrelated to the book) he wrote that the watercolorists were "clever enough to recognize the white man's limitations and his inability to grasp the significance of Indian art; and they accordingly present their subjects in the white man's way. It must seem fairly stupid to them to represent in this manner only an instantaneous flash of a single aspect of an action, without continuity. For instance, an Indian is puzzled at a picture of a man shooting a deer. The deer is in the position of running and the man prepared to shoot, but nothing happens. The Indians would dramatize such an episode in pantomime or present it in symbols so that the completed action would be unmistakable and the deer either dead or escaped."[28]

Many of the reviews of *Indian Stories From the Pueblos* were favorable. George P. Baker, writing for the *Yale Review*, said the stories were "told with almost the terseness and directness of folk tales [that is, spoken tales]. ... Mr. Applegate shows a real gift for swift characterization, and genuine humor of two kinds. First, he has his own kindly humor in writing of his Indian friends; but far more valuable is his gift at making the sly sense of humor, little recognized in the Indians by most of their observers, very clear." Baker noted that the book subtly fostered understanding of the Indian, and therefore "should not be neglected even by ethnologists." He went as far as to compare the book to D.H. Lawrence's *Mornings in Mexico*, stating "This book of Mr. Applegate's must now be placed side by side with that of Mr. Lawrence."[29]

Not surprisingly, several Santa Feans joined in the accolades. First was Alice Corbin Henderson, who reviewed *Indian Stories* for the *Santa Fe New Mexican*. She called the book "delightful and entertaining" and said, "whether or not one knows the author, I am sure that the reader will have a sense of the keenly interested, amused and sympathetic observer, who, loafing quietly in the background, has overheard the stories."

Her comments on Applegate's style mirror those Bynner made in the book's foreword. "To say that the stories have the accent of speech, not only in reported conversations, but in the whole style of telling, is to say that the style has an individual rhythm, which to ears and eyes accustomed to more cut-and-dried 'book writing,' may at first seem awkward in spots," Henderson wrote. "But it is really the same sort of thing that one finds in the narrative poems of Robert Frost, who, more than any other poet of our time, has captured the rhythm of speech, rather than of books in his verse. What one finds in Mr. Applegate's stories is, in fact, the sophistication of simplicity. Moreover, like Robert Frost, Mr. Applegate puts more in a paragraph than many authors can put in a chapter."[30]

Novelist Stanley Vestal, writing for *Folk-Say*, called the book "a remarkable contribution to the growing literature of the Southwest." "It will take a deservedly high place among those volumes which now for the first time in our history begin to appear—volumes in which the Indian is treated as a human being, and not a monster or a child," he wrote. "More than this, Mr. Applegate's book recognizes the distinction between the culture and nature of these Pueblo 'peasant' Indians and those others of the Desert proper and the Buffalo Plains. … To Mr. Applegate, Indians are *people*. He even dares to take us into the heart of Indian humor—an amazing feat, really, though he does it so simply that only one who has tried it can appreciate the achievement." Willard "Spud" Johnson reported that *Indian Stories* was "a best seller in the ancient city," surpassing Willa Cather's *Death Comes for the Archbishop* in local sales.[31]

The most negative commentary came from Mary Austin, whose review of *Indian Stories* for *The Nation* was mixed at best. On a positive note she wrote, "Mr. Applegate has given us a type of Indian tale which, if not unattempted by others, is in this case notable," adding later, "Frank Applegate has that rarest of gifts, humor, which endears the subject and leaves him the better loved for being laughed at." She praised his "unusual sensitiveness to the rhythms of Indian speech" and his "subtle, unenvenomed satire," and concluded that the book was "too freshly drawn and too amusingly true to the qualities of tribalmindedness to be allowed to lapse from the growing literature of the Indian."[32]

Several of Austin's comments, however, seem unduly harsh, given her friendship with Applegate. "Mr. Applegate shows himself naively unfamiliar with the literary convention of storytelling, which is a pity since by his failure to achieve the absolute and compelling form he is due to lose several of the best of his anecdotes," she wrote. She criticized him for presenting diluted versions of some tales, specifically the myth in the story "Montezuma." Applegate began the tale, which attributes Pueblo origins to the great Aztec leader (and thereby explains the significance of the Pueblo Indians' Matachines, a dance drama), with this caveat: "The following myth I received from a Tewa Indian of one of the upper Rio Grande pueblos, and I have made a free translation of what he told me. It is a myth that has gradually evolved. A part of it is very old and pagan; other parts, through Mexican influence, have been added within the past hundred years or so, and there can also be detected in it some elements of missionary teaching."[33]

Austin found Applegate's disclaimer insufficient. The purity of myth was of great importance to her, and she chastised Applegate for relating the tale while knowing full well that the link between the Pueblos and Montezuma was not made until after the story of Montezuma had traveled north from Mexico to the Pueblos, after the Spanish conquest. Austin considered this a grave offense, writing, "It is when Mr. Applegate attempts to render the myth of the Indian that he leads the reader unfamiliar with the material slightly astray. Of the esoteric myths of the Pueblos there is practically nothing obtainable. Of the exoteric or secular myth there is little that has not been so added to and infused with alien matter that, as quoted by Mr. Applegate, it becomes largely misleading." She also noted that Applegate's account of why the Navajo do not eat fish (in "The Little Fish of San Juan") "is merely a Pueblo guess at a custom which seemed to them to require explaining. The Navaho themselves have another account of the business and the ethnologists still another."[34]

Throughout the review Austin made it clear that in the field of Pueblo folklore, she was the expert, Applegate the novice. Although her letters to him bespoke a true comradeship, she believed that Applegate's understanding and knowledge of Pueblo and Spanish culture was not nearly as sophisticated or extensive as her own. Her arrogance and air of superiority excluded no one, not even her "dearest friend." Nor was she satisfied with his talent as a writer. In a letter to Arthur Davidson Ficke, Austin elaborated on her views concerning Applegate's writing and her role in it:

> You are quite right in supposing that he does not yet know anything whatever of writing as an art. It is an interesting experiment that I am trying with him, to discover to what degree the technique acquired in one art can be transferred to another. I try not to impose upon him any bias for a more formal method of expression. The only thing I am afraid of is that he will have too much success just at the start, which will check his development. The book … is not without merit, as you will see. I was as strict with him as I dared to be about the fundamentals of Indian life, but I really advised him against publishing so soon in book form. A lot of it does not stand up, and I am not sure that he will be able to discriminate on his own account between the leads that are worth following and those that are not.[35]

Applegate must have taken Austin's criticism in stride, for he continued to collect and write down tales. Given his interest in Spanish Colonial art and the religious practices of Spanish villagers, it is not surprising that he began to collect Hispanic folktales as well as Indian ones. "The Buried Treasure of Cochití," which appeared in *Folk-Say*, combines the two as it relates one of the "gorgeous stories of buried treasure" still common in today's Southwest. In Part I of the piece Applegate offered tales of Indian "magic" and the Hispanics' belief in magic in a straightforward manner, without passing judgment. In Part II he presented the legend in the voice of an "intelligent Indian of Cochití, who has been three times governor of that pueblo."

The tale of how a Cochití cacique buried treasure under a creek may have been well known among folklorists of the time. It is both humorous in its story of a "very funny Indian" who leads Mexicans on a wild-goose chase and tragic, for the storyteller notes that Spanish soldiers tortured and slaughtered many Indians who failed to lead them to gold. The story is also ironic, for the soldiers kill the cacique and his assistant, who buried the treasure, before learning its whereabouts. It ends with Applegate asking the Indian storyteller matter-of-factly, "Do you think there was much gold buried by the cacique under the water?" and recording the Indian's response. Applegate accepted the tale at face value and reported it objectively.[36]

Although many of Applegate's stories convey a stereotypical view of wily, clever Indians (often at the expense of foolish Anglos), they also reveal his affection and admiration for the natives. And implicit in the tales is the fact that Applegate was close enough to some of the Indians that they comfortably confided in him. They liked and trusted him well enough to reflect with him on the silly ways of Anglos they encountered and to explain to him, as best they might, their religious rituals. He in turn treated them as individuals worthy of respect, singling out one as "intelligent … sincere and serious," referring to another as "my Indian friend," and to a third as "a dear friend."

The cacique and other storytellers in the folktales were such a part of Applegate's life that he wrote of them casually, using phrases such as "One Mexican told me … " and "Another descendant of the Spanish Colonials told me … " Looking at such phrases as literary devices, the effect is threefold. First, they tell the reader that the characters are actual people speaking in their own voices, an impression enhanced by the use of dialect. Additionally, the phrases leave the reader feeling that he or she is privy to "inside information." Thirdly, by using narrators with distinctive voices, Applegate gives the reader a sense of the tales being spoken rather than written. This is no clearer than in his colorful tale, "The Apache Kid," which introduces the reader to a character straight out of the Old West:

> I was having an ice cream soda at a little table in the luxurious corner drug store at Mesa, Arizona, one warm evening last January, while across the table from me sat Jack Fraser, "having the same." It would have been much more in keeping with Jack's looks if instead of that tall glass of frothy, insipid nonsense he had had on the table before him an old black bottle half-full of "forty rod."

Applegate described the old miner as having "the sort of mustaches that all old-time Westerners should have, large and sandy and drooping, so that no heed need be given by the wearer of them to the expression of his mouth even in the most exciting poker game." It is Jack Fraser who tells the reader the story, for Applegate attested, "I spoke to him about the Apaches and asked him just how bad these Indians had really been. And later that evening I set down what he told me as nearly in his words as I could remember."

Was Jack Fraser a real person or an invention of Applegate's imagination? Like other preservers of folktales, Applegate was more of a chronicler than a fictionalist, so Fraser likely did exist. (The Apache Kid certainly had existed and had been the subject of tales since the 1880s.) But Applegate's tales were screened through his own perceptions, and he made a conscious decision to introduce narrators into various stories. He understood that the use of other voices lent an aura of authenticity to the unfurled tales, largely due to the fact that the narrators' way of speaking—the cacique's in "The Buried Treasure of Cochití," for example, or Fraser's in this tale—differed greatly from Applegate's own storytelling voice. Take these quotes from Fraser in "The Apache Kid":

> "… All of 'em had heard of Geronimo and how bad he was, and they thought every Apache was just the same way, but for every Apache that was bad there were a hundred harmless ones. But that didn't make no difference with the whites, though, and no peaceful Apache could go about without some white fool taking a shot at him, and that made more bad Indians than anything else."

> "… he just settled it the Indian way and killed the feller himself."

> "… he took to the mountains and went 'bad Indian,' and when he did go bad he turned vicious all over."

Fraser's voice is that of a rough, Western miner, not an artist from back East, and who better to tell the tale? [37]

Applegate took the use of an outside narrator to the extreme in "A Hopi Visit to California," which ran in *Folk-Say*. In this tale the Indian narrator—a Hopi chief named Lolomi who considered Applegate "a dear friend"—speaks through a letter, which in turn had been written down by his Anglo-educated son-in-law. Thus, the humorous travelogue comes to the reader through three filters, much in the way family tales are passed down through generations. The narrator's manner of speaking, as translated by the letter writer, contributes a great deal of humor to the piece:

> " … We stay that first night at the lady woman house and sing and eat there too and the next day she show us thing she have and do it is very many and nice and we are glad to see it, for she got many things and automobile and oranges. We stay one night more at house of lady woman like before and next day we go to another place and see some kind of things I do not know what are, but we are glad to see anyway. …"

The Hopi visitor screened his perceptions through the familiar, describing unfamiliar objects as "things," unfamiliar sites merely as "places." Likewise, he knew of automobiles but not of ships, so he described a ship as "a kind of sheeps." His voice is foreign to Anglo literature, and the white reader can't help but be amused by it, although the Hopi narrator no doubt gave the account in all seriousness. The voice is quite different from that of the Indian speakers in Applegate's other tales, which he wrote in a grammatically correct style with no run-on sentences. Applegate may have been having a good-natured joke at the Hopis' expense by telling this story in such a manner, but the story also illustrates clearly how little the amenities of white culture meant to the Indians, and so by inference it criticizes contemporary materialistic white society. [38]

Applegate died in February 1931, before he could finish his second book of folktales, which the J.B. Lippincott Company intended to release that autumn. He was able to complete much of the book, however, for he sent Austin 10 of the stories in late January 1931 and told her a few days later that he had "two or three others that are not typed yet." Austin helped Alta Applegate put the book together, but exactly how much work she did on the stories is not known. "I could and did finish the *Native Tales*," she maintained. "We had worked together so long and so completely in each other's confidence, with such free interchanges of material that I did not find it at all difficult to do." In a letter written in October 1931 she mentioned that she had been working with Walter Goodwin to prepare the book for publication. [39]

An article in *New Mexico Magazine*, however, noted that Alta contributed to the collection as well, stating, "Work on the book was almost completed when Mr. Applegate died. The little that was left to be done has been completed by his widow. In the years that Frank Applegate wandered in New Mexico she was constantly at his side. They visited together in the more outlandish places in the state. The stories he heard she also heard. The little left to be done on the book, she was quite qualified to give it." [40]

Because five of the stories in the book, which was titled *Native Tales of New Mexico*, first appeared in *Folk-Say* and *Southwest Review*, one can compare the different versions to detect changes from Applegate's original text. Although all five stories contain minor alterations, such as revisions in punctuation, between the journals' versions and the book's version, two stories show more significant changes. In the book version of "The Buried Treasure of Cochití," three paragraphs that provided additional accounts of enchanted treasure were deleted. Also, the words "Indian of Cochití" were changed to "Cochiteño." [41]

Although Applegate appears to have changed the text himself, Austin undoubtedly influenced his choice of words, for she previously had coined the word "Puebleño" to mean Pueblo Indians. Astonishingly, the Indian narrator himself is quoted as using this term. The introduction to the book version of "The Apache Kid" includes more biographical information about Jack Fraser than did the version that appeared in *Folk-Say* (lending credence to the theory that Fraser was an actual person), and some of Fraser's words were altered to sound even more colloquial—"a-staying" for "staying," "havin'" for "having," "a-clearing" for "clearing." [42]

Applegate had divided the stories into "Spanish Tales" and "Indian Tales." A list of stories typed up after his death indicates he completed 10 of the Spanish tales and five of the Indian tales. Another three Spanish tales and three Indian tales are listed as "Unedited." One of the stories listed as such, called "Near Apotheosis," was not included in the book (and no manuscript has been found); another, "A Visit to California," does not appear in the book but had previously been published in *Folk-Say* as "A Hopi Visit to California." "Sandía the Tragic," which was not on the list but was published in *Southwest Review*, is included in the book (although it is not really a folktale), as are two other stories not on the list, "Interim" (called "How Saints Are Made" when it appeared in *Southwest Review*) and "The Ironic Sense." Letters from Austin to Ansel Adams indicate that Applegate had finished about two-thirds of the book before he died, and that she spent only a week on the manuscript before sending it to a typist. However, examination of the manuscript indicates she rewrote the endings to five of the stories – "Dead Men Tell No Tales," "The Miracle," "Poco Loco," "The Lost Child of Zia," and "Navajo Nieces" – sometimes adding several pages of new copy to each. [43]

In the introduction to *Native Tales of New Mexico* Austin treated Applegate far more generously than she had in her review of *Indian Stories From the Pueblos*. "Nobody knew [the Hispanics and Indians] and their tales better than Frank Applegate; knew them both in their separateness and their distinctions and their interweavings," she wrote. "He had neither preferences nor prejudices, but took them all in for their folk quality, their common denominator of humanness. He knew them with tenderness and humor, extenuatingly, as he tells them, as they were told to him. He tells them better than they were told to him because he never forgets their derivations, their sources, whether in Indian or Castilian stock, and because he had the story teller's appreciation of form and continuity."[44]

Like *Indian Stories From the Pueblos*, *Native Tales of New Mexico* contains tragic stories, humorous stories, and ironic tragi-comedies. Applegate wrote the Spanish tales in a style different from that of the Indian tales. Most of the Spanish tales are presented in straight narrative fashion with third-person narrators, while most of the Indian tales are written as first-person accounts, with Applegate either telling the stories or introducing an Indian narrator, and other Indians speaking through conversational quotes. Additionally, nearly all of the Spanish stories are humorous, while even the most amusing Indian tales contain tragic elements. The book also includes several folkloric essays, such as the aforementioned "Sandía the Tragic."

Many of the stories recount ancient legends that had been passed on to Applegate, but uncovering the purest form of a legend could be difficult. Applegate included an apology in introducing the tale of "San Cristóbal's Sheep." In writing the story, he said, he had attempted to gather together fragments of a well-known tale, "carefully collected, here and there, in the old Spanish settlements throughout the Rio Grande country." He added, "there were still small bits of it missing. These have been restored, but the restorations add nothing of importance to the tale and only serve to give it continuity."[45]

Other legends were presented by a first-person narrator, a voice of authority. "The Founding of Hano" is an Indian friend's tale of the tribe's forced move to the Hopi reservation in Arizona. In "The Ironic Sense" another friend explains why the Hopi village of Walpi is perched high on a cliff.

Treasure-hunt legends are the subject of several tales, including the aforementioned "The Buried Treasure of Cochití." "Dead Men Tell No Tales" and "The Mystery of Manzano" both discuss the burial of treasure under churches. In "Enchanted Gold" a Spanish friend of Applegate's, Lupe Romero, speaks of instances when Indian magic produced enchanted gold mines. One of the stories referred to is a variant of the legend "The Tale of the Lost Mine," about a mine near Córdova.[46]

Two of the native tales are about Tomacito, the New Mexican version of Tom Thumb, who performs mythical acts of kindness and heroism. Applegate described him as "a mixture of the native Santo, and the Indian 'little man,' which many gifted members of that race are supposed to carry tied in their hair, to advise them what to do in emergencies."[47]

Folklore is not only the stuff of legend, however, and *Native Tales*, like *Indian Stories From the Pueblos*, contains stories dealing with current or recent events. Some are set in the late 1800s, such as "Interim," an account of Billy the Kid's visit to a Spanish village and the goodwill gesture he performed there. Others are contemporary, such as "The Miracle," which takes place in 1929 and even refers to a Spanish Colonial artifacts dealer in Santa Fe. Quite a few focus on the Indians' adjustment to modern times, such as "An Indian Divorce," in which a Hopi couple, learning of the Anglo ritual of divorce, applies it to their own domestic dispute, and "Navajo Nieces," a humorous look at polygamy.

The more serious tales tackle themes previously addressed in *Indian Stories* such as the conquest of the Pueblos by Spanish soldiers and Franciscan friars and the brutality of whites toward Indians. "Poco Loco" mentions how the flight of Spanish settlers from hostile Indian lands resulted in overpopulation and overproduction on arable land. "The Lost Child of Zia" refers to Zia as the poorest of the pueblos and notes, "An American farmer of the most industrious sort would be unable to maintain the minimum family … on all the land that the Government has allotted for the use of this whole pueblo." Here, Applegate mentions that he was "invited to come to a grand thanksgiving ceremony and dance," and that, since the Zias were one of the most "forlorn" of the Pueblos, "I did not think they had much to be thankful for, but I accepted the invitation."[48]

The Spanish conquest of New Mexico is told from both the Hispanics' point of view and from the Indians'. Whereas the Indian narrator in "The Founding of Hano" refers to the "Long Gowns," or Spanish priests, who "tried to make us quit our own religion and become Catholics," the Hispanic protagonist in "The Mystery of Manzano" speaks of the "old time Spanish padres [who] bled and were martyred to save the souls of the savage Indians from hell."[49]

Two stories deal with the forced removal of Indian children from reservations and their placement in boarding schools. In "The Lost Child of Zia" the "lost child" referred to is a girl who was taken from the pueblo without the adults' knowledge and sent to boarding school. Applegate pondered the tragic outcome of this action and felt shame at the ways of whites (see Chapter 11). "Hopi Susanna Corn Blossom," on the other hand, treats the tragic situation with gallows humor. Applegate began the tale with a bluntly critical assessment of the practice. The title character is sent by an Indian agent,

> along with other Hopi children, a hundred miles by wagon to the nearest railroad and then by rail to a far-away Indian boarding school in California. This school had much the character of a prison reform school and Susanna was kept a prisoner there for eight years and was not once allowed during all that time to visit her people, to speak a word of her native language, or to practice drawing a single pottery design taught her by her mother. At this school the teachers tried in every conceivable way to make an imitation American girl of Susanna. She was deprived of her cultural inheritances while nothing was supplied to take its place. American middle class culture was held up before her as an ideal to be striven for, and the culture of her own people was belittled in every way possible.[50]

Her education leads to ruin when, upon returning to the reservation, she becomes promiscuous and bears children out of wedlock. But the school has also liberated Susanna, and she contentedly raises her three illegitimate sons in the face of the tribe's scorn.[51]

The "Spanish tales" have little of the gravity of the Indian ones. Many of them are comical, and the few serious ones have happy endings. Taken as a whole, they convey a stereotypical impression of the rural villagers as easily fooled innocents whose profound religious faith guides most of their actions.

Several stories focus on the Hispanics' relationships with saints and the saints' importance in their everyday lives. "Tricks of the Trade" tells how a greedy priest (the historical figure Padre Antonio José Martínez) duns money from a particularly stingy town by praising its patron saint. "No Calamity Equals a Bad Neighbor" is a humorous tale about San Ysidro, patron saint of farmers, that is based on a well-known legend. The treasure hunter in "Dead Men Tell No Tales" hides the Santo Niño (Baby Jesus) from a santo of San Antonio, vowing not to return it until the treasure's whereabouts is revealed to him. Other tales feature incidents set on feast days when villagers honored their patron saints. Holy personages are frequently mentioned in passing, an indication of their intrinsic importance in Hispanic culture.

"San Cristóbal's Sheep" is a classically Catholic 17th century tale of suffering and redemption. A widow fights off the unwanted advances of a townsman. The spurned man sets his sheep on her crops, and she prays to San Cristóbal to send the man over a cliff. Her wish is granted, and the widow is racked with guilt for her evil desire. Her confessor tells her that as a penance she must gather the man's sheep and "lead them throughout the province of New Mexico, to every village and to every settlement, and wherever you may find a person in dire poverty or worthy of charity, you shall give that one a single sheep … with the blessing of San Cristóbal." By doing so, the woman is rewarded by being reunited with her long-lost son and receiving the blessing of the saint.[52]

The Spanish tales merit reading for their insights into Spanish traditions and the rural villagers' way of life. They contain many homey details that enliven the characters and settings. Villagers cook tortillas on an iron griddle over a stove, raise a little livestock and grow chile, beans, and corn. Afternoons are time for siestas and discussions of politics with friends in the town plaza. After the church, the plaza is the most important location in town, site of dances, parties, and other community gatherings. A typical New Mexican village room is described in "Interim":

> It was a long room with white-washed walls and the low ceiling was supported by heavy round vigas cut from young pine tree trunks. In one corner was a small fireplace with horseshoe-shaped opening, within which a pot of stew was simmering. Near the center of one side of the room stood a low table above which a single candle in a tin wall sconce burned, dimly lighting the table and the interior of the room.[53]

Burros were an essential part of rural life as well as life in Santa Fe, for their woodcutter owners used them to haul firewood from the hills into the towns. Applegate was fond of the animals and frequently included their dark-colored, perky-eared figures in his watercolors. To him the burro represented the rural, the pastoral, the idyllic "old ways" that were vanishing all too quickly. He thought them similar in character to their Spanish masters, for whom the summer was time for relaxation, the winter for work.

Burros take center stage in "Burros" and "Old Juan Mora's Burro." "Burros," an essay that Applegate intended to use as a preface to the latter story, examines the animal's lot in life. Applegate's descriptions created vividly picturesque images of Old Santa Fe. "During the afternoons of sunny winter days you may see groups of these little animals with wood racks on their backs drowsing, ears pendant, in unfrequented alley ways, while their lords and masters are foregathered in the plaza, with as much

of their body areas as possible exposed to the warming sunshine of New Mexico," he wrote. Applegate imagined the burro spent the summer on vacation, "gorging on bloated dahlias," but come winter, he believed, the animal was content to realize "real work is to be done."[54]

The burro could be a nuisance, because he knocked over garbage cans and consumed gardens. The narrator reflects on "the moonlight gambols he shared with you during the past summer over your front lawn–you, with flowing nightshirt classically draped about your form, pursuing and he goatishly kicking up his heels."[55]

A burro stars in "Old Juan Mora's Burro," a sweet, funny tale about the close friendship between an old man and his pack animal. When the burro falls down a well, the man is so distraught that he climbs down to join him, and together they share a bottle of whiskey, with comical results. The old man and the intelligent animal are vividly drawn, and it is not surprising that "Old Juan Mora's Burro" served as the basis for a puppet play performed at the 1934 Fiesta. Applegate considered the story one of his best, and a book on Southwestern literary history called it "one of the priceless literary folktales of the country."[56]

Alcoholic beverages play a part in a surprising number of the Spanish tales, while in the tales of Indians (whom it was acknowledged even then suffered problems with alcoholism), drinking is rarely mentioned. In "The Mystery of Manzano" the townsfolk operate stills, and a stranger uses brandy to inebriate the villagers so he can steal their treasure. The man and the burro in "Old Juan Mora's Burro" get drunk together. The thwarted treasure-hunter in "Dead Men Tell No Tales" quells his disappointment by drinking. The residents of San Antonio in "The Miracle" are "mellowed by a drink or two" and witness a drunken fight. The husband in "Tomacito and the Burro" wants to sell his burro to buy whiskey. The evil bandit in "Interim" plans to intoxicate the dancers at a dance. Judging from its prevalence in the stories, one unfortunately would conclude that drinking and drunkenness were intrinsic to village life.

As in *Indian Stories From the Pueblos*, the Indian tales in *Native Tales* shed light on Indian traditions and culture. "Hopi Susanna Corn Blossom" explains a Hopi christening ritual of rubbing cornmeal on the baby. "The Lost Child of Zia" gives a description of the pueblo village and the women's pottery skills. In "An Indian Divorce" the couple battle over the dietary staples of cornbread and mutton stew.

Applegate had planned to illustrate the book with photos by Ansel Adams and his own sketches. *Native Tales* instead was illustrated with five of Applegate's richly colored watercolors, depicting the New Mexico landscape, rural Hispanic towns, and an Indian pueblo (see Chapter 6). The American Institute of Graphic Arts selected the book as one of 50 released in 1932 that demonstrated "book-making excellence" with a design that was "strictly appropriate to [its] literary or artistic contents."[57]

Native Tales of New Mexico received several negative reviews—more than *Indian Stories From the Pueblos*, but it was also reviewed by more publications. Critics considered the book slight and insignificant. *The Nation*, in which Austin's harsh review of *Indian Stories* had appeared, complained that Austin's introduction to the book "promises more than the author can fulfill, and the tales will not be likely to captivate those who cannot add to these scenes a long and affectionate familiarity of their own [with New Mexico]."[58]

The *New York Evening Post* panned it for the same reason: "No one is likely to be as repelled by Frank Applegate's informal and humorous anecdotes of New Mexico as by the extravagance of the claims made for them. The disproportion between Mary Austin's introduction to the present volume and the stories themselves is great. … It is a commentary on regionalism as a literary movement that the most successful of these stories succeed in spite of the syrup of local color poured so heavily over them." *Scribner's* praised Austin's introduction and noted Applegate's ability, as "one of the best friends of the Indians of the Southwest," to learn from the Indians "things which are generally withheld," but considered the stories "mostly interesting without being vastly important."[59]

Native Tales did receive a number of positive reviews. *The New York Times*, whose art critics had lavished praise on Applegate's sculptures and paintings, called the book "the most delightful collection of true folk tales and legends that the reviewer has seen in some time," and concluded, "each tale is in itself a work of art." An additional review in *The New York Times Literary Supplement* cited Applegate's ability to write humorously, comparing the story "Old Juan Mora's Burro" to that of "the best of modern Provençal story-tellers." The review also noted "more careful and welcome attention to form" than had been evident in *Indian Stories From the Pueblos*.[60]

Celebrated literary critic Burton Rascoe praised the "ingenuous charm of Mr. Applegate's literary style," noting, "They are not always from the same source; he might remold and select a story as it came from two different narrators. This is the work of an artist. Mr. Applegate was an artist."[61]

Alice Corbin Henderson contributed a glowing review to the *Santa Fe New Mexican*. "More than anyone else who has written of them, Frank Applegate gives the feeling of the native Spanish people of New Mexico," she wrote. "He was equally at home with his Indian neighbors, without either that condescending kindliness, or that sentimental idealization which so often characterizes the attitude of the Anglo who 'discovers' the Indians for the first time. … One gets a veritable cross section of New Mexican life through concrete characters that have a homely familiarity for those of us who live here, but with that sharp verification that comes from an artistic presentation. It is like looking through an old album and recognizing forgotten friends or landscapes."

Henderson praised Applegate's "straightforward simplicity of style," continuing, "The Anglo-Indian or Anglo-Spanish conversational idiom used is an achievement in itself. It is so entirely natural that the casual reader would never suspect the difficulty involved, or the restraint that has avoided any 'laid-on' colloquialisms." She considered *Native Tales of New Mexico* "richer in experience and finer" than *Indian Stories From the Pueblos*.[62]

Applegate left several writing projects unfinished at the time of his death, including a book on New Mexican architecture and the Spanish Colonial arts manuscript that he and Mary Austin were writing (see Chapter 14). His daughter, Betty, completed one project, an article titled "Los Hermanos Penitentes," which appeared in the October 1931 *Southwest Review*. The article, a detailed account of the structure of the Penitente moradas (or chapter-houses), the history of Penitentes in New Mexico, their religious services, and practices such as the marking of flesh with a sharp instrument, flagellation, and crucifixion, was "based mainly on unpublished studies of Frank Applegate."[63]

Applegate's two books can be found in many libraries. The Rio Grande Press of Glorieta, New Mexico, reprinted *Indian Stories From the Pueblos* in 1977. Publisher Robert B. McCoy called the book a "genuine classic of Southwestern Americana," and stated, "It is far too good a book to lie fallow another 40 years, nearly forgotten. … It is a soft and gentle book, perhaps bittersweet, touched with masterful whimsy and edged here and there with an evanescent and most delicate sarcasm."[64]

Modern-day historians have criticized the Anglo folktale collectors for the same reasons they criticize Anglo efforts to preserve other aspects of Indian and Hispanic culture: the Anglos set the parameters, and the tales are told from the Anglo viewpoint for an Anglo audience. The intellectuals believed it fell to them to appreciate the poetry inherent in the Native Americans' and Hispanics' everyday existence—in their religions, their local legends, even in their household objects. The sense of superiority inherent in this belief made Indians and Hispanics desire to "take back" their heritage. In the late 1930s, Hispanic writers such as Cleofas Jaramillo, Nina Otero-Warren, and Fabiola Cabeza de Baca Gilbert began publishing their own folktales, cookbooks, and personal reminiscences. By doing so, "the Spanish-American elite sought to preempt what they viewed as the shallow and inaccurate work of Anglos."[65]

Yet these writers may not have found an audience for their work among Anglos had not Applegate and others written down stories first. Through all his writing, Applegate attempted to educate Anglos about the native peoples of the Southwest and offer valid reasons why their cultures should be preserved. One can read his essays and folktales for their humor, their stoic depiction of tragedy, and their cultural insights.

The serious issues Applegate addressed were important to many of the Santa Fe art colonists, and by reading Applegate's articles and stories, one gains insight into their artwork and their shared beliefs as well as his own. The wheat-plowers in John Sloan's "The Threshing Circle," for example, are more than picturesque anachronisms; they are poor peasants who subsist on back-breaking labor. The snake priest in Applegate's "Hopi Snake Dance" is a subject of great respect and honor among his people, not merely a dramatic personage.

Additionally, as the *New Mexico Historical Review* pointed out in its review of the reprinted edition of *Indian Stories From the Pueblos*, the tales have value as a contemporary expression of the artistic and literary renaissance of the 1920s.[66] The awakening of the Anglos to Indian and Spanish culture, their realization that Indian and Hispanic art had beauty and value, encompassed folktales as well as visual art, drama, and music. In the same way they wanted to preserve the old methods of pottery-making and chip-carving, so Applegate desired to tell the tales "before too much of the source has been wiped out."

Endnotes

1 Publisher's preface, *Indian Stories From the Pueblos*, 1977 edition.

2 Austin, "Frank Applegate," *New Mexico Quarterly* 2:3 (August 1932): 215. Austin to Ina Sizer Cassidy, Jan. 19, 1927, Cassidy Family Papers, Box 1, Folder 2. Quoted by permission of The Bancroft Library, owners of the Cassidy Family Papers, [ca. 1897-1965]. BANC MSS 67/1 p.

3 *Southwest Review* 12 (Oct. 1926): 23-27.

4 "New Mexico Backgrounds," *Southwest Review* 14:3 (Spring 1929): 351-359.

5 *Southwest Review* 15:3 (Spring 1930): 310-316.

6 Applegate incorrectly states the Sandías returned to the pueblo in 1762, when in fact they returned over a period of years in the 1740s. See Ferguson, "The Acculturation of Sandía Pueblo," master's thesis, University of New Mexico, 1931, 22-23.

7 *New Mexico Highway Journal* 7 (April 1929): 26. Courtesy of *New Mexico Magazine*. For an explanation of the term "Poor Lo," see Taft, *Artists and Illustrators of the Old West*, 300-301, note 49.

8 Ibid.

9 FGA to Austin, Feb. 5, 1929, Mary Austin Collection, Huntington Library. Applegate, "Citizens of the Desert," *New York Herald Tribune*, March 10, 1929, sec. 11, 20. Austin had criticized Crane's support of sending Indian children to day schools away from the reservations. Crane responded by calling Austin a "tender sentimentalist" and stuck to his guns. See Crane, *Desert Drums*, 373.

10 *The Survey* 66:3 (May 1, 1931): 156-157. At editor Paul Kellogg's request, Austin edited the article before its publication; see Austin to Alta Applegate, Feb. 15, 1931, Applegate Papers.

11 FGA to Austin, Feb. 5, 1929, Feb. 11, 1929, Mary Austin Collection, Huntington Library, AU 998. Carr in "Santa Fe and Taos Take on Luster As Stamping Ground for Literati," *Los Angeles Times*, June 9, 1929, states that Applegate was still working on the book at that time. Goodwin worked with other writers in Santa Fe; see Austin to Witter Bynner, April 4, 1934, Mary Austin Papers, Center for Southwest Research, MSS 31 BC, Box 1, Folder 1.

12 "The Folk in Literature," *Folk-Say* 1929, 12-15. Austin in Applegate, *Native Tales of New Mexico*, 8.

13 FGA to Dobie, Dec. 7, 1929, J. Frank Dobie Papers. FGA to Carhart, Oct. 16, 1929, Applegate Papers. Major and Pearce, *Southwest Heritage: A Literary History with Bibliography*, 136.

14 All citations from *Indian Stories From the Pueblos* are from the first edition, copyright 1929, J.B. Lippincott Co., Philadelphia. List price $3.50. Reprinted with permission of HarperCollins Publishers. The Applegate Papers contain the complete manuscript of *Indian Stories*, including multiple drafts of many of the stories.

15 *ISP*, 5.

16 *ISP*, 9-10.

17 *ISP*, 17.

18 *ISP*, 114, 125.

19 "Artists See Snakes!" *Santa Fe New Mexican*, March 6, 1925, 1.

20 *ISP*, 38.

21 *ISP*, 41. The authors do not know which characters Applegate gave pseudonyms and which he named with their actual names, with the exceptions of the names of the artists and chief in this tale and Kenneth Chapman's name in the story "Ago Po." See also p. 209, note 8.

22 A manuscript copy of "San Juan de los Caballeros" showing Applegate's editing of his work is in the Applegate Papers. A note on the side reading, "Cut the historical part," has been crossed out, with the words "Leave it in," written underneath, followed by the initials "E.S.H." (Elizabeth Sage Hare), so Hare apparently had some hand in editing it.

23 *ISP*, 69, 70, 76.

24 FGA to Austin, March 1, 1929, Mary Austin Collection, Huntington Library.

25 A manuscript copy of "A Hopi Quarrel," showing Applegate's editing of his work, is in the Applegate Papers.

26 Based on stylistic similarities, the authors believe that "Cochití Ancient Hunting Dance" was painted by Julián Martínez and "The Mountain Lion Pursuing a Deer" by Awa-Tsireh.

27 McCoy, publisher's preface in *Indian Stories From the Pueblos* reprint. Applegate noted on the manuscript for "San Juan de los Caballeros" that he wanted the Corn Dance painting to run with it, indicating the paintings were not placed randomly in the text.

28 Applegate, "New Mexico Backgrounds," 354.

29 "The Pueblo Indian," *Yale Review* 19 (1930): 410-411.

30 Henderson, "Applegate's Tales from the Pueblos Living, Human Folk-stories," *Santa Fe New Mexican*, Oct. 10, 1929, 4.

31 *Folk-Say* 1930, 424. *Santa Fe New Mexican*, Feb. 8, 1930. Mary Austin also reported that the book was selling very well in the West; see Austin to Arthur Davidson Ficke, Nov. 6, 1929, Mary Austin Papers, Center for Southwest Research, MSS 31 BC, Box 1, Folder 5.

32 Austin, "Pueblo Stories," *The Nation* 129: 3359 (Nov. 20, 1929): 597.

33 *Indian Stories From the Pueblos*, 171.

34 Austin, "Pueblo Stories," 597-598. For additional reviews of *Indian Stories*, see Brenner, *New York Evening Post*, Nov. 30, 1929, 8; *Boston Transcript*, Nov. 30, 1929, 7.

35 Austin to Ficke, Nov. 6, 1929, Mary Austin Papers, Center for Southwest Research. Ina Sizer Cassidy recalled that Austin went into a rage because she could not get Applegate to write the book as she thought it should be written. See Cassidy's notes about Mary Austin, 1933-34, Cassidy Family Papers, Carton 5, November 28, 1933.

36 *Folk-Say* 1930, 212-218.

37 *Folk-Say* 1931, 330-337. At one time, the story was titled "Charlie Dobie"; see manuscript in Applegate Papers. For more on the Apache Kid, see Hayes, *Apache Vengeance*.

38 *Folk-Say* 1930, 84-87.

39 FGA to Austin, Jan. 26, 1931, Jan. 30, 1931, Mary Austin Collection, Huntington Library, AU 1016. Austin, "Frank Applegate," 217. Austin to Mrs. Meredith (Elizabeth Sage) Hare, Oct. 2, 1931, Applegate Papers.

CHAPTER 13:
FROM BRUSH
TO PEN:
APPLEGATE
THE WRITER

[40] "Southwest Bookshelf," *New Mexico Magazine*, March 1932, 2.

[41] *Native Tales of New Mexico*, 116. All citations from *Native Tales of New Mexico* are from the first edition, copyright 1932 by J.B. Lippincott Co., New York. Reprinted with permission of HarperCollins Publishers.

[42] *NTNM*, 206, 210. Manuscript, Applegate Papers. "The Mystery of Manzano" features the word "Chihuahueñan" as well.

[43] Story list and manuscripts, Applegate Papers. *Southwest Review* 17:2 (January 1932), 199-208. Austin to Ansel Adams, March 13, 1931, March 21, 1931, Ansel Adams Correspondence. The Applegate Papers include the outline for another story, "Don Amador Santiago de – [*sic*]," and pages from three tales that apparently were not finished: "San Ildefonso," "José Roybal," and "Tomacito at the Governors Palace." Given the comments in *New Mexico Magazine* about Alta having worked on the stories, it is possible she may have been responsible for the altered endings.

[44] *NTNM*, 6.

[45] *NTNM*, 239.

[46] Briggs and Vigil, eds., *The Lost Gold Mine of Juan Mondragon*, 194-195.

[47] *NTNM*, 153. The incomplete "Tomacito at the Governors Palace" in the Applegate Papers tells how Tomacito was to fight a mouse who was eating up the laws at the Palace of the Governors. The "little man" resembles "Big Fly" of Navajo myth, who assists people in times of trouble, often sitting on their ear or shoulder and whispering to them. See Wyman and Bailey, "Navajo Indian Ethnoentomology," 131.

[48] *NTNM*, 195, 198.

[49] *NTNM*, 17, 35.

[50] *NTNM*, 171.

[51] The Applegate Papers contain three scenes from a dramatic version of the Susanna story.

[52] *NTNM*, 245-246. Writer Raymond Otis, who had been a friend of Applegate's, turned "San Cristóbal's Sheep" into a play, "The Sheep of San Cristóbal," which was performed by the St. Francis Players in 1937. See Nestor, *The Native Market of the Spanish New Mexican Craftsmen*, 45.

[53] *NTNM*, 127.

[54] FGA to Austin, Jan. 26, 1931, Mary Austin Collection, Huntington Library. *NTNM*, 61, 62.

[55] *NTNM*, 61.

[56] *Santa Fe New Mexican*, Aug. 25, 1934. FGA to Austin, Jan. 26, 1931.

[57] Austin to Adams, March 13, 1931, Adams to Austin, March 17, 1931, Ansel Adams Correspondence. "Applegate Book Given Honor by Institute," undated clip from unidentified newspaper, Applegate Papers. The cover price was $2.50, according to a 1933 price list from the Villagra Book Shop (Weigle and Fiore, *Santa Fe and Taos: The Writer's Era*, 179). This was $1 less than *Indian Stories From the Pueblo* had sold for, possibly due to the Depression.

[58] *The Nation*, 135 (Sept. 28, 1932), 290.

[59] Cantwell, *New York Evening Post*, May 28, 1932, 7. *Scribner's* 92:5 (November 1932): 19.

[60] Walton, "The Folk Tales of New Mexico," *The New York Times Book Review*, June 5, 1932, sec. 9, 2. *The New York Times Literary Supplement*, Dec. 8, 1932, 945.

[61] Rascoe, "The Book of the Day," unknown New York newspaper, 1932, Applegate Papers.

[62] Henderson, "The New Mexico That We Love: Frank Applegate's Posthumous Book," *Santa Fe New Mexican*, May 20, 1932. For additional reviews of *Native Tales*, see Sergeant, Review of *Native Tales of New Mexico*, Books, May 29, 1932, 3; "Old New Mexico," *Time*, June 13, 1932, 51; Raines, *Writers and Writings of New Mexico*, 15-16.

[63] Applegate, Betty, "Los Hermanos Penitentes," *Southwest Review* 17:1 (October 1931): 100. As Betty recalled to Gretchen Beall, Mary Austin had insisted she write the article and would not rest until it was completed.

[64] Publisher's preface, *Indian Stories From the Pueblos*, 1977 edition. This book has been reprinted by several other companies as well.

[65] Wilson, *The Myth of Santa Fe*, 153.

[66] Szasz, *New Mexico Historical Review* 54:2 (April 1979): 159.

14 The Spanish Colonial Arts Book

In the late 1920s Frank Applegate and Mary Austin collaborated on a project that overshadowed the final years of both their lives, a book covering all aspects of Spanish Colonial art. Who better to produce such a work than Applegate and Austin, who shared a respect for the art, an interest in its history and the passion to preserve it? And to illustrate it, they commissioned photographs from an unknown, energetic young photographer named Ansel Adams.

In hindsight the success of the project appears guaranteed, given Austin's reputation, Applegate's expertise, and Adams' talent. But the saying that events have a way of conspiring against us proved true in this case, and despite earnest efforts on the part of many people, not least Applegate, Austin, and Adams, the Spanish Colonial arts book was never published.

Spanish Colonial art was a subject waiting to be explored in the 1920s. While Austin and writers such as Charles Lummis and Aurelio Espinosa had studied Spanish folklore and language, and archdiocese records documented the existence of santos in church collections, no one had yet investigated the origins of Spanish Colonial art, for several reasons. Because the early craftspeople lived in rural villages some distance from the Southwest's population centers, their work was relatively unknown. Since most of the work was made for villagers' homes and churches, it had scant chance of coming to Anglo attention. Before the artists and writers came to New Mexico, most of the Anglos who were aware of the artwork and furniture considered it artistically crude and of little or no value. They found the religious work appalling to their Puritan beliefs about idols. It remained in the possession of Hispanics and the Catholic Church until dealers and collectors began to discover it.

While buying up santos and handmade furnishings, Applegate and the other collectors naturally began to gather information about the pieces, such as how they were made and by whom. Applegate was undoubtedly the most avid collector of both objects and facts at that time. His entry in the 1930-31 edition of *Who's Who in America* noted he owned one of the largest collections of Spanish Colonial art in the United States. After his death, the *Santa Fe New Mexican* said his collection "is easily the finest in existence, and no man was better informed on the subject." By the late 1920s his expertise on Spanish Colonial art, especially the religious art, was so highly regarded that journalists often sought his advice when writing about it. He found one writer especially lacking, reporting, "what she knows about [santos] is less than a vacuum and quite as important." He considered a

255

locally published book on santos "misinformation to the last detail" and was concerned that writers of little ability or knowledge were planning books on the subject.[1] It is not surprising that he would want to write down what he had learned about the art to set the record straight and for his own posterity.

Applegate and Austin had discussed writing a book on the Spanish Colonial arts for some months before they outlined the project. It grew out of a book Applegate was thinking of writing that focused exclusively on santos.[2] An outline for Applegate and Austin's book, originally called *The Saints in New Mexico,* indicates that Austin was to contribute chapters on the Spanish settlement of New Mexico and the Spanish-New Mexican culture at that time, the Spanish culture of present-day New Mexico, the iconography of santos, music and poetry, and folk dramas and literature. Applegate's chapters would include an introduction to native New Mexican art, a discussion of the Indian influences on the art, and the areas of Spanish Colonial handicrafts, woodworking, metal work, leather and straw work, weaving and dyeing, embroidery, architecture, altar pieces and murals, and domestic and ecclesiastical furniture. Together he and Austin would write a chapter on the Spanish Colonial influence on the art and culture of the Southwest.

To illustrate the book, Applegate was to contribute drawings of "racial types, original types of santos, decorative design, initials, letters, tail pieces, etc." At Austin's suggestion Ansel Adams, then better known as a classical pianist, would provide photographs of New Mexico towns, architecture, furniture, old mission churches, and interiors. As Austin saw it, the book was to be "two-thirds photographs."[3]

Adams, a native Californian, first came to New Mexico in the spring of 1927 with his friend and patron Albert Bender and was instantly beguiled by the landscape and people. Although he already had done some excellent work as a photographer at Yosemite National Park, Adams was still uncertain whether his future lay with photography or music. Bender encouraged him to pursue photography. He introduced Adams to Austin and suggested they collaborate on a book about the Southwest.[4]

Austin recruited Adams for a book on Taos Pueblo as well as the Spanish Colonial arts book. She offered Ansel and his wife, Virginia, the use of part of her home while he worked on the books. Adams was thrilled and quickly set about making plans to return to Santa Fe. "While the cold weather lasts I shall do as much as I can with the reproductions of the old santo's [*sic*], etc., and then when the spring comes, we shall get about the country," he told Austin. "I approach this work with reverence; I feel that association with you in any work is a great honor, and it is a privilege indeed to enter on so fascinating a task under such delightful relations with you and Frank Applegate."[5]

In December 1928 Applegate told an acquaintance the book on the Spanish Colonial arts would be completed "in the near future."[6] Unfortunately, Austin's ability to work on the book was hampered by her chronically poor health and by previous commitments to several other projects. It was more than a year before she began to write her chapters.

Yet the ambitious project began to assume concrete form in March 1929, when she reported to Applegate that she had interested the Yale University Press in publishing the book. In a letter the previous month, however, she had warned him that she had no time to start a new project. She had signed a contract to write another book, which would require two years' work, and meanwhile was working on her autobiography, *Earth Horizon,* and on the book *Taos Pueblo.* She told Applegate and Adams she could not possibly work on the Spanish arts book on more than an occasional basis anytime in the foreseeable future.[7]

Paying Austin's warning scant attention, Adams and Applegate enthusiastically proceeded with their own work on the project. In the spring of 1929 Ansel and Virginia lived in an apartment at Austin's home while he shot photographs for the Spanish Colonial arts book and for *Taos Pueblo.* Together with

Applegate, "bumping over ruts and down arroyos in an old flivver, he went to the Spanish villages in the mountains photographing ... the Penitente shrines and chapels, festooned with lace and paper roses, the santos, always vivid and intense, the hand-painted chests, the Chimayó blankets on bed or floor, the smoke-blackened fangs of adobe holding simmering pots of chile, the adobes fitting into the hills." The photographs attest that among the places he and Applegate visited were Chimayó; the Santa Cruz and Tesuque churches; Santo Domingo, San Ildefonso, Cochití, and other pueblo towns; the Puyé cliff dwellings; Chaco Canyon; and Córdova, where Adams photographed the woodcarver José Dolores López. Adams photographed items from Applegate's collection as well as objects in homes, churches, and museum collections. He also made portraits of Frank, Alta, Betty, and their pets. At Austin's suggestion, Adams sent a handful of proofs for the Spanish Colonial arts book to Malcom Davis, an editor at Yale University Press.[8]

On June 1 Applegate, Austin, and Adams signed Adams' contract for the proposed book, by this time called *Spanish Colonial Arts in New Mexico.* Under its terms, Adams would receive $4 for each photograph up to 50, then $3 apiece for the next 100 and $2.50 for the following 100. As Austin later pointed out, Adams was the only one of the three who was assured of earning anything from the book, for she and Applegate stood only to gain upon publication.[9]

While working on the Spanish Colonial arts book, Adams and Applegate decided to collaborate on a second book focusing exclusively on New Mexican architecture. Austin later recalled Applegate was especially interested in interior decoration, stating that he undertook the book at her suggestion and that it was to be about "the whole history of the House, as it had evolved in New Mexico." Adams shot photographs for the architecture book while shooting Spanish Colonial arts photos and sent several architectural photos along with the Spanish Colonial arts prints to Davis at Yale. Applegate asked Austin to intervene with the press and help get the architecture book published, and she

complied.[10] A ruptured appendix cut short Adams' stay in the Southwest, and he returned to California for a few months.

Davis sent Adams' prints on to Austin. When Austin received the prints, she angrily fired off a letter to Adams informing him that he had committed a grave error:

> The business began by my suggesting that you could illustrate ... a book that Frank Applegate and myself had in mind to do. ... Later, when I found that my publishers were going to insist on the autobiography, I wrote you that I would not be able to do the Spanish book for two or three years, and could not, therefore, give it any further consideration at present. ... Therefore, when I returned from New York and discovered that you had not only come with the intention of going right on with the Spanish book, but that you had already, without consulting me, or inquiring whether it would make any difference in my plans, arranged to do a book with Mr. Applegate from which, of course, I could expect no profit whatever [that is, the book on New Mexican architecture].

Austin went on (after this sentence fragment) to explain how she had pulled strings with the Yale University Press to get them to consider the architecture book, and told Adams he had interfered with their negotiations.

> Now no publisher cares to do business on any proposition in which there is a division of direction. ... About a week before you wrote to them the Yale Press had asked for further time, and I had naturally extended the time. I had also asked them to allow the photographs to be seen by a magazine editor who had written me for illustrative material. ... I am now put in the embarassing position with both these men of having taken up their time and attention with matters over which I apparently had no control.

"You and Mr. Applegate may find yourselves in the position of having no publisher for your book," she said, adding, "the illustrator is always a secondary consideration with the publisher. … About the Spanish Arts book, as I have repeatedly told you, I can give it only very limited attention at present. … As far as … the book you are doing with Frank, I don't want to hear any more about it."[11]

Austin's strident letter surprised Adams, whose request that Davis send the proofs to Austin had been made with the best intentions. But he humbly apologized for the misunderstanding in a telegram, followed by a letter. In a second letter Austin accused Adams of "meddling" by contacting Davis at the Yale University Press. "You have held up the whole matter, which I was pressing to a successful conclusion, for what may prove to be six months or a year, for I have refused to move further until Frank has the illustrations well in hand." Only after a distressed Adams contacted Davis and Davis explained to Austin that he sent her the prints of his own volition was she placated. Applegate also assuaged Austin's feelings on Adam's behalf.[12]

Most frustrating to Austin was that the book illustrations had become her responsibility, when they were to have been Applegate's. "One of the difficulties has been that Mr. Applegate is less experienced than I thought him in the matter of illustrating," she told Adams. "He has not known how to take hold of matters as efficiently as I had hoped. As soon as I get him straightened out he will have charge at that end, and I will be relieved of it entirely."[13]

Adams sent a batch of prints for the Spanish Colonial arts book to Austin in late August. Austin told Adams that she and Frank "have gone over the new prints and made the first discard. There will be others as time goes on. He will write to you about that. Please do not write to me about it anymore. That is his job, as the publishing end is mine, and I can not be bothered about it."[14]

Adams found Austin's remarks about the Spanish Colonial arts book puzzling. "I have always thought, as the contract mentions us three in collaboration with the potential publisher, that you were equally interested; otherwise I should not have troubled you in any way," he told her. He had good reason to be confused, for on the one hand, Austin was declaring no intention of working on the book, while on the other, she had signed his contract, was helping Applegate edit the photos, and was telling Adams to make sure he photographed the old medicine woman of Tesuque.[15]

In April 1930 Austin returned to Adams the photos for the book on New Mexican architecture, which the Yale Press had sent her. According to Austin, Applegate had decided "he was not at all prepared to write the book on Architecture."

"I never really supposed that he was," she confided, "but it was something he had to find out for himself, so we are now at work on a book on Spanish Arts, which is going very well. It will be, at the rate Frank works, two years before he can settle down to the book on Architecture."[16]

By the end of the month, Austin had decided that Applegate was doing a poor job at selecting the subject matter and arranging photos to illustrate the Spanish Colonial arts book. "I am afraid he has overlooked a great deal that ought to have been done," she told Virginia Adams. A few weeks later she asked Ansel Adams to return to Santa Fe and again complained about Applegate. "It is extremely difficult to get Frank to dig in to the work and plan in advance what has to be done. We ought to have all the illustrations in before next October. I don't wish to butt in on Frank's part of the job, which was to supervise the illustrations, but I would like to know if he is at work on it."[17]

Austin's letters indicate she considered Applegate lazy and slow, and compared to Austin herself, who was known to work at a whirlwind pace when in good health, he may have appeared so. After all, Applegate had had seven months to arrange the shooting of the photographs once he discerned exactly what Austin wanted. Captions writtten in Applegate's hand on the backs of Adam's photos indicate he was actively working on the illustrations however, and the recollections of others do not paint Applegate as slothful. Family members recalled that he could work faster than anyone once he set his mind to it. The *Atlanta Argus* noted early on his capacity for "hard work and study." In his obituary, the *Santa Fe New Mexican* remembered him as "a hard worker with hand and brain."[18] Applegate was spreading himself thin during these years, as his projects included helping to save the Santuario de Chimayó, fighting the spread of outdoor advertising, teaching, working with the Indian Arts Fund, and coordinating numerous activities for the Spanish Colonial Arts Society. It is possible that Austin simply needed to take charge of affairs involving the book in the same way she took command of most everything else in her life and the lives of others.

In any event Applegate continued researching the Spanish Colonial arts. His passion for the subject was so strong that he tackled the research with a missionary zeal. "When we are gone, except for this book there will be no record of how things really were," he told Austin. He soon became, as *El Palacio* called him, "the leading authority on the subject" and began to give lectures on what he had discovered. His fluency in Spanish aided in his efforts to learn about the art, for it gave him immediate access to relevant documents (if there were any) and to the artisans' descendants themselves.[19]

According to the book outline, Austin was to complete a chapter on the iconography of saints, but Applegate studied this subject thoroughly and wrote a chapter on santos. To research the subject, he needed to look no further than his own collection, for a partial list of items from it shows he sometimes owned dozens of depictions of the same saint. He found the Hispanics' reverence for the saints somewhat amusing and was charmed by the customs surrounding them. In March 1929 he told Austin he had identified about 80 different saints.[20]

Eventually Applegate was ready to begin writing his manuscript chapters. In July 1930 Applegate reported to Austin, "I have been getting up at five and six every morning for a couple of weeks to work on Spanish Colonial Arts and have been getting a good deal done at it. I'm finding it a little easier to arrange things as I work more, but it is no snap at that."

Paul Bernat, the wool supplier for the Spanish Arts Shop artisans, planned to use a chapter on weaving and others written by Applegate in connection with an exhibit on "Craftsmen at Work" in Boston.[21]

Adams returned to New Mexico in June 1930 and stayed with the Applegates while he finished shooting photos. He photographed items from the Spanish Arts Shop, including embroideries and woodcarvings. Adams was to supply 130 photographs of furniture, textiles, tinware, santos, churches, and other items. Some of the surviving photographs are rather straighforward and documentarylike, including pictures of carved chests and other pieces from the Spanish Colonial Arts Society collection in the Palace of the Governors and the Spanish Arts Shop. Others, such as his moody interior of a Penitente morada and several images of bultos, reveal his awakening talent and his "respect for the objects' inherent quality and meaning." In October 1930 the Spanish Colonial Arts Society paid him $25 for five photographs. The photos (three interior shots of the Applegates' house and two of colchas) ran uncredited in the December 1930 *Ladies Home Journal,* with cutlines written by Applegate (pp. 71, 103, 205).[22]

Work on the book proceeded, and Austin told Adams in October 1930 that she and Applegate "are both so buried in our books that I have scarcely seen him since you were here." That December she had a premonition that something would happen to the book, as she later told Elizabeth Sage Hare, "and I pushed him very hard to get all of his part of the book on paper, so that I could correct it and make sure that it was in proper form." With Applegate's sudden death in February 1931, the project came to an abrupt halt. Austin informed Adams of Applegate's death, and added, "I have no special news about our business here [that is, the book] and no desire to write about it. Frank's death will make great changes in my plans, but I do not know now just what changes." In Adams' sympathetic response, he emphasized his willingness to assist her in any way possible.[23]

Austin now had an additional reason to complete the book—to do right by Applegate—and she quickly got to work. "Frank had completed the technical work, the part I couldn't have done by myself," she told Adams a month after Applegate's death. "I mean he had got it all on paper. I will now have to write the whole book from first to last." She added that Alta Applegate would help her with indexing and illustrations. She told Hare that Applegate had left "complete notes on all the various arts" and that she would have to put the book "into literary form." Despite Austin's earlier complaints, Applegate had taken control of arranging illustrations and selecting their subject matter before his death. However, he had not organized the photographs, and after he died Austin and Adams had no idea which photos he had wanted to use.[24]

At one point, Austin found herself at odds with Alta, for she reported to Adams:

> One of those young English writers who come here, on the make, got a hold of Alta and tried to persuade her to let him have the material about the Santos, which he meant to write up for magazines. He also wanted to use a lot of the photographs, but I put my foot down firmly. I know nothing of this young man, and in any case I shall want to keep the magazine rights in my own hands. Alta does not understand about those things, and seems to be rather vaguely under the impression that the magazine rights do not amount to anything so far as you and I are concerned. I had to convince her that Frank and I had an option on the negatives that were taken from [sic] the book and that she must call off her young man. She won't, of course, intentionally make us any trouble. She doesn't realize at all how many second rate writers there are buzzing around any bit of good material.[25]

The dire financial circumstances created by the Depression hurt the publishing business, and the Yale University Press broke its contract for the Spanish Colonial arts book in 1932 "owing to the financial shortage." "I am thinking it is only a postponement, and that I shall be able before a great while to get money enough to go on with it," she told Virginia Adams. "I shall not let go of it until I am certain that there is nothing to be done about it."[26] Austin succeeded in convincing her publisher, Houghton Mifflin, to take on the book.

Although Austin planned to work on the book during the summer of 1932, another two years passed before she was able to report to Adams that she was "finishing up" the Spanish arts book. "I wanted to get the manuscript finished, so that if anything happens to me, it won't be lost," she wrote. She planned to have it completed within a few weeks but did not finish the work until shortly before her death on August 13, 1934. A tribute to Austin noted that the manuscript had gone to Houghton Mifflin just two days before she died. She left the bulk of her estate to the Indian Arts Fund and stipulated that the Spanish Colonial arts manuscript should become the property of Alta Applegate.[27]

Acting on behalf of the Spanish Colonial Arts Society, Alice Corbin Henderson asked T.M. "Matt" Pearce of the University of New Mexico English department to work on the manuscript, and he agreed. Pearce soon discovered that the material would need serious revision before it could be considered publishable. What he had been given was the work of two individuals who wrote in completely different styles and tones, which he somehow had to merge. Houghton Mifflin advised Pearce "that the material on history [that is, Austin's work] be separated from the material dealing with the arts and crafts [or Applegate's work]."[28]

When Austin told Adams, soon after Applegate's death, that she would "have to write the whole book from the first to last," she implied that Frank had merely left her with notes, which she would have to turn into prose. She reiterated this in a tribute to Applegate, stating that Applegate had left her "with the completed notes of his part of the book." Applegate had left behind more than "completed notes," however. A partial copy of the manuscript contained in his personal papers reveals that he had written two or three chapters on Spanish

Colonial arts in general, a chapter on santos, a chapter on painting, several chapters on chests, and chapters on tinwork, tables, silver, ironwork, weaving, embroidery, leatherwork, cochineal dye, blankets, cupboards, and chairs. Although some of the chapters are in rough form, most of them are more or less complete. There is no indication on the rough drafts that Austin did any work on Applegate's chapters, although Alta's handwriting appears on some of the pages.[29]

Pearce found that Applegate's chapters were, if not in publishable form, at least fairly complete, but Austin's contributions presented problems. "This manuscript of Mary's is full of inconsistencies which I am striving to iron out," he told Alice Corbin Henderson,

> such as where she says the colonials depended on the Indian crafts for the first century here and brought with them few of the arts of Spain, and then writes of early artisans carving chests from their memories of ones seen in Spain; in several spots she has written Mexican when the Applegate notes show that the text is speaking of New Mexico. And then her fill-ins with what the Indians must have been doing and what the Spanish immigrants must have been like— all suppositious and largely guesswork. I've written a foreword which I'll send up to you soon; then I've worked out a good division of the material and begun to put it together. I really think that is the answer if I can do it—get it done, I mean. It is fairer to Applegate, rather than to unload a lot of speculation on his really excellent detailed description of the arts and crafts. However, for fear that doesn't work out, I'm now editing the manuscript, as it stands, trying to make it consistent with itself and Applegate's notes, and correcting slips of statement that are obvious.[30]

Henderson proposed that "Mary's historic part ... condensed and corrected" be used only as an introduction to Applegate's material on arts and crafts.[31] Copies of the manuscript show heavy editing and major revisions of Austin's sections of the book.

Meanwhile, Adams continued to wait patiently to receive payment for the accompanying photos. In addition to the $25 he had received from the Spanish Colonial Arts Society in 1930, he also may have been paid for the use of a photo of a Spanish Colonial chest in the August 1933 issue of *Theatre Arts Monthly* that accompanied an article by Austin. In keeping with the terms of the book contract, Adams hoped to make $2.50 to $5 for each print, or $250 for 70 to 80 of them. Elizabeth Sage Hare originally planned to cover the costs of Adams' photographs but by 1935 had reconsidered. Alta Applegate told Pearce that Adams might take less and asked Pearce to include the cost of the photos in a grant application he was preparing. Adams' photos were included in the submission of the final manuscript.[32]

In April 1937 Pearce gave a copy of the (presumably completed) manuscript to Kenneth Chapman of the Spanish Colonial Arts Society, who had assisted him in writing it. Chapman contacted the American Council of Learned Societies to inquire if grant money was available for the manuscript's publication— specifically, to pay Pearce and cover the cost of the photos and the services of a typist. Pearce did receive grant money, and the Spanish Colonial Arts Society paid Pearce $40 in 1937 and $10 in 1939 for his efforts. He also received aid from Alice Corbin Henderson, New Mexico Senator Bronson Cutting, Mary Cabot Wheelwright, and Alta Applegate.[33] However, Houghton Mifflin rejected the manuscript.

"The book on Spanish arts still hangs fire," Alta Applegate told Mary Hunter, Austin's niece, in 1939. "I get all enthusiastic over it then a time comes when I fear for it—but for the faithfulness of Dr. Pearce I would have given up long ago and he has worked hard to edit it and keep it Mary & Frank. If it is finally published I shall be eternally grateful to him for all he has done."[34]

By November 1939 the manuscript was in sufficient form that both Alta Applegate and Walter L. Goodwin, Jr.— who had helped Applegate publish his books of folktales with J.B. Lippincott, and who was by this time the president of the Rydal Press—thought it publishable. "I think you have done an excellent job in getting the material together in the form it now is," Goodwin told Pearce. Unfortunately, the Rydal Press did not have the money to print it, which Goodwin estimated at about $3,000. Although he was certain money could be raised to augment the Spanish Colonial Arts Society funds (which stood at about $750), the money was not forthcoming.[35]

Pearce revised the book further, and it was retyped in June 1941. He contacted the University of New Mexico Press, which determined the book would be too expensive to print. The Laboratory of Anthropology also considered publishing it at this time. Pearce again sought grant money from the American Council of Learned Societies, but this request was turned down. The next year Spanish Colonial Arts Society members tried unsuccessfully to solicit funds from the University of New Mexico's School of Inter-American Affairs and from wealthy private individuals. In 1944 Spanish Colonial Arts Society treasurer John DeHuff unsuccessfully sought aid from another foundation. By 1947 Chapman and Pearce were discussing the publication of part of the book as chapters in a scholarly publication, but that, too, failed to materialize. Despite Pearce's continuing efforts, the manuscript was never published. As late as 1965 he wrote that he had believed the manuscript "just as good as it could be" by the time he finished it.[36]

Adams stored the Spanish Colonial arts photographs in a vault for many years. In 1964 he contacted E. Boyd, curator of Spanish Colonial arts at the Museum of New Mexico, to see if the museum had any interest in the photos. "It would be fine if I could realize some profit out of these pictures because it cost a lot in time, effort and expense to make them and nothing has been realized from them," he wrote. "But if there is no feasable [sic] way to use them … I could probably present them to the Library of Congress or your Museum which might offer the opportunity of a tax advantage." She assured him the museum was quite interested, and that his photos "covered a vanished period" and "would certainly have cultural value," but the correspondence produced no

results. The University of Arizona Press was still interested in publishing the manuscript as late as 1982.[37]

Since the 1930s scholarly research into Spanish Colonial arts has surpassed what was documented in the Applegate-Austin manuscript. Roland Dickey's 1964 *New Mexico Village Arts* offered a thorough description of the art forms. E. Boyd dug deep into the history of Spanish Colonial art and contributed a wealth of books and articles. William Wroth, formerly with the Colorado Springs Fine Arts Center, Boyd, and other writers have extensively researched santeros. While Austin and Applegate's research proved of some value to these authors, if their manuscript is someday published, it likely will serve more as a historical artifact than a research tool.

T.M. Pearce considered Adams' photographs for the manuscript "the finest collection of photographs of the Southwestern Spanish Arts in existence." Unfortunately, the prints Adams made were only proofs, for he intended to make fine-quality prints once the ones to be used in the book had been selected.[38] However, if the photos do, indeed, have historical value, then perhaps the manuscript might best serve as a source of descriptive passages for them. As one who was told that "the illustrator is always a secondary consideration," Ansel Adams surely would appreciate that irony.

Endnotes

[1] *Who's Who in America* 1930-31, 191. "Frank Applegate Dies Suddenly at Home," 5. FGA to Austin, March 1, 1929, March 6, 1929, Mary Austin Collection, Huntington Library, AU 1007, 1008. An article in the Jan. 14, 1931, *Albuquerque Journal* referred to Applegate's collection as "the largest," but the reporter likely was going on Applegate's word. The writer Applegate was referring to was Elizabeth DeHuff, who wrote *Indian Detour Couriers' Instructional Bulletin,* no. 31, and "Santos" for the Hispanic Society of America; see Salazar, "Ansel Adams and Spanish Colonial Arts," *History of Photography* 22:2 (Summer 1998):168, n. 17. DeHuff had asked Applegate to read over the *Indian Detour* article prior to publication, and he was highly critical of it; see FGA to Mary Austin,

n.d. (probably Feb. 9, 1929), Mary Austin Collection, Huntington Library.

2 Adams to Austin, June 13, 1928, Austin to Adams, Oct. 23, 1928, Ansel Adams Correspondence, Ansel Adams Archive, Center for Creative Photography, University of Arizona.

3 Mary Austin Collection, Huntington Library, AU 507-508. Adams, *An Autobiography*, 65. Austin to Arthur Davidson Ficke, Nov. 6, 1929, Austin Papers, Center for Southwest Research.

4 Newhall, *Ansel Adams, The Eloquent Light*, 48.

5 Newhall, 54. Adams to Austin, n.d., probably December 1928, Ansel Adams Correspondence.

6 FGA to Carl Zigrosser, Dec. 6, 1928, Zigrosser Papers.

7 FGA to Austin, March 15, 1929, Mary Austin Collection, Huntington Library. Austin to FGA, Feb. 11, 1929, Mary Hunter Austin Collection, Bancroft Library. Austin to Adams, Aug. 30, 1929, Ansel Adams Correspondence.

8 *Santa Fe New Mexican*, April 10, 1929. Newhall, 60. Adams Archives. Adams to E. Boyd, Oct. 7, 1964, E. Boyd Collection. Adams to Davis, April 14, 1929, April 19, 1929, Ansel Adams Correspondence. The portraits of Frank are on pages 192 and 236. The photo on page 236 also appears in Adams, *Photographs of the Southwest* and uncredited in Carlock, *History of the Carlock Family*. The negatives are in the Adams Archives.

9 Contract; Austin to Adams, Aug. 30, 1929, Ansel Adams Correspondence.

10 Austin, "Frank Applegate," *New Mexico Quarterly* 2:3 (August 1932): 216. Adams to Davis, April 14, 1929, Austin to Adams, Aug. 30, 1929, Ansel Adams Correspondence. Austin wrote an introduction for the book on "the House," which is in the Applegate Papers. In her novel *Starry Adventure* (1931), the character of Franklin K. Marvin, an architect, works on just such a book.

11 Austin to Adams, Aug. 30, 1929, Ansel Adams Correspondence.

12 Austin to Adams, Sept. 9, 1929, Davis to Adams, Sept. 9, 1929, Ansel Adams Correspondence. FGA to Ansel Adams, September 9, 1929; transcription in Augusta Fink Papers, Box 1, Folder 36.

13 Austin to Adams, Sept. 6, 1929, Ansel Adams Correspondence.

14 Austin to Adams, Sept. 9, 1929, Ansel Adams Correspondence.

15 Adams to Austin, Sept. 3, 1929, Austin to Adams, Sept. 18, 1929, Ansel Adams Correspondence.

16 Austin to Adams, April 9, 1930, Ansel Adams Correspondence.

17 Austin to Virginia Adams, April 29, 1930, Austin to Ansel Adams, May 8, 1930, Ansel Adams Correspondence.

18 *Atlanta (Ill.) Argus*, Feb. 19, 1915. "Frank Applegate Dies Suddenly at Home," *Santa Fe New Mexican*, Feb. 13, 1931, 5.

19 Austin to Alta Applegate, Feb. 15, 1931, Applegate Papers. *Santa Fe New Mexican*, Nov. 26, 1930.

20 Taylor Collection list, Colorado Springs Fine Arts Center Archives. FGA to Austin, March 15, 1929, Mary Austin Collection, Huntington Library. Today about 160 separate subjects are known.

21 FGA to Austin, July 16, 1930, Mary Austin Collection, Huntington Library, AU 1014. Paul Bernat to FGA, June 1, 1930, Paul Bernat to Preston McCrossen, Sept. 19, 1930, Spanish Arts Shop Correspondence, Spanish Colonial Arts Society Papers.

22 Adams to Austin, May 29, 1930, Ansel Adams Correspondence. Adams to Helen McCrossen, n.d., Correspondence/Applegate-Austin Manuscript, Spanish Colonial Arts Society Papers. "Photographs for Spanish Colonial Arts in the U.S.," Adams Archives. Salazar, 164. Spanish Colonial Arts Society Canceled Checks, 1930-31, Spanish Colonial Arts Society Papers. "Southwestern American Colonial Interiors and Fabrics," *Ladies Home Journal* 47:12 (December 1930): 58. Austin told Adams that she and Applegate had sold the photos to the *Journal* in Austin to Adams, Oct. 11, 1930, Ansel Adams Correspondence. It is not known if Adams received additional payment from the magazine, or only the money from the Spanish Colonial Arts Society. Captions on the backs of the photographs are in Applegate's hand. The photo of the morada appears in Eldredge, et al., *Art in New Mexico*, 134.

23 Austin to Adams, Oct. 11, 1930, Feb. 14, 1931, Adams to Austin, Feb. 22, 1931, Ansel Adams Correspondence. Austin to Mrs. Meredith (Elizabeth Sage) Hare, Oct. 2, 1931, Applegate Papers.

24 Austin to Adams, March 13, 1931, Aug. 25, 1931, Ansel Adams Correspondence. Austin to Hare, Oct. 2, 1931, Applegate Papers.

25 Austin to Adams, July 8, 1931, Ansel Adams Correspondence.

26 Austin to Ansel Adams, April 21, 1932, Austin to Virginia Adams, April 29, 1932, Ansel Adams Correspondence.

27 Austin to Adams, March 10, 1934, Ansel Adams Correspondence. Austin to Hare, Oct. 2, 1931, Applegate Papers. Sergeant, "Mary Austin: A Portrait," *Saturday Review of Literature* 9:8 (Sept. 8, 1934): 96. Fink, *I-Mary*, 253.

28 Pearce to Adams, Oct. 25, 1971, Ansel Adams Correspondence. Pearce to University of New Mexico archivist, Oct. 18, 1976, Pearce Papers, Box 2, Folder 20.

29 Austin, "Frank Applegate," 217. Unpublished manuscript, Applegate Papers. The Center for Southwest Research at the University of New Mexico's General Library contains several copies of the manuscript as well as several chapters in Applegate's hand. The Mary Austin Collection at the Huntington Library contains an outline and several chapters. The Cassidy Family Papers contain several chapters and the Cassidy file at the Museum of New Mexico History Library contains manuscript material as well.

30 Pearce to Henderson, Feb. 25, 1937, Pearce Papers, Box 2, Folder 31.

31 Undated note from Henderson attached to copy of Spanish Colonial arts manuscript in Applegate Papers.

32 Austin, "Folk Plays of the Southwest," *Theatre Arts Monthly* 17:8 (August 1933): 607. Adams to Alta Applegate (with note from Alta to Pearce), Aug. 6, 1935, Pearce Papers, Box 2, Folder 23. Pearce to Adams, Oct. 25, 1971, Ansel Adams Correspondence. Copies of the photos and negatives are in the Ansel Adams Archives at the Center for Creative Photography, University of Arizona.

³³ Pearce to Henderson, March 19, 1937, Pearce Papers, Box 2, Folder 31. Donald Goodchild to Chapman, April 2, 1937, Correspondence 1937; Spanish Colonial Arts Society Bookkeeper's Ledger 1930-36, General Fund, Spanish Colonial Arts Society Papers. Weigle, "The First Twenty-Five Years of the Spanish Colonial Arts Society," in Weigle, ed., et al., *Hispanic Arts and Ethnohistory in the Southwest*, 195.
³⁴ Alta Applegate to Mary Hunter, Sept. 28, 1939, Mary Austin Collection, Huntington Library, AU 992.
³⁵ Goodwin to Pearce, Nov. 8, 1939, Pearce Papers, Box 2, Folder 23.
³⁶ Spanish Colonial Arts Society Canceled Checks, Spanish Colonial Arts Society Papers. Pearce to University of New Mexico archivist, Oct. 18, 1976,

Pearce Papers, Box 2, Folder 20. Weigle, "A Brief History of the Spanish Colonial Arts Society," in Pierce and Weigle, eds. *Spanish New Mexico: The Spanish Colonial Arts Society Collection*, Vol. 2, 30. Joaquin Ortega to Ina Sizer Cassidy, April 1, 1942, Pearce Papers, Box 2, Folder 23. Goodchild to Pearce, Dec. 12, 1941, Pearce Papers, Box 2, Folder 23. DeHuff to Alta Applegate, et al., May 1, 1944, Pearce Papers, Box 2, Folder 23. Chapman to Pearce, Jan. 14, 1947, Pearce Papers, Box 2, Folder 23. Pearce to Sallie Wagner, March 31, 1965, E. Boyd Collection.
³⁷ Adams to Boyd, Oct. 7, 1964, Boyd to Adams, Oct. 15, 1964, E. Boyd Collection. Gregory McNamee to Adams, Sept. 3, 1982, Ansel Adams Correspondence.
³⁸ Weigle, in Weigle, ed., et al., 195. Salazar, 166.

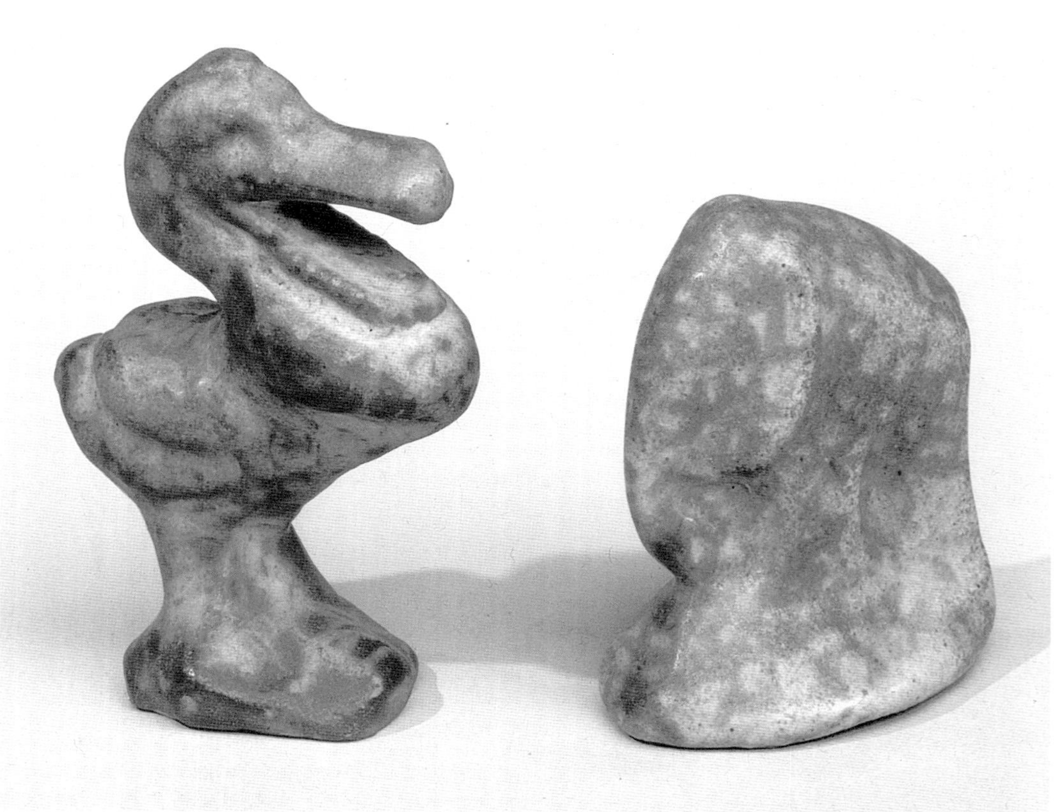

Pelican and *Elephant*, ceramic figures. Collection of Gerald Peters Gallery. Photograph courtesy of Gerald Peters Gallery, Santa Fe.

15 Death of a Renaissance Man

The issues of Indian rights and billboard blight obsessed Frank Applegate during the last months of his life, as he participated in a public demonstration supporting the former and stealthily took action against the latter. The two incidents illustrate the radical turn Applegate's politics had taken by this time, while the excitement they produced may have contributed to his premature demise.

The year 1931 opened with the Santa Fe artists and writers in a state of rabble-rousing indignation, stemming from the fact that John C. Collier, the secretary of the American Indian Defense Association and a former ally of the artists and writers, had become the Santa Fe equivalent of Public Enemy Number 1. The rift between Collier and his fellow Bursum Bill opponents had widened throughout the 1920s. Collier dated the split to the spring of 1923, when he fired defense association attorney Francis C. Wilson for supporting a bill nearly identical to the Bursum Bill, which again would have taken away Indian land rights. Wilson was friend to and attorney for many in Santa Fe's art scene, including the Applegates, and belonged to many of the same organizations.[1]

In 1924 the American Indian Defense Association fought for the passage of the federal Pueblo Lands Act, which gave non-Indian settlers "squatters' rights" to land they had lived on for at least 20 years but compensated the Indians for the land. The artists opposed the statute, for they believed it would alienate the Pueblo Indians from their Hispanic neighbors. Collier's support for the Pueblo Lands Act quickly died as the Pueblo Lands Board, which included former New Mexico Territorial Governor Herbert J. Hagerman, began to enact the statute's provisions, for the act did not compensate the Indians for their water rights. The artists and writers' fears were realized as well because the rural Hispanics, who earned their livelihoods by raising livestock, ended up with land they could not graze sheep and cattle on, while the agriculturally based Indians received land they could not grow food on.[2]

In *John Collier's Crusade for Indian Reform,* Kenneth Philp claims an additional reason for the artists and writers' opposition: "The passage of the Pueblo Lands Act had caused a great amount of dissatisfaction from both Anglo and Spanish-American settlers, who had lost land improvements and inheritances from their forefathers. These settlers had been forced to spend their savings paying attorneys to defend the titles to their lands, and they supported Hagerman's low awards to the Indians." Philp implies that the artists and writers supported the rights of "landed" Anglos and long-established Spanish families over the Pueblo Indians. His arguments merit consideration, especially when one recalls the earlier charges of "vested interest" levied against artists and writers who opposed the Bursum Bill in 1922-23 and fought against the cultural center in 1926. In both cases, members of the opposition were accused of wanting to protect their own land holdings. A positive result of the debate over the Pueblo Lands Act was that it increased the artists and writers' awareness of the Hispanic villages' vanishing culture and may have been the catalyst that led them to start preservation efforts.[3]

The artists and writers again clashed with Collier beginning in 1927 over the American Indian Defense Association's proposed Indian Arts and Crafts Bill, also called the Leavitt Bill. Indian Arts Fund members publicly opposed the measure, which would have expanded the market for Indian wares, believing such action premature. "They doubted whether the Indians needed an expanded market for their arts. More important than establishing a wide market was developing a method of persuading the Indians to produce art. It would be folly to spend money that compelled the Indians to engage in quantity production." Mary Austin thought the bill was designed to create "another little Indian bureau to deal with Indian art, in precisely the same manner that Indian education has been dealt with in the past."[4]

Members of the Indian Arts Fund considered themselves the supreme authority on affairs concerning Indian arts and crafts, just as members of the Old Santa Fe Association believed themselves infallible in matters of Santa Fe architecture. Austin chastised Collier for not consulting with the fund before supporting the arts and crafts bill, and imperiously advised him to join the Indian Arts Fund. The artists and writers' lack of support contributed to Collier's failure to get the bill enacted into law.[5]

In 1930 Collier spoke out against the Simms Indian Bill, which would have given Pueblo villages a court of appeal from the decrees of their tribal governments. The *Santa Fe New Mexican* and the artists and writers favored the appeals court concept, and the newspaper cited instances when tribal elders had used their decision-making powers for personal gain: "Indian youths from Jémez who unwisely came to dance at the Santa Fe Fiesta without permission of the village cadi were deprived of their lands as a result, and are still without them. Indian boys educated at government schools who try to use tractors on their farms—unromantic though the tractors be—are similarly punished."

The *New Mexican* accused Collier of having ulterior motives for opposing the bill. "His outburst [in Congress] is based on the theory that the Indian Bureau is still framing up on Poor Lo with the object of despoiling him of his ancient liberties, religion, and customs. Collier however has everything to lose by elimination of subjects for crusades, as that is his living, hence his failure to admit that any change has taken place in the purview or policies of the Bureau or that a new dormitory and hospital were built at the local Indian school. To concede any improvement is to shorten his job by so much." The editorial went on to stress, "This is no brief particularly for the Simms bill, but against Collier's cheap misrepresentation."[6]

Finally, Collier incited the art colony's ire by calling for public hearings against Hagerman, the special commissioner to the Navajos. Hagerman was active in several organizations to which the artists and writers belonged, including the Old Santa Fe Association and the Indian Arts Fund. Collier accused Hagerman of "improper conduct" involving oil leases. Speaking before a U.S. Senate subcommittee in January 1931, Collier testified that in 1923 Hagerman had sold Navajo oil property to friends for $1,000 and that these friends later sold the property for $1 million. He accused Hagerman of wresting control of the oil properties from the Navajos and of mismanaging Pueblo lands. Hagerman refuted Collier's charges, yet his previous testimony before the U.S. District Court in New Mexico had revealed cases in which, as a member of the Pueblo Lands Board, Hagerman had seriously undercompensated the Pueblos for land taken by their Hispanic neighbors. As Collier saw it, Hagerman "had given away the Indian title to great areas, had given away Indian water rights, and had denied to the Indians the compensation which the Pueblo Lands Act had intended."[7]

One would assume the artists and writers who were longtime supporters of the Indians would attack anyone who deprived them of oil-rich lands. Instead, they backed Hagerman, believing the charges against him unfounded. The Eastern Association on Indian Affairs and the New Mexico Association on Indian Affairs (to which many artists and writers belonged) analyzed the charges, and their findings unquestioningly supported Hagerman.[8]

In an editorial titled "Duped!" E. Dana Johnson reiterated the theme of his earlier commentary:

> Mr. John Collier ... is dependent for his livelihood on keeping the public convinced that the Indian bureau is rotten, always was rotten, and always will be rotten. This is his program, his agenda, his business, and his meal ticket. It will be fatal to his personal interests to have the Bureau reform, and will make useless the peculiar and remarkable talents which he has developed as a muck raker for a salary. ... The present hearing has revealed the complete ascendancy of this agitator over the senate committee on Indian affairs and the completeness with which he has deluded and duped them. ... The senators have accepted his weird and fantastic tales implicitly and unquestioningly, with no attempt to check up the facts on the ground. ... Quite regardless of Hagerman, who seems to be amply defended, this general situation is fraught with the greatest danger to any practical reform in the Indian service. So long as the senate committee remains thus strangely hypnotized by this professional agitator and fails and refuses to examine into the facts free from his insidious influence, so long will improvement in conditions be more or less paralyzed.[9]

The *Santa Fe New Mexican*'s coverage of the Hagerman affair exacerbated the community's already-intense animosity toward Collier. Applegate mentioned the situation to Austin, whose ill health and need for eye surgery had forced her to remain in New York between lecture series. "People in Santa Fe are very much stirred up over Collier's attack in the Senate (through [North Dakota Sen. Lynn] Frazier) on Gov. Hagerman," he wrote. "Even both houses of [the] state legislature passed and sent to [the] senate strong denouncement of this attack. I doubt if Collier would be exactly safe in Santa Fe just now."[10]

The Senate voted to remove Hagerman from the Indian Bureau payroll, but he later was reinstated. On February 10 a group of artists and writers, Applegate among them, formed a noisy motorcade to meet Hagerman's train at Lamy and escort him back to Santa Fe. With them they carried an effigy of Collier made by Andrew Dasburg and Will Shuster. Willard Nash, dressed as an Indian and beating a drum, sat on the radiator of the first car in the procession, with the effigy tied atop the second car.[11]

Returning to town, the group proceeded to a tree on the corner of Lincoln and Palace streets and hanged the effigy of "Demijohn" Collier, holding a sign which read, "Wanted: Indians to Attend My Councils." Witter Bynner composed a verse for the occasion, which hung on a large sign next to the effigy. Entitled "Collier Foxology," it read: "Praise God from whom all blessings flow–Praise God for Indians here below, No Matter who may pay the cost, without the Indians I'd be lost–Whoever really helps the tribes receives my curses and my jibes; and there for [*sic*] Mr. Hagerman I try to hurt you all I can–If there were many more like you I should have nothing left to do–Love for the Indians is my boast yet I love John Collier most–Amen."[12]

In retrospect the Collier "hanging" was a typical, if minor, event in the history of the Santa Fe art colony. It illustrates the artists' love of spectacle, talent for drumming up publicity, and ability to turn anything into a party. The incident had some dramatic results, however. It severed any remaining ties Collier had with the community, save for a few friends. And the excitement it produced likely put a strain on Applegate's heart, which, unknown to all, was weakening.

CHAPTER 15:
DEATH OF
A RENAISSANCE
MAN

Applegate's array of activities continued at their usual busy pace. In mid-January he gave a presentation on Spanish Colonial art to the Art League of New Mexico in Albuquerque. During the last week of January, he mailed 10 new folktales to Austin, who was going to help him place them in magazines. Austin had suggested that Applegate hire an agent, but he rejected the idea, stating that he already had contracts for the second collection of folktales and for the book on New Mexican architecture. On February 9 Applegate celebrated his 50th birthday, and mentioned having "lined out a lot more work"; that is, outlined the areas he planned to research for future writing projects.[13]

Meanwhile, Applegate was rehearsing for a starring role in the Santa Fe Players' production of the well-known drama *The Monkey's Paw*. The one-act play by W.W. Jacobs tells the story of an elderly couple who receive a magic monkey's paw, on which they may make three wishes. Their first wish tragically leads to their son's death. The grief-stricken mother wishes that the son will return from the grave. The father, played by Applegate, realizes the horror that awaits if their son returns, and with the last wish commands him back to the grave.

During play rehearsals Applegate occasionally raved about the recent installation of billboards in a canyon near Santa Fe, according to family members. His frustration over their proliferation despite his efforts had only increased over time. On the morning of February 12, family members say, Applegate enlisted the aid of William Penhallow Henderson, and together they went out to the canyon and tore down the offending eyesores, in an act of vandalism that was never prosecuted.[14]

That afternoon Applegate had a long conversation with Philip "Ted" Stevenson, the playwright and novelist who had played Applegate's son in *Hindle Wakes* and was directing *The Monkey's Paw*. Stevenson was a man after Applegate's own heart, a socialist who "believed that machines in socialized industries can be made to free the worker for folk arts, by time saving and energy saving instead of wasting both time and energy in competitive warfare for profit." The two men discussed their respective writing projects, and Frank fretted over Austin's health.[15]

In the evening Applegate took part in a long dress rehearsal at the Rialto Theater, just off the Plaza. As Stevenson recalled a few days later, "I told him that he had acted better than ever in his life before, and he answered, with a pleased smile, that he knew it—he could feel it—and that the play would have a powerful effect on the audience the next night. ... he seemed especially happy and exhilarated."[16] Shortly after 11 p.m. Applegate left the theater and walked home. He sat down in an easy chair in front of the fireplace. At about midnight, Alta was awakened by labored breathing. Thinking her mother had taken ill, she looked in on her, then went downstairs and found Frank slumped over in his chair.

"Frank Applegate Dies Suddenly at Home," blared the banner headline on the front page of the next day's *Santa Fe New Mexican*. Although he had appeared to be "in perfect and rugged health," his heart had stopped, and the doctor indicated it may have been weak for some time. The suddenness of his death and his relative youth fueled speculation, and the fact that he was playing a highly emotional role in *The Monkey's Paw*, a play about death, was lost on no one. The *Santa Fe New Mexican* went into considerable detail about Applegate's dramatic part, feeding a rumor that it contributed to his heart attack.[17]

Applegate's death stunned his family and friends. Upon learning the news, Austin dashed off a note to Ansel Adams: "This is to tell you the sad news of Frank's sudden death yesterday of heart failure. ... I am overwhelmed with grief."[18]

Stevenson wrote to Austin in New York:

> I feel impelled to write you something about the tragedy ... for no clear-cut reason, unless it be that I think I can tell you certain things that no one else knew. The strange set of coincidences that surrounded his end so seized on people's imaginations that they seem to have forgotten all else. But

all this has been aired sufficiently by the gossips and the newspaper. As you can imagine, words cannot express my regret at having asked him to do a part so highly emotional that it must have contributed to the cause of his death. One may make the excuse of ignorance—apparently no one in his family had any suspicion that his heart was weak—and yet the sense of responsibility remains, leaden and obscure. To be sure, Frank himself was more than willing to take the part. … He postponed a prospective trip to Arizona and California in order to play the role. … Occasionally in the evenings he would remark that he was tired.

Stevenson mentioned his last conversation with Applegate.

It was then that he spoke of you, with immense affection, and with regret that you should have to be ill in New York. He said he hoped you would be able to give up lecturing and come back to Santa Fe where you had been so well, especially lately. He looked forward to your return, when he intended to persuade you to this course. We also discussed the books on which he was working, and his plans and mine for future writings. He wanted me to read his stories as soon as he had got them in shape, and he offered to help and advise me in regard to a book I had outlined to him—to lend me reference books, find me a place to live in Córdova for a while, etc. In short, he was entirely and typically himself—concerned for those he cared about, ambitious, energetic, helpful and thoughtful.

I am glad I had that hour with him, for I had admired Frank a long time on the basis of really stingy contacts, and on this occasion I felt closer to him than I ever had before. He had a large, solid simplicity about him which I love, which seems to me rarer in artists than in commoner folk, yet which to my mind contributes more to artistic significance than brilliance of intellect or technical dexterity. Anatole France's negative conclusion was right: great men have not small souls. I think Frank would have liked [Theodore] Dreiser, and Dreiser would have liked him; they seemed to be built on the same scale, and their resonance to the shocks of life proved a similar soundness.

What a great pity that Frank should have left so much work unfinished! For I feel that he had only just found his true course, and I agree with him that, as he himself said on his birthday a week ago, although he was fifty he was more fit to carry through a strenuous programme than ever before. He had learned enough of discipline, and had forged a philosophy competent to bind art and life successfully together.[19]

Austin proposed that Frank's ashes be saved until she, herself, died, so they could be mixed and scattered together. Not surprisingly, Alta rejected the suggestion. Funeral services were held February 16 at Santa Fe's Episcopal Church of the Holy Faith, although neither Frank nor Alta was Episcopalian. Applegate was the first of the art colony's permanent members to die, and the list of pallbearers who attended him indicates the extent of his friends' and neighbors' affection. The actual pallbearers were William Penhallow Henderson, John Gaw Meem, Dr. Harry Mera, Jesse Nusbaum, Witter Bynner, Gustave Baumann, Dick Riley (a neighbor and copy editor for the *Santa Fe New Mexican*), and Andrew Dasburg. The honorary pallbearers included E. Dana Johnson, Philip Stevenson, Will Shuster, Willard Nash, Fremont Ellis, Josef Bákos, John DeHuff, Kenneth Chapman, Gerald Cassidy, Howard Coluzzi, Herbert Hagerman, Francis C. Wilson, James McMillan, B.J.O. Nordfeldt, writer Raymond Otis, Raymond Jonson, Edgar Lee Hewett, Preston McCrossen, Sheldon Parsons, Carlos Vierra, Randall Davey, James Seligman, state Attorney General Miguel Otero Jr., Datus Myers, Dr. Frank Mera, painter Albert Schmidt, Theodore Van Soelen, and a dozen others.[20]

Equally noteworthy is the fact that the Zia Indians held a ceremony for Applegate at their pueblo. The *Santa Fe New Mexican* described it as "a sort of tribal memorial ceremony," continuing,

CHAPTER 15:
DEATH OF
A RENAISSANCE
MAN

"This is an extremely unusual occurrence in the case of a white man and indicative of the high place held by Applegate in the regard of the Indians." Additionally, "a Pueblo Indian accompanied by his wife and child also went through the ceremony of the Indian blessing while the body lay at the house on the Camino prior to the funeral," and "sorrowing Spanish-speaking neighbors" filled the house as well. Frank was the first of the nine children of Lina and A.A. Applegate to die (his mother outlived him by 10 years), and his brother Archie and Archie's wife, Edna, traveled from Illinois to attend the service.[21] Applegate was buried in Santa Fe's Fairview Cemetery, in a grave marked with a simple plaque.

Applegate's death had a profound effect on many of those who knew him, not least Mary Austin. She dramatically called his demise "the greatest calamity that could have happened to the country that knew and loved him." Her belief in life after death gave her strength, and soon after his death she told Alta she hoped "Frank will manage to get through to us" to help them complete his work. That October she told another friend, "I still feel that he might come back any day." More than a year after his death, in June 1932, she noted to an out-of-town friend, "I miss Frank Applegate more every day. I can never think of his death as anything but a regrettable incident which ought not to have happened."[22]

Ansel Adams was away skiing at the time of Applegate's death and did not learn of it for more than a week. "I am shocked beyond telling by this unfortunate event," he told Austin. "There is really no use of saying anything, for my regard and affection for Frank was very deep, and nothing I could say or write could ever express my emotion. He was a magnificent friend and a truly great person. ... Everything possible should be done to assure continuance of Frank's great work for the preservation of the real Southwest."[23]

Friends and colleagues paid numerous tributes to Applegate. John Sloan, writing from New York, called his death "a great shock and a great loss to old Santa Fe."[24] Henry Nash Smith, editor of the *Southwest Review*, told Austin:

One of the most vivid memories of my short visit to New Mexico was our meeting with him at your house and at his. After we got back to Dallas, we had so much to say about Frank Applegate that our friends almost began to joke with us about our admiration for him. I do not believe I had ever met a man for whom I had more respect. We are keenly aware of the gap which his death must make in the Santa Fe community and in fact in the cause of American arts and letters.[25]

For José Dolores López the news of his "brother Frank's" death was "the biggest and greatest sadness for my heart and for all my family." "We feel a great sorrow for mother Alta Applegate," López wrote. "Knowing about this I went to the church and tolled the knell for mama's great burden. I will never forget Frank for his decisions and affection he had for me and my family. ... For me my loud voices [of grief] have overcome me, and I can't find anyone ... I held more esteem for."[26]

Writer Norman MacLeod said he felt "as if a rugged, beautiful portion of New Mexico were suddenly effaced" and called Applegate "the type of man that made northern New Mexico a wonderful place to live in." Applegate's hometown paper, the *Atlanta Argus*, stated, "He had not yet reached the peak of his career and we feel that the combination of a keen intellect, his artistic tendencies, his enthusiasm, and his great capable hands would have led him on to greater achievements."[27]

Austin helped Alta Applegate put together the book of folktales on which Frank had been working when he died, which came to be called *Native Tales of New Mexico* (see Chapter 13). Some of the reviews for *Native Tales* contained tributes to Applegate. *The New York Times Literary Supplement* called Applegate's death "a serious loss to students of New Mexico."[28] Mrs. J.B. Montgomery McGovern, reviewing the book in the *New Mexico Quarterly*, said she had learned during her residence in Santa Fe "that where definite knowledge of customs, either Spanish-American or Indian was desired, Frank Applegate was the man to seek. And Mr. Applegate was as generous in his sharing of knowledge as he was painstaking and accurate in its acquisition. He was never foolishly sentimental, any more than he was ever unkindly critical or coldly unsympathetic, in his attitude toward the Spanish-Americans. … The same balanced attitude of seeing things 'steadily, and seeing them whole' was noteworthy in Frank Applegate's discussion of the Indians of the Southwest."

The review concluded, "Just why a man of the brill[iance] of Frank Applegate should have been snatched away in the cruelly tragic manner that was the case, from a career of creative usefulness, when the career was apparently little more than beginning, is one of the questions to which no answer can be vouchsafed better than the one characteristic of the land which he loved, and of which he wrote: 'Quien sabe?'"[29]

Perhaps the most eloquent eulogy came from the Indian Arts Fund, which passed a resolution stating, in part: "The death of Frank G. Applegate … brought to an end a life dedicated to beauty, its creation and preservation. … In fostering the developments of native arts and crafts his work was tireless, unselfish, and wise. In all human contacts he left the impress of his genial and kindly personality to a lasting degree. He was selflessly ready to lend a hand to the ambitious artist, whether the artist was American, Mexican or Indian, and his efforts to perpetuate the vanishing treasures of Spanish colonial art will live enduringly. A builder in the broad sense, his works have given inspiration in high places and low; his example of generous helpfulness will be long remembered."[30]

Endnotes

[1] Collier, *From Every Zenith*, 153.
[2] Forrest, *The Preservation of the Village*, 57-58. Philp, *John Collier's Crusade for Indian Reform*, 110-111.
[3] Philp, 110-111. Forrest, 59.
[4] Philp, 102. Stineman, *Mary Austin, Song of a Maverick*, 176.
[5] Schrader, *The Indian Arts and Crafts Board*, 34, 38.
[6] "The Simms Indian Bill," *Santa Fe New Mexican*, June 12, 1930, 4.
[7] "Collier Testifies at Hagerman Hearing," *Santa Fe New Mexican*, Jan. 30, 1931, 1, 5. Philp, 104. Collier, 154.
[8] "Brief Digest of the Analysis of Charges," Hagerman Papers.
[9] *Santa Fe New Mexican*, Jan. 31, 1931, 4.
[10] Austin to Alta Applegate, Feb. 15, 1931, Applegate Papers. FGA to Austin, Jan. 31, 1931, Mary Austin Collection, Huntington Library, AU 1016.
[11] Philp, 110. *Santa Fe New Mexican*, Feb. 9, 1931, Feb. 11, 1931. In 1932, Congress again removed Hagerman from the federal payroll, this time for good. See Philp, 111.
[12] "Towns/Santa Fe/Events/Collier Hanging" file, Museum of New Mexico Photo Archives. Applegate is visible in several of the pictures. Weigle and Fiore, *Santa Fe and Taos: The Writer's Era*, 125. Andrew Dasburg's letter to his son, Alfred, dated Feb. 17, 1931, corroborates Applegate's involvement in the Collier hanging. See Andrew Dasburg and Grace Mott Johnson Papers, AAA, Reel 2046.
[13] *Albuquerque Journal*, Jan. 14, 1931, 6. FGA to Austin, Jan. 26, 1931, Mary Austin Collection, Huntington Library. "Frank Applegate Dies Suddenly at Home," *Santa Fe New Mexican*, Feb. 13, 1931, 5.
[14] See Richard Applegate to Gretchen Beall, Jan. 17, 1988, Applegate Papers. Other family members corroborated this story orally and noted Henderson's involvement in interviews with the authors, including nephew Albert Hieronymus.
[15] Pearce, "Rockefeller Center on the Camino," *New Mexico Quarterly Review* 5 (1935): 85. Stevenson to Austin, Feb. 16, 1931, Mary Austin Collection, Huntington Library, AU 4786.
[16] Stevenson to Austin.
[17] "Frank Applegate Dies Suddenly at Home," 1, 5.
[18] Austin to Adams, Feb. 14, 1931, Ansel Adams Correspondence.
[19] Stevenson to Austin.
[20] Stineman, 201. "Funeral Rites for Applegate Held on Sunday," *Santa Fe New Mexican*, Feb. 14, 1931, 4. "Applegate Funeral," *Santa Fe New Mexican*, Feb. 16, 1931, 2. Although Austin's suggestion may fuel speculation that Austin and Applegate were romantically involved, it should be noted she made the same offer to Witter Bynner the year before. See Bynner to Austin, March 31, 1930, Mary Austin Collection, Huntington Library. In 1937 Austin's ashes were buried, alone, on Mount Picacho, near Santa Fe.
[21] "Indian Rites for Applegate," *Santa Fe New Mexican*, Feb. 18, 1931, 2. "Applegate Funeral." "Frank Applegate Dies Suddenly," *Atlanta (Ill.) Argus*, Feb. 20, 1931, 1.

[22] Austin in Applegate, *Native Tales of New Mexico*, 8. Austin to Alta Applegate, Feb. 15, 1931. Austin to Mrs. Meredith (Elizabeth Sage) Hare, Oct. 2, 1931, Applegate Papers. Austin to Mrs. Thomas Wood (Helen) Stevens, June 30, 1932, Mary Austin Collection, Museum of New Mexico History Library.

[23] Adams to Austin, Feb. 22, 1931, Ansel Adams Correspondence. Adams printed the photos on pages 192 and 236 for Applegate family members and friends after Frank's death.

[24] "Village Gossip of Santa Fe," *Santa Fe New Mexican*, March 2, 1931, 4.

[25] Smith to Austin, March 13, 1931, Mary Hunter Austin Collection, Bancroft Library, Box 110.

[26] López letter, Feb. 19, 1931, Spanish Colonial Arts Society Papers. The letter's recipient is unknown, but judging from the rest of the text, it probably was Preston McCrossen at the Spanish Arts Shop. Translation by Brenda Romero.

[27] MacLeod, "From the Pueblos," *Laughing Horse* 19 (Summer 1931): 28. "Frank Applegate Dies Suddenly."

[28] Review, Dec. 8, 1932, 945.

[29] Review, *New Mexico Quarterly* 2:3 (August 1932): 269, 274.

[30] "Frank Applegate, A Builder," reprinted in *Atlanta (Ill.) Argus*, July 31, 1931, 1.

FRANK APPLEGATE OF SANTA FE

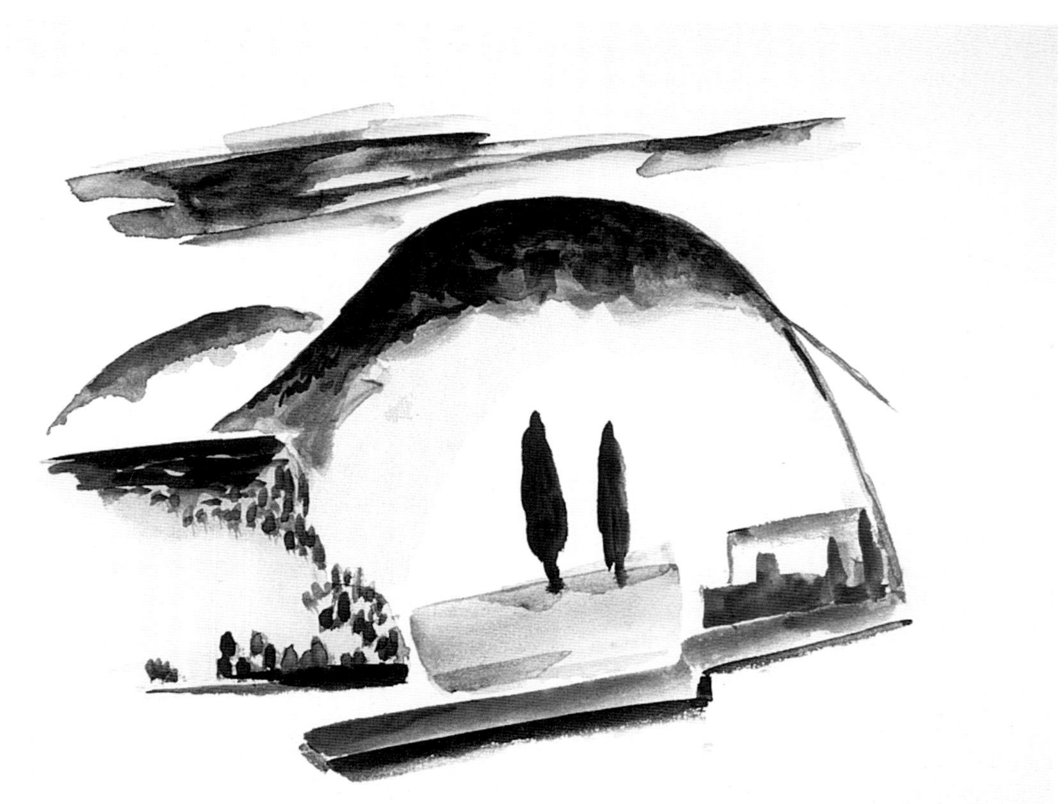

Untitled, watercolor, 8½" by 11½". Private collection. Photograph courtesy of Gerald Peters Gallery, Santa Fe.

272

Epilogue: The End of an Era

Alta Applegate continued to live in the de la Peña House after Frank's death, and she turned his studio into an apartment.[1] She frequently spent months at a time visiting relatives in Illinois and elsewhere, but remained in contact with Santa Fe friends, including Ina and Gerald Cassidy and Ansel and Virginia Adams, and actively participated in the Spanish Colonial Arts Society during the 1930s.

Shortly after Applegate's death the Spanish Colonial Arts Society, mindful of the earlier sale to Alice Bemis Taylor, arranged to purchase from Alta "the very choicest" pieces from Applegate's collection of santos. "It is the general opinion among the members of the Spanish Colonial Arts Society that the collection should be kept in Santa Fe as a memorial to Frank Applegate and the valiant work he did for the society," wrote Marjorie Schmidt, arts society member and wife of painter Albert Schmidt. "As there is nowhere in Santa Fe any representative collection of santos available to the public, this one will be a valuable asset to the city and will increase the interest of the place to all inhabitants and all visitors." The items were appraised at $1,500, Alta Applegate agreed to a price of $1,200, and Austin set about trying to raise the money, soliciting funds from Mabel Dodge Luhan and Elizabeth Sage Hare, among others. "Alta asked the Society to make a selection and has made us a price on them far less than she could get by selling them separately to collectors," she told Hare.[2]

In April 1932 Austin told Ansel Adams, "I succeeded in raising enough money this year, to make the first payment. Alta has been very lenient with us, and I am still hopeful of being able to raise eventually the whole amount; but it is very hard sledding."[3]

The Applegate Memorial Collection was installed in the Historic Museum at the Palace of the Governors. It consisted of 18 bultos, 16 retablos (including a painting on hide), and a hooked altar cloth from the Córdova church. Witter Bynner, James MacMillan, Andrew Dasburg, and Mary Wheelwright selected the articles. Among the bultos were a Trinidad, two San Ysidros, San Antonio, San José, a Penitente-style crucifix, and a fragment of a larger figure of Christ. The retablos included a Santiago, San Juan Joven, San Cristóbal, two San Gerónimos, and a Cristo Crucificado. Ten representations of Nuestra Señora ranged from those done in a medieval style to ones modeled after local women. The altar cloth depicted the flight into Egypt by Mary, Joseph, and baby Jesus. The *Santa Fe New Mexican* reported that "subscriptions are coming in with gratifying liberality which insures that before long the collection as a whole will become the permanent possession of the society, which holds it in the trust for the people of New Mexico. … It is a fitting memorial to Frank Applegate, whose work in this field is thoroughly deserving of so notable a memorial." Alta Applegate received $500 for the collection in 1932 and the remaining $700 in 1933.[4]

In April 1931 the Palace of the Governors displayed two religious paintings on skin that had hung in an abandoned San Ildefonso Pueblo church. Applegate had bought them from a local auto wrecking company owner as one of his last purchases for the Spanish Colonial Arts Society. The September 5, 1931, edition of *El Pasatiempo*, a supplement to the *Santa Fe New Mexican*, included many photographs of items in Applegate's Spanish Colonial arts collection and praised him in the text. At this time Alta donated his collection of authentic blanket patterns to the society.[5] Drawings of pieces from the collection also appeared in the *Spanish Colonial Furniture Bulletin* issued by the New Mexico Department of Vocational Education in 1933.

The Museum of Fine Arts hosted a retrospective memorial exhibition of Applegate's artwork in May 1934. Although it included two alcoves of paintings and a display of his books, the exhibition spotlighted the area of expertise less familiar to Santa Feans, ceramics and sculpture. The show included decorative tile, nudes, sculptural groups, vases, animals, plates, and two sculptured mice, the same mice that first captured *The New York Times*' fancy in 1914. "The whole is altogether delightful, amazing in its variety, apparently the cunning hand of this master-craftsman could do anything with clay and glaze, and color, with china and porcelain," a reviewer said.[6]

In January 1936 Alta sold most of the Applegates' collection of Pueblo pottery to Alice Bemis Taylor, who had opened the Taylor Museum (later the Colorado Springs Fine Art Center) in Colorado Springs several months before. The purchase included 137 bowls, jars, and canteens from the various pueblos, as well as a Jémez medicine bundle and Hopi prayer and altar sticks.[7]

Many of the articles Mary Austin published in the next several years mentioned Applegate, as if she needed to acknowledge posthumously his importance to her. In a letter printed in the June 27, 1931, issue of the *Saturday Review of Literature*, for example, she commented that Applegate knew more about New Mexican linguistics than anyone. In the article "Mexicans and New Mexico," which appeared in *The Survey* in May 1931, she cited his ability to treat the Indians fairly when buying their crafts. She penned a tribute to Applegate for the August 1932 *New Mexico Quarterly* in which she praised "the penetratingly simple quality of creativeness which was the least appreciated of his personal characteristics."[8]

As Austin's health declined, she relied increasingly on Alta and Betty Applegate to care for her. Betty recalled having to bathe Austin and that she would sometimes gorge on food immediately after assuring her doctor that she was following her diet.[9] One scholar believes that Applegate's death led Austin to ponder obsessively on her own death, "wondering if she would live long enough to finish her life story and plaguing whoever would listen with a litany of morose predictions." Austin completed her autobiography, *Earth Horizon*, and Alta Applegate hosted a party to mark the occasion of its publication in December 1932. She also gave a tea for Austin in June 1933.[10]

Austin continued to work on various projects and tour the lecture circuit. She intended to complete Applegate's book on New Mexican architecture, which at his death amounted to nothing more than a few notes.[11] Austin was overburdened with work, however, and the architecture study was never written. She died on August 13, 1934.

Betty Applegate worked as a reporter for the *Santa Fe New Mexican* and was active in local theater until her marriage to Rupert McClung in 1939. The McClungs moved to Denver, and when Alta's health began to fail, she moved in with them. Shortly before Alta's death, she and Betty sold off some of the remaining items from the Applegates' collection of Spanish Colonial and Indian art and artifacts. The Museum of New

Mexico acquired a Rio Grande Valley blanket; a Pueblo katsina, manta, and rain sash; a Hopi man's robe and a woman's dress; an Acoma dress; and two Jémez skin paintings. Additionally, Betty donated a Santo Domingo storage jar, a Pueblo woman's belt, a hair tie, a wicker-work basket, and a number of periodicals. The Historical Society of New Mexico purchased a painted chest, a carved table and two carved, hanging dish cupboards. Alta also made several donations of Indian items to the Indian Arts Fund, among them a bowl, jars, baskets, clothing, blankets, several pieces of battle gear, and weaving tools.[12]

Alta Applegate died in Denver on July 29, 1944. The *Santa Fe New Mexican* reported her death on the front page, noting the "important though self-effacing part" she played in her husband's endeavors, and calling her "the patient, untiring helpmate." Her pallbearers included Albert Schmidt, T.M. Pearce, and Dr. Harry Mera, with other artists and writers listed as honorary pallbearers. She was buried next to Frank in Fairview Cemetery.[13]

In 1941 the Historic American Building Survey, a division of the National Park Service, chose the de la Peña House as "one of the eight Santa Fe buildings of historic importance to the United States." Photographs of the house taken in 1937 were placed in the Library of Congress.[14] Betty McClung sold the de la Peña House shortly after her mother's death. She had no children and died July 23, 1990.

* * *

The Great Depression changed forever the Santa Fe that Frank Applegate knew and loved. Gone were the wealthy art patrons and any chance of an artist's earning a living from art. Members of Los Cinco Pintores and others in need of money rented out their increasingly fashionable adobe homes and lived in cheaper dwellings. Will Shuster moved his family to a homestead northwest of town, while other artists took refuge in their studios and in tents.[15] Santa Fe's extensive growth during the 1920s had made the Camino del Monte Sol much less remote than it had been when the painters first built their "mud huts" on it.

Even established non-controversial painters such as Gerald Cassidy felt the Depression's effects. Cassidy's hardship occured early on, for he wrote in a letter in 1931: "I have been obliged to borrow additional funds on my house to meet living expenses and buy paint materials, and since the first of the year Mrs. Cassidy has taken paying guests into the house in order to pay our grocery bills." He added that $2,000 worth of "sold" paintings had been returned to him after the 1929 stock market crash. Mary Austin noted that year, "We have not had any suffering and very little unemployment, but the tourist crowd has fallen off so in the last two years that there is very little money in town, and as for the poor artists, they have had nothing at all, and the writers are not much better off."[16]

Ironically, the Depression also helped sustain the arts in New Mexico, because it spawned the Public Works of Art Project, which hired painters, sculptors, designers, and craftspeople to create art for public buildings and parks. It was replaced by the Works Progress Administration's Federal Art Project in 1935. The FAP received federal funding under the WPA for projects in music, drama, art, and literature. Among the many artists and writers these projects employed were Ina Sizer Cassidy, Will Shuster, and William Penhallow Henderson.

Shuster credited the federal arts projects with stimulating the public's interest in art. "I think the great interest that we have in art today is probably due largely to the work that was done under … the two programs," he said in 1964. "American art was presented to the people. They hadn't paid any attention to it before." Average people began to appreciate art and even tried to make it themselves, Shuster said.[17] The WPA also helped minority artists such as Hopi artist Fred Kabotie, and funds from the Federal Art Project went to purchase and exhibit woodcarvings by José Dolores López and his son George.

In addition to the Federal Art Project, the New Deal also produced the New Mexico Department of Vocational Education, established in 1932. Under the direction of Brice Sewell, the bureau used funds acquired from New Deal agencies to set up community handicraft centers. These efforts eventually made many Spanish Colonial Arts Society efforts unnecessary, but the society continued to run the Spanish Arts Shop for a few years. It closed in October 1933, although the Native Market of Spanish New Mexican Craftsmen run by Leonora F. Curtin (later Paloheimo), which opened in June 1934, provided an outlet for Hispanic crafts until 1940. Additionally, in 1931 Preston and Helen McCrossen opened the Kraft Shop, which employed Hispanic weavers and dealt exclusively in weaving.[18] The Spanish Colonial Arts Society met rarely during the remainder of the 1930s. Curtin led an attempt to renew interest in it in 1938, but it remained largely inactive until 1951, when E. Boyd succeeded in reviving the group. The society's collection went on long-term loan to the Museum of New Mexico and later was installed in the Museum of International Folk Art. Ground was broken for the Society's own museum in 2000.

The Indian Arts Fund thrived for many years. The Indian Fair, which took place annually during Fiesta, evolved into the Southwest Association on Indian Affairs' Indian Market, an event held independently of Fiesta. Financial problems led to the merger of the Laboratory of Anthropology with the Museum of New Mexico in 1947. The School of American Research received the Indian Arts Fund collection in 1969. Called "the most impressive array of southwestern Indian art in existence," it is housed today in the Indian Arts Research Center in Santa Fe. As Applegate and others had wished, the research center's reason for existence remains the edification and enlightenment of Indians.[19]

In retrospect the efforts of the artists and writers of the 1920s to preserve Indian and Hispanic cultures and aid the people have received both praise and condemnation. Erna Fergusson, writing two decades after Applegate's death, believed the artists could not help but ruin their New Mexican predecessors:

> Altogether the artists' greatest gift to New Mexico was respectful appreciation. Out of this grew the effort to save the old arts and to aid their further development. But artists were to kill the things they loved. Even as the Philistines they deplored, artists felt the great American urge and went into business. A group of them opened the Spanish and Indian Shop in Santa Fe, and artists were now to be met in the pueblos talking a weak-willed Indian into selling ceremonial objects, or in Spanish villages tempting a family's neediest member into giving up the chest that had traveled the Chihuahua Trail.[20]

Even disregarding the racism implicit in Fergusson's statement—the idea that Indians and Hispanics lacked the strength of character to stand up to demanding Anglos—the veracity of her claim is debatable, for, as noted earlier, Indians and Hispanics were often quite willing to part with old objects in exchange for useful cash. These were not rich people, however, and the Anglos could not help but take advantage of them to some degree, just as an antique dealer today takes advantage of a seller when buying items for 10 cents on the dollar.

Business—"the great American urge," as Fergusson called it—had to play a part in the revival, because economics—improving the livelihoods of the "natives"—was the great motivator that led Applegate and the others to reintroduce native crafts in the first place. T.M. Pearce, discussing "the economic side of the regional movement in the Southwest" in 1935, noted that Applegate's and Austin's efforts had "figured impressively toward self support of small communities through crafts." "The economic aspects of Southwestern regionalism both in merchandising novelty and stressing special industries is not to be dismissed," he wrote.[21]

Digging for Native American artifacts, as the Anglos often did, is illegal today, and many modern-day Americans, including some in government, have developed a respect for Indians' sacred religious objects. Fred Kabotie had his wish (see Chapter 11) granted posthumously in 1997, when under the Native American Graves Protection and Repatriation Act the School of American Research returned to the Hopi Tribe 25 cultural items that Applegate had collected in 1925. The items included those Kabotie had seen in the museum in the 1920s. According to the notice of repatriation, the items "are sacred objects needed by traditional religious leaders for the practice of traditional Native American religion," which have "ongoing historical, traditional, and cultural importance central to the Hopi tribe, and could have not been alienated by any individual."[22]

The legacies of the Santa Fe art colony of the 1920s have been debated, discussed, and criticized by scholars in many fields. Was the colony merely a group of "disappointed people protesting against reality," as sculptor Grace Johnson, who lived in Santa Fe in the mid-1920s, saw it? She was not alone in this sentiment. In an essay Pearce refuted a claim that Anglos who settled in New Mexico in the 1920s were "defeated by life and eager to escape it":

> None of the leaders here as I have known them answer to [this] description except D.H. Lawrence and perhaps his Southwestern hostess [Mabel Dodge Luhan]. C.F. Lummis, Frank Applegate, Eugene Rhodes, Mary Austin—to name only four of those who have led— can with little justice be said to have been "defeated by life and eager to escape it." That in more directions than one, each of them embraced life to its fullest, and founded almost schools of followers, present day Southwestern archaeology, crafts, literature, ideology, and phraseology will testify.[23]

Although the Santa Fe colony endured longer than most of the country's other aesthetic communities, many critics of art and literature believe that Santa Fe's artistic legacy never lived up to the promise of the talents who made their homes there. Most of the artists and writers who settled in New Mexico achieved only regional fame, and many of them have been forgotten. Raymond Otis, in a letter to the *New Mexico Sentinel* published in 1937, speculated on Santa Feans' inability to produce first-rate work, speaking in part from his own experiences as a writer:

The lure of sociability in Santa Fe is a dangerous thing. One's friends are close at hand; associations are frequent and intimate, for there are relatively few distractions. This is a threat to the creative life.

Everybody has more or less genius for sociability. A person attempting serious work in Santa Fe must guard against his genius for friendship. His attempts to coddle his talent for sociability into submission to his wish to create, too often take the form of telling his friends what he is doing, or plans to do. "Now I am writing a novel. Now I am going to write a play." From there his loose talking proceeds to a telling of the muddled contents of his brain about the novel or the play, and the ultimate dissipation in thin air of all the idea contained—which with some discipline and work might have been shaped and evolved into something worth while.

This is the thing which stigmatizes and nullifies most of the work done in Santa Fe. The creating of anything here tends to become a community effort. Individual genius is hardly ever given a chance to express itself. Community expression is well and good in its place, but it has no place in art, for if art is anything at all it is the reflection of the scene and the time in the brain of one individual capable of transmuting it. When more than one person enters the arena of creation, all of its issue loses its significance as art, and it becomes a tour de force—mere entertainment. Even in a collaboration, which is not the ideal form of creation, if anything that is art emerges from it, that part is the product of one of the workers, and not both.

One sees so much of this—oneself is guilty of it so often that the heart grows sick. For it is hard to work alone in a place where one's friends are solicitous and criticism is non-existent. That is the great disadvantage of attempting to make Santa Fe one's work-place. It is a play-place, and any place like it is more or less the same.[24]

Santa Fe was indeed a play-place, and the artists and their art suffered for it. John Sloan knew this, so he lived in New York most of the time, and he told friend Will Shuster early on to "give way to any feeling of aloofness that may find its way into your temperament" when in pursuit of the artistic muse. Witter Bynner knew it, and his frustration at being labeled second-rate may well have been the reason he once poured a beer over Robert Frost's head.[25] It is no mere coincidence that New Mexico's most famous painter, Georgia O'Keeffe, eventually settled in a remote community some distance from Santa Fe and Taos.

However, the "community effort" that Otis commented on did have a place in Santa Fe, in the area of preservation. More so than the art they created, the legacy of the artists and writers of 1920s Santa Fe lies in the city itself. Edgar Lee Hewett suggested as much in 1940, by which time, thanks to the public works projects of the New Deal, Santa Feans had finally begun to appreciate the artists in their midst:

> Art has rescued the state from the commonplace and made it conscious of its own fine character. The arts have kept Santa Fe from becoming an "up-to-date" burg and made it unique and beautiful among the capitals of our country. … Artists and writers constitute only a small percentage of the population [of Santa Fe] but their influence is wherever you look. … In arousing in the minds of our people consciousness of the beauty of this Southwestern land, in restoring this heritage of history, tradition, poetry, folk life, a priceless service is rendered to our state and its people.[26]

Through the Old Santa Fe Association, through their numerous and successful efforts at preservation, the artists and writers succeeded, as much as was possible, in keeping Santa Fe a "City Different." Their efforts also helped to preserve Indian and Spanish culture in the face of Americanization.

Frank Applegate's name and work have faded from memory, in part because his active life precluded aggressive self-promotion. The Santa Fe artists "spent a lot of their time becoming active in civic affairs rather than developing the patrons and contacts outside of [the] area that would have led to a larger-scale promotion of their careers."[27] Without public commissions or purchases of their work by important museums, artists' reputations rarely survive their demise, and Applegate's reputation was no exception.

An appreciation of Applegate's work has been late in coming partly because Alta and Betty Applegate took most of his paintings and sculptures from Santa Fe when they moved to Denver. The artwork remained in storage for decades. In the late 1980s Betty sold the bulk of the collection to a Santa Fe art collector and dealer, and the work has only come to light since then.

If what constitutes an artist is the act of creating art—using skill and imagination to create unique works, taking tools to materials and investigating their unlimited potential—then Applegate was truly a great artist. He had the ability to pick a medium—be it adobe, clay, oils, watercolors, wood, or words—explore its possibilities, push its limits and produce something beautiful, and he encouraged other artists to do the same.

Applegate's most important legacy, however, is the one he shares with the other writers and artists of the 1920s. Their appreciation of the uniqueness of Santa Fe's ancient adobe buildings, historic churches, and communal plaza gave them the foresight to keep the city from becoming another Strawberry Point, Iowa. Applegate's and the others' work in the Indian Arts Fund and Spanish Colonial Arts Society fostered an appreciation for the ancient arts and helped ensure their continuing evolution.

An artist's work lives on after his death. As long as someone still sees it, hears it, reads it, the artist achieves an immortality not earned by lesser mortals. Today, visitors tread Santa Fe's narrow, winding streets to marvel at the spectacular adobe homes, million-dollar properties born from those simple "mud huts." They visit the Museum of Indian Arts and Culture and the Museum of International Folk Art and see the contributions of the Indian Arts Fund and Spanish Colonial Arts Society. They head to the Museum of Fine Arts to study the paintings of the Santa Fe and Taos artists. And if they want to see a statue of a pioneer mother, they go to Albuquerque.

And everywhere in Santa Fe, inscribed invisibly, are the words, "Frank Applegate was here."

Endnotes

1 *Santa Fe New Mexican*, March 24, 1931, 2.

2 Proposed letter from Marjorie Schmidt, Spanish Colonial Arts Society Miscellaneous Minutes, 1930-1934; John DeHuff to Austin, Sept. 12, 1932, in Spanish Colonial Arts Society Canceled Checks, 1933-34; Spanish Colonial Arts Society Papers. Austin to Mrs. Meredith (Elizabeth Sage) Hare, Oct. 2, 1931, Applegate Papers. Austin to Mabel Dodge Luhan, Sept. 16, 1932, Luhan Papers. Austin to Hare states that Alta originally asked for $1,500.

3 Austin to Adams, April 21, 1932, Ansel Adams Correspondence.

4 Austin to Hare, Oct. 2, 1931, Applegate Papers. "Frank Applegate Memorial Collection in Old Palace," *Santa Fe New Mexican*, n.d., Applegate Papers. Spanish Colonial Arts Society Canceled Checks, 1932-33, Spanish Colonial Arts Society Papers. Some of these pieces are in the possession of the Spanish Colonial Arts Society, but the whereabouts of most of them is unknown.

5 *Santa Fe New Mexican*, April 30, 1931. "Artes Nativos de Nuevo Mexico," *El Pasatiempo*, Sept. 5, 1931, 5.

6 "Memorial Exhibition of Applegate's Books," *Santa Fe New Mexican*, May 16, 1934, 1. "Memorial Collection Shows Remarkable Versatility of Artist, Writer, Applegate," *Santa Fe New Mexican*, May 18, 1934, 6.

7 Taylor Collection list, Colorado Springs Fine Arts Center Archives. Judith Burdick to Gretchen Beall, Jan. 5, 1995, Applegate Papers.

8 "New Mexico Spanish," *Saturday Review of Literature* 7:49 (June 27, 1931): 930. *The Survey* 66:3 (May 1, 1931): 45. "Frank Applegate," *New Mexico Quarterly* 2:3 (August 1932): 213.

9 Authors' interviews with Gretchen Beall. For corroboration see interview with Leonora Curtin and Leonora Curtin Paloheimo, September 9, 1967, Augusta Fink papers, Box 1, Folder 30.

10 Blend, "Women Writers and the Desert: Mary Austin, Ina Sizer Cassidy, and Alice Corbin," (dissertation, University of New Mexico, July 1988): 182. Pearce, *Mary Hunter Austin*, 61-62.

11 Austin to Adams, March 13, 1931, Ansel Adams Correspondence.

12 "Dispersal of Frank Applegate Collection," *El Palacio* 51:1 (July 1944): 132-33. Indian Arts Fund to Alta Applegate, June 10, 1944, Indian Arts Fund Papers.

13 "Mrs. Applegate Dies in Denver," *Santa Fe New Mexican*, July 31, 1944, 1. According to Betty Applegate McClung, Ina Sizer Cassidy placed flowers on Frank and Alta's grave each Memorial Day. See undated note from Betty McClung to Gretchen Beall, Applegate Papers.

14 Historic Santa Fe Foundation, *Old Santa Fe Today*, 46.

15 Robertson, *Los Cinco Pintores*, 9. Dispenza and Turner, *Will Shuster*, 64-66.

16 Cassidy to Mrs. J.H. Palmer, Feb. 12, 1931, Cassidy Family Papers, Box 13. Quoted by permission of The Bancroft Library, owners of the Cassidy Family Papers, [ca. 1897-1965]. BANC MSS 67/1 p. Austin to Hare, Oct. 2, 1931, Applegate Papers.

17 Shuster interview with Sylvia Loomis, July 30, 1964, Shuster Papers, AAA, Reel 277, transcript, 11-12.

18 Taylor, "Arts and Crafts in the Santa Fe Style," paper presented at the Winterthur Conference on the Decorative Arts, Wilmington, Del., 1990, 33-34. Weigle, "The First Twenty-Five Years of the Spanish Colonial Arts Society," in Weigle, ed., et al., *Hispanic Arts and Ethnohistory in the Southwest*, 192. Kardon, ed., *Revivals! Diverse Traditions*, 262.

19 Constable, "Hidden Treasures," *Santa Fe Reporter*, Feb. 9, 1994, 11. Truettner, "The Art of Pueblo Life," in Eldridge, et al., *Art in New Mexico*, 82. In 1999 the school transferred ownership of 97 percent of its collection to the Museum of New Mexico.

20 Fergusson, *New Mexico*, 373.

21 Pearce, "Rockefeller Center on the Camino," *New Mexico Quarterly Review* 5 (1935): 84-85.

22 "Notices," *Federal Register* 62:133 (July 11, 1997), from the *Federal Register* Online. In 2000 the school gave the Zia Tribe a headdress Applegate had collected in 1925; see "Notices," *Federal Register* 65:41 (March 1, 2000), from the *Federal Register* Online.

23 Grace Johnson to Nancy Lane, Oct. 20, 1928, Andrew Dasburg and Grace Mott Johnson Papers. Pearce, "Rockefeller Center on the Camino," 86.

24 Reprinted in Weigle and Fiore, *Santa Fe and Taos: The Writer's Era*, 138.

25 Sloan to Shuster, March 1, 1922, Shuster Papers, AAA, Reel 277. Wilbur, ed., *The Works of Witter Bynner, Selected Poems*, lxv.

26 "A List of Prominent Artists and Writers of New Mexico," *Santa Fe New Mexican*, June 26, 1940, 1.

27 Bullandy, *Images From Santa Fe and Taos*, 12.

EPILOGUE: THE END OF AN ERA

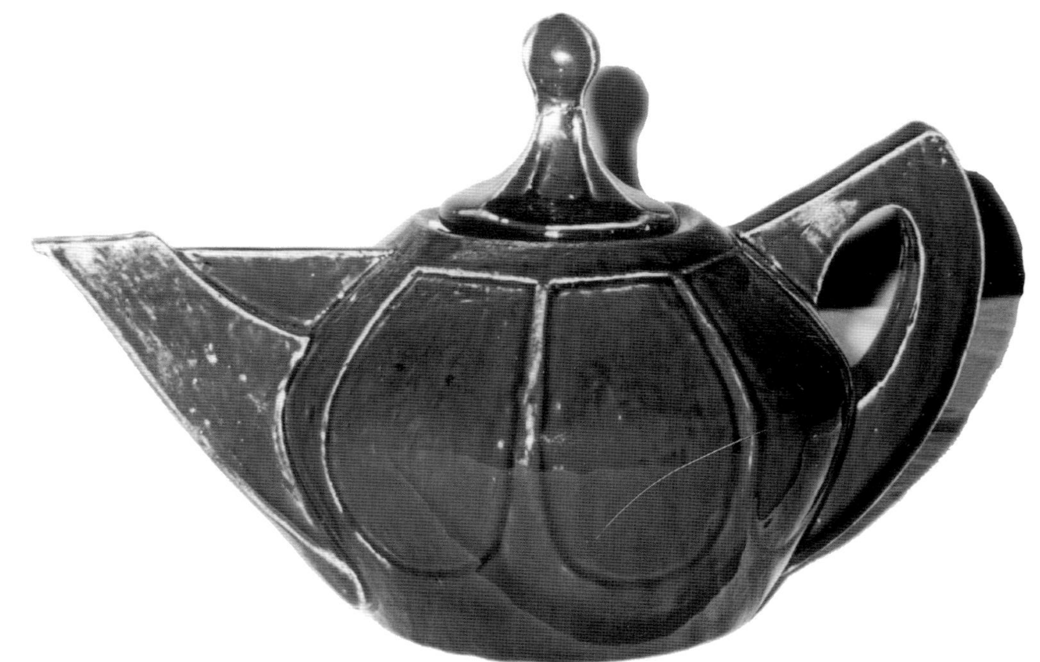

Teapot. Private collection. Photograph courtesy of the owner.

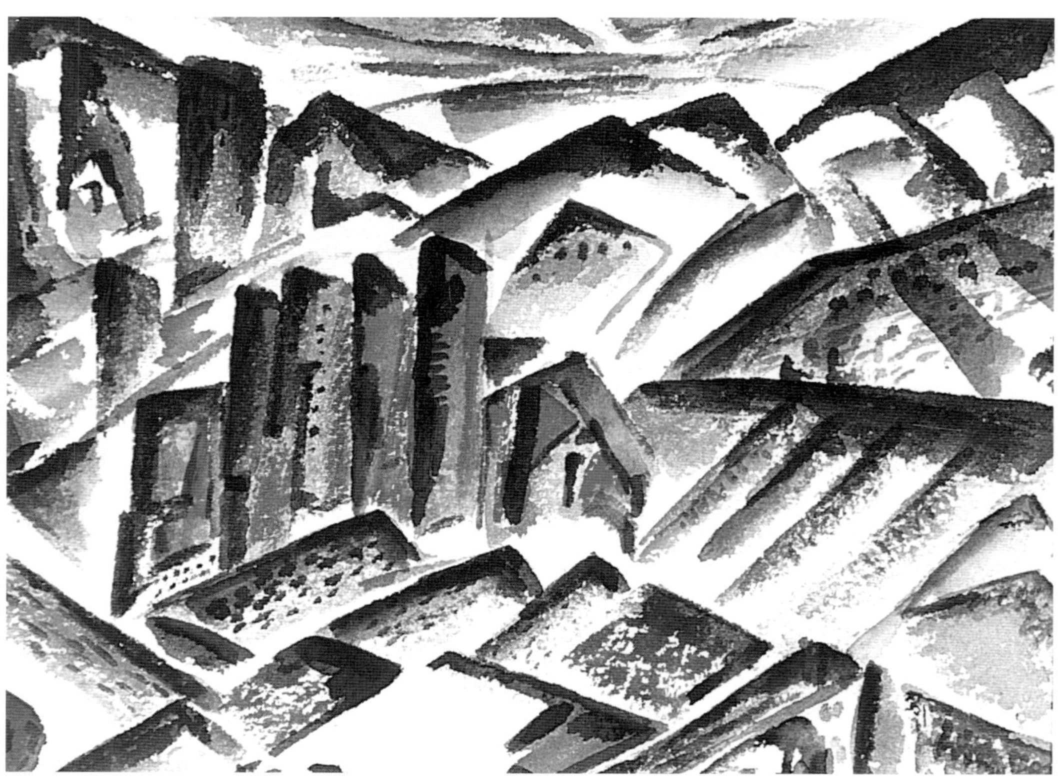

Valley, N.M., watercolor, 5" by 8½". Private collection. Photograph courtesy of Gerald Peters Gallery, Santa Fe.

Bibliography

Writings by Frank Applegate

Atlanta (Ill.) Argus, Feb. 8, 1907, March 29, 1907, April 19, 1907, April 26, 1907, May 24, 1907, July 12, 1907, July 19, 1907, July 26, 1907, Oct. 4, 1907, Nov. 8, 1907, Nov. 20, 1908, April 29, 1910, July 15, 1910, July 22, 1910, Aug. 5, 1910, Aug. 12, 1910, Aug. 19, 1910, Sept. 2, 1910, Sept. 16, 1910, Sept. 23, 1910, Sept. 14, 1923.

___ "Citizens of the Desert." Review of *Desert Drums* by Leo Crane. *New York Herald Tribune*, March 10, 1929, sec. 11, 20.

___ *Indian Stories From the Pueblos*. With foreword by Witter Bynner. New York: J.B. Lippincott Co., 1929. Also second printing, Glorieta, N.M.: Rio Grande Press, 1977.

___ (As told to Tom Howard), "If You Buy Antiques." *New Mexico Highway Journal* 7 (April 1929): 24-25+.

___ *Lincoln (Ill.) Daily Courier*, June 1, 1907.

___ *Native Tales of New Mexico*. With introduction by Mary Austin. New York: J.B. Lippincott Co., 1932.

___ "New Mexico Backgrounds." *Southwest Review* 14:3 (Spring 1929): 351-359.

___ "Spanish Colonial Arts." *The Survey* 66:3 (May 1, 1931): 156-157.

___ "Tourists and Art." *Southwest Review* 12:1 (October 1926): 23-27.

Essays and stories from *Indian Stories From the Pueblos* and *Native Tales of New Mexico* reprinted in:

Becker, May. *Golden Tales of the Southwest*. New York: Dodd, Mead & Co., 1939.

Botkin, B.A., ed. *A Treasury of Western Folklore*. New York: Crown Publishing Inc., 1951.

Folk-Say: A Regional Miscellany. Norman: The University of Oklahoma, 1930. 84-87; 212-218.

Folk-Say: A Regional Miscellany. Norman: The University of Oklahoma, 1931. 330-337.

Fulton, Maurice Garland, and Paul Horgan. *New Mexico's Own Chronicle*. Dallas: Banks, Upshaw & Co., 1937.

Major, Mabel, and T.M. Pearce. *Southwest Heritage: A Literary History With Bibliography*. Albuquerque: University of New Mexico Press, 1972.

Schaefer, Jack Warner, ed. *Out West; An Anthology of Stories*. Boston: Houghton, Mifflin Co., 1955.

Sonnichsen, Charles L. ed. *The Laughing West: Humorous Western Fiction Past and Present*. Athens, Ohio: Swallow Press, 1988.

Southwest Review 15:3 (Spring 1930): 310-316.

Southwest Review 17:2 (January 1932): 199-208.

Primary sources

This book could not have been written without aid from Applegate's niece, Gretchen Hieronymus Beall. Beall interviewed Applegate's daughter, Ruth Elizabeth "Betty" Applegate McClung, on numerous occasions in the 1980s. She also compiled notes based on her own recollections and those of other family members and conducted research in anticipation of someday writing a book about Applegate. Her discussions and correspondence with the authors were invaluable, as was her sharing of the Applegate Papers with them. Upon completion of this book, the papers were donated to the Center for Southwest Research, University of New Mexico General Library, which already owned some of Applegate's papers (MSS 97 SC).

Other primary sources:

Adams, Ansel. Ansel Adams Archives, Center for Creative Photography, University of Arizona, Tucson, Ariz.

Applegate, Albert Angelo. "Recollections of A.A. Applegate." Unpublished. Atlanta Public Library, Atlanta, Ill.

Archives of American Art, National Gallery of Art, Washington, D.C.

Archives of the Pennsylvania Academy of the Fine Arts. Microfilm.

Bákos, Josef and Teresa. Papers, reels 663, 1215. Transcribed interview, conducted by Sylvia Loomis, April 15, 1965, 26 pp.

Dasburg, Andrew, and Grace Mott Johnson. Papers. Microfilm.

Gratz Collection, Historical Society of Pennsylvania. Microfilm.

Kuhn, Walt. Papers. Microfilm.

MacGinnis, H.R. Papers. Microfilm.

Mowbray-Clarke, John and Mary. Papers, reels D169, D169A.

Shuster, Will. Papers, reels 169-177, 277. Transcribed interview, conducted by Sylvia Loomis, July 30, 1964, 24 pp. (The Museum of Fine Arts, Santa Fe, N.M., retains the Shuster Papers, but the authors read most of them on microfilm at the AAA. If the authors cite an item found at the MFA, it is so noted in the footnote.)

Woodward, Sidney C. Collection. Microfilm.

Zorach, William and Marguerite. Papers. Microfilm.

Austin, Mary. Collection. The Huntington Library, San Marino, Calif. All quoted material reproduced by permission of the Huntington Library.

Mary Austin Collection, Museum of New Mexico History Library, Santa Fe.

Mary Hunter Austin Collection, Bancroft Library, University of California, Berkeley.

Mary Austin Papers, Center for Southwest Research, General Library, University of New Mexico, Albuquerque. MSS 31 BC.

Brooklyn Museum Archives. Painting & Sculpture Exhibitions: 1925 Watercolor Exhibition.

Bynner, Witter. Papers. Houghton Library, Harvard University, Cambridge, Mass.

Cassidy, Gerald P. and Ina Sizer. Family Papers BANC MSS 67/1 p. University of California, Berkeley, Calif. Quoted by permission of The Bancroft Library, owners of the Cassidy Family Papers, [ca. 1897-1965].

Center for Southwest Research, General Library, University of New Mexico, Albuquerque, N.M.
    Applegate, Frank. Papers. MSS 97 SC.
    DeHuff, John David and Elizabeth Willis. Papers.
    Fink, Augusta. Papers
    Meem, John Gaw. Papers.
    Pearce. T.M. Papers.
    Pearce, T.M., ed. Unpublished manuscript on Spanish Colonial arts, Frank Applegate and Mary Austin, authors. In Pearce Papers.

Colorado Springs Fine Arts Center Archives, Colorado Springs, Colo. Alice Bemis Taylor Collection documents.

Denver Art Museum, Denver, Colo. F. H. Douglas Papers, Department of Native Arts.

Dobie, J. Frank. Papers. Harry Ransom Humanities Research Center, The University of Texas at Austin, Austin, Texas.

Henderson, Alice Corbin. Collection. Harry Ransom Humanities Research Center, The University of Texas at Austin, Austin, Texas.

Hodge, Frederick Webb. Manuscript Collection. Braun Research Library, Southwest Museum, Los Angeles, Calif.

Laboratory of Anthropology, Santa Fe, N.M.
    Indian Arts Fund. Papers.
    Kidder, A.V. Correspondence.
    Laboratory of Anthropology. Correspondence.

Luhan, Mabel Dodge. Papers. Beinecke Rare Book and Manuscript Collection, Yale University, New Haven, Conn.

Metropolitan Museum of Art Archives, New York.

Morse, Dorothy Applegate. "Memories of Uncle Frank." Unpublished. In Applegate Papers.

Museum of Fine Arts, Houston. Archives.

Museum of New Mexico History Library, Palace of the Governors, Santa Fe, N.M.
    Cassidy, Ina Sizer. Correspondence.
    Dihl, Ruth Kelsey. Papers, in Nichols Collection.
    Ellis, Bruce. Collection.
    Fairview Cemetery Collection.
    Hewett, Edgar Lee. Papers.
    Historical Society of New Mexico Collection.
    Indian Arts Fund Collection.
    Johnson, E. Dana. Papers.
    McGee, Norman. Collection.
    Museum of New Mexico History Bureau Collection.
    Old Santa Fe Association. Papers.
    Pueblo Land Matters. Papers.
    Santa Fe and Taos Artists. Papers.
    Taos Society of Artists. Official Society Papers.

Museum of New Mexico Museum of Fine Arts Library
    Applegate, Frank G. Biographical file.

Museum of New Mexico Photo Archives
    Portraits/Frank Applegate/Betty Applegate.
    Towns/Santa Fe/Events/Collier Hanging.
    Towns/Santa Fe/Homes/de la Peña.
    Towns/Santa Fe/Homes/Frank Applegate.
    Towns/Santa Fe/Streets/Camino del Monte Sol.

New Mexico State Records Center and Archives, Santa Fe, N.M.

Boyd, E. Collection.
Hagerman, Herbert. Papers.
Spanish Colonial Arts Society. Papers.
Wilson, Francis. Papers.

Pennsylvania Academy of the Fine Arts Archives, Philadelphia.

University of Illinois Archives, Champaign-Urbana, Ill.

Zigrosser, Carl. Papers. Annenberg Rare Book & Manuscript Library, University of Pennsylvania, Philadelphia.

Secondary sources
Books

Adams, Ansel. *An Autobiography.* Boston: Little, Brown & Co., 1985.

___ *Photographs of the Southwest.* New York: Graphic Society Books; Boston: Little Brown & Co., 1976.

Adams, Clinton. *Printmaking in New Mexico, 1880-1990.* Albuquerque: University of New Mexico Press, 1991.

Adams, Philip Rhys. *Walt Kuhn, Painter.* Columbus, Ohio: Ohio State University Press, 1978.

Adriani, Götz. *Cézanne Watercolors.* Translated by Russell M. Stockman. New York: Harry N. Abrams Inc., 1983.

Amon Carter Museum of Western Art. *Quiet Triumph: Forty Years With the Indian Arts Fund, Santa Fe.* Fort Worth: Amon Carter Museum of Western Art, 1966.

Atlanta Women's Club. *A History of Atlanta, 1853-1953.* Atlanta, Ill.: Stewart-Finks Publishing Co., 1953.

Austin, Mary. *Earth Horizon.* New York: The Literary Guild, 1932.

___ *The Land of Journey's Ending.* Tucson: University of Arizona Press, 1983.

___ *Starry Adventure.* Boston: Houghton Mifflin, 1931.

Bartlett, Katharine. "A History of Hopi Pottery," in Frederick, E.C., ed. *Hopi and Hopi- Tewa Pottery.* Flagstaff: Museum of Northern Arizona, 1990.

Batkin, Jonathan. *Pottery of the Pueblos of New Mexico, 1700-1940.* Colorado Springs, Colo.: The Taylor Museum of the Colorado Springs Fine Arts Center, 1987.

___ "The Taylor Museum: A Tribute to Folk Culture," in Kerstetter, Josie De Falla, ed. *Colorado Springs Fine Arts Center: A History and Selections from the Permanent Collections.* Colorado Springs, Colo.: Colorado Springs Fine Arts Center, 1986.

Belshaw, Michael. *Camino del Monte Sol Architectural Historic Survey.* City of Santa Fe, 1984.

Bennitt, Mark, ed., *History of the Louisiana Purchase Exposition.* St. Louis: Universal Exposition Publishing Co., 1905.

Berman, Avis. *Rebels on Eighth Street: Juliana Force and the Whitney Museum of American Art.* New York: Atheneum, 1990.

Boyd, E. *Popular Arts of Spanish New Mexico.* Santa Fe: Museum of New Mexico Press, 1974.

___ *Saints and Saint Makers of New Mexico.* Santa Fe: Laboratory of Anthropology, 1946. Revised edition, edited by Robin Farwell Gavin, with appendix by Charles M. Carrillo. Santa Fe: Western Edge Press, 1998.

Briggs, Charles L. *The Wood Carvers of Cordova, N.M.: Social Dimensions of an Artistic "Revival."* Albuquerque: University of New Mexico Press, 1989 (paperbound edition).

___ "The Role of Mexicano Artists and the Anglo Elite in the Emergence of a Contemporary Folk Art." In *Folk Art and Art Worlds: Essays Drawn From the Washington Meeting on Folk Art,* organized by the American Folklife Center at the Library of Congress, edited by John Michael Vlach and Simon J. Bronner. Ann Arbor, Mich: University of Michigan Research Press, 1986.

Briggs, Charles L., and Julián Josuá Vigil, eds. *The Lost Gold Mine of Juan Mondragón: A Legend From New Mexico Performed by Melaquías Romero.* Tucson: University of Arizona Press, 1990.

Brody, J.J. *Indian Painters and White Patrons.* Albuquerque: University of New Mexico Press, 1971.

___ *Pueblo Indian Painting: Tradition and Modernism in New Mexico, 1900-1930.* Santa Fe, N.M.: School of American Research Press, 1997.

Brown, Lorin W., with Charles L. Briggs, and Marta Weigle. *Hispano Folklife of New Mexico: The Lorin W. Brown Federal Writers' Project Manuscripts.* Albuquerque: University of New Mexico Press, 1978.

Brown, Milton W. *American Painting, From the Armory Show to the Depression.* Princeton, N.J.: Princeton University Press, 1970.

___ *The Story of the Armory Show.* New York: Joseph Hirshhorn Foundation, 1963.

Bunting, Bainbridge. *John Gaw Meem, Southwestern Architect.* Albuquerque: University of New Mexico Press, 1983.

Carlock, Marion Pomeroy. *History of the Carlock Family and Adventures of Pioneer Americans.* Los Angeles: William B. Straube Printing Co., 1929.

Carswell, John. *Lives and Letters: A.R. Orage, Beatrice Hastings, Katherine Mansfield, John Middleton Murry, S.S. Koteliansky, 1906-1957.* London: Faber & Faber, 1978.

Cash, Marie Romero. *Santos: Enduring Images of Northern New Mexican Village Churches.* Niwot, Colo.: University Press of Colorado, 1999.

Chapman, Kenneth M. "The Pottery of Santo Domingo Pueblo." In *Memoirs of the Laboratory of Anthropology, Vol. 1.* Santa Fe: Laboratory of Anthropology, 1938 (1953 reprint).

Chauvenet, Beatrice. *Edgar L. Hewett and Friends: A Biography of Santa Fe's Vibrant Era.* Santa Fe: Museum of New Mexico Press, 1983.

___ *John Gaw Meem: Pioneer in Historic Preservation.* Santa Fe: Museum of New Mexico Press, 1985.

Coe, Ralph T. "Native American Craft." In *Revivals! Diverse Traditions: The History of Twentieth-Century American Craft, 1920-1945,* edited by Janet Kardon. New York: Harry N. Abrams Inc. and American Craft Museum, 1994.

Coke, Van Deren. *Andrew Dasburg: His Life and Art.* Albuquerque: University of New Mexico Press, 1979.

___ *Nordfeldt the Painter.* Albuquerque: University of New Mexico Press, 1972.

___ *Taos and Santa Fe, the Artists' Environment, 1882-1942.* Albuquerque: University of New Mexico Press, 1963.

Colby, Virginia Reed, and James B. Atkinson. *Footprints of the Past: Images of Cornish, New Hampshire and the Cornish Colony.* Concord, N.H.: New Hampshire Historical Society, 1996.

Collier, John. *From Every Zenith: A Memoir.* Denver: Sage Books, 1963.

___*Indians of the Americas.* New York: W.W. Norton & Co. Inc., 1947.

Comfort, Charles Haines, and Mary Apolline Comfort, eds. *This is Santa Fe.* Santa Fe, N.M., 1955.

Crane, Leo. *Desert Drums: The Pueblo Indians of New Mexico, 1540-1928.* Boston: Little, Brown & Co., 1928.

Craven, Wayne. *Sculpture in America.* Newark, Del.: University of Delaware Press, 1980.

Czestochowski, Joseph. *Arthur B. Davies: A Catalogue Raisonné of the Prints.* Newark, Del.: University of Delaware Press, 1987.

Davidson, Abraham. *Early American Modernist Painting, 1910-1935.* New York: Harper and Row, Publishers, 1981.

DeMille, Agnes. *Dance to the Piper.* Boston: Little, Brown & Co., 1951.

Dispenza, Joseph, and Louise Turner. *Will Shuster: A Santa Fe Legend.* Santa Fe: Museum of New Mexico Press, 1989.

Doyle, Helen MacKnight. *Mary Austin, Woman of Genius.* New York: Gotham House, 1939.

Dunn, Dorothy. *American Indian Painting of the Southwest and Plains Area.* Albuquerque: University of New Mexico Press, 1968.

Elliott, Malinda. *The School of American Research, A History.* Santa Fe, N.M.: The School of American Research, 1987.

Evans, Paul. *Art Pottery of the United States.* New York: Feingold & Lewis Publishing Corp., 1987.

Falk, Peter Hastings, ed. *The Annual Exhibition Record of the Art Institute of Chicago, 1888-1950.* Madison, Conn.: Sound View Press, 1990.

___ *The Annual Exhibition Record of the Pennsylvania Academy of the Fine Arts. Vols. II and III.* Madison, Conn.: Sound View Press, 1989.

Fergusson, Erna. *Dancing Gods.* New York: Alfred A. Knopf, 1931.

___ *New Mexico: A Pageant of Three Peoples.* New York: Alfred A. Knopf, 1951.

Ferrell, Robert H., ed. *Dear Bess: The Letters from Harry to Bess Truman, 1910-1959.* New York: W.W. Norton & Co., 1983.

Fink, Augusta. *I-Mary: A Biography of Mary Austin.* Tucson: University of Arizona Press, 1983.

Forrest, Suzanne. *The Preservation of the Village: New Mexico's Hispanics and the New Deal.* Albuquerque: University of New Mexico Press, 1989.

Fosdick, Raymond B. *John D. Rockefeller, Jr., A Portrait.* New York: Harper & Brothers, 1956.

Frank, Larry. *New Kingdom of the Saints: Religious Art of New Mexico, 1780-1907.* Santa Fe: Red Crane Books, 1992.

Friedman, B.H. *Gertrude Vanderbilt Whitney.* New York: Doubleday & Co., 1978.

Garmhausen, Winona. *History of Indian Arts Education in Santa Fe.* Santa Fe: Sunstone Press, 1988.

Gerould, Katharine Fullerton. *The Aristocratic West.* New York: Harper & Brothers Publishers, 1925.

Gibson, Arrell Morgan. *The Santa Fe and Taos Colonies: Age of the Muses, 1900-1942.* Norman: University of Oklahoma Press, 1983.

Gish, Robert. *Paul Horgan.* Boston: Twayne Publishers, 1983.

Green, Harvey. "Culture and Crisis: Americans and the Craft Revival." In *Revivals! Diverse Traditions: The History of Twentieth-Century American Craft, 1920-1945,* edited by Janet Kardon. New York: Harry N. Abrams Inc. and American Craft Museum, 1994.

Hagedorn, Hermann. *Edwin Arlington Robinson.* New York: Macmillan Co., 1938.

Hayes, Jess G. *Apache Vengeance: True Story of Apache Kid.* Albuquerque: University of New Mexico Press, 1954.

Henzke, Lucile. *American Art Pottery.* Camden, N.J.: Thomas Nelson Inc., 1970.

Hieronymus, Lynn. *Eminence: A Steeple Above the Prairie.* Privately published, Atlanta, Ill., 1988.

Historic Santa Fe Foundation. *Old Santa Fe Today.* Albuquerque: University of New Mexico Press, 1972.

History of Logan County, Illinois. Chicago: Inter-State Publishing Co., 1886.

History of Logan County, Illinois. Lincoln, Ill.: Logan County Heritage Foundation, 1982.

Homer, William Innes, with Violet Organ. *Robert Henri and His Circle.* Ithaca, N.Y.: Cornell University Press, 1969.

Horgan, Paul. *The Centuries of Santa Fe.* New York: E.P. Dutton & Co., 1956.

Houghland, William, ed. *Mary Austin: A Memorial.* Santa Fe: Laboratory of Anthropology, 1944.

Houghton, Stanley. *Hindle Wakes.* London: Sidgwick & Jackson Ltd., 1912.

The Illio. Champaign, Ill.: University of Illinois, 1904-1906.

Iowa, Jerome. *Ageless Adobe: History and Preservation in Southwestern Architecture.* Santa Fe: Sunstone Press, 1985.

Jenison, Madge. *Sunwise Turn: A Human Comedy of Bookselling.* New York: E.P. Dutton & Co., 1923.

Kabotie, Fred, with Bill Belknap. *Fred Kabotie: Hopi Indian Artist.* Flagstaff: Museum of Northern Arizona, 1977.

Kardon, Janet. "Within Our Shores: Diverse Craft Revivals and Survivals." In *Revivals! Diverse Traditions: The History of Twentieth-Century American Craft, 1920-1945*, edited by Janet Kardon. New York: Harry N. Abrams Inc. and American Craft Museum, 1994.

Keen, Kirsten Hoving. *American Art Pottery, 1875-1930*. Wilmington, Del.: Delaware Art Museum, 1978.

Kelly, Lawrence C. *The Assault on Assimilation: John Collier and the Origins of Indian Policy Reform*. Albuquerque: University of New Mexico Press, 1983.

Kraft, James, gen. ed. *The Works of Witter Bynner, Selected Letters*. New York: Farrar, Straus, Giroux, 1981.

___ *The Works of Witter Bynner, Prose Pieces*. New York: Farrar, Straus, Giroux, 1979.

LaFarge, Oliver. *Laughing Boy*. New York: Literary Guild, 1929.

___ *Santa Fe: The Autobiography of a Southwestern Town*. Norman: University of Oklahoma Press, 1959.

Levin, Elaine. *The History of American Ceramics*. New York: Harry N. Abrams Inc., 1988.

Lorenzo de Cordova (Lorin W. Brown). *Echoes of the Flute*. Santa Fe: Ancient City Press, 1972.

Loughery, John. *John Sloan: Painter and Rebel*. New York: Henry Holt and Co. Inc., 1995.

Ludington, Townsend. *Marsden Hartley: The Biography of an American Artist*. Boston: Little, Brown & Co., 1992.

Luhan, Mabel Dodge. *Movers and Shakers*. New York: Harcourt, Brace & Co., 1936.

Major, Mabel, and T.M. Pearce. *Southwest Heritage: A Literary History With Bibliography*. Albuquerque: University of New Mexico Press, 1972.

Marlor, Clark S. *The Society of Independent Artists: The Exhibition Record, 1917-1944*. Park Ridge, N.J.: Noyes Press, 1984.

Martin, Wallace. *'The New Age' Under Orage: Chapters in English Cultural History*. Manchester, England: Manchester University Press, 1967.

Mather, Christine, ed. *Colonial Frontiers: Art and Life in Spanish New Mexico: The Fred Harvey Collection*. Santa Fe: Ancient City Press, 1983.

Meem, John Gaw. "Preface." In Historic Santa Fe Foundation. *Old Santa Fe Today*. Albuquerque: University of New Mexico Press, 1972.

Miller, Joseph. *New Mexico: A Guide to the Colorful State*. New York: Hastings House, 1953.

Modernist Themes in New Mexico: Works by Early Modernist Painters. Santa Fe: The Peters Corp., 1989.

Museum of New Mexico. *Handbook of the Collection, 1917-1974*. Albuquerque: University of New Mexico Press, 1974.

Neff, Emery. *Edwin Arlington Robinson*. New York: W. Sloane Associates, 1948.

Nestor, Sarah. *The Native Market of the Spanish New Mexican Craftsmen, Santa Fe, 1933-1940*. Santa Fe: The Colonial New Mexico Historical Foundation, 1978.

Newhall, Nancy. *Ansel Adams, the Eloquent Light*. Millerton, N.Y.: Aperture Inc., 1980.

Pearce, T.M. *The Beloved House*. Caldwell, Idaho: The Caxton Printers Ltd., 1940.

___ *Mary Hunter Austin*. New York: Twayne Publishers Inc., 1965.

Pearce, T.M., and Telfair Hendon, eds. *America in the Southwest: A Regional Anthology*. Albuquerque: University of New Mexico Press, 1933.

Perlman, Bennard B. *Painters of the Ashcan School: The Immortal Eight*. New York: Dover Publications, 1979.

Philp, Kenneth R. *John Collier's Crusade for Indian Reform, 1920-1954*. Tucson: University of Arizona Press, 1977.

Pierce, Donna, and Marta Weigle, eds. *Spanish New Mexico: The Spanish Colonial Arts Society Collection*. Vol. 2, *Hispanic Arts in the Twentieth Century*. Santa Fe, N.M.: Museum of New Mexico Press, 1996.

Raines, Lester. *Writers and Writings of New Mexico*. Las Vegas, N.M.: New Mexico Normal University Department of English, 1934.

Reich, Sheldon. *John Marin: A Stylistic Analysis and Catalog Raisonné*. Tucson: University of Arizona Press, 1970.

Robertson, Edna C. *Los Cinco Pintores*. Santa Fe: Museum of New Mexico Press, 1975.

Robertson, Edna C., and Sarah Nestor. *Artists of the Canyons and Caminos*. Layton, Utah: Peregrine Smith Inc. 1976.

Robinson, William H. *Under Turquoise Skies*. New York: Macmillan Co., 1928.

Schimmel, Julie. "The Hispanic Southwest." In Eldridge, Charles, Julie Schimmel, and William H. Truettner. *Art in New Mexico, 1900-1945: Paths to Taos and Santa Fe*. New York: National Museum of American Art, Washington, D.C., and the Abbeville Press, 1986.

Schrader, Robert Fay. *The Indian Arts and Crafts Board: An Aspect of New Deal Indian Policy*. Albuquerque: University of New Mexico Press, 1983.

Seymour, Tryntje Van Ness. *When the Rainbow Touches Down*. Phoenix: The Heard Museum, 1988.

Sikorski, Kathryn A. *Modern Hopi Pottery*. Logan, Utah: Utah State University Monograph Series 15:2, 1968.

Sloan, John, and Oliver LaFarge. *Introduction to American Indian Art*. New York: Exposition of Indian Tribal Arts Inc., 1931.

Smith, William Jay, ed. *The Works of Witter Bynner: Light Verse and Satires*. New York: Farrar, Straus, Giroux, 1978.

Spanish Colonial Furniture Bulletin, compiled by the New Mexico Department of Vocational Education, Brice H. Sewell, State Supervisor of Trade and Industrial Education, 1933.

Sprague, Marshall. "Colorado Springs Fine Arts Center, Its Formative Years." In *Colorado Springs Fine Arts Center: A History and Selections From the Permanent Collections*. Colorado Springs, Colo.: Colorado Springs Fine Arts Center, 1986.

Stark, Gregor, and E. Catherine Rayne. *El Delirio: The Santa Fe World of Elizabeth White*. Santa Fe, N.M.: School of American Research Press, 1998.

Steele, Thomas J., S.J. *Santos and Saints: The Religious Folk Art of Hispanic New Mexico*. Santa Fe: Ancient City Press, 1994.

Stineman, Esther Lanagan. *Mary Austin, Song of a Maverick*. New Haven, Conn.: Yale University Press, 1989.

Taft, Lorado. *The History of American Sculpture*. New York: Macmillan Co., 1924.

___ *Modern Tendencies in Sculpture*. Chicago: University of Chicago Press, 1921.

Taft, Robert. *Artists and Illustrators of the Old West*. New York: Charles Scribner's Sons, 1953.

Taggett, Sherry Clayton, and Ted Schwarz. *Paintbrushes and Pistols: How the Taos Artists Sold the West*. Santa Fe: John Muir Publications, 1990.

Taylor, Lonn, and Dessa Bokides. *New Mexican Furniture, 1600-1940*. Santa Fe: Museum of New Mexico Press, 1987.

Titiev, Mischa. *The Hopi Indians of Old Oraibi: Change and Continuity*. Ann Arbor: University of Michigan Press, 1972.

Truettner, William H. "The Art of Pueblo Life." In Eldridge, Charles, Julie Schimmel, and William H. Truettner. *Art in New Mexico, 1900-1945: Paths to Taos and Santa Fe*. New York: National Museum of American Art, Washington, D.C., and the Abbeville Press, 1986.

Udall, Sharon Rohlfsen. *Contested Terrain: Myth and Meanings in Southwest Art*. Albuquerque: University of New Mexico Press, 1996.

___ *Modernist Painting in New Mexico 1913-1935*. Albuquerque: University of New Mexico Press, 1984.

___ *The Santa Fe Art Colony, 1900-1942*. Santa Fe: Gerald Peters Gallery, 1987.

___ *Spud Johnson and "Laughing Horse."* Albuquerque: University of New Mexico Press, 1994.

Van Buren, Deborah. "The Artists and Their Works." In *A Circle of Friends: Art Colonies of Cornish and Dublin*. Dublin, N.H.: University Art Galleries, University of New Hampshire, 1985.

Wade, Hugh Mason. *A Brief History of Cornish, 1763-1974*. Hanover, N.H.: University Press of New England, 1976.

Weigle, Marta. "The First Twenty-Five Years of the Spanish Colonial Arts Society." In Weigle, Marta, ed., with Claudia Larcombe, Samuel Larcombe. *Hispanic Arts and Ethnohistory in the Southwest: New Papers Inspired by the Work of E. Boyd*. Santa Fe: The Spanish Colonial Arts Society and Ancient City Press, 1983.

___ "A Brief History of the Spanish Colonial Arts Society." In Pierce, Donna, and Marta Weigle, eds. *Spanish New Mexico: The Spanish Colonial Arts Society Collection*. Vol. 2, *Hispanic Arts in the Twentieth Century*. Santa Fe, N.M.: Museum of New Mexico Press, 1996.

Weigle, Marta, and Kyle Fiore. *Santa Fe and Taos: The Writer's Era, 1916-1941*. Santa Fe: Ancient City Press, 1982.

White, Robert R., ed. *The Taos Society of Artists*. Albuquerque: University of New Mexico Press, 1983.

___ "The New Mexico Painters," in *The New Mexico Painters*. Santa Fe, N.M.: Gerald Peters Gallery, 1999.

Who's Who in America. Chicago: The A.N. Marquis Co., 1930-31.

Wilbur, Richard, ed. *The Works of Witter Bynner, Selected Poems*. New York: Farrar, Straus, Giroux, 1978.

Wilder, Mitchell, and Edgar Breitenbach. *Santos: The Religious Folk Art of New Mexico*. Colorado Springs, Colo.: The Taylor Museum of the Colorado Springs Fine Arts Center, 1943.

Wilkinson, Burke. *Uncommon Clay: The Life and Works of Augustus Saint-Gaudens*. San Diego: Harcourt Brace Jovanovich, 1985.

Wilson, Chris. *The Myth of Santa Fe: Creating a Modern Regional Tradition*. Albuquerque: University of New Mexico Press, 1997.

Wroth, William. *Christian Images in Hispanic New Mexico*. Colorado Springs, Colo.: The Taylor Museum of the Colorado Springs Fine Arts Center, 1982.

___ "The Hispanic Craft Revival in New Mexico." In *Revivals! Diverse Traditions: The History of Twentieth-Century American Craft, 1920-1945*, edited by Janet Kardon. New York: Harry N. Abrams Inc. and American Craft Museum, 1994.

___ "Hispanic Southwestern Craft Traditions in the Twentieth Century." In *Hispanic Crafts of the Southwest*, edited by William Wroth. Colorado Springs, Colo.: The Taylor Museum of the Colorado Springs Fine Arts Center, 1977.

Wyman, Leland C., and Flora L. Bailey. "Navaho Indian Ethnoentomology." In *University of New Mexico Publications in Anthropology, No. 12*. Albuquerque: University of New Mexico Press, 1964.

Zigrosser, Carl. *My Own Shall Come to Me*. Privately published, 1971.

___ *A World of Art and Museums*. Philadelphia: The Art Alliance Press, 1975.

Zorach, William. *Art Is My Life: The Autobiography of William Zorach*. Cleveland: World Publishing Co., 1967.

Magazine articles, journal articles, selected newspaper articles

Adkins, Lynn. "William Penhallow Henderson and Southwestern Indian Art." *El Palacio* 93, no. 2 (Winter 1987): 23-33.

Agee, William C. "Rediscovery: Henry Fitch Taylor." *Art in America* 54 (November 1966): 40-43.

"An All-Star Sales Force." *New Mexico Highway Journal* 7, no. 4 (April 1929): 31-32.

"Annual Art Exhibit: Artists of the Southwest." *El Palacio* 23, no. 11 (Sept. 17, 1927): 298-301.

Applegate, Alta. "From New Mexico." *Atlanta (Ill.) Argus*, Feb. 10, 1922, 2.

Applegate, Betty. "Los Hermanos Penitentes." *Southwest Review* 17, no. 1 (October 1931): 100-107.

"April Follies by the Artists." *El Palacio* 14, no. 8 (April 16, 1923): 124.

"Art at Home and Abroad: The MacDowell Club Exhibition." *The New York Times Book Review and Magazine*, Nov. 22, 1914, sec. 5, 11.

"Arthur Szyk Miniatures; The New Mexico Painters." *American Art News*, Dec. 12, 1925, 5.

"Art-in-Trades Club at Waldorf-Astoria." *El Palacio* 15, no. 9 (Nov. 1, 1923): 149-150.

"Artists at San Juan Dance." *El Palacio* 13, no. 2 (July 15, 1922): 23.

"Artists Headed for Santa Fe." *El Palacio* 13 (reprinted from *The New York Times*), 1922, 168-169.

Austin, Mary. "Folk Plays of the Southwest." *Theatre Arts Monthly* 17, no. 8 (August 1933): 599-610.

___ "Frank Applegate." *New Mexico Quarterly* 2, no. 3 (August 1932): 213-219.

___ "Indian Detour." *The Bookman* 68, no. 6 (February 1929): 653-658.

___ "Mexicans and New Mexico." *The Survey* 66 (May 1, 1931): 141-144+.

___ "New Mexico Spanish." *Saturday Review of Literature* 7, no. 49 (June 27, 1931): 930.

___ "Pueblo Stories." Review of *Indian Stories From the Pueblos. The Nation* 129, no. 3359 (Nov. 20, 1929): 597-598.

___ "The Town That Doesn't Want a Chautauqua." *New Republic* 47, no. 605 (July 7, 1926): 195-197.

Baker, George P. "The Pueblo Indian." Review of *Indian Stories From the Pueblos. Yale Review* 19 (1930): 409-411.

Barker, Virgil. "The Season Opens." *The Arts* 4 (1923): 213-214.

Bernstein, Bruce. "From Indian Fair to Indian Market." *El Palacio* 98, no. 3 (Summer 1993): 18+.

Boyd, E. "Celso Gallegos." *El Palacio* 60, no. 5 (May 1953): 215.

Boyer, Hazel. "Work of Santa Fe Painters Praised at San Diego." Reprint of article from *San Diego Union* in *Santa Fe New Mexican*, June 28, 1924, 7.

Brandt, Beverly K. "Worthy and Carefully Selected: American Arts and Crafts at the Louisiana Purchase Exposition, 1904." *Archives of American Art Journal* 28, no. 1 (1988): 2-16.

Brenner, Anita. Review of *Indian Stories From the Pueblos. New York Evening Post*, Nov. 30, 1929, 8.

Breuning, Margaret. "New Mexico Painters." *New York Evening Post Literary Review*, Sept. 25, 1926, 10. Reprinted in *Santa Fe New Mexican*, Oct. 7, 1926, 5.

Briggs, Charles L. "What Is a Modern Santo?" *El Palacio* 79, no. 4 (March 1974): 40-48.

Buffalo (N.Y.) Fine Arts Academy. "Collection of Works By New Mexico Painters." *Academy Notes* 19, no. 1 (January-June 1924).

Buffalo (N.Y.) Fine Arts Academy. "Exhibition of Contemporary American Sculpture at the Albright Art Gallery." *Academy Notes* 11, no. 3 (June 1916).

Bynner, Witter. "A City of Change." *Laughing Horse* 11 (September 1924): 1-5.

___ "Indian Drumbeat in the Southwest." Review of *Patterns and Ceremonials of the Indian Southwest* for *The New York Times Book Review*. Reprinted in *Works of Witter Bynner, Prose Pieces*. New York: Farrar, Straus, Giroux, 1979, 247-249.

___ "It's Our Fiesta." *Santa Fe New Mexican*, Sept. 6, 1929, 5.

Cahill, E. Holger. "America Has Its 'Primitives.'" *International Studio* 75 (March 1922): 80-83.

Cantwell, Robert. Review of *Native Tales of New Mexico. New York Evening Post*, May 28, 1932, 7.

Carr, Harry. "Santa Fe and Taos Take on Luster As Stamping Ground for Literati." *Los Angeles Times*, June 9, 1929.

Cassidy, Ina Sizer. "Art and Artists of New Mexico: Frank G. Applegate." *New Mexico Magazine* 12, no. 6 (June 1934): 29, 49-51.

___ "Art and Artists of New Mexico: The Little Theater in Santa Fe." *New Mexico Magazine* 16, no. 10 (October 1938): 25.

___ "Beginning of Greater Art Colony on Camino Monte Sol." *Santa Fe New Mexican,* Oct. 29, 1921, 2.

___ "I-Mary and Me: The Chronicle of a Friendship." *New Mexico Quarterly* 9, no. 4 (November 1939): 203-211.

"Chappell School of Art." *El Palacio* 18, no. 9 (May 1, 1925): 211.

"The Chappell School of Art." *El Palacio* 19, no. 4 (Aug. 15, 1925): 63-65.

Chenoweth, Olive. "A Visit to the Cliff Dwellings." *Atlanta (Ill.) Argus,* Aug. 11, 1922.

"The College of Literature and Arts at the Louisiana Purchase Exposition." *University of Illinois Press Bulletin* 40 (Feb. 22, 1904): 1. In University of Illinois Archives.

Comstock, Helen. "W. Langdon Kihn." *International Studio,* October 1925. Reprinted in *El Palacio* 9, no. 10 (Nov. 16, 1925): 214.

Constable, Anne. "Hidden Treasures." *Santa Fe Reporter,* Feb. 9, 1994, 11-15.

"Cultural Center of the Southwest." *El Palacio* 20, no. 9 (May 1, 1926): 171-181.

"December Exhibits." *El Palacio* 23, no. 22 (Dec. 3, 1927): 571-572.

"Dispersal of Frank Applegate Collection." *El Palacio* 51, no. 7 (July 1944): 132-133.

Drohojowska, Hunter. "The Southwestern Aesthetic: Gerald and Kathleen Peters in Santa Fe's de la Peña House." *Architectural Digest,* June 1992, 106-111+.

Dunn, Dorothy. "Awa-Tsireh: Painter of San Ildefonso." *El Palacio* 63, no. 4, 108-115.

Dunne, Brian Boru. "Inaugural Ball Breaks All Records for Gor[g]eousness." *Santa Fe New Mexican,* Jan. 3, 1923, 1.

___ "Raymond Jonson Winner of Underwood $500 Art Prize." *Santa Fe New Mexican,* Sept. 15, 1925, 2.

Edgerton, Giles. "A Group of Brilliant New Mexico Painters." *Arts and Decoration* 20 (December 1923): 15+.

El Pasatiempo, special supplement to the *Santa Fe New Mexican,* Sept. 5, 1931. Articles featured: "Antiquedades Coloniales Espanolas Son Muy Bonitas," 7; "Artes Nativos de Nuevo Mexico: Un Tesoro Cultural Mas Precioso del Pais," 4-5; "Celso Gallegos, Fabricador de los Santos de Bulto," 6; "Muebles Tipicos para la Casa y el Jardin," 8.

Ewing, Robert. "William Penhallow Henderson: A Contemporary Appreciation." *El Palacio* 93, no. 3 (Winter 1987): 12.

"Exhibit by Santa Fe Society Artists." *El Palacio* 19, no. 1 (July 1, 1925): 18-21.

"Exhibits at Denver." *El Palacio* 22, no. 25 (June 18, 1927): 536-538.

"Exhibits of Etchings and Prints." *El Palacio* 20, no. 2 (Jan. 15, 1926): 51-52.

"February Exhibits." *El Palacio* 28, nos. 1-4 (Jan. 4-25, 1930): 13-15.

Fergusson, Erna. "Laughing Priests." *Theatre Arts Monthly* 17, no. 8 (August 1933): 657- 662.

"The Fiesta Art Exhibit." *El Palacio* 13, no. 8 (Oct. 16, 1922): 98-100.

"Fiesta Event: The Spanish Colonial Arts Society." *El Palacio* 29, no. 3 (Sept. 2, 1930): 105-106.

"Fiesta Exhibition." *El Palacio* 15, no. 6 (Sept. 15, 1923): 98-100.

"The Folk in Literature." Introduction to *Folk-Say: A Regional Miscellany,* 1929.

Frederick, Frank F. "School of Industrial Arts, City of Trenton." *Journal of the American Ceramic Society* 6, no. 1 (January 1923): 115-116.

___ "The Trenton School of Industrial Arts." *Keramic Studio,* January 1918, 187.

"The Galleries in May." *El Palacio* 14, no. 11 (June 1, 1923): 169-170.

Gibson, Arrell Morgan. "Native American Muses." *New Mexico Historical Review* 56, no. 3 (July 1981): 285-302.

Hare, Elizabeth Sage. "The Wood Carver of Cordova." *Travel* 81, no. 1 (May 1943): 20-21+.

Hawthorne, Hildegarde. "Santa Fe Becomes the Eden of Authors." *The Literary Digest International Book Review* 4, no. 2 (November 1926): 739-741.

Henderson, Alice Corbin. "Applegate's Tales from the Pueblos Living, Human Folk-stories." *Santa Fe New Mexican,* Oct. 10, 1929, 4.

___ "An Indian Goya Who Amazes Artists." *Literary Digest,* Oct. 17, 1925, 45-46.

___ "The New Mexico That We Love: Frank Applegate's Posthumous Book." *Santa Fe New Mexican,* May 20, 1932.

___ (Anonymous, Alice Corbin Henderson.) Review of *Native Tales of New Mexico. New Mexico Magazine* 10, no. 6 (June 1932): 28.

Hewett, Edgar L. "Native American Artists." *Art and Archeology,* March 1922, 107-109.

"Historical Society Lecture." *El Palacio* 29, no. 9 (Oct. 15, 1930): 325.

"Immigrant in America Competition." *American Art News,* Nov. 20, 1915, 7.

"In the Pueblo Style of Santa Fe." *House and Garden* 55, no. 9 (August 1929): 94-95.

"Independent Group Shows 1,180 Works." *American Art News,* March 7, 1925, 3.

"Indian and Spanish in Santa Fe." *House and Garden* 55, no. 4 (April 1929): 116-117.

"John Curtis Underwood Prizes Awarded." *El Palacio* 19, no. 7 (Oct. 1, 1925): 146-147.

Johnson, Willard "Spud" (referred to as "the editor"). "Index to First Lines." *Laughing Horse* 12 (August 1925): 33-34.

___ "Spud, Laffin Hoss Editor, Takes Brief Look at the Modernists." *Santa Fe New Mexican,* Feb. 13, 1924, 6.

"Julian and His School." *American Art News,* Feb. 23, 1907, 4.

"June Exhibits." *El Palacio* 22, no. 23 (June 4, 1927): 506.

Laughlin, Ruth. "Santa Fe in the Twenties." *New Mexico Quarterly Review* 19 (Spring 1949): 58-66.

"Loan Exhibit: Two Santos Placed on Exhibit in Museum Loaned by Colonial Arts Society." *El Palacio* 30, nos. 19-20 (May 20, 1931): 252-253.

"Los Angeles." *American Art News,* Aug. 11, 1923, 7.

"Los Angeles Museum's Western Painters Exhibition of the West." *El Palacio* 17, no. 3 (Aug. 1, 1924): 56-57.

"Los Cinco Pintores." *Artists of the Rockies and the Golden West,* Summer 1979, 66-69.

"Los Cinco Pintores." *El Palacio* 11, no. 9 (Nov. 1, 1921): 111.

"Los Cinco Pintores." *El Palacio* 11, no. 11 (Dec. 1, 1921): 139-140.

"Los Cinco Pintores." *El Palacio* 13, no. 10 (Nov. 15, 1922): 131-132.

McAllister, Dorothy. "The Santa Fe Fiesta." *El Palacio* 11, no. 6 (Sept. 15, 1921): 78-81.

McBride, Henry. "Masterly Art Not Yet Fully Appreciated: The New Mexican Painters." *New York Sun,* Dec. 12, 1925, 9.

McCrossen, Helen Cramp. "Native Crafts in New Mexico." *School Arts Magazine* 30, no. 7 (March 1931): 456-458.

McGovern, Mrs. J.B. Montgomery. Review of *Native Tales of New Mexico. New Mexico Quarterly* 2, no. 3 (August 1932): 269-274.

MacLeod, Norman. "From the Pueblos." Review of *Indian Stories From the Pueblos. Laughing Horse* 19 (1931): 27-28.

"Marvels of Modeling from Pellets of Clay." *The Crockery and Glaze Journal,* May 28, 1909, 21-22.

Melrose, Frances, "Famed St. Gaudens Family Left Its Mark on Denver," *Rocky Mountain News* (Denver), Nov. 26, 2000.

"Moderns at the Montross Gallery." *Arts and Decoration,* May 1915, 285-286.

Mowat, Jean. "The Artist in the Southwest." Reprinted from *Chicago Evening Post* in *El Palacio* 20, no. 10 (May 15, 1926): 194-200.

Murray, Marion. "Art in the Southwest." *Southwest Review* 11, no. 4 (July 1926): 281-293.

Nelson, H.C. "Strenuous Art Season Looms Ahead." *New York Sun and Globe*, Oct. 6, 1923, 9.

Nestor, Sarah. "Viewpoint: An Interview with Alice Henderson Rossin." *El Palacio* 93, no. 2 (Winter 1987): 15-19.

"New Art Society in the Southwest." *American Art News*, Aug. 11, 1923, 2.

"New Group Joins New Mexico Artists." *American Art News*, Oct. 25, 1924, 1-2.

"New Mexico Painters." *American Art News*, Oct. 13, 1923, 2.

"The New Mexico Painters." *El Palacio* 15, no. 2 (July 16, 1923): 32.

"New Mexico Painters." *New York Evening Post Literary Review*. Sept. 25, 1926, 10.

"New Mexico Painters in Boston." *El Palacio* 21, no. 9 (Nov. 1, 1923): 247.

"New Mexico Painters in New York." *New York Evening Post*, reprinted in *El Palacio* 16, no. 2 (Jan. 15, 1924): 31.

"Not Coming to Santa Fe." *El Palacio* 24, nos. 20-21 (May 19-26, 1928): 409.

"Notable Art Exhibit." *El Palacio* 16, no. 6 (March 15, 1924): 99.

"November Arts and Architecture." *El Palacio* 25, no. 20 (Nov. 17, 1928): 323-325.

"November Exhibits." *El Palacio* 23, no. 20 (Nov. 19, 1927): 515-517.

Oaklander, Christine I. "Clara Davidge's Madison Art Gallery: Sowing the Seed for The Armory Show." *Archives of American Art Journal* 36, nos. 3-4 (1996): 20.

"October Art Exhibits." *El Palacio* 25, nos. 14-17 (Oct. 6-27, 1928): 267.

"Old Art in New Forms." *New Mexico Association on Indian Affairs Bulletin*, No. 8. Reprinted from *New Mexico Magazine*, 1936.

"Old New Mexico." Review of *Native Tales of New Mexico*. *Time* 19:24 (June 13, 1932): 51.

Parmelee, Cullen W. "History of Ceramic Education at the University of Illinois." *Journal of the American Ceramic Society* 6, no. 1 (January 1923): 97-104.

Pearce, T.M. "Rockefeller Center on the Camino." *New Mexico Quarterly Review* 5 (1935): 84-87.

"People and Places." *New Mexico Magazine*, August 1967, 34.

Peters, Helen. "Madonna of the Trail." *New Mexico Magazine* 71, no. 12 (December 1993): 48-54.

Podmore, Harry. "A Little Journey to Picturesque Morris Heights." *Trenton (N.J.) State Gazette*, May 27, 1921.

Popejoy, Tom L. "Analysis of the Causes of Bank Failures in New Mexico, 1920-1925." *University of New Mexico Bulletin* 1, no. 1 (Oct. 1, 1931).

Rascoe, Burton. "The Book of the Day." Review of *Native Tales of New Mexico*. Unknown New York newspaper, 1932. In Applegate Papers.

Read, Helen Appleton. "Pueblos of Distinct Cubist Lines." *Brooklyn (N.Y.) Daily Eagle*, Oct. 26, 1924. Reprinted in *Santa Fe New Mexican*, Oct. 30, 1924, 4.

"The Reader's Guide." *Saturday Review of Literature* 9, no. 6 (Aug. 27, 1932): 70.

Review of *Native Tales of New Mexico*. *The Nation* 135 (Sept. 28, 1932): 290.

Review of *Native Tales of New Mexico*. *The New York Times Literary Supplement*, Dec. 8, 1932, 945.

Review of *Native Tales of New Mexico*. *Saturday Review of Literature* 8, no. 5 (July 9, 1932): 832.

Review of *Native Tales of New Mexico*. *Scribner's* 92, no. 5 (November 1932): 19.

Riis, Edward V. "Brooklyn Museum Opens Gallery; Fine Exhibitions." *Brooklyn (N.Y.) Eagle*, n.d. 1925. In Brooklyn Museum Archives.

Rönnebeck, Arnold. "Applegate Exhibit at Denver." *El Palacio* 23, no. 21 (Nov. 26, 1927): 540-544.

___ "Santa Fe Painters and Their Art." *Rocky Mountain News* (Denver), June 19, 1927, drama section, 3.

Salazar, Theresa. "Ansel Adams and Spanish Colonial Arts." *History of Photography* 22, no. 2 (Summer 1998): 161-168.

"Santa Fe Art School." *El Palacio* 27, no. 10 (Sept. 7, 1929): 123.

"Santa Fe Artists at Los Angeles." *El Palacio* 15, no. 4 (Aug. 15, 1923): 61-62.

"The Santa Fe Meeting." *El Palacio* 28, nos. 10-25 (June 15, 1930): 109-117.

Sergeant, Elizabeth Shepley. "The Journal of a Mud House." *Harper's Magazine* 144-145, nos. 862-865 (March-June 1922): 409-422+.

___ "Mary Austin: A Portrait." *Saturday Review of Literature* 9, no. 8 (Sept. 8, 1934): 96.

___ Review of *Native Tales of New Mexico*. *Books*, May 29, 1932, 3.

___ "The Santa Fe Group." Reprinted from *Saturday Review of Literature*, Dec. 8, 1934, in Weigle, Marta, and Kyle Fiore, *Santa Fe and Taos: The Writer's Era, 1916-1941*. Santa Fe: Ancient City Press, 1982.

Shuster, Will. "Los Cinco Pintores Enlivened Art Colony." *Santa Fe New Mexican*, Sept. 23, 1951.

"Society." (Article on a talk given by Applegate.) *Albuquerque Journal*, Jan. 14, 1931, 5.

"Southwest Bookshelf." *New Mexico Magazine* 10, no. 3 (March 1932): 25.

"Southwestern American Colonial Interiors and Fabrics." *Ladies Home Journal* 47, no. 12 (December 1930): 58.

"Spanish Colonial Arts: Mr. Applegate Speaks Under Auspices of Historical Society of New Mexico." *El Palacio* 29, no. 21 (Dec. 5, 1930): 329-332.

"The Spanish Colonial Arts Society." *El Palacio* 29, no. 3 (Sept. 2, 1930): 105-106.

Stevens, Clifford. "Celso Gallegos: The Santero of San Ysidro." *Viva* (in the *Santa Fe New Mexican*), Jan. 13, 1974, 6.

Szasz, Margaret Connell. Review of *Indian Stories From the Pueblos* (1977 reprint). *New Mexico Historical Review* 54, no. 2 (April 1979): 159.

"Taos Paintings Win Praise Here." *Houston Express*, April 10, 1931.

"Thirteenth Annual New Mexican Art Exhibit." *El Palacio* 21, no. 6 (Sept. 15, 1926): 160-163.

"Three New Exhibits." *El Palacio* 14, no. 8 (April 16, 1923): 123.

Townsend, James B. "The Pennsylvania Academy of Fine Arts Exhibition." *American Art News*, Feb. 1, 1908, 2.

Van Stone, Mary R. "The Fiesta Art Exhibition." *Art and Archeology* 18 (November-December 1924): 225-240.

"The Very Latest at Montross Gallery." *American Art News*, March 27, 1915, 2.

Vestal, Stanley. Review of *Indian Stories From the Pueblos*. *Folk-Say*, 1930, 424.

"Walls Tumbled, Roofs Leaked But Artists' Houses Still Stand." *Albuquerque (N.M.) Journal* (North), Feb. 4, 1984, E-7.

Walter, Paul A.F. "Biennial Report of the President, 1930-1931." *New Mexico Historical Review* 7 (Jan. 19, 1932): 183-186.

Walton, Eda Lou. "The Folk Tales of New Mexico." Review of *Native Tales of New Mexico*. *The New York Times Book Review*, June 5, 1932, 2.

Ward, Leah Beth. "Los Cinco Pintores." *Albuquerque (N.M.) Journal* (North), Feb. 4, 1984, E-6.

"Water Colors at Brooklyn Museum." *Christian Science Monitor*, May 6, 1925.

White, Robert R. "The New Mexico Painters, 1923-1926." *Southwest Art*, May 1986, 76-81.

"Who's Who in American Art: N.E. Montross." *Arts and Decoration*, July 1915, 435.

Wolf, Arthur H. "The Indian Art Fund Collection of the School of American Research." *American Indian Art Magazine* 4, no. 1 (Winter 1978): 32-37.

"The World of Art." *The New York Times Magazine*, Dec. 14, 1924, 9.

"The World of Art: The Architectural League." *The New York Times Book Review and Magazine*, April 3, 1921, 20-22.

Zorach, William. "The Background of an Artist." *The Magazine of Art*. 34, nos. 4-5 (April-May 1941): 162-168, 234-239.

Other newspaper articles

Atlanta (Ill.) Argus, April 1891-July 1931.
Boston Transcript, Dec. 12, 1923, Nov. 30, 1929, June 25, 1932.
Buffalo (N.Y.) Evening News, Jan. 5, 1924, Jan. 12, 1924, Jan. 26, 1924.
Buffalo (N.Y.) Truth, Jan. 12, 1924.
Chicago Daily News, Feb. 20, 1924.
Christian Science Monitor, Oct. 6, 1923, Jan. 24, 1931.
Dallas Morning News, Oct. 21, 1928.
Houston Post-Dispatch, Oct. 26, 1930.
Las Vegas (N.M.) Optic, May 12, 1926.
Lincoln (Ill.) Daily Courier, April 22, 1898-Dec. 6, 1907.
Lincoln (Ill.) Times-Courier, Jan. 14, 1905.
Memphis (Tenn.) Commercial Appeal, Feb. 24, 1931.
Memphis (Tenn.) Press-Scimitar, Jan. 30, 1931.
New York Herald, March 26, 1915.
New York Herald Tribune, Oct. 26, 1924, Sept. 5, 1926.
New York Sun, Dec. 12, 1925.
The New York Times, Nov. 20, 1914, March 26, 1915, Nov. 3, 1915, Dec. 3, 1915, Jan. 13, 1916, May 3, 1916, Nov. 8, 1921, Nov. 19, 1921, Oct. 3, 1923, Oct. 21, 1923, Dec. 13, 1923, Nov. 2, 1924, April 26, 1925, April 29, 1928, July 16, 1928, Oct. 22, 1928, Feb. 23, 1930, Dec. 11, 1932, Nov. 21, 1962, Aug. 19, 1970.
New York Tribune, Nov. 13, 1915.
(Norman) Oklahoma Daily, Oct. 13, 1922, Oct. 19, 1922, Oct. 26, 1922.
Norman (Okla.) Transcript, Oct. 19, 1922.
(Oklahoma City) Daily Oklahoman, July 18, 1926.
Rocky Mountain News (Denver), Nov. 6, 1927.
Santa Fe New Mexican, Aug. 25, 1921-Feb. 16, 1931, May 20, 1932, Aug. 10, 1932, May 18, 1934, June 26, 1940, July 31, 1944, Sept. 23, 1951.
Springfield (Mass.) Republican, Dec. 15, 1929.
The Times of London, Dec. 8, 1932.
Trenton (N.J.) Evening Times, Feb. 17, 1931.
Trenton (N.J.) State Gazette, May 27, 1921, Jan. 15, 1923.
Trenton (N.J.) Sunday Advertiser, Sept. 22, 1907 through 1921, Jan. 15, 1923.
Trenton (N.J.) Sunday Times-Advertiser, Feb. 7, 1915, Nov. 22, 1959.
Trenton (N.J.) Times, June 2, 1942.

Exhibition catalogs

Albright Art Gallery. *The New Mexico Painters: Exhibition of Paintings, Prints, Pastels, Etchings*. Buffalo, N.Y., 1924.

Brooklyn Museum. *Catalogue of an Exhibition of Water Color Paintings, Pastels, and Drawings by American and Foreign Artists*. Brooklyn, N.Y., 1925.

Brooklyn Museum. *Catalogue of an Exhibition of Water Color Paintings, Pastels, and Drawings by American and Foreign Artists and Miniatures by the Brooklyn Society of Miniature Painters*. Brooklyn, N.Y., 1931.

Brooks Memorial Art Gallery. *An Exhibition of the Works of the Artists of Santa Fe and Taos*. Memphis, Tenn., 1931.

Buffalo (N.Y.) Fine Arts Academy. *Catalogue of an Exhibition of Contemporary American Sculpture, Held Under the Auspices of the National Sculpture Society*. Buffalo, N.Y., 1916.

Bullandy, Vivian. *Images From Santa Fe and Taos*. Gerald Peters Gallery, Santa Fe, March 27-April 26, 1992.

California Palace of the Legion of Honor. *Catalog of the Southwest Exhibition*. San Francisco, 1928.

Corcoran Gallery of Art. *Eleventh Exhibition of Contemporary American Oil Paintings*. Washington, D.C., 1928.

Friedman, Marilyn. *Marguerite and William Zorach: The Cubist Years, 1915-1918*. Manchester, N.H., Currier Gallery of Art, 1987.

Kevorkian Galleries. *John Mowbray-Clarke*. Foreword by Amy Murray. New York, May 7-June 7, 1919.

Los Angeles Museum Exposition Park. *Catalogue of an Exhibition of Paintings by Artists of New Mexico*. Los Angeles, June 6-Sept. 10, 1923.

Montross Gallery. *New Mexico Painters*. Catalog of the exhibition. New York, 1923.

National Collection of Fine Arts. *Pennsylvania Academy Moderns, 1910-1940*. Introductory essay by Richard J. Boyle. Washington, D.C.: Smithsonian Institution Press, 1975.

Pennsylvania Academy of the Fine Arts. *Catalogue of the 23rd Annual Philadelphia Water Color Exhibition and the 24th Annual Exhibition of Miniatures*. Philadelphia, 1925.

The Phillips Collection. *Men of the Rebellion: The Eight and Their Associates*. Washington, D.C., 1990.

Selections from the Estate of Josef Gabryel Bákos. Santa Fe: The Peters Corp., 1992.

Other

Blend, Benay. "Women Writers and the Desert: Mary Austin, Ina Sizer Cassidy and Alice Corbin." Dissertation, University of New Mexico, July 1988.

Eastern Association on Indian Affairs and New Mexico Association on Indian Affairs. "Brief Digest of the Analysis of Charges Made By John Collier Before Sub-Committee of the Committee on Indian Affairs, U.S. Senate, January and February, 1931." Hagerman Papers.

Federal Register, July 11, 1997, Vol. 62, No. 133. Notices, p. 37280. From the Federal Register Online via GPO Access (wais.access.gpo.gov).

Federal Register, March 1, 2000, Vol. 65, No. 41. Notices, p. 11079. From the Federal Register Online via GPO Access (wais.access.gpo.gov).

Ferguson, Marjorie. "The Acculturation of Sandia Pueblo." Master's thesis, University of New Mexico, 1931.

Frank, Ross Harold. "From Settler to Citizen: Economic Development and Cultural Change in Late Colonial New Mexico, 1850-1920." Dissertation, University of California, Berkeley, 1992.

Gaither, James Mann. "A Return to the Village: A Study of Santa Fe and Taos, New Mexico, As Cultural Centers, 1900-1934." Dissertation, University of Minnesota, 1957.

Greenlee, Diane. "An Untitled Watercolor by Frank Applegate in the Colorado Collection at the University of Colorado, Boulder." Unpublished paper, University of Colorado, n.d. Applegate Papers.

Indian Arts Fund Bulletin. No. 1, 1925. Santa Fe: Indian Arts Fund. In Bruce Ellis Collection, Box 390, Folder 6.

Land records, Bucks County Courthouse, Doylestown, Pa.

Land records, Santa Fe County Courthouse, Santa Fe, N.M.

Mathes, Maria. "The Walter Mruk House of Los Cinco Pintores." Unpublished paper. Courtesy Maria Mathes, Santa Fe, N.M.

Museum of Fine Arts (Houston) Bulletin 7, no. 8 (November 1930). In Museum of Fine Arts, Houston, Archives.

Museum of New Mexico Fine Arts Library. *Exhibition History, 1917-Present*.

Reeve, Kay Aiken. "The Making of an American Place: The Development of Santa Fe and Taos, N.M., As an American Cultural Center, 1898-1942." Dissertation, Texas A&M University, 1977.

Santa Fe Chamber of Commerce. Santa Fe and Vicinity Map, 1925.

Taylor, Lonn. "Arts and Crafts in the Santa Fe Style." Paper presented at the Winterthur Conference on the Decorative Arts, Wilmington, Del., 1990.

Wolff, N.S. "John Mowbray-Clarke and His Work." Paper in Mowbray-Clarke Papers.

Index

Numbers in **boldface** refer to illustrations

ALSO FROM LPD PRESS

ARCHBISHOP LAMY: IN HIS OWN WORDS
EDITED AND TRANSLATED BY THOMAS J. STEELE, S.J.

THE COMPLETE SERMONS OF JEAN BAPTISTE LAMY: FIFTY YEARS OF SERMONS (1837-1886)
[ARCHBISHOP LAMY: IN HIS OWN WORDS]
EDITED AND TRANSLATED BY THOMAS J. STEELE, S.J.

SEEDS OF STRUGGLE HARVEST OF FAITH
THE PAPERS OF THE ARCHDIOCESE OF SANTA FE
CATHOLIC CUATRO CENTENNIAL CONFERENCE
THE HISTORY OF THE CATHOLIC CHURCH IN NEW MEXICO
EDITED BY THOMAS J. STEELE, S.J., BARBE AWALT, & PAUL RHETTS

OUR SAINTS AMONG US: 400 YEARS OF NEW MEXICAN DEVOTIONAL ART
BY BARBE AWALT & PAUL RHETTS

THE REGIS SANTOS: THIRTY YEARS OF COLLECTING 1966-1996
BY THOMAS J. STEELE, S.J., BARBE AWALT, & PAUL RHETTS

SANTOS: SACRED ART OF COLORADO
EDITED BY THOMAS J. STEELE, S.J.

HISPANIC NEW MEXICAN POTTERY:
EVIDENCE OF CRAFT SPECIALIZATION 1790-1890
BY CHARLES M. CARRILLO

CHARLIE CARRILLO: TRADITION & SOUL/TRADICIÓN Y ALMA
BY BARBE AWALT & PAUL RHETTS

TRADICIÓN REVISTA: THE JOURNAL OF TRADITIONAL & CONTEMPORARY
SPANISH COLONIAL ART & CULTURE
BARBE AWALT & PAUL RHETTS, PUBLISHERS

LPD PRESS
2400 RIO GRANDE BLVD. NW PMB 213
ALBUQUERQUE, NEW MEXICO 87104-3222
505/344-9382 FAX 505/345-5129
EMAIL PAULLPD@AOL.COM   WWW.NMSANTOS.COM